SOMETHING LOST
BEHIND THE RANGES

Something Lost Behind The Ranges

THE AUTOBIOGRAPHY OF

John Blashford-Snell

HarperCollins*Publishers*

This book is dedicated to
LAL SHERMAN,
a remarkable lady and a great friend

HarperCollins*Publishers*
77–85 Fulham Palace Road,
Hammersmith, London W6 8JB

Published by HarperCollins*Publishers* 1994
1 3 5 7 9 8 6 4 2

A catalogue record for this book is
available from the British Library

ISBN 0 00 255034 2

Photoset in Linotron Pilgrim at
The Spartan Press Limited, Lymington, Hampshire

Printed in Great Britain by
HarperCollinsManufacturing Glasgow

CONTENTS

MAPS

ILLUSTRATIONS

between pages 246–247

Operations Drake's flagship, *Eye of the Wind*, off Jersey.

Young explorers in the swamps of Panama.

Barbara Price (Martinelli), a very effective recce officer on many expeditions.

The flying trapeze on the walls of Fort George.

During his visit to the Fort George Volunteers in 1982, HRH The Prince of Wales takes a ride in the Avon Searaider.

Operation Raleigh, 1985:
Sir Walter Raleigh, flagship of Operation Raleigh, and the expedition's brigantine *Zebu* rendezvous off the Turks and Caicos Islands.
Venturers constructing the Canadian sub-igloo off Grand Bahama.
Shaving in the snow on the slopes of Mt Xixabangma, Tibet, 1987.

With some of my greatest allies: General Sir John Mogg, Ambassador and Mrs Walter Annenberg, and Graham Walker.

An Executive Expedition: the microlight sets out on a dawn recce in the Kalahari.

Raja Gaj, king elephant, 11′ 3″ at the shoulders.

Mongolia, 1992:
American banker Pamela Stephany and my pal Nokhoijav near Mt Somboros.
Ann Tweedy Savage with her camel, Basil, west of Hovd.
Lindsay Griffin with shattered leg in the helicopter with Richard Snailham and Dr Jan Kemmis.

Victoria and Julian fly away in the Royal Engineers' balloon 'Sapper II' after their wedding.

ACKNOWLEDGEMENTS

WRITING BY CANDLELIGHT in the Gobi, and trying to stop the sweat dripping all over the paper in the jungle or the winds of the high Altai blowing the manuscript away, I have struggled to put down an account of some of the events of my first fifty-six years. It is also a story of the endeavours of an army of people all over the world who have befriended and helped me.

I am especially grateful to Eddie Bell and Michael Fishwick of HarperCollins, who didn't even blink an eyelid when an elephant accidentally mucked up my right hand, forcing me to have an operation before I could continue writing.

Over the years I have had expert help from my chums, including Ann Tweedy Savage, Mike Cable, Andrew Mitchell and Richard Snailham in recording the events of many of the expeditions described and I am quite sure I will have used their words in some places. I trust they will forgive any plagiarisms.

I am also indebted to the Council of the Scientific Exploration Society for its kind permission to use some material from the books on Operations Drake and Raleigh. The photographs have come from numerous sources, but there are many good ones by Chris Sainsbury who accompanied us for twelve years. My thanks also go to Jane Harvey of Canon UK and to Eileen Swift of Nikon UK for keeping my own cameras, cine and still, operational and to Jessop's for their generous help with photographic gear.

The Avon Rubber Company conveyed me safely by land, sea and river for twenty-five years and I am most grateful to Gordon Morris and his staff for their kind assistance in preparing this book.

I have been most fortunate to have the support of most efficient and charming PAs: Sue Fyson, Rosh Allhusen, Pam Baker, Betty Starling, Sara Everett, Margot Barker, Sally Harris, Sue Farrington, Melanie King, Peta Lock, Nadia Brydon, Barbara Carlisle, Sally Cox and, now, Carol Turner. Their contributions have been enormous and their friendships have meant much to me.

The assistance and backing of Harbourne Stephen, formerly Managing Director of the *Daily Telegraph*, has been immensely valuable and the advice of my friend, Jennifer Watts, on literary matters is greatly appreciated. I'm especially indebted to Sally Cox who worked at the word processor in sand- and hailstorms in Mongolia, whilst Anne Cooke and Judith did a huge amount of the transcript back in Britain. Lal Sherman and Julian Matthews have also done much to help as 'readers'.

There has simply not been space to mention all those who have played important parts in the various activities I have described and I ask their forgiveness. However, I must record my special gratitude to Ambassador Walter Annenberg and General Sir John Mogg for their marvellous support and wise counsel over many years.

JOHN BLASHFORD-SNELL
September 1993

SOMETHING LOST
BEHIND
THE RANGES

ONE

———∘∞∘———

Happy Days

CLUTCHING THE MAORI war spear alongside, Jacko and I wormed our way through the long grass, still damp with dew. The great cat must be very close and we hardly dared to breathe. Inching the spear forward and with the sun rising behind, I lifted my head very slowly over the stalks. There, only ten feet away, our quarry crouched, his evil green eyes fixed on me. Changing my hand-grip I rose and hurled the heavy weapon with all my strength. But the killer leapt sideways and the blade thudded into the ground. In a trice, Jacko, my pet monkey, was in hot pursuit. Alas, the enormous ginger tom-cat that had so recently devoured one of my mother's rabbits escaped.

The spear had come from New Zealand where my parents spent their early married life. Jacko was an ex-regimental mascot, whose tail had been shut in the NAAFI canteen door, making it permanently crooked, thus he detested anyone in khaki. We had much in common; like me Jacko was mischievous, loved eggs, hated cats, pulled little girls' hair and screamed with rage when he couldn't get his own way. Together we went on safari through the 'jungle' of orchards and rose-gardens. The long grass behind the church became our Serengeti in which lurked a fearsome lion, obligingly played by the over-fed tom. On sighting our prey, Jacko would chatter excitedly and with Tarzan-like whoops we would give chase. Sometimes we both got too near and were badly scratched for our pains, but it added greatly to the realism.

At this time the family lived in a Herefordshire rectory, but maintained strong links with Jersey. My father had been born there in 1903, the son of a sea captain. He had a good brain and during his time at the island's public school, Victoria College, had intended to try for a commission in the Indian Army. In his final year, however, he decided to enter the Church and in due course attended a theological college in Essex. Here he met the beautiful daughters of the squire, George Sadler, and in July 1924 at a dawn ceremony in St Helier Parish Church, Jersey, he married the elder, Gwendolen, and they took ship to join the pioneering population in New Zealand where he was ordained.

My mother, like all her family, was a great character. Full of fun, loving life and adventure, she claimed a strange assortment of forebears, including Louis XV, Oliver Cromwell and Judge Jeffreys. My father's ancestors were largely seafaring people and their graves are found in the West Country and the Channel Islands. I believe our name originated from a family of Snells at the village of Blashford in Hampshire. Indeed there is a Snell Lane in the village today.

After twelve years of travel, Father became rector of a busy parish on the outskirts of Hereford and here it was that I arrived in October 1936. Father was a leading figure in local affairs, the council, the RSPCA, the Territorial Army and, of course, the Church. Our home was the centre of the parish activity, and everyone who called, be he duke or dustman, was given a cheerful reception.

At first I was a shy child, but this timidity rapidly disappeared and I learned to make friends easily. My babyhood was marred by a shrivelled left arm, the result of a difficult birth. It was only the attention of our old family doctor and my mother's persistent strapping of the offending limb that eventually induced it to grow properly. Gwen had a great love of animals, which we all shared, and seeing her bandage up a sparrow's broken wing in later years, I could imagine her treating me in exactly the same way. She certainly had plenty of opportunity to practise her healing because, in spite of being well-built, I suffered from a host of ailments.

Father's involvement with the Army had originated in the OTC in Jersey, and during his time in New Zealand he had been the padre of the Southland Regiment. As war-clouds gathered over England, Pa, or 'Bish' as his friends knew him, foretold the coming conflict, and made himself unpopular in many quarters amongst those who refused to face facts. However, his reputation as a fiery, forthright preacher was well-known and this, coupled with his infectious good humour, won him a wide circle of friends, especially amongst the more radical. As a boy, I met many dashing soldiers, who told of hair-raising adventures and it is not surprising that from my earliest days I longed for a life of travel and excitement.

At home we were surrounded by animals: horses, donkeys, cows, dogs, cats, foxes, rabbits, guinea pigs, tortoises, pigeons, chickens, budgerigars, a parrot and the monkey. Today it would probably be classed as a private zoo and, to the local children, it was just that. The dogs usually included Alsatians, which at least twice saved my mother from serious injury. The first occasion was at night while driving down a narrow Jersey lane. She came upon another car blocking the road, with its headlights blazing. Hooting produced no reaction and Gwen was about to reverse when a hand came through the open nearside window and switched off the ignition. The black Alsatian bitch sitting on the back seat caught it in her mouth, and it was only with some difficulty that Mother managed to prise the teeth apart. A day or two later, a farm worker was admitted to hospital, severely mauled, saying he had been bitten by a dog in a field. The police thought otherwise, but no charges were pressed. He lost the hand through gangrene.

Another time Mother was mistaken for the St Helier Prison governor's wife and was attacked by a demented escaped prisoner. The faithful Alsatian almost killed him, and Father arrived in the nick of time to break a priceless antique vase over the rogue's head. Bish was the prison chaplain at the time and much liked by the inmates, and on discovering his dreadful error, the would-be murderer wrote Gwen a letter of apology and complimented her on her guard dog!

Without doubt she had an extraordinary power over animals. As the years went by I saw her calm a mad, half-starved dog that had been locked in a caravan without food for a week, and mend the broken limbs of countless small creatures that people brought to her, often after a vet had pronounced them beyond help. Accepting these cures as being perfectly normal, it was not until I reached manhood that I realized many of them were almost miraculous. Perhaps they were. She seemed to know just the tone of voice to use to each particular animal, the right expressions, where to touch or hold them and never to show fear, although at times she must have felt it. 'They smell fear, you know,' she would say. 'Dogs immediately sense someone who is frightened.' My attempts to imitate her methods have been fairly successful, although my skill could never compare with hers.

It is to my deep regret that I did not know my maternal grandmother, Ferdie. By all accounts she was a great personality with many attributes, including being an accomplished shot. One summer afternoon the village ladies had gathered for tea on the terrace, when Ferdie spied a large carrion crow perched vulture-like some seventy yards away on the pheasant pen. With accustomed nonchalance, she summoned her butler, Wootton, and asked him to bring the rook rifle. A few minutes later, hardly interrupting conversation, she raised the weapon to her shoulder and despatched the predator!

My grandfather, George Sadler, was a large, jolly man and reached 300 pounds in his prime. His house was always full of wild men, who, by all accounts, were the scourge of the county. The stories of their escapades are legendary: George killing an escaped circus python with a tractor or collecting a runaway bull on the bonnet of his new Armstrong Siddeley as the enraged beast fled down Braintree High Street; or, returning from a hilarious shopping spree in London with a trick truncheon (one side of which was sorbo rubber) and, happening upon the vicar, a nervous introvert, who was taking sherry with my grandmother, raising the club and bellowing, 'The Philistines are upon you,' and striking the cleric over the head. Unfortunately he had neglected to use the soft face and the poor man was downed on the spot!

One night during the Great War, Wootton tapped on the door of my grandparents' bedroom and announced that an enemy dirigible was hovering over the park. Immediately the household was woken and while the governess led the ladies to the summerhouse, George climbed to the roof with the keeper. There, for all to see, like a giant cigar, was a Zeppelin, poised 1,000 feet above the hall. Possibly to aid its navigation, it was dropping flares which illuminated the surrounding countryside with an eerie green light. The opportunity to strike a blow for England and defend his heritage was too strong for even George, who had not seen a day's military service, to let pass. Rifles and ammunition were passed from the gun-room and, encouraged by the ladies, he engaged the enemy. History does not relate whether it was the squire's gunfire or some whim of the German airman that saved the village from destruction. However, on learning that the raiders had eventually been destroyed by the Royal Flying Corps, George wrote to the Secretary of State inviting the brave aviators concerned to join him for a celebration of their joint victory. To everyone's joy the visit was arranged and instructions given for the large paddock to be used as a landing-ground. Alas, the field was a little short and the biplane ran into the fence, snapping its propeller.

'Never mind,' cried Grandfather, 'Wootton will go to London and get you a new one.' The squire's teenage daughters had already caught the eyes of the handsome pilots. 'Don't hurry back,' urged Gwen, slipping Wootton a half sovereign. A great party was enjoyed by all and I still have half a propeller as a memento.

During World War Two, the Hereford Rectory became a centre of activity and was the local Air Raid Precaution (ARP) Headquarters (HQ). Sand-bag blast walls were built across the front of the house, an Anderson bomb-shelter was installed and the study became the control-room. Nearby an RAF station had opened and a regiment of Indian Cavalry with horses camped on the racecourse. At night a band of portly gentlemen armed with shotguns and pitchforks patrolled the parish on bicycles. The Home Guard, as it was named, was led by our churchwarden, the redoubtable Captain Faulkner. For a small boy it was very exciting and I wished I could grow up quickly and rush off to fight, but, if the posters that adorned the walls were anything to go by, it was likely that the Germans would come to me anyway.

I cannot remember exactly the date that it happened, but I recall a summer's afternoon in my playroom. Hereford housed an important ammunition factory and air-raid alarms were not uncommon. The sirens had wailed on and off all day and the thump of anti-aircraft guns was clearly audible to the east. A new sound caused me to stand on a bench and peer out of a high window. Low over the fields a green-and-grey, twin-engined aeroplane was gliding earthwards. A trail of black smoke streamed from one engine and the other was emitting a spluttering roar. Above, in close formation, two Spitfires followed, the red-and-blue roundels on their wings standing out clearly. Through the smoke I saw emblazoned on the fuselage of the bomber a black cross. I did not see it crash, but the ting-a-ling of the fire engines and the Home Guard speeding by on bicycles told me the bomber was down nearby. In the study Bill Bailey, the duty warden, picked up the phone. 'By the Canny Brook,' he shouted, 'they've got one of the Jerries alive.'

Only a short time elapsed before I confronted our prisoner. He was a tall, slim warrior, although, in retrospect, he was probably barely out of his teens. Dressed from head to foot in a black flying-suit with a silver eagle and a swastika on his breast, he looked impressive. A mass

of straw-coloured hair fell untidily over his pale face. By the door
stood Captain Faulkner, his twelve-bore levelled menacingly.

'Were you in that bomber?' I enquired.

'Yes,' he said without emotion in perfect English.

'Now you'll go to prison,' I pointed out.

'But not for long,' he smiled.

The significance of the remark was lost on me, but the men in the
room stiffened. At that moment a khaki fifteen-hundredweight
utility full of burly military policemen swept up the drive. 'Auf
Wiedersehen,' said the German with a sad look as he was escorted
away.

Everyone was terribly cross that I had even spoken to him. There
was no love of the Boche in our house. Jersey was occupied, and, for
all we knew, everything that Father's family had possessed was now
German loot. My godmother, Aunt Jess, had served as a Red Cross
nursing sister in France in 1914 and her aged father and brother were
still in Jersey. Cut off from her beloved island, Jess nursed wounded
troops and spent her spare moments filling bombs with TNT at the
armaments' factory. After the war I learned how Father Le Brun had
defied the enemy. When their military band passed beneath his
window, the cantankerous and supposedly bedridden old man had
emptied his chamber pot over them, shouting as he did so, 'Les sales
Boches'. His arrest was only averted by his housekeeper's protest that
he had TB and was insane.

Mother spent much of her time helping welfare organizations and
ran the parish whilst Pa was abroad with the 53rd Welsh Division.
Granny was left to run the house and attempt to keep me in order.
She was a grand little lady, very Victorian with a stubborn Jersey
personality. Married twice, first to a John Blashford-Snell, she was
again a widow and thought to be on the look-out for a third husband.
The war years were hard, but she managed to relieve the tension with
a wee nip of Scotch from a bottle concealed in her boot cupboard. I
discovered that she also kept her false teeth in a weak solution of
brandy.

Early education at Miss Gibson's School for Girls and Young Boys
became a nightmare when we were forced to go through 'wedding
ceremonies' every break-time with the older pupils. Nor did I enjoy
acting. In the school play *Robin Hood*, being of ample girth even at
such a tender age, I was cast as Friar Tuck and had to prance on stage
addressing Maid Marian with the words, 'Behold I am the brave Friar

Tuck'. Strangely, even now I sometimes mix up my Fs and my Ts. On this occasion it caused great embarrassment to my mother.

Sadly, Jacko had now developed a liking for birds, which he feathered and ate alive. As he aged, long fangs protruded from his mouth and, one day when teasing him, I was bitten to within half an inch of my jugular vein. Wisely, Mother decided he must live in a cage, but he frequently escaped and still managed to terrorize our neighbours. His exploits were renowned, but eventually he rather overdid it by climbing into the machine-gun post outside the ARP HQ. He swivelled the ancient Maxim at the curate, who did not approve of Jacko anyway, and liked him even less when he was forced to dive for cover into the freshly-manured rose-garden. Ironically, my erstwhile chum was shortly despatched by a local farmer in, of all things, a monkey puzzle tree.

However, I had other animal friends to console me. There was Brutus, the huge St Bernard, who adored being dressed up and always won the prize for the best-attired dog at the church fête. He did not travel well and I will never forget one epic journey from Hereford to Tenby, moving in the wake of a long military convoy. Bish was chaplain to the unit and the presence of German aircraft added excitement to the trip. However, in the small green Hillman car was Granny, her cat and parrot. The bird was green, swore, belched and bit. Neither Aunt Jess nor Brutus, who were with us, liked the revolting creature and to show its distaste my canine pal vomited over everyone. At this moment some bombs fell nearby and we dived into a ditch. The huge dog landed on top of my grandmother, who was clutching her cat, and the parrot escaped, sadly only temporarily.

Back home I set about turning Brutus into a gun dog. Unfortunately he couldn't differentiate between rabbits, cats or small dogs and once ate a poor, deaf, old Pekingese in the act of cocking its leg on the war memorial. I tried to comfort its grief-stricken mistress, pointing out that the end had been both quick and painless and, anyway, the Peke had had a good innings. Furthermore I mentioned that my 160-pound pal, who now sat dejectedly beside me, dribbling in dismay, felt strongly about dogs of oriental origin desecrating a British war memorial. My reasoning was not appreciated.

By now the rectory was being used to house twenty attractive nurses and Mother, seeking to add a little sparkle to their lives, invited the Commanding Officer of a nearby American Air Force unit to send along some of his men for Sunday afternoon tea. It was my duty to welcome them at the front door and as such receive the copious quantities of candy that our gallant allies carried. The scarcity of chocolate made this a highly-prized trade good. Tea was served in the drawing-room and soon the airmen were fascinating the ladies with tales of America. One huge sergeant named Tex came from Texas, where, he informed us, everything was larger, faster, stronger and better than anywhere else in the whole wide world. He was a very big man and I feared for Mother's bone china tea cup, which was completely encompassed by his vast hand. I noted that no one contradicted Tex. When the hot crumpets, a special treat, were produced the door rattled. Brutus had a passion for crumpets and had learned to open doors by seizing the door knobs in his great jaws. Tex was in full flow when it swung open to reveal the awesome sight of a massive St Bernard, strings of saliva hanging from his cavernous pink mouth.

'Gawd, what a dog,' cried the Texan.

'Oh, that's only the pup, wait until you see his mother,' said Gwen, refilling the tea cups.

One crumpet later the enormous creature sat obediently, its bloodshot eyes fixed upon the rapidly emptying plate. The girls were now exchanging sly glances with our guests so I felt I should provide a little distraction. A stock of pheasants' feathers were kept by the fireplace for cleaning Father's pipe. Deftly slipping one along the carpet I was able to flick it back and forth across Brutus's testicles (a little trick I had learned from the verger's daughter). Within a few moments conversation began to die away as all became aware of the St Bernard's enormous erection. Then my Mother caught sight of the offensive item.

'Filthy beast,' she shrieked, hurling a cushion and ordering him out.

'Hey kid, do that next Sunday and we'll double the candy ration,' said Tex as he left.

Meanwhile my faith in the Home Guard had diminished and, unable to play a more active part in the war other than run messages for the ARP, I decided to raise a small private army to defend the parish. Recruiting was easy. Before the war Mother had laid in a plentiful stock of tinned pineapple and other mouth-watering delights. These, plus our fruit orchards, and the abundance of cuddly pets, attracted hordes of children. From this host I was able to select some thirty loyal followers of both sexes. We had our headquarters in an old stable, shared with a pet fox, and from here would sally forth against the enemy, which, in the absence of German paratroopers, was provided by a rival organization of uncouth lads, whose main occupation was to raid the apple crop. Epic battles involving dozens of children raged back and forth across the countryside. Our weapons included catapults, grenades, Molotov cocktails and even a ballista (copied from a history book) to hurl evil-smelling dead cats.

By the time I was fourteen, the need to defend the parish from Hitler had long receded and my schooling was making serious inroads into the conduct of the campaign. However, early scientific education and a patriotic local chemist gave new impetus to our activities. We had managed to construct a lethal cannon, mounted on an old invalid carriage, and, worse still, a great mortar fashioned from a brass church candlestick that could hurl a one-pound projectile 200 paces.

It was a bright summer's afternoon when our heroic little band, already suffering depletion as some members, whose voices had broken, showed more interest in the choir girls than their military duties, made its last stand. After the first engagement, the scrumpers, as the fruit-thieves were known, used all their low cunning to draw us to one side of the churchyard, whilst a nimble group scaled the eight-foot garden wall and wrought havoc amongst the Cox's Orange Pippin. These were similar tactics to those used by Prince Rupert at Marston Moor to raid my ancestor, Oliver Cromwell's baggage train. We were not unprepared. Concealed in a yew hedge was the invalid carriage cannon and in a trench by the rhubarb bed sat the mortar. The two possible escape routes through the allotments were liberally sown with mines, consisting of Kilner jars filled with a fearful mixture of chemicals and acid. Leaving a handful of archers and air riflemen to deal with an enemy feint, I joined the artillery and catapulteers. There were now some fifteen scrumpers looting the best fruit. 'Now, Hitchen,' I hissed in the ear of my master gunner, who applied his illicit cigarette to the touchhole. The cannon roared, hurling half a pound of dried peas across the kitchen garden. Even as the carriage was careering backwards, I heard the screams of the enemy, but noted with some dismay that we had at least one innocent victim. Meredith, the gardener, rose phoenix-like from the spinach patch, clutching his posterior and mouthing a dreadful oath. But he who hesitates is lost, and, having gained the advantage of surprise, we followed it up with a volley of missiles and charged the enemy. As expected, they ran into the minefield. At least half turned back, were seized and dragged to the potting shed for unspeakable torture by the choir girls. Meanwhile, the mortar came into action to cut off the survivors. With a loud crump, it fired a bundle of fizzing fireworks inside a tin can high into space. Alas, the senior chorister's aim was hasty and the bomb overshot, to explode immediately behind an old lady, who with her little dog was hidden in the long grass. Scared witless, dog and owner fled, clearing two stiles with extraordinary ease. The next shot landed on the rectory roof and brought down an avalanche of tiles. I accepted the chorister's resignation, apologized to Meredith, released all my prisoners unharmed and offered to pay for the roof as soon as I could negotiate a loan from Mother. It was to no avail. Father, now a JP, spent a week calming the populace and my private army was disbanded.

It is ironic that much of my military service was spent at the receiving end of missiles very similar to those with which I had disturbed that peaceful shire. Father decided the Church was not my vocation and thereafter encouraged me to join the Army, where my destructive nature might be put to good use. But this was some years off, and in the hope of keeping me out of trouble I was despatched to the sparsely-populated Welsh Mountains where lived an indulgent nature-loving aunt and uncle. Here too I learned to appreciate wildlife and the countryside. However, I had been taught to shoot at the age of nine, and, when Father returned from the front and, in spite of family protests, thrust a .45 Service Revolver into my hand, I roamed the hills blazing away at rabbits and collecting wildflowers to my heart's content. It was not long before I shot both myself and the village idiot and learned a useful lesson on gun safety.

I sometimes longed for the sea, and so we regularly visited relatives on the south coast. I met retired Ship's Captain, Great-uncle Albert, in his garden by the Solent. As I was brought forward to be introduced by a timorous cousin he sat, enormous in his deck-chair, a flowing grey beard cascading over his massive chest. Raised to his eye was a naval telescope. The old sea dog growled with a voice that had sent fear through a thousand square rig sailors. 'So it's young John, is it?' and, without looking down, 'What ship's that?' he asked, swinging the lens to a sleek destroyer seaward bound. 'Nice lines,' he muttered, 'I like nice lines.' His telescope had moved to some scantily-dressed girls, bathing on the far shore. 'See the world,' he roared, fixing me for a moment with a twinkling, reddened eye, and then turned his attention back to the ladies.

My 'Just William' existence progressed throughout prep-school in sleepy Worcestershire, where my voice broke early, enabling me to learn poker in the commoners' stalls. At home for holidays, my musical enjoyment was confined to playing a drum, which made Brutus howl, a ghastly and unsociable noise. So I turned my attention to the church organ. The organist was unsympathetic and, in a mood of sullen revenge, I took a dead rat that Granny's cat had been gnawing and popped it down one of the organ pipes. With evil glee, I sat in the choir stalls next day, awaiting the awful note that would result from the rodent rattling on the reed. There followed a very strange sound. Then, oh horror, it flew out and landed on a choir girl's lap. 'Eeee,' screamed the maiden and, unseen, I seized the carcass and secreted it in my hassock. They scolded the poor girl. No one believed her innocence, but I was encouraged because the rat had lasted to be played another day.

Father, believing that I was a useless waster, encouraged me to do something positive to help at home. Therefore, with reluctance, I agreed to rise before dawn on Wednesdays and ring the church bell for mid-week communion. The searing cold in the unheated rectory bit through me like an Arctic wind as I stumbled through the snow to open the heavy vestry door and tug the aged bell-rope. Even a nip of the sideboard brandy failed to fortify me and I knew that, if I were to survive, I must find a better solution.

It came to me like a vision – indeed, it may have been divine providence that showed the way. The great bell was within view of my bedroom window and a round of .300 rook rifle fired from my bed would produce a ring to waken the dead. Twenty shots and we had filled five pews but, alas, the resultant ricochets may have had more to do with it. As the last of the faithful scampered into the cover of the church porch, Father, in a biblical rage, reminded me that it was a house of peace. Nevertheless, he realized that we must move forward with the times and thus, by the next holiday, a gramophone and loud-speaker system had been installed to give a rendering of a slightly tinny version of 'Bow Bells' and other well-known peals. Not only did this increase the congregation, but when I turned the volume up to full power we even pulled in a few of the rival vicar's flock. Whilst fellow clerics muttered disapprovingly in the cathedral cloisters about progressive parsons, Pa enjoyed a full house.

By now I had become friendly with the milkman's dark-eyed daughter. This temptress dared me to put a certain disc on the machine. Thus, the parishioners were greeted with a jolly ballad, 'Captain Brown, Captain Brown, he played his ukelele as the ship went down'. In a final defiant gesture, I turned up the volume to the deaf-aid system for the last few bars, which sent the rows of pensioners bouncing in their seats.

It was perhaps understandable that my parents should send me to school as far away as possible. Thus, in 1950, I arrived at Victoria College, Jersey. Granite-built, it stood fortress-like above St Helier. In the high-windowed classrooms generations of Channel Islanders, including Father, had studied hard to gain places in the establishments of the Empire and also, for the chosen few, a venerated position in the dignified local government, the States.

Studies at Victoria were made tolerable by the many unofficial extra-mural activities available for the adventurous. Some of my contemporaries preferred to gain early experience with the French maids, but, for me, the great attraction was the maze of underground tunnels left behind by the German army of occupation. The island abounded in a liberal quantity of ammunition, mines and weapons. Years later, during my training as a sapper officer, I discovered how lucky we had been to survive our experiments with assorted explosive devices.

Bish had made his mark at Victoria and had become its first Scout Master. I joined his old troop, but soon found the attractions of the Combined Cadet Force irresistible. Joining the brutal and licentious military, I was able to indulge my love of shooting, and so with the school team made the annual pilgrimage to Bisley.

While Hans Hass and Jacques Cousteau were making headlines in the new world of underwater adventure, my friends, Adrian Troy and Tony Titterington, and I were seeking the great grey conger eel amongst the seaweed and rocks of Jersey's treacherous coastline. Our adventures were numerous, and when I regaled my mother with them she must have been horrified, but she simply smiled encouragingly and helped me to buy a powerful harpoon gun to continue the battle.

Tony was the mechanical genius and he converted German submarine escape apparatus into underwater breathing equipment. We should have used soda lime to re-purify the air but, being short of funds, employed caustic soda. To test the device I was lowered off St Brelades Harbour wall, a net full of house bricks tied to my waist for ballast. 'Give two tugs when you want to come up,' said Tony, as the sea closed over me. After a few minutes the oxygen tasted awful so I pulled hard on the safety line. To my horror it came snaking down from the surface. It wasn't tied to anything and the attention of my handlers had been distracted by a couple of girlfriends. In desperation I fought to untie the net but the knot was immovable. With head spinning I therefore climbed the harbour wall like an underwater mountaineer. It took a terrible time, and, when I had scaled the fifteen feet, I emerged blue in the face! 'Oh well, back to the drawing board,' grunted Tony.

To turn our minds to safer activities our headmaster created a compulsory debating society. Thus, all sixth-formers had to learn to speak in public, a valuable training that has stood many an old-Victorian in good stead. To liven up our debates, a mock election was held. At once an evil bunch of us formed the 'Neo-Fascist' party. 'Nellie' Le Geyt became poet laureate and composed party political ballads, whilst Adrian, Bungle Colson and John Gwyther became henchmen to myself as 'Blashford von Schnell', the dictator. The population of Jersey was more than mildly surprised to see our Nazi uniforms, armbands and steel helmets. However, it was not until our storm-troopers raised a fourteen-foot German banner over the school that the patient head intervened. Nevertheless, for weeks the election campaign raged with its incredible dramas and satire, mainly centred on the controversial problem of the emancipation of the mole. Mass meetings were held and hecklers dragged off screaming by my black-shirts to the showers, where they were treated to a cold wash-down fully clothed! Party songs were sung at midnight sessions in a secret beer cellar. It was all great fun and, to everyone's horror, we almost won the final election.

I loved schooldays, but my great failure was with the opposite sex. Girls did not seem to appreciate bombs, guns, underwater fishing or my dancing. The ones that did were singularly unattractive.

Much of the school holidays I spent with the Territorial Army. Father was chaplain of a Monmouthshire gunner regiment and thus I learned the intricacies of anti-aircraft defence. Most members having served in the war regarded the time at training camps as holidays.

Regular officers, who had the misfortune to be posted to the various gunnery stations we visited, lived in dread of our arrival.

Of course there were occasions when the regiment excelled. One such was the visit of the Lord Lieutenant. By the time he arrived, monocle in eye, thrashing his breeches with his riding crop, we were feeding heavy shells into the guns. With deafening noise, our twenty-four 3.7s hurled tons of high explosive at a red canvas sleeve being towed half a mile behind an RAF Mosquito fighter-bomber. Rich Welsh voices screamed orders. Acrid brown smoke drifted over the firing point, obscuring the bright summer sun and glimmering sea. The Australian pilot of the aircraft encouraged us with a running commentary over a loud-speaker system.

In the hot stuffy radar wagons, the operators followed every move of the little green blips, indicating the path of aircraft and target. It was the operator's job to 'lock on' the rearward blip, which was the moving sleeve, and thus direct the gunfire. We were a mixed-sex unit and it was not uncommon for the male controllers to arrange their shift with a female soldier of their liking. By coincidence a red lamp glowed outside each wagon during firing, prohibiting sudden entrance which would spoil the operator's night vision. Under these darkened conditions and with a pretty girl beside you, it is easy to imagine how even the most ardent gunner's attention might wander. 'You're dropping short, cobber. Wow, that's a good 'un!' came our pilot's voice, as his Mosquito droned to and fro.

The Lord Lieutenant, enjoying the sun, and clearly happy to smell cordite, watched the regiment sweating in the heat. Everything was going terribly well and it must only be a matter of time before someone actually struck the sleeve. The beer tent was sited conveniently near and ice-cold ale awaited the traditional celebration that would follow a direct hit. Perhaps the temperature in the radar wagon was too high or Private Jones too passionate; we shall never know. Suddenly the Mosquito disappeared amidst a welter of shell bursts.

'Cease fire, cease fire,' shrieked the safety officers, as the plane began to spiral downwards.

The loudspeaker system had gone silent. Then, to our intense relief, the Australian pilot spoke. Most of what he actually said is unprintable. But he ended, 'Remember I'm pulling this f . . . ing thing, not pushing it.'

'How about some gin, sir,' suggested our quick-witted colonel.

The official party stomped off to the mess, whilst we gunners tittered and the Australian managed to land his plane, full of holes.

Our camp was plagued with rats from the tip on the outskirts of a small town. I was appointed the rodent NCO and, armed with Sten gun and torch, did nightly battle against the loathsome creatures on the stinking dump. Although I expended a fair quantity of ammunition, it was to little avail, and so I decided on more drastic action. Approximately sixty pounds of old explosive had been lying around the magazine for several years and the quartermaster sergeant was delighted to be rid of it. I spent a whole day burying it in the centre of the tip. With all the noise of gunfire, I reckoned another bang would go unnoticed and, as the rats were most active after dark, awaited a night exercise before touching off the charge. To my consternation, the blinding flash and thundering roar were much more spectacular than any gunfire. Refuse and rats rained down for half a mile. Passing the village chapel next morning, I found the preacher pointing to dead rodents on the roof. 'A message from Heaven,' he proclaimed with religious fervour.

Those fortnights at firing camp were the times when I really grew up. And it was from here I mounted my first expedition, into the Welsh mountains. A schoolfriend, Cliff Le Quelenec, and I set out from my uncle's cottage at dawn one August morning, carrying rucksacks bulging with camping equipment. The packs were badly balanced and it was almost impossible to stand upright. On our heads were Australian-style bush-hats and we each carried a four-foot ash-staff. I had a revolver with which to shoot rabbits when inevitably our rations had gone and starvation threatened.

The first day was sheer hell and by afternoon our feet were raw and shoulders aching. A mountain mist dropped suddenly upon us and within minutes we were utterly lost. So we camped for the night, but next day visibility was as bad as the first. By late afternoon we were following some sheep along a narrow track when, to my astonishment, I saw my colleague sink waist-deep into a pool of bright green slime. The sheep scattered and ran back to dry ground, leaving us in the middle of a very treacherous bog. There was no point in looking around for help – we had seen no one all day. Cliff, in spite of his considerable strength, was quite unable to move. Slipping off my cumbersome rucksack, I unwound the eight-foot toggle-rope we both carried. 'For God's sake, hurry,' was all he said, as I tossed him the free end. The ground shook like a jelly, so to spread my weight I lay face down. We both pulled hard, with the result that I began to slide towards him. 'It's no good,' he shouted, a note of fear in his voice. 'I can feel the bloody stuff sucking me down.'

'Can't you get your own rope off?' I asked, but I realized that if he took his arms off the surface, he would probably sink right under. Overhead a lone buzzard circled, oblivious to our plight, and the sheep baa'd contentedly. 'Wait,' I said, 'I've got an idea.' Crawling back to my pack, I undid the waist and shoulder straps and buckled them together. It gave an extra six feet of line. Sliding back across the oozing surface, I joined it to the toggle-rope. It was just sufficient to enable me to get behind a hummock of grass that stood like an island in the swamp. Now we had an anchorage and I began to pull. I'll swear nothing happened for ten minutes. The sweat was being forced out of our pores and neither of us said a thing, but went on pulling. Suddenly it was a little easier and to my great relief I realized that, inch by inch, Cliff was beginning to move towards me. Thirty minutes later we lay laughing together on the mountainside. For a further ten days we marched on, exploring ancient ruins, crossing fast-flowing streams, being chased by bulls and getting lost time and time again. When eventually we emerged, we were thinner, fitter and wiser for our experience.

I managed to pass the entrance exam to Sandhurst and, with a year to kill, took every opportunity to broaden my knowledge, whilst remaining at school to debate, shoot, swim underwater and take a few A levels. By the time I left Victoria I had grown to love Jersey and have regarded it as home ever since.

Sandhurst meant going to the bottom of the ladder again. However, Britain still had an Empire and we hoped for a life of adventure and travel, engaging in the numerous bushfire wars. The basic training brought one down to earth with a bump and we did all those useful character-building activities like floor-scrubbing, boot-bulling, spud-bashing, bed-packing and cutting grass with nail scissors. Cursed, chased and screamed at by baying drill sergeants, we learned and re-learned our military skills for sixteen weeks until, suddenly, we were officer cadets, fit to enter the Academy proper. Now we were cursed, chased and screamed at by more senior officer cadets and thus the process started again. But if we survived, and most did, we came away from that famous establishment with its motto 'Serve to lead' firmly fixed in our minds. It was a grand finishing school, often likened to a third-rate university, where the Officers' Training Corps had been allowed to run wild.

The two pleasant years at the Academy passed quickly. I had to work hard to get into the Royal Engineers, but nevertheless I had time to make hundreds of new friends and enjoy the lighter side of life. There were the famous Sandhurst rags, such as when we chained the cannon wheel to wheel across the London road causing traffic jams. Doubtless today we would be prosecuted. The bright lights of London were a great lure and, in our senior terms, there was increased freedom to visit the capital. By working hard one leave, I managed to buy a Triumph motorcycle, which worried my parents so much that they quickly helped me purchase a bone-shaking old BSA sports car. 'Rigormortis' was far more lethal than the motorbike but, because it had four wheels, was considered safer. 'Don't laugh, Madam, your daughter may be inside,' proclaimed a notice on the boot. Indeed, some of my girlfriends' parents were so horrified by the machine that they gladly lent me their own cars for evenings out. A family friend with a reputation for wild living was quick to understand the pressing needs of a Sandhurst cadet. 'Wouldn't it help if you had a flat in town?' he enquired after a good dinner. 'My company has one in Jermyn Street. It's always free at the weekends.' I accepted the offer with alacrity and thus began a splendid era of parties that the late Rosa Lewis, in whose famous Cavendish Hotel the apartment lay, would have approved.

I now found the opposite sex more receptive. One in particular, a lady soldier, was more so than most and we saw a lot of each other. On the night of her Commissioning Ball I set out with a friend in Rigormortis. It was a crisp, clear March evening as, bedecked in black tie and silk scarves, we sped past Frensham Pond. Because the headlights gave out such a poor light, it took me several seconds to realize that my front wheel had mysteriously become detached and was proceeding in front of us towards the pond. Out of control, the car ran down a sandy bank and stopped abruptly in a pool of black mud. Fortunately a convoy of Austin 7s and sundry wrecks belonging to other cadets saw our plight, and within a few minutes we were on our way to the ball once more, this time seated less comfortably on a spare tyre attached to the boot of an aged Riley. Even so, I was a little late for the dinner and my first meeting with

the dignified and upright colonel, whose daughter I was escorting.
He was clearly not impressed by my dishevelled appearance and an
immediate request to borrow his car.

TWO

Travel and Adventure

'CHRRRIST,' GASPED Lieutenant Joseph N. Beerbecker Jnr. 'We're on fire.'

This was my opinion too, but it was only when my curiosity about the black smoke belching from an engine had got the better of me that I had woken my fellow passenger.

The pilot's loudspeaker cut in, 'Hear this, hear this, we have a malfunction in our starboard engine and are returning to base.'

Aboard the USAF transport plane we sat tensely as the grey Atlantic waves swept by beneath, and felt a huge sense of relief as the American coastline appeared. Fire engines racing alongside stifled the fire with jets of foam as the plane halted.

Back on terra firma I said a short prayer of thanks that my career in the Royal Engineers had not ended before it had really begun. Indeed it was not a year since our fresh-faced batch of young officers had gathered at Chatham to learn the black arts of sappering. For nine months we had built bridges, laid mines, dug trenches, fired demolitions, surveyed roads, driven bulldozers and pumped water.

'By the time we have finished with you,' stated the mild-mannered, pipe-smoking warrant officer, 'you will be fit to tackle any obstacle in the world.'

'Sappers', we were informed, 'are all mad, married or methodist,' and there was certainly a number of Royal Engineer officers who lived up to this reputation. Such men, we noted, were often well-decorated and would have blushed had they heard some of the legends told of their deeds. It was they who encouraged us, possibly because they felt that even we might invent some fiendish engine of war or act irrationally, but courageously, in battle. Mess nights beneath the portraits of Gordon, Kitchener and Napier reminded us of the illustrious heritage of eccentric generals. Determined to live up to our reputation, we once derailed an army train by accident and blew up a row of washbasins in the mess. The authorities were amazingly patient, although we drove one instructor after another berserk. 'There has never been such an ill-behaved course,' stated the adjutant. But discipline and self-control did not seem to go with independent thought, and the practical application of unconventional ideas.

Being only thirty miles from the West End, the austere barracks did nothing to dampen our spirits. My Jowett Jupiter sports car had a fine turn of speed with torsion-bar suspension, which enhanced its cornering, and I enjoyed trying to beat the record from London. My twenty-first birthday party was celebrated in a cellar in Gray's Inn Road. It was a well conducted orgy and so impressed were the police, when inevitably they arrived, that they returned later, off-duty, to join in the fun. Although some superiors regarded us as irresponsible, immature idiots and told us so frequently, there were others who tended to encourage our exploits.

A posting to a field squadron on active service in Cyprus came at the end of the course, and we had six weeks' leave, which I determined not to waste. My girlfriend from Sandhurst days was in Singapore and her letters gave vivid descriptions of Malaya. Given my deep-seated desire to travel, I decided to go to the Far East. Forty-two days were quite enough to get there and back. A friendly MP said he knew someone in the Royal Air Force who might help, if I would carry out a few despatches. Thus, early on a July morning, I boarded a glittering silver RAF Comet and set off on a trip that did not turn out quite as planned.

Firstly, the flight was prolonged because of mechanical problems and I experienced my first tropical heat. Then, on arrival in Singapore, we learnt of a revolution in Iraq and the RAF air route's closure. We had been the last plane through. This was tricky. The civil airfare was £350, over a year's pay. I just had to catch that troop-ship to Cyprus. However, after several enjoyable weeks and the failure of all attempts to get home westward, I turned my attention to reaching England via America.

The US consul in Singapore was sympathetic. He said that if I could get to Clarkfield in the Philippines, there was a chance that the USAF might lift me to the States. Thus it was that I found myself, drenched to the skin in a leaking Royal New Zealand Air Force freight plane butting through a heavy tropical downpour over the South China

Sea. Eventually we reached the jungle-clad mountains of the Philippines. The resident RAF liaison officer explained my plight to his taciturn opposite number.

At last the heavily-built American major spoke. 'You've a problem, boy,' he said, drawing hard on his cheroot, 'but maybe we can help. You come to the party tonight and tomorrow we'll figure what we can do.'

In the morning I learnt that the first difficulty was for a non-US national to remain on the air-base for more than seventy-two hours without contravening some greatly-respected regulation. The resourceful Major Harry had solved this even before I met him at 0730 hours.

'You've just become a UN observer,' he exclaimed, passing me a large cup of black coffee. My 'papers' bearing the crest of the House of Commons had impressed our allies far more than they had the RAF. 'We'll always try to help guys on a special mission for the Pentagon,' he said, 'and I guess that's the sort of duty you're doing.' I did not contradict him.

The Americans overwhelmed me with kindness, but after ten days I was still there and, despite all efforts, some red tape still blocked my progress. It was at the end of the morning when the office staff was leaving for lunch that Liz, the secretary in the outer office, invited me to her twenty-first birthday party that night. She had left before I realized that I knew neither her surname nor where she lived. Hearing my predicament, Major Harry gave a low whistle and then very slowly said, 'Man, you've just struck gold. She's the general's daughter.' Arriving at the residence wearing my tropical dinner jacket, I was greeted by the commander of the 13th Pacific Air Force in his braces. His huge hand gripped mine as he skilfully manipulated a barbecue spit with the other. To the strains of Sinatra, he told me with relish of the wonderful times he had enjoyed in London during the war.

'How long are you staying, young man?' he said, filling my glass with a liberal quantity of 'Old Crow'. I told him my problem and he promised to sort it out.

The fifty-six sets of orders that I was handed next day authorized my travel from Clarkfield Air Base, Philippines, to Burtonwood in England via America. It was a long flight in the comfortable Constellation with stops at Wake and Guam Islands, where thanks to the general's signals I was ushered into the VIP lounges and entertained royally. I could only assume that the wartime parties in London must have been very good. At Honolulu the aircraft was diverted to the civil airport, where an impressive array of grass-skirted girlies and Hawaiian bands greeted us. On discovering that we were not the anticipated tourist flight they disappeared, grumbling, into the night.

The last leg was passed in oblivion, thanks to a monumental party and I still felt slightly jaded when we arrived late at night at Travis Air Force Base, California. To my dismay the general's liberal supply of signals had dried up. However, there was a plane flying east in two days' time and, if I cared to stay at the officers' club for a couple of nights at ten dollars a time, I could catch that. Stringent British foreign currency restrictions and the total inadequacy of a second lieutenant's pay had reduced my ready cash to three dollars, ninety-five cents, hardly sufficient to keep one in essential body liquid for forty-eight hours. At this point a kindly negro sergeant mentioned that a giant C130 transport plane was en route for New Mexico and, what was more, the pilot was an RAF officer on secondment. Flight Lieutenant Hicks was sipping grape-juice at the bar when I acquainted him with my problem. He seemed delighted to meet another Briton and readily agreed to add me to the load of pineapples being flown to some highly secret destination in the desert. Soon after take-off I climbed into a bunk and slept soundly until we reached a place that really sounded like the wild west – Albuquerque.

On landing I was invited to join the crew for breakfast and Hicks persuaded his merry men to part with their loose dollars in exchange for my British cheque. Whilst we were doing this a man in white overalls approached and asked about the C130's radio. Without paying him much attention, the operator said it was 'all fine', but that the aircraft was open if he wished to inspect it. The crew then went off to change, leaving me to finish my coffee.

The white overalled technician returned and said in an angry tone, 'That radio's not working and you know it! How in hell's name am I going to speak to the President of the United States?'

I looked up in bewilderment and tried to explain that I was not a member of the crew. He stormed off, clearly very angry, muttering that I was a spy from Russia.

When Hicks got back I said, 'That chap was here about the radio again – he wants to speak to the President.'

'Oh well,' said Hicks, only mildly interested, 'I expect he'll come back.'

Obviously the whole matter was of no importance and due to my lack of comprehension of American terminology and vocabulary, quite above my head.

At the flight operations desk they attempted to get me a lift eastwards, and while we were enquiring about aircraft timings the overalled gentleman reappeared.

'I want to speak to the President,' he boomed at the sergeant who was helping us.

'You wait your turn, man — jeez, sit right over there and wait your turn.'

The fellow turned puce with rage, went over to a drinking fountain and pressing the knob, yelled, 'Get me the President.'

Conversation in the flight operations ceased. Even Hicks looked surprised and the desk sergeant said, 'Excuse me, sir, I think we may have a problem.' He picked up the telephone and said, 'Air Police.' The man was still in consultation with the President (down the water pipe) when the police seized him.

'Who is he?' I asked Hicks.

'Oh! Just some nut escaped from the local lunatic asylum.'

There were no Air Force planes going east that day, so I decided to buy a ticket to Denver in Colorado where I might pick up a USAF flight to Washington next day. I was about to leave the air base when the desk sergeant thrust me a piece of paper. 'You'll need that to get out of the main gate,' he said, 'our security is pretty tight here.' Outside the civil airline office, legs crossed and smoking a pipe, sat the first Red Indian I had ever seen. He eyed my brown shoes, long stockings, khaki shorts and stared fixedly at my officer's cane.

'How,' he grunted.

Unconsciously raising my hand in the sign of peace, I replied, 'Very well, thank you,' and went inside.

I sat in the shade awaiting the plane. The Indian watched me, sucking and puffing at his empty pipe. The temperature rose. At last he spoke. 'What that stick for?'

Could I say a symbol of authority? A British Army tradition, we exchange them for a baton on promotion to Field Marshal, or the bloody dress regulations say I've got to carry it? 'You may have heard of General Gordon?' I enquired. The Indian nodded solemnly. Perhaps the Americans had a Gordon too, better be careful what I say, he probably butchered the Blackfeet or whatever tribe this gentleman belongs to, I thought. 'Well, General Gordon led an army of Chinese soldiers many years ago. A stick like this was the only weapon he ever carried in battle. The enemy believed it to be magic, and it so inspired his men that they never lost a fight.'

The Indian nodded. 'Plenty good wood,' he wheezed.

At Denver, I followed the usual procedure of telephoning the nearest USAF Base. In this case it was the Air Force Academy. Within minutes a car arrived and a major ushered me into an office to await the arrival of the colonel. Coffee was produced, my papers checked and we began talking about England.

'Say, who won the FA Cup last year?' he asked. I am not a keen disciple of football and simply could not remember. 'How about cricket? How's the Test Match going?' he went on. I only played rugby and he looked a little disappointed.

Suddenly the door burst open and a large, red-faced man in a short-sleeved shirt and Bermudas stepped in. 'Well, what do you think?' he demanded.

'Oh, I think he's genuine, Colonel,' said the major.

The colonel pumped my hand and apologized for an 'interrogation'. 'Can't be too careful,' he emphasized. 'Now, James here will see you have all you need and we'll hope to get you on that flight tomorrow. Any friend of General Morman's is a friend of mine.'

Hurray for General Morman, I thought, as I tackled a giant T-bone steak with James. Unfortunately he had arranged for me to attend an all-night 'orgy' at the nearby nurses' home and so I was not in the best condition as I waited for my next plane. I decided Old Crow really lived up to its name! A buckskin-clad six-gun-toting sheriff with two bloodhounds arrived to hunt for a deaf-mute child, lost in the Rockies. Someone introduced me.

The sheriff, with a grip like a gorilla, shook hands and said, 'Howdy, partner.'

'Do you think you've a good chance of finding the boy?' I asked.

'Yep,' he drawled. 'If the bears don't first.' Everyone around nodded and muttered, 'bears'.

When the plane finally arrived it was a special, plushly furnished aircraft of the Presidential Flight. Most of the passengers were members of an army golf team returning from a tournament. They had a highstake poker school in progress, but I declined their offer of a game. Next to me sat an enlisted man, reading a comic.

'Do you play golf too?' I asked.

'No, I'm going home on special furlough,' he replied.

'Oh! compassionate leave,' I said.

'Yes, you might call it that,' he replied. 'Papa attacked Moma with an axe last night.'

'Really, how awful, I am sorry, is she badly hurt?' I asked.

'Yep, I guess so, he chopped her head clean off, darn it,' he said sadly.

At Washington the general's signals had done their stuff and I was taken on a conducted tour of the capital by night, before flying on to Macquire Air Base, near New Jersey. With luck I would arrive in Britain two days before the troop-ship left for Cyprus. I sent a telegram to my depot regiment and settled down to write my diary as the four-engined transport lifted off. We had only been airborne for twenty minutes when an engine caught fire. Back at the base I discovered that a plane was leaving for Paris that afternoon, which would be better than waiting another twenty-four hours whilst our aircraft was repaired. A helpful movements officer said that he would try to get me transferred and went off to see his supervisor. He returned with an uneasy expression. 'The major says you've to see him,' he said.

The major, a harassed man, looked as if he carried the troubles of the world in his briefcase as he flicked through my papers. 'The 13th Air Force can't issue orders for you to travel to England,' he said, his voice rising. The phone rang – he answered it – 'You're – ' he started but the phone rang again, and whilst he spoke the light on a silent red phone glowed.

Two aides bumped heads as they seized it. 'Yes, sir,' they said four times. It was obvious that war was about to break out so, apologizing for being a nuisance, I gathered up my documents and was backing out when the major screamed, 'Not so fast – I know what you are – you're a deserter – and those orders of yours are no good here.'

The movements officer looked embarrassed. 'It's been a busy day,' he said.

'Do I look like a deserter?' I asked him.

'Well, I couldn't say as I've never met an English deserter,' was his slightly unhelpful reply.

I felt very much like Alice in Wonderland. However, I guessed that the overworked staff officer would be off-duty the next day, if he had not suffered a coronary beforehand. I was still on the passenger list of the original plane and, keeping well out of sight, hopped aboard at the last minute.

Our only stop was Goose Bay in Labrador, where contrary to my expectations I was not arrested. It was bitterly cold and sleet was falling, and I felt rather foolish in my khaki shorts and shirt, so headed for the transit lounge. A fur-clad figure shuffled past with a trolley. He stopped suddenly, spun round, looked and said slowly, 'Gee, you must be British.'

When we got to Prestwick I found that by chance a USAF Dakota was going down to Burtonwood. As I climbed aboard the pilot said, 'This bird's got a sick engine. You'd better wear this,' handing me a parachute. We arrived safely, and the Yank couldn't understand my profuse thanks. There wasn't time to tell him how the USAF had devoted so much effort to getting a very junior officer 12,000 miles to catch a boat.

The band was playing on the quayside as I staggered up the gangplank with numerous items of hastily packed luggage. I waved goodbye to my parents, remembered to shout a brief word to my father about a parking summons that I would not be there to receive and bumped into several chums from Sandhurst days.

'Hello, Blashers – you look brown, where have you been?'

'Let's have a beer and I'll tell you.'

I was fortunate to join a Cyprus-based unit in September 1958. The 33rd Field Squadron was commanded by an energetic, unconventional major, who gave his subordinates a free rein with the minimum of supervision and the maximum support. Our regiment was in a tented camp on the foothills above Limassol. My troop consisted of fifty-four sappers, mostly National Servicemen with no great love of the Army, but they were a tough, spirited and hardworking gang who got into trouble continuously.

'Why did you throw the NAAFI juke-box at the manager?' I asked one of my sinners.

'Well, sir, I put a five-piastre piece in and nothing happened. "You've been done," my mate told me. At that moment up comes manager bloke, so I hands him juke-box to see if he can get me five piastres out.' The manager, allegedly struck by a flying 200-pound music machine, was in hospital with multiple injuries.

We usually supported one or more infantry battalions, and roared about in our own little fleet of trucks and armoured vehicles, armed to the teeth with a variety of weapons and explosives. Like all small units acting independently on active service, we had our fair share of adventure.

One dark night a patrol discovered a hole that had been cut in the rock surface of a mountain track. Obviously it was intended that a mine should be placed here later. It was decided to booby-trap the hole to give the EOKA bomber a rude shock and I was ordered to lay a suitable device. Accordingly, I fashioned a fiendish little bomb and placed it in position. Being aware that if it did not function someone would have to remove it, I marked the place with a strand of green plastic-coated wire, bound round a tree five paces away, and then made a detailed sketch map of the area.

Unfortunately, when the campaign ended some months later, I was ordered to dispose of it. It was after dark when we reached the area. With no need for secrecy, we drove up the moonlit track. Since my last visit, a great many trucks had used the road and the surface was hard-packed. To make matters worse, I could not see any sign of the green wire. Nevertheless, I found the area and my driver, Corporal Cutler, began to search with a mine-detector.

'Nothing,' he grunted. 'Not a thing, sir.'

'Not surprising,' I replied. 'There's very little metal in it anyway and we put it eighteen inches down.'

There was one slight depression that fitted my bearings and distances, so I ordered the vehicle to back off and, whilst Cutler held the torch, I probed the soil. It was solid rock, but suddenly my prodder penetrated something rather soft.

'I think we have it,' I murmured. 'Feels like the edge of the hole that the terrorist cut.'

Cutler's face was as usual expressionless. We had been through a number of anxious moments together and he never showed any emotion. I located a slab of rock, the size of a book. 'It's under here – and I remember this stone,' I remarked.

The wind rising from the Mediterranean sighed in the fir trees and I felt a shiver of excitement run down my spine as my fingernail touched something metallic. Must be the release switch, I thought. Now I've got to get hold of the tongues and hold them together whilst Cutler lifts the slab. Then he inserts a safety-pin and, hey presto, we are home and dry. But I couldn't get at the tongues, the soil around the bomb was packed solid. 'Not worth fooling with this,' I said. 'Let's blow it.'

A moment later the corporal returned holding one miserable stick of the almond-smelling explosive. 'That's all there is,' he said, handing it to me together with a detonator and a length of fuse.

'Oh! well, that should do,' I replied and tamped the charge carefully into the hole about the bomb. We sheltered round a bend in the track whilst the fuse burned. 2,000 feet beneath us the moonlit ocean glittered and the lights of the coastal towns twinkled amongst the olive groves.

The explosion was not very loud and, as soon as the debris had stopped falling, I walked forward. The stone slab had gone and there was no evidence of the bomb. Funny, I thought, expecting to find something and thrust my hand deep into the warm soil at the bottom of the crater. To my horror Cutler's torch revealed a hideous string of mechanism, fuse and explosive dangling from my hand. Our charge had failed and, as I watched, the release switch shifted a fraction. It was only held together by the glutinous soil and now the tongues were opening.

'Down!' I yelled, pitching the whole thing over the cliff.

A split second later the explosion shook us. 'You all right?' I said.

'Sir,' said Cutler.

'Have yer done then?' asked my batman, Rampling, as we reached the Land-Rover.

Rampling was one of the most amusing and yet courageous soldiers I ever met. A born comic from Preston, where his mother made confectionery, he was also the troop medical orderly. I reckoned that even if a chap were dying, Rampling would make him laugh.

A few days later I was on reconnaissance in the Troödos mountains. My party consisted of the Land-Rover, driven as usual by Corporal Cutler, and the Daimler armoured scout-car, driven by Sapper Oran, with Rampling as his crewman. We rounded a bend and saw a Royal Marines Commando vehicle parked on the verge. The driver was punching out the remains of a smashed windscreen and an officer was tying a dressing around a gash in his forehead.

'What's wrong?' I asked, pulling up.

'I wouldn't go through that village if I were you,' he said, indicating a cluster of red-roofed buildings nestling in the foothills beneath us.

'The road's barricaded with huge earthenware jars and when you try to move them they stone you to blazes from the roof-tops,' he explained.

'Did you open fire?' I asked.

'No, not a man in sight, usual trick, just women and children.'

To avoid the village would mean a detour of over sixty miles and I had another job to do that evening. Explaining the situation to my group I said, 'Oran, you lead the way in the armoured car. If the road is blocked, don't stop, just smash through. We'll be right behind you in the Land-Rover.'

'Good luck,' nodded the commando officer, as we sped off down the dusty road towards the village. We were still half a mile away when the chanting of 'Ee-oo-ka, Ee-oo-ka' reached our ears.

Cutler pulled on his goggles and I drew my revolver. Turkeys, dogs and chickens scattered as we roared into the narrow street, flanked by the vine-bedecked coffee shops. Not a soul in sight. At the narrowest point in the road, an unbroken line of earthenware jars formed a solid wall. 'Keep going,' I roared, as the brake lights on the armoured car flickered, but Oran needed no encouragement and, with a loud crunch, hit the jars. The Daimler disappeared momentarily in an explosion of pottery, olive oil and grain. The bits were still falling as we followed through the gap. From the roofs astonished faces peered down. We sped on and were still in the village when, to my consternation, Oran stopped. At once I realized why. We had taken the wrong turning and were now in a dead end. There was hardly room to turn round but, as I leaped out, Rampling was there directing the driver.

In record time we were facing outward. A huge crowd of villagers were moving slowly towards us. My stomach felt very queasy and I remembered the awful stories of similar incidents when troops had been caught by hostile crowds. There were four of us and at least a hundred of them. The crowd was silent, grim-faced, determined. Not a man in sight. Just dark-skinned women in the traditional black dress of the Cypriot peasant. The fact that we had just destroyed a large amount of their winter food stock did nothing to endear us to them. Their leader was a wrinkled old woman, carrying an axe in her bony hand. She knew she had us cornered and like a cat with a mouse was enjoying the scene. Even if we fired, we couldn't stop more than half a dozen before they seized us. My only other thought was to charge them with the vehicles. The consequences were too horrible to contemplate.

'You must disperse or we shall open fire,' I said in as stern and authoritative a voice as I could manage.

The old woman, standing twenty-five yards away, spat a long stream of filthy green phlegm in reply.

'Oki,' roared her comrades edging nearer.

'Here, will you hold this?' Rampling thrust his rifle into my hand.

'What on earth . . . ' I began to ask, but he was already ambling towards the crowd.

He reached the old crone and, looking forever like an English Bobby on duty at a football match, placed his hands on his hips and said loudly, 'You can't do that here, Mom.' The witch looked bewildered.

'Come on, I'll take ruddy axe,' said the lad from Preston and, grasping the razor-sharp weapon, turned to the crowd and waving them back said, 'Now I've got to get back to camp for tea, so if you'll just clear the road, we can all go home.' To my astonishment, they obeyed.

'Come on,' yelled Rampling and signalled us forward. 'Tata, sorry about the oil jars, but thou shouldn't park them on busy highway, you know,' he grinned, as he leapt aboard the armoured car.

We got almost fifty yards before the crowd recovered and ran screaming after us with sticks and stones. Thanks to the cool courage of this extraordinary soldier, we escaped.

Back in camp two hours later I called him over. 'You did well, Rampling, thank you very much,' I said.

'Ay, it was good laff, wasn't it?' He grinned and shuffled off to persuade the cooks to give him a late tea.

Years later, instructing at Sandhurst, I tried to impress on cadets how fortunate they were to lead men who would be untroubled by disaster, unflattered by success, who would face adversity and danger with the same cool courage, sparkling with a unique brand of ready wit.

As the winter set in I was ordered to support the 3rd Battalion, Grenadier Guards, who had been sent to quell the terrorist-infested Panhandle district. Thus on a wet evening we found ourselves harbouring in broken country. Our sections were quickly deployed to the rifle companies whilst I established my small headquarters near Battalion HQ. The first thing and, indeed, one of great import-ance, was to site the thunderbox.

'Where would you like it, sir?' asked my transport corporal.

'That spot by the trees looks well drained, nicely concealed and has a pleasant view,' I replied. So my fine oak portable lavatory was erected under a Karib tree so that, when enthroned at dawn, I could survey the mountains of Turkey forty miles distant.

The next day the corporal reported that the thunderbox must be moved as it was 'full up'.

'Full up,' I gasped, 'with only five of us here?'

''Fraid so, sir. It's them Guards sergeants using it.'

This was an insult of the highest order. An officer's thunderbox is a very private thing; although I allowed my own soldiers access to it, it was a gross insolence for outsiders to intrude. The proximity of the device to the Guards sergeants' mess was clearly too great a temptation. Regretfully I ordered it moved westward, some sixty paces.

Alas, next morning it was found to be 'full' again. This really was too much, and I was of a mind to report the matter when the corporal, a devious but ingenious man, suggested an alternative plan to dissuade trespassers.

'You may recall, sir, we captured some home-made explosive yesterday,' he smirked. 'Might I suggest that we place a minute quantity, with a simple booby-trap switch, beneath the toilet, to be operated by anyone seating himself thereon?'

The idea appealed. 'What about us?' I inquired.

'We shall leave a safety pin nearby. All engineers, before seating, must replace the pin,' he replied.

It was an hour after dark and I was on duty in the battalion operations room when I heard a dull 'boom' followed by a cry of 'Medical orderly, medical orderly'. When the padre relieved me, I asked what the medic had been called for.

'Oh! one of the sergeants sat on a stove; bit singed, I gather!' replied the vicar.

Back at our lines, I found my men grouped about the thunderbox, or the remains thereof. The hessian screen lay on the ground and the shattered timbers were scattered around. The black plastic seat was fifteen feet away and the roll of soft white paper trailed sadly across the field. The pungent smell of explosive was heavy in the night air.

'About 2100 hours, sir,' reported the corporal, 'Rampling and I perceived a light bobbing across the field. "Stand to, lads," I says, "here comes the enemy." We sees the light go behind the screen and a few second later there is a bloody big bang.' The wreckage told the rest. 'Then there's t'bloke rolling about in t'smoke,' said Rampling, in his strong Lancashire accent, continuing the tale. 'He can't get up quick like, cos 'is trousers is round 'is ankles and 'ee's lost 'is belt.'

'Was he badly hurt?' I enquired with concern.

'Well, 'ee was making bit of fuss like, but I think it were just shock,' replied Rampling.

It took all next day to rebuild the thunderbox but it was never the same. A week later, after a long cordon and search operation, most of the battalion regrouped at the main camp. My sections came in and, having arrived in the middle of the night, were not familiar with the layout. Unfortunately a sapper was discovered on the Grenadiers' commanding officer's thunderbox by the battalion adjutant, with whom I had already crossed swords on other matters. 'One of your wretched men is on the colonel's thunderbox,' he screamed. I was tired and considered that there were more important things to worry about at that moment. 'I'm sorry,' I grunted, but the adjutant continued to rave. 'For Pete's sake,' I retorted, 'I am always finding Guardsmen on my thunderbox and I have a way of dealing with them.'

For a moment I thought he would have a seizure. 'You, you, you have a way of dealing with a Guardsman?' he stammered.

'Yes,' said I, 'we blow them up.'

Then the colonel entered.

'Sir, Blashford-Snell has been blowing up Guardsmen,' blurted out the adjutant.

'Really?' said the CO, looking mildly interested.

I explained what had happened, hoping that I sounded more confident that I felt.

'Hmm,' muttered the senior officer, looking stern. 'Can't have that, can we?'

'Certainly not,' snapped my tormentor with obvious satisfaction.

Poking me with his walking stick the Colonel said slowly, 'Your punishment, young man, is that you must write the story for our regimental magazine.'

My next assignment was to help a gunner regiment sent out from Britain in the infantry role. Their commander was a great character and insisted that I run a course on terrorist weapons. This was designed to teach all ranks the techniques employed by EOKA, and one lesson was devoted to homemade bombs. We had with us a quantity of captured chlorate. The class, consisting of most of the officers and NCOs from regimental headquarters, had gathered around as I showed them how simple it was to mix the chemicals to produce an explosive.

The lesson was adjourned for lunch and, afterwards, we found that owing to the heat the chlorate had solidified from a fine white powder into a number of solid lumps. I needed powder to make up a small bomb. Without thought, I picked up a safety-match box and used this to pulverize the lumps. The phosphorous particles on the striker surface at once combined with the powerful oxidizing agent and I saw a thin wisp of smoke – just in time to hurl the entire box, containing about twenty pounds, behind me. With a great 'whoosh' and a brilliant yellow flame, it ignited. I sat down rather heavily, my NCOs scattered in all directions and the class dived for cover – all, that is, except the colonel.

'Get up, get up, you idiots,' he scolded. 'Don't you know every sapper demonstration begins with a bang? Come on, Blashers, stop fooling around, get on with it.'

My face was blackened, my eyebrows had disappeared and my trousers were full of small holes; however I attempted to smile and continued as if the whole thing had been intentional.

In 1959 EOKA surrendered and peace descended. Now was the time to create a friendly atmosphere. The Underwater Section which I now ran was sent to the ancient city of Paphos to seek evidence of an extensive port, thought to have sunk beneath the waves during an earthquake.

So it was that I stood with a group of soldiers in the Paphos museum, whilst the curator recounted the history of this famous area. The men shuffled, sniffed, coughed and scratched; archaeology was not a subject close to their hearts.

'So you see, each year many, many ships came from all over the Mediterranean bearing young maidens.' The men's eyebrows rose.

'He's on about skirt,' whispered a lad from Leeds, waking his pal with a nudge in the ribs.

'Ough!' grunted Sapper Robins, taking an instant interest in the lecture.

'The young women were unmarried,' explained the curator, 'it was necessary that they should be virgins.' Even Rampling was awake now. 'They left their ships at anchor in the port and walked up through a place we call the beautiful gardens, where they made offerings of terracotta figurines. At Kouklia there was a great temple, in the centre of which was a fifteen-foot phallus. This is a model of the original,' said the curator, tapping a four-foot black monolith. 'It is said that so many maidens came to be initiated that some had to wait here until the winter.'

'Bet there weren't no shortage for ordination in them days,' muttered Rampling.

Complete with a 100-ton flat-bottomed open-decked Royal Engineer Z craft, thirty-five soldiers, piles of diving equipment, plus an eager Army Public Relations Officer, the expedition arrived at Paphos. The introduction of a spot of ancient sex into the task was a splendid catalyst and the men set about their work with enthusiasm. Thus, for a few weeks during four summers, the army surveyed the seabed and brought up tons of pottery, marble, glass and metal.

One of our earlier finds was the wreckage off the Moulia Reef of a man of war, whose carronades lay scattered in shallow water. We had just raised the last of five large cannons and the wind was freshening as I took a last look round in case we had missed anything. Flipping along over the rocky bed, I came to a ravine and peered down. Something smooth, grey and round like a metallic cylinder lay across the sandy floor of the cleft. I turned round slowly. What on earth . . . ?, I thought and, jackknifing my body, I slid down into the crevice.

On the seabed I found myself staring into a low cave. The cleft was simply a large crack in the roof. The grey cylinder now looked about twelve inches in diameter and got thicker as it disappeared into the gloom. Grasping the rock, I pushed myself down and under the ledge. For a few moments all seemed black then, as my eyes grew accustomed to the dark, I perceived movement. A small cloud of sand billowed up. To my left the cylinder moved, or I should say twitched, and, at the same time, the floor of the cave slid forward several feet. Still puzzled I stared in and it was another few moments before I realized I was hovering between the roof and the back of a giant stingray. An arm's length in front, I could make out the gentle mound of its head, and behind me stretched the huge tail that had first attracted my attention. I guessed it was ten feet across.

Why did it stay so still? Perhaps it had been stunned by the explosions earlier that day? Hardly daring to breathe for fear that the rattle of my valve would disturb it, I inched backwards from the black hole. Before I reached the ravine it twitched again, but at last I was back in the light and speeding to the surface.

'What's that in the crack?' shouted Corporal Jones, who had been watching my descent.

Tearing out my mouthpiece, I yelled back, 'The monster of the Moulia Rocks – it's a bloody great ray.' Only a couple of evenings before, we had listened to the fisherman of Paphos telling us of a terrible creature that lived on this reef, destroying their nets and threatening boats.

'If you kill it,' they promised, 'we'll buy everyone a beer.'

'Prepare a five-pound charge,' I shouted. 'Tell Christos to come and see, we'll need him to give evidence if we're to get that beer!'

Christos, our Cypriot boatman, swam over and, donning a mask, kicked his way down to the monster's lair. He came back ashen and convinced. Five minutes later the sea erupted as the charge detonated.

'It is far too big to be killed by you,' laughed the fisherman, in spite of Christos's assurances. We never did get our beer.

In August 1960 I returned to England and married Judith, now home from Singapore. My new partner was an excellent swimmer and became the general manager of the underwater expeditions. Solving the mystery of Paphos became an obsession. We searched and searched and then, towards the end of one particularly gruelling day, I made a discovery that sent the adrenalin racing through my bloodstream and almost led to disaster as I was struggling to bring up a heavy, inscribed marble slab.

The needle on the pressure gauge was approaching the danger zone. After a few more deep breaths the air supply would stop abruptly and I knew the aqua-lung had no reserve. I cursed my stupid stubbornness for causing me to neglect a basic safety rule of diving that would now probably cost me my life.

Letting go of the slab, I fought to control my breathing and watched the precious artefact twirling down into the tangled seaweed. For ten minutes I had struggled, using up far too much air, to bring it up from its watery grave forty feet below. I had found it jammed between rocks near the infamous Moulia Reef and felt certain that the inscription would provide a valuable clue to the origin of the great port.

Above me the late afternoon sun glittered on the waves, and as I rose quickly to the surface still the air held out, although the needle was now right against the stop. I hardly dared to glance at the gauge. I had ditched my fourteen-pound weight belt on the seabed, so I tried to control the ascent with my breathing. 'Too fast, too fast,' I kept saying as I rose in the cloud of bubbles. I felt a twinge in my leg but, thankfully, I had not been down long enough to risk the dreaded bends.

As I surfaced, the valve went clunk, signifying the end of the precious supply. Tearing the mouthpiece out, I sucked in air and sea water. The sun was blinding and the strong wind blew the short waves into my face. Looking down, I noticed with interest that the seabed was sliding past. Two more mouthfuls of water left me feeling horribly sick and an awful rattling noise came from my chest. A red film was clouding my vision. Don't panic, think. I repeated my own advice, but I felt terribly tired and even thought was an effort. To get a good mouthful of air, I turned over on my back and, at the same time, tried to release the useless aqua-lung. One shoulder strap come off at once, but the other was stuck. Now I was drifting with the current straight towards the foaming outline of the reef. How ironic that the rocks, whose earlier victims I had been investigating, should claim me as well.

Suddenly the strap came undone and the tanks dropped away, leaving me free to swim with what strength I had left. Rolling over I noticed that the seabed was only twelve feet below. I still had a chance, and in the far distance the bridge of Z 11 was rising and falling in the swell. Any instinctive cry for help would have only wasted valuable energy, so I tried to swim, my leaden legs doing little against the current. The waves breaking on the jagged rocks were clearly audible. Each second their boom grew louder. Two hundred yards, I thought. Five minutes if I'm lucky. What a damned silly thing to do, leaving the other divers and going off alone after some antique tombstone. Again I tried to swim, but my legs refused to answer. 'Conserve your energy for the reef. There's still a chance of clinging onto a rock, if you can get through the outer breakers,' said optimism. 'Some hope! You've seen the dragon's teeth, they even slice you open if you touch them in calm conditions,' replied pessimism and realism together. 'You're a bit off course,' said another voice and I turned my head to see one of the expedition's boats about thirty yards away. Kneeling in the bows was the public relations officer, who had come out to cover the story. Drowning men are supposed to relive their past in the last few seconds, but I must confess that I had been too busy trying to survive.

However, the evidence of the existence of the port was found inconclusive and, before I had to return to Britain in December 1961, I decided to have one last thorough look to see if we could unravel the mystery. Operation Aphrodite II consisted of a task force of boats, vehicles, light aircraft and the faithful flagship, Z 11. Almost a hundred soldiers and civilians were involved. The Royal Navy made some preliminary soundings for us and the RAF flew special sorties with infra-red cameras. The people of this quiet corner of Cyprus were awe-struck by the incredible effort the British, who had now given them independence, were putting into solving some ancient legend. The press was also interested and the expedition needed a special public relations section to deal with the growing number of enquiries.

At last I was told someone was coming to help with the archaeology and, to the joy of our merry men, a delightful and very attractive lady arrived. Whether it was her charming personality or the undersized bikini I'm not sure, but productivity increased tenfold and the deck was soon piled high with ancient artefacts. A few days after the start of the venture, I realized that at least three of our members were vying with each other for her favours, which, in fairness, I must say she kept to herself. Even so, at the end of the first week, I had to rebuke two of my colleagues for quarrelling, and that evening asked her as discreetly as possible if she wouldn't mind wearing a one-piece costume. Giving me a delicious smile, she said in her husky voice, 'Well, John, which piece would you like me to wear?'

Although we never did solve the mystery of the lost harbour, we made one important discovery. Many of the older folk at Paphos had told me a tale of a great cannon believed to have disappeared in the sixteenth century. When the Turks had ruled Cyprus, they had a garrison in the square fort on the harbour wall. It was said that on top of the battlements they placed a huge cannon. Reportedly this piece was able to hurl a ball to any part of the town and thus the Greek Cypriots lived under constant threat. Eventually there was a revolution, the Greeks captured the castle and butchered the garrison. Like many before it, this revolt eventually failed but, when the Turks returned to Paphos, the great gun had gone. With customary ruthlessness, they took numerous prisoners and, in an effort to discover the whereabouts of the cannon, burned and tortured them to death, but the cannon was never found.

Everyone thought that the gun had simply been lowered over the battlements into the water and we had already made exhaustive searches of the seabed beneath the fort. We found a few cannon balls, but no gun. To throw a shot into the town, it must be a sizeable piece and would probably weigh several tons, not easily moved over land. If the cannon were not in the immediate area of the fort, the Greeks had probably dragged it away into the town, but then it was most likely that the Turkish inquisitors would have located it. Where on earth could it be hidden? Everyone in the port had his own theory. One thing was sure: the great gun had vanished without a trace. Perhaps it was all a myth.

Thus, when two police officers who claimed to know the where-abouts of this legendary gun arrived, I was pretty sceptical. However, it was a hot night, Greek music echoed from the bar and overhead the cloudless sky glittered with twinkling stars, and I was in a benign mood. They sat down, the barman brought ice-cold Keo and we toasted each other. After a long pause, one said slowly, 'You know about the great gun?' I nodded, passing him the dish of salted nuts. 'I have seen it,' said the other, looking very solemn.

'Where?' I enquired, still sceptical.

'It is near here, on the other side of the headland, very close to the shore,' he gestured. 'I can show you the place, sir.'

It was 1600 hours next afternoon with the worst heat of the day over when we boarded our tug and set out on yet another quest for the long-lost cannon. I was not very hopeful, but the sea on the Moulia Reef was too rough for diving and it seemed a useful way of keeping in training. Rounding the headland, we followed the constable's direc-tions to the sheltered beach. 'Getting pretty shallow,' cautioned the helmsman. Fifty yards ahead the waves rolled over a reef. 'We can't go in much closer,' I said over my shoulder to the policeman. 'Where do you reckon it is?'

'There, just beyond the rocks,' he said pointing at the line of black shadows. The tug rolled in the gentle swell.

'Drop anchor, we'll swim in.' With a splash, half a dozen divers jumped in and, fanning out in an extended line, began to flipper slowly towards the shore. For about ten minutes we searched. There was nothing but bare rock and sand. Suddenly Corporal Jones's excited voice rang out above the sound of waves. 'It's here, it's here,' he yelled, 'a damned great gun.' And there indeed it was. At first, all we could see was the breech sticking up about eight inches above the sand. It was lying in four feet of water and, within a few minutes, we had uncovered two feet of it. It was certainly big. It had been protected by the sand and the heavy black metal bore no growth or encrustations. I was surprised to see it was so plain and, seizing the boss, I pulled myself down for a closer examination. There were no inscriptions, but it was obviously an iron cannon – and so large that it was unlikely to be a ship's gun.

'What a monster,' said the excited public relations officer. 'How are you going to lift it?' That was the problem – it was buried at an angle of forty-five degrees. Landward and seaward were low reefs. It must weigh at least two tons and would need strong lifting tackle to move it. To get our landing craft above was out of the question.

Walking onto the beach and standing in the warm white sand, I looked around. Just inland rose the massive natural rock slabs in which were carved the 'Tombs of the Kings' and running down from them was a narrow pathway. This track was very old and made a relatively smooth route through the rock formations. Did the Greeks drag the gun down this, I wondered, and then somehow push or float it out to its grave? 'We'll blast a channel through the inshore reef, then we'll bring the recovery vehicle ashore from Z 11 and try to get it over the headland to this point. Next we'll run out the winch cable for divers to fix to the gun, then heave ho and it should be like pulling a tooth,' I explained to the team.

So at dawn next day, our divers laid the charges. The wind was up and a heavy swell made work difficult. Several sappers had to be treated for lacerations after being swept against the reef. On shore the massive Scammell recovery vehicle had already run out its heavy steel cables. Z 11 lay 200 yards out, providing communications and refreshments. By 0800 we were ready to fire the first demolition; the police cleared the area and the fuse was ignited. Suddenly, low overhead, came an Army Auster aircraft containing several senior officers who had flown down to witness the operation. It banked sharply over Z 11 and came straight over the beach. Frantically I waved it away as the spluttering fuse burned down. With a dull roar, the charges exploded, sending a column of spray straight upward at the Auster, which, none the worse for a drenching, flew straight on!

One more bang, then the cable was fixed and the winch took up the strain. The explosives had done the job and in a few minutes the onlookers could see the great black, iron cannon in the surf. Inch by inch it was dragged like a stricken whale to the beach. 'Can't find any sign of a carriage,' said Corporal Jones, emerging from the surf as I took a closer look at the gun. How many poor devils were torn apart or roasted alive to preserve this secret, I wondered. Eight feet long and weighing over two tons, our prize was carried in triumph to Paphos port. That night Cyprus Radio credited us with solving the mystery. I knew, however, that to leave the metal exposed to the air would ruin it in no time, so we lowered it into the harbour to await the construction of a special preservative bath.

Eight years later Judith and I went back and walked amongst the ruins on the headland. Some spectacular discoveries had been made since our expeditions and, to our amazement, we found that we had been camping only inches above a wonderful mosaic floor of a villa. But although Paphos had gained much in its knowledge of the past, the present political situation had greatly deteriorated. Now Turks and Greeks lived behind barricades, and the houses bore the signs of civil war. Takis, the museum curator, found us in the Crusader Castle overlooking the harbour. 'Welcome, welcome,' he said, embracing me. 'Have you seen your great gun? It is in a place of honour on the quay.'

We strolled into the little port and at once saw the cannon, mounted on a carriage in front of the local Cyprus Navy HQ. I raised my camera. A sentry rushed over. 'It is forbidden to photograph military weapons,' he explained politely.

'Things have changed,' apologized Takis.

Elsewhere in Cyprus we had made other discoveries, but, of course, there was the military side to the diving that usually meant hard work under difficult conditions. One morning the military port office rang. 'John, we're in trouble,' said the commandant. 'Some idiot has run our mobile crane into the harbour. It's effectively blocking the slip and we've no crane big enough to lift it.'

It seemed the only way to move it was to pass a cable beneath and then partly sink Z craft on either side, fasten the cable to them and refloat the craft. The only snag was that the machine was lying in liquid mud. Securing the crane's jib to the dockside, Sapper Ellis and I slid into the chilly water. I used a hose-pipe to 'tunnel' through the mud. Ellis handled the steel-wire cable which we were to pass beneath the mobile crane. The mud closed about us as we felt our way through the tangled mass of struts and cables. It was pitch black.

Communicating by hand signal we descended slowly and I hosed away the solid lumps. I guessed we were right beneath the crane when I felt a slight increase in pressure on my ears. I could not see my depth gauge, but I realized at once what was happening. The machine was sinking deeper into the mud, pushing us down with it. I held my breath. The clatter of Ellis's valve stopped also. The slow, relentless movement of the steel-work was obvious. Only our efforts beforehand had masked it. We had to get out of this death-trap with all speed. I tried to go forward, but came upon an impenetrable barrier that was probably a wheel. I could either go down and try and come up beyond it or retreat the way we had come. At least I knew the way back was clear. The mud was getting thicker and movement against it was an effort. I touched Ellis and gave the signal for 'going back and up'. He seemed to understand. I remembered that I was still clutching the hose, and it was now vital for survival. Suddenly the crane gave a jerk which frightened me stiff. I must move faster, I thought, so I slid one shoulder under the hose and passed the nozzle down towards my feet. Then, gripping it between my knees and hands, I began to tunnel backwards, following my lifeline. Something tightened around my thigh. It felt like a small octopus but I couldn't move against it and as I struggled it tightened. I felt it, coarse and rough. It was simply a loop of rope into which I had stuck my foot. Laboriously I went forward, freed my leg and started back again.

It seemed like minutes, but was probably only a few seconds before I found my nylon lifeline rising. Feeling above me all the way, I began to ascend. Once I hit a loose cable and a surge of panic returned. Was I still under the crane? The water was jet-black and I saw nothing until I surfaced. As the mud drained from my facemask, Ellis came into view beside me. 'Bloody hell' was all he said.

'Sorry about that,' shouted the port officer. 'One of the strops slipped on the jib, but you'd have been all right – we had another one anyway.'

'Thanks for telling me,' I murmured into my mouthpiece.

We got the cable under at the second attempt and I went home. Judith was waiting. 'Come on,' she smiled. 'Don't look so fed up – let's go underwater fishing this afternoon.'

*

Our Mediterranean diving activities also extended to examining the ancient harbours of Apollonia and Leptis Magna in Libya. However, it was not the African shoreline that attracted me, but the desert. The desolate, magnificent Sahara had not changed in 4,000 years. The population was still largely coastal or at the few oases. The maps bore the tempting words 'relief data incomplete'.

Libya stretched over 500 miles deep into this wilderness. All one needed was time, a few Land-Rovers and fuel to be able to explore areas where few, if any men, had trodden before. We quickly learned to navigate by sun compass, de-bog vehicles with pierced metal planks called sand channels and mend every possible break-down. Our forays into the dun-brown wasteland were enlivened with visits to oil-rigs, where rare and glorious hot baths, ice-cold beer and inch-thick steaks were available. The oil men had not yet penetrated far into the desert, but they always seemed glad to see us at their lonely, but well-stocked camps.

Near the coast where our predecessors, the Desert Rats, had fought desperate, but finally victorious battles against the Afrika Korps, one moved with caution. Much of our work here was clearing mines that remained in abundance.

It was late one afternoon and we hadn't seen a mine for miles. I was impatient to get back for a swim in the warm sea, so, instead of walking slowly ahead of my Land-Rover, eyes peeled for evidence of a deadly device, I'd decided to sit on the bonnet as we drove slowly. 'If I shout, stop immediately,' I told my sapper driver. We had been going for almost an hour when a movement right in front of the offside wheel caught my eye. 'Stop,' I yelled and shot off as the brakes slammed on.

The baby tortoise tucked his head in his shell as I reached for him. It was then I spotted something else. He was on top of a set of three rusty prongs. 'Back off very slowly and keep in your own wheel tracks,' I ordered the mystified driver, my heart pounding. Once the Land-Rover was away I pocketed my little friend and gently cleared the sand from around the German S mine. Slipping a safety pin into the igniter, I checked for booby traps and lifted the heavy pot. It was in perfect condition.

'Cor, what's that?' asked my soldier.

'Anti-personnel Jumping mine,' I replied. 'Step on it and it bounces up six feet, explodes and showers ball-bearings for a hundred yards.'

'Charming,' he muttered, but it had been a close call. Back in Cyprus, I planted a special spinach patch for my tiny friend who was christened 'Churchill'.

In 1961, on an expedition deep in the Sahara, we had been held up awaiting spares for a broken-down truck. At last they arrived and we headed home. 'Do you mind if I go on ahead?' I asked the expedition leader.

'No, by all means,' said Bob in his usual cheerful tone.

'I'll keep to the main track and come up on the radio schedules as usual,' I assured him. So saying, I set off in my well-laden Land-Rover with Sapper Smart at the wheel and Corporal Smith as navigator. We made good time and by noon had cleared one hundred and thirty miles. Hissss went our nearside front tyre. Smart swore.

I unbuckled the spare tyre, then ran it towards the punctured wheel. The driver was standing silent and grim. 'Well,' I said, 'let's get on with it.'

He looked very dejected as he uttered the awful words, 'I lent my box spanner to Higgins last night.'

It took several seconds for the full meaning of this statement to become clear. The desert Land-Rovers were fitted with a special hub to which a rope could be attached and provide the vehicle with a simple capstan. However, with these on, it required a long box spanner to undo the wheel nuts. 'There must be another way,' I protested. We turned out our kit, but there was no way to unscrew even one nut. We were stranded.

'Four gallons left,' said the corporal and I knew he was talking about water.

'Plus the water bottles,' I added.

Silently and trying to avoid unnecessary activity, we laid out the fluorescent air identification panels in the form of the emergency signal, prepared flares, made a shelter along the side of the Land-Rover and crawled beneath. Our radio was not working well and therefore it was no surprise when we failed to make contact by dusk. After the day's scorching heat, the blissful cool of the night was a welcome relief.

When the first flush of panic passed, I had wanted to call Smart every name under the sun. However, eight hours later my anger had subsided and I concentrated on trying to evolve a plan that would save us. We had broken down on the edge of the mile-wide track and it was quite possible that the convoy would find us. But they only had to be 500 yards eastward and they would pass behind a low ridge, missing us completely.

That night, lying in the depression I had dug in the sand, I awoke to hear a rattling metallic noise nearby. There was no wind, yet when my eyes opened to peer out across the moon-lit desert, I could see nothing. That's strange, I thought, and there it was again. I instinctively drew my Walther pistol from my bedroll. As I scanned the desert, from behind a low hillock, one of our discarded tin cans rolled into view. It was rolling over and over as if propelled by a strong wind, but the night was still. As I pondered this, the can suddenly stopped and then rolled back the way it had come. I'm going mad, I thought. Then it changed direction and came towards me. My God, a haunted tin can, probably something they put in the rations.

The shining object was only ten feet away now, rolling this way and that, when I raised my pistol. The sharp crack rang out in the still air, the bullet threw up a spurt of sand a couple of inches from the can, which instantly accelerated away. I fired again. The can stopped rolling and, to my amazement, a desert rat hopped out – clearly annoyed at having his feast disturbed.

At daylight, I rose stiffly to find the radio still silent and, although I went through all the drills a dozen times, I could get nothing; altering the setting of the aerial didn't help either. However, just in case others could hear us, I sent an SOS signal giving our position. The sun was up when I gave up fiddling with the knobs.

'What shall we have for breakfast?' asked Smith.

'I don't mind,' I replied, 'but let's have it quickly before the heat hits us.'

Lying under the shelter I made a mental check of our emergency actions. Flares ready, ears alert for noise of aircraft or vehicles, air-identification panels out. Remaining water, now down to two-and-a-half gallons, carefully stowed in the shade. All other sources of liquid checked, we lay in silence, the beads of sweat growing on our filthy skin and turning into rivulets, which ran into the sand. God, how we smelt. On the move we had not noticed it, but now it was becoming unpleasant to be near anyone else. Somehow one's own odour was bearable, almost fascinating, but anyone else's was disgusting. Sleep was impossible, so I tried to read, but a voice in my head kept saying 'There must be a way out'. Rather like shipwrecked sailors on a raft, I mused. It's the waiting that is the worst.

At noon the sun was right overhead, and to reassure ourselves we took a fix with the bubble sextant. It simply confirmed that we were about 120 miles south of the coast. The nearest water was seventy-five miles away. We discussed walking out, but realized this was hopeless. Stay with your vehicle, was the great cry.

Smart was looking very sorry for himself. After all, it was his fault we were in this predicament. But then I had asked if we could go on ahead and alone. Corporal Smith was truly without any blame and looked the most cheerful of us all. We delayed lunch until mid-afternoon to avoid working in the full heat. 'These boiled sweets certainly help to lessen the thirst,' I remarked. Smart passed me another, and I began to remove the paper. We all heard it together, like a distant rumble of thunder.

'Three-tonners,' yelled Smart. 'It's the convoy, I knew they'd find us.' Our flares streaked upward, but I still couldn't see the trucks, whose noise was quite clear. Oh God! They must be just the other side of the ridge. The Corporal was already tearing towards it, when I heard another engine and, spinning round, saw a Land-Rover bearing down on us.

The goggle-clad face grinned. 'Having a spot of bother?' our rescuers enquired.

We had all learned a lesson.

THREE

Adventurous Training

O N 28 MAY 1962 a terrible tragedy occurred in the former German Army storage tunnels in Jersey. Two teenagers from my old school were killed by a concentration of poisonous gas, reported as a mixture of cyanide and methane, set off by decomposition in the damp tunnel.

Eventually it transpired that the boys had been overcome by carbon monoxide produced by the smouldering remains of some old pit props set afire underground by youngsters who had visited the passages the previous day. The victims died as they struggled to reach the open air through a narrow passage dug beneath the concrete plug that had sealed the tunnel. Would-be rescuers were struck down by mysterious vapours wafting from the entrance. Rumours of wartime cyanide gas were soon circulating, holidaymakers cancelled bookings and hoteliers screamed for action.

The local government – The States of Jersey – quickly called upon the Ministry of Defence to investigate. There were few Jerseymen in the Royal Engineers and thus I found my time at the Junior Leaders Regiment interrupted by this unusual and exciting job. Our task was to examine all the old German underground works on the island and, equipped with the original maps, my small team sailed from Weymouth on a ferry loaded with apprehensive tourists.

As we had expected, the German map had been drawn with Teutonic thoroughness and, guided by my pal, Tony Titterington, with whom, as a boy, I had spent hours exploring some of these very tunnels, we set to work. The mysterious shafts were rumoured to contain everything from Nazi treasure to Luger pistols.

Several tunnels were as large as a London tube station and, lined with ferro-concrete, looked very similar. However, others had bare granite walls, dripping with water and often blocked by roof falls.

There were stories of Russian prisoners being cemented into the walls when they died at work. There was no doubt that the piles of jagged rock that we found hindering our exploration had almost certainly entombed workers and soldiers alike. However, many of the tunnels had been completed and were now filled with untidy heaps of military hardwear – helmets, anti-tank guns, bazookas, machine guns – everything lay scattered by the hands of generations of small boys seeking souvenirs. There were more lethal items – the occasional shell and drums of flame-thrower fluid. Working our way forward over the debris, we surveyed, checked roofs, examined equipment and searched for any unknown passages that might conceal especially dangerous items.

'I feel just like a bloody mole,' said my cockney sergeant, stripping off his emergency oxygen breathing-apparatus, miner's helmet and lamp after six hours underground. 'Funny smell in the place ain't there, sir?'

'Yes,' I admitted, pulling a crumpled packet of filter tips from my pocket.

'I'm not sure what it is – it smells familiar, but I can't place it.'

'Well, it didn't show up on the test papers,' said Tony, who'd joined us.

One of the soldiers had found something. 'Do you think it's this stuff that's smelling?' he asked, handing me a grey rocklike lump. One sniff confirmed that it was. 'There's barrels and barrels of it in one of the side tunnels,' he remarked.

We passed the lumps around and eventually tossed one away. It landed with a soft plop in a pool of rainwater. To our amazement, the puddle began to bubble and boil, giving off a pungent vapour – I flicked my lighted match at it. 'Pop' went the gas, igniting with a bright orange flash. 'My God!' said the sergeant, still holding a lump. It was calcium carbide and the tunnel was full of highly inflammable acetylene gas. We stubbed out our fags and moved away from the entrance rather speedily. The Germans had obviously used this for emergency lighting and, in case any other little nasties turned up, I decided to get some expert local advice.

A number of Jersey quarrymen had been forced to work for the Germans. Virtually enslaved, they were given a little potato soup and black bread at dawn each day, then marched under armed guard into the growing labyrinths. Together with prisoners of war, and anyone else the Hun could press into service, they laboured in the darkness with pick and shovel until well after dusk. Many who had survived the ordeal were now dead, but those who still lived would never forget the years in this underground hell, the terror of the roof falls, the screams of the injured and the endless passages down which they shuffled, half starved and cold, knowing that, if they as much as paused, a jackboot would come crashing out of the darkness to drive them on.

'You know, you could smell a German and you learned to step out when you passed him,' said my visitor. Charlie was a small quarry-man who had spent two years there. He and several friends had come to advise us on a particularly difficult tunnel, where a massive rock fall had blocked progress. Scrambling together over the fallen granite and rotting pit props, we reached a dead end. 'Reckon they gave up here,' grunted my guide. 'I can't say exactly what happened 'cos I was working in the main passage when this lot came in – but I'll never forget the rumble when she went – then the dust and the yelling.' The pale yellow beam of my lamp lit the lined faces of the grim-looking men.

The next day, I was already in the tunnel when the two quarrymen – Charlie and his mate – groped their way towards me. 'I've found an air-shaft that we may be able to squeeze through and get behind the rock fall,' I told them. With much grunting, we heaved ourselves forward on our stomachs inch by inch through the narrow passage. Not the place to suffer from claustrophobia, I thought, moving aside a fallen pit prop and worming my way into the shattered passage behind the rock fall. The wood, sodden and rotten, broke away in my hand and I cast a furtive glance at the unsupported roof. The tunnel was littered with debris; a bottle, a broken spade, a rusty drilling rod, then our lamps shone down the passage and we saw another rock fall. Tree roots hung from the roof like giant fingers.

'Must be pretty near the surface,' said Charlie and I nodded, looking round. The other quarryman stood watching with us and said nothing, but nodded in agreement. He was slightly shorter than Charlie and I guessed a little older, but I was hardly in the mood for conversation and we only exchanged a few words.

Having inspected the chamber into which we'd crawled, I said, 'Well, that's it – let's get out of here.' So we wriggled back through the ventilation shaft into the main tunnel and I led the way to the entrance. Just as the welcome blast of fresh air hit us, I remembered my maps that I'd put down before entering the narrow passage.

'Blast!' I swore. 'Go on, Charlie – I'll just nip back for my millboard.' A few minutes later, when I emerged, the soldier whose job it was to check everyone in and out ticked me off on his list.

'Everyone out then?' I asked.

'Yes, sir,' he replied, swinging back the metal grid over the entrance.

'Oh! Which way did Charlie and his mate go?' I asked, thinking I should buy them a beer.

'He's gone off on his bike,' said the sentry, 'but I didn't see no mate.'

'You must have,' I remarked tetchily. 'You know, the chap who came in with him.'

'Charlie went in alone, sir, and no other civilians have been in this afternoon.' The hair stood up on the back of my neck. Yet I knew there'd been a second man. Hell, I'd spoken to him!

'Are you sure?' I questioned.

'Quite sure, sir,' replied the soldier pushing his notebook towards me to emphasize the point.

Five minutes later I found Charlie in the pub. 'Where are your chums today, Charlie?' I said, trying not to seem concerned.

'Couldn't get away from work,' he muttered, wiping the frothy beer from his cracked lips. 'Like a drink?'

'Yes,' I said, 'I would very much.' I had several!

Back at the Regiment trying to train young sappers in the face of an ever tightening defence budget was a frustrating business but it did bring me into contact with the Outward Bound Organization when I spent some time as a temporary instructor at their Ullswater School.

Thus it was in the bitter winter that I trudged around the Lake District, trying to prevent twelve young boys from smoking, talking after lights-out and reading pornographic literature. The only way to do this was to work the little blighters so hard that they practically fell asleep on their feet. As part of the process there was a rather insane tradition at the school that demanded you rose before dawn, stripped naked, ran through the woods onto a jetty to plunge into the freezing lake. There was a limit to everybody's patience, I explained to the warden. I would be lashed helpless into a mountain-rescue stretcher and dangled upside down over a thousand foot drop. I would survive without cigarettes or whisky for ten days. I would collect moss and lichen on the nature trails and even press flowers in books, but I quite categorically refused to be seen belting down a woodland path starkers, pursuing a dozen naked little boys.

The warden thought me unreasonable, but I stood my ground. I agreed that if it would satisfy him, I would enter the water in military uniform and with dignity! So, next day, I waited whilst long lines of youngsters, hell bent on improving their characters, dashed screaming into Lake Ullswater. Then, at a regulation quick march, dressed in full combat kit and fortified with four swigs of illicit cherry brandy, I marched off the jetty. I felt I had registered my protest and won my point.

It was something that the warden wrote about me that caught the eye of a well-known sapper, Colonel (later Major General) John Cowtan. He was then the senior Royal Engineer at Sandhurst, and in 1963 I was invited to return to my former haunts as an instructor – poacher turned gamekeeper! The Army had started a new scheme, and on arrival I was appointed as an Adventure Training Officer. The Commandant, then Major General John Mogg, explained my task. 'Your job is to get as many as possible of these young men overseas for the benefit of their character and the least possible detriment to the Empire.'

'Yes, sir,' I said and went away to try to find an office.

The helpful College Sergeant Major provided me with the old bootroom, and placed a world map on the wall sticking the title TRAINING AREA above it. By 1400 hours he'd produced tables, 'six-foot, with blanket army grey' to cover it and a chair 'folding flat'. When I explained that my visitors might be invited to sit down, a second chair arrived. By tea I had cabinets, 'filing, grey, one', and I enquired about a telephone. For the first time the Sergeant Major looked worried, but eventually produced a field telephone with handle which I turned to attract his attention in an office seventy-five yards away. I would give the number required and he would hold the field telephone to his GPO device. I planned global expeditions thus for several weeks until my own phone arrived.

In the summer of 1963 I went along to help fellow sapper, David Hall, who was leading an expedition of cadets in the far south of the Libyan desert. Historically, this is a fascinating area, for it was here that a famous British Army Unit, the Long Range Desert Group (LRDG), had fought a magnificent hit-and-run campaign against the

Italians during World War II. Our task involved important mapping and scientific work directed by David, who was already a legendary figure in desert exploration. He was happy to leave me to handle the administration.

On one re-supply run from our remote base to the oasis of Kufra, I had a strange experience. There were three of us in my Land-Rover when we set out before the glowing orb of the sun rose to destroy the glorious cool of dawn. How I loved that blissful couple of hours! Quite why we went with only one vehicle I cannot recall, but it was an easy run on what was by now a well-trodden trail, and we had a radio. We made good progress and in the afternoon were bowling along at about seventy m.p.h. on the flat, hard sand. The cars were always piled high with kit, and panniers of wire-mesh hung out of both sides. In these we carried our rations, sleeping-bags and personal belongings. The back of the Land-Rover was fitted with a dozen tightly-packed jerry cans of petrol. Water, not petrol, would be carried in the jerry cans at the front – in case of a collision. Smoking in or near vehicles was strictly forbidden for obvious reasons. The good old army-issue boiled sweets were great thirst-quenchers and John, my navigator, turned to get some from a pannier.

'Fire!' John had screamed the dreaded word. If you stop a moving vehicle that is on fire suddenly, the flames may come back and – woomph! – that's the end, but by keeping going, one might just keep the fire away from any fuel cans. 'In the pannier – the bedding's alight!' he yelled.

The wind, such as it was, was blowing from behind so I pulled the wheel over to the left to keep the flames from the cans and we halted gently enough to avoid spilling any fuel. Hurling survival gear away from the car, we leapt out, tearing at the burning bedding. The other crewman had already dragged to safety a can of precious water in case the vehicle blew up with all our supplies. Using the pathetic little fire extinguisher and some hastily-dug sand, we smothered the fire. A hard bump had bent our exhaust pipe upwards, pointing at the bottom of the pannier. Fortunately the only loss was a sleeping-bag, but it had not been a pleasant experience. We stopped shaking, repacked, had a few good gulps of water and drove on in silence.

I'd wanted to make Kufra by dark, but now we hadn't a hope. At dusk we reached some low rocky hills, really just big piles of jumbled broken stones with numerous narrow passes running through them. The map wasn't very precise so I chose one at random, which turned out to be a little west of the usual route. The sand was soft, and in the failing light we bogged down several times. Heaving the sand channels back aboard for the third time I said, 'We should be able to get some shelter amongst these rocks,' and my weary crew readily agreed that it was none too soon to call it a day. None of us felt like cooking, so we munched a few hard-tack biscuits smothered in raspberry jam and washed them down with a mug of coffee. The night was clear and before turning in I went to commune with nature.

Squatting beneath the stars I swore I heard the sound of a voice. The first time, I looked back towards the dull outline of the Land-Rover. The second, thinking one of the crew had called, I said loudly, 'Just a minute.' Back at the car, I asked, 'What's the matter?'

John was already asleep, his colleague looked up and said, 'Nothing, why?'

'Didn't you call?'

'No,' he replied.

'Funny,' I yawned, 'must have been the wind.'

I woke just after dawn, with a shiver and a bursting bladder. Standing up, I shook off the sand, rubbed my eyes and stretched stiff limbs in the half-light. I was only partly awake when I saw something odd. About sixty yards away was a truck, or rather the remains of one, and all around it were scattered bits of equipment, dark against the white surface. I walked over to the Chevrolet, for even at this distance I recognized the familiar shape of the LRDG raiding vehicle. The debris consisted of cartridges, grenades, mortar bombs, broken rifles and parts of a machine gun. Thirty feet to one side by a low mound lay a small wooden cross and pieces of splintered wood that had probably been another. Similar vehicles were 'parked' along the rock walls of the pass. Some had engines missing, all appeared to have been blasted apart by a single explosion in the back. A self-destruction charge, I guessed.

Combing the area, we made an interesting discovery high amongst the rocks; a faded canvas British Army haversack, containing a rusty Kodak camera and a toothbrush. Nearby were scattered a pile of empty .303 cartridge cases. I now believe it was here that the LRDG's T Patrol was destroyed by its Italian opposite number, the Auto-Saharan Company based at Kufra. According to W. B. Kennedy Shaw in his book *Long Range Desert Group* (HarperCollins), a running fight developed on 31 January 1941, when the Italians, with a heavily armed motorized patrol and three aircraft, caught T Patrol advancing on Kufra, in the valley of the Gebel Sherif. Following the battle a New Zealander, Trooper R. J. Moore, and three colleagues had remained undetected amongst the rocks of the waterless hills. Almost everything they needed for survival had been destroyed. They were wounded and all the wells within 200 miles were either in enemy hands or filled with stones. The situation seemed hopeless. However, they managed to salvage a two-gallon tin of water and, scorning any idea of walking a mere eighty miles north-east to surrender at Kufra, they buried the dead, then turned and marched south towards their allies. The Free French Army's positions were known to be several hundred miles away across almost waterless desert. Their remarkable and heroic escape, over an astonishing distance, was typical of the soldiers of one of the finest special forces ever raised. Three survived and their leader, Trooper Moore, was found by the French walking steadily after ten days, having marched 210 miles. He was awarded the DCM for his leadership and courage.

We tidied up the grave, re-erected the crosses, saluted, stood silent for a moment and drove off towards Kufra. I reported the matter in Benghazi and later heard that the Imperial War Graves Commission had visited the site. But I never discovered the origin of the strange voice.

Since childhood my godparents, Lord and Lady Forester, had encouraged my adventurous spirit with tales of big-game hunting and excitement in distant lands. Cecil Forester had commanded the Royal Horse Guards. When I asked him the origin of the German Maxim gun, mounted at Willey Hall, he always smiled and just said 'Something my regiment picked up in the Great War.' After his death I learned he had captured it single-handed. He had lived a wonderful life in the days of the Empire, hitch-hiking from Cape to Cairo, exploring the Congo and, above all, devoting himself to the service of others. He was much respected in Shropshire where he helped many and pursued his hobbies as a naturalist and sportsman. He lived out his final years in the other land he loved – Africa – and finally died peacefully in Rhodesia in 1977. The patience and understanding this kindly man showed me as a small scruffy schoolboy were to be a lasting inspiration.

During World War II the Foresters had been hospitable to His Imperial Majesty, Haile Selassie, Emperor of Ethiopia, during his exile in Britain. The Emperor never forgot this kindness and thus a door was opened that changed my life. When my godfather wrote requesting his support for a Sandhurst expedition, there followed four highly adventurous visits to this little-known land of mountains, bush and desert.

Meanwhile I continued with my other duties at Sandhurst. Cadets were first given theoretical tactics training in the model rooms, where toy tanks and symbolized units could be moved about with little chance of making some costly and irrevocable error. It was here that I was the unwitting perpetrator of a near disaster. The chief instructor was to lecture on the nuclear battle and asked if I could make a miniature atomic bomb that could be exploded on the model.

'Certainly,' I replied, 'a small charge of powder fired electrically should do the trick.' So, pouring the contents of army fireworks known as thunderflashes into a flowerpot, I disguised it with a paper house and connected it by cable to a switch on the lectern. I explained the firing procedure to the delighted chief instructor, who felt sure it would impress several visiting officers. I wedged a round tin lid firmly in the top of the flowerpot in case anyone should knock it over before it was required, and I instructed the clerk to remove this obstruction before the lecture. Unhappily he was taken ill.

When some seventy officers and cadets had seated themselves on the tiers of chairs overlooking the cloth model, the chief instructor began. 'Before you, gentlemen, you see the 1st Battalion, the Loamshires, and their vehicles,' he stated, indicating a cluster of Dinky toy tanks and plastic symbols. 'They are holding this ridge,' he continued, his pointer stabbing at a sausage-shaped bump, where the hessian had been raised with balls of newspaper. 'The enemy, the Fantasian Army, are here,' he said, dumping a pile of ominous-looking red tanks at the edge of the model. 'They may use nuclear weapons at any moment.'

Allowing the full impact of his words to sink in, he paused before pressing the firing button. The effect was devastating. With a blinding flash and a deafening bang, the innocuous looking 'village' in the centre of the battlefield exploded. Cadets were struck by toy tanks and plastic soldiers. Shrapnel from the flowerpot peppered the audience and the colonel seated in the front row had the fluff scorched off his battledress trousers by the resultant fireball, which also singed the black labrador curled up at his feet. A mushroom cloud of white smoke rose quickly to the ceiling, then, like atomic fall-out, descended, choking the shell-shocked spectators. Coughing and spluttering cadets hurled open windows, the dog fled and the stand-in model room clerk, a civilian of timid appearance but with unquestionable initiative, seized a stirrup pump and extinguished the burning hessian. It was ten minutes before the smoke cleared sufficiently to allow the lecture to continue. There can be no doubt that the demonstration was a success, but I was not asked to repeat the performance.

Sandhurst encompassed every conceivable type of activity. One of my responsibilities was the pistol club, where I was able to teach aspiring marksmen. An aspect of the training was the combat course, which was designed to enable cadets to engage fleeting targets under battle conditions. It was extremely realistic and one of the noted shots was a young man called David Bromhead, whose acute accuracy was to be useful on many occasions.

Preparations for the 1964 Ethiopian expedition were progressing well. Cadets were trained to catch and preserve various scientific specimens. Under the direction of Natural History Museum staff we pursued adders and grass-snakes over Army training areas and caught small rodents in box traps. One over-enthusiastic cadet, trying to anaesthetize a shrew held by a colleague, drove the hypodermic needle clean through the animal and paralysed his friend's arm for several hours.

In early August we set out. One party which included a number of overseas cadets went ahead on the first available RAF aircraft. It flew to Aden in South Yemen, leaving the rest of us to follow a week later. In spite of the impending arrival of Emma Jane, Judith was determined to come with me. The Aden Brigade commander offered to find useful employment for the early arrivals and despatched them up country to see some action.

At one small fort a group of dissidents opened fire from the hills. As the garrison took posts, bullets pinged and ricochetted amongst the stone sangars. The range was at least 1,000 yards and no one could see the enemy. Suddenly the machine-gun on the watch-tower opened up with uncanny accuracy, flushing the tribesmen from their position and sending them scampering away amongst the rocks.

'Jolly fine shooting,' commended the commanding officer, who happened to be visiting. 'Who's on the gun?'

'A Sandhurst cadet,' replied the company commander.

'Must congratulate him,' said the colonel, climbing the tower.

Reaching the platform where the cadet lay behind the machine-gun, he said, 'Glad to see they're teaching you to shoot so well at Sandhurst.'

'Thank you, sir,' murmured the cadet turning about, his ebony face and flashing teeth set in a broad grin.

Slightly taken aback, the CO asked, 'Which regiment are you joining?'

'Oh,' smiled the young man. 'I'm not in the British Army.'

Arriving in Aden a few days later, I was greeted by an impressive array of rather worried staff officers, who hastened to explain the terrible oversight that had caused them to employ a member of another army in the cause of what local propaganda would call 'British Imperialism'. I promised to talk to the cadet.

'Oh! I enjoyed it,' smiled the African when I explained the problem, 'but our President will never know!' then added rather wistfully, 'I suppose I can't get the campaign medal now?'

In Addis Ababa I found my godfather's letter had paved the way and we were invited to the royal palace. His Imperial Majesty stood erect behind his desk. One by one we entered and shook his out-stretched hand, murmuring 'Votre Majesté', and giving a short, formal bow. There was something very powerful about the tiny figure, who could only have been just over five feet high. His alert, brown eyes seemed to penetrate my innermost thought. Not a man to be misled, I felt. Closely-cropped wavy hair led down to a grey moustache and a short, neat beard. His skin, a light brown, was paler than many of his countrymen. Described as the mouse with the jaws of a lion, his gentle, kindly appearance did not deceive me. I knew I was standing before one of the most supreme Christian warrior kings the world had ever known.

'How is your godfather?' The soft voice and perfect English took me by surprise.

'Very well, Your Majesty, and he sends you his good wishes,' I spluttered.

'He has a beautiful house in Shropshire. Are the rhododendrons in flower?' mused the Emperor. I was amazed how much he remem-bered of his stay at Willey Park. 'What do you wish of me?' he enquired, becoming more formal and addressing us through his interpreter.

'Permission to collect scientific specimens in your country, Your Majesty,' I replied.

His answer in Amharic was made without waiting for the interpreter to translate. 'His Imperial Majesty says it shall be so and he will send with you a liaison officer from his army.'

We bowed out of his presence. Outside one of the cadets muttered, 'Well, he's the nearest thing I've ever seen to a deity.'

Captain Marcos Berhanu Haile sat silently beside me in the early morning as we bumped over the waterfilled potholes on our way south. Leaving the city behind, we came to open country. Marcos slipped a shining revolver from beneath his great-coat and held it in his lap.

'Expecting trouble?' I asked.

'In this country I always expect trouble,' he replied ominously, but by evening we had seen nothing worse than several bad traffic accidents. There were few vehicles on the gravel roads, but the previous week Ethiopia had changed to driving on the right. It appeared that only half the drivers had heard the news!

After two days the road reached the town of Soddu. Here we refuelled and drove down into the rift valley. I hoped the road would take us towards the Kenya border, but our information was poor and I had been unable to discover how far it actually went. We did not have to wait long for the answer. Quite suddenly the gravel surface deteriorated and our heavily laden one-ton Land-Rover supply truck came to a grinding halt, axle-deep in mud. It took half an hour's pushing, shoving and towing to free it from the grip of the black cotton soil. Then another vehicle got stuck, then another. Local villagers looked on in amazement. They could not understand why we should make so much effort to press on – around the next bend was the impassable Hamasa River in full flood.

We camped in a small clearing near the road, where a stream flowed down to Lake Abaya and from here began our exploration of the rift valley. The Hamasa had still to be crossed so we attempted to build a raft. Alas, the available wood was too heavy and the device would not even support one man. There were crocodiles nearby and we learned that two Italians had been swept away in the swift currents recently. It was therefore with some trepidation that we piled our clothes and rifles on our heads and, clutching a fixed line, inched our way through the rapids. Marching into the bush on the far side we soon found tracks of lion, pig, antelope and hyena. Splitting into small parties we each took an area of countryside and began to seek the animals that the Museum had listed.

Mid-afternoon we spied a greater kudu browsing a quarter of a mile away. A short, easy stalk got me to within 200 yards. It was not possible to get closer so, taking careful aim, I sent a high velocity round crashing down the valley.

Breathless, I reached the antelope. It was down but not dead. Oh, hell! I thought, Why did I have to shoot it at all? My second bullet killed it instantly and, in order to take a perfect skin for the museum, we worked with great care. It was not a pleasant sight and soon the trees around us were heavy with hideous black vultures. Various parts of the body were required to be retained and the skull was removed intact. Inside the beast we discovered a complete foetus, apparently of considerable biological value, which we preserved in formalin in a large plastic tub. Finally we cut a haunch for our supper and then stood back to allow the vultures to clean up. Carrying the bloody items back across the Hamasa that night was a little worrying. Crocodiles were supposed to go for blood!

The local governor, His Excellency Wolde-Semait Gabre Wolde, was a most progressive man. Educated in Britain, he was striving to build up the province, and with determination and energy seemed to be doing a good job. He was always helpful and so I was delighted to be able to do something for him.

'There's a lion killing the cattle near here,' he told us. 'I should be grateful if you could get rid of it.'

So that afternoon we drove to the area and met a local guide. Dressed in a blue sports jacket and loin cloth, he also wore a large gold ear-ring, indicating that he had killed a lion single-handed. Following him closely, we soon came on fresh spoor, which led into dense bush. Marcos and I were ahead with the guide. Two cadets, David Bromhead and Andrew Penny, were ten yards behind us.

We reached some thick bushes, from which came the sound of a low cough and the guide gesticulated wildly, pointing and shouting, 'Oola, oola!' I could see nothing, nor could Marcos. Turning, I made a silent sign to David to discover what was happening. As if to answer, he flung up his rifle and, at the same moment, a great yellow shape leapt over me! 'What on earth . . . ' I gasped.

'A bloody great lioness,' replied David. 'She looked round one side of the bush, whilst you looked round the other.'

The guide and Marcos were already in pursuit, but our quarry had disappeared and, after a fruitless search, we headed back to our Land-Rover.

'Look, on the track!' whispered David. We stood rooted to the spot. For there, by the vehicle, lay the lioness, stretched full-length in the evening sun. A few feet away in the grass two cubs played. Cunning old thing, I thought, she's doubled back. I raised my rifle, but the sight of this beautiful beast and her young was too much. We sat down cursing that no one had a camera. Even Marcos, an experienced hunter, agreed we should not kill her, so we decided to have a cigarette and then, if she had not moved, we would try to out-flank her and reach the Land-Rover.

But suddenly a shepherd boy appeared strolling nonchalantly up the path towards us, oblivious of the great cat obscured from his view. Jumping up, Marcos yelled, 'Ambessa, ambessa!' The boy stopped with an expression of surprise. He saw nothing wrong and then, peering round the Land-Rover, caught a glimpse of the hind quarters of the lioness. Like a Walt Disney character, he leapt with one bound into a tree and scrambled to its highest and rather precarious branch. The lioness eyed him with mild interest.

'Keep together, safety-catches off, and we'll walk towards her,' I said, trying to sound confident. We were twenty-five yards away – which is not far when one remembers a charging lion can do 100 yards in four seconds – before she moved. Then, with a yawn, she stood up and ambled to the roadside. The guide flung up his rifle, but luckily his shot was wild and in a flash the lioness and her cubs had gone.

'You are extraordinary people,' said the governor, shaking his head sadly. 'How would you feel about killing a fox in England that had taken all your chickens and left you with nothing to eat for four months?' I felt like explaining the British attitude to foxes, but we apologized for our failure and went out to cull some bush-pigs that were destroying crops. No one minds shooting an ugly beast!

The thorn scrub was teeming with pig. I managed to get close to one small herd and shot a good eating-size sow, when unfortunately the bush around erupted with pigs, running in every direction in mad panic. Tek Negussie, a handsome Ethiopian cadet, pushed Judith up a tree to save her from one – a deed which she has never forgotten and, as a result, she regards all Ethiopians with the uttermost gratitude. Elsewhere, Marcos had shot, in the nick of time, a monster boar that had ambushed him and our other lady, Kay Thompson. Kay, ever intrepid, was left sitting on the carcass with Marcos's pistol while he went for assistance to carry the beast out. He was gone several hours, night fell, and the pig twitched once or twice, but she was still sitting on it when we eventually reached her. She did admit to smoking several cigarettes!

There was one part of our mission which was of great import-ance. The British Museum had charged us to find Osgood's swamp rat. Only one specimen of this strange black-and-white rodent had ever been collected and this was kept in America. The Museum badly needed one of their own. Pictures of the creature were reproduced and distributed all over the suspected locality, near Lake Tana, north of Addis Ababa. Through the driving rain of the wet season, we headed up into the highlands. Around us, the bleak plateau was populated by tall, proud Amharas, who lived in neat, round tukuls.

The only real break in the scenery came at Shafartak, when we reached the Blue Nile Gorge and in the space of three miles dropped 4,000 feet. Lunching at the bottom, we watched the Blue Nile, heavy with brown silt, swirling by beneath the bridge. Climbing back on to the plateau, we drove to Debra Marcos, the capital of the province of Gojjam. There we were guests at the governor's palace and were treated to a gigantic feast of raw meat, enjerra and wat. Enjerra, the traditional unleavened bread, has the appearance and consistency of a dirty rubber bath mat. The wat is a very hot meat sauce. The Ethiopians believe that by adding peppery spices to the raw meat it will cook in your stomach!

Dressed in tweed jacket and cavalry twill trousers, the governor plied us with Black Label whisky. That night I lay awake listening to raw meat and Scotch churning over in my stomach and also in Judith's! 'What did you think of the Blue Nile?' I asked her.

'Not very blue' was her sleepy reply.

'No one has ever really explored it, you know. There are supposed to be some terrible rapids and the world's most aggressive crocodiles.' She yawned. 'I wonder if it could be navigated with rubber dinghies,' I mused. Judith was already asleep.

Our base camp was set up in a community centre by the Piccolo Abbai River, said to be the origin of the Blue Nile or Great Abbai, and it was to here that the local people came in response to our offer of fifteen dollars reward for an Osgood's swamp rat. We combed the countryside, laid hundreds of traps and dealt with dozens of snakes, antelopes, small mammals and birds that were brought daily to our camp. Many were interesting and we purchased these, but there was no sign of Osgood. We had failed and felt miserable about it.

One day I awoke as dawn was breaking to hear something rustling in the corner of our cell-like room. Sliding the heavy Smith & Wesson from its holster on the bedpost, I levelled it at a biscuit packet in the corner. Maybe a cobra, I thought, one had been seen near the building. The roar of the revolver in the confined space was deafening. Judith shot up with a yell and a surprised rat hopped out of the biscuits. Alas, it was not Osgood's and the bullet, penetrating the wall, ricochetted down the corridor giving the expedition a rude awakening.

On Lake Tana our fishermen had been very successful and made a fine collection. Our dispirited band of rat-catchers needed an outing, so we all went up to Bahadar, partly to fish, but also to view the great falls of Tisisat, where the Blue Nile tumbles 150 feet into its canyon. The mist thrown up by the falls may be seen for miles, hence the name Tisisat, 'smoke of fire'. I watched the river cascade over the polished black basalt with a mighty roar, a fish eagle called and brightly-coloured birds flitted amongst the luxuriant green growth swaying gently in the drifting clouds of spray. The power and majesty was awe-inspiring.

'I know what you're thinking,' said Judith, who had been watching me.

'Do you?' I smiled and said slowly, 'It might be possible with rubber boats.'

On returning to England, we took our specimens to the Museum. Everyone was delighted with them, and I had just started to apologize for our failure to obtain Osgood's swamp rat, when the mammalogist cut in. 'After you left, we looked into the question of Osgood rather more carefully and we've decided that the rat he discovered in Ethiopia is exactly the same as one that is found in the Congo, so it isn't really a rarity after all. It was just an unusual distribution.' I stared in blank amazement. How could I tell him of the days and weeks spent searching every inch of the swampy bogland! How could he understand our feelings of failure at not discovering the bloody rat?

Ethiopia had some hidden tricks that did not emerge until after we had returned, when eight of us got malaria in spite of taking the regular dose of Paludrine. Nevertheless, the expedition was highly successful and immediately I began planning a follow-up. Next year I had to do my staff college exam, but in 1966 perhaps I could get beyond the Hamasa.

The Sandhurst Ethiopian Expedition of 1966 was designed to be a joint-service venture. Over fifty officer cadets and scientists of many nations would take part in a study of the archaeology, veterinary and zoological aspects of the rift valley between the Hamasa River and the Kenya border. We would leave after the summer term.

As adventure training officer this was my busiest term. Twenty expeditions were going off and as their departure grew nearer, so the urgency for administrative arrangements to be finalized increased. My office grew chaotic as cadets staggered in and out with animal traps, underwater equipment, mountaineering gear, rifles and mosquito nets. There was very often a good piece for the local press and the *Camberley News* often rang on Monday mornings to enquire if there were any interesting stories. On one particular day I had to confess that nothing special had happened in the previous week. As I was speaking my yellow Labrador, Kinder, waddled in. To my amazement, she was carrying a stuffed mongoose in her mouth.

On the telephone, the reporter was pleading, 'Are you sure there is nothing we can write about?'

'Well, my dog has just brought in a stuffed mongoose,' I said and laughed.

'Where did she get it and what does it look like?' he asked. He was most anxious to photograph the unusual sight, admitting that they were very short of news. The idiotic dog, terribly pleased with herself, continued to waddle round and round the office, snorting. The reporter and a photographer arrived, took copious pictures of Kinder parading on the lawns. I had no idea where she had found this trophy, probably in a dustbin. 'What are you going to do with it?' he asked.

'Oh! I'll probably stick it up on the training area and teach cadets how to recognize different animals,' I joked.

When I returned from an overseas trip a week later, our public relations officer (PRO) greeted me in great excitement and explained that, following the *Camberley News* story of my dog and the mongoose, almost all the national press now wished to descend on Sandhurst and photograph the expedition in a mock jungle. They supposed that I would have sewn the woods with a liberal quantity of stuffed animals.

'But I only said that as a joke!' I protested.

'Never mind, but now you must carry it out. It will be a wonderful thing for Sandhurst,' ordered the PRO.

For several weeks I searched desperately for stuffed animals and, in the end, all I had was a leopard's head, a pair of pottos and the mongoose. It was a warm Sunday afternoon when the media descended en masse. I had laid on all sorts of interesting demonstrations. A special raft was constructed to ferry a Land-Rover over the lake. A light mortar fired a line and grapnel into the dense vegetation on one of the islands demonstrating how to get a rope over a crocodile-infested river. The fact that the grapnel broke away from its cable and landed in Camberley was fortunately overlooked. But my efforts were all to no avail, they simply wanted photographs of the stuffed animal safari. We duly obliged and bewildered cadets crawled through the trees looking for the leopard and the pottos. The following Monday almost every national newspaper gave it wide coverage, which strangely the staff at Sandhurst regarded as a good thing to enhance the Army's image! Also, to my great surprise, funds began to come in and help to make the expedition solvent. So perhaps Kinder's mongoose had been worthwhile after all and I'd learned that in the silly season the press love an unusual tale!

The plan was to make the expedition main base in the rift valley at the southern end of Lake Abaya, near the developing town of Arba Minch. At this point, the valley is extremely narrow and clearly defined. It is almost exactly 4,000 feet above sea level, with mountains rising in steps on either side to a height of over 13,000 feet. It contained many lakes, swamps and areas of dense jungle, and in 1964 I had noticed that the flora changed rapidly with altitude. The new expedition was going to encounter areas of scrub, grass land, rain forests and, in the highest regions, a topography not unlike Dartmoor.

Reliable weather information was scarce, but I made our plans to deal with the worst situation; heavy rain on the mountains causing a rapid rise of the many rivers that flowed into the lake. The only motor track in the valley ran from north to south along the west side of Lake Abaya, and was dissected by numerous rivers. One of these was the Hamasa.

It was clear that we would have considerable engineer problems, and thus I appointed Officer Cadet Bill Bullock as the 'chief engineer' and he formed a small team of potential sapper officers.

One way to get the vehicles across the river was to fit flotation bags to their sides. These could be pumped up by a device fitted to the exhaust system. The disadvantage of this method was the vulnerability of the bags and the fact that the wheels of the vehicle hung down into the river and could catch onto boulders or rocks beneath. I also investigated something called the Bubble. This consisted of a fabric hemisphere connected by a trunk to an industrial compressor, which filled it to slightly above atmospheric pressure and caused it to hover. A vehicle could be suspended on wire strops inside the Bubble and, provided some directional force could be applied, it should be able to cross rivers. However, the problem was where to put the compressor and, although this method was considered seriously we felt the need for more research and development before taking a Bubble to Africa. There were various swimming vehicles, including an amphibious Land-Rover, with a boat-shaped hull, driven along by a propeller running off the rear differential. Inflatable bags gave additional buoyancy, but once again the wheels hung down in the water to catch snags. It was also extremely difficult to get it out of the river and up a steep bank.

Finally we turned to the well-tried idea of a raft. There were various methods involving oil-drums, ground-sheets stuffed with grass and even tarpaulins wrapped right around the vehicles. Boats were too bulky to carry and so I managed to persuade the Daimler Company to build us a light, air-portable raft of fibreglass and polyurethane. This was designed by Bill and the material only weighed two pounds per cubic foot. With its cellular construction, it floated well. The raft consisted of five pontoons made up of the polythene blocks bolted together and coated with a strong, fibreglass skin. Wheel channels were moulded on top, outriggers were fitted to either side, connected to the structure by reinforced fibreglass tubes. It was designed to carry a laden, quarter-ton Land-Rover plus three people. Ramps were made of hard wood. The raft could be carried on the roof of two Land-Rovers and assembled in forty-five minutes by six people. Light-weight nylon rope, aluminium anchorages and blocks enabled it to be used as a ferry.

The sixty-strong team that set out in July 1966 included a zoologist, a young vet and a doctor, who specialized in gynaecology! In the field we were joined by an escort of some fifteen local police. The bulk of the stores and vehicles had come over from the army base in Aden.

To our relief we found that the rains at the Hamasa River had not been heavy, and the vehicles crossed the wide ford with little difficulty. In the late afternoon of the second day we established our base camp as planned beside the Lake. The weather was excellent, with a noon temperature in the eighties and no sign of rain. But the mosquitoes devoured us at night.

We had been in the camp for a few days when, to our amazement, a certain officer cadet strolled in. He had missed the plane in England, having overslept, and we had left without him. On his own initiative, he had got himself to Aden, hitched a lift across the Red Sea on a dhow and come up the railway to Addis Ababa. Here he had managed to beg some money from the Defence Attaché and got a local plane to Arba Minch. On the way he had discarded almost all that he had, except one of the special water filter pumps with which he was entrusted. It was a splendid show of initiative and I forgave him!

From our base we explored the rift valley, and usually found the people friendly. However, once we were confronted with what might have been a nasty situation. We had camped near a large village. Supper had been served when suddenly the silence was broken by the sound of drums. In a flash, Negussie was on his feet and disappeared into the surrounding bush. The noise got louder. He returned and whispered, 'I'm not happy, the last white men they saw were the Italians, who dropped the chief out of an aeroplane over the village. We must find out what is happening. Will you come with me?'

Clutching our rifles, we set off into the night. I earned a quick rebuke when I tripped, but most of our sounds were drowned by the thunder of the drums. Clearly the villagers were getting worked up. At the stockade, leaving the police corporal and myself to cover him, Negussie went forward to the gate. Through the fence we could see a huge fire burning with half-naked figures leaping about and jumping through the flames. Around them the crowd ululated and the drums beat faster and faster. Negussie paused for a moment listening intently. He came from the north and I doubted he would understand the language. Like most Ethiopian officers, he was smartly dressed and even when working for long hours, in the rain and the mud, always managed to look as if he had just come off parade. Suddenly we saw him push open the gate and stride in. The drums stopped at once and the ululating ceased. He held up his hand, his pistol still in its holster. I could understand a little of what he was saying. 'I am an officer of the Emperor. His Imperial Majesty's friends are camping near here. What is all this noise about?'

A wizened elder in a leopard's skin shambled forward and in a whining, pleading voice talked for several minutes. Eventually Negussie nodded, said something in Amharic, turned and strode out of the compound. At once the drums thundered louder than ever and the ululating began again. I thought it a pretty cool act for, had they been hostile, he wouldn't have lasted long.

'It's all right,' he smiled, 'they're having a celebration for the return of their chief, who is expected back tonight with a new wife.'

This was not the only time that Negussie's courage impressed me. Early one morning he came with Bill and me to examine the shores of Lake Abaya. It was barely light when we left camp and at the water's edge walked out along a partly-finished jetty to get a better view. I led the way. We carried oddments of reconnaissance kit as we hopped from the top of one timber pile to the next, never more than a couple of feet above the water. Almost at the end of the jetty I saw what I thought was a tyre, with the tread just on the surface of the water.

'Is that a tyre or could it be a crocodile?' I asked. As if to answer, Negussie used a surveyor's pole to press down in the centre of the object. It sank without movement, and bobbed up again. A tyre, we all thought, and took another pace forward. At that moment, he repeated the process. With a crash a leviathan rose from the depths. It was just like St George's dragon! The tail came crashing round splintering the timber just beneath my feet. At the same time it launched itself at Negussie, who, being extremely agile, leapt to the top of a convenient pile. The beast then turned on me and with his mouth wide open, displaying serried lines of yellowing teeth, tried to get my leg. In one hand I held my rifle and in the other a theodolite. There was no time to aim. Flicking the safety catch off with my thumb, I thrust the weapon into the gaping mouth and pulled the trigger. The jaws closed about the barrel as the gun went off. Blood spurted at me, and at that moment the others pumped in more shots. Bullets flew everywhere and, with an awful gurgling sound, the slimy beast slid back into the black water.

'Grab it,' yelled Negussie, and seized the tail. It took us nearly an hour to get the carcass ashore and carry it to camp in triumph. It was a lesson I'm not likely to forget. Crocodiles will very often attack after you have stepped over them and not when you are about to.

The scientific work was going well. The zoologists captured and preserved a great number of species, including fish, snakes and many large mammals. The field laboratory had the appearance of a witch's cave. The collection of smaller animals was also growing steadily. Indeed in the world of zoology these were probably more important because they were less known. Everyone who had a spare moment was sent out to catch frogs, toads, mice and rats.

We had located an isolated area of grassland alive with large game. Behind it rose a steep escarpment, and on the other side was the lake and elsewhere swamps and rivers cut it off from the rest of the country. It was part of our programme to survey new areas for wildlife conservation, which included this district. To get there we had to cross a difficult little river called the Cullufu. The raft was quickly constructed and we were about to ferry a vehicle across, when downstream, some hundred yards away, a large herd of cattle had come to water. Suddenly the cattle gave startled tongue and scrambled back up the bank, as the herdsmen rushed down, screaming and waving spears. I was mystified. What was wrong? The centre of attention seemed to be a great white bramah bull, now standing with its tall heavy horns raised at the water's edge. His legs were set deep in the mud and he seemed to be struggling to draw something out of the river, the muscles of his powerful body contorted in effort.

'He's got something in his mouth,' gasped a cadet. Through binoculars I saw there was something, but it was not in the bull's mouth, it was round it – the jaws of a huge crocodile. Remorselessly the reptile was dragging the animal into the river. I put up my rifle but, with the demented herdsmen dashing round the struggling beast, dared not fire. If we crossed the river, we might have saved it, but the sight of the massive croc did not encourage quick dips. While we watched impotently, the reptile won the dreadful tug of war and, with its thick, squat legs working like pistons and its scaly tail thrashing the water into foam, pulled its victim into the shallows. Suddenly the bull was down, the froth turned red and, still kicking frantically, it disappeared in the turbid brown stream. The rest we could imagine. The croc would place the carcass in its underground lair or beneath a rock on the riverbed until it had putrefied sufficiently for its liking.

A rare species of mongoose was believed to exist several days' march from the end of the road and I decided to leave the Land-Rovers and proceed on foot. Two army drivers would remain with them and I guessed that as soon as we disappeared they would indulge in an orgy of sunbathing and drinking. To keep them gainfully occupied I handed out two large plastic tubs and indicated a nearby mosquito-ridden swamp.

'The British Museum is in urgent need of small green frogs. By the time I return I expect these to be full,' I said.

'Sir,' they replied in a tone verging on dumb insolence.

Three days later I marched into camp and, as expected, the soldiers were dozing in the shade. 'Frogs,' I bellowed.

'In tub,' said one.

To my astonishment both containers were crammed with writhing green frogs. 'How on earth did you do it?'

'Oh, was nuffin really, just a bit of hard work,' they replied with assumed modesty.

My opinion of these two rogues mellowed and I recommended them for promotion! It was long after the expedition that I discovered their method. They would go to a native village with a copy of *Playboy*. As soon as the local men had gathered round, they would open the centre pages and permit a quick peep, and then say 'Three frogs, one look'. Thus encouraged, the natives would rush off to collect as many frogs as they could to earn another look.

The expedition over, we had to get all our zoological specimens back to England. Although we had done our best to preserve them, the presence of some large, slightly putrefying reptiles in a hot, stuffy aeroplane en route from Aden to UK did not endear us to the RAF, and one of the planes had to make an unscheduled landing at Malta when the stench became overpowering. There can't be many pilots who can claim to have been forced down by a crocodile!

We returned via Addis Ababa, where we were greatly honoured to receive an invitation to meet His Imperial Majesty once again. The invitation was extended to everybody, and I wondered whether the court realized just how many of us there were. In Ethiopia protocol demands one bows to the Emperor three times. Once when you enter, again halfway up the red carpet and finally when right before him. On leaving his presence one repeats the process in reverse. No problem, you may think, for well-drilled officer cadets, but Haile Selassie had a population of lions roaming the throneroom and I could imagine a terrible incident that might result if a cadet, walking backwards, should fall over one of the royal beasts. I consulted

Tommy, an Ethiopian working at the British Embassy, who gave me the solution.

'You will notice,' he said, 'that we cast ourselves down very low when bowing to the Emperor, pressing our foreheads upon the carpet.'

'Steady on,' I said, 'we're British you know – a stiff little bow is all that is usually required.'

'I'm not suggesting you be obsequious,' replied Tommy, 'but if you cast yourself down low you can look between your legs and see the lions lurking behind you.' By this means sixty officer cadets and two ladies in skirts successfully entered and left the presence of His Imperial Majesty.

The Everest of Rivers

THE EMPEROR'S EYES TWINKLED. 'I should like you to explore my Great Abbai,' he said in a firm quiet voice. 'Who knows what animals and minerals you might find there?'

This was like asking an average hillwalker to climb Everest. Playing for time I replied, 'I will look into the possibilities, Your Imperial Majesty.'

Back in Britain I was posted to the Royal Military College of Science at Shrivenham to do fifteen months' technical training. The fiery commandant, Major General Napier Crookenden, had heard of the Emperor's request. 'Quite a challenge, good for morale, just what the Army needs,' he enthused. 'Of course we must do it, we'll need a committee. I'll be Chairman and you can be Secretary. I see no need for anyone else.' So Haile Selassie's chalienge was accepted and I embarked on the expedition that changed my life.

The infamous Blue Nile or Great Abbai River cuts a 5,000 feet deep gorge through the highlands of Ethiopia, forcing its way through the mountain wilderness to spill out into the sun-soaked plains of the Sudan. Until 1968 this sinister canyon had remained virtually unknown, although the actual source of the great river is a spring that bubbles up in a bog south of Lake Tana.

The first Briton to view this source was the adventurer, James Bruce. Visiting Ethiopia in 1771 he wrote of 'people who anointed themselves not with bear's grease or pomatum, but with the blood of cows, who instead of playing tunes upon them wore the entrails of animals as ornaments and who, instead of eating hog meat, licked their lips over bleeding living flesh'. For my part, whilst seeking Osgood's elusive swamp rat, I had tramped many miles and been eaten alive by mosquitoes in this region.

For its first eighteen miles after Lake Tana, the Blue Nile is wide and shallow, flowing through swampy water-meadows and around numerous islands. But there are long stretches of dangerous white water and several small waterfalls. At Tisisat the river suddenly drops with a thunderous booming over the second-biggest falls in Africa. There, the huge volume of water is compressed into the narrow sheer-sided gorge and, for almost a hundred miles, the torrent races through this cleft before the valley opens out. However, the river is still at the bottom of a great gutter in the Ethiopian Highlands and 10,000 feet above it towers the cloud-swathed Mount Choke. From here on, the river alternates between rocky cataracts, dangerous shallows and stretches of flat water populated by hippo and large aggressive crocodiles.

As far as I could find out, the first attempt at navigation was made in 1902 by an American big-game hunter with three especially-designed steel boats. After only three miles these were swamped in a cataract and the expedition abandoned. In 1905, a Swede called Jesson came upstream from the Sudan. He only got his boat to the Azir River where he met hostile natives and retreated.

In 1926, Major R. E. Cheeseman, the British consul in North West Ethiopia, tried to follow the course of the river by foot. His survey work was invaluable but, due to great difficulty experienced in moving along the banks, he was soon forced up onto the high plateau. In 1955, Herbert Rittlinger and his wife, with a small party of Germans, attempted to canoe down the river. They had with them a number of ladies who, by all accounts, were rather attractive and liked to paddle along in the nude. However, crocodiles are no respectors of persons. Their canoes were attacked and the party driven from the river.

One of the best organized expeditions was mounted in 1962 by the Canoe Club of Geneva. Six experienced canoeists set out in two large Canadian-style boats. They started, as many have, from the bridge at Shafartak and after much effort reached a point near the Sudan border. There they camped on an island and whilst asleep were fired on by bandits. Two died but the rest escaped in one canoe. The next attempt was by Arne Rubin who became the first man to travel along the Blue Nile from Shafartak to Rosiares. During our research, we corresponded with this plucky Swede, who in 1965 had navigated this stretch in a Kleeper canoe, alone! It was a splendid achievement. The next year, he returned with a friend to attempt the upper reaches of the river, but after fifty miles of hair-raising adventure their canoe

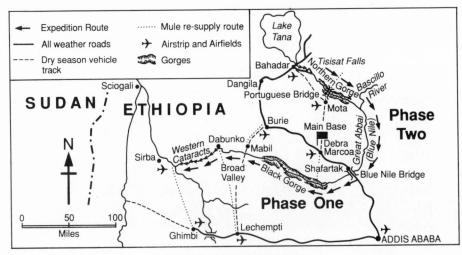

BLUE NILE EXPEDITION

was smashed on jagged rocks in the Northern Gorge and they had to walk out.

There have been other expeditions; in March 1968, a small British team, attempting the river in rubber boats, came to grief in a short distance after the bottoms had been torn off their craft. It was a salutary warning, and I realized that if one were to navigate this river it must be done when there was plenty of water.

None of the previous explorers had been able to examine the banks or carry out any scientific research, so we hoped that our expedition would be of value both to science and to the people of the region.

Much of the river was unmapped, and there was little reliable local knowledge, but on an early reconnaissance visit to Ethiopia I met numerous 'experts', who had told me some of the elements of mystery that surrounded this fearsome river.

There was said to be a great swamp alive with crocodiles – 'crocodilicus Niliticos', the most terrible man-eater of all Africa! Had not the Queen of Sheba sought the advice of Solomon because of the depredations of a monster croc? And it was a fact that an Austrian gentleman had recently been seized by one of these powerful reptiles and dragged down into the Nile, bleeding and screaming, under the eyes of his wife. The crocodiles were said to reach ten metres in length, but this I considered an exaggeration. However, if there were such giants, where did they hide? Where was the legendary swamp, infested with mosquitoes and leviathans?

There were many who told tales of radioactive gas, claiming that the intense sun heated the black basalt so much that radioactive vapours oozed out and, being heavier than air, dropped to the bottom of the canyon. There the gas was thought to collect in pockets, bringing a slow death to every living thing it touched. Animal corpses were reported to have been found in such places. If the Blue Nile Gorge had such gas, might it have radioactive minerals? Were there great deposits of uranium awaiting discovery?

Geologists told of extensive lakes being formed when landslides of rock, loosened by erosion and earthquake, crashed into the river, forming instant dams and creating waterfalls over which a frightening volume of water cascaded, making it totally unnavigable. Yet if valuable minerals were present in the gorge, it would be extremely useful if mining companies could use the river as a road. Doubtless this thought had occurred to the Emperor when he asked us to explore it. Apparently wildlife was plentiful and dangerous. There were rumours of huge leopards, and the lions, Ethiopia's national beast, were said to be the largest in Africa. Herds of buffalo and elephant were reported to abound to such an extent that the Ethiopian Wildlife Department was eager to see if there really was a mysterious untouched natural nature reserve.

Snakes were another hazard. One species, a small grey viper, was thought to be present, in millions! The little reptiles attacked humans (very unusual) – the bite, a neuro-toxin bringing immediate paralysis and painful death. Local hunters advised that we should wear strong breeches and high leather boots whilst smearing our legs with an ointment of dubbin and tar! I had come across an island in a swamp near Lake Tana in 1964 on which we'd captured several dozen little grey snakes so perhaps there was something to this tale. Giant pythons were said to thrive in the Northern Gorge and an earlier explorer had apparently grabbed one by the tail in error whilst following a path beneath the Tisisat Falls.

The legend of the Queen of Sheba popped up all the time. It was said that following the First World War, an ex-Royal Engineers officer had discovered an amazing cave system full of gems that could only be reached by overcoming a forceful underground river. The Ethiopians are well-known for carving churches and dwellings from solid rock and one tale told of a 'lost' tribe of white people living in a subterranean town, somewhere in the gorge. There were also stories of apemen who attacked travellers. Everyone talked of the canyon as the home of the most murderous bandits, and several travellers reported hearing spine-chilling screams echoing about within the walls during darkness.

My friends at the Natural History Museum reckoned the hippo might be more dangerous. 'Give them a wide berth, my boy,' cautioned one scientist.

'How far away should we be?' I asked.

'Oh! about a quarter of a mile,' he suggested. As the river is rarely more than 150 yards wide in its upper reaches, this would not be easy. 'And avoid them in the mating season, they might mistake your rubber boats for an attractive female,' my friend advised, but he wasn't too sure when that would be, and added that he'd be grateful for any information on the sex lives of the Nile hippo.

The water was said to carry the dreaded bilharzia, which the river brought down from Lake Tana, but no one was sure if it really did exist in the turbulence and that was something we had been asked to investigate. Rumours of alluvial gold and vast copper deposits all added to the reputation of the area and I wondered why the Ethiopian police had made such an effort to prevent a small British expedition from entering the Northern Gorge. All this only served to heighten my curiosity. There must be something there.

No accurate information on river conditions was available. But as up to eighty inches of rain falls annually in the mountains, mainly in the summer, I expected the Nile would be in flood in August and the level beginning to drop in September. On the plateau the rain would be heavy and vehicle tracks extremely difficult to say the least. At the higher altitude the temperature would be around 60°F at midday, but down on the gorge bottom it would rise to at least 80°F. We could expect nights in the mountains to be extremely cold but the great advantage of attempting a navigation at this time was that the higher water should cover the rocks.

Chris Bonington, the British mountaineer, who was to accompany us as photo-journalist on behalf of the *Daily Telegraph Magazine*, described the area as 'the last unconquered hell on earth' and 'the Everest of Rivers'. This caused some mirth at the time, but we were later to discover that it was not so much of an exaggeration after all.

To organize a scientific investigation of the area presented me with something of a dilemma. It would cost a great deal of money to get the scientists into the difficult region, enable them to work, keep them alive and get them and their specimens out again in one piece. It would also mean sending a lot of people there just to back them up. To get the money, the resources and the necessary assistance for the project we had to catch the imagination of the Army, the press and industry. At the same time, I would have to recruit servicemen and civilians who understood the needs of the scientists, their idiosyncrasies and demands.

My first recruit was Richard Snailham, a Civilian Lecturer at Sandhurst. I knew him well and found him one of the most amusing and likeable men I had met. It was Richard who was to become the Chief Nilographer, reading up everything he could find about the area and helping to write the prospectuses and begging letters that we put out to gain sponsorship and support. He would also write the official history of the expedition and act as Treasurer.

My second in command was to be Nigel Sale, of the Royal Green Jackets. I believed that this thorough, slightly serious officer would be a good antidote to my own character. One of the most important people would be the Chief Engineer. Here we required, not a fresh-faced, Sandhurst-trained subaltern with bags of enthusiasm, but an experienced, bold and imaginative engineer who would be prepared to tackle any obstacle with the minimum of resources and manpower. For this post I selected Jim Masters, a quiet forty-year-old officer from Somerset whom I knew I could depend on at all times. Having served together in Cyprus I respected his depth of experience and expert knowledge. To lead the White Water Team, I chose Roger Chapman, an instructor at Sandhurst. A Captain in the Green Howards, he possessed boundless vitality and dogged determination. He would have the unenviable task of navigating the most difficult stretches.

In total the team would consist of seventy servicemen and civilians from Britain and Ethiopia and the scientists were to include an archaeologist, an ornithologist, the medical officers and a host of zoologists. I was simply the conductor of a large, highly-motivated orchestra. Now we had to play.

Shrivenham was an ideal place to launch an expedition. Judith and I moved into a tumbledown camp nearby, took over a host of buildings and, together with the amusing Lance Corporal Henry of the Royal Engineers who had volunteered to accompany me, we made up the expedition headquarters. The excellent scientific and technical facilities at the College were of great value.

The expedition was divided into two phases. The plan was to set up a base at the hilltown of Debra Marcos, roughly at the centre point of the expedition area. From here we could radiate outwards attempting to navigate the river first from Shafartak to Sirba, when the water level was highest. On that phase we should use alloy assault craft powered by forty horse-power Johnson outboards.

For the second phase from Lake Tana back to Shafartak, we needed boats that would stand up to the tumbling white water in the narrow gorges at the head of the river. Arne Rubin told me he believed that only inflatable craft could survive these terrible rapids. So I planned to use Avon rubber yacht tenders. The company thought I was insane but kindly agreed to provide six, payment being deferred until the publicity value was assessed. In the end they were delighted with the result and charged us nothing.

Re-supply would be by small overland parties dragging mules through the mud on the high plateau, before descending into the baking hot gorge. More supplies would arrive by parachute from an Army Beaver aircraft.

Months of training and preparation now followed. Every spare moment was taken up by the expedition and the thankless task of raising £15,000 in cash. We tested boats on the wild rivers and, on the sandy areas of Aldershot, we trained with Army packhorses. Boats were selected, boats were rejected, boats were modified and finally, with days to go, boats were packed.

In March 1968, I was able to visit the river and carry out an air reconnaissance. Flying low in a single-engine plane, I went the length of the lower gorges. Seeing it in the dry season I was impressed and, although we found no large swamps, I observed whole regiments of crocodiles rushing into the water as the aircraft roared overhead. There did not appear to be any obstacles in the river itself that we could not overcome in the wet season although there would be some challenging rapids. However, weather did not permit an air recce of the unknown Northern Gorge.

We returned to England in time to explain the whole thing to Her Majesty the Queen and His Royal Highness Prince Philip during their visit to the Royal School of Military Engineering at Chatham. 'You will be very careful,' cautioned Her Majesty, looking at the photographs of the cataracts. Meanwhile the Prince was advising Jim Masters on modifications for the boats.

Very sadly my mother, Gwen, my staunchest of allies, died suddenly in April. Apart from family upheavals, the expedition problems seemed to multiply but whenever I became depressed, I forced myself to go on, because that is just what she would have advised. Throughout all this, Judith, my jolly, supportive wife, had a great deal to put up with, but she too urged me forward.

Our preparations were complete by the end of July. Then, at the eleventh hour, I had an accident that almost knocked me out of the expedition. During the boat training in Wales, I fell heavily onto my right knee. It was excruciatingly painful and I could hardly walk. 'Rest it for a month and then start taking gentle exercise,' said the doctor. I acquired a stout walking stick and a supply of crepe bandages and prayed hard. We flew into Addis Ababa on 31 July.

Our advance party had already achieved administrative miracles. Considerable help was forthcoming from the US Army Mapping Mission and various Ethiopian Government Departments. We were able to move our personnel and stores to Debra Marcos on 2 August and set up the base in pouring rain. Flying ahead of the main column, I went forward with our chief pilot, Major Alan Calder, in the Beaver, reaching the grassy airstrip above the town at the same time as a tropical squall. High winds and rain clouds were sweeping across the flat green landscape as Alan fought with the controls and tried to land. Six times he made his approach and six times pulled away at the last minute. Fuel was beginning to run low and there was not enough to get us back to Addis Ababa. 'Here we go!' he yelled through the intercom as we went in for the seventh time. Ahead, strolling slowly across the strip, a herd of white cows appeared. Alan swore and the next moment we were over the top of the cattle by a hair's breadth and, with a bump, our wheels hit the ground. The crosswind swung the Beaver from one side of the strip to the other, but fortunately there was nothing in the way and we slid to a halt.

The true violence of the storm was apparent as we tried to open the doors; they were almost wrenched off in our hands. At the end of the airfield sat a silver and red Ethiopian Army helicopter, rocking in the heavy gusts. Climbing out to meet our allies, I ran through the torrential downpour. Huddled inside the chopper were half a dozen soldiers, with bandaged heads and limbs. The pilot, a young Amhara in a bright orange flying suit, grinned and slid open a small panel of perspex.

'Good morning,' I shouted above the noise of the wind.

'Hi,' he replied, with an American accent, 'who are you?' I explained that we were a British Army expedition, come to examine the Blue Nile Gorge. 'Gee, I thought you were reinforcements,' he added. 'Say, don't you guys know there's a war going on?' He pointed to the wounded soldiers whom he was about to evacuate when the storm abated.

I had heard that there was some minor internal problem in the province of Gojjam, but I had not been informed of the serious nature of the conflict. It seemed that the people of the region had risen up with one accord against what they considered the dastardly imposition of something called Income Tax. Clearly, we had some sympathy with the rebels. But in protest they had turned to slaughtering the tax collectors and now the Army was trying to sort out the rebels. We had landed in the middle of a small civil war.

As soon as the rest of the party arrived, I went down to visit my old friend the Governor. I had last seen him four years ago in his mud-walled palace. On arrival I noticed how few people were around, there was not even a guard on the main gate. Walking up to his office I found the door open and to my surprise saw a police corporal seated at the Governor's desk smoking a cigar. 'Tanastalin,' I greeted him.

He looked up equally surprised and said in halting English, 'Good morning.'

'Where's the Governor?' I enquired.

'He's gone,' said the corporal, 'and I go too.' He hastened to explain to me that the town was soon to be attacked by some 3,000 heavily-armed rebels who were out for the Governor's blood and, indeed, that of anyone connected with the administration.

'Well, before you leave,' I asked him, 'will you be so kind as to let me have some letters that I can send out to the various chiefs to grant us assistance and passage through their tribal areas?'

'Ah, yes,' he said, 'the Governor left these,' and, to my astonishment, he produced a sheaf of letters which he proceeded to hammer with the official rubber stamp. Messengers were summoned and each was handed a letter for an appropriate chief. Bowing their way out from the corporal's presence, the runners made off at high speed towards the great river. I was given more letters of authority and assured that all would be well.

Back at camp, I explained to the bewildered expedition that we were in a very hostile area and that the town was likely to be surrounded by a large number of armed tribesmen, hell-bent on blood, who would undoubtedly sack it and, having done so, might turn their attentions to us. 'Ah well,' said the quartermaster, 'we'll build a zoriba, that'll keep them out.' The zoriba, all of two feet high, was made of thorns and even the small boys who plagued us had no difficulty in hopping over it. The effect was undoubtedly intended to be psychological.

The final preparations and air reconnaissance took a few days. Polaroid photographs of the obstacles were used at the briefings. Mules and donkeys for the re-supply teams had been made available as a result of the Governor's letters, stores were packed, the aircraft flying schedule was detailed and all was made ready. The die was cast. We moved down into the gorge to meet the Nile.

On 7 August, twenty-two of us in four assault boats started on the 275-mile voyage from the great bridge at Shafartak to Sirba. There was no turning back, our engines would not overcome the current. For three weeks we battled through the cataracts, stopping at selected points for scientific investigation. Specimens were taken out of the gorge by mule parties, who likened their journey to the ascent of a never-ending ladder in a Turkish bath. The steep slopes were covered in loose rocks, concealed by elephant grass up to twelve feet high. Midday temperatures could soar to around 90°F and the humidity could go to eighty-five per cent. At night we shivered as the temperature dropped thirty degrees and on many mornings low cloud hung in the gorge blocking out the early sun.

The cataracts were certainly pretty challenging and we found places where enormous rocks, weighing thousands of tons, had crashed into the gorge, but there were no waterfalls. Jim's modified assault boats got us through. Although the crocs were large, they never exceeded twenty feet and only displayed aggression on one occasion. Beaches littered with mica and 'fool's gold' caused momentary excitement, but we found no caves full of gems. The tribesmen were generally friendly and even a couple of bandits we found spying on us turned out to be amicable.

It happened at the first camp at the junction with the Guder River whilst our scientists ranged about their demi-paradise on the sides of the gorge. Two tall upright bronzed men stalked one of our patrols for several hours until our people, tiring of the game, reversed the process and herded them down to our camp. Attired in old Italian Army tunics festooned with accoutrements of leather worn over faded loin cloths, they spoke no English. On their right shoulder they carried a blanket and in their left hand a thin five-foot staff. On the other shoulder was slung a heavy Russian rifle (*circa* 1898), almost certainly captured at the Battle of Adowa. Their hair was anointed with rancid butter which smelt revolting.

Taken off guard, I couldn't think of anything suitable to say to a couple of inefficient bandits. So I offered them a Mars bar. They eyed it suspiciously, as a pair of black carrion crows might examine an unusual but possibly tasty morsel in an English field. I urged them to eat and eventually one of them shot out a long scrawny hand and grasped the confectionery. He sniffed it without expression and handed it to his comrade who did the same. They looked at each other and then, eyeing me, nodded their approval before handing the bar back again. I broke it in half and gave them a piece each, at the same time eating some myself. They tasted it with care and then nodded again. So I gave them the rest of the bar.

In the middle of the interview Lieutenant Telahoun Mekonnen, our liaison officer from the Ethiopian Navy, came in from a reconnaissance. Immaculately dressed in his uniform he stepped ashore and, sighting our visitors, his jaw dropped noticeably. 'I must speak to you,' he whispered, and leading me to one side explained that it was his painful duty to shoot these men immediately. Could I lend him my revolver as his own pistol had not yet arrived from Naval Headquarters. I felt sorry that we should need to despatch our two visitors so soon, as it was quite possible we would learn much about the river and the flora from these two wanderers in this lost world. Telahoun insisted that he should shoot them and one of our police guides urged him to take off their ears to return as evidence to Addis Ababa. But in the end I prevailed on him to spare us the embarrassment of an incident so early in the expedition. The two policemen who had accompanied us from the bridge looked positively terrified by our visitors and I noticed that the swarthy bandits regarded our other Ethiopian friends with nothing short of contempt and scorn. Anyway it was time to sail so I took the opportunity of shaking them both by the hand and giving them some old plastic bags. They bowed politely and, thanking me in Amharic, strode back up the slope, smiling and clutching the gifts.

We scoured the precipitous sides of the canyon, but detected no smell of any gas, radioactive or otherwise. However, the zoologists made many important discoveries, but although we *saw* no giant leopard or lions, we heard these cats roaring at night. As far as any lost tribes were concerned, all the rumours pointed to the Northern Gorge.

Plans for the second, most difficult and longer phase of the expedition from Lake Tana to Shafartak were already under way. Perhaps the answers to many of the Blue Nile's mysteries lay in those unmapped vertical-sided canyons which no white man had seen. The first fifty miles were obstructed by raging white water cataracts and the river party would move in the inflatables. We were all novices at this game, learning as we went. Looking back on those days it is interesting that all our river-exploring techniques developed from that expedition.

Meanwhile the archaeological team was making an exciting discovery. On the southern shore of Lake Tana they found a small fortress which defended a peninsula from the mainland. The moat, ramparts and gatehouse were soon revealed from beneath the tangled growth that had gradually crept over them in the passing years. It had undoubtedly been constructed at about the time of the Portuguese arrival in Ethiopia. But the inhabitants had long gone – there was no lost tribe here.

The White Water Team, anxious to get started on its journey into the Northern Gorge, quickly formed a small corps d'élite of nine men in the three especially-constructed boats aptly named Faith, Hope and Charity. Flying over the route, Alan Calder reported that there were many more crocodiles than expected, some of them 'huge', and therefore we decided that Captain John Wilsey, a tall, handsome officer in the Devon and Dorsets, should take an assault boat and come upstream from the Blue Nile bridge to meet us somewhere near the Bascillio junction. He could then escort us in his alloy craft through the most heavily-infested area.

The way ahead of the Avons was foaming white water for many miles. By the first afternoon they had met the full force of the cataracts and realized that, with only paddles, they were powerless to do more than keep the bow head on the waves. The fury of this untamed river was more powerful than anyone had imagined and very soon the team was battered, bruised and often half-drowned. To make life more difficult, there were parts of the river where it widened out and flowed through hundreds of channels. The problem was to know which one to take. The edge of the river was a swamp with no firm ground for some distance and this meant that camping for the night was a long and tedious business.

While the team continued downstream, I flew to the hilltop shanty town of Mota and prepared a new group to meet them at the fifteenth-century Portuguese bridge deep in the sinister Northern Gorge. In contact by radio, I discovered they were having more than their fair share of thrills and spills. Far from being stimulated, some were becoming very frightened. Dividing themselves into hawks and doves, some wanted to go on, others to pull back and they argued amongst themselves nonsensically. All I could do was to make one or two unpopular decisions and try to help them sort themselves out. Having done this, they then pressed on with much more caution towards the great falls at Tisisat where the boats were roped over.

In the Northern Gorge the cataracts became even more dangerous so Nigel went ahead to run the re-supply groups who were now stationed along the lip of the canyon. It was soon found that the boats could not stop and therefore they needed early warning to pull into the bank before a cataract. Then if there were sufficient water they would ride it down but if the rocks showed through, they had to portage the boat round the side, a laborious and difficult task especially in the bottom of this vertically-sided chasm.

Leaving Mota in the cool of early morning we went down into the gorge; a long straggling column of mules and men taking with us fresh boats, engines, stores, weapons and ammunition needed for the final part of this epic journey. The last couple of miles' descent was an interesting example of how mules can be used successfully in this terrain. The path was barely wide enough for a man to walk and yet these sturdy beasts carried on with their heavy loads. Suddenly we came to the edge of a cliff and saw a narrow little path plunging down to the river. I could see beneath me the rickety structure of the old bridge. The central stone arch had been replaced with local timber and as I watched, a small herd of cows were driven across. Some masonry tumbled away into the swirling brown water and I was amazed that it had stood so long. There was something eerie about the gorge at this point. It was damp, dark and silent, except for the swish of the river racing under the bridge. We had been forced to come here because it was the only place for many miles where there was a track that led down to the Nile and a bridge across it, however rickety. Here I awaited the arrival of the white water team.

Each evening the radio brought news of the various sections and I knew that Roger Chapman's men were only a few miles away.

They were very tired and many were suffering from infected bites and cuts. It would be a relief to have them back with me as I felt that one or two, lacking imagination, were allowing their courage to lead to rashness.

However, at the old bridge, we had plenty of problems to occupy our time. The tribesmen obviously resented our presence and each day grew more insistent that we should leave. Stores were in short supply and money was running out. I was more than a little worried about the rains, for, if they stopped early, the river would dry up rapidly and maroon us. Time was not on our side.

Everywhere the expedition was showing signs of nervous strain. Whilst working a simple flying-ferry across the torrent, I was swept overboard and came close to drowning. 'Our luck seems to be running out,' muttered one of my friends that night. I slept badly and at dawn was blowing the fire into life when I heard running feet on the trail down the gorge.

Scattering pebbles, Roger rushed in. 'Ian's dead,' he gasped. Strangely the words did not surprise me. 'Swept away, nothing we could do.'

It was early and the sun had not yet reached us. Teeth chattering, we gathered around to hear the terrible news. I took Roger aside and we sat quietly on a great, black basalt slab in the shade of the high cliffs, while he told the story. He spoke in a low voice, his tanned, muscular body glistening with sweat: he had run most of the way to bring me the news, when he could not get through on the radio.

Late on the previous day the battered, exhausted members of his team had reached the Abaya Canyon. Here the mountain torrent carves a thousand-foot deep gash in the highlands and cascades down a tortuous rock-strewn path to join the Blue Nile near the ancient bridge. For weeks they had struggled against the mighty river and, at last, in the Northern Gorge, had come upon a stretch of rapids too fearsome for even these stalwarts. On my orders they had let the boats go through the raging water unmanned, to be collected by my own group a short distance downstream, at the crumbling, old bridge. The towering, vertical cliffs had forced them to march west to find a route to my position. Alas, this narrow track had led across a tributary to the Blue Nile – the Abaya. Now it was a racing brown torrent, swollen by the rains, cascading over black eroded rocks, swirling and eddying with an ominous hiss.

Thus in the late afternoon they had started to cross. Alastair Newman, known for his nerves of steel and lack of emotion, had been the first in and taking a great leap had swum with fast, powerful strokes to the far side. He carried with him a line of red climbing rope and, clambering out onto the rock ledge on the far bank, called out for another man to assist him. It did not look difficult and they were anxious to be over before dark. After all, they knew that I was only a few miles ahead with fresh men, new boats and supplies.

Corporal Ian Macleod of the Black Watch and SAS volunteered to go next. I had taught him to swim underwater in the sheltered coves of Cyprus years before: this wiry and popular Glaswegian was one of our toughest and most resourceful members. As well as being a thoroughly professional soldier, he had a scholarly air and was an accomplished linguist. Ian was a man who spoke no ill of any other and no one spoke ill of him. He had not been well, following a narrow escape and bad battering in the rapids above Tisisat a week earlier. However, apart from a bandaged knee, he showed no sign of his ailments. It was typical of this rugged Scot that he would always volunteer for the dirtiest job. With a rope lashed securely to his waist, he lowered himself into the rushing water and struck out for the far shore, only forty feet away. On the warm rocks his colleagues rested their aching limbs and waited for the ropeway to be completed.

At first all went well, but suddenly, as Ian was about to reach the bank, the rope went taut and he disappeared beneath the surface. Seconds later he bobbed up. His friends, aghast and realizing his plight, gave more slack to enable him to reach the far side, but at once the line went taut again. The rope was being carried downstream by the speeding current, or perhaps a submerged tree had struck it and was dragging it along the river bed. Whatever the cause, Ian was drowning, being pulled under by the lifeline. His friends tried to play out more rope praying he could reach the far bank. For a moment it seemed as if he had made it, but then the river washed over him and he disappeared, still struggling for his life.

Roger was already ripping off his clothes. Someone hurled a semi-inflated life-jacket to Ian, it missed and floated away tossing in the turbulent waves. Others, realizing that he desperately needed just a few feet more of slack line, yelled, 'Cut the rope.' A jackknife was tossed across the river to Alastair and he began to saw through the tough fibres. Roger dived in and reached Ian, forcing the drowning corporal above the surface. Still the rope anchored them against the jetting current. Then it parted and at once the two men spun downstream through the tossing brown waves of the cataract. Roger, fighting with all his massive strength to gain a grip on the bank, could be seen struggling as he was swept along beside the polished, ebony boulders, one arm, muscles bulging, crooked around Ian. Dashing along the bank, the men leapt from rock to rock trying to keep pace. Now Roger had an arm around a finger of rock and was trying to pull Ian from the water. But the current pounded them relentlessly and by now Ian was unconscious. Ahead was a small waterfall, only a ten-foot drop, but with jagged rocks at its base; their chances of survival would not be high if they were swept over. Roger's face was red and contorted with effort, Ian's ashen and grey. Suddenly his limp body was seized by some unseen force and he was dragged relentlessly downward. In a second he had gone. Once his head bobbed above the surface, but after that he disappeared over the waterfall and was never seen again.

On the bank the exhausted men summoned every last ounce of energy and raced down the narrowing, boulder strewn ledge, desperately hoping to catch a glimpse of Ian and be able to reach him. It was all in vain. The ledge soon ended and they were forced to stop. Ahead they could see the river disappearing into a black abyss, into which the water tumbled with a terrible roar.

Chris Bonington, his voice broken with emotion, said, 'We can't get any further, he's gone.' Gulping in the warm humid air, his weary companions nodded agreement and all turned back. As darkness fell, they rigged up an aerial ropeway and crossed, to spend a damp, cold night huddled amongst the rocks. Their minds and bodies had reached a point of exhaustion which sleep would barely alleviate. To make matters worse, the deep canyon prevented radio contact with the rest of the expedition. Roger knew I was only five miles ahead, but he also knew that we were virtually captives of the tribesmen. To the dispirited white water men, it seemed that the bottom had fallen out of their world. Any hope of continuing the expedition seemed out of the question, indeed some even wondered if they would survive.

This was the story Roger told me. I found myself issuing the orders for an emergency helicopter search. I seemed to do it almost mechanically and, after a moment, realized that my mind was running on two tracks at once. One of the signals officers was already calling base and the intelligence officer was asking me short, sharp questions, to which I gave automatic answers, which must have been subconsciously thought out minutes or perhaps days before. The other part of my mind was saying, 'Poor Ian, a search is hopeless.' I remembered my own desperate struggle in the grip of the river only the previous morning. Having finished giving orders I stood deep in thought, looking at the milk chocolate coloured water racing under the old bridge. How many disasters had this awful place seen, I wondered.

In the early afternoon a small US Army helicopter landed on a broad ledge above our camp. This caused a great stir amongst the locals, but we were extremely glad to see him. Leaving his crewman at our camp, the American pilot flew me up and down the gorge, travelling as slowly as possible so that I could scan the innocuous looking water and the rocky banks for any sign of Ian. Once something did catch my eye. It was a football bladder, obviously released from a wrecked Redshank. It could only have escaped if the tube had been torn open and this could only have been done by a crocodile. There were several huge log-like reptiles sleeping on the sandbanks.

Turning up the Abaya Gorge, we saw the terrible conditions into which Ian had disappeared and there, still camped on the ledge, were Alastair and Garth. They waved slowly, as if to say, 'It's no good, you're wasting your time.' We made a final sweep of the immediate area and, with fuel running low, turned for Mota. As we rose out of the chasm the engine gave an unhealthy cough. We dropped a few feet and the pilot started to sweat profusely, although it was quite cool in the aircraft. We were too low for safety, only 100 feet above the ground that was now rising rapidly to meet us. The engine coughed again and the American grunted something unintelligible over the intercom. By his actions I gathered we were going to land. Skilfully he brought us in on a small patch of grass beside a low bluff, and whilst the rotors continued to thrash around, he sprang out and began to tinker with the motor. Satisfied, he climbed in again, grinned and gave a thumbs up. We flew up to Mota without incident.

On the bumpy little airfield outside the tin-roofed town that nestled amongst the eucalyptus trees, I saw the twin-engined Otter aeroplane. This was also from the US Army and had carried the fuel for the helicopter up from Addis. Time was precious if I wanted another flight before dark, so as soon as the chopper was re-fuelled, we flew down to the gorge again, dropping over the lip of the plateau as if it were the edge of a coral reef, into the abyss beneath. More crocodiles were in evidence but more alarming was the increase in the number of tribesmen gathering about our camp at the bridge. All were well-armed and waved their rifles excitedly. Was this the vanguard of the force of 3,000 rebels that local chiefs had assured us would attack unless we moved away quickly? I had dismissed this as gross exaggeration at the time but now I was not so sure, and wondered how long forty of us with sporting rifles, shotguns and revolvers could hold out in the exposed bed of the canyon against an attack by so many. Nigel Sale and his party, with one injured man, were still out in the Abaya region, making their way to the bridge. The problem of searching for Ian was rapidly being overtaken by a far more desperate situation involving the safety of the whole expedition.

The river was running too high for comfort and I did not want to sail on until it had dropped another two feet. We only had enough boats to take ten men and their equipment. Many of the survivors of the white water team were injured or sick and quite unfit to proceed by river. Ahead lay the worst crocodile-infested stretch yet and I wanted John Wilsey to reach the Bascillio Junction with his relief force before I set out to study the one part of the Blue Nile which was unmapped, unexplored and unknown. It would be a difficult enough stretch of water without interference from rebels and, as we had our last look for Ian, I felt I was sitting on a powder keg with the fuse burning shorter each second.

By the time we landed on the ledge above the camp, my plan was made. Get the walking wounded, sick and other persons up to Mota as quickly as possible. Gavin Pike, a robust young cavalry captain, who had been with me before in Ethiopia, would take these men out; I prayed the rebels would let them pass. Nine of our fittest would sail on with me to survey the last stretch and meet John Wilsey at the rendezvous. I would tell Nigel by radio to make for Mota direct and not come to our camp. All I needed was about four hours to organize this. As I clambered out onto the short grass I noticed two young warriors with their rifles unslung and pointing vaguely in my direction. Trying to appear unconcerned, I thanked the pilot and said just loud enough for him to hear, 'I think we've got trouble here, I'll get your crewman up, but keep your engine running.' A precipitous goat track, a foot or so wide, led down the cliff face to the camp. One of the warriors followed me, his rifle aimed at the small of my back.

Mesfin, our Ethiopian Government liaison officer, came over and whispered quickly, 'I cannot do anything more with them.' In camp everyone looked worried and watched with drawn faces. The tribesmen were in a truculent mood.

When in doubt, confuse the enemy! 'Good,' I said loudly. 'Thank you, Mesfin, please tell the Chief I have been to Mota and I bear important news for all the tribe, but first I must prepare some notes, then I will come and tell them all about it.' Hoping the interpretation of this white lie and ensuing questions would keep the warriors busy for a few minutes, I seized the confused American crewman.

'You've got problems, Captain?' he asked.

'Yes, but with luck you can get out as soon as I start speaking to the tribesmen. Go to the Chief of Police at Mota and get him to come here as fast as possible and sort out these old gentlemen and their people. You are our only hope, so do all you can. Also, please tell my head-quarters what is happening.' With that I turned, and, replacing my beret with the pith helmet, I strolled over to the stone bridge and, whilst Mesfin interpreted, gave a long harangue about Ian's death, the search, our scientific work, the medical aid I had brought from Mota for the treatment of all ills, and how grateful we were to the tribesmen for looking after us. I threw in the names of Haile Selassie, Churchill and Wingate for good measure, and I was still speaking when the helicopter lifted off the ledge and soared back towards Mota. My audience barely seemed to notice.

To endorse the speech, I announced that there would be a sick parade in ten minutes for the tribesmen. Then, grabbing Ian Macleod's medical kit, I told Corporal Henry to gather together all the spare pills and potions he could find. Together we set up a clinic on the bridge.

The queue of evil-smelling patients stretched fifty yards. They jostled for places, and minor punch-ups took place between the warriors to get to the head of the queue. Our meagre resources were totally inadequate for anything more than token treatment. Our proper medical officer was himself sick at base and Ian, who had been our best medical orderly, was dead. Treating the tropical sores and eye diseases as best we could, we gave out aspirins for tummy aches and Henry's remedy for the numerous malingerers was a Horlicks tablet sellotaped over the painful area. In the case of a particularly unpleasant brave, he administered two dozen powerful laxative tablets with a drink of water. He then told the young warrior to run home as fast as possible, lie down and await results! He never saw him again.

As night fell we held a simple memorial service for Ian. Many a tear rolled down a tanned face. We had lost a good friend.

I then gave the orders for the next day. Gavin would take out the overland column. Nigel had already been diverted. I would lead the new group downriver to investigate the last unexplored part of the gorge and eventually meet John Wilsey. We would take most of the guns and ammunition from the others. I had a feeling our need might be the greater. However, everything depended on the tribesmen letting us leave. But I had sent out word to the muleteers of Mota to bring their beasts to the bridge the following morning.

At darkness the chiefs and their followers retired to the top of the gorge and fortunately there was so much preparation to carry out that our minds were fully occupied until sleep took over. Once during the night our sentries woke me. A noise had been heard twice on the track above the camp, but the early warning necklace of stone-filled cans strung across the path had not rattled. Probably a hyena.

The misty dawn was cold and damp when the tribesmen returned. Hardly had the sun appeared over the cliff when we heard the helicopter. The Police Chief of Mota, Captain Mulena Alamu, strode into view, smartly dressed in a freshly laundered uniform, peaked cap, shiny boots, black Sam Browne and bearing a .30 carbine and revolver. He walked amongst the chiefs, smiling and greeting them; a diminutive figure, confident and authoritative, just like his Emperor. Crossing the bridge, he spoke with Begemir Province chiefs, who had remained on their own side. Then he made copious notes in a large official book. In no time, this efficient law officer had sorted out the problem with commendable tact and diplomacy. I spoke to him through Mesfin and, as he left, I followed up the cliff path to the waiting chopper. Glancing around to make sure he could not be overheard, he said to me in perfect English, 'It is all right for you to continue, but keep your guns handy and a good watch at night.'

'Where did you learn English?' I said in genuine surprise.

'England,' he hissed, and climbing into the cockpit shouted, 'Tanastalin,' and was gone.

At the bridge we remained under guard. However, following the visit of the gallant captain, we were treated with a new respect.

Miraculously the mules arrived on time and the overland party was soon shouting farewell as it started up the steep ascent to the high plateau. They did not have an easy journey: ambush parties met them throughout the route, and at each stop there was much argument and discussion before they were allowed to pass. The entire province was in turmoil and the rebels were said to be marching on Mota.

Back on the river, we prepared to sail next day. The Beaver made an air drop of supplies, but many of the items that were free-dropped fell onto rocks and were badly damaged. With foresight, the packers had placed the whisky inside new socks, so at least we were able to wring out the remains of a few precious drops! Circling above, Alan told me of more tribesmen massing in the mountains, and the Beaver had been fired on. We really were in a boiling cauldron and I wondered if our overland party would reach Mota.

My first problem was to overcome the fears and anxieties of the team, who were apprehensive about the conditions ahead. Reconnaissance by air does not always give a true picture of river conditions, and we had been lulled into a false sense of confidence several times. *I* knew we could do it, but the men needed a lot of persuading. They had not seen the Army recce boats in rough water and, of the six sent from Britain, only two had been found fit for use. Nevertheless, I had no doubt that these craft would manage the rapids.

It was 21 September. The temperature at 0800 hours was 74°F; rain had fallen during the night. We awoke cold and wet on our rocky beds. My knee, injured during the pre-expedition training, was stiff and the pain under my armpits told me that the poison from infected rope burns on my hands was spreading. Somehow the antibiotics had ceased to work, and anyway we had only a few left.

My helmsman was Sub-Lieutenant Joe Ruston, Royal Navy. Joe, a rugged, amiable person, was an engineer, and his quick wit and good humour made him an ideal companion under such arduous conditions. He and I were to scout ahead in the recce boat *Semper* and warn the two engineless Redshank inflatables of forthcoming hazards. An ingenious mechanical engineer, John Fletcher, brought up the tail of the fleet with the second recce boat, *Ubique*, and with him was our crocodile expert, a young zoologist named Colin Chapman.

The recce boats were both equipped with nine-and-a-half horsepower motors and could hold against the current, which enabled them to manoeuvre more easily than the Redshanks. Even so, they were not as robust as the Avon. But if anything went wrong, the recce boats would come to the rescue, or if we were attacked by crocodiles, they had the heavier weapons necessary for defence. Colin was certain that the crocs would not attack, but I remembered he had said there were none north of Tisisat and one had strolled into our camp above the falls!

Many tribesmen were still with us, having spent an equally wretched night wrapped in their voluminous shammas. As I dipped the blunt razor into a mess tin of tepid water, a fish eagle screamed its yodelling call into the canyon of the Blue Nile. The river simply hissed and bubbled as it swept on its way. Our guards, seeming to sense our imminent departure, eyed us suspiciously and shuffled nearer like optimistic vultures, hoping for gifts of surplus food. I wondered if they would really let us go.

A Close-run Thing

'GO, GO, GO,' I SHOUTED as we pulled into the current, and in seconds our little fleet was borne away by the swirling flood. One or two of the guards raised their rifles as if to fire but our sudden departure had taken them by surprise and we were out of sight before they recovered.

Rising early we had gone about our usual chores as if everything were normal. Most essential items had been stowed in the boats under the cover of darkness, and we left a pile of boxes which had given them the impression that we were not going anywhere. The river gave us an exciting ride and at times I judged it prudent to come into the bank to use the roping technique past a particularly difficult cataract. We shot through most rapids in grand style! Hitting big waves, we were drenched, but the old recce boats did remarkably well and our confidence grew.

Antelope stared from the banks and birds rose in dismay as we flashed by. The crocodiles were well hidden for we saw none. Perhaps the engine noise drove them to shelter in the murky depths. High on the hills white-robed figures gave shrill cries, announcing us from mountain top to mountain top. At water level the black basalt was so polished that it looked like marble. Scribbling in my log I recorded that the river width varied between thirty and fifty yards, and in the rapids we were moving as fast as nine knots. The Redshanks paddled on steadily, and it quickly became apparent how useful the powered boats were in escorting, guiding and towing the paddled craft.

We were able to inspect a place where Major Cheeseman believed the river had changed course. There was every sign that this happened, but the water level was sixty feet below the old bed so it must have happened long ago. In fact Cheeseman's original map was correct, but the copies and reproductions showed the river in the earlier course. We updated the map and passed on, looking all the time for evidence of minerals and people. As we journeyed on into the most fantastic vertically-sided gorges, the water hissed between the cliffs like a stream of liquid brown mud. These sheer walls, which rose from the water for 100 to 200 feet, appeared to be limestone capped with volcanic rock. Towards late afternoon we reached some vertical lava pillars, standing in mid-river. This gave me our exact position, as I recognized them from the air reconnaissance. I felt instinctively that if we were to find a clue to the mystery of the Northern Gorge, it would be in these sinister canyons, through which I knew no white man had sailed.

Suddenly we caught sight of a roughly-built dwelling, perched high on a cliff on the Gojjam bank. This was a niche in the rock, closed off by a stone wall. A doorway in the wall had a timber frame. Was this evidence of a lost tribe? Waving our Ethiopian flag, I signalled the other boats to pull in to the shore. Stumbling along the rock-strewn beach, we sought a route inwards, but then Joe called out, 'Hey, there's a man there.' At the top a lone figure stood watching us intently. He did not return my wave, but regarded us in sullen silence. Then, without warning, he became agitated, shouting and waving us away. I thought this unusual as Ethiopians are most punctilious about returning greetings. However, it could be that he lived alone in the dwelling and thought us to be raiders, although I doubt if raiders would bother to fly the Imperial Ethiopian flag! But tax collectors might! So, after a short inspection, we sailed on through the vertical rock walls, our voices echoing unnaturally and for some way we were completely enclosed in the massive slot.

A sharp bark to our left surprised us and there, scampering amongst the rocks, was a party of hideous old men clad in grey fur coats. Or that was what it looked like! 'Hamadryas baboons,' called Colin. The boats slowed, cameras clicked, the baboons screamed with rage and one quite deliberately threw a small stone. They really did look human. My God, I thought, so those are the mysterious ape men! It was easy to see how a legend of a lost tribe could be based on a colony of Hamadryas, living in crevices on these remote cliffs. I was still making notes when Joe said, 'Look at those caves, surely they're man-made?'

Passing by on our right were two large openings situated in the rock face about thirty feet above the water. At the same time, a small cove containing a stream and some low trees appeared on the left. It was probably the Tammi River. 'Pull in to the beach!' I yelled.

It was the most pleasant site we had found to set up camp so far. The stream had cut a narrow gorge, which ran back some fifty yards behind the beach. The little river formed a beautiful waterfall as it entered the cleft, spurting out from the terrace above and sending clouds of spray to gather rainbows in the last rays of sunlight. The water in the stream was clear and slightly warm. Lichen and ferns grew out from the cliff in profusion. Beneath the trees was a plentiful supply of firewood and a clear area in which to erect our bashas.

Across the Nile the cave entrances gaped at us, one semi-circular, the other triangular. They were partly blocked by a well-built wall of rough stones. That was certainly man-made, but there was no evidence of any inhabitants and, as I studied them with my binoculars, I wondered how we could gain access. There was an overhang immediately above the caves and the only possibility seemed to be to ascend from the river bed. This was a job for our rock climbers. We all felt excited and yet slightly apprehensive. After our adventures of the past weeks I wondered what fate had in store for us now.

In no time our tents were pitched on a sandy ledge amongst the trees. While supper was cooking, Garth and David, our 'zoologists', went on a lizard hunt. John Fletcher repaired the transom on his boat, which had been damaged during the day. Chris and Roger discussed a plan for getting into the caves on the morrow. Richard filled several more pages of his notebook. Joe was working on the engines. Alastair, Colin and I cooked up an awful mess of sardines and rice. After supper I strolled up the narrow canyon behind our camp and there I made another discovery. Jumping across the stream, something green caught my eye. I stopped and looked back. The bed was littered with bright green rocks. 'Copper,' I said aloud. Sure enough, the stream bed contained lumps of copper oxide, apparently carried over the waterfall at the end of the canyon. Picking out a few specimens I resolved to return next morning to seek the source.

Darkness fell rapidly but, in spite of our exertions, spirits were too high to sleep and we talked for several hours. It had been a good day. After weeks of painfully slow progress, we had covered seventeen miles in five hours and conquered the worst of the rapids below the Portuguese Bridge. We had made these intriguing discoveries that might unravel some of the mysteries of this mighty river. Furthermore from now on we should have a relatively easy voyage, although there might be the odd sporting stretch of water to keep us on our toes and, of course, there were always the ubiquitous crocodiles!

I did guard from 2200 hours until midnight, spending the time writing my log by the light of a guttering candle. The night was quiet, warm and dry, and our camp seemed safe from interference. I had much to record and ponder. Were the caves in fact entrances to tunnels leading to an extensive subterranean settlement? Did the Hamadryas baboons live there? How could we get in? Once inside – would the baboons attack us? Was the presence of the copper significant? Perhaps the caves were mine shafts? I felt a great surge of excitement sweeping through me – after all these months we seemed on the verge of a great discovery. No other white men had been here which explained the lack of knowledge of the region.

A sudden puff of wind blew out my candle and I was about to relight it when I heard a sound on the beach, so I remained still and listened. There it was again – the crunch of shingle. My fingers eased the long barrelled Smith & Wesson from its holster as my left hand gripped the flash light. Flicking on the beam I scanned the beach. Nothing moved and I relit the candle to continue writing. I was in mid-sentence when I heard the voice. Unmistakably it said, 'Be very careful in the morning.' The hairs on the back of my neck rose, but I didn't jump up, in fact I was rooted to the spot. My mother's voice? I heard nothing more, but I was wide awake and alert. That warning caused me to review our plans.

My concern now centred on the crocodiles that lay ahead. From the air I had seen some monsters; certainly many more than we had seen elsewhere on the river. Scientific advice had told us that the crocodiles would now either be far up the tributaries, or well down the river beyond Shafartak. But they were still here. This was why I had despatched John Wilsey with three men to come upstream from Shafartak to meet us. However, he'd had a great many difficulties and we had not made radio contact for several days. But Main Base had managed to pick him up and learned that two of his outboards had blown up under the terrific strain of forcing the rapids. A third engine, dropped from the Beaver, had disappeared into the Nile when the parachute failed to open. Unfortunately this load also contained the team's rations so they must now be pretty hungry. Our last spare outboard was on its way to them by American helicopter. I knew

John wouldn't give up, and I could easily imagine him straining every muscle to get his boat to the Bascillio Junction.

Base also told me that the assault boat team had reported an alarming increase in the number of crocodiles and strongly advised that we should not proceed past the junction without the alloy boat as escort. Until we met John, I had a simple plan of defence against the crocs. We'd try to avoid them, remembering the bite one had taken at an assault boat the previous month, but each craft was to carry a sandbag full of stones for use as a deterrent. If all else failed, we would open fire with our heaviest weapons and thrash the water with paddles. Colin, who had been working on crocodile surveys in Ethiopia for several years, considered an attack to be most unlikely. Nevertheless I always had the heavy Mauser rifle ready, just in case. I prayed that if we met an angry thirty-foot croc, this would stop it.

Healthwise we were not in bad shape. Most people's cuts and lacerations were now healing or at least the infection was not spreading. My own injuries were giving little trouble; the knee hurt occasionally but I could dispense with the walking stick. My torn hands were of more concern. The nylon rope that had cut through to the bone during my earlier rescue from the river had led to an infection that sent a jabbing pain to my elbow joints and armpits, but with constant cleansing and dressing I hoped to keep going for another week. As the moon rose over the gorge I thought again about the voice, 'Be very careful in the morning'.

Heavy rain fell while I slept and at dawn the baboons' barking chorus roused us from our moist sleeping bags. We wolfed down breakfast and, while the air was still cool and with the canyon in deep shadow, started to explore the caves. Joe lightened *Semper*'s load to the minimum and, with his engine racing against the current, took Chris Bonington across the river. Festooned with rope and climbing equipment, the mountaineer stood in the swaying boat. Joe brought his craft with throttle wide open against the cliff and, as we watched apprehensively from the other side, Chris studied the rock face, then he sprang upwards, found hand and toe holds and started climbing. Had he slipped he would have plunged into the turbulent river. In a minute or so he was in the cave and lowered the rope, which Roger, coming across next, secured as a fixed line. Richard was the last to go and soon all three climbers were safely inside the cavern. Quickly and with some regret they discovered there was no tunnel and the cave uninhabited.

'The place is full of pottery and basket work,' yelled Chris. Joe ferried their archaeological finds back to camp, while Roger shot a small bat for the zoologists. It appeared that we had discovered some ancient refuge, probably deserted for many centuries. The floor was deep with bat dung giving off a nauseous smell, but the remains of an old leather rope provided a clue to how the former dwellers had got in. Perhaps in the dry season there was a ledge beneath the entrance.

Just before midday the party returned and we spread out their discoveries to photograph. Gazing down at the potsherds, bones, fire carbon and aged leather rope, I heard a distant whooping cry. This was the usual way that one Amhara shepherd signals to the next, but it was repeated and sounded excited. I couldn't read the strange language, but I had heard our guides use it often enough to realize that the tone had much to do with the message. 'I think we'll have a quick lunch and press on,' I said.

'What, and leave the caves only half explored?' complained my chums with obvious disappointment.

'Yes,' I said crossly, 'just grab a Mars bar and let's pack up and go.' I had intended to continue the exploration in the afternoon. Quite why I suddenly changed my plan, I'll never know. The tone of the shepherd's cry would not have been sufficient by itself. Something made me uneasy. It would take us at least thirty minutes to pack up and load boats, and I simply felt we must move.

I was so entranced by the beauty of the waterfall behind the camp that I decided to take a quick snapshot before we left and record the site of the copper. In the little canyon it was cool and pleasant and I spent a few moments deciding which would be the best angle. The sharp crack and the shower of chippings from the rock face made me duck instinctively. I looked up. There, at the top of the bluff, a hunter, silhouetted against the blue sky, stood clutching his rifle and watching me. 'Look out, you idiot, you nearly hit me,' I shouted in anger and, ludicrously, in English. The man opened the bolt to reload and I suddenly realized that was exactly what he was trying to do. Instinctively my right hand flew to my holster, but I had taken off my belt a few moments before when going to commune with nature. My revolver was on my pack in the camp.

My feet hardly touched the ground as I raced back down the gorge, leapt over the stream bed and rushed into camp. I don't think I've ever run so fast in my life. 'Blashers, running?' said the look on the faces of my friends, but before they could speak, I shouted, 'Hurry, we must get out quickly, just grab everything and get into the boats.' We moved fast, and I had just loaded my pack on to *Semper* when a horn sounded several short, strident notes. A second later a bullet smacked into the shingle a foot away and I looked up to see the cliff top on the far side of the river alive with some thirty armed tribesmen, their white shammas billowing in the wind. They were only sixty yards away!

A wild fusillade of shots followed, ricochets whined off the rocks and spurts of water sprung from the river. Our attackers waved their weapons and screamed blood-curdling war whoops. Up on high ground beyond the cliff top I could see long lines of tribesmen coming to join them. Obviously the lone rifleman had given the game away too soon. Perhaps my appearance with the camera had surprised him, but what on earth had prompted the attack? This was not the moment for analysis. We ran for cover under the trees.

Army training in dealing with hostile crowds brought to mind the words 'minimum force'. I seized the loud hailer and dashed out on to the beach. One man seemed to be the leader and, addressing him, I boomed out, 'Tanastalin, tanastalin, we come in peace and are your friends.' To my relief, the firing ceased and Geronimo, as he was instantly nicknamed, bowed low in the customary Ethiopian manner. I realized that they had never heard a loud hailer before so I hoped to gain time by keeping him talking. After all, they could not reach me. Having completed his bows, the man deliberately raised his rifle and fired at me from the waist. The bullet came uncomfortably close, showering me in pebbles. In another attempt at appeasement, I again told Geronimo in my few words of Amharic that we came in peace and offered him a Mars bar! Once more the firing and stone slinging stopped – Geronimo bowed.

'John, for God's sake let's fire back,' yelled Garth.

'No,' I said, 'must try minimum force first, just let me attempt to get them talking.'

'You'll get yourself shot standing out there in your bloody white hat. It's not bullet proof, you know,' said another voice.

But the tribesmen were clearly a little confused and, as I spoke, they held their fire. Meanwhile the team packed vital kit.

I tried to switch my mind on to track two again. To stay and argue would give us time, but we would be slaughtered once we tried to run the gauntlet on the river. Right, if we did not want to end with squeaky voices, at best, we must escape. Perhaps they would stop shooting and we could slip away. I doubted it. My heavy rifle was securely packed in *Semper*. Garth's shotgun was in his boat also. David had a .22 rifle, and my own hand gun was a Smith & Wesson .38 Special and I knew how to use it. We could put up a pretty good show if only we had more ammo and some cover. At 180 feet a good pistol shot will register a fair score on a man-size target. But I did not want to fire.

As the tribesmen argued and the loud hailer impressed them more, I shouted rapid orders to the team. 'We are going out by boat, Redshanks first, keep in under the far cliff for cover. Joe, go upstream and draw their fire. If they start shooting, zigzag. John, escort all the Redshanks downriver. Joe, pick me up when the rest are clear, we'll regroup half a mile downstream. Colin, you and I will give covering fire, but only on my order.'

I was interrupted by the sudden arrival of several boulders the size of overgrown footballs crashing through the trees. The cliffs behind us were also alive with the enemy. What coordination! If only they could shoot straight, we'd be dead. Rocks, sling-shot and bullets rained down again as our attackers screamed and yelled. They were not just trying to frighten us. Already the Bejimir tribesmen behind were beginning to descend into the gorge. In a few moments we should be fighting hand to hand. We must leave now.

'Get ready,' I yelled, using the loud hailer to overcome the noise of the gun fire.

'We'll all be killed,' shouted Chris. 'We can't go out there. Call for an air strike, it's suicide.'

'I'm bloody well giving orders here,' I said. 'Shut up and do as you're told.' For many it was a baptism of fire and for all of us frightening.

The rifle fire was now very heavy and it seemed incredible that the inflatables lying in the open had not been hit. 'To the boats,' I cried. Joe was out first, he showed no regard for his own safety and, as the storm of shot and stone raged about him, he calmly pushed his craft into deep water, then, shaking his fist, he sped upstream to draw the enemy fire. I watched him for a second and thought, 'In the best traditions of Nelson, I only hope he survives.' I suppose we all assumed that being a naval officer he would be rather good at this.

John Fletcher and Colin Chapman were in *Ubique*, and ready to escort the Redshanks on their way downstream. One Redshank was launched and being paddled furiously for the relative safety of the far cliff. The surface of the water danced with plumes of spray from the missiles. At any one time six or seven rocks could be seen in the air and many struck the boats. It will be a miracle if we can come through this, I thought. The second Redshank was caught up in some reeds by the beach, the crew struggling to get it into the main stream. I was alone on the beach. Around me lay the scattered remains of our camp. Gripping my .38 Special I looked up to the Bejimir cliff. As I did so, a bullet hit the beach between my legs. The firer stood on a rock slab twenty-five yards away in the Tammi gorge, working the bolt of a short Italian carbine. Raising my revolver, I fired whilst he was reloading. Slightly to my surprise, he doubled up, dropped his rifle and ran up the cliff path. I probably only hit his weapon, but gave him quite a fright. I turned my attention to a group higher up, who carried long barrelled rifles of an early vintage. One shot drove them to cover and, hearing a clang of stone striking metal, I spun round to see a jerry can of fuel standing on the shingle. Nearby lay the precious artefacts collected so laboriously from the caves.

But now Joe was planing downstream, sending pale brown spray up in a fan behind the boat. Weaving in and out of a pattern of missiles, his revolver clutched at the ready, he yelled, 'Get aboard.' Seizing the can of petrol, I regretfully left the artefacts and, racing across the beach, I was up to my knees in the swirling water before *Semper* reached me. Half-falling over the side, I collapsed into the boat. At once, Joe gunned the throttle and we hurtled across the river. The sky above was full of rocks and sling shot. Several lumps, the size of tennis balls, struck the inflatable's tubes and bounced off with a loud 'pong'.

Forty yards ahead I could see the Redshanks now coming under aimed fire. Using his engine, John Fletcher was pushing them downstream. 'Fire,' I cried, and from *Ubique* came the crash of Colin's .45. I swivelled to face the Gojjam bank. Geronimo was there, standing in full view atop a buttress of rock. I saw his rifle kick and a bullet sent a shower of water over me, missing the boat by inches. Joe's tense face was pointed ahead. 'Chris has been hit,' he said. Oh God, what a mess, I thought.

Geronimo was trying another shot as I took aim. 'Hold us steady, Joe,' I yelled. The Smith & Wesson roared and my bullet struck the rock six feet beneath the white robed target: his went on towards the Redshanks. In the time it takes to squeeze the trigger, I fired again, but three feet too low. Rock chips flew downwards towards the swirling current. My last shot came almost at once. Geronimo's head jerked up as he reeled backwards and with his arms outstretched as if seeking support, fell from sight. I turned to face his followers, but they were now hiding behind the rocks, their rifles silent. Only the odd long range shot whistled after us and splashed harmlessly into the river.

During the battle, Joe had calmly taken Chris's Redshank in tow. Now the injured photographer was seated, blood running from a stone wound in his back and trickling down the side of the boat, but he was not badly hurt and already his camera was ready. 'Look left,' he cried. Joe and I, our guns still in our hands, spun round to face the next enemy, click went Chris's camera. I suppose it may have looked authentic! It was 1210 hours. The whole incident had lasted only ten minutes.

For several miles we towed the Redshanks. The gorge gave way to sloping hillsides, plantations of maize and a few huts. Great square blocks of basalt lay like islands in mid-stream, the results of massive avalanches. When I judged we had gone a safe distance, we halted to reorganize. As I dressed Chris's wound, Joe set up the radio and I scribbled a message for base. 'Sitrep. Attack on camp by forty natives from both banks with rifles, rocks and slings. Fire was returned in self-defence. No enemy casualties. Bonington minor injury. Do not cause flap over this. Tell base all OK, but much kit lost. Do not release to press.' I hoped that this statement would keep the whole matter at a very low key, and this was the reason I had not mentioned Geronimo or any other enemy casualties. The Racal radio was fitted with a twelve-foot rod. Such aerials are only designed for short distances but, to our utter astonishment, base, almost 100 miles away and with Mount Choke (13,000 feet) between us, answered our first call.

We cruised on throughout the afternoon. Whoops and shouts followed us from the hills. 'Here come the tax collectors,' they probably said. Eventually all was silent, but I knew that dozens of unseen eyes were watching and, sitting with the big Mauser on my lap, I scanned the high ground through binoculars. Crocodiles were appearing here and there on the banks, but they made no aggressive movement. I estimated we had covered twenty-five miles since the ambush and felt that we had probably out-stripped any pursuit. Darkness usually fell at around 1830 hours, so it was as well to stop an hour or so before this. At 1700 we were still some three miles north of the junction, when I saw another canyon ahead. The walls were much wider apart than the previous gorges and I recognized a pinnacle of basalt leaning out from the Gojjam cliff in the far distance. I had noted this on the air reconnaissance and remembered it marked a short stretch of small rapids and also the start of a longer stretch of vertical cliffs. If we got into any difficulties in those rapids, darkness would probably catch us in that gorge. We drifted on downstream coming upon a long, low, shingle island. A small patch of trees and scrub grew in the centre. There were a few driftwood logs that could be used for defences and there were no crocs about – as far as I could see. The current was quite fast and even the narrow channel on the right contained deep water. Around the island the river banks were largely devoid of cover and the nearest high ground was at least half a mile back. It seemed a reasonable defensive position and probably the best we should find for miles. It will take a determined bunch to attack us here, I thought. Crunching ashore on the pebbles, we pulled the boats up and established camp under the trees in the centre of the island. In order to get the radio equipment nearby Joe sailed *Semper* into the narrow channel, mooring to a tree.

We were sipping a brew of hot sweet tea that Richard Snailham had cooked up when we spotted three boys swimming diagonally across the river from the Bejimir side. Any bitter feelings we had felt after the ambush had now abated and we waved a friendly greeting to the brave newcomers, who treated crocodiles and the swift current with such contempt. They came out of the water and stood at the edge of the island, their smooth athletic bodies glistening with water. They looked like shy young girls for they were stark naked except for a small silver Coptic cross on a string around their necks. These people had probably known Christianity when our ancestors were painted blue. Unlike most natives we met they seemed timid and hesitant and simply stared at us. Eventually our gestures and offers of small gifts tempted them to come into the camp and, once there, they lost all shyness. I doubt if they were older than fourteen. They spoke a dialect none of us understood and even Colin, whose Amharinya was better than most, could not get through to them. They seemed quite amicable and we presented them with aspirins, plastic bags and Mars bars. Like all Ethiopian young men, they displayed considerable curiosity towards our weapons and, when they swam home a few minutes later, I felt rather uneasy about this interest. Was it the normal respect for guns, which are a status symbol in this wild land, or was there more to it? I was still pondering when Joe called me for supper. We had been forced to abandon some of our rations at the Tammi, but although on a reduced scale, the meal was adequate.

As it grew dark I held the usual briefing and outlined the plan for our defence and possible withdrawal should we be attacked that night. We arranged to have two sentries on duty at all times and built a rough zoriba or thorn fence around the camp. Colin and I were carrying ministar flare launchers which we would keep loaded and close at hand. Each man was given his responsibilities, and ammunition was distributed. Being Sunday, after orders we held our usual service. Richard selected a hymn from the Army Prayer Book and just then it began to rain. Everyone huddled under my basha and we sang, 'Now thank we all our God, with hearts and hands and voices . . . ' The words seemed appropriate.

The night was very black and, apart from the patter of the rain and the hiss and gurgle of the river, all was silent. I wrote up the log, penned half a letter to Judith and then lay fully dressed on my sleeping bag. I undid the laces but kept my boots on. Positioning my flashlight nearby, I cleaned and checked my battered old revolver and laid it beneath the pith helmet which served as a pillow. Next I oiled the Mauser and loaded the magazine before placing it in its plastic tube. This I pushed inside the sleeping bag. The final act was to dress my throbbing suppurating fingers and swallow an anti-malaria tablet. It was just after 2200 hours when I blew out the candle and sank into a deep sleep and as usual snored like a pig!

In the distance I heard yells and shots. A faraway voice shouted, 'Stand to, stand to,' but it was all a dream. Or so it seemed for a long time, which, in fact, could not have exceeded three seconds.

As I came to, my hands groped for the ministar launcher. The shots and war whoops were very close, and somewhere a hunting horn was sounding short blasts. Tearing open my shirt pocket I felt for the pen-sized device and, rolling out of the basha, I thrust it upwards and tried to manipulate my swollen fingers to fire it. 'Crack' went the tiny cartridge as the flare curved through the sky lighting up the island and the river. The shingle beach was alive with shining black bodies advancing on the camp. One figure, carrying a short spear or a sword, was only fifteen yards away chasing Roger towards the zoriba, trying to stab him. My hand was searching for my gun as I saw David, our second sentry, crouched by a tree. He brought up his .45 and its flash and roar came together. In the last light of the dying flare, I saw the leading attacker stop as if he'd hit a glass wall, then sink to his heels and roll over backwards. A hole the size of a dinner plate gaped in his back. Another flare rose into the sky almost at once, fired by Colin and in its light I buckled on my belt and drew my revolver. As I put up another ministar, a volley crashed out from the camp. 'They're coming through the trees!' I heard someone shout. 'For heaven's sake, guard the boats,' yelled Chris.

It was now 0105 hours and bullets from the enemy side were hitting the camp. Suddenly a figure came blundering through the scrub. It was pitch black. My gun came up and I was about to shoot John Fletcher when I heard him say, 'Joe's down by *Semper*.' It was not until this moment that I realized that the heaviest fire was coming from the river bank on the Gojjam side. The bandits' covering party had been in position there all the time and was now trying to pick us off in the dark. I let go another flare, horizontally this time, aimed at the next rifle flash and, to my delight, saw half a dozen white robed figures scampering away in panic. Meanwhile the raiders were still on the north end of the island and trying to work their way through the scrub.

'I'm firing into the bushes,' I yelled, not wishing to risk the chance of an accident with one of our own men. There was no reply and, advancing a few yards, I waited. Low voices muttered about twenty yards ahead. More firing and whoops on my right showed that Roger and his party were busy by the boats. Then I saw a definite movement a few yards ahead, one or probably two men, I thought. Someone was calling out in the local tongue on the bank. The figures showed again and I blasted two quick shots, deliberately aiming low in the scrub. With much noise of breaking undergrowth and grunts, the bandits fled through the bush.

'Beach is clear,' came the cry from the right.

'Garth,' I shouted.

'Yeah,' came back the faint Australian accent.

'Take David and recce forward up the island, see if there are any of them still here. We'll switch our fire to the covering party.'

Alastair Newman had joined me and, together with ministar and revolver, we took on the bandits on the mainland. The tactics were simply to watch for a gun flash, put up a flare in its direction and get off a couple of quick shots whilst the target was illuminated. Joe was already packing up the radio equipment. 'The aerial's caught in the branches,' he muttered, 'I'll have to climb the bloody tree and sort it out.' As most of the shots from the enemy were passing over our heads through this particular tree, it would be a hazardous undertaking, but the radio was of little value without it. He started to climb up the thorny trunk and I heard hoots of laughter from the bandits. I'll swear there was a clink of a bottle, and I realized that the gentle thudding I'd heard earlier was a ramrod being driven down some ancient musket barrel. To confirm my impressions, there was a bright flash, a 'boom', and a cloud of white smoke jetted out from the trees. A six-inch nail or some similar object crashed through the branches near Joe, who swore loudly. A few minutes later he jumped down. 'Got it,' he gasped, 'see you at the RV,' and, clutching the radio, aerial and his machete, he staggered down to *Semper*. Then continuing to ignore his own safety, he pushed off into the channel and drifted silently downstream between the firing lines. Although there was no moon, the night seemed to be getting lighter as my eyes became accustomed to it. It was possible to distinguish large objects, especially on the water, and I saw the bandits only twenty yards away from Joe. The fire fight continued for another fifteen minutes and slowly all of us pulled back to the pre-arranged rendezvous at the far end of the island. Roger had brought the boats down the shore and was joined by Joe in his inflatable from the other side.

Alastair and I pulled back to the defensive position last. There was a low shingle bank, but we were close to our boats and had a completely clear field of fire. Everyone was there. Garth reported the island free of enemy. Ammunition was quickly redistributed, we had three rounds left for each .45 and, although we had more liberal quantities for the other weapons, we were not well off. I checked each man's arc of fire and, coming to Richard, said, 'You cover from that bush to . . . '

'John,' he interrupted quietly, 'I feel there is a small point I should raise at this juncture.'

'What on earth is it?' I said tersely.

'I haven't got a gun,' he replied. I found it difficult not to burst out laughing. Richard, as gentle and unassuming as ever, was clutching his Swiss Army penknife. 'Would you like your pith helmet back now?' he said. Guarding it like an Imperial Eagle of Rome, he had carefully concealed it from view throughout the battle.

It was now 0200 hours and I planned to hold out until just before dawn, then slip away when the light was sufficient for us to see the way through the cataract approximately a mile ahead.

The bandits' shooting was as bad as their tactics and field-craft were good, so I doubted if they would be able to hit us as we moved downriver. I could probably discourage them from following too closely with my rifle. But it meant holding them off for another three and a half hours at least. They were brave men and I suspected well-primed with alcohol. It is difficult to estimate the numbers involved, particularly as we were fighting at night, but I believe a reasonable approximation would be forty to fifty, against ten of us.

There was only occasional firing from the bank and this we returned with the rifle to conserve revolver ammunition. Once I thought I saw a figure swimming the channel between the island and the mainland. If indeed it was a man, my shot must certainly have worried him.

At 0300 hours Richard reported a growing movement on the mainland opposite his post. I listened and could hear a lot of muttering and shuffling amongst the bushes. The bandits were probably massing for another attack, so I put up a flare which revealed nothing. 'If they make another determined attack we shall have to withdraw,' I said, 'simply not enough ammunition.' No one questioned this, but all wondered how we could negotiate the rapids in the dark. I gave instructions for the withdrawal and, to avoid revealing our movement to an enemy cut-off party, who might be lurking downstream, I said that no engines were to be used except in dire emergency.

The silence was broken by the short, sharp notes of the hunting horn. Just as we had heard earlier. I put up another flare and, in its light, I could see groups of robed figures moving forward through the trees on the far bank. They were coming again.

'Right, man the boats,' I whispered loudly and, firing several shots at the massed bandits, clambered into *Semper*.

'Life-jacket,' said Joe, thrusting one at me as he pushed us into deep water. 'By the way, I think we've been hit somewhere up front, we've got a frightful leak,' he remarked, and I felt the soft, squashy forward tubes of the boat. As we pulled away from the island, I rummaged about and found one of the foot-pumps. Fortunately, it was easy to connect to the valve and as I sat I used one foot to keep the pump going, whilst my hands were free to paddle.

We reached the far bank and at once the current forced us against some trees. 'Push clear quickly,' came Roger's urgent warning, 'or we'll be dragged under the branches.'

We had only been on the water for a short time when the whoops and horn blasts announced that our evacuated position was under attack.

'We've got a good start,' I said to Joe, but he was too worried about his craft to notice the events behind us.

'Keep pumping, we're losing air fast,' he said.

To help keep together, each recce boat took a Redshank in tow and it was in tandem that we reached the cataract. Ahead, in the blackness, we could hear its thunder, but saw nothing. As we raced towards it at some six knots it was an eerie, unnerving experience. The terrifying noise got louder and louder. In daylight we could have chosen the best route through the white water, but now we had no idea whether we were coming upon a small waterfall, a huge rock in mid-river or some shallow rapids that would tear our hulls open, like a knife through butter. Straining my eyes ahead, all I could see was inky blackness. To our left *Ubique* and its Redshank were now invisible.

The water hit us without warning. The Redshank under tow was completely engulfed. A second wave swept over and the rapidly deflating front tubes almost bent double. I lost the foot-pump in the chaos and heard Joe yelling, 'Can't go on like this!'

'Ok, let's use the engine to run into the bank,' I screamed back, 'but we'll have to cut the Redshank loose.'

'Can't make it,' called Joe to the boat behind, 'we're going ashore for repairs . . . Casting you off, pull in further down, good luck.' At least they'd have a better chance without us. The tow-line parted and at once they were swallowed up in the darkness and the raging river.

Our outboard started almost immediately and, with superb seamanship, Joe took the sinking craft astern and out of the main stream. We thumped into a shingle bank and I shot out backwards onto the shore as Joe killed the engine. As I landed, something slightly blacker than the pebbles slithered off into the water – I'd almost fallen on a crocodile! For a few moments we sat still with drawn revolvers, listening for any enemy, but the noise of the cataract drowned everything. Suddenly from the darkness, two shapes loomed up. It was *Ubique* and her Redshank. They landed ten yards away and we heard their horrific story of a capsize in mid-cataract. David and Richard had both gone overboard and were only saved by a miracle. Much kit had been lost including the vital box of rations. We were now soaked to the skin and very cold. 'Where's Chris's boat?' said Colin. As if to answer him, a light appeared flashing dimly down river. The signal, in morse, read OK. So they were safe too! Back upriver our camp was still burning, small showers of sparks cascading skyward as our enemies vented their wrath on all we'd left behind.

Joe had discovered *Semper*'s trouble, a leaking valve which was easily cured. Someone passed round a handful of boiled sweets and we cracked one or two nervous jokes.

Making a quick reconnaissance, I discovered to my relief that we had landed on a featureless shingle bank, separated from the mainland by a fast-flowing stream. However, we dared not show lights or speak loudly, as the bandits could not be far away. Thankfully cloud still covered the moon. We worked quietly in the dark to refit the boats and it was about 0415 hours when John Fletcher lost the nut that held on the propeller of his engine. It had slipped from his wet hand into the river. Without this, the propeller could not be secured and therefore the engine was useless. John tried everything his resourceful mind could dream up, but it appeared there was no solution. As a last resort he mixed a paste of Araldite in a tobacco tin and glued the propeller on to the shaft.

'How long will it take to set, John?' I asked.

'About an hour and a half if I can keep it dry,' he replied.

'You reckon that we can sit here in daylight, do you?' I exclaimed.

'No, I realize we must push on, and if necessary I'll lash a plastic bag over the propeller when we go. We'll just have to hope that it will set and paddle meanwhile,' he answered. Fitters, like John, are worth their weight in gold on expeditions!

An hour later the sky began to lighten and, casting off once again, we skirted round the tumbling cataract and picked up the missing Redshank and crew downstream. The dawn was fantastic. The growing light revealed an incredible view of towering cliffs, giant boulders and natural limestone arches painted shades of brown, pink and yellow. The river was like a mirror, much wider now and slower, only a gentle wave or two disturbing the surface. Nevertheless I kept the rifle handy and watched the cliffs. We passed Bascillio Junction, but I reckoned John Wilsey must be further south.

Along the banks we could make out the shapes of dormant crocodiles, and it was not until the sun began to reach the gorge that they started coming out to inspect us. We watched warily, occasionally hurling a rock to deter them. However, they kept their distance and at 0700 hours Joe managed to raise base on the radio. Once again it was a miracle of communication, for he was only using the twelve-foot rod.

I had just spoken to Nigel, the deputy leader now safely at base, when I saw Joe's mouth open. 'Oh, my God,' he said. Looking up, I saw a leviathan of a crocodile literally galloping with its legs extended. The giant reptile plunged into the water and came speeding straight at us, its great head causing a bow wave. I simply yelled 'Crocodile attack!' into the microphone and leapt for my rifle. The huge twitching tail propelled it like a torpedo as I aimed the Mauser at a point midway between its evil yellow eyes.

'Don't shoot,' shouted Colin, 'he's only curious, he'll stop short.' If you're wrong, my friend, I shall kick you off the cloud when we meet in Heaven, I thought. The huge creature closed to within eight feet of the boat, when, without as much as a splash, it dived and passed beneath us, its scales rubbing the hull, only to surface on the far side. It then cruised alongside for about twenty-five yards, giving me a chance to estimate its size, which was even bigger than our boat. At a conservative guess I would have said fifteen feet in length! Suddenly it had disappeared beneath the muddy water, this time for good.

Base was trying to contact us on the radio. 'Sorry for that interruption,' I said, giving a brief outline of the battle. 'Don't get the authorities all worked up yet. Give me a chance to get well clear before Haile Selassie's jets come thundering in to deal with the bandits.'

'They've got troops standing by to be helicoptered in and get you out,' replied Nigel, 'and John Wilsey is twelve miles south of Bascillio Junction.'

'Fine, but we need ammunition and food in that order, so may we have a drop when we meet John?' I went on.

'Our stocks of rations are almost out,' retorted Nigel. 'What has happened to all of yours?'

'Oh, I gave them to friendly people around here,' I replied sarcastically.

We switched off the engine to save fuel and drifted for a while. More crocs swam out to investigate, but Colin was right, they always stopped short. However, I could see how any inexperienced person would assume they meant business and open fire long before they had got within eight feet. It was 0815 hours as we rounded a bend and saw the dark green assault boat. A great cry of joy went up and I stumbled ashore to shake John's hand. For several hours crews swapped stories.

Cataracts grew bigger, bandits and aggressive crocodiles multiplied. John himself had a great tale to tell. For seven days he had struggled upstream, his boat leaping rapids like a giant salmon. No one had ever brought any form of powered craft so far up the Blue Nile before. It was an incredible achievement.

Having washed, shaved, cleaned our guns and re-fuelled, we ate a meagre breakfast. Food supply was very short, but at mid-morning the Beaver came roaring into the gorge and dropped several bundles. They only had one parachute left and that was used for the petrol and ammunition. The rations came in by freedrop and, sadly, the pack burst, scattering its contents far and wide. They were all the supplies they had left at base. This consisted of some packets of biscuits, a bag of rice, sardines and cheese, plus a four-gallon plastic container of whisky! 'Well, at least we can lay on a cocktail party,' joked John. The whisky container was leaking, so we had liberai gulps before setting off in a euphoric haze to study the last part of the river.

The remaining time passed quickly and a new menace hit us: mosquitoes. The dry season was approaching and already the trees were turning brown and the river beginning to drop. We had started picking the chewing gum repair patches off the petrol cans, but the hunger pangs got unbearable and eventually we persuaded Colin to shoot one of his beloved crocs. With a single accurate shot he took out a seven-footer, killing it cleanly with the big Mauser. 'Joe,' I said, 'you're a Naval officer, you're bound to be good at croc skinning.' So my helmsman got to work and we ate the tail. To starving men, cooked in some candle fat, it tasted delicious.

It was 24 September when we sailed from our camp on the Uolaka junction and began the final run to Shafartak. On the radio we heard that quite a reception awaited. It was hard to realize that we had got through, and now, after nearly two months, it was almost over.

Sitting in the boat as we made that last day's run, I began to make notes for my report to the Emperor. No lost tribe, just some unsociable apes and a large population of reluctant tax-payers. No radioactive gas or uranium as far as we could tell, but very likely a good deposit of copper. The crocs were certainly huge, but nothing above eighteen feet had been seen. Although there'd been massive landslides, there were no waterfalls below Tisisat and, in the wet season, inflatable boats could navigate from the Portuguese Bridge to the Sudan if His Imperial Majesty so desired!

At 1620 hours the Beaver came skimming over the river and we knew we were close. Ten minutes later we ran ashore and the champagne corks flew. A large lady from Texas was amongst those who had come out from Addis Ababa to see us arrive.

As we staggered up the beach she turned to her husband and said, 'These guys must be crazy.'

'Hush dear,' he replied, 'they're British.'

Escapism

THE KING'S ARMY was crossing the open ground some six hundred yards in front. In the summer's sunlight the cavalry, infantry and camp-followers of the Royalist forces were a colourful sight. The breeze carried the sound of drum and fife as well as the oaths of the gunners, sweating on the drag ropes as they heaved the great culverins over the ankle-deep grass. Sir William Waller, my commanding officer, dressed in puritan black, his hand resting on a fine silver-embellished pistol, glanced casually towards the clump of trees, where I sat upon the sixteen-hand grey charger, and nodded. I acknowledged the signal and, turning about, cantered to the rear, rounded a leafy bush and faced my Ironsides.

Sixty or so stood by their horses, their black lobster helmets glinting, orange sashes standing out against their drab leather coats. There was not a cigarette, not a pair of dark glasses, not a wristwatch, nor indeed any vestige of the twentieth century.

'Ironsides, mount,' I yelled, and at once the troopers sprang into the saddle. 'Captain Muir,' I shouted. 'Pray advance thy horse beyond yonder ditch, whence you will see the malignant host. Then thou shalt take them in the flank, for they do presume to cross our front.'

'It shall be so, sire,' replied the young cavalry commander.

'We'll ride with you,' I called, as the horses began to trot.

'On the right, then,' replied the good Captain. Emerging from the trees, the Ironsides shook out into five ranks of twelve. 'Draw swords,' came the order.

Visors dropped as we splashed over a shallow brook, passed through gaps in the hedge and entered a large meadow, at the far end of which the enemy was still moving slowly to the east. They saw us when we were four hundred yards away, trotting forward in good order and they began to run out cannon and form square. I could see Prince

Rupert's cavalry behind the foote, trying to find a way through the confused ranks.

'Ironsides, charge,' screamed Johnnie Muir.

At once every trooper brought the flat of his blade down on the rump of the horse in front. The tight box of cavalry rocketed ahead with the thunder of hooves. We bent forward, grateful for the cooling wind. Even to stand in forty pounds of armour, leather and thigh boots is no joke on a summer's day.

Screaming like banshees, we scattered two gun crews, kicking over powder barrels and slashing down a standard before whirling right to circle behind the enemy and rejoin our friends. What tremendous fun, the wildest schoolboy dream come true!

'Ow!' I spat, as something very hard hit my upper arm, a stinging blow. 'What the hell was that?'

'A tennis ball, my lord – one of ours,' said Frances Copping, my ADC, raising her visor and mopping the perspiration from her brow. Sure enough, in the middle distance the line of trees where we had started was masked now by drifting clouds of smoke, as the Round-head artillery engaged the army of King Charles.

'There,' cried a gunner, 'let's see how they like this – Fire!' Propelled by a thunderflash, a tennis ball whistled down the meadow. His earlier shots had been high, but this one struck a small enemy cannon, whose fuse was already burning. The gun spun and dis-charged itself at its crew. A great cheer went up from the Army of the Lord, as we sometimes called ourselves. Cromwell's men were enjoying the artillery duel. Their next shot hit the breech of an enemy culverin and bounced about amongst the gun crew, causing a standard-bearer to drop his colours. Thus encouraged, the Vicar General ordered the Twenty-third Psalm and the Roundheads sang.

The final act of the day was the inevitable head-on clash of the Foote – as chance would have it, on a narrow bridge. The cavalry stood back as the rival mobs, no regimental order remaining, beat hell out of each other! One poor fellow lost his teeth to a pike butt – 'Well, he shouldn't have joined if he couldn't take a joke,' commented Sir William (alias author and historian, Professor John Adair). Eventu-ally the stentorian bellow of ex-commando Brigadier Peter Young, Captain General of the Sealed Knot, brought a stop to the bloodbath. We all shook hands and limped back to our respective camps. The five thousand spectators trooped home, having had twenty-pence-worth of fun.

Peter had started the Sealed Knot in the spring of 1968, and in no time the brigadier had formed an army. Many of his friends, always ready for a spot of colourful fun, joined. Promotion was rapid and by the time I reached Marston Moor in June 1970, I was a 'General of Engineers'. Beneath all the amusement, there was a serious purpose to our activities. By restaging the battles on the original ground, using authentic equipment, those interested in the history of warfare could appreciate the difficulties faced by the forces from which developed the modern British Army.

Both Roundheads and Cavaliers had regiments of horse, foot, dragoons and traynes of artillery. Our membership included people from every walk of life. Girls fought as men and acted as camp-followers: on the Roundhead side, Judith and Kay Thompson organized a nursing corps, known as the Sisters of Chastity! Alas, Judith was later dismissed for drinking wine upon the field of battle.

Recruiting was no problem. Those with the sense of the theatrical obviously preferred being Cavaliers, for the glorious uniforms, if nothing else, although the simple, more modest armour and leather of the Roundheads had a definite appeal and was certainly less expensive. The recruiters for the Army of the Covenant were ever ready to point out that many attractive damsels rode with the Royalist cavalry 'and will be ours by right of conquest, for, as according to history, we always win'.

The battles were usually staged so that a local charity could benefit from the large crowds that flocked to see the carnage. Was this not the attitude of Rome in its decline? However, although our casualties were not uncommon, they were rarely serious. Beer flowed like water and demure young ladies cast inhibitions to the wind and flirted outrageously with men whom they scarcely would have glanced at in twentieth-century garb. It seemed that once we donned our costumes, we left today's world far behind. A 'wench' was carried off to hospital at Plymouth with a strained back.

'How did you do this?' questioned the doctor. 'I had to be raped by a Roundhead,' she explained, 'but, whilst trying to catch me, he fell off his horse and squashed me flat.'

Officers had no real authority but discipline was surprisingly good, although we always considered the Cavaliers rather unruly and issued strict warnings to our Ironsides against 'brawling, duelling, bear- and bull-baiting'.

At the re-enactment of the first battle of Newbury (20 September

1643), I took the part of Sir John Merrick, whose Parliamentary artillery had played an important role in the battle. I persuaded a dozen fellow students from the Staff College to join in, including a United States Army major, George Smolenyak, who had recently fought in Vietnam. George, dressed as a puritan officer, was in the thick of the fight during which his fibre-glass helmet was topped by a Cavalier's sword! Emerging battered, bruised and truncated, he was heard to mutter, 'Gee, Vietnam was never as dangerous as this!'

Judith and I have often given unusual parties, and in 1970 with some pals we held a Viking Blot (an early Scandinavian drinking 'orgy' and fertility rites) at Hawley Lake, the Royal Engineers' watermanship training area in Hampshire. Here we set up a marquee and hired an extraordinary all-electric musical group equipped with a sort of portable water organ. We decked out two thirty-five-foot whalers as Viking ships and moved in a vast quantity of wine.

Whilst we were setting this up, the Sealed Knot was amusing the crowds at the Sandhurst Horse Show. At the height of the battle, our friend Ken Monk, playing his usual part of the Vicar General and extolling the Roundheads to spare no one, but to do the Lord's work and smite the malignants with all their might, was ridden down by a Cavalier. Looking much the worse for wear, poor Kenneth was carried off to a waiting Army ambulance. When he came to his senses he was at the Cambridge Military Hospital in Aldershot.

'Rank?' enquired the orderly.

'Vicar General,' groaned Kenneth.

'Name, sir?' said the soldier with new respect.

'Monk,' replied Kenneth.

'Date of injury?'

'11 September 1646,' said Ken.

'How exactly did it happen?' asked the orderly, more than a little puzzled.

'Ridden down by cavalry,' said Ken, in his soft Welsh voice.

Looking at the form, the orderly wrote in the remarks column 'Mind wandering', and sent him off for head X-ray.

It was nearly 2230 hours before they finished setting his broken arm and Ken was able to change into his costume as the High Priest of Wodon and persuade the army to despatch him by ambulance to the 'orgy'. The dancing girls, a dozen nubile nymphs fresh from being 'raped' on the Sandhurst lawns in the cause of charity, were now attired in sealskin bikinis and cavorting in an erotic dance that set the men's pulses racing. Just as Ken arrived, a duel resulted in one guest being run through the hand with a sword, so the ambulance did not have a wasted return trip.

As the extra strong Danish beer flowed, the party got into its stride. The Viking ships raced up and down the lake. A few guests who had foolishly come in suits of chainmail almost drowned. Finally we auctioned the slave girls for charity and, when a thick mist descended, the party dissolved into chaos as guests tried to find parked cars and, having done so, attempted to drive them. I will never forget seeing Richard Snailham, dressed as Diogenes, and wearing a barrel, trying to climb into his Triumph sports car.

I spent what remained of the night collapsed on a bearskin in the marquee. At dawn, very stiff, with a wicked headache, I stepped over my prostrate friends, and staggered out. There was a terrible scene of desolation. Broken weapons, sealskin bikinis, Viking regalia and empty bottles. The smoke from the fires drifted vertically upwards in the still air and beyond I could see the ships, one demasted, riding at anchor on the misty lake.

Seeking some privacy to attend to the most pressing business of the moment, I strolled off into the rhododendrons. Still dressed as Wodon, with two-horned helmet, beard, cloak, skins and sword, I was eagerly watering the flowers when I sensed I was not alone. Looking up, I saw a wide-eyed, bespectacled fisherman, complete with green waders, landing net and rod, gaping at me from twenty yards off. His Jack Russell, one leg raised, also stared. 'What ho!' I bellowed, waving the sword with my free hand. To my amazement, the poor fellow turned and fled. I often wonder what he told his psychiatrist!

Much of my time at Staff College was unofficially devoted to planning explorations and, although the idea of pushing paper in the MOD did not greatly appeal, I opted for a posting to Whitehall knowing that it would be immensely valuable to understand the workings of the Civil Service. I found that if handled correctly, this much-maligned body of dedicated people could really be most helpful, especially to expeditioners.

I found myself in trouble early on whilst attempting to oil the wheels of a conference dealing with defence estimates, by ordering chocolate biscuits for coffee break. My claim to the finance branch

Cuddly pets attracted recruits to my small private army at Hereford. (Guinea pig on J BS's shoulder.)

My parents always visited me at Bisley. (*Daily Telegraph*)

CCF exercises in Jersey were all the more realistic when played out amongst the old German fortifications. (*Jersey Evening Post*)

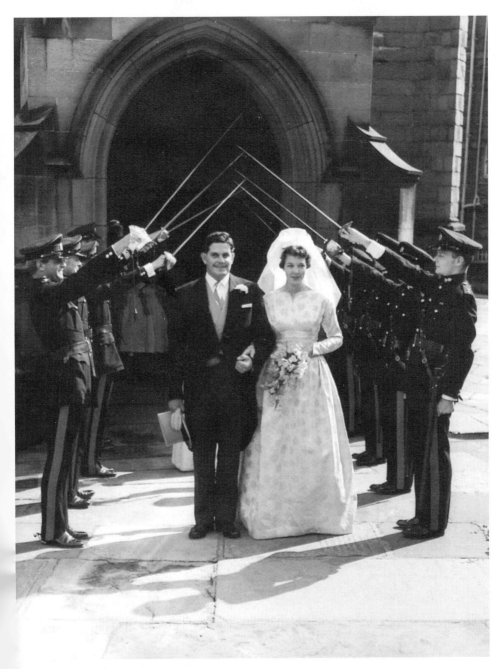

Judith and I were married in Chester in August 1960. (The Guard of Honour booby-trapped the exhaust pipe of the car we drove off in. It was blown off with an enormous explosion an hour later! We survived!) (*Fotocraft*)

Washing the expedition at an oasis in the Libyan Desert, 1963

'Roaring Meg' in action with a Parliamentary battery
of the Sealed Knot. (*Soldier Magazine*)

Captain Jim Masters, the Sapper
officer who played such a vital role
in many of our expeditions. (*MOD*)

THE BLUE NILE
EXPEDITION, 1968.

Right: After the second battle it was
a miracle that we managed to
raise base on a simple rod aerial.
JBS and Joe Ruston in the RE recce
boat *Semper.*

Below: The Army Air Corps
Beaver swoops low over Captain
John Wilsey (now General Sir John
Wilsey) to drop ammunition and
much needed supplies.
(*Chris Bonington*)

THE DARIEN GAP EXPEDITION, 1972.

Above: Ernie Durey and his unstoppable engineers forcing the Land-Rover Pathfinder through the Darien jungle. (*Scientific Exploration Society*)

Below: Rafting across the Tuira in a stretch of fast current with the indispensable Avon M650 rig. (*Daily Telegraph*)

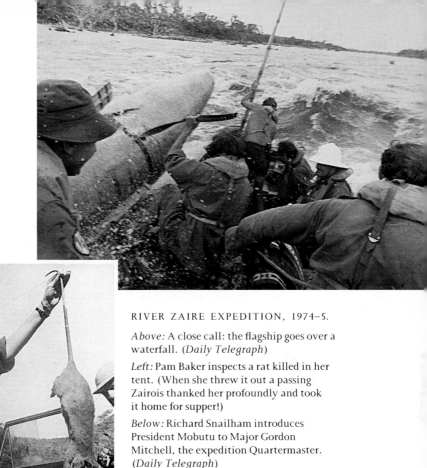

RIVER ZAIRE EXPEDITION, 1974–5.

Above: A close call: the flagship goes over a waterfall. (*Daily Telegraph*)

Left: Pam Baker inspects a rat killed in her tent. (When she threw it out a passing Zairois thanked her profoundly and took it home for supper!)

Below: Richard Snailham introduces President Mobutu to Major Gordon Mitchell, the expedition Quartermaster. (*Daily Telegraph*)

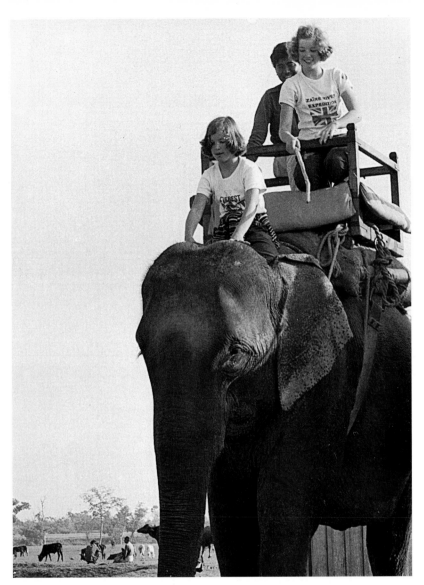

My daughters Victoria
(*left*) and Emma learn to
control elephants during
a family expedition at
Tiger Tops in Nepal.

Ruth Cartwright
(*née* Mindel) finds Monty
rather lively at an
Operation Drake selection
weekend. (*SES*)

for ten pence was rejected out of hand with the comment, 'Biscuits, chocolate, are for generals. Other officers only qualify for biscuits, plain.' However a colleague got £10 from Peterborough for the story and took me out to lunch.

There were countless files to be studied, many of which had been in circulation for decades. I was given one concerning a claim for compensation from an irate householder who complained of a wartime concrete bunker, complete with coastal artillery piece, that was still in his garden. As a housing estate had grown up around the weapon he pointed out that to fire it would certainly cause fatal casualties amongst the population of Little Piddling-on-Sea and demanded that we should remove it or pay compensation. The correspondence had flowed since June 1945 and one could trace the steady decline in the poor fellow's health. The Ministry letters were sympathetic, but unhelpful. Sometimes they blamed the economy, sometimes another ministry, and finally the local council for having erected houses around the gun emplacement. However, offers of help were made from time to time, such as 'The matter is under review by the Engineer-in-Chief and it is hoped that the defences in question may be demolished by explosive charges with the minimum damage to your property', or 'As the removal of the block-house is now considered impractical, perhaps you would wish to make an offer to purchase it.'

There was the usual crop of letters to the Member of Parliament concerned, and about once every twelve months a really abusive one from the tortured victim himself. When this happened the Ministry rolled itself up, hedgehog-like, in a protective ball and refused to reply, thus forcing the complainant to eat humble pie and write an obsequious plea to obtain an answer. Of course, staff officers changed every two years and so the Ministry was constantly being revitalized whilst the complainant grew more frustrated. When he finally expired, a loose minute on the file suggested that the matter should now be passed to the antiquities department of the Ministry of Public Buildings and Works.

The telephone rang for the hundredth time one morning. Grabbing it, I said, 'One minute, please,' and signed the letter that my sergeant was holding in front of me. Scowling at the aged, chipped, black telephone with barely concealed malice, I wondered which lost cause this call would ask me to support.

The voice sounded polite and hesitant. 'Some friends and I have a small exploration problem on which we should value your advice. Could you lunch with us next Thursday?'

A good meal would be more than welcome. 'Thank you very much,' I said, 'where shall we meet?'

'The Hispanic Council at Canning House,' came the reply.

I had heard of this organization: Anglo-Latin-American relations, trade, cultural and economic links. I had become very interested in South America whilst acting as rear-party officer for the Roraima Expedition, which had explored the site of Conan Doyle's Lost World that summer. The mystery of Colonel Fawcett's disappearance also intrigued me, but I wondered why anyone should want to consult me on exploration in South America. I had never been there.

Following the success of the Blue Nile expedition and on the advice of the Sandhurst Commandant, then Major General John Mogg, a group of us had founded the Scientific Exploration Society (SES), to organize and encourage scientific exploration worldwide. This charitable organization was to become the driving force behind many major expeditions.

In 1969 we ran our first project to investigate a strange blindness as well as the fauna and flora of the remote and little-known Dahlak Islands in the Red Sea. The team had returned in triumph. Freddie Rodger, our eye surgeon, decided that the blindness was largely caused by the intense ultraviolet radiation, and, what was more important, he believed that in many cases a cure might be possible. I felt a deep satisfaction from helping these simple, unselfish people who, possessing few worldly goods, had shown us kindness as great as anyone could expect in our own world. Already the SES was establishing a reputation for tackling challenging but worthwhile expeditions.

Lunching at Canning House, Colonel Julian du Parc Braham, eyeing me through his monocle, asked, 'Have you ever thought of driving from Alaska to Cape Horn?'

'No, but I do not imagine there would be much of a problem, simply a question of time and petrol.'

'Then you do not know about the Darien Gap,' he said sharply. I didn't!

I learned from the British Darien Action Committee that the Pan-American highway system, 17,000 miles long, from the snows of Alaska to the deserts of Southern Chile, is a bloodstream with many arteries, feeding twenty-three nations with trade, tourism and the exchange of ideas. But it was not complete. In the middle, at the Isthmus of Darien where the Atlantic almost meets the Pacific, there was a tiny block, a thrombosis that stopped the flow of lifeblood between North and South America – a mere 250 miles of hills, jungle and swamp that had so far beaten the highway engineers of both continents. This was 'El Tapon' – the 'Stopper', or the Darien Gap.

Tim Nicholson, the committee's secretary, explained that a bill recently passed by the United States Congress would provide two-thirds of the $150 million dollars needed to build a road across the barrier. President Nixon himself had commended it. But words were one thing, action another. The area was receiving publicity through being the site for alternative projected routes for a new Panama Canal, but the road was a poor relation. A spark was needed to fire men's imagination and translate words into the deeds so desperately needed by the nations concerned.

This spark, the Colonel said, had been lit by the Darien Action Committees of the United States, Panama and Colombia. Now they were seeking support for a pioneering British expedition to try something never before accomplished because of the natural hazards: to drive specially-equipped vehicles all the way from the Arctic Circle to southern Chile, traversing the Darien jungle and swamp for the first time. Other hazards and obstacles it would meet included almost perpendicular razor-back ridges, bridgeless rivers, wild beasts, reptiles and insects in profusion. The expedition, he claimed, would bring a dream a step nearer to completion by providing the publicity and 'spark' needed to get money for the road-builders.

My hosts explained their plan to send a party of six in two Land-Rovers to tackle the journey in the coming December, and they wanted my advice. There seemed to be no real difficulty in getting from Alaska to Panama and from Colombia to Tierra del Fuego. The problem was the Darien Gap. Several expeditions had reached the Panama-Colombian frontier, but then ran out of time and were caught by the rains which came in April. The most difficult part of the obstacle was the Atrato Swamp, almost the size of Wales, which nearly severs South from Central America. Clearly the promoters considered the British mad enough to take up the challenge.

It seemed to me that, to be successful, an expedition from the north must get its vehicles to the frontier in time to cross the swamp before the rains. The team must then have a proven method of crossing the morass and know a feasible route. I wondered if it would not be better to tackle the swamp first, by going from Tierra del Fuego to Alaska, but the committee lacked any real information about the swamp and their knowledge of the Darien jungle was pretty sketchy. My advice was that they make a thorough reconnaissance at the same time of year in which they proposed to tackle the obstacle. This meant postponing the expedition for twelve months.

A week later, Tim Nicholson telephoned to ask if I knew a suitable person to do the reconnaissance. So I began to look for a determined, self-sufficient SES member with a keen eye for observation and the stamina of an ox. Brendan O'Brien at twenty was a wild, tough, well-travelled Irish daredevil. His amusing, easy manner and winning smile helped him to get on with people, who rarely took him seriously. Having recently overtaken a police car at enormous speed on the wrong side after a London party, he accepted the post without hesitation and, after some rushed training in Spanish and field engineering, set off for Darien in January 1971.

While our stalwart friend was hacking through the jungle, I did a little research into the type of vehicles and equipment that might be used in the Gap, assuming that, as a result of Brendan's reconnaissance, the committee decided that the project was feasible. At this stage I was simply an adviser. Then Tim telephoned me again.

'The leader's been posted to a new job,' he said with apprehension in his voice. 'Would you be interested?'

My curiosity was already aroused and, subject to the Army's blessing, I agreed. I realized this was going to be a hard fight even with a good team and the best equipment.

Recruiting began at once. Rosemary Allhusen, a charming and highly efficient young lady, with enough self-sufficiency and determination to put half a dozen men to shame, volunteered to be my PA. Rosh, as everyone called her, had a real love of adventure, and experience of handling horses that was to be of considerable value. We worked well together. Even so, I must have driven her mad and I'll never know how she put up with me.

In April Brendan returned, thin and haggard. For two hours I listened to his story and examined his photographs. In the end he said, 'Well, there it is. I think you can do it, but don't ask me to come with you.' With that he rushed off to the Hospital of Tropical Diseases, leaving me to reflect on the magnitude of the task.

For several days two voices argued inside me. One said, 'It will be bloody horrible; snakes, insects, heat, rain, jungle, swamp and what's more – very costly. The General Motors expedition, with all their careful planning, well-tried vehicles and generous funding, could not make it. How on earth do you think you can do it? Back out now with dignity.' The other voice said, 'Difficult yes, uncomfortable certainly, but nothing's impossible. A flexible plan, good logistics, sound equipment and a carefully chosen team could do it. What a challenge.'

The weather pattern dictated that we should move from north to south in the dry season, a purely relative term, which could be assumed to run from mid-December to mid-April. To fit this time-table, the vehicles should leave Alaska in early December and they would probably reach Tierra del Fuego in May.

The permission and support of the Governments of Panama and Colombia would be essential. The help of the US Forces in the canal zone could be extremely valuable and, furthermore, political clear-ance was required to cross frontiers. Lastly, it would cost at least £25,000 in cash, in addition to the generous support in kind from the British services and other sponsors.

I told this to the organizers, now renamed the British Trans-Americas Expedition Committee (BTAE), and added that it would take about six months overall and my team would be around sixty, including scientists. I insisted that the expedition must have a scientific programme. It was of little real value just to get the vehicles through; we must explore the region as thoroughly as possible. So we planned to undertake important investigations of a zoological, botanical and geological nature in what was, by any standards, a remote and inaccessible area. This task would be an urgent one, in view of the ecological disruption which might follow on the construction of the highway. I also believed it was important to study the local people before their lives were changed forever.

My studies of various types of all-terrain vehicles showed that, whilst an amphibious tracked vehicle would be best for the Darien Gap, it would not be able to maintain the high speed on metalled roads necessary for the easier parts of the journey. It simply had to be a reasonably fast, light-weight, economical and robust wheeled vehicle. I talked to Ministry of Defence experts and examined reports on a wide variety of vehicles that might fit the bill. We decided an up-engined Land-Rover was required.

So I asked Captain Gavin Thompson, a cavalry officer with rallying experience in the Americas, to head our vehicle section and he now advised that the newly-produced Range Rover might be an answer to the problem. The Rover Company was confident that the more powerful brother to the famous Land-Rover would indeed be the best vehicle and was enthusiastic about the opportunity for some valuable publicity for the new car. They agreed to lend us two Range Rovers, my only worry being that they weighed twice as much as Land-Rovers. But Gavin, whose knowledge of vehicles I respected, was impressed by the power and pointed out that this more than compensated. Jim Masters and Ticky Wright, sappers of the Blue Nile team, had joined the new venture. 'Well, if it won't swim, we'll have to make it float,' they muttered, and phoned the Avon Rubber Company to discuss making an inflatable raft that would carry such a load. Jim thought it a hell of a weight to get over the narrow ravines, and sought advice from the Royal Engineers (RE) bridge experts on the construction of special alloy ladders that could be carried on roof-racks, and laid over ravines. Meanwhile, Rover tested a Range Rover with various types of tyres and other fittings that might make it suitable for the expedition.

'We need something to carry the cordage, tools, explosive, jacks and equipment for the engineers,' said Jim at one of our many meetings. 'Must keep the weight on the vehicles to the minimum.'

'I was hoping to get mules for this,' Keith Morgan-Jones, our massive Army vet replied, 'but you can't get them for love nor ruddy money in Panama and, because of foot-and-mouth, they won't permit them to be brought in from elsewhere. Only packhorses are available and they don't carry more than 120 pounds.'

So off we went for more advice. The MOD engineer equipment branch produced details of a tracked, motorized wheel-barrow called a Hill-Billy. In no time, trials of equipment were going on all over Britain. Our experts examined the Range Rovers, Hill-Billys, rafts, power-saws, outboard-motors, radio and food. The rations were, as usual, Kay Thompson's department and she also took up the reins as general manager and PRO. She and Rosh got on terribly well and were the nucleus of my staff in London. A steady stream of articles began to appear in many newspapers at home and abroad. Television and radio also took up the story, but, alas, having educated Britain to the horrors of Darien, we found that people believed the project was doomed to failure, and were not inclined to give us the support we now needed badly.

'Look John,' said an old chum in the media business, 'I've put this project of yours to everyone I know – they all say the same – you've bitten off more than you can chew this time. If it's half as bad as the press reports, it's obviously impossible. Anyway, no one in Britain cares very much about a road through Darien.'

But on the other side of the Atlantic, people did care. Ultramar Inc generously offered to supply us with free fuel, the Explorers' Club in New York helped us to recruit scientists and the governments of Colombia and Panama suddenly began to take a considerable interest in the project. The Latin America desk of the Foreign and Commonwealth Office was tireless in its efforts to assist, as were the British Embassies throughout the Americas.

From the United States came a letter of good wishes from President Nixon and from the US Canal Zone came welcome offers of support. I felt we were really getting somewhere at last, and when the Canadian Broadcasting Corporation bought the North American television rights, we reached our minimum fund-raising target. Funds and grants came in from British sources as well. While some learned societies regarded the whole affair as a commercial publicity stunt, certain to fail, it was noticeable that a number of enlightened organizations put their faith in us and backed the expedition to the hilt. Prominent amongst our supporters was the Natural History Museum. I have always found the executives of the museum very keen to take opportunities to further exploration with natural history objectives. Members of the museum staff, Dr Philip Burton (ornithologist) and Mick Baachus (entomologist), were to form a scientific section with Jerry Carter, a young geologist, Robin Hanbury-Tenison, sociologist, and Dr Al Gentry, a botanist working in Panama.

Colonel Peter Reid, a cavalry officer with an interest in natural history, would oversee the scientific work. Another keen ornithologist was the Army's Engineer-in-Chief, Major General Caldwell. The general had joined the BTAE committee at the outset. As the senior officer on the committee, he did a splendid job in helping us to get assistance and full-scale support from the Royal Engineers. Captain Ernie Durey, a well-fed, energetic forty-year-old sapper, with much experience of crossing obstacles, joined our team on the general's recommendation.

So the expedition assembled: sappers, infantrymen, cavalrymen, pilots plus an army doctor and his SRN wife. A dentist, a vet, scientists and secretaries, Americans, British, Latin Americans and a Gurkha. In all, fifty-nine men and five women to join another forty or so persons in Darien.

In October 1971 we announced our plan. Our aim was simply to take two Range Rovers from Alaska to Cape Horn (or as near to it as it is possible to drive), making a scientific study of the Darien Gap en route.

In early December, a six-man driving-team would set out from Anchorage in Alaska, aiming to reach Panama City in early January. There they would be joined by the main body of the expedition. Our column would enter the jungle with David Bromhead's recce team scouting ahead, finding a route for Jim's sappers to clear for Gavin's vehicles. My HQ would bring up the rear with the supplies carried on Keith's horses. Outside the Gap, Major Kelvin Kent, my intrepid deputy leader, another Jerseyman, would organize our re-supply by air and river. Depots were to be established in the Gap or on the coast, and a main base would be set up in Panama.

The Avon raft would get the vehicles across the rivers and through the liquid portion of the Atrato Swamp. I intended to airlift recce parties ahead of the expedition, so that they might have adequate time to examine the ground, especially the great swamp. The Colombian Navy promised a gun-boat to act as a floating base on the Rio Atrato and both the Panamanian and Colombian armies would send soldiers to escort us in their territory.

The scientists would accompany the expedition's main body or set themselves up independently in the area, whichever suited them best. Hopefully their work would contribute to the protection of the environment in the future. I hoped to reach the far side of the swamp by mid-April, when I believed the rains would start. We should all go to Bogota, and, having sent the Range Rovers on to Tierra del Fuego, the rest of us would return to the UK.

Put like this now, it sounds very simple. Basically it was, but above all else, it was the most flexible plan I could devise. In spite of Brendan's recce and all the information we had gathered, I still felt that there were far too many unknowns. Planning the attack on Darien was like preparing to assault a strong enemy position in war. Staff College training advised a commander to outnumber the opposition three to one. I knew that in this case the odds were very much reversed and the only way we could win was to concentrate our force at one point and maintain it for at least three months.

By December all was ready. The advance liaison officer, Captain Paul 'Arrangement' Arengo-Jones, had already arrived in Panama to make initial preparations and await the end of the rains. Meanwhile, feverish activity had been going on at Rover until the last minute, but eventually the cars were loaded into the RAF Hercules and despatched to Anchorage.

In mid-December came the awful news that one car had suffered a bad crash on Alaska's ice-bound Alcan highway, which would certainly prevent the vehicles reaching Panama before 10 January. Paul signalled ill-news from Panama – the rain was still falling hard with no sign of a break. Christmas was beset with worries, and I realized that I had become so consumed by the forthcoming campaign that I was now a real bore to my family.

At the farewell party the Minister for Defence said the expedition was the most ambitious ever undertaken by the British Army. It made me feel terribly responsible. It was a cold, wet dawn when I climbed shivering into the cavernous belly of the Hercules, feeling very tired, unfit and more in need of a week's holiday than three months in one of the most unhealthy regions on earth.

The Stopper

THE TURQUOISE BLUE SEA showed momentarily through the clouds, then, as the Hercules altered course for Tocumen airport, a range of low green hills protruded through the cotton wool. At first the jungle of Panama looked peaceful. Facing inwards again, I fastened my seat belt, gazed across the mound of equipment and awaited the landing.

The belly of the giant freighter was largely filled by the dismembered Beaver light plane. Its wings folded alongside, it rocked gently on restraining chains, like some giant tethered insect. Around were dozens of boxes and crates, some labelled 'hazardous – with care', others 'fragile – this way up', and all bearing the words 'Operation Darien'. The weariness that had dogged me for the past weeks had gone. I now felt revitalized, alert and ready to go. Perhaps it was the welcome sleep I'd had while crossing the Atlantic, or the long-awaited sight of the jungle. Whatever, quite suddenly everything became very clear.

When the great tail door swung down a blast of humid tropical heat drew rivulets of sweat from every pore. Paul was there, and Kelvin, plus, praise heaven, the two Range Rovers. 'Everything's under control, John,' said Arrangement-Jones. 'The Ambassador's car will take you to his residence where you are staying.' I thanked the crew of the RAF Hercules, which, to the astonishment of our Panamanian friends, was already giving birth to the Beaver.

His Excellency, Dugald Malcolm, was an honorary president of the expedition and, as a one-time regular soldier, the Ambassador understood both the diplomatic and military viewpoints of the project. Sipping whisky in his air-conditioned study, I realized how very fortunate we were having such an ally and supporter at the startline.

Everyone in Panama wanted to know of our plans and volunteered candid opinions about the Darien Gap. I had a strange feeling of being treated with a certain respect, rather as one might regard somebody who had once had a nervous breakdown and would shortly end up in an asylum!

Some say the first few days of an expedition are the worst. However, thanks to the advance party, all went remarkably smoothly. The Guardia Nacional (Panama's Defence Force) was most cooperative, and customs and immigration formalities were waved aside. The US Forces in the Canal Zone bent over backwards to help and provided us with a base, transport, vital jungle boots, hammocks and a one-day course at their Tropical Survival School. Further flights of passengers and freight came in on time and the task force quickly took shape. There were only two problems. Packponies, so necessary as load-carriers, were proving difficult to obtain and, most serious of all, it was still raining hard.

Captain Peter Marett, our intelligence officer, searched Panama for detailed information on the Gap and the weather we could expect. Nothing new emerged, surprisingly little was known of the mysterious forest beyond the city bounds.

As we held a press conference the lightning flickered and the rain fell in sheets. I hoped my replies sounded confident. Luckily, their attention switched to the ladies. The smartly dressed girls, fresh from swinging London, did not match the conventional idea of hearty women explorers. Did we but know it, they were every bit as mentally rugged and tough as their Victorian forebears.

Our first forward base camp was established in an army training camp on the edge of the actual Gap. Near here at the 'Wild West' town of Canitas the Pan-American highway ended as a dirt track. We hung our mosquito nets on the bunk beds and crawled onto the straw-filled mattresses.

Dawn at the Centro Instrucćion Militar (CIM) seemed to come very early. I was awoken from a deep sleep by the most hideous din. My watch showed 0430 hours, yet blaring from the camp public-address system was a continuous arrangement of martial music. Did our allies realize what they were doing? Heaving myself up, I rushed over to the guardroom. Fortunately I had grabbed my pith helmet, for I suddenly found myself involved in a military ceremony. The guard, immaculately dressed in starched fatigues, presented arms, as their national colours were raised. Dressed in a colourful sarong, wearing flip-flops and my white helmet, I was at least able to stand to attention and salute.

The orderly officer marched over and with a smart salute said, 'Buenos Dias, Major.' With halting Spanish and convincing gesticulations, I explained that his music was driving me mad. The officer looked embarrassed and gave a sharp order. The din ceased immediately. Ah! peace, perfect peace. I thanked him in French and staggered back to bed.

'That was probably their national anthem and they'll shoot you later,' growled the massive Morgan-Jones from behind a pile of saddles.

There was not a moment to spare during those hectic days. The sappers prepared the tools of their trade, the doctor made arrange-ments for the inevitable casualty evacuations, the scientists liaised with their opposite numbers in Panama and organized the safe custody of specimens, while Kay sorted out the tons of rations and 'goodies'. The vehicle party, helped by an expert from Rover, prepared the cars for the coming ordeal. The team from the Canadian Broadcasting Company arrived, a rugged pair of thoroughly profes-sional film-makers who fitted in well.

Peter had arranged a reconnaissance programme, and we set off with David Bromhead, our chief recce officer. Soon we were racing through the cold morning air, the roar of that powerful engine taking us up and above our base camp. Now for the first time I saw the Darien Gap. We turned above the airstrip and headed east-south-east. Beneath us was gentle countryside, rolling green savannah, dotted park-like with trees and herds of white cattle. The town of Chepo, with its galvanized iron water tower, slid by under the port wing. Beyond, the sun glinted on the thick brown coil of the Bayano river, glistening like a giant snake. Canitas consisted of a scatter of white boxes in a square of red earth.

We tilted down as our pilot, Captain David Reid, turned the Beaver once again. Now the grassland was patchier and the green darkened as it thrust up towards us. A mist that had lain in sausage-shaped clouds at treetop level began to clear. The true shape of our enemy now showed, yet from 500 feet it still looked innocuous. The steep ridges were thickly forested; in between, the trees appeared to be more widely scattered. All rose straight-trunked, some bearing

THE DARIEN GAP EXPEDITION

umbrellas of foliage at their tops, others white and bare, with branches that reached up like spread fingers.

We dropped to have a closer look. The altimeter still read 400 feet even though we seemed to be brushing the tallest trees. I looked again at the green carpet and realized that what we had first seen was merely the primary jungle – the real problem lay below it. The giants emerged from an undergrowth so thick that, even from a modest height, it looked solid. This secondary jungle flourished most luxuriantly where the big trees were sparse and let the sun in.

We descended towards the Bayano and flew about 100 feet above the water, over one of the long, narrow outboard-powered canoes or piraguas that serve as river transport in the isthmus. Faces turned up and arms waved. Further on the neat, rectangular, palm-leaf roofs of an Indian village clustered on the bank but, strangely, not a soul was in sight. We climbed to 1,500 feet and headed for the northernmost area of the two mountain ranges that flank the Darien. Our eyes searched the ground for any sign of a track. There was none. From the air the hills did not at first appear to be too steep, but this was deceptive: when we got low we saw that climbing them would be no easy task.

The smaller features, such as rivers, which twisted and turned under the green canopy were hard to distinguish. There were few villages marked on the map: only the occasional dwelling dotted along the riverbanks. I had to discover the best place to cross the Bayano, so we flew up and down the riverline until our fuel was almost exhausted. Several points looked possible but all would require rafting and the current was certainly not slack. Then we saw a track deep in sticky black mud leading to the river. So this must be it. We headed home. A further reconnaissance team moved into the Gap on 17 January and eventually located the crossing point.

Our main body was meantime assembling its vehicles, stores and packhorses in Canitas. Two days later, in drenching rain, we loaded the animals. The track ahead was ankle deep in mud but we could wait no longer. So, for the first seventy-two hours we marched in terrible conditions through the heat and mud of the open pasture-land. We camped with our hammocks slung between the trees, cooking on damp wood fires. As yet the mosquitoes were not a plague but, nevertheless, we always hung nets above our beds.

The Bayano was no mean obstacle, a 150-yard-wide coffee-coloured stream flowing at over four knots between jungle-covered banks. However, the sappers were confident and skilled, and in three hours they had got men, horses, vehicles and equipment all safely to the other side. The Avon inflatable raft again proved its worth. We looked ahead into the darkening jungle of the Bayano valley, the track still fairly clear, but covered in black, adhesive slime.

Each day we marched further into the forest in a long straggling column. Our prison, for that is what it seemed, was illuminated by a dull green light, which at times gave an almost translucent appearance to this eerie world. Great trees rose up like pillars reaching for the sun, which beat down on the canopy some 150 feet above. Lianas and vines hung in a tangled mass to catch projecting horse-loads and to trip the unwary. The ground was a mat of leaves, and underneath we found a layer of humus, from which grew thick undergrowth. Visibility was rarely more than thirty yards and, all the time, the jungle resounded to the drip, drip, drip of the condensed humidity and the occasional crash of some giant tree falling at the end of its life. When the rain came it usually fell in torrents, turning the track into an instant quagmire. The thick black mud, ravines, gullies and dense jungle were augmented by the fast-flowing rivers, patches of poisonous palms and stinging plants. Then the sun would emerge, imparting a ghostly appearance under the dripping canopy. This was my first impression of the hot and humid Darien jungle and, after even a week, it seemed that we had been there forever. Our advance along our 300-mile uncharted route was at an average of three miles a day, a gruelling pace. It was easy to see how the ill-fated Scots colony, established on the coast of Darien in 1699, had perished from disease and hunger.

Going to bed was a tedious business. Firstly, we placed a waterproof cape above our mosquito nets to form a shelter and the guy ropes were thoroughly spread with insect repellent. Then the procedure involved unpacking a set of dry clothes from a plastic bag; peeling off the stinking wet day-clothes while balancing precariously on another bag; and wringing out the worst of the moisture and popping them into yet another bag to form a pillow. Then we paired up and aided by torch and mirror examined our bodies for thorns and septic cuts. We got the thorns out with tweezers and applied liberal quantities of antiseptic to the sores, before climbing into slightly drier night-clothes and ensuring that every item of equipment was suspended by an insect-proof cord above ground level. Now came the hop into the hammock. Great care was essential if one were not to plummet out the other side. Next one pulled on a flimsy sleeping-bag and positioned the pillow so that day-clothes, although soaking wet, would at least be warm in the morning. Finally, I always sprayed inside my net with a liberal dose of insect repellent, which usually put me to sleep as well!

The damp jungle chilled us to the bone by the early hours. I began to notice the effect of the strange environment on my friends and in my log recalled:

> I have noted that on previous expeditions people looked forward to mail. I think, on this one, it is heightened by the jungle's claustrophobic effect which not only isolates one from civilization, but also from the sun and light. Daily we advance through a tunnel of dense vegetation.

Our sweat-soaked clothes rotted on us. Leather equipment grew mould, even the special self-draining canvas and leather jungle boots began to fall apart. The mosquitoes, gnats and flies became a constant plague. There were inch-long black ants whose bite hurt like hell for hours, stinging caterpillars and, in the river, electric eels. The heat and humidity were oppressive, and the nights brought little relief. Clusters of aggressive and vindictive hornets nested in hollow trees and swarmed out to meet anyone who disturbed them. I have never seen insects so vicious. Two stallions were among the herd. Randy, a bad-tempered beast, kicked and bit, so I took him myself. I thought he was under control until, without warning, the stupid bugger bit a hornets' nest. I fled and Randy bolted. We both had multiple stings. He didn't do it again! Within seconds a well-ordered column could turn into chaos under attack from hornets. Rosh became seriously ill when she developed an allergic reaction to one such assault. She had collapsed, unconscious in the jungle, when Keith found her and it was his rapid action that got her to safety and probably saved her life. Centipedes and black scorpions also took their toll, whilst spiders as large as dinner plates were fearsome to behold.

When brushing against the foliage we constantly picked up ticks that, almost unnoticed, buried their teeth into one's flesh with such tenacity that they often had to be removed by the medical officer. On the other hand, the snakes were usually shy and it was not until later that we came across more aggressive varieties. The larger animals were rarely dangerous but on one occasion we came face to face with a beautiful black jaguar on the jungle track. Other cats included ocelot and margay, and, surprisingly, we saw many large deer.

The white-lipped peccary, a small wild pig, was a different matter altogether. Unlike his timid cousin, the white-collared variety, this vicious beast was much feared and avoided whenever possible. They moved in the twilight areas of the darkened forest in sounders of up to 200. At night in the impenetrable darkness only the noise of their snorting and rooting gave us warning of their approach. A machine gun would have had little effect on the concentrated rush of these ugly tempered creatures and once they completely wrecked a camp, scattering the terrified horses into the jungle. Our revolvers and shotguns were useless in such an onslaught.

Not surprisingly Sunday services were well attended and with Keith as choirmaster, the sappers, who loved to sing, would give throaty renderings of 'Guide me, O Thou Great Redeemer' and other appropriate hymns.

These Royal Engineers had been especially selected for their experience and stamina. Many were old hands at jungle-bashing but among them were two seventeen-year-olds from the Junior Leaders Regiment at Dover. Neither had been outside England before but, like other youngsters on the trip, put up a fine show. Also working as an engineer was an eighteen-year-old civilian, Simon Wilson, who had just left school. He obviously enjoyed being with the soldiers because on return to England he joined the Army! Thus started my ideas for later projects.

Our team also included Robin Hanbury-Tenison, an expert on the South American Indian and chairman of Survival International; one jungle expert was Gurkha Sergeant Partapsing Limbu. The Hon. Charles Keyes, grandson of the famous Admiral, was an interpreter and navigator and we had soldiers from many regiments.

In the beginning we moved in a complete body with the leading recce team working some five to ten miles ahead. Another reconnaissance team worked about two miles in front marking the trail. Behind this came the first engineer section to cut a track some ten feet wide, using machetes, power-saws and dynamite. They cut their way forward and when they reached a ravine they bridged it with the special aluminium ladders, two of which were carried on each car. These ladders, devised by Jim, could be linked together and were vital for bridging and rafting. We used them over 400 times throughout the expedition. The second engineer section used Tirfor jacks, blocks, tackles and the capstans of the cars to their absolute limit to drag the Range Rovers up the steep and slippery slopes.

Finally the animal transport and Expedition HQ brought up the rear of the column. Rations, petrol, radios and medical supplies made up the bulk of the packhorse loads. Meanwhile the scientists moved independently about the expedition area. From time to time they came in to join the column before once again disappearing into their jungle demi-paradise in their quest for knowledge.

Kelvin brought in supplies by boat, helicopter, parachute, pack-ponies and porters. In all, over ten tons of rations, 15,000 gallons of petrol, 2,400 cans of beer, and 80,000 cigarettes, plus sacks of horse fodder, boxes of dynamite and mail were delivered by these means. These vital items mostly came from our support base in the Pacific coastal town of La Palma. It was not always easy to find us, so to help our pilots gas-filled balloons were launched on the end of a string to come bobbing up above the tree canopy. These fluorescent orange markers were accompanied by a firework display of rockets. Even so, searching for a small party deep in the forest was a difficult task.

Expedition members had been picked for their compatibility, physical fitness and expertise. However, as our problems increased and the going became more difficult the inevitable minor squabbles and signs of nervous exhaustion, more common in mountaineering, became apparent. The girls rose highly in our estimation, for, in spite of living under the same trying conditions as the men and being expected to work the same hours, do guard at night, pull the horses through mud, push boats up rivers and beat off the hordes of insects, they retained their good humour, rarely complained and always looked smart. Indeed, they added tone and often brought common sense to cool a heated argument. Kay was a tower of strength, even writing to those who did not receive letters. Limbu, whose wife was in Nepal, got few. After Kay complained to his regiment he got two mail bags' full, while the rest of the expedition received one! Back in Britain, the 7th Gurkhas CO had issued an order 'all men will write to Limbu'.

The rations designed especially for the project by the MOD were very good and, thanks to Kay's efforts, other food was provided by numerous kind sponsors. The climate, which was usually between 90° and 100°F with eighty-five per cent humidity, made us long for fresh, crisp salads, but the dehydrated food, especially the sliced apple, was a fine substitute. To vary the diet, we also ate local dishes, which included jungle fruit, iguana, fish, monkey, snake and wild turkey. Just as we were breaking camp one morning two Cuna girls arrived. Earlier our doctor, John Richardson, had treated one of their babies for a skin rash. The child was now cured and they had come to thank us. I could not understand Cuna, but it seemed the young spider monkey they carried was a gift. Intending to release it as soon as they were out of sight, I accepted the little fellow. But one of the girls took it back and, slipping a knife from beneath her dress, smiled very sweetly as she slit its throat. Blood splattered everywhere when she pushed a sharp stick up the monkey's bottom and out of its mouth to enable her to roast it for me on the embers of our fire. She looked terribly hurt when I declined but she and her sister ate it themselves!

But now the rains had stopped and the lack of water became a problem. We had to resort to slicing open vines and drinking from them, filtering the water from slimy pools, or having it delivered by parachute.

A strange recruit was an American hobo who was fleeing the Inland Revenue Service. He had heard in Miami that the British were building a four-lane highway to South America and had decided to reach an aunt in Caracas via this road. Soon he lost our trail and was near starvation when Choco Indians found him. Fortunately he had studied their language and, whilst he recovered in their village, learnt what they knew of us. Apparently we were led by a tall and superior yellow-skinned Indian, which must have been Limbu and our cars were so light we could toss them over rivers! But the item they admired most was our magic box through which we communicated with our God. Whenever we needed anything, they said, we simply erected this little green altar in a clearing with a spike pointing to heaven, then we twiddled knobs and spoke to God. If he didn't reply, we shook the altar and sometimes kicked it. Eventually God replied and we'd ask for whatever we needed. A great bird then delivered copious quantities of powerful firewater. Some we put in the cars and the rest we drank before advancing with renewed energy. A nice description of a radio call for a para-re-supply!

In the atrocious mud we had only done thirty miles in seventeen days. All our vehicles were casualties. To the sappers' delight, we had abandoned the Hill-Billys: the mud had oozed into their tracks, and set like concrete. Then our heavily-loaded Range Rovers, with their immense power, began to break their differentials every few miles, sending gear teeth right through the casing and the floor, just like shrapnel. They ground to a halt at the Piriati River. Determined that the expedition should not fail, the Rover Company fought to solve the problem, flying out an expert from Britain with a massive load of especially manufactured parts. Geoff Miller was lifted by helicopter into the jungle, where he worked non-stop in a makeshift workshop. We were now weeks behind schedule: it was a race against time.

The climate and pace were beginning to tell, and eventually thirty members had to be evacuated by helicopter, light aircraft or boat because of illness. Dr John Richardson and his energetic SRN wife, Suzie, fought a constant battle to keep us fit. To maintain the momentum we needed large numbers of Indians, who, with their long machetes, could continue to hack through the jungle, and it was to the Cuna village of Ipeti that I now turned for manpower. My log records the meeting with the chiefs:

Travelling silently upstream in the dark, skilfully propelled by two braves, we were greeted by others at the entrance to the village and taken up to the council chamber. We entered the low, smoky building, lit only by many glimmering lamps set on little tables, beside which sat the women, embroidering and smoking from conventional looking pipes; olive-skinned children, mostly naked, scampered about the floor. Up towards the roof, sitting on top of the tiered seats, as in a government chamber, sat the few men of the village who were not out earning their living in some distant part. In the centre of the room was a long bench which faced two hammocks set at right angles. On these swung the wrinkled old chief and his deputy. Our own interpreters, rather like the defence counsel in a court, sat on the right. We felt like prisoners in the dock. With me were Peter and Sergeant Limbu.

After the customary greeting, very, very slowly came the questions. It was so slow because everything had first to be translated from English into Spanish and from Spanish to Cuna. The chief would then put any major decisions to the entire village and a vote was taken. Eventually we learned that we were allowed to hire twenty men at the reasonable price of $1.50 per man, per day. They asked us how we would communicate with the people who could speak no English or Spanish. I must confess I was stumped for a moment, and then said, 'I

have a Gurkha!' 'How prudent,' replied the Chief, not really understanding what a Gurkha was. Limbu just smiled.

The Chief then asked about our work and got me to design an
airstrip, which I did on the back of an envelope. He was particularly
keen that his people should become educated, for he saw this as a
means of advancement. He was naturally worried about the Bayano
Dam, and what would happen to his hunting grounds and, indeed, to
his village if the resultant lake spread up the Ipeti. Finally he
questioned us about England. 'Are there Indians in your country, and
do they have schools?' I replied that there were Indians and that they
all went to school. He said, nodding his wizened old head, 'Ah, it
must be a good country.' They described their political problems, and
how they had voted for a man who had promised much, including a
school, but nothing had happened. I told him such injustice also
occurred in Britain.

After dark the jungle, viewed from the river, becomes a towering
wall of blackness, broken only by fireflies. At night the creatures of
this luxuriant world come forth to hunt and feed and, as we paddled
against the current, the noise of the beasts reached an awesome
crescendo. Frogs croaked, monkeys screamed and chattered, and
birds flapped loudly in the tall trees. My torch revealed pairs of red
eyes glowing from the bank where small caymans waited expectantly
in the shallows.

I placed Limbu in command of a Cuna working party, and the
column struggled on to Torti. The mud was the worst yet, horses sank
in, loads came off, hornets attacked and tempers flared. One horse
became so badly stuck that it took Keith and the sappers nineteen
hours to extract it, only for the wretched animal to run back in again!

In early February base was set up at Torti. The 500-yard airstrip was
the nearest point to the stricken vehicles, where I could air-land the
heavy axle assemblies by Beaver. To get them to the Piriati would
need a daunting porterage operation. The only real answer was to
helicopter the spares direct to the cars. Kelvin would have to use all
his ingenuity to achieve this. I had complete confidence in my
deputy, but it was as well to be prepared if choppers could not be
obtained. So I sketched out yet another contingency plan in my
notebook which was already filled with a mass of illegible hiero-
glyphics.

Torti had ample grazing and water but beyond this point we would
be climbing out of the Bayano valley, leaving behind the sea of mud.

The way ahead was by contrast dry and almost waterless. By radio David reported several formidable obstacles, many fallen trees and large numbers of aggressive peccary. He said the insects and snakes seemed more plentiful. Even the Indians avoided this region and it was difficult to find guides. We needed water, dynamite, more engineer tools and power-saws to cut the trail through to a ranch on the Gulf of San Miguel – called Santa Fe.

It was early morning when, marching ahead of the column, I heard an unusual sound – a heavy diesel! Five minutes later we rounded a bend in the path and came face to face with a gigantic yellow bulldozer. 'Oh you great big gorgeous creature,' I said, slapping its steel tracks. The operator, a stocky little old man with dirty blond hair, spoke Spanish with a guttural accent. Using the expedition dictionary that Rosh had written, I discovered he was opening a new logging trail and for some of its length would be using our route. Musing on our good fortune I noticed the operator looking at me in an odd way.

'Americano?' he enquired.

I told him I was a British army officer and he paled slightly. So, for fun, I said, 'You are from Germany?'

He muttered, 'Many years ago, I come here in 1933,' and jumping into his seat went clanking off down the trail.

The horses suffered terribly from the vampires, which attacked at night, biting their necks and injecting them with anti-coagulant to make the blood easier to drink. The horses' screams kept us awake and they grew weak through loss of blood. Then 'Scouse' Yeun, a Chinese Liverpudlian Lance Corporal in the Royal Engineers, came up with a plan. He cut up a pink parachute and made a protective nightshirt for a badly bitten animal. Eye and nostril holes were cut and the horse hobbled for the night. 'Well done, Scouse,' we said after an undisturbed night, but at dawn the horse had gone. Searching for it along the trail, we came upon some terrified Indians who explained that the previous night they had been celebrating the fertility rites; the dancing girls were whirling faster and faster and the purpose of the gathering was about to be achieved when a pink apparition had walked in and ruined everything. They supposed it to be a sign sent by their ancestors to rebuke them for evil and licentious living. When they discovered it was our horse, they were not best pleased so I let them keep it.

On 7 March we reached the dirty old riverside town of Yaviza.

While the Range Rovers were being repaired, the column had lengthened to more than 100 miles, so to help speed up the advance we bought a second-hand Land-Rover in Panama for use as a pathfinder. It was flown out in the belly of a giant USAF helicopter, and used to support the leading engineer section.

Time was against us. Every day counted if we were not to be defeated by the onset of the mid-April rains. But by 20 March we were at Boco de Cupé and the Range Rovers were on the move. At the front, the reconnaissance patrol was working over a wide area desperately seeking the best way through some seemingly impassable terrain known as the Devil's Switchback.

When the rains started again we were lashed with the full fury of the elements to an extent which few of us had ever witnessed. When this happened we were still crossing the Devil's Switchback. Here it was that whilst trying to hurry our reconnaissance we suffered a severe setback by going straight up a 'one-way street'. This led to an impenetrable hilly barrier and, because the Beaver had damaged its tail wheel and was being repaired, we failed to find this out by an air reconnaissance. Thus for ten days we floundered and struggled to conquer the Pucuru heights. I had even hired all the prisoners from the local jail, including several murderers, to cut for me. I guessed they feared the Indians more than us and would not flee.

In the wet I turned to Charlie Thompson, a friendly and helpful Negro. 'Is this the rains, Charlie?' I asked.

'Rains, man,' Charlie shook his grizzled old head, down which the water cascaded, and smiled. 'No sir – this is jus' hoomidity!' But he told me that the main rains were preceded by a few days of the small rains. Then, some two to three weeks later, the proper rains would start. I looked at my battered map and wondered how much good luck we could count on. And it was at this point that Panamanian Sergeant De Leon told me of a place named Cruso Mono, where the Indians dragged logs down to the river.

If a heavy log could come down, a vehicle might be winched up, I thought. But it could only be reached by river, so we took a gamble and motored the cars up the bed of the river Tuira. This was possible because the water level was still low in spite of the downfalls. When we reached deep pools the raft was called in and used to ferry the cars to the next shallow. However, it was not without incident. We were towing the laden raft upstream when, to my horror, I saw it rear up like a stricken beast. A helmsman yelled, 'She's going, lads, get away, get away, we're going over.' The tow rope from my piragua slackened as the raft and its swaying Range Rover spun out of control in the foaming water, engines racing and men plummeting over the side. Water was pouring in through a two-foot gash in the hull of one pontoon.

Like a whaler's longboat, my piragua, with which we had been towing the raft across a fast flowing stretch, was dragged backwards by the stricken grey 'whale'. Sergeant Major Ticky Wright, boat expert and formerly a helmsman on the Blue Nile, was still aboard. My Panamanian boatman, Canito, realized what must be done and sliced through the tow rope with his machete. Somehow the raft was still upright. Men were struggling in the water, clearly visible by their bright life-jackets. Downstream it spun, but by a miracle it seemed Ticky was winning control and he rammed the wreck into a shingle bank. The survivors had reached the river's edge and were clinging on to the trees, few had the strength to climb out: they had been working for hours in the blistering heat and, for some, every step with their feet raw from 'jungle foot' was agony. With his usual skill Canito swung the thirty-foot canoe around and we picked them up. Some laughed nervously, some grinned, others looked very shaken and, in spite of a shade temperature of over 80°F, they shivered. Everyone was safe and the vehicle had been saved; but the raft, ripped open by a rock, was crippled and would need extensive repairs.

Nevertheless we got all cars to Cruso Mono and, winching them up a sixty degree slope, reached the smugglers' trail to the Colombian frontier. A young sapper collapsed with acute appendicitis in Paya, the last village, and there followed one of several dramatic helicopter night-time rescues by the USAF 'Jolly Green Giant'.

Half a mile from the border-plinth on the Panamanian side, we found a rusting red car, a sad reminder of the ill-fated Chevrolet expedition that had reached the frontier over ten years before, only to turn back. Now it lay, a rotting hulk, trees growing up through the engine compartment and an ants' nest in the boot. As we poked sticks into the interior a highly venomous coral snake slithered from beneath the remains of the back seat and a large black spider scuttled from the dashboard.

There had been several narrow escapes from serpents. When I was holding our ornithologist on my shoulders so that he could feel in a bird's nest, a coral snake slide along his arm and into his shirt: luckily this was not tucked in and the reptile dropped out, past me, onto the ground. On another occasion a six-foot bushmaster sank its teeth into the rubber heel of David Bromhead's boot. Its fangs stuck fast and, as it writhed, David blew its head off with his Smith & Wesson. Near the frontier Limbu had a lucky escape when a huge bushmaster reared up behind him. It struck twice, but each time the Gurkha took a pace forward for his next swing at the vegetation and the snake missed. Behind Limbu there was Ruby, a Colombian prisoner who spoke no English and no Gurkhali. Limbu spoke no Spanish and therefore Ruby's timely warning went unheeded. However, he raced up, pinning the reptile down with a forked branch, but could not hold it. Limbu spun round and with a continuous swing of his razor-sharp kukri beheaded his attacker.

On 6 April we closed the base at Paya. A Colombian mule-train was joining us and Keith Morgan-Jones, his job done and now four-stone lighter, waved goodbye as he set off downriver in Canito's piragua. With him went Kay and others to help at Panama City, and then fly over to join us in Colombia. Charles Keyes took our faithful packponies back to sell them to the kindest homes possible. Many years later I was to see their descendants at Boca.

I presented the young Cuna chief with a splendid all-steel British axe. He looked rather sad and a tear welled in his eye as he gripped my hand. 'Come back one day, Quebracha,' he said.

'What does that mean?' I asked.

'Axebreaker – name of hardest wood in the forest – it's a compliment,' said De Leon.

'Don't tell the sappers that,' I retorted.

This was a significant moment in the expedition, the curtain was dropping on an act; teams welded together by their battle against nature were breaking up after a long time. The old cast had hardly dispersed before the new actors came on stage.

'Buenos Dias,' said the living image of Mussolini in a sombrero. Francisco, muleteer extraordinary, strode into our camp at the head of his column. His massive, muscular beasts dwarfed our ponies. 'If you are ready, my mayor, I will load mules,' said Francisco firmly, and we stood back to admire his skill. 'The mules will march by themselves, you go ahead. I will meet you at Palo,' said our self-assured friend. Enormous trees soared skyward for over a hundred feet. An occasional ray of sunshine filtered through the canopy, but for the most part the forest floor was a gloomy green world, through which flittered electric-blue butterflies and tiny humming birds.

Above us raucous macaws, big-beaked toucans and brightly coloured parrots clucked and called with ear-splitting shrieks. The air was heavy with the scent of blooms that I had not seen when moving on my feet because of the need to pick a path with care.

From muleback I could observe brilliant flowers, beefsteak plants and thousands of tiny creatures who lived in this vast overgrown hot-house. We reached Palo at 1350 hours and, apart from the broken-down concrete plinth that marked the frontier, the little clearing was empty. We were to meet the Colombians at 1400 hours, so I walked forward to photograph our four-man headquarters with the Union Jack, which the American hobo was clutching incongruously.

It was 1400 hours precisely when the jungle around us moved. I looked up to see that we were facing the Colombian Army. A platoon of swarthy, purposeful soldiers in camouflage uniform, their weapons spotlessly clean, watched us in silence. From their midst an officer stepped forward, and said, 'Captain Sierra of the Fourth Brigade Infantry,' clicking his heels with Prussian precision and saluting. 'Welcome to Colombia.' His sergeant major seized our Union Jack. I was certain that we had committed some unpardonable breach of international law, but he put my mind at rest saying, 'It is your right to carry your flag into Colombia, according to the Treaty of 1821.' This was true, but I was surprised that our friends were so well briefed. The sergeant major then asked if he might be allowed to carry the Union Jack into his country as indeed the Duke of Wellington's veterans had done when they came to support the colonists in their bid for freedom 150 years before. Thus we marched downhill into the thickening jungle of the Atrato valley.

Kelvin and the Pathfinder group were already a day ahead and going well, and that night we reached the riverside camp of the Colombian Commander, Major Alberto Patron. We ate a communal meal with our allies and enjoyed the first of many cups of superb local coffee. Alberto briefed me on the campaign that was being waged against the communist guerrillas throughout the more remote regions of Colombia. 'I think the Atrato is too unhealthy a place – even for the communists,' said the unusually fair-haired officer, 'but we must take precautions; seven soldiers were killed in an ambush near Barranquillito last week.'

So far the Darien Gap had thrown everything at us except bandits so I checked my revolver carefully that evening. From here on the going got wetter but a new spirit had come into the team and nothing could stop us now, not even the swamp the size of Wales that lay ahead. I had every faith in Alberto and his soldiers, some of whom were members of the original team sent to meet us when a terrible tragedy occurred. The Colombian gunboat that was to support our crossing of the Atrato was lying off the small port of Turbo. Our liaison officer, Captain Jeremy Groves, was with a party of six Colombian servicemen heading out to join the vessel in one of the ship's boats when it was pooped by a large wave and sank immediately. The only survivors were a Colombian officer and Jeremy. The remaining five Colombians had been drowned or sucked down in the mud of the mangrove swamp that fringed the shore nearby. Nevertheless, our friends produced another team within a matter of days and continued to back us wholeheartedly until the very end. So on 10 April Expedition HQ was established for the last time. By coincidence it stood on a 'peak in Darien' looking out, not across the Pacific, but over the steaming green morass of the Atrato swamp. We were two weeks behind schedule and the promised rains had begun. It was a desperate race to cross the remaining fifty miles that no motor vehicle had ever traversed.

Working ahead of us for some weeks, Sapper Captain Richard Summerton had discovered a possible route through. Much of the area was liquid with a coating of water weed, in which lived countless mosquitoes, many snakes and the occasional alligator. To break through we used our raft, which was undoubtedly the most successful single item of equipment we possessed. Forcing a way through the matted weed was a hellish problem. We tried cutting with machetes, pulling on it with grapnels, and eventually used necklaces of dynamite. The side benefit of the latter method was some good fish breakfasts. Indeed the swamp was teeming with huge tarpon. As we forced our way, the foul stench of rotting organic material rose up. In some places logs had mixed themselves in with the weed to form more obstacles and these we smashed with dynamite or sliced through with the outstanding Husquvarna power-saws. Gradually the number of trees began to increase, strange unearthly shapes, growing up from the swamp around us which was only populated by huge birds, lizards and giant otters. It had the appearance of a primeval forest and was totally uninhabited by man. On one occasion my piragua capsized. Luckily it did not sink, because apart from a muddy bank nearby there was nowhere to swim for safety. Whilst bailing out the boat we were supported by our life-jackets and, although we lost some valuable equipment, we managed to reboard the boat and continue our journey, somewhat shaken, very wet and rather smelly.

Eventually the cars were placed on a firmer crust. This slippery surface of matted vegetation and soil would be flooded when the rains reached their height. Now, however, it was about three to four feet thick and would stand the weight of our vehicles fitted with extra wide Firestone tyres. The area, which was forested, had the construction of a giant sponge and you could see numerous holes going down from the surface into the liquid mud. Doubtless it was up these shafts that the water would rise and flood the area. We were told by engineers and surveyors that they had lowered a drum full of concrete on a wire into the swamp and at 1,000 feet they had not yet reached firm bottom. Many parts of this incredible area looked solid, but one day when landing from a float-fitted helicopter I climbed gingerly out onto the surface. Immediately the area within fifteen feet gave slightly and I had the wobbly feeling of standing on a giant blancmange.

On 23 April the sun set with its usual livid orange glow and as it did so a party of ragged, filthy men and women, mules and vehicles emerged on the far side of the vast bog. Their eyes were hollow and their faces drawn, their bodies a mass of bites and sores and their feet were in an indescribable condition, but somehow as they staggered up, dragging, heaving and pushing their vehicles on to the northern end of the southern section of the Pan-American Highway, they managed to smile.

After ninety-nine days in the jungle and swamps of Darien, we had broken through. It was St George's Day. That night a storm surpassing anything we had experienced previously hit the little town of Chigorodo where we slept. As we bailed out our accommodation, Alberto said, 'Now, John, the real rains have come; you made it by ten hours.'

There was always danger round the corner. And on the last day Ticky and a sapper almost lost their lives when returning to Turbo with the gunboat. They were working on the raft tied alongside the ship, which was moving at approximately five knots. Suddenly, something struck the front of one of the inflatables and without warning the bow of the raft doubled up and water swept over it. Both men were hurled into the river and sucked under. They found themselves bumping along the rusty, flat hull and suddenly being spun with enormous force by the screw. Fortunately the gunboat had lost one propeller the previous week, which saved them from a horrible death. Nevertheless, they were extremely fortunate to be hurled out into the wake, having lost all their clothing and watches, with only superficial bruises and cuts, to be hauled aboard.

In Medellin we were received with warm hospitality, and found a message of congratulations awaiting us from Her Majesty the Queen. More parties, a triumphal motorcade and a ceremony at Simon Bolivar's statue followed in Bogota. Checked and serviced, the Range Rovers drove on.

Complete success came later, on 9 June 1972, when Jeremy Groves sent 'Mission Accomplished' from Cape Horn.

In Mexico they had met desert conditions and in Guatemala the Pan-American Highway became a rutted track. They beat the Darien Gap and then climbed into the high Andes. In May 1972 they sped on through South America, crossing more mountains and once again meeting desert in Chile. Here they covered 2,375 miles in four days, and one day made 800 miles cruising at ninety m.p.h. on a desert road. In the Gap they had only averaged three miles in a day.

As they neared their goal, they hit snow and ice once more. Many mountain passes were blocked and it took five long days to break through this last obstacle. On one occasion they had to cross a lake on a Heath Robinson local raft to avoid the blocked passes. At Cape Horn the engines were switched off after seven months and 17,000 miles.

We won the special gold medal presented by The Darien Action Committee for being the first vehicle expedition to make a complete crossing, including the Atrato swamp. The project was hailed by governments and sponsors as a notable success but there had been many times during the journey when we found it hard to believe that we could win, but still we pressed on. Common sense and logic would have made us give in a hundred times. Indeed, it had been an incredible adventure, accomplished by determination, flexibility, excellent equipment and good practical engineering, coupled with generous backing from sponsors. Our track has become known by the Indians as the Carretera Inglesa – the Englishman's Road – and they use sections of it to travel to market.

Later we learned the Highway would go ahead and follow our path. However, I sincerely hoped that the road-builders would spare a thought for the animals, the people and the flora of this strange land, whose environment would now be changed forever.

EIGHT

The Beavers

'GOOD MORNING, SIR,' snapped the wiry Scot. 'Sergeant Major Donald reporting.' Standing in front of me was the erect figure of my new squadron sergeant major. Had I not already heard that he was a very high-grade soldier, I should now have guessed that here was someone with fire in his belly. Although greying hair and weather-beaten features made him look rather older than he was, his twinkling eyes were those of a man young in heart and spirit.

'Do sit down,' I said. 'How do you like the idea of joining 48th Field Squadron?'

'Very much,' he replied sharply, the bristle of his short moustache twitching.

'Any reason in particular?' I asked.

'Weell – they say that you're a wee bit of a mad bugger and so am I, so I think we'll get on together,' he said slowly with a broad grin. I decided I liked Sergeant Major Donald.

We both enjoyed being with the squadron. Following the Darien adventure it was time for some conventional soldiering and this was going to be much more enjoyable than driving a desk in the War Office. The squadron had been raised in Canada so its symbol was the beaver; a busy little chap who spends his life eating, sleeping and mating whilst mucking up people's gardens. He epitomized the spirit of our unit.

It was a bitter February morning when we came ashore at Belfast Docks. We were to provide engineer support to the British troops, covering some 2,000 square miles of the Ulster border counties. One of our major tasks was searching for terrorist arms, explosives and equipment and for this purpose we had formed a special search troop. It was a difficult, hazardous and unpleasant task. Houses were often

booby-trapped and a 'tip-off' on the robot telephone system could be a
lure to get us into a trap. I needed my best leader for this troop and,
without hesitation, appointed the sergeant major.

The squadron worked around the clock building defences, hunting
for mines, clearing obstacles, manning boats, patrolling the streets
and searching, searching, searching. From time to time we got shot
at, usually by a sniper, unseen behind a darkened window or a leafy
hedge. Mines exploded beneath vehicles, and on one occasion it was
only a short stop for tea that saved me from being blown up by a 300-
pound bomb, placed in a culvert. Tragically it got a Ferret armoured
car a few minutes ahead of us, killing a young officer.

However, there were also lighter moments. In one village an old
lady had been observed carrying out plates of food, having looked
furtively around to place them under an upturned bucket in her
garden. Suspecting an IRA gunman was concealed in a hide we raided
the property only to find a sleepy tortoise under the bucket.

In Ulster I met the most friendly, hospitable people in the world,
but I also met the most bigoted and unreasonable. I saw hatred that I
would have hardly believed possible in the United Kingdom, and I
saw love and compassion beyond compare. I came away as perplexed
as the day I arrived, but sadly I left a good friend behind.

Donald's Goblins, as we knew the search troop, had quickly gained
an enviable reputation for their dogged determination and skill. For
fourteen weeks the rugged Scot encouraged and led his men from one
success to another. In the face of danger Ian Donald set the highest
example of courage, initiative and leadership and his happy manner,
devotion to duty and tireless efforts were an inspiration to all. It gave
me a tremendous thrill to watch this team at work. One could not
help admiring the cool, matter-of-fact way they searched, cheering
themselves up with a continuous good-humoured string of obsceni-
ties, knowing all the time that they were a prime target for the
bomber and sniper.

On 24 May 1973 they had been engaged on a variety of searches
since well before dawn. It was a bright, sunny afternoon in South
Armagh, when they found the first collection of bombs and booby-
traps in a post office. Leaving an expert to deal with these, the Goblins
moved on to examine a house that was thought to contain another
bomb. The infantry had already cleared the council estate of civilians
and children. The semi-detached dwelling was surrounded by a small
low-walled garden and stood at the end of the street. The border was

100 yards away. It all looked innocent, but Donald trusted nothing. Rightly, he decided to blow a hole in the rear wall. Doors and windows are likely sites for booby traps. Thus he deployed his men to minimize the risk and began a methodical search of the garden.

'No one is to enter the house until I am satisfied that it is safe.' So saying, he moved forward alone to clear a safe lane across the lawn. 100 yards away women in curlers, grubby children and sullen men watched in silence. On the hills around, red-bereted paratroopers scanned the hedgerows for any sign of a terrorist, and over the border the Irish Garda watched too. To the Goblins it was just another job. There were always these tense minutes when someone must go forward by himself and it was usually Ian Donald who did so. Two of the team were circling the house, their cautious movements watched by other sappers from behind the village store. On the lawn the sergeant major inched his way probing for the concealed menace and feeling for trip-wires. Only fifteen yards from the back door, he paused and looked up.

At that moment the house disintegrated into a mass of flying slates, bricks and splintered timber. The distant roar of the explosion was heard in the sand-bagged police station at Crossmaglen, where Lance Corporal Szade, one of the search team commanders, was waiting with his men. Long before the first radio message came through, they all felt a dreadful foreboding.

At Castle Dillon the rising trout were sending concentric ripples over the mirror surface of the lake. At my desk as I finished off some paperwork, the operations room intercom crackled, 'OC, sir – there's been an explosion near Crossmaglen – we've got Corporal Szade on the phone.' The hair on the back of my neck rose a little. I knew Szade would only use a telephone if it was a real emergency. The line was bad. The NCO had no definite information, but he could not raise the sergeant major on the radio.

In minutes I boarded the helicopter, hurtling over the lush green countryside. The village of Cullaville appeared in the distance and, as we got nearer, I could see the little estate littered with debris. A burst waterpipe was sending up a fine spray from a pile of rubble that had been the end house.

Donald was lying in the garden, partly covered by wreckage; he had died instantaneously. In the road outside, a sergeant in the Parachute Regiment, who had chanced to walk down the street, had been killed by a piece of flying timber, but thanks to the care with which their leader had positioned them, the remainder of the search team had survived.

We waited until nightfall before getting him out; just in case there was a second device, possibly rigged to be fired by remote control. Thus it was 2300 hours, when, crouching behind the garden wall, we carefully pulled aside the wreckage with a length of rope. With my heart thumping I crawled over the lawn and reached out to touch his hand. It was cold and stiff with rigor mortis, but his pistol, loaded and cocked, was held in a vice-like grip. It took several minutes to prise the fingers apart and release the weapon before carrying the shattered body out of the ruins to the waiting Saracen armoured vehicle. I collected his sheath knife and holster for his sons and then wrapped him in a blanket, before giving him a final salute. I knew that the army had lost an outstanding soldier, Margaret Donald had lost a fine husband, and I had lost a friend I was not likely to forget.

In June 1973 we handed over to 11th Field Squadron – its commander, my old friend, Major Dick Jarman, waved us farewell. 'Look after yourself, Dick,' I shouted. Three weeks later he too was killed by a bomb.

But by now the Beavers were deployed in warmer climes in Belize. On my way back home to Yorkshire, I planned to rest at the Scientific Exploration Society base in Wiltshire. The white-walled Tudor farm was bathed in pale moonlight, the shrubs and trees of the garden cast strange shadows on the concrete patio. As the big Volvo's engine died, I stepped out into the chill English night air. 'Brrr,' I shivered, as I strode over to the kitchen door. 'Keys in the letter box,' I remembered Jim Masters' instructions, 'We'll be back in the morning.' My friends Jim and Joan were wardens of the base and having just flown in to RAF Brize Norton I was to sleep here; with some snow over much of Northern England, I didn't fancy a long drive after my eight-hour trans-Atlantic flight.

The door swung open and warm air spilled out to greet me. The neon light flickered, revealing a note, a newspaper and a bottle of J&B on the scrubbed kitchen table. 'Welcome John,' read the message, 'help yourself. Please use the bedroom at the top of the stairs. See you tomorrow.' Pouring a good measure of man's best friend, I flicked open the *Daily Telegraph* and started to catch up on the news. My heavy diver's watch read 1930 (New York time) and, having just caught up five hours, I was not the least bit tired. The glass of Scotch was getting low when I heard the coughing – it was right above me. How odd, I thought, looking at the oak-beamed ceiling – then remembered. Heavens, it must be Michael – and I've woken him up. Michael, Jim's teenage son, slept in the room above the kitchen and, although his parents were out, I guessed Michael had come home early, used his own key and gone to bed. So I put away the Scotch and tiptoed up to my bedroom where the long hours of travel quickly had their effect.

Waking up with the sun, I stretched, yawned, climbed reluctantly out of bed and tottered off to the bathroom to shave and bath. The internal walls in the farm were barely partitions and with the creeky, irregular wooden floors every noise was audible. I could hear Michael dressing in his room and later, as I wallowed in the steaming bath, I saw his shadow cross the frosted glass door, followed by the 'clump, clump, clump' as he descended the narrow wooden stairs. As I dried myself, he returned and as he passed the door, I called out, 'Morning, Michael,' but there was no reply. Once dressed, I phoned Judith and announced my return. Michael was still moving about in his room.

Suddenly, there was the sound of a key in the lock and in walked Jim and Joan. 'Sleep well?' they enquired.

'Yes – super, and bless you for the J&B, you know my taste.' We chatted for a moment and then, as Joan put on the coffee, I said, 'I'm sorry I disturbed Michael last night.'

She looked at me in a strange way. 'Michael?' Joan asked.

'Yes,' I said, 'upstairs.'

Her brows narrowed. 'John,' she said very slowly, 'Michael has not been here for six weeks – he's away at college.'

'Then who on earth's upstairs,' I said, 'because he's still there?'

In a flash we were at Michael's room. The bed was not even made up – there was just a plain mattress on the springs. I felt rather cold and the hairs on the back of my neck lifted. We checked the entire house from top to bottom. All doors and windows were locked from inside. Other than the one in my possession, Jim had the only other key. I must have been alone.

'Leave the coffee – you'd better have something stronger,' said Jim. 'We've got a story you'd better hear.'

The tale they told was all the more amazing because of the personalities involved. Jim and Joan are two of the most practical, down-to-earth people I've ever met. To hear them talking of the mysterious events that had been going on at the farm for the past year left me feeling uncomfortable. It was like finding a life-long teetotaller stoned out of his mind!

For some time the family had experienced strange noises, movements and finally seen a silver-haired lady in Michael's bedroom. Jim, a stolid West Country man, is not the sort to make a fuss. One of their most dramatic sightings had occurred quite recently. Jim had been alone in his indoor workshop with the door open when he became aware of a cold feeling. He turned around and there stood a man – medium height, ruddy complexion, fifty-ish, dressed rather like a farmer. As Jim gasped in astonishment his visitor wore an inquisitive smile, as if to say 'What are you doing?' Then he was gone – quite literally into thin air. Jim, as an ex-parachute engineer and used to rapid action, reacted at once. Dashing out of the room, he checked the doors and windows. All were locked from inside – there was nobody else in the house.

There was no more to tell. However, the farm belonged to a friend of mine who knew of no previous history of haunting, no accounts of terrible deeds, no tales of unrequited love, but he promised to ask around. Several months later, I called in on him. 'Oh, by the way, John,' he said, 'You remember the silver-haired lady – well I've found out something.'

'Go on, tell me more.'

'Well, there was a lady who fits that description; her husband was employed on the farm some years ago, and she died in that bedroom. But from natural causes, no murder or anything. But,' he went on, 'you'll remember the man Jim saw, well, that seems to be her husband. The funny thing is he's still alive and lives about ten miles away!' I had another whisky and went off to tell Jim and Joan.

Our next destination was rather warmer.

The desert Sultanate of Oman lies in southern Arabia with its province, Dhofar, bordering on the Indian Ocean. This coastal territory separates South Yemen, better known as Aden, from the oil-rich Persian Gulf, where in 1974 six giant tankers passed each hour through the narrow Straits of Hormuz carrying the precious lifeblood for the West. Since the British withdrawal from Aden, the former colony had become a Marxist base and was actively supporting a rebel war in Dhofar. The rebels' strategic aim was the Gulf; Soviet arms were sent in and local revolutionaries received training in China and Russia. The oppressive rule of Said bin Taimur, the aged sultan, complete with his long-standing alliance with the Imperial British and the poverty-stricken Dhofaris were ideal ingredients for communist propaganda. The People's Front for the Liberation of the Occupied Arabian Gulf had grown from various rebel groups and initially made good progress. Against them stood the poorly equipped Sultan's army, consisting of barely 1,000 combatants, including a large number of Baluchi mercenaries and a few seconded British officers. In 1970 the situation changed.

It was a quiet July afternoon in Salalah: the still air in the yard of the Sultan's palace was hot and humid. Unnoticed by the household slaves, the local Wali's son, a handful of Omani Askers, plus an amusing soldier of fortune named Spike, entered the labyrinth of passages that led to the private apartment of the charming old tyrant. At first they were unopposed but suddenly the royal bodyguard discovered the intruders. Shots rang out, ricocheting off the thick stone walls. Dashing through the dark corridors, Spike came to a heavy door, behind which he assumed lay the Sultan's room. Flinging it open and yelling 'Your Majesty', he found himself looking down the barrel of a tripod-mounted machine-gun with its owner in the act of pressing the trigger. 'Clackety-click' went the weapon as it failed to feed a round into the breech. 'Christ,' swore Spike and, dealing swiftly with the opposition, dashed on to the next room. The door was locked and the answer to 'Your Majesty?' was a burst of shots through the wooden panels. 'Oh bother,' said Spike (or words to that effect). He was just wondering what to do next when a shot was heard within, instantly followed by a shriek of pain. Bursting in, he found the Sultan hopping around holding his foot! Whilst trying to reload his pistol the ruler had accidentally shot himself. Spike, who knew the old man well, helped him to the courtyard where a Land-Rover rushed him to hospital. Within minutes it was all over. Said bin Taimur signed a letter of abdication in favour of his Sandhurst-trained son, Prince Qaboos, and an RAF aircraft flew him to Britain where he lived out his last few years in a private suite at the Dorchester.

The new Sultan immediately set about strengthening his armed forces and turning the tide, and at the same time the Beavers underwent some hard training on the North Yorkshire moors. In December 1973, in freezing blizzards, we practised our tasks and got fit. 'Just imagine it's sand, lads,' grinned Sergeant Major Cox, Donald's replacement, as we stumbled about in the snow and cursed this new jaunt, which they were convinced 'bloody Blashford-Snell' had dreamt up to keep them away from the fleshpots of Ripon.

In a fleet of RAF transports, we left Britain, still in the grip of winter, for the deserts of Dhofar. At last a hazy coastline loomed ahead. Miles and miles of sandy beaches stretched as far as the eye could see. Breaking waves rolled in from the deep green ocean to pound the shore, upon which we could make out the dun-coloured houses of Salalah. Roaring in low over fertile gardens, the Hercules wasted no time circling the airfield and so risking a burst of enemy fire. In seconds we were down and taxied quickly between a line of oil drums filled with sand to give protection against shrapnel. The men's eyes screwed up in the intense glare as the sun scorched our skin.

Although the province was largely a wasteland with barren mountains and just an occasional oasis, the plains of Salalah are an exception. This is because from June to September the southwest monsoon blows in from the sea. Known as the Khareef, it produces clouds that precipitate water onto the Qara Hills, filling the rivers that flow on to the Salalah Plain, and giving rise to spectacular waterfalls and raging torrents. When this happens the desert blooms into stunted jungles, lakes and rolling downlands of lush grass.

The Dhofar Brigade whom we were to support was commanded by a tough, dynamic officer with a grand sense of humour. I counted myself fortunate to serve under Brigadier Jack Fletcher. Briefing me in the small headquarters on the edge of Salalah airfield, his sun-tanned hand moved deliberately across the map. 'In the eastern and central areas the enemy have been driven back and now we must hunt them out. We also need to convince the tribesmen that we are offering a better life than communism. So that's one of your jobs: to help us win over their hearts and minds. But I also want you to improve our defensive positions and living accommodation on the jebel before the wind and damp of the Khareef hits us in June. Then . . . ' He paused to uncover a separate map and waited whilst the roar of a departing flight of Strikemasters subsided. The new map showed the mountains to the west. 'Now to where you can have a real field-day,' smiled Dynamite Jack, as he was known. 'The Hornbeam defensive line runs through these mountains. It's designed to stop enemy getting personnel and supplies to the eastern and central areas. We've started to wire it, but before the monsoon you must create the most deadly obstacle you can devise. The problem is that the line is thirty miles long. Wire is on its way, but mines are still in short supply. I can't spare many troops to help you and only helicopters can reach the hilltop positions. The Northern Frontier Regiment is holding the line with a battery of guns in support. I suggest you pop down and see Brian Ray* and then let me have your plan, in say two days' time. And, by the way, do you know anything about finding water?'

'I'm ready to try,' I replied.

'Good. Well, you'd better see what you can do for Simba.' He pointed out an isolated position where a battalion held a rocky bastion right on the frontier with South Yemen. They were completely surrounded, shelled and mortared daily, and relied entirely on helicopters to lift in their supplies of everything, including water.

As I left the Brigadier's office a staff officer greeted me. 'We're here to help you, but you may be able to assist us,' he said. 'Can you build air-portable ration stores?'

In another room the commander of the Sultan's Air Force handed me a glass of iced lemonade and asked if we could construct landing pads for a squadron of Wessex helicopters that were expected in ten days' time. I got back to my windowless office at Umm Al Ghwarif with enough work to keep an engineer regiment going for weeks, let alone a small squadron. Peter Page, my wiry, energetic second-in-command, whose immediate ambition was to get a place on the forthcoming Army Everest Expedition, cleared the layers of freshly blown sand from the operations room table and we sat down to study the map.

As we worked on the deployment plan Jack Walker, our quartermaster, began to list all the nails, timber, sheets of 'wriggly tin†', explosive, cement, hand tools, barbed wire, mines and vehicles that we were going to need. In such an unsophisticated country as Oman the job of obtaining these was no easy task. Everything was 'on order' or 'on the high seas somewhere' or would 'arrive tomorrow, Insh'allah‡'! On the rocky jebel even sand was in short supply, and if concrete was required in the defensive positions, we had to deliver cement, water and sand to the site by aircraft!

Victory in this war depended just as much on the logistic back-up as on the skill and courage of the front-line troops. However, before we

---

* Lt-Col J.B. Ray, MBE
† Corrugated iron
‡ If God wills

could serve effectively alongside the Sultan's men we needed to acclimatize, and thus I planned a week's intensive training aimed at getting the Beavers used to working in the blistering heat and building up a protective tan on their skin. We did PT on the beach, swam in the surf and zeroed our weapons on a nearby range. Each day we exposed our bodies to the merciless sun a little longer and rapidly the lily-white torsos turned a deep brown.

On the fourth day we mounted a simple operation with the aim of building a corrugated iron school at a coastal village seventy miles east of Salalah. The people, mainly fisherfolk, had been resettled on a flat plain separated from the rebels and the rest of Dhofar by the towering peaks of the jebel. Using a fleet of box-like Skyvan transports we flew men, tools, stores and water over the pale brown crags and canyons. The terrain was stark, awe-inspiring and frightening. In this desolate land mere survival against the elements is a battle itself, without the added complication of deadly human enemy.

Winging our way through the great gorges we rounded a bend to find the green ocean waiting. The mountains fell away in vertical buttresses as we dived steeply onto the short air-strip. Skyvan engines have an unusual characteristic of not changing pitch as they land and it was therefore comforting to realize that we were in fact slowing down. Men and children poured out from the shacks to meet us and, without bidding, began to cart all our equipment towards the school site. The area was peaceful and no rebels had been seen in recent times, so the work progressed rapidly. As the school went up, Sergeant Major Eddie McGee of the Army Physical Training Corps put his knowledge of the area to good use. Chatting up the locals in a Yorkshire dialect of Arabic, he found that one youngster had fallen backwards onto a broken bottle, which had gone right up his rectum. When Eddie arrived the boy was in a terrible state. The villagers, having no proper medical facilities, had covered the dreadful wound with camel dung, believing it to be antiseptic. Whilst this was going on the leader of these poor people thanked us for the school, presented me with a pair of ibex horns, to which putrefying meat still clung, and asked why we had not provided desks, chairs and a blackboard! Leaving the troop to finish the job I flew back to Salalah, taking with me the prostrate bottle-squatter from whom most of the manure had been removed, and also my rotting trophy. It was not the most pleasant of flights.

Being in a Muslim country we worked on Sunday; Friday, or Jummah, is the day of rest. On the jebel we laboured seven days a week, but when in Salalah the squadron usually spent Jummah by the sea. White women were almost unknown in Dhofar and the Arab ladies lived in purdah, so relaxation was centred around fishing, swimming, boating, football, eating and drinking. The sea yielded up a fascinating array of marine life. Spanish mackerel and crayfish became welcome additions to our menu. Nevertheless caution was advisable when swimming because of the high population of potentially dangerous giant Indian rorqual whales; 100 feet long this dorsal-finned monster is the largest living animal. Lying close beneath the cliffs they blow spouts of water skyward and it was said that at night they utter near-human cries. Saw-fish, stingrays, octopus, monster groupers and aggressive moray eels were frequently encountered, whilst the much-feared hammerhead sharks mingled with the playful and harmless dolphins amongst the inshore reefs. However, in spite of such a population of predators no one was attacked. For my own part I should have loved to explore some of the archaeological sites of this ancient land. Only a few miles east of our base camp lay the ruins of Sumuran. The temple of the moon-god Sin had stood here in 1000 BC, guarding the stores of frankincense that were distributed by camel-train to every corner of Arabia and even to parts of the Roman Empire. Alas, there was no opportunity for an expedition but I made notes for a future visit.

As the monsoon approached, our ramshackle camp, with its limited air-conditioning, became a paradise and a cold beer a dream. In the relative cool of the evening we planned our operations, whilst out on the Salalah Plain the artillery thumped as the men of the outer defences engaged fleeting targets located on radar. In the Muscat Regiment mess I was made most welcome and often joined Spike, the soldier of fortune, for a glass of malt and a chance to pick his brains. No one knew more about this complex campaign than he and no one else had survived being blown up in a Land-Rover by a Russian anti-tank mine three times!

On one operation Mastodon, my faithful bulldozer, hit a mine whilst improving a road. By a miracle, and thanks to the steel anti-mine plates, the operator escaped unhurt. However, this represented fifty per cent of my dozer force so recovery and repair was essential.

Mines were an ever-present threat. Both British models left behind in Aden and modern Russian versions were present. However, some were buried too deep to be effective and we surmised that this had been done by a surrendering enemy who, after his conversion to the Sultan's cause, could suddenly 'discover' the mine and claim the generous bounty offered! A favourite place for dreaded Russian anti-personnel mines to be placed was in an old sangar, a rock-walled defensive position. Sangars littered the province but you entered a long-disused one at your peril. Visiting the hospital one day I saw a Baluchi soldier brought in without legs, hands, face or genital organs after stepping on one of these. Yet he lived!

By the middle of March our men had become experienced desert hands, bronzed and dusty, and they moved from one defensive locality to another providing essential engineer support. We seldom saw the elusive enemy, although undoubtedly they watched us and, when you least expected, there would be the crack of a high-velocity round or the crash of a mortar bomb. They were always 'out there somewhere' in the shimmering dun-coloured hills. Usually only the eyes of the Firquat, the irregular troops of the Sultan's army, many of them ex-rebels and some with brothers still in the opposition, would pick out our hidden foes. We grew to rely on the Firquat to warn us of an enemy presence, but even they slipped up sometimes, as one of our sections discovered.

A ramp down a steep escarpment was being built by the faithful bulldozers, assisted with liberal quantities of plastic explosive, when an aged tribesman approached some sappers. He jabbered away in Jabali and, when our lads shook their heads and said 'Sorry, Johnnie, don't speak the lingo', he became most excited and appeared to be pleading with them. 'No bakshish, now, go on, push off, will you,' they retorted. Thus the poor fellow went from group to group without success. Eventually he found an Omani NCO of the escorting infantry platoon who certainly did react. The man was a rebel trying to get someone to accept his surrender!

Relations with the Firquat were never easy. Proud men and traditional fighters, they had few material possessions, but believed it their right to have everything provided for them. They seldom carried any water of their own and on operations they would often demand that the Sultan's regular soldiers should give them some. If this were refused they would sulk and become childish, saying, 'You do not like us, you will not give us water, see, you are not our brothers after all.' The jundee* who had carried his precious water for miles could

* A regular soldier in the Sultan's army.

hardly be expected to sympathize. Of us the Firquat demanded 'wriggly tin' and building materials for their houses and even the use of bulldozers to improve their villages! Yet they fought well and had to be encouraged.

I often met the Firquat at the defended oasis named Tawi Atair. As was the case with most such areas, the occupation depended on a water source, but Tawi Atair was unique in that the precious liquid was brought up from an underground lake at the bottom of a massive sink-hole. One of the first tasks of the Royal Engineers in Dhofar had been to install a submersible pump to raise the water up an iron pipe and thus fill drinking troughs for the livestock. This had been done before we arrived but we had to maintain the pump.

Access to the caverns was gained by first descending some 300 feet into a huge cavity of rectangular cross-section with the long axis running approximately east-west. Then there followed a hair-raising journey down a 270-foot vertical pipe which our predecessors had installed, welding on bars to act as rungs at intervals. Peter Page's mountaineering expertise was extremely valuable. Descending into the hole, we could see a number of old, dry water-beds running down the sides. Finally at the base of the shaft there were many entrances to cave systems, some of which led into huge underground lakes. We explored one of these and found water depths down to 110 feet. Small, almost translucent fish, which I imagined to be blind, were seen swimming at various levels. With our chums at the British Museum in mind, we tried to capture some but failed miserably. They might be blind but they always managed to elude our divers.

From the amount of driftwood discovered in the cavern, it would appear that at the time of the rare heavy rains the whole shaft must fill up to a higher level of approximately sixty feet. Running water could be heard falling within the caverns and we decided that even if we installed a second pump there was little danger of running the incredible source dry. There was only one pump in position and, if that failed, the numerous cattle, goats and camels that relied upon it would die. So it was that the sappers set to and installed a reserve. Watched by curious weaver birds nesting inside the rim we lowered our paraphernalia. The worst part of the whole operation was climbing back up the iron pipe. One rung was missing at the precise point where we had to negotiate an overhang.

Throughout Dhofar water is the key to life. North of the jebel lay the greatest sand desert in the world, the Rubh Al Khali, or 'Empty

Quarter'. It stretches for 1,000 miles from the coast of Oman Island to Saudi Arabia. In this harsh region live the nomadic Bedu whose main interests are camels and simply keeping alive.

Patrick Brook's armoured cars prevented the enemy from crossing this enormous obstacle and reaching the jebel from the north. The Sultan's army also maintained one or two small defensive positions from which Patrick could operate and our main job in this area was to find water and build wells. Normally one was not disturbed by the enemy but on one occasion a section of sappers had been dismayed to discover that the aircraft they had been watching approach was not a friendly supply plane but an Ilyushin bomber. They took cover in their well and luckily the bombs fell wide. Back at home things were none too peaceful either and shortly after we arrived in Oman we learned that the IRA had bombed our camp in Yorkshire! However, they managed to get the whole place redecorated far more quickly than otherwise and my quartermaster was able to account for years of deficiencies!

On my recce to the Hornbeam line I was greatly impressed with this amazing terrain. Deep wadis separated the waterless mountain tops on which the soldiers of the Northern Frontier Regiment lived in underground bunkers. Having drawn up a plan with Brian Ray and received the brigadier's blessing we set to work. Firstly we had to complete the wiring and then thicken up the mine fields in between the infantry company positions. Thus I moved my tactical head-quarters to a heavily blasted summit named Ashoq. This mountain was occupied by B Company under a delightful Scotsman, Angus Ramsay. His second-in-command was Charlie Daniel, a Royal Marine who, with half the company and the mortars, held the end of a long ridge that stretched north for several miles from Ashoq. Standing on Angus's hilltop we could look south to the Indian Ocean and north to the skyline beyond which the Hornbeam line ended.

From the air I noticed how white the summit appeared. On close inspection I discovered this was due to the enormous number of direct hits received from Katyusha 122-millimetre missiles fired from as far away as seven miles by the Adoo. Angus kept a small museum of the remains of these onslaughts and an area of ground outside his command post was covered with rows of tail fins, shell splinters and shrapnel that he had picked up in the relatively short time he'd been there. A direct hit by a Katyusha could knock a rock-built sangar clean off the hill. To reduce this hazard we used our electrically driven drills to bore down into the soft rock and blast out deeper bunkers for the troops.

The Katyushas could usually be heard approaching and a lookout would shout 'incomer' on his walkie-talkie. All officers and NCOs carried these and thus would dive for cover. With luck you might have four seconds to act. It seemed extraordinary when considering how many rockets had landed on this position that they never caused a single fatality. Most injuries were due to people banging their heads and shins as they jumped into the holes. However, the enemy rocket crews did suffer (as we learned from Radio Aden), when the Strikemasters bombed the dust-cloud caused by the Katyusha's firing. The Adoo, as the rebels were called, were only about 1,400 yards away across the far side of a deep valley. At night we picked up their radio conversations on our own sets and Ashoq frequently received mortar bombs and recoilless rifle shells in addition to the missiles.

My first night with Angus was an alarming one. He kindly produced a bottle of Scotch which flowed freely while he briefed me on the situation. There was little room inside the rock-walled command post but I was quite comfortable on the floor. The first interruption of my night's sleep was the feeling that something smooth and warm was sliding over me. It was: a small grey sand viper. A few moments later a rat with Mickey Mouse ears bounded over my legs chasing the snake and then came fleeing back in the other direction as the viper pursued the rat. Relaxation was not easy under these conditions, but I had just dropped off when there was the most ear-shattering noise. I realized at once that heavy machine-gun in the next bunker had opened up. Forgetting rats and snakes I rushed out to see what was happening, only to hear Angus groan from his pit, 'Bet you it's foxes they're shooting at.' Outside, in the delightful cool of the night, I could see flares alight in the minefield and watched the tracer curving away into the distance. Eventually a somewhat sleepy Angus emerged to see what was going on. But he need not have worried because one of his Arab officers had the situation under control and after ten minutes of fireworks we returned to bed. An hour later the same thing happened again; this time Angus was a little concerned that it might be an attempted intrusion through the line and put down some mortar fire to deter visitors.

The sapper is a very adaptable chap and soon our men were completely integrated with our Arab hosts. Living and eating with them presented no problems although at best our men could speak only a little Arabic and few of the Omanis knew any English. I always enjoyed working with the Omanis. They were interesting people and some of their strange ways were fascinating. One soldier who was said to possess special powers could take a poisonous sand viper and place its head inside his mouth and then close his lips around the neck with no apparent ill effects. However, before he did this he put a spell, or hesp, on the creature.

The mine-laying was not made any easier by the presence of a large number of unmarked mines laid by previous occupants. I soon discovered that the planning figures so religiously stated in our manuals do not apply when you are dealing with live mines. I would recommend multiplying the theoretical timings by five if you are to get the right number of mines per man laid by soldiers who previously have only used plastic or concrete ones. One of Charlie Daniel's NCOs accidentally tripped one of our little toys during a skirmish. It was a fiendish device which, when activated, would jump into the air and explode at shoulder height, throwing shrapnel all around it for distances up to 100 yards. Known as 'jumping jacks', these were amongst the most deadly mines we possessed. However Charlie and his NCO were extremely lucky and got away with only minor scratches. Thereafter people treated the minefields with great respect.

A gruesome relic of an earlier attempt by the enemy to get through the line could be seen across the far side of a deep wadi. Through binoculars you could make out the whitening bones of a headless skeleton. Known to the soldiers as Jonah, this unfortunate fellow had been killed by a 'jumping jack' a few months before. Charlie had gone out to investigate and, while approaching, heard some noises and took cover. A few moments later he was able to witness the awful scene when a small pack of Arabian red wolves came stealthily down the track, avoiding the other mines with great care, and feasted on the corpse. Although some valuable papers and documents were recovered after this incident it was not possible to get the body out without risking life and limb in the minefield. This greatly upset our own Arab soldiers who believed that, although a communist, the man must still be a true believer and should be brought back for burial.

There were many nationalities involved in the war and the largest single foreign force was an Iranian brigade. Prior to the start of a thrust against the enemy I was with an Omani task force passing through an Iranian position. At sunset, as our dishevelled troops prepared supper, we became aware of a ceremony taking place at the Iranian Company HQ. A guard of honour assembled by the entrance of the hillside bunker, an immaculate jeep driven by a cleanly uniformed sergeant drove up and then the smartest major any of us had seen for weeks came out of the door, pulling on white gloves and adjusting his very dark glasses. Inspecting the guard he said a few words of encouragement. Clearly their commander was leaving for more comfortable nighttime quarters elsewhere. The Omani troops muttered darkly that they had little respect for their allies' military prowess. The major then inspected his jeep and, having found it to his satisfaction, decided to drive himself. The sergeant moved quickly into the passenger seat, the major revved up the engine, the guard of honour saluted and their commander reversed over them. 600 Omanis howled with mirth, literally rolling in the sand with tears running down their cheeks. Relations with the Iranians were not enhanced, but their support was pretty important.

Once I knew the mine-laying was going well I flew to the isolated position known as Simba. The cool early morning air left us shivering as we boarded the Iranian helicopter. Packed in with us were some 400 pounds of explosive, two drums of water and three sacks of smelly goat meat. The flight over the sea was as beautiful as ever and it was only a short while before we were approaching the enemy-held coast. Beneath us there were deep shadows in the steep-sided wadis and the stark dry hills stood out clearly in the first rays of the morning sun. Not speaking Persian, I couldn't understand the pilot's conversation with ground control but he had become rather agitated. Glancing up I was just in time to see two Strike-masters diving steeply past us towards the ground. We swayed in their slip stream and far below I could just make out the defensive positions and the narrow scar that must be the airstrip. The runway was clear, but in the broken ground on either side lay the wreckage of aircraft. Enemy fire had prevented the use of fixed-wing planes and so now all supplies came in by helicopter. I had lost sight of the Strikemasters when something else attracted my attention. Two white streamers were heading groundward and I realized that they were rockets fired from the leading fighter. The flash of the explosion followed almost at once and then I saw the other plane release its rockets before pulling up once again. Now we could see small puffs of smoke drifting about in a haphazard way on the position: we were flying into the middle of a bombardment.

Our pilot was in two minds about landing, but I gesticulated wildly, pointing at my load of explosives and the water, both of which were important for the defence of the garrison. The Iranian smiled again, this time a little nervously, and took us down in a tight spiral towards the landing pad. As the ground rushed up the puffs of grey smoke got bigger. Our shadow raced to meet us and the skids were barely on the rock when a Baluchi sergeant came running forward to help me lift down our lethal cargo.

As I jumped out he said in English, 'Good morning, sahib,' and saluted! 'I have a Land-Rover right here,' he added as we dragged the stores away from the helicopter, whilst the pilot yelled at us to hurry. As the last box was removed, the Huey rose in a cloud of dust and whirled skyward.

Now that we were no longer deafened by the engine noise, the crash of the mortar bombs and the thump of the guns were clearly audible. No time was wasted in loading the battered Land-Rover, and then, with the Baluchi at the wheel, as pebbles and debris rained down, we took off at a frightening pace along a bumpy track towards the battalion headquarters. On arrival the sergeant insisted on jumping out and opening the door, and saluted once again. A mortar landed fifty yards away as I dived into the cool darkness of the command post. Making my way through the labyrinth of sandbag walls, I came to the open-topped observation post where a British major was controlling the jets, guns, mortars and everything else by radio.

'Hello old boy,' he said with a smile. 'I'm rather busy at the moment – would you excuse me for a few minutes?'

I sat down on an aircraft seat that had been dragged from the wreckage of one of the planes lying by the runway, and looked up to see a mess orderly in a white jacket holding a silver tray on which stood spotlessly clean cups and saucers and a pot of coffee. A few minutes later the battle had ended.

'Well, that's this morning's show over,' sighed the acting battalion commander as he joined me for coffee. 'So you think you may be able to find some water for us?'

'I'll certainly try,' I replied.

'Good. Well, I've got a section of men who will go with you. Better have a long drink first though; it's quite a way and a good climb. And, by the way, be a bit careful – we've mined the wadi bed.'

Thus it was that, within the hour, our small party of engineers was stepping warily over the trip-wires, seeking any patch of greenery or damp sand which might indicate the presence of water. I was just examining a likely spot when there was a loud 'pop' behind me. Certain it was one of the wretched 'jumping jacks', I hurled myself flat. The Baluchi soldiers roared with laughter. It had only been a trip flare!

On our flight back from Simba we passed over an armed dhow of the Sultan's navy. The crew waved from the deck as the helicopter zoomed homeward. These ungainly looking craft were far more effective than they appeared. They carried recoilless guns on deck and at night would creep in under the communist guns, unseen on the darkened sea. By using their machine-guns they would draw retaliatory fire from the Adoo. Immediately an enemy weapon was pinpointed, the giant recoilless rifle would send its heavy shell whistling shore-ward. The back-blast was enormous and, as soon as it had fired, the dhow would make out to sea with all speed, usually followed by heavy mortaring from the shore.

It was 1130 hours on a June morning when we saw a mine explode in front of Ashoq. Immediately our artillery shelled the area, then Angus helicoptered forward to direct a strike by the jets. Although he was unable to see any sign of movement on the ground, he decided that a rapid follow-up was justified in the hope of finding enemy who might have been wounded. At 1700 hours the swirling mists were low with visibility being about 200 yards. Angus sallied forth in daylight and, trusting to the low cloud for cover, he left Ashoq with a thirty-strong patrol, including Charlie and Lieutenant Salim Said. In the fog they came upon a large force of enemy and fought a desperate close-quarter gun battle with every skill they possessed. Angus saved Charlie's life and although they lost several men they eventually managed to withdraw to their mountain top position, carrying their casualties with them. Clashes like this were typical of this bitter campaign.

There is no doubt about it, that working in the Scotch mist conditions of the Khareef was one of the most eerie sensations I've ever had to endure. It is quite different to that of being in complete darkness; somehow one felt that one was always being watched by unseen eyes peering through the drifting clouds.

Just north of Charlie Daniel's position was an enormous wadi called Jizalawt. It was a huge cleft in the mountains, over 2,000 feet deep, and in the early days we suffered a number of casualties due to heat exhaustion simply walking up and down the canyon. John Hoskinson, one of my troop commanders, had done sterling work in mining this natural route through the line. He was operating from the other side of the wadi with thirty of the toughest sappers you can imagine. Meanwhile I continued to work on the south side, seeding the minefield with a few special fiendish devices that were designed to be set off electrically from an observation post on the rim of the canyon. It was now a race against time. The monsoon had started early and our task was not yet complete. Thus we could not afford to stop for weather conditions.

One day I was halfway down the wadi side with a small party of sappers and Omanis when the clouds rolled in, reducing visibility to fifty yards. The temperature dropped and I felt a shudder go down my spine. But an even bigger one came a moment later when I heard the familiar 'crump' of mortars. The first bomb landed 100 yards away, and chippings and splinters showered around us. I grabbed my walkie-talkie, but couldn't get through as we were shielded from our friends by the wadi rim. To try to climb up the way we had come was now almost impossible. The rocks, dampened by the mist, were like a skid-pan and a slip could mean falling hundreds of feet. Quickly we concealed the rest of our devices under the rocks and tried to climb out, but for every pace we went forward we slid two backwards. There was only one thing to do: we tore up our shirts and, wrapping strips of cloth around our hands, began to pull ourselves up the barbed-wire fence that marked the minefield and led out of the gorge. It was a long, hard, nerve-racking business with the mortar bombs raining down from above. Each time I heard the noise of their descent I wondered where it was going to land. At the top Lieutenant Salim Said greeted me. They had been his mortars; a sentry on top of the mountain had seen enemy moving into the wadi below us. We had very sore hands but were extremely thankful.

Although we saw rather a lot of B Company, their neighbours, A Company, were also good friends. When we started work on the line the second-in-command, Ian Gardiner, a rugged marine, had been responsible for our escorts and safety and I had many dealings with Johnnie Braddell-Smith, the company commander, who advised on the mining of likely places to catch penetrating parties of enemy.

Johnnie was highly respected and beloved by his men, with a quiet manner that gave no indication of the fire that burned within. He was

a thoughtful, devoted and tolerant person with whom it was a
pleasure to serve. His knowledge and interest in the Omanis was
outstanding and in Salalah it was Johnnie's pleasure to go around the
barracks, talking and eating with the soldiers. As a result, he built up
an impressive store of knowledge about his men, their families,
homes, fears and aspirations. This deep interest in their well-being,
together with his wisdom and skill as a commander, inspired loyalty
and affection such as are rarely seen in a military environment. His
outstanding characteristic was his unflappability, which must have
contributed greatly towards his courage. But it was his ability to take
the sting out of the most formidable situations that we appreciated
most. There were many instances of this, but the most notable was an
action in the Wadi Sha'ath.

Intelligence had indicated that there were sixteen enemy based
immediately east of the Hornbeam line, where they were acting as a
reception committee for Adoo who succeeded in getting through our
defences. Accordingly A Company mounted an operation to hunt
them out. Thus four platoons, supported by mortars, moved into the
area and laid night ambushes. The following morning Johnnie sent
Ian and two of the platoons further east to take up new positions,
while he remained in ambush with the rest. At 1130 hours, about ten
Adoo appeared and were in the act of walking into Johnnie's killing
ground when Ian's half of the company came under heavy and
accurate fire further east. On hearing this, the enemy took cover,
avoiding being caught in Johnnie's ambush. Meanwhile his second-
in-command's forward platoon had taken up a position on a small hill
to the south of their initial position. Ian was moving with the rear
platoon on ground which was not to his advantage and he started
taking casualties straight away. The soldier on the general purpose
machine-gun was killed immediately and, of the party of four who
came to assist with the dead man, one was wounded and another
killed. In the face of such a heavy attack Ian's group withdrew
rapidly, leaving bodies and equipment in open ground. They
consolidated their position as best they could with the remainder of
the platoon, and Ian called Johnnie for help.

Johnnie had no idea of the enemy's strength, but it was apparent
that there were considerably more than the original sixteen. Subsequently intelligence indicated that up to sixty Adoo had passed
through the Hornbeam line very recently. Ian's forward platoon was
not in a position to afford direct assistance; it was having trouble of

its own anyway. To make matters worse communications had broken down. The intensity of the fire steadily increased, despite sterling work by the mortars and jets that had now come up to support A Company. Nothing could be done to prevent the enemy's flanking movements nor their looting the bodies. A Company was extremely keen to prevent this and the loss of a machine-gun with 500 rounds as well as a radio set would not have been to its credit.

By 1400 hours A Company were in the depths of despair. Now low in ammunition, they were being out-flanked and had sustained a further casualty. Ian Gardiner admits he had run out of ideas. If Johnnie did not come soon he would be of little use. But he did arrive. An agitated Ian exhorted him to position his troops with all speed. Diving for cover behind a rock, Johnnie regained his breath and offered his second-in-command a drink of water. 'Look,' said Ian, frantically explaining the situation. Johnnie fumbled in his pocket and produced a crumpled packet of Rothmans and asked for a light. So they lay there, the pair of them, without saying a word, and smoked a cigarette while bullets zipped overhead. Ian knew that everything would be all right.

The combined force now positioned itself where it could at least cover its casualties. Johnnie then organized a small party and, as our jets thundered in to strafe the enemy, led them to a hollow near where the dead lay. On the next air strike, the Omani soldiers ran to the bodies, dashed round them and back again! Patiently Johnnie had another word with the men, led them out again and brought one body back. All this time they were under fire. However, A Company's superior firepower was now beginning to have an effect. Ian felt it was his turn next, he couldn't leave Johnnie to do all the work, so he rushed out and recovered a second body with the help of another party of four. Meanwhile Johnnie, under aimed fire, sprinted forward and recovered both the machine-gun and the radio.

Perhaps one may be forgiven for believing that to risk life for such a comparatively worthless end was nonsensical. Indeed, looking back, Ian admits that his spine shivers. But it must be remembered that they had been told to recover the radio if at all possible and the Northern Frontier Regiment had never left a body for the enemy. To be the first to do so was unthinkable. Apart from anything else, they could never be sure that their friends were dead and the possibility of their being taken alive by the Adoo was a sufficient stimulus to drive everyone to almost any folly.

During my last week in the mountains I talked far into a night with Johnnie, sharing a bottle of Scotch. Little did I know that I should never see him again. When the long-awaited advance took place, the Sultan's army, reinforced with Imperial Iranian units, swept forward from the Hornbeam. The fighting was bitter and there were many casualties. In the forefront was Johnnie. He had been commanding a group of irregulars, the Firquat Tariq Bin Zaid, working with an Iranian task force.

On 10 December 1974 an Iranian battalion sought to establish a position about a mile to the south of its forward base, which was then on the edge of the tree-line. Johnnie led the advance through the trees at the front of a column of Iranians with complete disregard for his own personal safety. On reaching the objective he discovered the main body had somehow been separated and so he immediately returned along his route and successfully made contact with the missing troops.

Later that day the Adoo attacked the position with heavy small-arms fire and RPG 7 rockets which killed ten soldiers and wounded another. As soon as there was sufficient fire being directed against the enemy, Johnnie went forward to check the position. Moving stealthily around the company perimeter, he recovered the bodies of three Iranians thought to have been captured by the enemy. Those who watched him operate and organize the evacuation of casualties were greatly inspired by his personal example and tireless vigilance, which eventually enabled the column to withdraw without further losses, in spite of determined enemy attacks.

The next day the Iranian battalion sustained yet more casualties in its forward locations. Because of the proximity of the Adoo it was not possible to evacuate them by helicopter and so the indefatigable Johnnie continued to retrieve the wounded and dead under extremely dangerous conditions.

On Christmas Day he accompanied a patrol moving forward from another defended area to seize high ground near a main enemy position. They had gone 1,000 yards when the leading troops were attacked in thick trees. The Arab officer of the Firquat died in the opening burst of fire. A soldier picked up his body and attempted to carry it to the rear and, seeing that the man was having great difficulty, Johnnie handed his weapon to another and picked up the dead man himself. Shortly afterwards he was heard to cry out as he fell mortally wounded. The intensity of the enemy's fire was so great that it was impossible to recover Johnnie's or the Arab officer's bodies for some time afterwards.

It was perhaps typical of the man that he should have given his life attempting to bring in the body of a comrade whilst under deadly aimed fire from a ruthless enemy. His action typifies the magnificent courage and complete disregard of his own safety that he always showed*. Like so many who died in this little-known war, his gallantry and devotion to duty were beyond praise, and it was the deeds of such men that eventually brought victory to the Sultan and peace to this desert land.

In June 1974, as the swirling clouds rolled in from the Indian Ocean to cloak the jebel, I left Oman to face a different challenge: the great Zaire River.

---

* Major J. B. Braddell-Smith was awarded the Sultan's Gallantry Medal, posthumously.

NINE

━━━━◦◦◦◦◦◦◦◦━━━━

Dr Livingstone, I Presume?

'**D**R LIVINGSTONE, I PRESUME?' These immortal words were uttered by Henry Morton Stanley in 1871, and in 1943 they sent a shiver of excitement down my spine as I sat in Sunday school, attentive for once, listening to the gripping story.

David Livingstone, that remarkable Scot, had been found by a successful journalist who was to become equally famous as a dogged, determined explorer. Their meeting was an historic occasion, which made a deep impression on Stanley, and during their four months together he learned much of the old missionary's discoveries and hopes.

When, after his return to Britain, he heard of the doctor's death, Stanley said, 'May I be selected to succeed him in opening up Africa to a shining light of Christianity,' but his chief ambition was to pursue Livingstone's unfinished quest, the search for the source of the Nile. We now know that John Hanning Speke had in fact found the principal source at the Ripon Falls on the northern shore of Lake Victoria in 1862; however, twelve years later this was still disputed by many of his contemporaries. Livingstone was among them; he believed that the Lualaba River, which he had discovered west of Lake Tanganyika, might itself be the source of the Nile. To test his theory one must follow the Lualaba's course, and Stanley resolved to do just that. Backed by the *Daily Telegraph* and the *New York Herald*, he set out from Zanzibar in November 1874, with three other white men and 356 Africans. They carried an impressive quantity of weapons and the sectionalized wooden boat, which Stanley named *Lady Alice* after his fiancée, a Miss Alice Pike of New York.

Throughout 1875 the expedition pressed on across Africa, circum-navigating and surveying the great lakes, driving off attacks by hostile tribes and marching, marching, marching. In October 1876, Stanley and his now severely depleted party reached the banks of the Lualaba at Nyangwe. Already he had taken heavy casualties; his men were exhausted. He spun a coin saying, 'Heads, I go forward, tails I go back.' Apparently it came up tails twice, but Stanley decided to press on.

They had reached the Lualaba some 550 miles from its source, in the swamps of what is now southern Zaire. The Lualaba is not, of course, any part of the Nile but instead the headstream of the Congo. Together they form the mighty confluence, which flows across central Africa to the Atlantic. Stanley finally reached the Atlantic in August 1877. Two years later he returned to central Africa to play an important role in establishing what was recognized in 1885 as the Congo Free State. This was annexed by Belgium in 1908 as the Belgian Congo, and only in 1960 achieved independence as the Democratic Republic of the Congo. Finally, in 1971, after many internal vicissitudes, both republic and its great river were given their present names of Zaire.

No detailed scientific work was carried out on Stanley's expedition and, in the years that followed, the vast Congo basin remained largely cloaked in dense tropical jungle and was relatively inaccessible. Then, in 1970, Richard Snailham suggested that the SES should attempt to carry out a programme of medical and scientific research here in commemoration of Stanley's epic journey.

So it was that, whilst my attention was largely centred on the problems of the Darien Gap, I was also asked to lead the proposed expedition to Zaire. The late Prince William of Gloucester launched the venture at a dinner in the Grocers' Hall on 3 November 1971, the 100th anniversary of Stanley's famous meeting with Livingstone. It was a splendid party and superbly organized, thanks largely to the help of the *Daily Telegraph*. Then followed three years of hard, problem-studded planning.

Having digested the reconnaissance report prepared by Martin Romilly and Richard Snailham, we invited Major General Griff Caldwell to chair the expedition committee and battle with the unenviable task of raising the funds. Unlike military operations, the expedition had to pay for everything in advance. It was rather like going into battle, but with the added worry of raising money to buy ammunition. I could write a book on that subject alone, but in the end we left for Zaire £20,000 short of our target.

Whilst I had been in Oman, our London office had been run by my dear friend, Kay Thompson, and her daughter Jill. Without the help of Denis Lowry, Ken Monk and all Gestetner's, I do not know how we would have coped. But there were literally masses of people who came to our aid and unselfishly gave valuable help to the project.

My first major task was to select the team and its equipment. The Zaire is the seventh longest river on earth and the second biggest in its outflow, which averages 1,483,000 cubic feet per second! The country is the third largest in Africa, approximately the size of Western Europe, and it has one of the highest rainfall areas in the world. So the team grew, eventually reaching a total strength of 165. We selected our members from all over the world, mainly for their compatibility and industry. People with experience of Africa and those with a knowledge of French or the local languages were especially favoured. Our final complement included Americans, Australians, Belgians, Britons, Canadians, Fijians, French, Nepalese, New Zealanders and Danes. I also asked for a strong contingent of Zairois servicemen.

So many British scientists wanted to join the expedition that we ran a long series of searching interviews, conducted with great

ZAIRE RIVER EXPEDITION

patience by Dr Humphrey Greenwood of the Natural History Museum, who had long assisted the SES. The main problem was that, of the fifty scientists, all wanted to go in different directions.

The lady members were particularly interesting. Three were scientists. A charming Australian bacteriologist, Beth Haslewood, was married to Professor Geoffrey Haslewood, another expedition member. We had a French immunologist, and from Leicestershire came Dorothy Bovey, one of the leading painters of botanical specimens, who was to provide illustrations commissioned by Kew Gardens.

There were three nurses. Marie-Therese Guichard, or Fifi, was a sister with the British Army of the Rhine and a qualified State Registered Nurse: I discovered halfway through the expedition that this was for mental nursing, but perhaps that was appropriate. A well-built Canadian, Adrianne Damgaard, was also an SRN and a physiotherapist. She was to work wonders on many strained muscles in the months ahead, although one soldier complained that he went to Adrianne with a painful shoulder and came back with a broken neck! A happy-go-lucky blonde nurse called Pamela Baker spoke fluent French as well as some Lingala and Swahili. She was the daughter of George Baker, who, as Head of Chancery at the British Embassy at Kinshasa, had done much to help our reconnaissance team. Pam had the ability to work twenty-three hours a day without food and possessed a tremendous sense of humour and sympathy. I reckoned anyone who had known President Mobutu and the people of Zaire would be especially useful, so I made her my personal assistant.

My deputy was ex-Royal Marine Captain Mike Gambier, whom I had known for many years. Major Derek Jackson, a thirty-five-year-old rugged and ruthless administrator, became commander of the important logistic support group, with Gordon Mitchell, a tough Scots Guards major, as quartermaster. Naturally there were many ex-Darien hands, including Ernie Durey, the inexhaustible engineer who was to crack the land obstacles, and Jim Masters, once again in charge of the fleet. Captain Peter Marett joined in his former position as my intelligence officer. Advanced liaison in Zaire was assigned to a chum from Cyprus days, Major Tom Hawkins, and his able assistant Jim Winter. Both had been on a British Army training team in Zaire for several years, knew the people and spoke French. A galaxy of experts under Freddie Rodger, a leading authority on tropical eye disease, directed the medical research seeking a cure for 'river blindness'.

Air support was a vital factor. Here our good friend, Lieutenant General Sir Napier Crookenden, managed to obtain the assistance of the Army Air Corps, who once again provided a Beaver light aircraft. Gordon Mitchell worked long hours to amass over eighty tons of stores and supplies and, together with his aide, Dick Festorazzi, saw to its shipment to Africa. Whilst this was going on, the headquarters of the expedition had been established in my Whitehall cellar; in the end there were twenty-eight servicemen and civilians working in the small airless rooms fifty feet beneath the pavements.

1974 was not a good year to launch one of the most ambitious expeditions ever to leave Britain. Money was tight and the RAF desperately short of aircraft and civil air charter rates were soaring. The price of petrol was rising daily, as indeed was the cost of almost everything. British Army units were hard-pressed and could ill afford to spare good men for what some regarded as a swan. In Africa, political feelings were running high. The wind of change was sweeping through Angola and Mozambique. President Mobutu had recently nationalized the petrol companies in Zaire and former white settlers were leaving in droves. Thus the pessimism of Europeans in Zaire about our project was understandable. Nevertheless, we believed it could be done and planning continued. For political reasons, we decided to change our name from the 'HM Stanley Centenary Expedition' to simply the 'Zaire River Expedition', quickly abbreviated by the military to ZRE.

The old SES formula appeared to be working once again; a thorough scientific expedition with the added spice of an attempt to run a dangerous river. A varied research programme made it all objectively worthwhile, and the prospect of heroics on the water attracted the media and the commercial sponsors.

But our use of the Zaire River to move from Shaba (formerly Katanga) to the Atlantic with a vast team, equipment, stores and a variety of nationalities was no gimmick. There were few roads and little means of communications in Zaire and therefore the river was the only way. Indeed in colonial times the Belgians had inaugurated a steamer service throughout its navigable parts. Where cataracts intervened – below Kinshasa, at the Stanley Falls and the 'Gates of Hell' – they had built narrow-gauge railways around the obstacles.

But to move along the river, we had to find a way of getting through these cataracts, where waves could reach forty feet.

After some time on the Colorado River Jim Masters designed and assembled three giant thirty-seven-foot inflatable rafts. They only had an air pressure of two-and-a-half pounds per square inch, and one of the problems that worried us most was how to apply enough power to these flabby craft. In the end we fitted each with two forty-horsepower Mercury outboards. We were also provided with Avon inflatables and two rather unusual Hamilton water jetcrafts which Prince Philip had very kindly helped us to get from New Zealand. I believed that with this fleet we could tackle almost any rapid and if, in the end, we could not get through, then we should be able to portage. By starting the expedition in October we hoped high water levels would cover the rocks. Two of our giant inflatables were sponsored by companies, and were therefore named *David Gestetner* and *Barclays Bank*. Another was called *La Vision* by Mohammed Ali who was in Zaire for a title fight. She became my flagship.

Many of the lessons learned on the Blue Nile were remembered, and it was of great advantage having some of the old team with us. We could find no suitable river to compare with the Zaire, and no rapids to match its cataracts, so we could only hope and pray that our choice of boat was right. Our lives depended on it! The story of how we got the stores to Africa, through customs, overland and finally to where they were needed, is an epic in itself.

Once there, we would face a river almost as long as the distance from Ireland to New York, and the research groups and boat parties would be split up as if one team were in London, another in Athens and a third in Sicily. The lack of roads, railways, bridges and ferries did not help, but our support group was to work tirelessly to win the logistics battle. We hoped to link the various teams and the fleet on relatively old A14 radios. These were designed with a range of 350 miles and were hardly suitable for the distances anticipated. Nevertheless, great credit is due to the Royal Signals detachment who somehow managed to get our reports through to both the *Daily Telegraph* and the Ministry of Defence, in London. We established a rear base in the capital, Kinshasa, to liaise with the Zaire Army and Government, and to run a special expedition post office, set up by the Royal Engineers.

Linking this scattered force were three eight-man, mobile, forward support teams (FST), each commanded by an experienced officer. It was their responsibility to carry out advanced reconnaissance, establish good relations with the local people (who, after their experience of white mercenaries, were highly suspicious) and to move stores, scientists and specimens to and from the river. Each FST was responsible for one sector of the waterway. The whole operation was planned around the requirements of the various scientific parties but, because our experts could not be certain exactly where they would want to work, we had to be extremely flexible.

One hundred years before, Stanley had had a similar system but, lacking vehicles, had been forced to use 700 men marching parallel to the river to support him. Nor did Stanley have the Beaver aircraft we possessed. Fitted with the latest Sony video equipment and commanded by Cliff Taylor, a warrant officer in the Army Air Corps who had been with us in Panama, this robust six-seater was used for reconnaissance, parachute delivery of stores and aerial photography. One of its servicing team, Sergeant Ben Cartwright, had also been with us in Central America and had inscribed on its door the proud motto, 'Pas de problème'. Even so, local aviators did not envy them. Flying a single-engined aircraft out from Britain, over the Sahara, and spending four months operating above dense jungle with a countrywide fuel shortage, no diversionary airstrips, poor weather and few rescue facilities is no picnic. 'They'd never find you if you crashed in that cabbage anyway, so why worry?' smiled Flight Lieutenant Steve George, RAF, the second pilot.

In early September the advance parties began to deploy – Tom Hawkins with one group to Lubumbashi and Derek to Lobito – to extract our vehicles and stores from the hold of a cargo ship and ferry them up the Benguela Railway to Zaire.

The day before the main party's departure, my telephone rang and a voice said in poor English, 'This is Air Zaire, in Brussels.'

'Bonjour,' I replied with relief, for we had not heard anything for a considerable time from the company that was to fly us, and I was beginning to wonder whether they would turn up.

'Please may we have permission to land in your country?' went the slightly squeaky voice.

General Griff, who was sitting near me, grinned and nodded, so I simply said, 'Yes, when are you coming?'

'In about five minutes,' came the reply.

I was so staggered by this that I forgot to ask them where they were coming to, and it was Gatwick that got the shock when an enormous DC 10 thundered in over their runway completely un-announced!

Gordon had taken great pains to see that all our stores were packed, weighed and listed with meticulous care. Nevertheless we seemed to be considerably overweight. When our convoy reached Gatwick, the Zaire loadmaster rolled back his lips and waving aside any formalities of actually checking the cargo said, 'Stuff it all in, there is plenty of room.' Next morning four hefty guardsmen were still trying desperately to close the cargo doors against the bulging contents. However, we were soon airborne and as we undid our safety straps a smiling Zairois hostess came to me and said, 'Mon Colonel, may I have your permission to serve the champagne?' Like Stanley* I said, 'Who pays?' 'Oh, it is with the compliments of the company,' she assured me, and so they served champagne from Gatwick to Lubumbashi.

We stopped in Kinshasa to refuel with champagne and also to pick up one of our advance party, Captain Paul Turner, and our Zaire liaison officers (ZLOs). Paul, an energetic Hussar, had been in the capital for three weeks making final arrangements. As we flew on into the growing darkness of the African night I questioned the senior liaison officer, a Zaire parachute captain, about the Shaba region. 'It is a very bad place,' he warned. 'They eat people,' he said, tapping his pistol meaningfully. Few of our ZLOs had ever visited the far-flung province; indeed it was rather like expecting a Londoner to know all about Castile!

I spent most of the flight, when not drinking the excellent champagne, learning a speech from Pam. My French is abominable and so I had to write it out phonetically. The rest of the team enjoyed their last taste of luxury to the full!

It was long after dark when we touched down at Lubumbashi, and when the aircraft had stopped the doors opened to let in the hot blast of African night air. Striding out on to the top of the steps I prepared to deliver my oration. There was only one problem – the airfield was deserted! Only an attractive Zairois lady stood at the foot of the steps and so, bouncing down, I extended my hand and said, 'Enchanté, citoyenne.'

---

* When briefed by his employer, James Gordon Bennett, editor of the *New York Herald*, to go and find Livingstone, Stanley had asked, 'Who pays?' Bennett replied, 'Draw £1,000 now; and when that is spent, draw another £1,000 and when you have finished that, draw another £1,000, and so on; but find Livingstone.'

As she returned my smile I heard Derek's voice coming from the darkness. He was running towards me and hissed, 'Not her, that's the airport whore.'

'What on earth have you done with customs and immigration?' I said.

'Well, it's a long story, but they have all gone to a Burns' Night supper,' he replied.

'Burns?' I gasped. 'But I shouldn't think they have ever heard of the immortal bard in Lubumbashi.'

'No, no,' he admitted, 'but we are paying for the supper, so they have all gone.'

We set off towards our first base at the mining town of Kolwezi. Thanks to the kindness of various expatriates and the authorities, we were made welcome; not only that, we were given accommodation in, by expedition standards, superb houses. On the first night of our sojourn I was the guest at a dinner given by a local businessman. The meal was excellent and, as the assembled company made their way on to the verandah with their cigars and brandy, my host said quietly to me, 'Colonel, I have been in Africa a very long time and I know why you are here. I would not presume to question your orders for one moment but I do hope that when the time comes you will call on me for assistance.'

'But we are here for a long-range scientific expedition,' I explained.

'My dear Colonel, with the utmost respect, when you have been in Africa as long as I, and when you have studied world affairs with the same interest as I, a businessman, have been forced to, you will learn to respect certain people. It is my opinion that for a very long time the British have been underestimated, and I congratulate your government on its present plans.'

Nothing I could say would convince him that we were not the forerunners of a massive British army that was to seize the mineral-rich province of Shaba. I tried, but he simply replied, 'I have looked carefully at your organization; you have a colonel, there are a great many majors, and you have radios, vehicles and a light aircraft. There is no doubt that you have the outline organization sufficient to raise an army in Africa tonight.' After two brandies I gave up and we joined the assembled company on the verandah.

Two days later Tom Hawkins came to me with a serious transport problem and I instructed him to call upon this gentleman and request the use of his two large trucks.

'But those are the only vehicles he's got,' interjected Tom.

'I know,' I said, 'but just tell him I have need of them.' He did as I bade and came back to me with surprise written on his face. Our friend had provided them without question!

On Sunday 6 October Michael Gambier, Jim Masters and I flew south towards the Zambian border. Here we examined the river and selected a site to launch the boats and start the voyage. As we wheeled over the narrow stream, Peter Marett took Polaroid pictures. There was a slightly tricky fall within a few miles of our starting point which worried me, but not as much as the bumpiness of our ride which made us all violently ill. Jim managed to hold out to the last, but unfortunately the sick-bag was full up by then and when he could wait no longer it was explained that there was no room left in the paper envelope!

At the base morale was high and everyone eager to be off, but there was still a great deal of preparation to be done. Whilst Derek and his team slaved away bringing forward the stores to our depot, the command element continued with reconnaissance.

On 7 October we flew forward to view the rapids immediately north of Kolwezi. The initial expedition recce carried out by Richard and Martin in 1971 had warned that these were very likely to be impassable, and I saw two bad falls in an enormous gorge of reddish rock. Peter Marett named it the 'Red Gorge' and marked it on the map. There were many rapids and, of course, the dams themselves built to provide hydro-electricity for the copper-rich province. Portage would be necessary in a number of places until we came to the great mosquito-ridden swamps of Upemba. Here the problem would be navigation because it was difficult to locate the river's sinuous course.

Flying low we spotted hippo, elephant and buck along the riverbank and then, at Kongolo, the foaming Gates of Hell. The water was dangerously shallow, and until the jagged black rocks were covered I was doubtful if we could sail through. However, at the local airstrip the people assured me that the water would rise within the month. There was no aircraft fuel available here and we were forced to fly on towards Lake Tanganyika, and eventually landed shortly before dusk at Kalemie (formerly Albertville). Lake Tanganyika, like a vast inland sea, azure blue with long, palm-fringed golden beaches, glimmered beneath us. After a night in the modest hotel we awoke at dawn to find the streets outside lined with armed soldiers. As a flaming orange sun rose over the lake the troops moved off in vehicles on an operation, but the atmosphere was still tense. It was fortunate that we had a ZLO, and another useful asset was our special expedition arm badge which displayed the symbol of the Mouvement Populaire de la Revolution, which indicated that we were on the side of President Mobutu.

Flying back to Kolwezi across the rising hills and savannah we saw magnificent waterfalls and rapid-strewn rivers, all tributaries of the mighty Zaire. Small herds of game dotted the plain, and re-examining the area of the Red Gorge, I decided to deploy a bank reconnaissance group. The vast distances involved in this enormous country and the logistic problems of this expedition had been highlighted. This was no Blue Nile or Darien Gap, with a few hundred miles of difficult terrain to be overcome, but a seemingly endless land of mountain, swamp, river and jungle sweltering in the equatorial heat. I concluded that wherever possible we must move by water and, therefore, it would be necessary to increase the size of the fleet we proposed to assemble north of Bukama.

As we neared base I must have fallen asleep for suddenly I awoke with a searing pain on the right side of my head. My eardrum had burst, undoubtedly due to the rapid descent whilst suffering a mild head cold. The discomfort which followed was a wretched nuisance, especially as we had such a busy time ahead and as I was to speak that evening at a dinner given by the Lions Club of Kolwezi.

Everywhere we went people, both black and white, were friendly and hospitable. In fact, there was a considerable demand for us to show the films of our previous expeditions. Tom Hawkins' deep Scots voice was often heard haranguing the inhabitants in French on the terrors of the Panama Jungle. Indeed, by passing the hat round we were even able to raise some money for our depleted funds!

The first part of the expedition was to navigate the upper reaches of the river. So with our base still at Kolwezi, we proceeded downstream in the Avon inflatables, steered by long sweep oars and the occasional use of small outboard motors. At the Red Gorge some of the younger men wanted to try to get through in the boats. It was the old 'hawks and doves' situation of the Blue Nile, and I had to make it clear that we were not here to commit suicide but to get on with an expedition. The hawks grumbled but the doves appreciated this decision.

Meanwhile our whole team was being controlled by Tac HQ (tactical headquarters), which consisted of Peter Marett and Pam, together with Sam Qarau, a Fijian corporal of the Queen's Own Hussars, as signaller.

There were a few minor problems with our Zaire friends, who didn't really comprehend us at this stage, and several of the more politically inclined were highly suspicious. There was one in particular, who was wont to stir up trouble. Accordingly I instructed Peter, a prodigious walker, to take him on a forty-mile hike to examine the Red Gorge. Peter set off with our friend and returned two days later, carrying him. We never saw this gentleman again and the political problem ceased.

The river party, with its scientists, went on, crashing and tumbling through the foaming white water in the Katanga gorges. Mike Gambier told of a narrow escape when coming on a hippopotamus with her calf in mid-river. The hippo did not take kindly to this intrusion on her privacy, and charged. With her first bite she destroyed the bow, with her second she got the stern and with her last, she destroyed what was left amidships. After this you don't have a boat and Mike's Marines baled out into another craft. They almost left behind Basil Pratt, our Army padre, who was at that moment in communication with his head office! When they looked back they saw a very perplexed hippo which, having just eaten an inflatable boat, was suffering from a severe attack of wind.

Although many of our number were old hands, as always we brought in fresh blood, particularly junior officers and young soldiers. It was very comforting to see how well the team moulded together in these early and rather trying days.

At the small riverside town of Bukama the river was wide enough for us to launch the giant inflatables, which resembled outsized rubber mattresses. The minimum crew was only three, but each raft could carry up to thirty. In addition there was fuel, rations, scientific equipment, radio sets, line-carrying rockets, engineer stores and tools, plus television cameras, artist's materials and medical stores to be stowed securely aboard. La Vision also carried a yellow fibreglass six-wheeled ATTEX amphibian. It was a useful two-seater vehicle, which allowed us to get about more easily in the swamps and along some of the flood plains.

The smaller craft in our fleet consisted of the close reconnaissance section's two Avon S400 boats, twelve-foot inflatables powered by forty-horsepower outboards. The section's task was to scout ahead of the big rafts and find a safe way through the rapids. Commanded by

Alun Davies, a cheerful captain in the Royal Regiment of Wales, they were a hard-working bunch who undoubtedly enjoyed the flexibility and speed of their little boats. In addition there was the engineer section commanded by Ernie Durey. This bunch of sappers was the greatest collection of piratical rogues on the river. They moved with their own boats and vehicles almost at will throughout the country. Their task was to ferry Land-Rovers across the rivers, build bridges, dynamite obstacles, transport scientists, collect fresh water and locate stocks of beer. All this they did very successfully but rather noisily.

From Bukama I hoped to reach Kinshasa, 2,000 miles away, without taking our rafts off the river. But sailing into the flat, treeless waste of the Upemba swamp I was extremely worried that the water in the Gates of Hell might still be too low for navigation. Stanley's boat, *Lady Alice*, had been built in sections so it could be dismantled. Our giant inflatables were collapsible, but the central float chamber, shaped like an elongated doughnut, weighed 750 pounds. Portaging would be a devil of a problem. I was also concerned about passing through the rocky Gates themselves, even though our padre assured me that with our sins they would be wide open! In the still water of the great morass birds wheeled around us and the occasional crocodile slithered from the muddy islets. But the ubiquitous hippo was a worry.

One evening a fearful tropical storm broke as we were making camp. Thunder roared and lightning flashed as the rain drove into every shelter. Crawling under a groundsheet I was soon drenched. The sound of music and the clink of a bottle was heard coming from *Barclays Bank*, moored nearby and, without further thought, I bounded across and landed on a small group huddled beneath a canvas, seeing the storm out with the aid of Neil Diamond and a bottle of Portuguese vinho verde. The shelter was barely sufficient to cover one person, but in spite of the discomfort we fell into a deep slumber. It must have been about four o'clock in the morning when an ear-splitting snort close at hand awoke us. There in the moonlight, only feet away, was the glistening body of a gigantic bull hippo enraged because we were blocking his only exit from the river. Already our ZLOs were rushing from their bashas, cocking automatic weapons, but Dick Festorazzi thrust the loud-hailer into my hand and said, 'Try that, it might have the same effect on him as it does on us.' Pee-eep-pee-eep screamed the device as I flicked the siren switch to full volume. With a startled roar, the beast fled up river. At dawn the sodden, weary fleet continued its voyage.

Sailing at night we certainly saved time but it also created other problems. Once, when proceeding after dark, I noticed one of our lady members making her way towards the stern. This had been set aside for privy purposes because we had no loo and to go into the bank would only mean dumping those in need up to their chests in mud! Suddenly the night was split by an awful scream; I thought that the poor woman had fallen overboard. But when she returned to the 'bridge' I discovered the real reason. A ZLO, unable to understand English and thus the briefing I had given earlier, had chosen to sleep in the scuppers at the stern of the craft.

'What on earth happened?' I asked.

'Oh! How the hell do you expect me to see a Zairois on a dark night?' she retorted.

Each day our scientists would explain their work to us. This was most helpful because on such an adventurous project it is easy to forget that the results of lasting value are those achieved by the experts. Captain Scott had said of his last polar expedition that he believed it was primarily a great scientific project, with the Pole as the bait for public support. Similarly, I believed that, although the navigation of the river was most important, the newsworthy challenge was also necessary to gain funds for the entire operation. Several of our scientists had been unable to obtain financial grants and thus we also needed to raise money for them.

Although immediate results are not easy to obtain, some of the subjects under scrutiny were fascinating. One project concerned the mountain gorilla. These enormous creatures can reach thirty stone and are found in the high altitude forests of Zaire. Tac HQ had been seeking information on their whereabouts and, one night in a small bar, Pam met a local official who claimed to know all. However, we had no map with us and it was difficult to find out exactly where he thought they resided. The quest was not made any easier by this gentleman having consumed a considerable amount of beer; as he did not speak English, I left him being interrogated by Pam. Later I found her with her back pressed hard against the bar. The Zairois was attempting to describe where we might find the gorillas using the map of Africa on her T-shirt. 'For God's sake get me out of here before he reaches the Cape of Good Hope!' she hissed.

Jeremy Mallinson, right-hand man to Gerald Durrell at the Jersey

Zoo, was eventually treated to a rare opportunity when he spent five days in close proximity to a large family of mountain gorillas in dense forest. Whilst there, one enormous male, who had been named Casimer, suddenly gave a deep roar and, beating its chest, charged to within six feet of Jeremy before calling off the attack! These bluffing tactics are well-known in gorillas and Jeremy stayed just long enough to get a very splendid photograph.

On the river our geologists studied the rocks. Zaire has a great wealth of minerals, and in some places we saw whole hills of what looked like solid copper. Meanwhile, the fish team sought their specimens with nets and lines and spent many hours each day trying to collect samples for the study of fish bile, but in desperation had to get the sappers to speed up the work with the aid of a little dynamite. Dr Roger Sweeting, a research fellow at Sir John Cass College, was concerned with parasites; he also managed to acquire two black kites, which he named Biggles and Cromwell.

At Kongolo there were a great many problems. The giant inflatables were using up to ten gallons of petrol per day and there was simply no more to be had anywhere. Somehow Derek had borrowed a train, filled it with fuel and, doubtless contravening numerous regulations, had got it to the river. So when I arrived I found a base already established with adequate supplies for us to tackle the Gates of Hell. Meanwhile the sappers were still battling to get the overland convoys through on the terrible roads from Kolwezi. To complicate matters, Cliff Taylor had been badly burned when a petrol cooker exploded. He looked a terrible mess, but thanks to Dr Ian Young's skill, he was back in his cockpit within a week.

On our way north we had passed through Mulongo, where we had met two charming missionaries, Mary Goodsell, who had come out from Britain forty-four years previously, and Dolly MacDonald from Australia who had been there for a mere twenty-eight! Together they ran the Protestant mission and were extremely hospitable to us. Everything looked serene and peaceful and there I enjoyed one of those blissful periods of relaxation that are, alas, a rare privilege for expedition leaders.

At Mulongo I became increasingly concerned about the threat from terrorists in the forests near the rapids. The local battalion had suffered many casualties and its CO warned me to be prepared for trouble. He hinted darkly that we were prime targets for ambush as we went through the worst rapids. The Zaire Army, foreseeing trouble, had issued us with a large consignment of arms which Gordon Mitchell had wisely decided to keep under his control in large boxes labelled 'Scientific Instruments'! However, I now decided to issue these 'instruments' and chose another mission as the distribution point. This had been the site of the most horrible massacre on 1 January 1962 when twenty-two priests had been taken out, had their throats cut and, it was said, had been cooked and eaten by rebels. When the inhabitants saw us receiving weapons they suspected that retribution was nigh and fled! However, as a result of our gunboat diplomacy, no one had to use a weapon in anger, nor were we fired on at any time. Nevertheless, a few months after we had left the area, Jane Goodall, the chimpanzee expert, had her camp attacked in Tanzania and a number of her students kidnapped and held to ransom. So the terrorists got their publicity after all, but not at my expense.

In spite of our misgivings the Gates were not such a severe obstacle as we had feared. One native, clearly convinced we were going to our deaths, simply stood looking down and made the sign of the cross as we passed through the foaming water between the reefs of black rocks. Our boats proved to be as robust as we had hoped and we sailed on, enjoying a slightly bumpy, but otherwise uneventful, ride in what could have been very dangerous water.

On 10 November we emerged from the final cataract of this stretch. Marc Smith, our young river-runner from the Colorado, was disappointed that the water had not yet really tested his ability, and even talked of going home. I was able to persuade him that the dangers and hazards of the Livingstone Falls that lay ahead would test the bravest of us.

As we passed downriver the banks were crowded with brightly-clothed villagers cheering and waving excitedly. They had come from miles around to see these, the first boats ever to sail through the rapids, and as it was midday we pulled in for our lunch. Chiefs came on board and were offered lemonade powder and Army biscuits, thinly spread with Shipham's paste! The greeting over, they announced that their people wished to sing to us. Squadron Leader Mike Barnard, our musical navigator, found it too good an opportunity to miss and unwrapped his saxophone to give a rendering of 'Sweet Sue', which the people applauded enthusiastically.

That night we camped on a grassy bank looking across a slow-moving river, almost 1,000 yards wide, to a low ridge in the east. It was from this point that Stanley had first viewed the river in 1876 when his expedition had almost crossed two-thirds of Africa. As we turned powdered egg into omelettes at breakfast, the chiefs arrived by canoe. These thirty-foot-long craft were each propelled by twenty paddlers who worked in unison, chanting as they dug in their blades. Boats like this had attacked Stanley, but to us the natives showed nothing but kindness. Indeed the fresh rations that they brought were a welcome change from dehydrated food.

On the fleet the pets multiplied. Ken Mason, the expedition's leading humorist and an ace photographer from the *Daily Telegraph*, had bought for Pam a small grey furry bushbaby named Tiddlypush. Being nocturnal, it was a useless pet, for when, in daylight hours, we wished to play with it, the creature was sound asleep up a tree. At night when we were trying to rest, the wretched beast was bounding about and usually tried to get into one's sleeping bag and do something unspeakable. Thus, to remove Tiddlypush from harm's way, Pam kept it inside her shirt. One day when she was interpreting a rather truculent chieftain, I noticed to my amazement that the man's eyes had suddenly come out on organ stops! The reason was simple: Pam's bosom was heaving up and down in a most remarkable fashion and then, suddenly, the goggle-eyed creature emerged from her neckline. The chief fled and we had no more trouble!

On 13 November we reached the village of Nyangwe, near where Stanley had launched *Lady Alice* after his march from Zanzibar, and where Dr Livingstone had lived for almost a year, trying in vain to persuade the local people to take him downriver. After witnessing a most dreadful slaughter by Arab slavers, the doctor had marched back to Ujiji on Lake Tanganyika where Stanley had found him, sick and weak, in 1871. In the field behind Nyangwe were graves of Belgian soldiers who had died fighting in the Force Publique, which Stanley had set up in the 1880s to defend the new Congo Free State. Ironically, these men had perished whilst driving out the slavers under the infamous Tippu-Tib, who had supported Stanley in 1876. As we stood in the long grass viewing the monument and its simple plaques, there was a movement on the brickwork. A thin green snake rose from the grass and slithered up to the top of the plinth, coiled itself and raised its head to hiss menacingly at us. We left the tombs with their sinister guardian and returned to the river.

Snakes were by no means uncommon. On one occasion, spotting one swimming across the river, I shouted to Bob Powell, commanding a nearby recce boat, 'Catch it!' He did, with the aid of a plastic bag and a paddle, and on getting it into the boat found that he had landed a spitting cobra, which can throw its venom with accuracy for some eight feet. Three men ended up in the water and the snake stayed in the boat!

Thanks to the ever-watchful eye of our fleet's medical officer, John Chapman-Smith, we were always alert for disease. We were riding one of the biggest sewers in Africa, and all drinking water had to be filtered, boiled and sterilized: indeed it was safer to drink whisky. Nevertheless, fevers did occur and Pam, having nursed a Gurkha suffering from chicken pox, caught the bug herself. For days she lay beneath an improvised canopy that Jim Masters erected on the flagship to shield her from the relentless African sun. Others went down with various maladies and for a time we looked like a hospital ship.

Meanwhile we pressed on towards Kindu, scene of more tragedies of the 1960s, for it was here that the drug-crazed Simba rebels had started their revolt, through which they eventually seized large areas of the country. The hard-working Commissaire du Zone greeted me with a bottle of Scotch and entertained us royally.

We always made enormous efforts to ensure good relations with the locals when we docked in any small town. Captain Kabe, a Zaire naval officer, would often say to me, 'John, I think I shall go ashore to look into Naval matters'. He normally returned at dawn, usually with two attractive girls on his arms, and to 'Naval matters all right, Captain?' would reply with a great grin 'Number one, number one'.

Early one day our 'Orders Group' assembled on the rubbery deck of La Vision. I noted the absence of one of our senior Z LOs.

'Slept ashore last night,' muttered Tom Hawkins, 'I'll find him.' A few moments later Tom confronted the concierge at the local hotel. 'Où est le Capitaine?' he demanded.

'Numéro neuf,' whined the terrified woman.

With barely a tap on the door, Tom thrust it open revealing our Zaire officer entwined with a lady. His speedy reaction was extraordinary for, leaping out of bed in his underpants, he exclaimed, 'Ah Captain, have you met my sister?' Thereafter, whenever we approached any riverside town, we would enquire, 'Got any sisters here, Captain?'

From time to time in our travels local officials would make the normal gesture of offering me, as commander of the expedition, the gift of a few local ladies. I had learned most of the excuses in my book – 'My religion doesn't permit', 'I am not feeling very well', 'My wife would not approve' – but, in one particular town, when I had exhausted all possibilities, Pam suggested that I hand the matter over to one of our able Zaire sergeants. I explained to him the cause of my embarrassment and asked if he could help out. 'Mais certainement, mon Colonel,' he replied. Next morning the sergeant in question arrived at Tac HQ, saluted, and explained that he was ready to provide his services in the cause of the expedition whenever required. As a result I escaped many a tricky situation and had the most faithful senior NCO of the Zaire Army!

In the Steps of Stanley

O N 14 NOVEMBER a solid wall of tall trees rose suddenly on both banks. We had passed through bush country and were now entering jungle. At Kindu our entomologists and Gurkhas set up a camp in the tropical rain forest. The scientists were sampling the flying insects at different levels between the top of the trees and the ground. They believed that this would give them the first overall indication of the composition, vertical distribution and richness of the flying insect fauna of the rain forest canopy in central Africa. Such knowledge is essential in order to assess the importance of the forest as a natural resource. Working closely with a team of Zaire scientists, who had been sent on the orders of the president, our experts set electrically-powered ultraviolet light traps to collect the insects at different heights above the ground. In order to get the traps up into the trees a small team of sappers was employed as climbers.

As we approached the site there was an anguished cry. Rounding the bend in the forest trail, I was just in time to see Sergeant Mick Hough hurtling through the air to land with an awful thud at the base of an eighty-five-foot tree. 'Don't touch him,' cried Fifi the nurse when we rushed to his aid. As we gathered round his limp body, Mick stirred. 'F***ing hell' he said several times and stood up! As he was a parachute engineer no one was surprised, but we later discovered that he had suffered a minor brain haemorrhage and a split liver. The fact that he survived was a miracle.

At ground level they discovered many interesting creatures, including fascinating butterflies, colourful moths and some highly dangerous snakes, including a deadly forty-two-inch gaboon viper, the bite of which gives you approximately three seconds to hand your best friend your wallet!

Supplying these groups in the forest was never easy and usually involved long difficult journeys by Land-Rover or parachute drops from the Beaver. Nevertheless they ate quite well, making up the deficiencies of their diet with monkeys provided by the ZLOs. It was never a taste I enjoyed. Once I bought them a bottle of whisky. The scientists' eyes lit up with glee. It was unfortunate that the water they used to top up the liquor had been tainted with formalin; the lot were almost pickled for posterity!

Back at Kindu, Derek's logistic team was working hard to keep the whole show on the road. Many frustrations were overcome, including one when a train started off in the wrong direction and no one could speak the same language as the engine driver. On another occasion a thief stole a video battery and was caught by a Zaire sergeant. Justice was done immediately and seen to be done, for the poor fellow was thrashed mercilessly in front of us before being taken off to the magistrate for sentence. As the battery had expired anyway, I sent a note to the court asking for clemency for the wretched man. The magistrate respected my wishes and only gave him a year's penal servitude.

In a remote village 400 miles away, Freddie Rodger, as senior medical officer, was leading the medical research team investigating many diseases, including river blindness*, which afflicts more than two million in Africa. It was a pathetic sight to watch the queues of people outside the head man's straw hut awaiting examination; some blind, many already heavily disfigured by the subcutaneous lumps from which the worms hatch. The only light relief was the arrival of four Pygmies, who politely declined Freddie's invitation to have their eyes looked at on the grounds that he would be able to glimpse their souls! The research was directed at finding clues towards a cure for the disease, which they already knew is caused by the bite of a black fly known as Simulium Damnosium. Freddie was there to find where onchocerciasis was most prevalent, and the background of each person was thoroughly investigated, even down to the number of wives.

At Kindu we refitted the boats from the quartermaster's train. In a railway siding guarded by Zaire soldiers stood a 'wagon-lits' and a collection of closed trucks. The quartermaster paraded up and down with a large stick. Men approached at their peril, but when the custodian of all we possessed decided that an issue should be made, it

* The results of this work are in *Onchocerciasis in Zaire*, edited by F. C. Rodger (Pergamon, 1977)

was a great moment. A huge bunch of keys was produced and, like a medieval jailer, Gordon would stride up to the selected wagon. The heavy steel doors would slide open, revealing a host of goodies. Few were permitted the privilege of actually entering the inner sanctum.

Meanwhile over the radio to Kinshasa I heard that the jetboats had arrived early. The New Zealand team under Jon Hamilton was anxious to get on with the job of reconnoitring the Livingstone Falls. Time spent in reconnaissance is never wasted, especially on expeditions, but I was not yet prepared to have an FST deployed that far ahead. Already our force was spread over 1,000 miles. However, the jets were there and so I reorganized our support groups.

To the west of the Zaire, zoologist Sinclair Dunnett and a tough marine named Bob Hudson were seeking the rare pygmy chimpanzee on the Lomami River. We would receive faint radio reports from them, but in spite of the most terrible privations they had not yet found the elusive creatures. We supplied them by air and kept our fingers crossed that nothing serious would occur, for they were well outside the range of any immediate help.

In Kindu I met the charming president of the local Luncheon Club, who mentioned that she also ran the cinema, nightclub and brothel. When she invited me to dinner the next day, I enquired if I might bring with me one or two friends (for safety!) and so, accompanied by Pam and Captain Kabe, went to her house the following evening. The lady and her sister, their hair arranged in spikes, basted liberally with rancid butter, had prepared a meal of traditional Zaire dishes. We were halfway through dinner when I felt something touch my leg. It was more than that; it was quite clearly a hand which, very gradually, worked its way up the inside of my trouser leg. I was slightly alarmed and, looking across to the lady's sister opposite, was intrigued by the fact that both her hands were on the table. Eventually when the fingers had almost reached my knee I could stand it no longer and shot my arm under the table to grasp whatever it was. Out came a tiny chimpanzee dressed in a sailor suit and furious at having been disturbed.

'Ah, you have found poor Sophie,' said madam.

'She must be a very young chimpanzee,' I replied.

'No, no, she is very old,' insisted the lady.

Thus it was that whilst Sinclair and Bob were undergoing a most trying expedition, I had found a pygmy chimpanzee under a table in Kindu!

When the fleet moved to Ubundu under Mike Gambier I went off to see Freddie to cope with the administrative problems that now plagued us. Finally I flew on to Ubundu in the Beaver and landed just before half light to be met by Joe Tuwai, another of our cheery Fijian NCOs. Motoring along a forest trail to the town, we came upon a group of large black apes. For a moment I thought we were facing gorillas but they were almost certainly wild chimpanzee, and, as I leapt out to follow them up, they disappeared, chattering, into the bush. Their coats of hair were much thicker than is usual with captive creatures.

Near Ubundu was a Christian mission headed by the lively Father Augustine, the only survivor from a Simba attack during the revolt. Everywhere we went on this stage of the journey there were reminders of the civil war: burnt-out tanks, crashed aircraft, destroyed bridges and ferries and deserted hospitals and churches. It was a sad scene although President Mobutu's government was trying to restore this area to its former levels of prosperity.

The Stanley Falls starting at Ubundu consist of a stretch of some seven cataracts over a distance of fifty miles. The usual reconnaissance had been carried out by air, land and river, and, in spite of local stories that the river went underground, we did not expect too much trouble. How wrong we were.

Ken Mason was snapping members of the flagship's crew as we passed through some moderate rapids. Suddenly all hell let loose.

'Look out,' yelled Peter Marett, who had seen that we were about to plunge into a yawning fourteen-foot-deep chasm which inexplicably had opened up in the riverbed.

Already one of the Avon dinghies was in the boiling pit being hurled about like a cork in a washtub. The giant raft on which I was riding came crashing down the slope and a huge wave swamped our engine, hurling the helmsman off his feet. A wall of water struck the bow, sweeping away stores, including a number of waterproof camera boxes that had been lashed in with 1,000-pound-breaking-strain wire. Decking boards splintered beneath us as the great raft flexed and twisted in the cauldron. 'We're breaking up,' someone cried.

With no engine we were trapped in the hole, being pounded by mountains of brown water that spun us around so that one lost all sense of direction. Then we were thrown clear to drift into slack water. It was a great relief, but behind us the second Avon had already gone into the swirling funnel and I'd just time to see Richard Snailham's bearded face aghast with horror as he held on for dear life. *Barclays Bank*, the second big boat, skilfully avoided the hole, but the *David Gestetner* went straight in. We watched anxiously as she stood on her bow. Oh God, she's going over, I thought, but miraculously the giant fell back into the pit and escaped.

Next day, we went to a village and tried to send a message offering a reward for recovery of any lost kit. Although they had no telephones we found that the local talking drums were quick and efficient and for the equivalent of fifty pence you could get ten minutes on a talking drum during the cheap period! The sweating drummers claimed they could communicate up to thirty miles by night and twenty by day. We thought it compared pretty favourably with our own radios or the GPO!

On Friday 29 November we crossed the equator. At lunchtime we held a small ceremony and drank a toast to mark this epic point in our journey. That night we camped amongst some limestone outcrops. The jungle contained old plantations, and wild lemons were plentiful. There were also some interesting caves in the area; in one we found a great many initials which, according to local legends, included some carved by H. M. Stanley himself!

The recce reports of the Stanley Falls were good. Having met Bill Coleridge's FST in Kisangani the manager of a local brewery had kindly come out to greet us by road with a large quantity of his products. The party that ensued was memorable and put us in a good mood to meet the Falls next day. Thousands of townspeople crowded onto the bank to cheer the fleet through. As each boat slipped over the six-foot drop into the heaving waves, a great cry went up from the shore.

'Mobutu oyeah,' we shouted over the loud-hailers.

'Mobutu ooyeeah,' echoed the watchers.

The Avons were hurled high by their impact with the waves, but the big rafts ambled through, all except *David Gestetner*, which delighted the onlookers by demolishing one of the fifteen-foot-high fish traps in mid-river. It was a great day; we had now reached our halfway mark and the brewery kindly saw that the occasion was suitably marked when we came ashore.

In the town our signal section, who had flown ahead, had already set up a high radio mast trying to contact the BBC in London. Sergeant Alan Cobb, our rear base radio operator in Kinshasa, had arranged the details and now we were to attempt the impossible: a link-up from the jungle to Broadcasting House. Early one morning I sat by the set as our signallers fiddled with the knobs. At last there came the clear voice of someone at Catterick in Yorkshire. 'We're connecting you with the BBC now,' it said.

Various pips and squeaks followed and then a clearly audible woman telephonist in Broadcasting House was heard to say, 'I am sorry, dearie, but the number's engaged, you'll have to ring back.'

'Madam, I am in the middle of Africa,' I screamed into the microphone.

'I can't help that, you'll have to call back,' she said, and the line went dead! Thus ended our attempt to communicate with the nation.

Over the next 1,000 miles of wide, slow-flowing river Stanley had fought great battles, but the Zairois were overwhelming us with their traditional hospitality. It was as well that our relations with them were so good for Roger Chapman's life was suddenly at stake. He had been taken ill on the afternoon of Thursday 5 December with what was thought to be peritonitis, and Vyvyan Jones, one of our surgeons, was extremely worried about his condition.

'Are you really proposing to operate in this bush hospital?' I asked.

'Well, if I don't, I think he'll die,' he replied.

That night they gave Roger a spinal anaesthetic, which meant that, although he felt no pain, he remained conscious throughout the operation. Roger with great Yorkshire wit happened to notice that the two surgeons working on him were John Chapman-Smith, an eye surgeon from New Zealand, and Viv, a gynaecologist from Swindon. He remarked that he hoped they had reached a compromise! However, by morning it was no laughing matter, for Roger was dying; the only chance of saving his life was to get him to a hospital where they could do a full laboratory investigation. The nearest was in Kinshasa, 1,000 miles away and, although our Beaver could have covered the distance in two hops, it was doubtful that there would be fuel at the end of the first 500 miles to get it the next.

At this point our guardian angel intervened and we managed to get the assistance of the local Zaire general. He ordered the nearest airliner to land at Kisangani airfield, which it did. John Benham-Crosswell, a para-sapper, surrounded it with his 'mercenaries' and the French pilots put up their hands in surrender. However, John explained that this was not a coup d'état but simply a question of borrowing their plane for a few hours.

We loaded Roger onto the DC4 which took off for Kinshasa without delay. Also on board was the faithful Sergeant Mulongo, who now needed treatment for VD. It was fortunate that we had Pam with us because she had worked in the President's Clinic in Kinshasa and knew the people concerned. Later, we heard that largely through the good efforts of Dr Bill Close, Pam's former boss and personal physician to the president, they had managed to save Roger's life, although not without a considerable struggle.

Meanwhile our fleet was once again under the command of Mike Gambier. I planned to send the boats on whilst I moved east into the Ituri Forest through which Stanley had marched to rescue Emin Pasha in 1888. In this dark land live the Pygmies and the strange okapi. Peculiar to this part of Zaire and only discovered around 1900, it is a type of giraffe with a backside like a zebra and a body similar to an antelope. I was keen to see the beast and badly wanted a few days away from the administrative nightmares. Accompanied by our photographers, and after driving 350 miles towards the Mountains of the Moon, we saw two fine bulls in captivity and were privileged to meet the Pygmies who hunt these strange creatures. In olden times the skin of the okapi was much sought after and reserved for chiefs. Apparently it was supposed to bring an endless supply of pretty young girls to those who sat on it!

With the Pygmies we tried to find and film this rare animal. Marching deep into the twilight forest with our tiny near-naked friends, we searched for days, and, although I was not lucky enough to see one myself, some members did get within twenty yards of them. The only creatures I met were far from gentle. On one sortie two Pygmies, Bongo, a Sandhurst-trained Zaire officer, Val Jones and I were moving along a narrow game-trail in thick jungle. Suddenly the leading Pygmy bounced past like a little chocolate-coloured rubber ball; close behind him was Lieutenant Bongo, who yelled, 'Run!': and behind him came a very angry jumbo, ears flapping and trunk raised. I leaped aside and just remembered to warn Val. Four irate elephants crashed past, scattering branches and leaves. They looked rather small and it was only later that I discovered they were the very dangerous variety that inhabit the Ituri Forest and are much feared by the locals. I couldn't imagine what had caused this unprovoked attack until I remembered that for some 3,000 years Pygmies have been sticking poisoned spears into jumbos' backsides.

The jungle hunts were arduous, but very exciting. To try to follow a Pygmy in the deep forest is not easy, especially if you are over four feet in height. The little warriors were quite superb hunters and very tough. Using their tiny bows they could transfix a cigarette packet at twenty paces with an arrow tipped with coagulant that will clot its victim's blood in seconds. During the search a hunter accidentally shot himself in the foot with an arrow, but luckily it was not poison-tipped; he went on to march seventeen miles with us that day!

When we returned to the village at night our hosts entertained us. We took turns at putting on dances and acts in our own language. Neither really understood the other but it was great fun. Ken Mason's songs made everyone hoot with laughter. Val did a Highland sword dance and Sam Qarau frightened the living daylights out of our tiny friends by drinking the contents of a paraffin lamp and then, with the aid of his lighter, blowing fire all around us.

From my point of view this short interlude was a chance to unwind. On an expedition there is rarely any rest for the leader and under extreme stress I find myself flitting between two characters: the stronger tries hard to defeat the weaker. The only noticeable result of this struggle is that my whisky consumption goes up! However, when the weaker begins to get the upper hand I find I may overreact to situations or exaggerate a problem. The difficulty is, as in war, to know which intelligence to accept. I believe it is essential to keep one's mind as open as possible to avoid blocking out unpleasant information. This is why I enjoy having a small group of trusted aides in my Tac HQ. Peter, with his methodical and cautious approach, was an ideal intelligence officer whilst Pam, with her knowledge of Zaire and its people, was a splendid adviser on the local situation. Sam could be relied upon to make us laugh under the most adverse conditions.

At work in the rain forest was Ken Joysey, a lean and enthusiastic zoologist, who was in hot pursuit of the West African otter shrew. There were no live specimens of this creature in captivity. Aided by the Pygmy bowmen, Gurkha soldiers and Sergeant Major Eddie McGee, Ken and our other zoologists probed deep into the Ituri. Eventually the Gurkhas managed to capture one. Back on the river our botanists were hard at work, studying amongst other subjects the spread of a notorious water hyacinth. Outwardly it is a pretty violet and green plant that was introduced from South America in 1914 as an ornament, but is now threatening to block parts of the great waterway.

On returning to our base in Kisangani I was able to review all the problems that faced the expedition whilst Mike sailed the fleet on towards Kinshasa. Ahead we faced a host of difficulties and our casualties were growing alarmingly as malaria, in spite of regular doses of Paludrine, took its toll. Dysentery, hepatitis, sundry fevers and ear complaints were reducing our force daily. I began to fear that we had too few to carry out the tasks necessary to reach the Atlantic.

On the political front the Zairois were extremely sensitive and we had to be very careful not to say anything that would cause offence. At Kananga there seemed to be a running problem between the British and the other nationalities in the medical research teams. In minor disagreementts the Zairois sided with the Belgians, with whom, of course, they had a common tongue. I was too far away to intervene but the irrepressible Freddy Rodger managed to lead this group effectively. The Zairois said he was 'another Stanley', because he made them work so hard!

The main reason for success on the river was the thorough reconnaissance and the good equipment. The Sony video was especially valuable and I believe we must have been the first expedition ever to use this equipment in the field.

Although the expedition's discipline was fair, I tried to avoid the larger towns wherever possible. It really would have been very useful to have had a regimental sergeant major to look after the number of soldiers. Officers tend to be rather hesitant about re-buking their men on expeditions, and I was constantly having to remind them about turn-out. The problem is that with the scientists bearded and long-haired it was difficult to enforce. However, there were no really serious personality problems. Indeed I cannot re-member an expedition where there had been so few difficulties of this nature. Furthermore the girls were a cohesive element on the expedition. Whilst Pan was nursing Roger in Kinshasa, Val had taken over as my PA and, with her Cordon Bleu training, was feeding us like fighting cocks. It was as well because morale was suffering through the lack and delay of mail in spite of the efforts of our army postman to get it speeded up. Another problem was the dire shortage of fuel and Land-Rover spares. Our transport was now virtually worn out.

The roads were generally poor and got worse as we proceeded north, and I noticed that the jungle was encroaching at an alarming rate. The railway companies, on the other hand, were extremely helpful and, wherever we could find ferries, the local authorities assisted. However, many of these had been destroyed during the civil war. The weather had been pretty good. We seemed to have dodged the rain along the river and yet had managed to get just enough water to navigate over the rocks. Mosquitoes were extremely rife in places as were the tsetse flies and other nuisances including scorpions.

On the whole the expedition was in good heart, although this was sometimes due to the supply of free beer! Several breweries along the river were about to be nationalized and thus were extremely generous.

Another problem was that, having left groups in Kisangani and Kananga, our communications were now stretched beyond range. Nevertheless the Royal Signals team somehow always managed to get through. The committee in London announced that in spite of our economies they had been forced to raise an overdraft and this we knew would take at least eighteen months in writing, lecturing and selling our philatelic souvenirs to repay once we returned to Britain.

So the whole expedition moved slowly on towards the Atlantic. Pam and I landed at Mbandaka to find our friends being royally entertained by personnel of the Wimpey Company. Alas, we had arrived too late for the party, but the recce section was waiting to take us forward to the giant inflatables, now motoring westwards. Neither of us felt particularly well one morning, waking with a mild fever and feeling very sleepy. I had intended to hold a conference of captains on the flagship, but the river was terribly choppy and we were constantly soaked, so I spent most of the day discussing our future moves with Mike. A great advantage of having such an able second-in-command was that I could bring him in to take over, allowing me to coordinate the whole expedition.

For three days my fever ebbed and flowed and I didn't think too much of it. Indeed I was more worried and frustrated because our radio communications were made difficult by constant interference from a Chinese station operating from the Congo Republic. On Saturday 21 December, I decided to move ahead with Alun Davies's recce boat to arrive in the capital ahead of the fleet. At Kinshasa I went straight up to Bill Close's house to see Roger who was then convalescing. Bill gave me a funny look and asked if I felt ill. 'A little hot,' I replied. He took my temperature, which was 104°F! Un-emotionally he informed me that I had malaria and in a flash injected me. In spite of feeling reasonably normal I found myself rushed back to the newly-established Tac HQ in the town where Adrianne and Val swabbed me down with icebags stark naked! It did the trick, for next day I was able to rise and greet the fleet.

Christmas never feels quite the same in the tropics but the European families there threw open their houses and did their utmost to entertain us. It was our only rest in four months. The sick were put into hospital and we prepared to tackle the huge cataracts that lay ahead. It was a time to relax and refit the boats for the battle with the great rapids of the Livingstone Falls. Richard Dorman, a wild Irish Guards ensign, caused a great stir by hurling himself fully dressed into the swimming pool of the Intercontinental Hotel, complete with a packet of soap powder, to get an instant bubble bath which filled the entire pool!

The complete New Zealand jetboat team now arrived and informed me that they had not a great deal of time left. They were very experienced river-runners and had already done an excellent recon-naissance for us of the Livingstone Falls, which proved extremely useful in planning this last phase. Long discussions went on far into the night. Captain Nigel Warren of the Gurkhas had been left with his FST at Kisangani to support the scientists working in that area and eventually withdraw them to the capital. Freddy was still at Kananga with his medical research team and contact with him was extremely difficult. On Christmas Eve we had a special dinner and I spent a short time at Bill Close's visiting Roger and returned in time for midnight mass, conducted by Basil Pratt. There were forty-one communicants and Basil had to use brandy and Christmas cake as wine and bread were absent.

By New Year's Day the boats had been made ready, engines tested, crews briefed and a great crowd gathered on the Island of Mimosa near the capital to watch our fight with Kinsuka, first of the thirty-two cataracts of the Livingstone Falls that cover more than 200 miles between Kinshasa and the Atlantic. Assisting us on much of the stretch were the two Hamilton water-jet boats. These 220–horsepower, fast and highly manoeuvrable craft were to be a vital part of the forthcoming operation. Stanley had said, 'There is no fear that any other explorer will attempt what we have done in the cataract region. It would be insanity in a successor.' Now I was to discover if he were right.

At 1100 hours *La Vision* passed easily through the narrows where the river had now been constricted from something like nine miles wide to one mile across. Running down a smooth tongue of water, the inflatables skirted the line of tossing twenty-foot waves that rose and fell in the centre of the river. Acting as rescue boats the jetcraft lay in the lee of weed-covered boulders. Gerry Pass and Eric Rankin, the *Survival*-Anglia television team, had been positioned on one of these tiny islands to get a really first-rate shot of the drama, which they did when *David Gestetner* appeared with her white ensign fluttering. On the shore an elderly English lady missionary, overcome with emotion, is said to have burst into tears and then fainted at the sight.

As the boat crossed the first fall, her stern engine struck a submerged rock which hurled it upwards off its wooden transom. The flaying propeller sliced through the neoprene fabric of the stern compartment, which deflated immediately. Aboard the jet we could see the great raft was being swept out of control into the angry wave towers that we knew must be avoided at all costs. In a second Jon Hamilton had opened the throttle and driven the eighteen-foot boat straight into the pounding mounds of coffee-coloured water.

Mike was in the water, his white crash helmet and red life-jacket showing clearly, as he bobbed amongst the flying spray. Our sister jet, driven by Ralph Brown, was already making for him with a scramble-net and Lieutenant Nigel Armitage-Smith was standing by to pull him in. The deafening roar of water and engines drowned all commands: everyone was acting instinctively now. *David Gestetner*'s skipper was trying to pass us a line, his face contorted as he yelled against the din.

Suddenly I heard Ken Mason yell, 'Watch out!' I looked up and saw an enormous wave had flung the crippled *Gestetner* forward and upward, straight towards us. For a moment she towered above, riding a fearsome wall of falling white water, and then came crashing down with a great 'ponk' right across us. For a second we were locked together in the tempest, but we managed to wriggle from beneath and circle our quarry once again. This time we succeeded in taking the line and were soon dragging the craft like a stricken whale towards Monkey Island. We were probably the first people ever to reach this large jungle-covered island.

The next day, with repairs completed, we set off downriver. Rapid followed rapid as we cautiously felt our way through the treacherous waters that gurgled and swirled between the banks of black rock. To get the necessary supplies into the boats meant relays of overland teams working outwards from the capital in our very tired Land-Rovers and a few Toyota trucks. Wildlife was not much in evidence but on 2 January we did come across some islands literally alive with huge bats. There were thousands of them festooning the trees and when I fired a flare from my signal pistol, the hideous creatures took off and showered us with their excreta. It is interesting that Stanley reported great flocks of birds in this area; I think that in fact he had seen these colonies of bats with a twelve-inch wing span. They were obviously of value to the Zairois because we could see nets set up on tall poles at the side of the river.

In the days that followed we shot more rapids and avoided the most ferocious waves and water I've ever met. For each the drill was the same: air reconnaissance by Beaver, then the jets would take the skippers ahead to examine the heaving inconsistent flood and the swirling whirlpools that went up to thirty yards across. On either side vertical cliffs of red rock rose for hundreds of feet and fish eagles shrieked their yodelling cries as we passed. Our support teams worked non-stop to get fuel and supplies to us over the deeply-rutted tracks.

On 6 January we reached Isangila, the falls that had forced Stanley to abandon his boats and march over the mountains towards the sea. Here I decided reluctantly to move the giant rafts overland as far as the Yalala Falls, leaving the jets and the Avon dinghies to tackle the ferocious stream alone. The giant craft simply hadn't got the power to manoeuvre in these rushing currents and boiling water. In no time, one of the dinghies was ripped open from stem to stern on razor-sharp rocks and Jim Masters was injured. It took 900 stitches and a gallon of Araldite to repair the damaged boat. Jim drank a little J & B and recovered!

It was late afternoon when our jets entered the relatively clear passage that would take us through the terrible Isangila cataract. We were halfway down when I saw two gigantic waves converging on our bows. With a crash they struck simultaneously, hurling the 3,000-pound boat upwards. I fell across Jon Hamilton, knocking him momentarily from the wheel, and out of the corner of my eye I saw Pam almost go over the side. Then as we hit the water again there was another hu e wave towering ahead of us. For a moment I thought we were done for. It was a monster. The wall of water smashed over us blotting out daylight; somehow we were still afloat. There was a strange silence; the engine had died. Ahead a line of black rocks rose like dragon's teeth on the lip of a fall and we were being swept straight towards them. Jon tried desperately to start the engine, his face creased with concern. On the third attempt it fired. It only stuttered for a minute, but it was just long enough for us to get into an eddy behind a huge boulder, where we could hold position whilst the electric bilge pumps baled us out.

Finally even the jets were halted by shallows and reefs at the Inga Rapid, but, with two more short portages and some excellent warping with long ropes, we got the amazing Avon recce boats through to the foot of the biggest obstacle in the entire river, the Yalala Falls. A mile of water boiling over terraces and through jagged rocks at frightening speed greeted us. Meanwhile our giant rafts had been carried by a Zaire army lorry to within two miles of the river. Here we regrouped. Some of us had marched over the Crystal Mountains just as Stanley's men had done and experienced the same elephant grass, endless rolling hills, ridges and sharp, suet-colour quartz rocks that give these highlands their name. We too stumbled and fell on the slippery boulders at the river's edge. Ken Mason suffered a badly ripped arm and I injured my back. Porters, descendants of the people who had helped Stanley, assisted us.

At last we all came to the Falls, where the sappers were already clearing a way for us to carry the giant boats down to the river. For three days we toiled in the blistering heat with pick, spade and crowbar, and some highly unstable dynamite, to clear the boulders and get the giant rafts to the water.

It was late at night when Pam, Ken and I set out in a Land-Rover with at least two broken springs. In the back were large boxes of sticky, sweating dynamite and a crate of whisky. The vehicle lights didn't work well and, as we motored along the rutted road in the night, Ken began to ask about the dangers of premature initiation. We soon convinced him that our journey was likened to that shown so graphically in the film, *The Wages of Fear*.

'Oh my God,' he said, seizing a bottle of J & B from the back and clutching it between his legs.

'What on earth are you doing?' asked Pam.

'Well, I may as well get drunk and protect my courting tackle at the same time,' rejoined our jovial photographer as we bounced along with our lethal cargo. Nervous tension made us roar with laughter and swig deep gulps of the bottle.

At this point Pam looked very much like a boy, with her hair covered in mud and her shirt in grease. In fact some Italian engineers whom we had met had referred to her as 'Fred the mechanic'. Earlier in the expedition a chief had greeted her with 'Bonjour, monsieur', but her confidence was restored when we discovered he was almost blind!

Finally, with sixty porters beneath each huge boat, we moved them like giant caterpillars down a 1,000-foot slope to the river. Here we joined up with the Avon dinghies that had been controlled by lines through the surging white water towards us. Now only three rapids barred our way to the sea, but with up to sixteen million gallons per second pouring through a gorge which had narrowed the river to a bare 400 yards, the power can be imagined. Indeed the depth here was probably about 140 feet at high water. The river seemed to be alive with great bubbles boiling up from the depths and erupting on the surface. Then as quickly as they came they were replaced by whirlpools and swirling currents.

Our porters, many of them Angolan refugees and some almost certainly Freedom Fighters, came with gifts of sugar-cane wine and fruit to see us off, but the river was not going to let us get away unscathed yet.

In the final rapid, *La Vision* was momentarily trapped in a whirlpool, being bent downwards and spun round and round with engines screaming. Before I could stop them coming down, Alun Davies's Avon was capsized by a fifteen-foot wave. The upturned boat with its crew of three clinging to it was swept towards a yawning whirlpool. The following recce boat saw the accident and its skipper Neil Rickards, a Royal Marine corporal, took his own small craft through the mountains of tossing water, and managed to get right into the whirlpool and circle around inside it, rather like a motor-cyclist in a 'wall of death' at a fairground. In the centre of this swirling mass, Alun's capsized Avon with its crew of three were still clinging on frantically to the lifeline. By going the same way that the water was revolving, Neil managed to get his craft alongside the stricken boat so that Bob Powell and Somue, one of the ZLOs, could pull the three men to safety. As they left he looked back and was just in time to see the up-turned craft disappear down the vortex. Downriver, I was surprised a few moments later, when the capsized boat bobbed up from the riverbed beside me. The engine was smashed, the floorboards wrecked and there appeared to be no survivors. But the crew had all been saved thanks to Neil's courage and skill, for which he was later awarded the Queen's Gallantry Medal and made one of Britain's 'Men of the Year'.

Two days later we reached the little seaport of Banana and at dusk our strange fleet, which had set out almost four months before in the centre of Africa, sailed into the setting sun. Basil, in cassock and surplice, held an improvised cross and beneath the flags of the nations represented in our team, he conducted a simple service. Under our hulls the water heaved gently. Strangely, it no longer tugged and pulled at us; there was no current, for we were now in the Atlantic.

There had been many difficulties in the years that it had taken to plan and execute this expedition. Manpower had been extremely hard to find, money was almost non-existent and we had a long struggle in the early days persuading our Zaire friends that we were not a bunch of mercenaries. However in the end it had all been overcome and we had managed to prove Stanley wrong; although perhaps we had been insane to challenge this giant amongst rivers. Stanley, and what he had accomplished, had always been in our minds. In fact I don't think we ever forgot him and were full of admiration for what he and his force had taken 999 days to do when they had crossed Africa from coast to coast and come out with only 115 survivors of the 350 who had set out almost three years before. No one could appreciate what this remarkable boy from the workhouse at St Aspeth had achieved more than ourselves.

On our return to Kinshasa we met and talked with President Mobutu about the problems that his country faced. We were able to thank him for the considerable hospitality and kindness that we had received in his land. All he asked of us was that on our return home we should tell people of his hospitality and do what we could to help them to understand Zaire and its difficulties. This I gladly agreed to do, because on no previous expedition had we been received with such wonderful treatment from a ruler, government and people of a country which had not always had much reason to thank white men.

Above all we had had a highly flexible plan. Naturally there had been tensions and there had been the usual vying between science and adventure, but it had worked and that was what counted. Now, when it was all over, there were bound to be those who would knock our success, but I have always found this is largely out of jealousy. I believe we succeeded because of our careful preparation, which had been carried out over a period of four years before we arrived with the main body in Zaire. The logistic support group had achieved an administrative miracle and how our doctors had kept us all so fit is beyond me. In fact, although over half of us did become casualties at one time or another, no one died.

We had a wonderful team. There were the young who had been brought up on the traditions of Outward Bound, and the excellent junior NCOs who had taken on enormous responsibility. There were also fine civilian leaders. Naturally people occasionally wanted to scratch out my eyes, but I have always accepted full responsibility on an expedition for everything that goes wrong and I expect people to grumble at me rather than at each other. This helps to keep the team together. Lastly, of course, our equipment had been magnificent. The Beaver aircraft and some of the innovations of the twentieth century had all worked, but the one piece of kit I shall never forget were the giant inflatable boats that had wobbled their way all those thousands of miles across Africa. And it was primarily due to them that the expedition was later to be awarded the Segrave Trophy for courage, initiative, skill and imagination in pioneering new forms of transport. One of the previous winning craft had been Concorde – on at least one occasion we had managed twelve miles per hour with the wind behind us!

Of course the final measures of our success were the medical and scientific results. I am not a scientist but simply, as a Royal Engineer, an 'obstacle-breaker' whose job it was to launch and sustain the experts in their selected areas to the best of my ability. The botanists from Leeds University had worked on the relationship of certain plants to mineral deposits and their work could well have important implications for the developing nations. Our study of the papyrus in Zaire may help developing nations to make use of this raw material for low-grade paper now that the production of newsprint from wood pulp has become so expensive. A means of clearing the river of the choking water hyacinth was suggested to the President during our final interview. Furthermore Professor Harold Woolhouse, our chief botanist, believed that with more research this protein-rich plant might be used as animal food.

Jeremy Mallinson's conservation-orientated work on the mountain gorilla has contributed to the protection of this rare beast and the fish team's results will certainly add to man's knowledge of fish evolution.

The anthropologist and geologists certainly had a field-day, whilst the entomologists' work should be of real value in the future understanding of the composition, vertical distribution and richness of the insects of the rain-forest canopy.

After the expedition Harold Woolhouse kindly said, 'We could never have undertaken this without Army support.' However, I felt the operation was only possible because of the expertise, teamwork and mutual respect that the Scientific Exploration Society had built up between civilians and servicemen of many nations. In short, I believe that the whole expedition had been a worthwhile project with a good mixture of science and adventure, showing that there were still plenty of people about with the same healthy contempt for difficulties and dangers such as Stanley and Livingstone had endured.

Leadership Training

'AND A MONSTER'S GOBBLING UP Mr Leggett's goldfish,' reported RSM Mansley completing his briefing on the disciplinary matters of the Regiment.

'Better increase the rations on future exercises,' I commented not believing a word.

'But it's true, Colonel, he's lost 3,000 and we've had a request to help from the constabulary.' Hank Mansley, a giant of a man with a laugh like a hyena, who had been on the Blue Nile expedition, was now my RSM at the Junior Leaders Regiment at Dover where future Warrant Officers and NCOs for the Royal Engineers were trained.

It transpired that Alf Leggett, a great character who ran a lovely Norman hall as a home for elderly folk, had a lifelong passion for goldfish. After an exciting career in the Royal Navy, he had sought more peaceful pursuits in a sleepy Kentish village and was renowned for his success as a fish breeder. He had recently noted a dramatic decrease in his pond's population. A local angling society was consulted. 'Could be a monster perch,' its members said, and set to with rod and line to catch the cannibal. However, in spite of their valiant efforts the goldfish continued to disappear. Alf and a policeman armed with shotguns spent the night in a tree waiting to blast the swine if it surfaced. But although they fired several times, no writhing monster appeared and eventually Alf fell out of the tree.

'Might be an eel,' suggested a professor of biochemistry from the Water Board. 'Or a heron,' said a senior police officer.

Only a handful of goldfish remained when someone mentioned that a lady had emptied her son's tank of tropical fish into a local stream. 'That must be it, then,' said the regulars in the village pub. 'All these mild winters and hot summers we have been having – whatever it is has grown and it's thriving on Alf's fish.'

The press, smelling a good story, was quickly on to it. Trade at the village pub increased and, once their gullets were suitably dampened, locals recalled forgotten tales of dark doings dating back to Chaucer. Meanwhile, Alf's former naval chums, reading of his difficulties, began to write in from all over the world. My RSM's uncle lived nearby and told Alf that there was only one thing for it, 'Call in the Royal Engineers!'

The RSM did a recce and reported that the willow-surrounded pond was set in a garden next to some glasshouses.

'A few pounds of plastic underwater would certainly kill anything there,' he said, 'but there is no safe place near enough to the pond from which you can see the demolition on firing.'

'We've got an exercise next week,' I replied. 'We could use one of the ferrets*, get it close to the water's edge and fire the charge electrically from inside the turret.'

As Judith and I swept through the manor gates I was mildly surprised to see a large number of cars. My Adjutant, Peter Enzer, led us across the beautifully mown lawns. Rounding a hedge we came face to face with a tall man in a deer-stalker hat clutching a .12 bore.

'Mr Leggett?' said I. But before he could answer, we were surrounded by a horde of press men. It was later reported that more members of Fleet Street had come to watch the attack on 'Jaws' (as it was instantly nicknamed) than had greeted President Carter on arrival in Britain that same day. Alf had risen to the occasion and provided a splendid lunch with lashings of booze to cheer on the reporters and, whilst I questioned him about the monster, the Junior Sappers got down to the mucky business of laying the explosive on the pond bed. Spencer Eade, the local Army public relations officer, was smiling gleefully as he strode up and down. 'Must have every national paper in the country here, John,' he enthused.

Whilst the charges were being laid the cameramen jockeyed for position. In the process a TV team crowded onto a small footbridge which, much to the joy of their rivals, collapsed, precipitating the luckless crew into the pond.

Finally all was ready. The Junior Leader who was to fire the demolition climbed into the armoured car, now being drawn up behind the hedge, its machine-gun pointing menacingly at the muddy water.

* Small armoured cars

'All clear,' came the shout from the sentries and, as the countdown commenced, the cameras were raised. 'Three, two, one, fire.' The roar was barely deadened by the water. Great spouts cascaded high into the sky, much of it drifting down upon us. The only immediate casualty was a duck that happened to be passing overhead and laid an egg in fright. A subdued cheer went up and champagne corks popped. The press, eager for a picture, was delighted when the odd dead minnow was discovered.

'Well, that should have fixed it,' I said, and we strode away for a welcome cup of tea in Alf's kitchen. As we passed a group of old ladies on the lawn I remarked, 'Good heavens, Alf, I should think they must have been scared out of their wits.'

'Stone deaf, all of them,' he winked.

But one old darling reached out and beckoned. 'Mr Leggett,' she wheezed. 'I think I heard something just then.'

Alf bent down and shouted loudly in her ear. 'Don't worry, dear, it was only an atom bomb they've dropped on London.'

'Oh, does that mean I shan't get my paper in the morning?'

Spencer had just put down the telephone. 'Oh well, you can't win them all,' he groaned. 'That was my boss at MOD on the line. He has just told me not to promote the story after all. I had to explain that it was too late, we'd done it. Apparently there is a programme on telly tonight critical of defence expenditure and he thinks that our story may not give the right image.'

He was right. The report carried by almost every paper in the country and many overseas, and told and re-told on television and radio, was far from serious, but it did show boy soldiers having the time of their lives. Recruits flowed in! Luckily for me a very senior General loved it and later the Prince of Wales asked how on earth it was that the Army managed to lay on such splendid publicity, and went on to enquire why it was that the Navy couldn't do the same! Giles drew two splendid cartoons for the *Daily Express* and the next term we had the biggest intake ever in the regiment. Later a huge perch was discovered, stunned, in a hole in the bank. Amazingly it recovered and now lives quietly in a Kentish reservoir – a rather nice end to a fishy story!

Of course, training is so much more interesting if it is fun, and there was no doubt that for the fit and motivated youngster the syllabus at Dover was tremendous. We trained on the moors and mountains of Britain and sent boys on Outward Bound courses, of special interest to me as I was now on the Outward Bound Council. I've always been a great believer in the work of this splendid organization founded on the four pillars laid down by Kurt Hahn: physical fitness, self-reliance, rescue and public service, and project work. All this fitted in extremely well with the training of the Junior Leaders.

Meanwhile the SES continued to develop and its list of successful ventures grew each year. Lectures given by members of expeditions were as popular as ever and also a useful source of raising funds. Dabber and Paddy Davies, who run Associated Speakers, a highly efficient lecture agency, did much to help us organize these, as did Barbara Snell who had another agency.

The world of expeditioning has no hierarchy, no ranks and few prizes. Most explorers are individualists and strongly resent being coordinated by anybody. But expeditions, if they are to be successful, must work as a team which, like a chain, is as strong as its weakest link. And there are risks. In August 1976 an expedition was decimated by the sudden eruption of Mount Sangay in Ecuador. Two died and two of my friends, Jan Iwandziuk and Richard Snailham, were severely injured. It was a miracle that anyone survived.

After Zaire, I found myself being asked to help organize many expeditions. I did this gladly and several of them achieved notable success. Squabbles broke out in some, but usually these were due to inexperience or lack of leadership. Some of the groups even got as far as fighting it out in the press! It was very like the nineteenth-century verbal battles between explorers. I do not blame the press. In fact, I have a great many friends in Fleet Street, so much so that I have often been accused of showmanship; but I would prefer to call it sales-manship. It doesn't matter how ambitious, worthwhile and well-planned your expedition may be, unless you can sell the idea to someone, you are unlikely to get the support to bring it to fruition. I believe that the two essential qualities of leadership are communication and inspiration. They are particularly applicable to expeditions.

Such was our liaison with the media that I was not altogether surprised to hear that, when I had been 'kidnapped' for the Thames Television programme, *This is your Life*, our detractors fancied the whole thing had been rigged! If they could have known the momentary fear I felt when I found strange people closing in on me and Éamonn Andrews' Irish brogue in my ear, 'Excuse me one moment, Colonel, we want you', they might have been more sympathetic. As it was, it was only by chance that I didn't hit him and bolt. When the truth came out I still felt like running, but was assured that many old friends were in the studio having a tremendous party and I couldn't really walk out on them. The evening was the greatest fun. Nobody burst into tears and everyone drank far too much. It was super to have so many chums present, including Charlie Thompson, the old Negro from the Darien, who had been flown across the Atlantic especially for the show. Confronted by a beefy Guardia sergeant saying 'You're wanted in Panama City', Charlie had been marched off to El Real jail to await a helicopter.

At Panama airport an Embassy Officer met him. 'Senor Thompson?' enquired the Briton. 'Si,' said Charlie, looking round for the gallows.

'Do you remember Major Blashford-Snell and a number of Englishmen coming to your village in 1972?' Reluctantly Charlie admitted he did. He'd never seen TV and the suggestion that he should fly to London to appear on a show was totally incomprehensible, but anything was better than garotting. That afternoon he was issued with a passport and a visa for seventy-two hours in Britain. 'Do you have any clothes?' asked the Embassy official, 'it is rather cold in London in October.'

Barefooted Charlie had only the patched shorts he had worn for five years, so he was given $20 to buy warmer garments. The money got him a straw hat, some flipflops and a cheap suit but no shirt. Thus clad he arrived at Heathrow. The lady who greeted him later told me that they were almost in London before she realized Charlie didn't speak a word of English and some hurried language lessons followed. I doubt Thames TV realized what they were taking on when they decided to feature the life of an Army explorer! Alas before the show they left Jim, Ernie and sundry other sappers in the Green Room with a table groaning with liquor. The results were predictable but somehow no one seemed to mind.

The SES has always made a point of including young people in its expeditions. On the Zaire we had had three sponsored teenagers – a business student, a police cadet from my home island of Jersey, and a river-runner from Colorado – funded by Mr Walter Annenberg, then American Ambassador in London. This proved such a success that it was enthusiastically agreed from then on to include such Young Explorers (YEs) on future SES ventures.

Thus we began to plan a series of worthwhile expeditions worldwide. From our meetings with international youth organizations, schools and universities, it had become abundantly clear that many youngsters felt the need to be stretched and challenged more severely than they could ever normally hope to be in modern society. Outward Bound and similar adventure training schemes did their best to satisfy this need and to provide imaginative outlets for natural aggression and excess energy, but for many they did not go far enough.

It was Prince Charles who had pinpointed the underlying cause of the youngsters' frustrations, and summed it up in one phrase when he told the House of Lords that what the young were really seeking were 'some of the challenges of war in a peacetime situation'.

It was all still a dream until David Bromhead and other chums in the Royal Regiment of Wales talked to the Prince at a mess dinner. Hearing their tales he asked to see me. His Royal Highness was especially concerned about the growing numbers of unemployed, bored and listless urban young and said, 'If you can do this for two or three youngsters, why not do it for two or three hundred?' Although momentarily taken aback by the prospect of planning on such a grand scale, I realized that this was simply a logical extension of what we had in mind, and would not only broaden the whole outlook of the project but also give it a far greater sense of purpose.

When I returned to Buckingham Palace a few weeks later I had a draft plan which, as it coincided with the 400th anniversary of Sir Francis Drake's great circumnavigation, had to be called Operation Drake. The Prince was fascinated and asked what he could do to help. When I suggested that it would give a tremendous boost if he were to become Patron he readily agreed. Not only would it be a very great honour but also it would endow the project with a prestige and credibility which would encourage the sponsors, on whose financial backing we were totally dependent. Furthermore, it would help to attract young people to take part. Although it was understood that the Prince's association could not be officially announced until the enterprise was financially viable and certain to go ahead, he was kind enough to send a discreet message of support in advance. It read as follows:

Colonel Blashford-Snell has explained to me the purpose behind 'Operation Drake' and I was most interested by its imaginative and adventurous approach. I hope therefore that it is given a chance to succeed, given all the ghastly problems that exist

with raising large sums of money nowadays. From my historical
studies I seem to remember Francis Drake managed to elicit
some discreet Royal support for his expeditions, but only if the
rewards from a little well-planned piracy were forthcoming!
Times have changed!

That message, with its characteristic touch of humour, was the key
factor that enabled the Operation to take off.

Our main priority now was to raise the £50,000 needed to launch
Drake with any confidence. That kind of sum is hard to come by at
the best of times and in a period of recession we reckoned it would be a
real battle. In fact, it fell into our laps at the stroke of a pen thanks to
the extraordinary generosity of one man.

Mr Walter Annenberg, a renowned philanthropist, noted for his
great foresight and imagination, has always found expeditions
intriguing. In view of this, it was with a thrill of anticipation that I
accepted an invitation to visit him at his home in Palm Springs to tell
him all about Operation Drake.

It was quite an experience. I arrived with Judith and daughters,
Emma and Victoria, to be met at the airport by a chauffeur-driven
limousine that whisked us to his estate on the outskirts of this
remarkable desert township, where he and his wife Lee lived with Bob
Hope and ex-President Gerald Ford as neighbours. As we passed
through the remote-controlled gates, we were impressed by the sheer
scale and magnificence of the place, which is really a private golf
course with a splendid modern house in the middle. A special guest
cottage in the grounds awaited us, and we were provided with a car
for transport between there and the main house!

I was just coming out of the shower when Emma rushed in to
announce that Mr Annenberg had arrived to see if we were comfortable. I poured him a drink and without any real preamble he said,
'Tell me about this Drake thing – and how much do you need to get it
started?' I outlined our plan and added as nonchalantly as possible
that we required about £50,000 before we could get under way. He
asked if I thought we could really pull off something quite so big, and
when I assured him that there was no reason why we should not,
providing we could get the finance, he paused for a moment and then
said, 'I'm not sure what the exchange rate is at the moment, but if I
give you $100,000, will that be all right?'

It was at that moment that Operation Drake became a reality, and from then on it all started happening at a whirlwind pace. My first task on returning to England was to assemble the nucleus of our executive team at our London HQ, which was housed in the Whitehall basement, known as 'Room 5B' or 'the dungeon'. This damp, dark, musty-smelling cellar two floors below ground level was a somewhat dismal place where daylight never penetrated and the atmosphere was permanently grey. But beggars cannot be choosers.

Among the stalwarts who gathered at this nerve centre was Jim Masters who had the key role as Head of Logistics and Personnel, which involved the mammoth task of moving hundreds of people and tons of equipment round the world for nothing, or next to nothing. One could not ask for a better man to tackle such a difficult and vital job. I had long respected Jim's ability to get things done. Also from the Blue Nile came Roger Chapman, whilst George Thurston, a tough and determined ex-Royal Marine, gave up a career in the Police Force to join us. A most capable lady, Ruth Mindel, was brought in to head up Procurement and Supplies and another old friend, Val Roberts, agreed to run the office. Andrew Mitchell, a young zoologist, came in as Scientific Coordinator, and Chris Sainsbury, my photographic expert for the past two years, gave up making films of Junior Soldiers and was appointed Chief Photographer.

There was one more very important post to be filled, and in securing General Sir John Mogg as our Chairman we had a real stroke of great good fortune. The General was initially a little reluctant, pointing out that he was greatly looking forward to a quiet life in his retirement. But he surrendered gracefully to my appeals after I assured him – with an absolutely straight face – that the position would involve no more than two or three meetings a year and a couple of pleasant trips overseas.

Of course, things did not work out quite as I promised, and he ended up spending most of his time guiding Operation Drake. Nevertheless, he seemed to enjoy every minute of it. As a former Deputy Supreme Allied Commander, Europe, his international reputation and contacts were formidable and as a respected figure of the highest calibre he brought added prestige to the project. On top of that, he has a rare ability to get on with just about anybody, including being perfectly in tune with the younger generation.

The money was coming in steadily, as more and more individuals and companies began to take up sponsorships or promise support in kind. A major boost came when John Whitney, the energetic

Managing Director of Capital Radio, reacted so enthusiastically to
the whole idea that he decided to sponsor ten young explorers from
the London area as well as giving regular coverage to the expedition.

At this point the Prince of Wales announced officially that he had
agreed to be Patron and at the same time promised not only to launch
the expedition on the 400th anniversary of Drake's voyage, but also to
be at the helm of our flagship when she sailed out of Plymouth a year
later. Squadron Leader David Checketts, the Prince's Private Secretary, also became an enthusiastic supporter and formed our Public
Relations Sub-Committee. Through him we got our PRO, Beth
Barrington-Haynes, who proved to be a tower of strength and became
an important member of our expanding HQ.

I felt I was riding a very fast horse in a steeplechase, and as we
cleared each fence our confidence grew. However, we had a long way
to go before the finishing post, and now the real work of selecting the
YEs had started. Following the announcement that anyone aged
between seventeen and twenty-five, who was fit, compatible, could
speak English and swim could volunteer, 58,000 applied for the 216
YE vacancies originally available.

I modelled the selection test on the Army's Regular Commission
Board, and I borrowed a useful volume on discovering personal
qualities under stress called *The KGB Handbook*. Basically we had to
get candidates wet, cold, hungry, miserable, frightened and furious as
fast as possible. We needed people who could work well under adverse
conditions.

The tests set up in many lands were devised to show up the
candidates' strengths and weaknesses. We hoped that in the end we
would have a well-balanced, mixed group. We wanted to be able to
put together in the field teams that might include, for example,
someone highly intelligent, well-educated and about to enter into
one of the professions, along with a young person from a broken home
who had possibly been in trouble with the police, and we were also
taking the physically disabled. Prima donnas would be rejected, but
we wanted some young adults with leadership potential who would
be prepared to place service before self and genuinely care about the
needs of others.

The batch of sixteen candidates – including three girls – who
arrived rather apprehensively at St Augustine's Priory, Kent, on a
bleak Saturday in February 1978 had no idea what to expect. They

had been told simply to report with the kit they felt they would need during a weekend's camp and a certificate of medical fitness! All they knew for sure was that they would be facing some stiff challenges both mental and physical.

After a general briefing and a kit inspection to check how sensibly they had prepared for the rigours of the weekend, they were led off into the woods, issued with tents and given half an hour to set up camp. They were then divided into two teams and marched off to Priory Pond for the first test, which had been carefully dreamt up with the sadistic intention of trying to ensure that everybody experienced the maximum discomfort at the earliest possible stage of the proceedings.

They had to imagine they were being pursued through the jungle by terrorists, that one of their number had been badly wounded and was a stretcher case, and that they had just one hour to get themselves and their casualty safely across the crocodile-infested river represented by the pond. They were supplied with a highly unstable canoe with a hole in it and some oil drums, planks and lengths of rope with which to construct a makeshift raft to ferry the heavily-bandaged casualty. We hoped they would fall in and most of them duly obliged! It sent shivers up the spine just to watch them floundering around in the icy water.

The Royal Signals had made some special recordings for me in Borneo but the scream of a gibbon coming incongruously from the centre of a rhododendron bush, mingled with the squawks of parakeets and other unmistakable sounds of the jungle which issued mysteriously from among the bare winter branches of a Kentish copse did not impress the soaked volunteers. It was snowing by then. 'Bloody brass monkeys if you ask me,' one muttered.

They were given no time to get their circulation going again before being rushed to another location where, having been divided into teams of four, they were to bridge a stream with a structure strong enough to take a Land-Rover. No sooner had this been completed, they were off to a local pool to prove that they could swim 500 yards and then, as exhaustion set in, they were told that they would now be going back to camp for a meal. The sighs of relief soon turned to gasps of anguish when they saw the menu. Hopes of being handed a tasty supper on a plate were cruelly dashed when they were given a freshly-killed, unplucked pigeon and a dead rabbit with its fur still on. If they were lucky, they got a few unappetizing mouthfuls of half-cooked, half-burnt flesh before collapsing cold, wet, tired and still hungry into their sleeping bags.

I told them they could sleep until 0800. Some actually believed me but, following the KGB's advice, we woke them at 0100 with flashing lights and brass band music and despatched them on a cross-country march to a map reference, where they were warned to expect to deal with some kind of emergency. But on arrival they were informed it was a false alarm and they could go back. By the time they had crawled into their sleeping bags once again, they were even more shattered, but still there was no respite.

At 0300 they were woken a second time and sent off to another map reference. This time they found that there actually was a staged emergency and they had to gather their scattered wits sufficiently to deal with it in a sensible fashion.

Now came the test of courage. I wanted to discover how they would behave when scared stiff. Andrew Mitchell pointed out that as everyone is usually frightened of some animal, that's what we should use. I watched the first two candidates equipped with bathroom scales and a torch searching a darkened upper room in the priory for a 'harmless creature'. At last Christine McHugh, a young police-woman, lifted a pile of sacks and leapt backward with a scream. Sliding out from beneath was a twelve-foot python, its tongue flickering in the torch light.

'Oh my God, I can't touch that. I hate snakes,' she cried.

'Think of your chance-of-a-lifetime,' I urged, so she picked up a cricket bat and tried to steer Monty onto the scales. It didn't work; his head went one way and the tail another, so she took a deep breath, bent down, picked up the writhing serpent and, wrapping it around herself, stood on the bathroom scales. That took guts and she gained her place on Drake.

Next time I changed the act and borrowed a hairy, black tarantula with which we played pass the spider. They all passed, so next I used a gorilla. Candidates were shown a very angry 400-pound mountain gorilla and were told they were being put in the pen with the one that had made him mad – his mate. They were to take her vital statistics with a measuring tape. In came the female, who was actually quite tame although they did not know it. Her keepers had taught her some tricks and, if she wanted a chocolate biscuit, all she had to do was to put her arms round the nearest human. If you had never faced an amorous lady gorilla this was pretty scary but worse was to follow. If she didn't get the biscuit quickly it meant you were hiding it in your clothes and this was terrifying!

We had some failures. One night I watched a test at a farm, where two young boys were being briefed by an Army sergeant. 'Right lads, I want you to go into that darkened stable, no torch allowed, feel your way around and identify the animal in there.' After a moment or two there was a loud 'moo' and the boys reported, 'You've got a cow in there.' 'Very observant,' said the sergeant. 'Here's a bucket and a stool, go back and milk it.' A minute later there was a loud clang as the bucket was kicked and a boy rushed out. 'Are you sure it's a cow?' he asked and, when the lights went on, there was a rather perplexed bullock. For some reason all the girls passed this and, in fact, we found a much higher percentage of women were being accepted.

After this intentionally demoralizing start, the unhappy campers were plunged into a new series of tests aimed at assessing mental prowess in their state of considerable exhaustion. It was interesting to note that, for many of the youngsters, the prospect of having to get up in front of an audience and speak for three minutes on any chosen subject proved far more gruelling than any of the previous hardships. This, together with various intelligence and observation tests and some shooting, to ensure the candidates could handle weapons safely, rounded off the weekend and the judges then had the task of deciding who should be given places on the expedition.

Our plan was really quite simple. Over two years a large sailing ship would circumnavigate the world westward via the Panama and Suez canals, carrying around thirty-six Y Es at a time and link up with expeditions in Panama, the Galapagos, Fiji, Papua New Guinea, Indonesia, Kenya and the Mediterranean. Every three months the teams of Y Es would change so everyone would spend some time on both land and sea.

Our tasks would be scientific research, environmental work and community aid projects in an adventurous setting: we would operate in remote areas and difficult terrain. This should encourage the pioneering spirit we sought to foster, but I needed a staff of experienced experts with the patience of Job and, through the SES, we recruited dedicated instructors from the Armed Forces, universities and other bodies worldwide.

Originally the flagship was to be the Dulverton Trust's beautiful *Captain Scott*, but suddenly the Sultan of Oman made an offer for the ship that the Trust could not refuse and I had a problem. We were

becoming desperate when I heard from my American friend, Allen
O'Brien. He had become co-owner of *Eye of the Wind* and had heard
about my 'Francis Drake scheme' through the SES Newsletter. He
wondered if I needed a 150-ton brigantine sailing vessel. Such a timely
offer seemed too good to be true. The ship was in Australia and due in
England in the summer of 1978 and would then be available. She was
not quite as big as we would have liked, but it was our only hope. We
wasted no time in arranging a charter.

Eye of the Wind was built in 1911 at a dockyard near Bremen,
specifically to ply the round trip from Germany to Argentina to
Cornwall and back. Nothing more was heard of her until 1923, when
she was bought by a Swedish concern. For the next forty-five years she
spent her winters trading cargo in the Baltic and the North Sea, and
her summers drifting for herring off Iceland. Badly damaged in the
late sixties by a fire which broke out while ice-bound, and after being
towed back to Gothenburg, she was left there to rot until a syndicate
of six enthusiasts found the burnt-out hull, bought and restored her.
This they did painstakingly, using church pews, oak panels from a
bank, a trawler's compass and old railway sleepers.

Despite all this admirable work by the syndicate – led by Londoner
'Tiger' Timbs and Leslie Reiter, who were to stay on board throughout
Operation Drake as Mate and Purser respectively – it became
frighteningly clear when we took delivery of the ship in August 1978
that she needed an awful lot doing to her. As well as fitting a new
engine, we had to carry out extensive alterations below decks to
provide adequate accommodation. In addition there was an
alarmingly long list of less fundamental but equally necessary repairs
and refinements.

Gloom and despondency began to set in as it became obvious that,
in addition to the astronomical costs of carrying out the work, there
was no way that it was going to be finished in the few weeks left
before we were due to depart. However, Prince Charles had said he
would sail her out on 22 October so with enormous help from the
Royal Navy and kind sponsors the work went on day and night.
Fundraising too was non-stop. Frank Taylor, Financial Controller of
Esso, had become our Treasurer and kept us on the straight and
narrow. Lectures, philatelic covers, book and film rights and
thousands of begging letters all played their part.

I have never hesitated to use a pretty face to further a cause which,
however good, will always sound much worthier when charmingly

explained by an attractive young lady. 'Blasher's Blondes' or
'Charlie's Angels', as they were variously known, played a vital role
in securing sponsorships, goods and services. This gang of beautiful
ladies, not always blonde, did a marvellous job of selling the idea of
Operation Drake. It was late when Ruth entered the dungeon looking
strangely dishevelled and flushed. Collapsing into a chair she eyed
her laddered tights and reported, 'Well, I've got you 3,500 cans of beef
stew and almost got raped.' She was nicknamed 'Rip off Ruth' ever
after.

The list of generous sponsors, many recruited by Prince Charles,
grew longer. BP came in with the fuel for the ship and Pan–Am
donated many free flights. Multinationals, like Unilever and BAT,
were marvellous and almost everywhere Gestetner backed us.
Around the world national committees were also working flat out. In
New York, Gordon White at Hanson Trust, with the help of the
British Consul, Gordon Booth, did an outstanding job in recruiting
and funding some fifty young Americans. In Australia, Denis Cordner
of ICI took up the challenge, whilst Jim Edwards backed us from
Nepal, and my pal from Zaire, John Chapman-Smith, handled New
Zealand. There were also supporters in Canada, Costa Rica, Fiji,
Indonesia, West Germany, Hong Kong and Kenya. My old school
friend Adrian Troy formed a Channel Island committee. We had
become a truly international enterprise.

'Well John, this looks like a splendid party,' smiled Barbara
Martinelli, one of Charlie's angelic American blondes, but I had no
time to think about my 42nd birthday that bright autumn morning as
we awaited the arrival of the Prince of Wales. Cheering, waving
crowds lined the waterfront and hundreds more people gathered on
Plymouth Hoe to give *Eye of the Wind* a wonderfully emotional send-
off as she headed out in the Sound with the Prince at the helm. It was
a magnificent sight as the beautiful, white-painted brigantine eased
her way gracefully out to sea. Guns fired, warships piped their
respects as she passed, and the armada of small boats that escorted her
out of harbour whoop-whooped their farewells. From her deck,
Capital Radio's David Briggs broadcast a live running commentary on
the departure, which to all intents and purposes seemed to get
Operation Drake finally under way. Not too many people were
aware, I hope, that this was not actually the case.

Like Francis Drake himself, we had got off to a false start. *Eye of the
Wind* certainly gave the impression of making a dignified and

dramatic exit, but she was actually being towed out to the break-water by a tug! There, with His Royal Highness at the helm, full sail was set and we appreciated the real beauty of our flagship for the first time. Once Prince Charles had been taken off by launch and then whisked away in a helicopter, and when the film and TV cameras had stopped rolling and the crowds had dispersed, she was towed back in again. The official excuse was that she had to undergo extensive sea trials before she could actually start the voyage, but the slightly embarrassing truth was that she was far from ready to sail. Her new engine, for which the Prince himself had generously paid half the £11,000 cost, was not yet in running order, and there was still much refitting to be done and equipment to be loaded. It had been a frantic race against time to get her into any sort of fit state, with everybody, including the first batch of YEs who had joined the ship a fortnight before, slaving twelve hours a day, seven days a week. A joke was circulating that it had been cut so fine that there had only been time to paint the side of the ship that would be facing the cameras and the crowds, and the other side had been left untouched! If people laughed a little nervously at that one, it was because it was uncomfortably close to the truth. The deck had certainly not been painted – that chore was not completed until we reached Tenerife.

It would have been a tragedy if we had been forced to postpone the formal departure. For one thing, it is doubtful whether Prince Charles would have been able to fit a later date into his crowded schedule, and that would have been a major disappointment robbing the occasion of much of its significance. Apart from that, it might well have been seen as an ill omen for the expedition. As it turned out everything went remarkably smoothly.

As *Eye of the Wind* left harbour, the Flag Officer, Plymouth, followed in his launch with General Sir John Mogg and the VIPs. We were just beginning to relax a little and breathe a few sighs of relief when I happened to glance at the Admiral and noticed with alarm that his knuckles were whitening as he clutched the brass rail. I followed the line of his stony gaze and experienced an awful sinking feeling as I recognized the Royal Standard fluttering in the breeze. The Royal Navy had most specifically requested that this should not be flown until *Eye of the Wind* was clear of the dockyard. Otherwise, naval protocol requires every ship present to parade bands and guards, and since it was a Sunday this would be rather awkward. Not wishing to interfere in any way with the sailors' weekend shore leave, we readily agreed to keep the Standard furled at the masthead until we were out of the dockyard. And yet there it was for all to see and we had barely left the shore. No sooner had Prince Charles stepped aboard than he asked Captain Patrick Collis, 'Where's my standard, then?' When our skipper explained why it was not being flown, HRH grinned mischievously and said, 'Well, let's break it anyway and see if they have got any bands and guards!'

The Prince's presence made the day a memorable one for everybody, but particularly the YEs who were delighted to find him charming, relaxed and informal. From the moment that he took the wheel of the ship with the remark 'All I need now is a parrot!' he was a tremendous hit with them. He chatted to them for over two hours and posed for photographs, showing an obviously genuine interest in what they were about to undertake. In the launch that transported him back to shore I found him bubbling with enthusiasm.

There was one anxious moment at the end. It centred around the provision of special private toilet facilities wherever an official Royal visit is being made. A particularly handsome prefabricated edifice had been erected near the helicopter landing pad. Sure enough, just before boarding the helicopter of the Queen's Flight the Prince decided to use it. An officer jumped forward smartly to open the door, only to find it apparently jammed. Increasingly harder and more frantic pulls failed to shift it. Clearly, it was locked. It emerged later that the attendant, under the impression that if the building was not required when the Prince first arrived then it would not be needed at all, had gone off with the key in his pocket.

When defeat was finally admitted, Prince Charles, who had been observing the proceedings with some amusement, turned to the senior officer present and enquired, 'Do you have a tree, perhaps?'

'I'm sorry, Sir,' stammered the officer, indicating a fallen elm nearby, 'I'm afraid we've just cut it down!'

'Oh, never mind,' murmured HRH. And as he turned to board the helicopter he said to the Admiral, 'I hope you find the key.' The Navy did not think it at all funny.

A special service of dedication had been held the previous day at the shore station HMS Drake. During the service the skipper of *Eye of the Wind* called on the congregation to ask for God's blessing on the ship with a time-honoured chant that dates back to the embarkation of the Crusaders in the thirteenth century. Among the prayers was the one written by Francis Drake himself on the day he sailed into Cadiz in 1587. Many of us offered up a few prayers of our own.

Prior to casting off the Prince had given a witty speech which ended with some advice for the YEs. 'I have a feeling,' he said, 'that those who take part in this particular expedition will enjoy themselves, but at the same time I expect there will be moments when they will wish that they were back home and had never volunteered for the thing in the first place. All I can say to them on that score is, just stick to it and when you get back you will find that rather like beating your head against a brick wall it's marvellous when it's over.' There were very few people involved with Operation Drake over the next couple of years who did not have occasion to reflect on the truth of those words.

TWELVE

Operation Drake

ENGLAND'S ECONOMY was in a pretty rocky state in 1577 when a West Country sea captain came up with a plan to set matters right. Basically it was to plunder the Spanish Main and return with the loot right quickly. Queen Elizabeth not only condoned Francis Drake's proposal but invested in it to the tune of £10,000.

So in December that year he set sail from Plymouth with five small ships, wisely not telling the crew the true purpose of his voyage. Had he done so, many would have jumped off. In fact he said they were headed for Terra Australia Incognita, or Sydney as it is known today.

Apart from a terrible storm off the Cornish coast which forced them to return for repairs, all was well until they reached Cape Horn. In the fleet there were two unions, the gentlemen and the seamen, and it was the former who caused the problem by refusing to pull with the latter. Thus Drake, a fair minded employer, dined with the gentlemen's shop steward, Thomas Doughty. Next morning they took communion together then he hanged him.

At this point two ships fled for home, two sank and Drake was left alone with his 100-ton flagship *Pelican*. As is sometimes the custom even today when a business venture runs into a spot of bother Drake changed the name and carried on. Thus *Pelican* became *Golden Hind*, and sailed up the west coast of South America where he met the lumbering Spanish galleons overloaded with treasure. With the aid of the eighteen bronze cannon, Captain Drake relieved the Spaniards of their cargo and, much to the annoyance of their King, headed up America's west coast to return to Plymouth via the north of Canada. A difficult enough feat today.

Stopped by the ice, *Golden Hind* came ashore to have her hull scraped of barnacles near where San Francisco now lies. Here the Indians rushed down to the beach, but worshipping white Gods, as many still do in California, they prostrated themselves at Drake's feet. He did nothing to disillusion them, and so that they should remember they were now part of New Albion or England he set up an inscribed brass plate in a tree. In its side they placed an Elizabethan sixpence bearing the image of their new ruler. In 1935 a truck driver proceeding along the freeway stopped to commune with nature and found the plate, but alas the coin had gone.

A prominent member of the Round Earth Society, Drake and his crew headed west, and reached the Celebes, now Indonesia, when in the middle of the night there was a loud crash: *Golden Hind* had hit an uncharted reef. Whilst the Captain fought to save the ship many of the crew took fright and the preacher, with less courage than most modern naval chaplains, called upon the Almighty, blaming their misfortunes on Master Drake and in particular the way he dealt with the shop steward at Cape Horn.

Meanwhile the skipper had thrown overboard the cheaper, heavier trade goods and finally eight of his guns, lightening the ship sufficiently for it to drift off the coral and float upright, undamaged in deep water. Then he summoned his men and for several hours preached them a sermon, at the end of which he produced a faded parchment and crying 'Behold I carry the Queen's commission' he shackled the preacher to a hatch and excommunicated him. Perhaps Drake was a mildly autocratic leader, but he was 15,000 miles from head office.

On Monday 26 September 1580, nearly three years after his departure, *Golden Hind* quietly entered Plymouth Sound. Drake reckoned it was Sunday, mysteriously he had lost a day! Knowing he had many enemies at home and having no news of the Queen, they came in unannounced out of the Channel mist. A lone fisherman, engaged in the usual local activity of looting his neighbour's lobster pots, spotted her first.

'Does the Queen live?' cried the red-bearded figure on the stern.

'Eye Sire, she do and she be well,' came the reply.

'Know you not 'tis I, Francis Drake, returned with North Sea oil in my hold – where the devil are the people of Plymouth?'

'No disrespect, Master Drake, but all those not dying of plague are at church praying they'll not get it.'

Unabashed Drake sent gallopers to London to acquaint the Queen with the glad tidings that he had brought home some £600,000 in booty, certainly the greatest treasure ever to reach England. It is said

Her Majesty was exceeding joyful at the news and despatched her auditors to greet them.

So the following year Drake and his ship came up the Thames to Deptford where Queen Elizabeth and her court came aboard. Demanding his sword, she ordered him to kneel. Fearing what she might do with it, Francis Drake obeyed, but his monarch passed the sword to the French Ambassador and said, 'Knight him.' Thus was cocked the greatest snook possible to the King of Spain.

A beautiful silver replica of the famous sword had been made for us by Wilkinson's and this we presented to Mr Annenberg, although he allowed us to carry it around the world on our ship and I produced this as I completed the historical briefing (with a little licence) of Drake's voyage.

'We're bound for the Caribbean,' I said, 'where he raided the Spanish Main and where he eventually died of dysentery. So for goodness sake, do watch the hygiene when we get ashore.' Then, I flew ahead to prepare the way.

Jeremy Groves and his advance party were already clearing an old landing strip at Caledonia Bay, Panama, where we had made some fascinating discoveries on earlier recces. During the Darien expedition I had flown over to the Atlantic coast to see if there was any evidence of the seventeenth-century Scots colony established at what is still called Caledonia Bay. It was pretty stormy when we reached the sea, but I could recognize the main features that appeared on the old maps and knew that below me lay the graves of several thousand courageous Scots who had defied the King of England in an attempt to gain a Scottish foothold in the New World.

So, in 1976 I returned with a few pals from the SES and the Explorers Club, to which I now belonged. Welsh seafarer Tristan Jones said he had met strange white people with names like MacDonald and Robinson lurking in the forest near Punta Escoces and we resolved to investigate.

On arrival we quickly discovered that the supposed lost Scots were in fact albinos or moon people, as they are known because their skin burns so badly in the sun that they tend to come out only at night. The San Blas islands, a Cuna stronghold, have a very high proportion of them, possibly due to inbreeding. They had probably acquired the Scottish surnames as a result of the colony.

Our first task was to find Fort St Andrew. So I marched through the coconut groves towards a promontory on which the old Scots maps showed the refuge. We found a stream of clear water running from the hills and I felt it should lead to our objective, but the vegetation grew thicker and the brook became a swamp so, moving inland again, I began to hack with my machete. Suddenly the ground dropped away steeply and I stumbled down into a shallow ravine. On either side the undergrowth fell back, revealing a clean-cut channel in the coral. There was no doubt this was the moat of Fort St Andrew.

Vince and Barbara Martinelli, two adventurous New Yorkers, followed the zigzagging ditch. Spoil from the moat had been used to build up ramparts; several bastion positions and a gateway were apparent. The vertically-sided moat, filled with sea water to a depth of approximately three feet, went right across the neck of the promontory with an entrance to the sea at one end and a mangrove swamp at the other. Searching the rampart, Barbara discovered glazed potsherds while Vince found a small cannonball. Our archaeologist, Gricelio, reckoned it was the type fired from a light cannon, which was probably the heaviest weapon the besieging Spaniards could have dragged through the jungle. Inside the fort there were depressions that might have been wells and a battery position for the guns commanding the harbour entrance. Broken pottery littered the ground everywhere.

But our recce was to have further success. A chance meeting with Father Ned Webster, the American Dean in the Canal Zone, had produced a crop of carefully researched information about the 'Lost City of Acla'. Acla had been built in 1516 by the Spanish Governor of the area, Pedrarias Davilla, and was only the second European township to be established anywhere on the American mainland. It was from here that Vasco Nunez de Balboa, the first European ever to gaze upon the Pacific Ocean, later set out across the isthmus, taking with him the dismantled parts of four ships which were to be reassembled on the other side. It was also the place where Balboa met an unjust end, when political conspiracy resulted in his being publicly executed in the main plaza.

Later the city declined and disappeared but Ned thought it was near Caledonia Bay. A helpful witch-doctor had told us of ruins on a nearby islet and, visiting the tiny outcrop of coral, we did indeed find pottery and bricks. 'Acla is supposed to lie between these two rivers,' I explained, 'and in fact this river is called the Aglatomate.'

'But they must have had a harbour,' said Vince.

'Yes,' I agreed. 'That's the mystery. There's a cliff, a reef or a mangrove swamp right the way along the coast.'

From the sea we couldn't even identify the two rivers. As we scanned the jungle shoreline with binoculars, the witch-doctor said, 'You want go there?'

'Can you get a boat through that reef, Ricardo?'

'Si,' he grunted. 'Es posible.'

Approaching the reef, we could see exposed heads of jagged coral projecting from the boiling surf. Suddenly I saw something that was only visible from very close in shore. There was a gap in the reef, which almost overlapped itself and, if you knew the way, you could slip safely into a sheltered cove on the far side.

On the palm-fringed beach dozens of Indian dugouts were drawn up whilst the owners harvested the precious coconut in the forest.

'Senor,' said Ricardo, 'there is a wall in the jungle, I see it as a boy.' Ricardo was easily sixty, so I was not too hopeful that he would actually find anything. Nevertheless, we split up, with one party going to the banks of the Aglatomate, whilst the other searched the shore and the Rio Aglaseniqua, the northern river.

Ricardo, Vince and I cut deep into a bamboo thicket which showed signs of flooding, but we found no walls nor any evidence of man. Back on the beach we discovered why the rivers had been invisible from seaward; during the dry season a high sandbar extended right across their mouths. However, it was late in the afternoon and I decided that it all looked like a wild-goose chase. 'We'd better get back,' I said.

'It here somewhere, I know, senor,' grumbled the medicine man.

We were about 200 yards from the boats when I heard the excited chatter of monkeys overhead and paused to watch them leaping through the tall palms. Suddenly a black, furry, feline creature, about twice the size of a domestic cat, leapt out of a tree, hurtled across the path and shot up a palm. It turned out to be a strange mammal called a 'high woods dog'. Ricardo wasn't interested; he'd met a small boy with a dog and was jabbering and pointing excitedly. The boy nodded and pointed. 'He knows, senor,' grinned the sage.

So we retraced our footsteps and then took a side trail leading deeper into the forest. After only a few dozen paces we were standing in a freshly burnt clearing. The boy pointed his machete at a tumbledown pile of stones running from one side of the clearing to the other. Apparently he had been burning the jungle to make space to plant coconuts, and had found the wall. I felt a surge of excitement as I called out to the rest of the team. 'Over here, over here, we've found something!'

Dan Osman, our doctor, and I measured the wall. It ran on a magnetic bearing of eighty degrees with an average width of eleven feet and a height of about three. A bastion appeared to project at right angles; between the wall and the sea Gricelio was already finding pottery and, most important, glass. Lines of stones appeared to mark the foundations of buildings.

'What do you think?' I asked our archaeologist.

'I think you have discovered Acla,' he said solemnly.

That night we sat in the sunset sipping our J & B, being eaten alive by mosquitoes and felt a great glow of contented excitement such as explorers only feel on very special occasions.

It was St George's Day. The rains were approaching so next day we canoed to the island of Mulatudo. Jose, an albino, kindly put us up in his tin roofed home and even found some beds and sheets. A few beers in the cantina and we were ready for sleep. Jose was smoking a cigarette in a dark corner of his verandah. 'Any mosquitoes?' I enquired. 'No mosquitoes, senor,' he replied and, thankful that I needn't unpack my net, I flopped on to the white sheet and the lumpy mattress. Slipping into oblivion I felt something prick my toe. Assuming it was an insect I kicked out and fell asleep.

The storm broke at 0115 hours and the monsoon rain upon the tin roof would have woken the dead. Then I realized my bed was wet. Oh, hell, I thought, the rain's coming in. As I rose to investigate I felt the call of nature and so, groping for my torch, I stumbled down the external staircase to the evil-smelling loo. The rain had ceased as I ascended again, but my torch revealed something that made me freeze. The stairs were dripping with blood. In six bounds I was in my room and, supposing murder to have been committed, seized my harpoon gun in defence. As I did so something brushed my hair, and, raising my torch beam, I saw a bat flitting around the room. Then the light caught the bed and to my dismay I found it drenched in blood which, even now, was dripping on to the floor and forming bright red pools. My legs were scarlet from the knees down. 'Ruth,' I hissed through the cubicle wall.

'What is it?' came a sleepy reply.

'You'd better give me a hand, I think I've cut a vein or something,' I whispered. Ruth Mindel padded in.

'Mind where you tread,' I cautioned.

'What on earth . . .' She stood looking at me in horror.

Dan arrived next. 'Hell, John,' he said, 'what did you do?'

I could remember nothing untoward except the prick in my toe just before I'd fallen asleep. Having cleaned me up Dan looked puzzled.

'I've never seen anyone bleed so much from such a tiny cut!' exclaimed the doctor. 'It's about a quarter of an inch long on your toe.' Then he added, 'Say, is there any history of blood disease in your family?' On being assured that there wasn't, he asked, 'Have you cut yourself recently?'

'Yes,' I replied, 'yesterday on my knuckle.'

There Dan found a perfect scab. So, dosing me with antibiotics and plastering up the cut, he left me to sleep.

At dawn the room looked like a slaughter-yard; interestingly the blood had still not congealed.

'John, I've made some enquiries,' said Dan at breakfast. 'I reckon that bat you saw was a vampire. Apparently the local people are often bitten; and because the creature injects you with a powerful anti-coagulant to make it easier for them to drink your blood, you will bleed profusely,' he explained.

Of course I should have remembered how our horses had suffered during the Darien crossing. 'There's only a four per cent chance of a bat carrying rabies,' Dan continued, 'but I suggest you start the shots the moment we get back to Panama City.'

Thus in the months that followed I was to undergo no less than three different series of anti-rabies injections, a total of thirty-two jabs in my stomach and backside. By comparison the bite was nothing, so I do hope that the bat got alcohol poisoning from his cup of my blood.

Now, two years later, fifty young explorers from six nations were to investigate these discoveries. To back up our scientific work, *Eye of the Wind* had a fully equipped marine biological laboratory aboard and from here Dr Patricia Holdway directed the programme. They had paused at the Caribbean island of St Vincent to carry out an urgent task with the University of the West Indies. Mt Soufrière, a fairly active volcano, had not had a major eruption since 1901 but in 1971 and 1972 a lava island had appeared in the crater lake.

So our youngsters dragged an Avon 3,500 feet up to its rim in order to float over to the island and assess its flora and fauna and make a thermometric study. They found it was much hotter and more lively than expected and on Christmas Eve beat a hasty retreat to warn the authorities. On Good Friday it erupted with terrifying violence and, had people not been evacuated thanks to the timely warning, there could have been heavy loss of life.

With back-breaking labour Jim Winter and the advance party cleared an old airstrip at the edge of Caledonia Bay and built a base camp. To get everything ready was a race against time: over 100 tons of stores had to be shipped from Colon to the Bay by our friends in the Guardia Nacional but finally it was done, right on schedule.

On 3 January 1979 Piper Robert Little of the Scots Guards cut a magnificent, if slightly incongruous, figure as he stood silhouetted against the palm-fringed headland of Punta Escoces in full ceremonial dress playing a lament in memory of his ill-fated countrymen of so long ago. It was a moving moment and I reflected that the lonely ghosts of Fort St Andrew must surely have appreciated the haunting sound of the pipes after 280 years.

The arrival of the Young Explorers was the occasion for a surprise visit by General Omar Torrijos, Commander of the Guardia Nacional and Dictator of Panama. Voluble archaeologist Mark Horton briefed him and finally fell silent. The tough General rocked back and forth in his chair sucking gently at his fat Havana. After several minutes of awkward silence there was a sharp bang; bodyguards hurled themselves into the mud, cocking weapons. Only the Dictator remained unmoved. My younger daughter, Victoria, had been given a cap pistol for Christmas which was smoking in her hand. Then louder and louder the great man began to laugh, finally his muddy aids picked themselves up and laughed too. 'Little girl,' he said, 'all this is very boring for you, yes?' Victoria nodded. 'Come,' he smiled, 'I'll get you a coconut.' So saying he removed his hat, boots and gun-belt and with astonishing agility shinned up a palm tree and picked her a large coconut which he then opened with a machete and handing it to her said, 'It's good, drink.' Everyone cheered and the General strolled off for lunch.

'Who is he?' hissed Victoria.

'Well, he's like the Queen of Panama,' I tried to explain.

'Doesn't look much like a Queen,' she grunted, wandering off with her coconut.

Torrijos was an impressive man and became a good friend of Operation Drake. His personal interest was enormously helpful and ensured the complete support of everyone in Panama. When jungle excavations were threatened by clouds of black fly, mosquitoes and falling coconuts that could kill, General Torrijos flew in a load of protective helmets and gallons of insect repellant and the work continued.

'Mad' Mark Horton worked non-stop to dig up the past. Although distantly related to that grand old man of archaeology, Sir Mortimer Wheeler, he actually reminded most people more of Magnus Pyke, as he waved his arms around and enthused wildly about some point of academic interest. His involvement in his subject was so total that virtually nothing could distract him. This was proved when he was giving our Chairman, General Sir John Mogg, and a party of visitors a guided tour of his excavations at Acla. As Mark rattled on, a long green snake slithered across the track a few feet in front of the General. My hand dropped to my holster but before I could draw, a Guardia major had his submachine gun up and blasted the beast to oblivion. The shattering noise was still echoing across the bay when, unabated, Mark continued, 'And furthermore . . .'

We knew the Scots had lost a supply ship *Olive Branch* which had burned to the waterline and sunk, after the ship's cooper had accidentally dropped a lighted candle while tapping brandy from the barrels in the hold and caused an instant inferno. The vessel had carried a mixed cargo including great quantities of bonnets, Bibles and clay pipes. Knowing it would be an historical treasure house, I got Tony Lonsdale, a very professional magnetometer expert, to accompany us and do a thorough survey. We concentrated our attention on an area close in to the shore on the eastern side of the bay, where it was thought the colony would have had its anchorage. Here, sure enough, readings soon indicated something fairly substantial. When the divers went down and probed in the mud, they made contact with wood and coral concretion.

The site was on a steep mud slope that dropped off the edge of the coral reef. At the shallow end there was live coral at a depth of six feet, while at the other end one could go down twenty-five feet before sinking into thick ooze. Underwater visibility was bad at the best of times and became non-existent once this silt was stirred up. Not quite what one expects in the Caribbean! The team used water jets and an air-lift suction pump, as well as shovels and buckets to clear glutinous mud, sand and coral fragments. After some considerable time, a piece of timber was prised out and brought to the surface for close examination by a marine archaeologist, who was able to confirm that it definitely came from a sixteenth- or seventeenth-century

European sailing ship. The next sample provoked even more excitement. It was immediately identifiable as a piece of deck planking, and it was badly burned on the underside, while the nail holes were charred right through. We soon realized that we had found a virtually complete ship and the evidence pointed to its being the *Olive Branch*, but it was another three weeks before final, indisputable proof was forthcoming. The breakthrough came when, after much careful probing, the divers uncovered a number of barrels, some of which were still intact. Down on the seabed, they sifted delicately through the silt that clogged the barrels while up above, on *David Gestetner*, the giant inflatable we had last used in Zaire that now served as a diving platform, the results of these painstaking labours were awaited with almost breathless anticipation.

The air of tension was further increased by a hair-raising incident. One of the divers, Warrant Officer Marc Moody, was down on the bottom, filling a bucket with silt in zero visibility when he felt someone moving around near him in the dark. There was a tug on the rope and the heavy pail was snatched away. Marc assumed that it had been hauled in by those up top but when he surfaced he was puzzled to find that this was not the case. Nobody knew anything about it and there was no sign of the bucket.

The disappearance remained a mystery until, shortly afterwards, the Guardia hauled in the fishing nets they had set nearby, and there, thrashing around in the mesh, was a number of sharks including two man-eaters – a five-foot Mako and a ten-foot Hammerhead. It did not take too much imagination to come up with a chilling possibility as to who or what might have stolen the bucket. The divers were understandably a little reluctant to work in the gloomy, pea-soup depths and every time something brushed unexpectedly against them they nearly jumped out of their wet suits. Even the excitement caused by the discovery of the barrels could not entirely take their minds off the spine-tingling thought of what might be nosing around them.

Meanwhile, the contents of several barrels were panned out like gold dust and passed up for examination. The first cask yielded a pronged fork and a few slivers of bone which suggested that it might have been part of a consignment of salt pork or beef; the next two were empty, and the fourth was full of nails. It was the fifth that provided the vital clue in the distinctive shape of three clay pipes that were identical to those found at Fort St Andrew – they even carried the same P and G initials, which, it was irreverently suggested, might stand for Porridge Gobbler.

Back on land, the total success of the historical and archaeological projects was nicely rounded off when Mark's unearthed evidence proved beyond a reasonable doubt that the Lost City of Acla had been rediscovered. By working in this remote, inaccessible spot, largely ignored by archaeologists in the past, we had filled in a few blanks of Panamanian history.

So throughout the dry season, a relative term in Panama, our army of Young Explorers worked on. There was medical research with the Cuna, zoological studies and further historical explorations deep in Darien. One of the most worthwhile projects involved ecological studies of the jungle canopy. Six miles inland a scientific base was established in the primary rainforest. Here, after building a helicopter pad so equipment and supplies could be airlifted in, Royal Engineers and YEs constructed a unique aerial walkway 100 feet up in the canopy, with observation platforms in each tree top. Botanists, zoologists, entomologists and an ornithologist were thus able to make detailed studies of the ecology. Tropical rainforests are cut down for timber at the rate of fifty acres a minute worldwide, but they do not regenerate. One step in solving the problem is to discover of what they consist and the role played by birds, animals and insects in their pollination biology.

Andrew Mitchell, having worked with me at Dover, knew what sappers could do and this enthusiastic zoologist suggested we construct walkways to investigate this unexplored area – 'where the great trees have their sex lives'. Mick Christy, a very tough engineer, built the construction of dexion and nylon strapping and arranged an ingenious system of lifts to raise visitors from the ground. The most important of these, General Mogg, marched seven miles through swamp and river and, to everyone's delight, was hoisted aloft to inspect the work. He wore the jungle green uniform in which he had commanded the Commonwealth Brigade in Malaya many years before, but his faithful boots collapsed at the camp so he gave them to a YE, who said he would boil them up if food ran out. It was a pretty remarkable achievement and left everyone, especially the Guardia who had never met a British General, impressed by his toughness.

However, a few days later when he bade farewell to their senior officers at the Citadel in Panama City, the Guardia surprised him.

Lying outside the Guard Room was a huge jaguar on a chain. 'I bet that fellow keeps the prisoners on their toes,' joked our General.

'Oh, yes,' replied a major, 'we put the big cat in one cell and don't feed him for a few days, then we put the prisoner in the next cell. There is a little door in between.' His gold teeth flashed. 'They usually talk!'

Back at the bay we decided it would be appropriate to celebrate Burns' Night. Haggis and copious quantities of J & B scotch were airlifted in and in the warm, moist night we toasted the immortal memory. Piper Little excelled himself as we danced and reeled beneath the stars. Our Panamanian guests were totally confused. Most had thought it a birthday party and came with presents. Towards midnight a Guardia gunboat sailed in and ran right onto a reef by our jetty. This caused much excitement whilst she was beached. The crew, who it seemed had already dined well, came ashore and the party went on. Towards dawn one of our visitors, an ugly little major, rather the worse for wear, seized my attractive blonde assistant, Sara Everett, and dragged her towards the bushes. Hearing her yell, I grabbed the wretch by his lapels and propelled him towards the sea. However, his pals intervened and apologized. Later I discovered his name – Emmanuel Noriega!

As the crossroads of the world, this little country housed a great number of interesting folk. At the end of our stay we were holding a meeting of Panamanian Y Es in a local hotel. Maps and charts were spread over the floor as we discussed future plans. Suddenly I became aware that a slim little lady in a large hat had come in. With amazing grace, she stepped over the papers and stretched out her hand. 'Hello.' She smiled. 'I just wanted to thank you for having my niece on the expedition.' It was Dame Margot Fonteyn. Her friendship in the years to come was immensely warm and helpful.

Whilst all our land-based activities had gone well we had major problems with *Eye of the Wind*. On arrival in Colon we needed a new gearbox. Obtaining one and flying it out had almost put us in the red – now I learned the anchor chain kept slipping because it was the wrong size for the 'gypsy' around which it wound. The ship was due to sail in a few days when Frank Esson, the new senior watchkeeper, arrived from Britain and achieved a miracle. He carried the 120-pound gypsy as hand baggage on a flight to New Orleans, bought a second-hand chain that fitted it and persuaded a

Panama Canal Company ship to carry it to Colon. The ship sailed through the canal on time.

However, our treasurer was forecasting imminent financial disaster. Back in Britain, General Sir John Mogg bumped into Prince Charles at Badminton and said he hoped he would not end up in the Tower if we went into debt. 'No, you'll probably go to Carmarthen Castle – that's mine and it's much worse,' replied the Prince of Wales.

From start to finish we lived from hand to mouth and, as inflation alone made a mockery of our original budget estimate of around £650,000, we constantly had to rev up our already frantic fundraising activities in order to keep up with soaring costs and to stop ourselves slipping back too far into the red.

So 'Charlie's Angels' and I set to work in America. In New York slow-talking Tulsa oilman John Linehan was an enthusiastic supporter and had spent some time in the jungle with us. He kindly let me use his New York office and provided many very useful introductions. He also helped to drum up a considerable amount of financial backing and threw a party for us which produced more donations. He himself presented me with $5,000 in typically flamboyant fashion, arranging for a radio-controlled jeep to roll to a stop in front of me, whereupon the bonnet lifted automatically to reveal a cheque! At such gatherings we sold, sold, sold and I began to feel like an old gramophone record when the needle became stuck. Whilst the angels were helping a well-fleshed stockbroker to find his wallet, I chatted to a charming young blonde who told me her family was 'into exploring'. Sara was soon to return to London and I would need a new PA, so I suggested my acquaintance might like the job. Just then my host introduced someone else and I learned I had been talking to Margaux Hemingway.

Meanwhile the expedition had moved on to Drake's Bay in Costa Rica where we erected a plinth to commemorate Francis Drake's earlier visit. By the time Eye of the Wind had reached the Galapagos, the skippers had changed and Mike Kichenside had flown in from Australia to take over the helm.

In the Galapagos the Darwin Research Station urgently needed a female land iguana. They only had males of this endangered creature. After a spirited chase, the youngsters managed to catch a female, which pleased a lot of male land iguanas and saved the species.

A hurricane had recently struck Fiji so the ship stopped there and we rebuilt a school. Another financial crisis was looming. In mid-Pacific Tiger Timbs discovered that vibrations in the propeller shaft had almost shaken the prop right off. They managed to fix it temporarily, but once in dry dock at Suva, they found a complete new prop shaft was required. 'Fourteen thousand dollars,' I groaned. Then we had an extraordinary stroke of luck. A producer from Columbia Pictures called me. 'We're remaking *The Blue Lagoon* in Fiji,' he explained. 'Could you possibly hire us your ship for a few days?' 'Certainly,' I replied, 'it will cost $14,000.'

On 5 September 1979 our gleaming white flagship sailed into Lae, Papua New Guinea (PNG). It was a sight no one will ever forget. There was a time when no sailing ship was welcome here. The approach of any such vessel to the reef-bound shores of the island was regarded with suspicion and hatred by the coastal villagers and landing parties could expect to be greeted by a hail of spears and arrows. This was hardly surprising, since, for many years, European visitors had only one use for the wild, remote and exotic land named by the first Portuguese explorers Ihlas de Papuas – Island of the Fuzzy-Haired – and that was as a source of strong young slaves to be carried off and sold on the world's lucrative labour markets.

Attitudes have changed since, and *Eye of the Wind* sailed in to a fantastic reception. However, although the people are usually friendly these days, the environment remains as hostile as ever. The island, second largest in the world after Greenland, is shaped like a giant turtle swimming in the South Pacific seas just above the northern tip of Queensland and is divided neatly down the middle by a straight north-south border, between the Indonesian territory of West Irian in the west and PNG in the east. It is an untamed tropical wilderness in which soaring mountain peaks rise out of stinking mangrove swamps, mighty rushing rivers gush through plunging rocky gorges, and baking arid scrubland gives way to wide delta quagmires. And, overall, it is shrouded in dense, impenetrable jungle, which is why it was still one of the least-explored areas on earth. The inaccessibility of the interior meant that nothing at all was known about it until the first aircraft flew over in the 1920s, and existing maps, compiled from aerial photographs, still contain blank spaces marked 'Cloud – Relief Data Incomplete', the modern equivalent of

mythical creatures, gogs and magogs, with which the old
cartographers used to fill the unknown areas that nobody had been
able to reach and chart.

It is not just the terrain that makes PNG so inhospitable. The
climate and the creepy crawlies – which seem to be bigger, nastier
and more plentiful than anywhere else in the world – add further
dimensions of discomfort and danger to life outside the few air-
conditioned townships. The feverish, steam-heat humidity of the
lowlands soon leaves one limp with exhaustion, and the catalogue of
lethal wildlife includes the world's largest crocodiles, enormous
pythons that can break every bone in a full-grown pig's body and then
swallow it whole, and small snakes just a few inches long with a bite
so poisonous that they can cause death within a matter of minutes.
There are outsize lizards, scorpions and spiders the size of your fist.
Mosquitoes, which, having had three doses of malaria, I regard as the
greatest threat of all, are also particularly virulent.

One way and another, it is a real battle against the elements to
survive in PNG. Everything stings or bites or causes rashes and
infections, and the best that twentieth-century technology can
provide in the form of salves, lotions and repellents seem powerless to
protect one's skin against continual attack. Your clothes rot and the
most rugged boots crack up in half the time it would take anywhere
else. Even my pith helmet, which for twelve years had kept me cool,
dry and safe from falling coconuts in some of the most God-forsaken
corners of the world, finally surrendered to the atmospheric extremes
of PNG and sprouted a terrible green mould.

I had always dreamed of leading an expedition here. One place that
fascinated me was the Upper Strickland River and, thanks to the help
of Gestetners, I had had an opportunity to do an air recce the previous
year. I had asked the local Defence Force Commander for his advice.

'That's a really mysterious area,' he said. 'Few have been there and
we'd love to know more about it, what the river's like, and the people,
and the animals and any minerals too.'

I went off to the Defence Force library to see if I could find some air
photographs – but there were none. 'Haven't got that far yet,' said the
Australian captain. 'It's a hell of a place to fly in.' So, clearly, if we
were to tackle this region, we would have to get our own photos.

The river falls 1,000 feet in seventy-five miles and, for much of this
distance, it is enclosed in a deep chasm, the Devil's Race. Low cloud
obscures the area for much of the year and thus, even an air recce was

unlikely to reveal what secrets lay beneath the swirling mists and the dark green rainforest. But I felt there must be a series of falls, or perhaps just one big fall on that course. If we were to explore the region we would need to use that river. 'If you get clear weather,' said a bush pilot in Port Moresby, 'it's because of high wind funnelling up the gorge – even the Army planes won't take it. You'll need a real power bird to get you through; if you hit that turbulence, you'll smash right into the rock.' Even if one survived a crash, the chances of being found didn't sound good, and the likely reaction of the tribes of head hunters (who were still thought to exist in remote regions) and crocodiles to an intrusion was not very inviting.

Barbara Martinelli was now seconded by Pan–Am as a recce officer on Operation Drake and somehow, as was her way, she managed to borrow a powerful light plane with a first-rate Australian pilot, Noel Frewster. We flew up to Wewak on PNG's north coast to try to make a low-level air reconnaissance of the high-altitude valley of the upper Strickland. Surprisingly, within a day of our arrival, favourable weather was indicated and Noel decided to have a try. Barbara had the still cameras and took the rear seat, whilst I held the Canon eight-millimetre cine in the front and flicked it on to 'slow motion'. The twin-engined Cessna 301, named Olivetti after the company who sponsored it in an air race, was an ideal aircraft for the job and we were soon climbing south into the towering peaks.

At 12,000 feet, we crossed a rocky ridge and winged our way through the crags of this little-known land. Suddenly, Noel pointed. 'Look, it's clearing,' he shouted. Sure enough, ahead of us the clouds were rolling back to reveal an emerald-green valley surrounded by towering cliffs and dark mountains. Barbara's camera was already in operation as I raised my cine. Noel took the Cessna through the valley 1,000 feet above the ground and we got a good view of the river winding its way fairly gently at first and then tumbling over rocky ledges in foaming fury before it plunged into the narrow, vertically-sided gorge. I felt the aircraft bank sharply and looked up to see a wall of rock racing past – very close. Blasts of wind shook the Cessna as it twisted and turned through the mountain pass. Noel gripped the controls, his face a study of concentration, beads of sweat running down his cheeks. 'Hold on,' he hissed through the intercom as the nose lifted over a jungle-covered ridge. Our bodies flattened against the seat back as the surge of power took us up, missing the trees by fifty feet. The tumbling brown river had almost disappeared in the

PAPUA NEW GUINEA: STRICKLAND VALLEY

dark green foliage which now covered the entire valley bottom and seemed to close over the top of the canyon. Eventually, we emerged from the mountains and saw the endless flat swampland of the lower Strickland ahead.

'That's fine, Noel,' I yelled. 'Can you take us back at low level?' The Australian made a funny face and we reloaded our cameras. The return journey was the most exhilarating flight of my life. Manoeuvring his aircraft like a fighter, Noel hurtled through the great cleft in that dark green wilderness. Barbara and I concentrated on filming, but the gravitational forces on some of the turns were such that my arms felt like lead and I could hardly lift the camera. Cliffs and jungle shot past the wingtips. We saw underground rivers emerging, huge caves, strange trees and then a single rope bridge strung across the river. So someone does live down there, I thought. Even so, there was no other obvious sign of any human habitation. Back at base that night, we celebrated and worked on our reports with enthusiasm, knowing that we now had the vital information which would enable Roger Chapman to tackle this river exploration task.

For the young people this was a wonderland and, even to the older folk amongst us, PNG was quite an eye-opener. The local government and people were magnificently kind and the expatriates did all they could to help. With their support we built aerial walkways in the jungle canopy, searched for minerals, mapped old wartime trails and combed densely forested mountains for the remains of long lost wartime planes. Our underwater team led by Royal Engineers and RAF divers charted Japanese wrecks, of which there was no shortage. The diving was exhilarating, deep, and once or twice, when sharks appeared, quite nerve-wracking. However, more worrying were the gigantic saltwater crocodiles or salties said to reach thirty feet that cruised the shallow lagoons.

Meanwhile Roger, Jim Masters and a foot recce party were preparing to take their Avons down the fearsome Strickland. The going was horrendous; as harsh and inhospitable as one is likely to find anywhere in the world. When not scrambling and hacking up and down almost sheer-sided ridges covered in dense undergrowth, one is picking a careful path across the limestone rock, so sharp-edged that the soles of the toughest boots will be shredded after a few miles. Even seemingly open areas, which appear from the air to be smooth carpets of green turf, usually turn out to be covered in kunai grass fifteen feet high, which is so difficult to cut through that a fit man can be reduced to sweat-soaked exhaustion within a matter of yards.

We had also learned that the interior tribesmen were often extremely primitive and their reactions to outsiders unpredictable. The early patrols had adopted a policy of sending ahead shouters – native guides who would go forward and bellow out advance warning of the party's arrival in the area and call in any tribes in the locality for a meeting. Salt and tobacco would then be handed over as a gesture of friendship and, once the ice had been broken, impressive shooting displays with rifles would be laid on to discourage any hostile notions. Although we were never attacked, we carried arms on the advice of the local Army, but more for protection against 'salties'.

I talked to all our outstations daily on a remarkably reliable radio net. One evening Roger came on loud and clear in great excitement. After telling me that they had been forced to make a hair-raising 3,000 feet climb up the side of Strickland Gorge, he said, 'We've found some people.' Then unusually bad conditions cut him out, but words like 'primitive', 'stone axes', 'no white men' came through and I knew they had achieved the ultimate goal in many armchair explorers' minds. Quite simply, he'd bumped into a lost or unknown tribe.

Next morning communications improved and I learned it had taken them nearly ten hours to claw their way to the top. They had to move with the utmost caution, hauling themselves up on vines, roots and the most tenuous handholds in the crumbling rock. By the time they eventually made it, they barely had the strength to rig their hammocks and swallow a hurriedly prepared meal of dehydrated food before flaking out. Then, striking inland in search of a suitable clearing in which to land the planned re-supply helicopter, they picked up an old hunting track and smelt wood-smoke. The patrol immediately crept further along the track until, around a bend, they glimpsed through the trees a small clearing in which stood two low, rectangular huts, with wisps of blue smoke filtering through the thatched roofs. Then, figures were seen moving about, and the sounds of children playing and pigs squealing floated across the forest. No settlements were thought to exist here.

At once Roger sent ahead two of his native Duna bearers – Harirega and Ayape – and when he saw that they received a friendly welcome, he led the rest of the patrol forward into the clearing. As he did so, Ayape pointed towards the man with whom he had been conversing in a strange dialect, and when Roger extended his hand, the small bearded fellow grasped it firmly and held on determinedly, clearly not wanting to let go. However, some of the men had seized the pigs and run off, whilst women and children lay down and moaned. There then followed a bizarre four-way conversation, English being translated into Pidgin – the nearest thing to an official language in PNG – so that Harirega could then rephrase the message in Duna for the benefit of Ayape, who was the only one familiar with the dialect spoken by the tribesmen.

In this tortuous way it was established that the village they'd discovered was called Tigaro and that the inhabitants were nomadic Pogaians. There were five families in the group which numbered fifteen altogether. The man who was hanging on to Roger's hand so affectionately was called Kiwanga, and the chief, who was away working in the village 'gardens', but was due back at sunset, was named Kemba. When he eventually made an appearance, he confirmed that nobody in his small tribe had ever seen a white man before – a fact which seemed to be rather amusingly borne out by the way in which Roger's white team members were subjected to close scrutiny and the occasional curious prod.

The fascination was mutual. Kemba and his people were clearly untouched by modern civilization. Their most sophisticated and prized possessions were two steel axe heads, which they had traded with other tribes in the Bulago Valley, where they had been originally introduced by one of the later Kiap patrols. Otherwise, they had only stone tools and implements and their other possessions were made from natural materials. Barbed or notched arrows of razor-sharp split bamboo were used with six-foot-long hardwood bows for the daily wallaby hunt. Some arrows had three or four prongs for catching birds or fish. The women appeared in the evening, carrying taro and sweet potatoes or 'Kau Kau' in 'bilums', net baskets hung from their heads. They wore only grass skirts, while the men covered themselves with a loin cloth in the front and, over their backsides, a hanging bunch of 'tanket' leaves known evocatively in Pidgin as 'arsegrass'. Most wore thin armbands, also of bark. Kemba, the chief, sported a necklace of large cowrie shells and a halfmoon-shaped 'Kina' shell on his dark chest. They existed on a diet of root crops grown in their forest 'gardens', augmented with whatever they could hunt down. Their precious domestic pigs were only slaughtered on very special occasions and are otherwise treated with loving care. The women walked around clutching piglets as if they were their own children and even suckling them in emergencies. Men guarded pigs more jealously than their wives and children and a tribesman once told me, 'Women and children very easy to make – pigs more difficult!'

Friendship was further cemented with gifts of salt and tobacco, and it was agreed that the patrol would spend the night in the village before clearing a landing-site for the helicopter the next morning. The villagers watched spellbound as my voice came through on the radio from base 350 miles away. Eventually, they grew bolder and fingered everything of metal, glass or plastic with child-like glee. Cigarette lighters and binoculars were considered quite amazing.

My arrival next day in a giant RAAF Chinook brought the Stone Age face to face with the twentieth century in the most spectacular fashion. The idea of a simple supply drop was changed because we decided that the patrol might as well take advantage of the situation and hitch a lift back to the banks of the Strickland. Alas, the stone axes had not cleared the last few feet of tree stumps and landing

Operation Drake's flagship, *Eye of the Wind*, off Jersey. (*Jersey Evening Post*)

Young explorers in the swamps of Panama. (*Chris Sainsbury*)

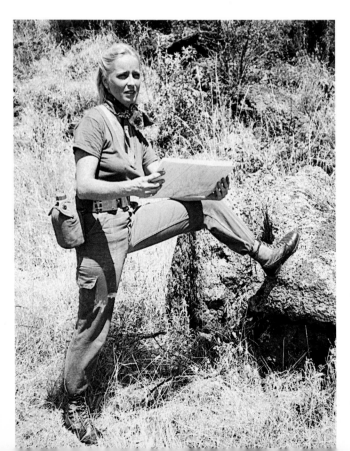

Barbara Price (Martinelli), a very effective recce officer on many expeditions.

The flying trapeze on
the walls of Fort George.
(*Chris Sainsbury*)

During his visit to the Fort George Volunteers in 1982, HRH The Prince of Wales takes a
ride in the Avon Searaider, now being used as a fast inshore rescue craft. (*Chris Sainsbury*)

OPERATION RALEIGH, 1985.

Above: Sir Walter Raleigh, flagship of Operation Raleigh, and the expedition's brigantine *Zebu* rendezvous off the Turks and Caicos Islands. (*SES*)

Below: Venturers constructing the Canadian sub-igloo off Grand Bahama. (*SES*)

Opposite: Shaving in the snow with Silva compass's mirror on the slopes of Mt Xixabangma, Tibet, 1987.

With some of my greatest allies: (*left to right*) General Sir John Mogg, Ambassador and Mrs Walter Annenberg, and Graham Walker. (*ORPL*)

An Executive Expedition: the microlight sets out on a dawn recce in the Kalahari.

Raja Gaj, king elephant, 11′ 3″ at the shoulders, browsing quietly near the Karnali.

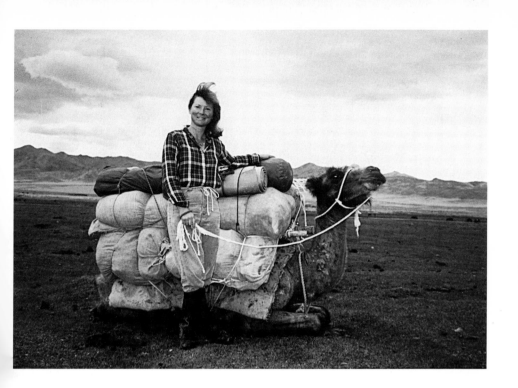

MONGOLIA, 1992.

Above: Ann Tweedy Savage with her camel, Basil, west of Hovd. (*Ian Robinson*)

Right: American banker Pamela Stephany and my pal Nokhoijav near Mt Somboros.

Victoria and Julian fly away
in the Royal Engineers'
balloon 'Sapper II' after
their wedding.

Airlifted from Mongolia:
Lindsay Griffin with shattered
leg in the helicopter with
(*left*) Richard Snailham
and Dr Jan Kemmis.

proved impossible, so we had to remain in the hover as our people struggled aboard. It was one of the most worrying ten minutes of my life, as the huge machine bucked and swayed in the jungle clearing. The 'Lost Tribe' stared in amazement at our monster, which might as well have been a space craft in a city dweller's backyard. Some wept with fear, but were so terrified that they were immobile. When they saw us pull the native carriers onto the open ramp, they thought the great bird was devouring them!

As the Chinook lifted off and rose above the tiny jungle clearing, with a deafening roar, the 100 m.p.h. downdraught from its twin rotors created a mini-hurricane that raised a swirling cloud of dust and whipped the surrounding foliage into a frenzy of dancing branches and wildly fluttering leaves. Fifteen near-naked brown bodies prostrated themselves on the ground, their hands clamped over their ears, their foreheads pressed to the earth, not daring to look up. As the scene receded, I peered down anxiously at the prone forms and wondered what must be going through their minds. Fifty years previously, when aircraft first arrived in PNG, similar encounters had given rise to the cargo cults among the primitive peoples, who understandably concluded that the strange white men who descended from the skies in the bird-like machines packed with wonderful goods must surely be gods. It was fascinating to speculate about the legends that might grow up around our meeting with Chief Kemba's people.

THIRTEEN

Strange Quests

'THERE ARE SEVERAL ACCOUNTS of a twenty-foot dragon that walks upright, breathes fire and eats men,' said my visitor. It was said to live in southwest PNG and was quite definitely not a 'saltie'! Although it sounded nonsense, the government was eager to find out if there was any truth in the tale. Having studied the more reliable reports, I decided to mount a search for what would undoubtedly be the longest lizard in the world.

We planned to base the expedition at Masingara, the village of my PNG liaison officer, Somare Jogo, and include Ian Redmond, a robust young zoologist. Masingara is just up the coast from the provincial capital, Daru, in the area generally considered the most likely haunt for any monster lizard.

Things got off to a suitably dramatic start even before my twenty-strong patrol reached Masingara, when we contrived to get lost in some of the most treacherous waters in the world. The Coral Sea is a wonderfully romantic name for a bit of ocean full of deadly reefs, strong currents and shifting shallows. We never really gave this a second's thought as we set out from Port Moresby, bound for Masingara in the MV *Andewa*, kindly provided by the government. The three-day voyage began well enough. Everybody was sunbathing on the afterdeck, while dolphins played in the bow wave and large juicy baramundi obligingly swallowed the hooks which we trailed out astern. It was around dusk on the second day that things began to go wrong. There was no sign of the lighthouse which was a vital landmark, and although we all strained our eyes through the growing darkness it was to no avail. At this point the skipper casually confessed that he never bothered with charts because he was used to sailing in waters that he knew like the back of his hand. Unfortunately, he had to admit, this part of the ocean was quite new to him and he really did not know where we were!

After haphazardly changing course a few times in the hope of finding some identifiable landmark, our position was even more confused. I did have a chart, but it was not a lot of help since we could not pinpoint our location. To make matters worse, the trawler's compass was not working. We were literally going round in circles, when Chris Sainsbury, the only real sailor amongst us, suggested that as we were in such dangerous waters it might be a good idea to throw a plumb line overboard just to be on the safe side, and this revealed the startling fact that we were over a sandbank with less than two feet to spare! The skipper inched into slightly deeper water before anchoring for the night in the hope that we would be able to get our bearings in the morning, when we would at least be able to see what we were doing. But I feared we were too far south and heading straight for the Great Barrier Reef.

Dawn broke to reveal that the water, which the day before had been the deepest blue, was now a murky, muddy brown, while large clumps of vegetation floated by in the strong current. This gave me the vital clue that we must be somewhere near the wide mouth of the Fly River and enabled us to chart a course which eventually led to Daru.

Whilst the good ship *Andewa* refuelled, I rushed off to find Somare and meet her uncle, Mr Tatty Olewale, OBE, the Premier of the Western Province. We found him at home having lunch, and reading from a gigantic leather-bound Bible, whilst his pet parakeet hopped about on his shoulder. The Premier rose to greet us with the words, 'Colonel, it is the Lord who has brought you to us.' After the adventure of the previous night, I was inclined to agree. In no time Mr Olewale summoned his brother, the head postman, who was able to tell us a great deal about Artrellia, as they called the dragon. The Premier wished us well and loaded us with small gifts, before sending us off with his niece, Somare, and a wizened old pilot, to guide us up the rivers.

Next day we anchored off Masingara and marched the half mile inland to Somare's well-ordered home village of traditional stilt-supported bamboo huts. There I was ushered by her brother, Seyu, towards a 100-year-old woman, who was the most senior citizen and who was said to know more than anyone about the Artrellia, having seen several in her lifetime. The white-haired old lady confirmed many of the things we had already heard: that these creatures grew to over fifteen feet in length; that they often stood on their hind legs and so gave the appearance of dragons or, to our minds, mini-dinosaurs; also that they were extremely fierce.

This last point brought much nodding from the village hunters, who made it quite obvious that they treated even the smaller six- or seven-footers – which they said were quite common – with the greatest respect. This came as no surprise, since we had already been told of an incident in another village where a captured Artrellia had smashed its way out of a stout cage and killed a large dog, before escaping. Now we learned that the creature's method of hunting was to lie in wait in the trees before dropping onto its victims and tearing them to shreds with its powerful claws. Apart from that, it possessed a very infectious bite as a result of feeding on carrion and this could bring death within a matter of hours. There were plenty of stories of men who had been attacked and killed by the Artrellia.

During the next few days, we split into four patrols and combed the surrounding jungle, but, although everyone we met understood immediately when we explained what we were looking for and claimed that they themselves had seen such creatures, the nearest any of us got to a sighting was when local dogs put up something that crashed off heavily through the undergrowth without showing itself. There was a flurry of excitement when we learned that dogs had killed a big lizard, but it turned out to be a three-foot monitor of a well-known species.

The Sunday before Christmas, I went to matins in the little village church. Singing 'Hark, The Herald Angels Sing' in Pidgin did sound strange, but the sincerity of these simple people was most impressive. Strolling out into the bright sunlight, I paused to talk to the vicar. 'Do you really believe in Artrellia?' I asked. He'd been educated in Australia and I reckoned he would be a sensible man.

'I know he exists, I sometimes wish he didn't, 'cos my people think him's a devil, like an evil spirit,' replied the pastor, 'but him just an animal, bad animal sometime.'

'Well, if we caught one, would it convince your flock that it was no evil spirit?' I asked.

'Sure.' He nodded his head.

'Then how on earth can we do that?'

'Oh, you fellows won't catch him – you makes too much noise

tramping around the bush – you needs good hunters,' he stated firmly and added as an afterthought, 'my choirboys is good hunters.'

'How much to hire the choir?' I asked.

'I needs a new church roof,' smiled the little priest, looking wistfully at the tattered thatch.

'How much will that cost?' I asked.

'Ten dollars,' was his quick reply. However, he suggested that I offer the reward at the village council that evening and in that way I'd get all the hunters helping. Ten dollars (or Kina) would be a month's wage.

'But don't tell dem fellows bout d'reward 'til seven o'clock,' he cautioned, ''cos I wants to leave at five – oh yes, and can you let me have some shotgun shells?'

Sure enough, the mere mention of money was followed by a mass exodus into the jungle of every able-bodied man, armed with everything from bows and arrows to an antique blunderbuss.

In the meantime, Somare showed us some interesting snakes that had been caught in a nearby swamp. They were almost jet black, more like eels, and apparently quite blind. Their skin lacked scales, but was covered in a mass of tiny pimples. Ian Redmond had never seen anything quite like these reptiles and Alan Bibby, our energetic TV producer, was anxious to film them being caught. 'That is not possible,' said Somare, looking very serious. 'They are only caught by the women at a certain time of year – it is a kind of ritual.'

'Goody, bags I go and catch some,' enthused my jolly PA, Margot Barker.

'I'll go too,' echoed Clare, the adjutant.

'Make sure you bring me a pregnant fully-grown female,' said Ian, with scientific motives in mind.

So we left the all-female expedition to its task.

On arrival at the swamp, Margot noticed the almost naked village ladies plunging into waist-deep mud covered by a thin layer of grass. The women chopped at the grass with bush knives, peeled back the top layer and, feeling around with feet and hands, found a great variety of lung fish, long-necked turtles, lizards and snakes. They hurled their catches to other ladies who waited on the bank. Margot learned that those on the sidelines were pregnant and were not allowed in the morass 'because they would drive away the mud-dwelling creatures'. Eventually Margot, reduced to battle order of bra and pants, plunged in, causing much consternation because only

pregnant ladies wore bras in Masingara. Eventually she felt something rather large squirming past her legs, and seized it. Out came a
very heavy, fully grown, black, eyeless snake – almost six feet in
length and full of eggs. So Ian got his wish. But Margot then felt
another serpent wriggling round her thighs – it felt thinner and much
more lively. Thrusting her hand back into the mire she grabbed it, or
rather it grabbed her, and in fact she was bitten four times by a rather
unpleasant diamond-headed snake about three feet long before she
got it out. Luckily, it wasn't poisonous.

Further and further our little ship penetrated up the unmapped
rivers. As we were reaching the head of navigation of one stream our
writer, Mike Cable, remarked, 'I doubt if any outsiders have ever been
up this far.' Rounding a bend, to our astonishment we saw ahead a
well-kept motor launch moored to the bank. The UN Development
Programme flag fluttered at its masthead and a shapely blonde in a
bikini was stretched across the hatch. 'Jesus,' breathed Mike, unable
to believe his eyes.

The blonde propped herself up on one elbow and said in broad
Australian, 'Goodday, mates.' I doffed my pith helmet and enquired if
she was alone. 'No, Bruce is down below trying to fix the freezer.'

At that point her colleague emerged. 'Strike a bloody light,' said he,
eyeing the premier Earl of Scotland (who had joined us on the quest),
a British Colonel and sundry others: as unlikely a bunch as you would
expect to meet up any tropical river.

'What are you doing?' we enquired when Bruce had produced some
ice-cold tubes of Fosters.

'A crayfish survey.'

'But there aren't any crayfish here,' said Ian.

'I know, mate, but don't tell the UNDP.'

We learned that Bruce recruited his assistant, as the blonde was
called, by advertising in a Sydney paper for 'Good-looking Sheila
required to accompany adventurous male on scientific survey in
PNG'. He then spent several weeks interviewing volunteers before
taking the selected lady back with him for the next season. It sounded
a good way to spend a few years.

Next morning Clare radioed to report that the vicar had managed
to shoot a big lizard somewhere deep in the forest and was on his way
back to Masingara with it. We returned at full speed and, by the time
we arrived, a large crowd had already gathered around a strange-
looking creature which was lying at their feet roped to a bamboo pole.

'It's alive,' muttered Mike Cable. Chris Sainsbury's cameras were already clicking as I handed the ten-Kina bill to the vicar, who assured me that this was Artrellia. Its dark green skin was flecked with yellow spots and its square head housed a set of needle-like teeth. The eyes twitched malevolently as it tried to squeeze itself out of the vines binding it to the pole, but the most impressive part of its anatomy was the claws. At the end of its short thick legs were enormous, black scimitars, quite out of proportion with the rest of its body. The tail was long and thin and twice the length of the body. I noticed the village dogs kept well away from the dying beast with its terrible talons. The mouth and tongue gave a red/yellow effect. 'Fire,' said the priest, and I saw at once how the legend had been started by the tongue darting in sunlight.

Ian pushed in the hypodermic and Artrellia passed quietly into death. As soon as it was safe to handle, measurements were taken. It was no dragon, but, even so, it was still a pretty fearsome looking specimen at just over six feet from head to tail. Once Ian had performed his postmortem, he was able to confirm that it was only a youngster which left plenty of room for speculation about what size an overgrown adult might reach. Meanwhile, a small patrol that had been keeping vigil beside a remote water hole, which we had been told was a favourite haunt of the creatures, came back with reports that they had seen several quite sizeable specimens coming to drink at night, but had been unable to get near enough to photograph them in the dark.

We did catch a glimpse of one monster with a head like a horse peering over a fallen log in the first light of day. Ian also made several sightings of pretty impressive adult lizards of lengths up to twelve feet, and from our specimen, we knew that Artrellia was indeed Salvador's Monitor (Varanus Salvadori), but no one had dreamed of the size to which these killers can grow. I was not surprised for in these little known tropical forests there are many tales of giant reptiles.

During our reconnaissance in 1978, we had come across a rather macabre, and well-documented story of an incident in Sulawesi. The *Indonesian Times* had reported that a farmer from Ongka Malino village at the foot of Mount Tinombala, Central Sulawesi, had been eaten by a twenty-foot python. The snake could not move because of its distended stomach. Monty, our own python, was thirteen feet long: I made a note to increase the accident insurance!

While the thought of coming face to face with a fifteen-foot lizard may be somewhat alarming, I doubt whether it would be quite so disconcerting as a run-in with an angry fifty-foot sperm whale, the most alarming experience I had during the entire expedition. It happened as I was aboard *Eye of the Wind*, after visiting our underwater team. A school of some forty whales was sighted, many of them leaping awesomely clear of the water, and we decided to get closer in order to film them. So, using an Avon, we approached to within thirty yards and, not wanting to disturb them, cut the engine. We got some excellent photos and were heading back to the ship when we saw three whales nearby and decided to get one last close-up. Frank Esson had volunteered to handle the engine. Now he shut it off and we paddled gently towards the leviathans. I was filming with my eight-millimetre cine which has a zoom lens, when I saw a gigantic tail rise out of the leaden sea, then fall and disappear with a great splash. Then, as I adjusted the zoom, a dorsal fin appeared, coming straight at us. 'Shall I start the engine?' asked Frank calmly. But I was concentrating on filming and, looking through the view-finder, felt strangely detached from the world around me. The dorsal fin came on. 'Shouldn't I start the engine?' shouted Frank, and, without waiting for an answer, he did. It was just as well because by now the bull whale's massive head was right beneath us and beginning to rise. The 'dorsal fin' was still fifty feet away. All we had seen was the fluke of its tail! Luckily the motor fired first time and we shot off its head and away, pursued for a short distance by the huge creature, its cavernous jaws and rows of molars rising in a ghastly scissor-like movement behind us. A second more and we would have been lifted out of the water and probably smashed to death by his tail. We were very happy to find ourselves back aboard *Eye of the Wind*, where the crew had enjoyed a grandstand view of the drama and thought it extremely funny.

On 22 January 1980 when our ship reached the island of Sulawesi, the advance party was already there and, thanks to an RAF airlift of stores from PNG, the base was ready. The pattern of our activities was different from the other land phases. Instead of being spread over a variety of unrelated projects, our efforts were concentrated almost exclusively on a single grand purpose: the preparation of a detailed and comprehensive management plan for the proposed nature reserve at Morowali. The inspiration for this came from ex-sapper John Blower, an old friend from Blue Nile days, who headed the National

Parks Development Project. He had drawn my attention to the fact that the Indonesian government had an enlightened attitude towards conservation and proposed to make five per cent of the country's entire land area into nature reserves and national parks. The one at Morowali was ready to go ahead as soon as the 2,000 square mile jungle wilderness in the southeast of the island had been surveyed and a proper plan produced, a daunting task, since the region was largely unmapped and unexplored. A project that promised to mix research, exploration and adventure in such a worthwhile way was very much in keeping with the SES's objectives. Furthermore Andrew Mitchell pointed out that Sulawesi was of paramount zoological interest since it lies on the Wallace Line, the watershed of animal life that separates Asia from Australia in the evolutionary process.

But I had foreseen that at this point I would need to spend time in London raising funds and planning ahead so, after consultations with John Blower and the Indonesian authorities, I asked Derek Jackson to lead the phase. All his logistic skills would be needed here.

Back in Room 5B Jim, George, Val, Beth and many others were labouring away, but we were all growing a little tired. Apart from the Drake work, I had an army job, rewriting the military 'bible', *Training for War*, which was somehow completed over the two years of the operation by my writing on planes and in every spare second. I wondered how many MOD authors had written about jungle warfare when actually sitting in one!

In the meantime, Judith and I had bought a charming sixteenth-century cottage in the village of Box, near Bath. 'The Old Dairy' was conveniently near the Royal School where Emma and Victoria were following in their mother's footsteps. I was sad that my supportive parents had now died, but although Lal and Tommie Sherman must have thought their daughter crazy to put up with the extraordinary lifestyle, they backed me to the hilt. It was as well because these were worrying times. Raising money was a nightmare and those at the front did not always appreciate that we simply did not have a crock of gold.

However, the Prince of Wales was elated by the success and was already encouraging us to do it all again! Indeed his enthusiasm, interest and help with the fund raising did much to keep us going. Michael Colborne, the Prince's secretary, was one of our greatest supporters and his quiet, sensible counsel was of enormous value.

*

Once the Sulawesi phase was completed successfully, we pressed on to Africa. When I first heard about the mysterious 'Lost World' of the Masai tribesmen that was supposed to exist at a volcanic crater less than thirty miles from Nairobi, I dismissed the idea with a cynical chuckle. I felt sure that somebody was trying to pull my leg. Either way, I was not about to announce a dramatic attempt to conquer the last remaining piece of unexplored territory in East Africa when the location was actually to be found within an easy Sunday afternoon drive of the Kenyan capital.

However, Gordon Davies of the Wildlife Planning Unit assured me that, although the outer crater of Susua was a popular spot, there was an inner crater that was far less accessible and within that was an unexplored plateau. 'I ought to know,' he said, 'I led the last expedition that tried and although we reached the top of the plateau, we were forced to turn back by the incredibly hard going and the lack of water. There was no way we could have gone any further. All other attempts have failed for the same reason. You'll need to build up stocks of water on the plateau or find some secret source if you're to explore it. Why don't you go and have a look for yourself – then you'll see the problem. It will be very useful to us if you can do it.' Gordon went on to tell me of strange lava caves that led outwards from the inner crater. It all sounded intriguing. If no one's been there, goodness knows what we might find, I thought, as I drove back to Nairobi.

As soon as I set eyes on the place, I understood exactly why it had remained so effectively cut off. It was a volcano within a volcano, but it was possible to get four-wheel-drive vehicles up inside the outer crater. However, a rocky and at times almost sheer-sided gorge, 1,000 feet across at its narrowest point and about 750 feet deep, separated the central uplifted raft of land from the rim of the inner crater like a gigantic dry moat of a huge castle. To get down into it and up the other side would require mountaineering techniques. On top of that, the terrain was murderous, jumbled lava rocks and boulders the size of houses, with treacherous crevasses in between, wicked thorn bushes that tear you to shreds if you are not careful and spear cactus with sharp, poison-bearing spikes, just like bayonets. And not a drop of surface water anywhere. A strange fact struck me. The central plateau and its moat was a mass of dark green vegetation, in stark contrast with the surrounding area, which was covered with thin yellow grass. Yet apart from the steam vents, the place was bone dry –

or was it? Was there some huge underground reservoir? Could this untrodden land hide some unknown species? An air recce revealed a strange conical feature on the southern side of the plateau that towered above the moat. On the summit were rocks, appearing unusually regular, which gave it the appearance of being man-made. We nicknamed it the 'Temple'. Could it be an ancient centre of ritual worship?

It was necessary to establish some kind of supply line across the gorge and the only feasible method of doing this was to rig up an aerial ropeway of tensioned steel wire on which a cable car could be suspended. But even if we could find a steel cable long enough, there was still the considerable problem of how to get it up there when there was at least a mile of boulder-strewn lava field between the point which Land-Rovers could reach and the edge of the crater. A 1,000-foot wire wound on a drum would weigh nearly a ton and it would be impossible to carry or roll over such rugged ground. Apart from that, I wondered how we were going to keep the advance party supplied with water once it started hacking its way across the plateau. In the kind of conditions and temperatures it would be encountering each man would require at least a gallon per day, maybe more, and there was no chance of it carrying sufficient quantities with it as it went.

After an air reconnaissance with our local chairman, John Sutton, we decided to go ahead. If it seemed like Mission Impossible, well, really tough challenges were just what we were supposed to be looking for. The Kenya Army could provide the explosives necessary to blast a path through the lava field along which we could roll the cable drum to the crater's edge, and to dig anchorages for the ropeway. Amongst our stores were cargo parachutes which could be used for water drops on the plateau from the Beaver aircraft which had been flown out to join us from Britain by veteran Army Air Corps pilots Mike Badger and Mike Somerton-Rayner, the Biggles Outfit as they were affectionately dubbed. As the preparations went ahead, including the setting up of a base camp, excitement and enthusiasm mounted. Gordon needed information on fauna, flora, water sources, caves, tracks, indeed everything there was to know to turn Susua into a unique wilderness reserve.

We decided to tackle the problem on two fronts: first there was to be the direct assault onto the central plateau across the moat. Later, we would explore the extensive lava tubes, a cave system close to the surface on the eastern side of the inner crater. I wondered if the strange long passages led up to the centre of the volcano.

There was a slight hiccup in our plans when the company supplying the cable confessed they had made a mistake and that the longest section they had was only 750 feet. However, Kenya Railways spliced two steel cables. John Leach, a highly experienced Warrant Officer in the Royal Engineers, took charge of the ropeway project and we dynamited a path through the lava, but it took a full ten-hour day of heaving, sweating and straining by our entire twenty-strong workforce to manhandle the heavy cable drum up to the edge of the crater. To make anchorages for either end of the ropeway, we blasted two narrow trenches, one each side of the gorge. In them we buried the trunks of cedar trees to act as anchors for the cable which had to be dragged by hand down into the moat and across to the other side before being tensioned. A team of the toughest YEs available helped John with this exhausting and potentially dangerous task. On one occasion the cable, which had become snagged, suddenly sprang free, hurling a youngster aside and catapulting another who was holding it fifteen feet into the air. Luckily he managed to hang on as the cable bounced him about above the rocks.

Everyone worked to get the stores and explosives over the moat; even our treasurer, ex-sapper John Hines, who was no spring chicken, was pressed into service. Barbara Martinelli, who had given up her holiday to rejoin the Operation, almost didn't go home when a football-sized boulder broke away from the top of the gorge and came crashing down the near-vertical slope. I heard a scream of 'Look out' and flattened myself against the side. Several small chippings struck my shoulders and with a crunch, crunch, crunch, a fifty-pound lump shot past a few inches from my face. To my horror, I saw it heading straight for Barbara, who was clinging to the fixed rope 100 feet beneath me. It was a miracle that it missed her.

Once the cable had been rigged and the first water cans and equipment were sent over on the little trolley, the exploration began. Through the long hot days, we toiled to hack a way forward across the plateau. The going was far worse than we'd imagined from our air recce. Huge chunks of rock lay scattered across the broken ground, covered in a sharp barnacle-like lichen that slashed fingers and knees. In between the giant boulders, the deep ravines caused more hardship and, everywhere, thorn trees and spear cactus threatened to catch the unwary. Once or twice we saw a much-feared death adder, one of

East Africa's most deadly serpents. 'Don't think much of this place – it's just like I imagine hell to be,' commented my Devon driver, Corporal Richardson, who compared everything with his native Exmoor.

Indeed, at times it was very like an inferno. We were over 6,000 feet above the sea and at night the temperature plummeted to frost level. At dawn we stood outside our tents sipping scalding tea and shivering, watching the steam vents on the plateau puffing their vapour into the clear air. Then, as the sun came up, the dry yellow grassland of the outer crater began to shimmer with heat and sweat pumped from our pores to stream down our bodies. Only the graceful movement of the giraffe to their feeding ground and the bobbing flight of the gazelle reminded us that this was Africa.

Our scientists spent the next two weeks carrying out a thorough survey of the flora and fauna on what Ian Redmond described as 'a unique ecological island'. Leaving the comfort of our base camp, the teams picked their way through the lava field, down into the moat and up onto the waterless plateau into a completely different world. The one fear that bothered me was that of a casualty on the plateau. How on earth can we get an injured man back to base, I thought. Thus, when Gordon Davies' son, Ben, went down with violent stomach pains and diarrhoea, I ordered up the strongest medicine we could get. The plateau was no place for an epidemic of the runs.

In the outer crater, there were scattered Masai villages where Barbara and Judith did their best to help with some first aid and medicine for the children. The people knew little about the plateau, for the Masai, courageous hunters that they were, would not go onto that land of spirits. We still wondered about the 'Temple' and each day brought our cutting teams nearer to it.

Our underground survey concentrated on the subterranean passages that had been created when the volcano erupted. The red-hot lava had spilled over and run down the mountainside. As the outside surface of this molten tide cooled and solidified, the inner core continued to flow, thereby creating hollow underground tubes that opened at intervals into large caverns. The network of passages, ranging in diameter from eighteen inches to thirty feet, was estimated to extend over five miles. Once used as a hideout by Mau Mau terrorists, there were now plans to turn them into a tourist attraction and it was with this in mind that some of the YEs helped local cave experts John Arkle and Jim Simon to survey and map the tunnel system.

John, an ex-soldier living in Mombasa, had one hair-raising experience when he and Jim penetrated far into the network. They had just wriggled their way through a long section of tunnel that was only eighteen inches high when they burst through into a large chamber. A shaft of sunlight was pouring through a small hole in the roof creating a pool of warmth on the floor of the cave in which was lying, fast asleep, an enormous fifteen-foot python. The two men tiptoed past and continued on their way up the next section of tunnel which turned out to be a dead end, and when they came back, the snake was nowhere to be seen. There was only one way it could have gone – down the eighteen-inch-high passage along which they had no option but to crawl. Their hearts were in their mouths as they inched forward, expecting to see at any moment the shadowy outline of the huge reptile rear up out of the gloom into the light cast by their lamps. In fact, they never did catch up with it, but John admits that the prospect of coming face to face with the huge serpent in such nightmarishly claustrophobic circumstances still makes his flesh crawl.

The system was an eerie place, full of strange shapes of solidified lava, some of these twisted like great ropes, others forming platforms at the sides of the passages and giving the tunnels an appearance of an underground railway station. Stalactites of lava hung from the roof on which musical notes could be rung. In one cavern we found the skeleton of a bull rhino. A gaping hole in the roof told the tale of its end and reminded us not to drive our Land-Rover carelessly through the bush above the passages. On another occasion, we discovered fresh leopard prints in the dust – going in, and we decided to go out!

Meanwhile, on the plateau the battle continued and flying low in the Beaver I saw something very odd. As Mike Badger swung the powerful plane over the cedar trees we came to a big clearing. We were looking for suitable parachute dropping zones and, as I glanced down, I saw an extraordinary animal. It was rather like an antelope, with a flash of white above the tail. My immediate reaction was to say 'waterbuck', but such a creature would hardly be likely to be living on a waterless plateau. Whatever, it was a biggish animal and it would need water. Later we were to discover other large mammals on the raft.

One day we came face to face with a group of approximately forty olive baboons on the track. Initially they showed no fear of us, probably because we were the first humans they had encountered. They appeared inquisitive and our yelling and shouting did nothing to make them move. Suddenly they seemed to feel threatened and two large males rushed at us with teeth bared. We had machetes, but no guns and the odds of getting away without injury were slim. Luckily, the two animals stopped short, and we decided not to push our chances and retreated back several hundred yards hoping that they would move along in their own time. We then tried throwing stones to scare them away, but soon discovered they could do this too! It was an hour before they moved off. In fact many of the female baboons acted in a strangely carnal manner towards us. Perhaps they thought we were rather attractive apes.

Hopes that the fiction of Conan Doyle's *Lost World* might come true with the discovery of weird and wonderful creatures, marooned there since pre-historic times, were not fulfilled. But the fact that there was a considerable amount of wildlife in this waterless zone was a puzzle in itself. The only source was from the steam vents, clearly visible at dawn, but later in the day, as the temperature rose, they were barely to be seen. However, early one morning as I rested atop a large boulder near one, my eye caught a movement below. A rock hyrax, a small rabbit-like creature with short ears, emerged from a crevice and crept up to a stone on the edge of the vent. Its nose twitching in the sulphur fumes, it began to lick up the condensed moisture. So smaller creatures could survive. But what about the large animals? While the survey path was cut, I began to seek for a pool, which I felt must be somewhere amongst the jumbled rock. However, Susua did not intend to give up her secrets easily and, after several abortive searches, I returned to base camp, battered, bruised and full of thorns. The mystery remains to be solved.

The most odd thing about the place was that whenever I was moving alone on the plateau I always had the feeling of being watched. I think it had something to do with the terrain, the huge rocks and boulders behind which it was easy to imagine all sorts of things lying in wait, and the many unexplained noises. It was quite common to hear a sudden crashing in the undergrowth without being able to see anything. The strangest noise of all was the ghostly whistling that was most noticeable at dusk. However, we discovered this came from the acacia trees that play host to a particular type of ant which nests in ball-like growths on the branches. These are full of holes made by the ants and wind blowing through them created the whistling.

It was desperately hard work to carry water forward from the head of the aerial ropeway. Using plastic sheets, we managed to collect a few pints of the precious liquid from the steam vents, but this was not nearly enough. However, by now, the Beaver was able to parachute water to us.

With the YEs to help him, Ian Redmond had been able to make several transects, noting the variety of animals and plants. The results were particularly interesting as the inner area of Susua has been effectively cut off from outside influences since it was created. After several weeks' back-breaking toil, these tough young people had blazed an eight-foot-wide trail for two miles from one side of the plateau to the other and up to its highest point at 6,850 feet where the Kenyan flag was ceremonially raised. Sadly the 'Temple' turned out to be a natural feature! Just a huge steam vent topped by unusual rectangular rocks, although it might easily have been used for Masai initiation rites. It then took three and a half hours to scramble back along the path that had been cleared, an indication of just how thick and impenetrable the virgin terrain had been.

Meanwhile our teams were excavating old Islamic ports under the direction of Mark Horton who still rushed about waving his arms. Around the great emerald Lake Turkana camel patrols were highly popular, whilst Ernie Durey of Darien fame built a magnificent 300–foot bridge at the Ark Lodge and we dug cattle dips and counted game from hot air balloons in the Masai Mara. Scientific studies were carried out in conjunction with the National Museums and everything was going rather well until tragically two YEs, Andrew Maara from Kenya and Richard Hopkins of Britain, died in separate motor accidents. For me this was a great sadness as I had always hoped to get through the venture without a fatal casualty, but alas the statistics were against us.

The Kenyan phase ended with a fascinating study of a giant cavern inside Mount Elgon, an extinct volcano on the Uganda border. It was said to be inhabited by elephants! Sixty years before, a farmer called Renshaw Mitford-Barbeton had entered Kitium Cave, and got a very nasty shock. Having edged cautiously through the wide, low letterbox-shaped entrance, he then penetrated right to the back of the 750-foot-deep cavern, crawling over fallen boulders, inching past narrow crevasses and skirting dark pools into which water dripped with echoing plops. It was as he prepared to make his way back out again that he suddenly realized with a start that he had company. He heard them long before he saw them, heavy, shuffling footsteps, a strange flapping noise, and some terrifying loud huffing and puffing. There was also a sound that seemed to him like the rumbling of giant stomachs. His mind boggled. Whoever or whatever they were, they had him trapped in the dead-end cave. He strained his eyes into the darkness beyond the range of his lamp and then gasped in amazement as he eventually managed to make out a group of huge shadowy forms in the gloom. It was a herd of elephants.

Mitford-Barbeton escaped unhurt when, after an hour that must have seemed to him like an eternity, the elephants left. However, we were to discover that his confrontation was no chance meeting, since the herds regularly visited the cave: they had beaten a well-worn path to the entrance. But why they should want to go out of their way to squeeze themselves into this one particularly inaccessible cavern had remained a mystery for many years – an even greater mystery than the legendary Elephants' Graveyard. Part of the problem was that it was impossible to see what they were doing in the darkness, and lights would scare them off and possibly start a stampede.

When Gordon Davies took John Sutton, Judith and me to Mount Elgon, we checked very carefully to see that the cave was uninhabited, and posted an armed game guard at the entrance. Following the beams of our head torches, we were soon deep underground when an appalling stench hit us. It was the unmistakable smell of decaying flesh and, on peering into a crevasse, we saw the cause. There, ten feet down, lay the putrefying carcass of a baby elephant which had stumbled to its death in the darkness. We pressed on, our lamps startling thousands of fruit bats that were hanging from the roof, so much so that they showered us with their droppings! Finally, we came to the pools, surrounded by recent elephant manure, and then we looked up and saw what attracted the great beasts.

All over the walls and roof were tusk marks – they had been mining salt. 'What an incredible story,' said John. 'Salt-mining elephants, it must be unique.' But it wasn't only elephants, for at much lower levels and in small side tunnels, I found the marks of wild pig, antelope and giant forest hog. Analysis of the minerals showed that it contained mirabilite, which has a mild purgative effect and probably helped the beasts' digestion. Clearly we were dealing with highly intelligent animals. Gordon felt that tourist viewing facilities could be provided by cutting a path up to the entrance and constructing an observation platform. We agreed to do this and carry out a survey of the cave itself to find out more about the frequency and duration of the elephants' visits. There was one thing about the cave of the elephants that still mystified me. I'd noted with an engineer's interest that the roof appeared to be supported by a single pillar, about twenty feet thick, but made of the same mineral salt as the walls. There were tusk marks on it, but very old ones. No fresh mining. Very strange, and it posed a question. Did the elephants, who after all are great engineers, know they must maintain this vital roof support, or was it pure chance? I like to think they did, for sadly some while later when a film team, encouraged by the SES, was making a documentary about Kitium, an earthquake collapsed the pillar and part of the roof fell in trapping an elephant. A very courageous Kenyan warden went inside and shot the crippled beast, risking bringing the entire roof down on top of himself.

By now *Eye of the Wind* was sailing north up the Red Sea or trying to against the most appalling head winds. John Hines, our tireless supporter, had gone ahead to Egypt to coordinate plans for a small task there and the Suez Canal transit. Unable to locate the vessel, he borrowed a MIG fighter from the Egyptian Air Force and roared past our flagship a few minutes later, but no one aboard deemed that 'our man in Cairo' was in it.

I was waiting for her at Alassio on Italy's Mediterranean coast, where she was to rendezvous with the Goodyear airship *Europa* and the Beaver for the last – and visually most spectacular – of our scientific projects. This was a unique experiment that involved taking simultaneous pollution samples from the sea and the air in and above the Gulf of Genoa, where the build-up of toxic trace metals in particular has been causing concern. The experiment, for which a sailing ship was perfectly suited since it would not itself add to the pollution, was to be carried out in cooperation with the UN Environment Programme as part of the Mediterranean Pollution Monitoring and Research Project.

Andrew, Barbara and I were to coordinate the experiment. The weather was appalling, but in the late afternoon the sky began to clear and I saw *Europa* approaching from the sea like an attacking zeppelin. The tubby silver 'cigar' looked really menacing as she flew low under the rain clouds and I felt that we were going back in time. The appearance of the high-winged Beaver, piloted by the two Mikes, added to this impression, and when dawn came, there, to complete the picture, was *Eye of the Wind* resting at anchor on a mirror-like sea 200 yards off the beach.

I felt slightly out of place standing there in desert uniform with a radio, whilst bikini-clad holiday-makers strolled by, but everything went like clockwork, even the weather turned out just the way we needed it for the four-day exercise, and it developed into a marvellously exciting international occasion.

We had thrilling moments too as the Beaver, with its leather helmeted crew, would seek the slow-flying *Europa* in the broken cumulus. Approaching from the south one afternoon, we saw the airship disappear into a bank of cloud some miles ahead and followed. 'Christ, where's she gone?' muttered Mike Somerton-Rayner as visibility dropped. The wings shuddered as he pushed through the cotton wool and then broke out. 'My God, she's turned back,' he yelled, pulling the Beaver's nose up and we roared over the great silver hull. In the cupola I saw Barbara's anxious face look up in surprise.

Our conferences in the hotel bar, our slightly luxurious 'base camp', were a hoot as the boffins of various nationalities discussed the research. 'Where do I find the Arno River?' asked Mike Badger at one briefing. 'You bomba da Italy alla de war and you ask now where is Arno . . .' exploded Professor Aristeo Renzoni of Siena.

On *Eye of the Wind* an oceanographer from the Saclant Research Centre at La Spezia studied temperature profiles across the Gulf using expendable bathythermographs, which relayed information from below the surface of the water to instruments aboard. Up above samples showed levels of atmospheric mercury contamination to be 280 times higher over Genoa than other non-industrial areas of the coastline. The airship proved a perfect craft for collecting the samples being able to float over potential pollution hotspots whilst special instruments 'sniffed' the air.

This brief episode was one of the highlights of Operation Drake. Everyone was struck by the great spirit of international cooperation, the tremendous energy which was put into coordinating a complex operation, and the feeling that something really worthwhile had been achieved. And there was a bonus in that the dramatic

newspaper and television pictures that flashed round the world
showing *Europa* hovering above *Eye of the Wind* gripped the public
imagination and did much to boost our image. The airship and the
brigantine even featured on the set of special stamps issued in Jersey
to commemorate the operation.

·On 13 December 1980 shortly before noon, *Eye of the Wind* passed
under Tower Bridge, with Kenyan Y E Mwingi Japan at the helm, to
mark the end of the great adventure. It was a wonderfully exciting
occasion for the tens of thousands who lined the banks of the river and
packed into St Katherine's Dock to witness the homecoming and a
very moving moment for the many youngsters from earlier phases
who had made the pilgrimage from as far away as New Zealand to be
in at the finish and to be reunited with the friends made during their
time with the expedition. As the ship covered the last few hundred
yards of the 36,000 miles she had logged altogether during her two
years away, Capital Radio's David Briggs broadcast a live commentary from a vantage point, halfway up the mainmast, while all
around him the crew lined the yardarms. A flotilla of small boats and
a fly-past by the Beaver and an R A F Hercules added an extra bit of
theatre and helped to ensure that the enterprise closed on a dramatic
note. At precisely 12.25 p.m. *Eye of the Wind* docked, to be greeted by
the Lord Mayor. It was all over.

For the Y Es who brought her home, the excitement was high to the
very end. After stopping off at Guernsey and Jersey, where thanks to
Adrian Troy's committee they were given a fantastic welcome, they
then encountered some of the worst weather of all, as a force eleven
gale blew up, and for six hours continuously the anemometer was off
the clock as the winds topped seventy m.p.h. However as our
Australian Chairman, rugby star Denis Cordner, who had made a
special flight to the Channel Islands to join the ship for the final leg,
said, 'I wouldn't have missed it for the world.'

My former C O, Brigadier Tony Landale, had organized the whole
of St Katherine's Dock into a massive exhibition with the ship at its
centre and it was here next day that Prince Charles came to meet the
young and our supporters. At the end our Patron said Operation
Drake was the sort of 'crazy expedition' that the British were
particularly good at organizing, and went on:

We have it somehow in our national make-up, the ability to
withstand with an amazing degree of good humour, the most

appalling conditions. The fact that on this occasion it was combined with scientific research and social projects showed the host countries that the British were keen on helping generally throughout the world. It can have done nothing but produce more good will and favourable reactions.

One of the elderly skilled craftsmen who serviced the ship was waiting to see me at Room 5B. 'It's about this 'ere invite,' he grumbled. 'You've asked me and the missus to meet the Prince of Wales.'

'Yes, of course,' I replied, 'I do hope you'll come.'

'But she's not my missus, we was never married,' he moaned.

'Well I'm sure . . .' I started to say.

'Oh no, that wouldn't do,' he chipped in, 'I'm going to take her out and marry her today.' And so he did, giving us one other little success for the venture!

FOURTEEN

Nothing Ventured,
Nothing Gained

NINETEEN-EIGHTY-ONE was not a happy year for Britain's inner cities. As dole queues lengthened the crowds of un-employed, frustrated and restless young grew and finally, on a warm summer's night, violence erupted on the streets. The police should not have been taken by surprise, for many of us associated with youth had warned of the explosive situation. At Prince Charles' suggestion Sergeant Major David Taylor and I had spent an evening with the Rastafarians in Wandsworth.

'You from the Fuzz?' hissed a dread-locked West Indian.

'These guys is in the Army,' said his pal.

'What you do there?' spat the questioner, pushing his face closer to mine.

'We kill people,' said the Sergeant Major quietly.

There was a short pause then a roar of laughter, 'Why man, that's great – have a drink.'

Then they told us a long tale of strained race relations and inter-tribal strife. When I suggested they go to Kingston-on-Thames for a job with British Aerospace, I was regarded as an idiot. 'You'd never get back to Wandsworth with your pay packet. You got to pass right through Red Tigers or the Black Hand,' they confided. Indeed, it seemed parts of Britain were becoming rather like PNG.

General Mogg passed our report to the Home Secretary but, by the time it was acknowledged, Brixton, St Paul's, Bristol, and Toxteth were burning. Many former YEs now involved in youth work did their best to restore peace, but the scars of that terrible summer were deep.

It was a Friday afternoon when the Director of Army Training rang me. 'John, what do you know of the proposal for a Youth Adventure Training Unit?' he enquired.

This was a paper exercise being carried out at the insistence of the Government, desperately seeking a solution to urban unrest. Like so many plans that circulate in Whitehall, it would be considered and later scrapped. The staff, with their long experience of fatuous ideas, had not taken it too seriously. 'Well, General, I believe it's a plan to take young civilians off the city streets and give them a new direction in life through a few weeks' outdoor activities under military experts,' I said, glad that I could recall the brief, and added, 'Frankly, it's unworkable.'

My boss raised his eyebrows. 'Well, maybe you can do something with it, because you are going to command this outfit. The Secretary of State, Mr John Nott, will see you on Monday. Have a good weekend.'

I rushed back to the office and shouted, 'No one goes home, meeting in ten minutes. Margot, get the files on that ruddy Army Youth Scheme,' and we got down to work. On Monday the Secretary of State smiled hesitantly. 'It's terribly important that this should succeed. If there is anything you need, just ask, you will be backed to the hilt.'

'How is all this to be paid for?' I enquired.

John Nott, like all cautious politicians, considered his answer carefully. 'Let the costs lie where they fall,' he said, and I repeated this to everyone who asked me. I was not over-pleased to be given command of this new enterprise. Nevertheless, I was determined to make the best of what seemed to be an impossible task to achieve in one year.

So it was that I took over the massive eighteenth-century Fort George near Inverness. It had been built after the last battle on British soil to keep the rebellious Scots in order. It seemed appropriate and was convenient to the Highlands for some really tough exercises. Recruiting 180 of the Army's top adventure trainers and assembling a fleet of vehicles, plus our dear old Beaver, I moved north with Judith and Max, the labrador.

The Fort George Volunteers, as we were named, took as their motto 'Nothing ventured, nothing gained'. When the doors opened in May 1982 and the first of 2,500 teenagers trooped in, the paint was still wet.

At once the Prince of Wales took an interest as did the press. We quickly became a political hot potato. However, I had Chris Sainsbury and several of the Drake team to help, plus an energetic new PA named Sally Harris, who typed like a machine gun. To my surprise the scheme was a success, and I learnt much about the needs of modern youth. I saw that the longer people were unemployed, the longer they were likely to remain so. It was a frightening statistic that in 1983 there were over 7.5 million Britons aged between seventeen and twenty-four and, of these, some 1.2 million were without work. Not only did they lack jobs, they were without any direction to their lives and, it seemed, any will to find one. Was this a product of the swinging sixties? Old values were being questioned, youngsters were reared with looser family ties, and parental discipline had slackened. Perhaps the sixties had swung too far. At Fort George the young showed they wanted challenges and inspiration, and during each group's two-week stay at that bleak establishment I saw a great change in them.

To help keep the Highlands tidy we got the volunteers to collect rubbish wherever they went and especially on the summit of Ben Nevis, Britain's highest peak. Never having climbed the mountain myself, I took Judith and Max to inspect the clean-up. There is an old pony track and normally it is possible to walk up. However, on this particular day, heavy snow had fallen and white-out conditions were setting in. Our rescue team was positioned halfway up and here I met one of the instructors.

'We've called the young off,' he said, 'getting a little tricky on top, but if you'd like to go on, Colonel, I'll come with you.'

On the pony track we exchanged greetings with four elderly gentlemen clad in heavy anoraks. A gale was blowing as we neared the summit but, to my horror, I saw a plastic bag with its contents spilling over the fresh snow. 'The little swine,' I roared into the wind, 'we sent them to clean up and they chuck their rations all over the place. Is it muesli or porridge?' I asked, as we tasted it.

'I'm not sure,' replied the instructor, 'seems a bit gritty.' Max sniffed it, but it was not to his liking. So I scooped up the mess and carried it home. Later, when we saw the rescue team again, they asked if we'd met the four gentlemen on the hill. I nodded.

'Did they tell you what they'd been doing?' asked the Sergeant. He went on, 'You see their father was a famous mountaineer in these parts; he died last week and they had been up to scatter his ashes.'

'If he tasted all right, he must of been a Gordon,' commented RSM MacDonald on our return to the Fort.

One cannot live in the Highlands without being aware of Nessie or the Loch Ness Monster. A few years before, when planning an army exercise, I had gone to Loch Morar and while I was attempting to rent a field for the base had met some extraordinary folk.

The air in the bar was heavy with tobacco smoke and the delightful aroma of malt whisky as we stood in a corner watching the dying sun sinking behind the Island of Rhum. 'Excuse me one moment,' said Adrian Shine through his dense red beard, as a thin man with a ruddy, weather-beaten face touched him on the sleeve. Tim Dinsdale, Corporal Thomas and I continued our conversation whilst Adrian talked intently with the newcomer at the other end of the room. A few moments later, our bearded friend returned and, with suitably furtive glances, spoke in a low voice. 'There's been a sighting,' he said, adding quickly, 'this afternoon – near the Chapel.'

I was faintly amused and they sensed it. 'I expect you think we've set this up especially for you,' said Tim, but I could tell from his expression that he hadn't and I felt that these people were deadly earnest and quite sincere. Already I knew that the Loch Morar Expedition was a serious attempt to solve one of the world's greatest mysteries and that this group of engineers and scientists were not the sort of people to gamble their meagre resources on something which they thought was a hoax or a myth.

'This man lives beside the loch not far from here,' said Adrian, a tinge of excitement in his voice. 'Apparently, his wife and her children watched a big hump moving about for several hours this afternoon, and he's agreed to allow us to question them.'

Although the hour was late, it was still daylight in this remote corner of the West Highlands and we set off at once for their lonely cottage. The lady who opened the door was worried and nervous, and welcomed us as if ushering in guests to a funeral. Her children sat or stood in the parlour where a low fire glowed in the hearth. They seemed stunned and overawed, but tea and cake were produced, and then expert monster investigator Tim Dinsdale and the expedition leader, Adrian, began their questioning.

The woman told her story, quite firmly and without a trace of emotion. She had been gardening in front of the cottage at about 2 p.m.; it was a fine clear day and the surface of the loch, some 200 yards away, was still. Suddenly, she heard a splash and, imagining it to be wild duck alighting, looked up, but what she saw left her speechless and clutching the hoe for support. About 200 yards out into Loch Morar, and therefore around 400 yards from her, was a great dark hump. 'So high it looked,' she said, indicating with her hand a vertical distance of about three feet. Then, full of fear, she did what every mother would do – called out to her children. They came running and saw it; the girls ran behind the house in terror, but the little boy, a tough lad, whom I guessed to be about twelve, seized a garden fork and raced to the shore. However, whatever it was took no notice of them. The amazing part of the story was how for almost three hours the thing submerged, surfaced, and darted hither and thither 'as if it were trying to catch fish'. Eventually it headed off up the loch leaving a big wake.

Tim questioned her with great tact, but with an insistence on detail. She'd lived there for fourteen years and had never seen anything like this before. The frightened woman knew the difference between salmon leaping, otters playing, ducks landing, floating logs, patches of weed and upturned boats. This bore no resemblance to any of these. She kept saying 'It was just like a whale.'

'How do you know what a whale looks like?' asked Tim.

'Because I'm the daughter of a fisherman,' was the instant reply.

Tim made her repeat the story – but her recall was faultless and except for one or two dimensions, her son's description confirmed it in every detail.

Sitting in the old armchair in the corner of that small sitting-room, I had no part in the proceedings, but was fascinated. When we arrived, the woman had asked us all what we did and made us swear that none of us was from the press. The thought of any publicity was totally abhorrent to her. This I learned later was because of a local superstition that says Morag, as Nessie's cousin, the Loch Morar monster, is known, was the harbinger of death, and this was confirmed by the sinking of HMS *Hood* during World War II, with many local men in her crew. It was said that on that fateful day, Morag had been seen rising from the dark peat-stained waters. Ever since then, its appearance has been regarded as an omen of ill fortune.

It was midnight when Tim switched off his tape recorder and we all stood up, thanked the woman and her family for their kindness and patience and strolled out into the twilight. In June, darkness only lasts for an hour or two this far north. The surface of the loch was still, nothing moved, there was not even a ripple.

How on earth could so large a beast inhabit a few square miles of water and remain unknown to science? But I had seen people interrogated and I knew that liars usually have a motive. I could see no reason for these simple folk to lie and I was quite convinced that they had been describing accurately whatever it was they'd seen. Many explorers claim that it's curiosity that drives them on, and I feel that this is an important motivating force in my life. Thus this mystery has always intrigued me. Later I discussed it at length with a fervent believer, Sir Peter Scott, and Adrian Shine, who had already made an important advance by establishing the existence of a food chain in the Loch, perhaps sufficient to support a large beast. The SES has always tried to support serious investigations, so I called my friend at Goodyear, Phyllis Angliss, who soon earned the nickname of 'Philatelic Phyllis' by marketing hundreds of special covers bearing the airship stamp of the Jersey Drake set to help fund the expedition.

By the time *Europa* appeared over Inverness Airport, a whole series of experiments had been organized. The youngsters of the Fort George Volunteers were delighted with the idea of a spot of monster-hunting from an airship, and we had assembled an impressive array of scientists. Adrian brought his 1907 Humber sailing barge to do sonar surveys, whilst Chris Sainsbury came along to film it and eccentric artist Bob Williamson produced a 1930 Puss Moth monoplane.

The weather looked promising on 2 June as *Europa* came obediently to her mast at Dalcross. Broadly speaking, the programme was to do two flights a day, dividing the time between the scientific research and surveillance over Loch Ness. As I knew from Alassio, airship flying is the perfect way to travel. The great bulbous creatures are relatively quiet; there's plenty of room in the cabin and not even seat-belts to restrict you. Visibility is marvellous and if you want extra air, just open a window. With a top speed of around fifty m.p.h. *Europa* usually cruised at thirty m.p.h. Although she could climb to 8,500 feet, the pilots preferred to operate under 3,000. She could cover 500 miles without landing, but as there's no lavatory aboard, you'd be pretty cross-legged by then!

As part of the scientific studies, the dispersal of sewage from Inverness into the Beauly Firth was studied by the Highland River Purification Board, who had red dye poured into the outfall, and then flying in the airship we photographed its movement on the ebb and flood tide. To us laymen, it seemed to show that it all flowed back to

Inverness when the tide turned! 'Good for the salmon,' commented
Chris, who was filming the experiment from Bob's Puss Moth.

Other scientists experimented with some very sensitive photographic and video equipment fitted on *Europa* and, clambering into
the eight-seat cabin of the massive craft, I sat up front with Enzo, the
pilot, whom I'd flown with in Italy. We pushed the aerial of the Army
radio out through the open window so I could talk to my mobile HQ
and also to Adrian on his barge.

Richard Snailham took the cine camera and climbed in next with
the scientists and their heat scanner. There was just time to brief the
team on their areas of observation before we slipped gently from the
mast and, with our engines ticking over, were walked to the take-off
position. Then, with an effortless roar, the twin engines pushed us up
at a steep angle into the blue sky.

We rose majestically and headed for Loch Ness. The engines,
sounding like a well-tuned motorcycle, purred away astern. We
approached the pewter water of the loch and moved down to
rendezvous with the sonar barge. The familiar sight of Urquhart
Castle, the sun lighting up its crumbled ramparts, appeared ahead.
Several motor coaches had brought dozens of tourists to swarm over
the ruin. 'They've got a bonus today,' said Richard.

The barge was already on station and, as we circled, Adrian opened
the throttle and began to creep along below us. Down in the spacious
hold, the scientists and operators scanned the screens as the sonar
probed the depths. In the half light, the steady stream of red, yellow
and green blips passed by like a slow-moving rainbow. Once, a tremor
of excitement went through the crew as a huge blip appeared. 'Side
echo,' muttered Adrian, ignoring it and scanning on. Above in
Europa we all longed to see a long, dark, leathery neck, or a massive
hump emerge dramatically from the surface – but nothing happened
and our joint patrol continued. Several times, we dived down to
examine unusual shapes in the water, but they were just sediment.

'High wind is bad for us,' said Enzo, as he swung the great silver
craft around over Fort Augustus and headed home up loch into the
freshening breeze. With engines droning, the airship slid over the
rippling waters 500 feet below, but by the time the white-walled
cottages of Dores appeared on our port bow, the wind had gone and as
we began to climb over the Caledonian Canal, we saw trouble ahead.
Beyond the swaying mooring lines that dangled from our nose, was a
rising grey wall stretching from the tree tops into the sky, a bank of

mist rolling in from the North Sea, brought by the easterly breeze. I could see from Enzo's expression that he was none too happy. Behind me, Richard looked up from his notes and raised an eyebrow; the scientists peered out into the swirling cotton wool as the mist began to envelop us and the engine note changed as we slowed. Enzo pulled the vertical elevator wheel back and the mooring lines swung in to meet us as our bulbous nose rose. The *Europa* was probing forward through the dense banks of fog at a few miles an hour. Our radio was dead; we were too far from control and Inverness Airport was now closed, but we could just hear Goodyear's base station as Enzo searched for the landing ground.

It's a weird feeling to fly in mist in an airship. With windows open and the billowing vapour drifting past, I quite expected to hear a fog horn. Suddenly, to my amazement, we were level with a seagull, which overtook this monster of the skies and flew on unconcerned. 'I believe we're over the Moray Firth,' said the pilot and we dropped lower until a patch of dark green conifer forest showed briefly below. Even the trees were wreathed in white mist. 'Blimey – it's down to ground level,' muttered someone. Navigating by beacon, we knew that the airfield must be near and so we crawled forward, a few hundred feet above Inverness-shire.

We were almost on the field, when the cloud base lifted a little and we saw the grass-edged runways. Enzo heaved the great wheel forward and our nose dipped towards the red-and-white mooring mast. Already, the ground crew was running through the long grass to seize the bow lines and guide us to the coupling. The engines gave one last triumphant roar and died. 'Phew,' said Richard. 'Quite exciting, yes?' said Enzo.

The next day was to be our last and Nessie had coyly refused to be enticed to the surface, or even within sonar range.

At 1455 hours on 7 June, I was manning our control radio in bright sunshine at Urquhart Castle, whilst *Europa* made her final sweep up the loch above the barge. It was a warm afternoon. Sally Harris had produced a good bottle of cold white wine for lunch and I was feeling that, even if we didn't see Nessie, it had been an enjoyable little expedition. Suddenly, I heard Adrian's voice in my headphones. 'Hello Zero, this is One – Contact. Over.'

'They've got a sonar target,' I yelled to Chris, whose cine camera was in action nearby. Already, a steady stream of bearings was being sent out from the barge to the airship. We could hear the higher revs of *Europa*'s engines as she closed rapidly with the barge.

By now, we could see the airship and the barge together about a mile southwest of the Castle. The huge silver craft hovered 250 feet up, just ahead of the barge. Tim Dinsdale was on the edge of his seat, peering down, but he knew from an experiment we'd made with a submerged dustbin lid that whatever it was would have to be within ten feet of the surface to be visible. In the twilight below decks the signallers tried to hold the contact in the sonar's beam. 'It was like chasing a bat on a dark night with a flashlight,' they said. For thirty minutes they kept it there, whilst it moved around the barge in a 300-yard diameter circle and, at one time, Adrian got his vessel within sixty-six yards. The horizontal display showed the target to be between forty and fifty feet below the surface, then it disappeared out of range just as suddenly as it had come. Tim saw nothing, which at least showed it wasn't a huge bubble of gas, or a decomposing log rising from the loch bed.

We were elated, and Adrian went on to get a total of thirteen major sonar contacts that year but the expedition taught us a great deal about Nessie-hunting, and we were greatly encouraged by the results. I feel that this is a very complex problem; however, by bringing together leading experts and the latest scientific techniques and equipment, we'd made an important advance. I firmly believe there is a case to answer at Loch Ness and not all those who claim to have seen something strange there can be branded as liars or alcoholics.

After the airship had departed, the *Daily Star* telephoned to ask if we'd like to try a hot-air balloon over the loch. Adrian and I had talked about this as a possible aerial observation post and I was delighted to give it a try. Greenall Whitley, a well-known brewery, kindly lent two balloons and we prepared to make the first such crossing of Loch Ness. It was all a bit of a spoof but the volunteers had some tethered flights and it would be interesting to see how powerless aircraft got on over the loch. The plan was for the wind from the north to take us out over Castle Urquhart when we should pick up the southwest breeze to blow us along the water to the eastern end of the loch.

At dawn a cheer went up as we ascended, a union jack fluttering from the basket. It was rather like rising in a lift. Beneath I saw Mike Gambier running after us waving his arms and shouting. The chase

Land-Rover keys were in my pocket! But I tied them to my handkerchief and dropped them into a huge gorse bush. Mike muttered a
dreadful oath. There was hardly a breath of wind as our propane gas
burners sent their fiery blast into the envelope and it took twenty
minutes for us to cover the two miles across the water. To demonstrate the control that was possible, our pilot touched down in mid-
loch and we drifted along on the surface of the water for a few
minutes before rising up again. 'How about the southwest wind?' I
enquired.

The pilot looked anxious. 'There doesn't seem to be any,' he
confessed, 'and we have not enough gas to get us over the mountain.'

We were drifting quite fast into some pretty inhospitable-looking
hills and so we returned to the water again to get Adrian to tow us a
short distance with a launch. When he released us we were opposite
a convenient clearing. However, as we cleared the low fir trees beside
a road we needed help on the ground and I threw down the drag rope
and shouted at a small tent that shared the clearing with a camper
wagon. 'Could you grab our line, please?' The tent flap opened and an
attractive, scantily dressed French girl stepped out and looked round
to see where the voice had come from. For a moment she saw nothing.
In the meantime, a rather older Scotsman in loosely tied striped
pyjamas had emerged from the camper, rubbing his eyes and then
they both saw our balloon and ran to take the dangling rope. At this
point, striped pyjamas' wife, in nightie and curlers, stuck her head
out of the camper window, failed to see us but found her beloved
jumping about with a lightly clad blonde. French boyfriend then
crawled out of the tent and, still on hands and knees, gaped in
astonishment at the unbelievable scene. A nasty international
incident was only avoided by the necessity for all to pull like mad to
get us down safely. Suddenly the girl seemed to remember she was
topless and let go, whereupon the balloon rose again lifting the
Scotsman up with it. 'Hold on,' I yelled and they all pulled again. This
time we landed and the balloon started to collapse across the small
country road. At that moment a milk float rounded the bend and in its
effort to avoid 'Greenall Whitley Beer' went into the ditch. The press
whose own balloon had landed rather more successfully nearby
appeared and I left the scene of devastation as quickly as possible.

In spite of the Falkland war our support did not dry up and the Fort
George scheme was indeed a great success. When the enterprise
ended, I was asked to find a number of volunteers to be interviewed by

the London press; amazingly, I couldn't find any in London who were still unemployed. Eventually a few took time off work to be interviewed, and one point was made by nearly all of them: they said they'd got jobs because of the self-confidence gained on the course.

As I had tramped the Highlands with the volunteers I had time to reflect on the lessons learned from Operation Drake. Some of the youngsters had been disappointed that their expedition was not as vigorous as the selection process, but clearly it would have been impractical, and also unfair on the slightly less aggressively daring souls, to turn every activity into a make-or-break challenge. The YEs had ranged from hard-bitten Zimbabweans fresh from fighting in the guerrilla war to teenage English secretaries who had never been away from home, so it was impossible to please everyone all the time. However, the maturity and capabilities of many did surprise me and, with the wisdom of hindsight, I regret that we were not able to give them more responsibility. The older ones, certainly, could have coped very happily with it. Furthermore, they objected to being called 'Young' explorers – only those over thirty want to be called young! Only one homesick youngster out of 414 gave up!

From the point of view of communications I owed a great deal to the Royal Signals and the companies who loaned the sets. I do not believe that any expedition has ever had such widespread links that worked so well under such adverse circumstances. To carry a briefcase-size radio, operating on a rechargeable dry battery with an aerial that one simply threw into a tree, and know that wherever we were one could usually speak to Room 5B, was very comforting.

I was also pleasantly astonished by the number of scientific discoveries. Even in my most wildly optimistic moments I had never anticipated that there would be so many important breakthroughs in zoology, biology and archaeology. It just goes to show what you can do when you have a lot of highly motivated young people with good eyes and strong legs. However, we had often needed field laboratories.

The gloomy atmosphere of 5B was not conducive to inspired and efficient work, and yet our team which led a mole-like existence in the cellar soldiered on superbly. They were the ones who had to deal with the crises, absorb the bad news and fight the endless, desperate battle for funds without seeing much of the fun at the front end. Inevitably, the strain sometimes showed and I often noticed, when in the field and on top of the world because things were going well, how glum the voices sounded over the radio from Whitehall. Their only consolation was the satisfaction of knowing that without them none of it could have happened. We could have done with a few more expert sailors at HQ. I do not think that those of us on land really understood all the problems faced by the flagship and, equally, I suspect that Mike Kichenside did not really appreciate just how difficult things were when viewed from the dungeon. Perhaps Prince Charles was thinking of the fund raising when he summed up expeditions as being like banging one's head against a brick wall –and that is as true for the organizers as it is for those taking part.

In November 1979 I was based in Papua New Guinea. The rain had stopped but the heavy night air was no cooler. As I walked up the steps of our wooden office, the radio operator was scribbling messages that crackled through from England. He looked up as I entered. 'George Thurston's on, says he'd like to speak to you.'

Slipping on the earphones, I heard George's distant voice.

Never a man to waste words, he came straight to the point. 'I had breakfast with our Patron this morning.'

'Good Lord,' I said, 'have we done something terrible?'

'Far from it. The Prince is rather pleased with progress and thinks we should do it all again – on a bigger scale.'

I took a deep breath and sat down.

Later that night, sitting on the verandah with my old schoolfriend, Nigel Porteous, over a Scotch, I told him of the message.

He said, 'Well, you'll need a bigger, faster ship.'

I listened intently while Nigel, a master mariner, put forward his ideas for a larger scale operation with a motor vessel as its flagship.

Drake, Sir Walter Raleigh's cousin, had been a fiercely nationalistic privateer. Raleigh was more of an internationalist, who tried to settle a society in a New World. It was felt that the new expedition should be named after him and, by starting in 1984, it would commemorate the 400th anniversary of the founding of English-speaking America in what is now North Carolina. Prince Charles liked the name, so Operation Raleigh it was, and with the Prince as Patron, the new and greater machine ground into action.

The aim was, quite simply, to develop leadership potential in young people through their experience of the expeditions. Our hope was that they would return home to give service to others. Having witnessed the inner city riots, it was clear to me that young leaders had a far better chance of communicating with the underprivileged than older counsellors or the police. Each venturer, as the youngsters came to be called, would spend approximately three months in the field. Weather charts dictated that we should go west and an invitation from Sir Jack Hayward to visit the Bahamas for our first expedition proved irresistible. But our first port-of-call would be in New York and on to the very site where Raleigh's colonists had landed in 1584, then south to the Caribbean, Central and South America before crossing the Pacific to Australasia.

The scientists were fascinated by what Indonesia had had to offer and we wanted to break new ground in Japan and Tibet. There were also interesting possibilities in Pakistan. Africa, of course, could not be missed from the route of any worldwide expedition, and after that we planned to spend time in South America before returning to Britain five years later, via the wastes of Arctic Canada.

Before anything could be set in motion we needed considerable financial backing. Once again our good friend Walter Annenberg stepped into the breach and provided the necessary seed money. The next essential was a dedicated, hardworking staff that could not expect much remuneration, and a team of experts to advise us on setting up an international venture. Thanks to the generosity of IBM, a giant computer was installed in the London HQ to pro-gramme finance, logistics and venturer selection.

A worldwide recruiting and selection system was set up to find young people, aged between seventeen and twenty-five, who were fit, compatible, spoke English (for safety reasons) and could swim well. They also needed to have leadership abilities and a willingness to place service to others before self. We planned to select 4,000 venturers. There was a danger that Raleigh might become an expedition for the elite and, to offset this, our selection procedure in Britain was consciously designed to help the less privileged, who lacked only the opportunity to reach their potential. As on Operation Drake this process included an interview and, for the finalists, a weekend in the wilderness where they were put through their paces under adverse conditions.

Publicizing Operation Raleigh in Britain began with a special television programme in which Prince Charles interviewed three ex-members of Operation Drake. His Royal Highness then called for volunteers. Candidates were advised to apply to any branch of the

Trustee Savings Bank, the only bank with branches in every part of the United Kingdom.

As with any non-profit-making organization, fund-raising was vital to our success. Although our commercial director, David King, and his friends in the City were striving to raise as much sponsorship as possible, the venturers themselves would help to fund the expedition. We calculated that if 4,000 young people brought in $5000 each, the expedition would have $20 million to spend over four years.

Applications poured in and the selection process went into full swing. Once again, eager youngsters faced the giant python in darkened rooms, handled hairy tarantulas and were made wet, cold, hungry, frightened and furious by turns so that we could discover just how well they would get on together. We also found many large companies prepared to send employees with us as part of their personal development policy.

Two vessels were acquired to support the enterprise. Our search for a sail training ship led us to discover the brigantine *Zebu*. She had begun life in a small, busy Swedish shipyard in 1938 and spent the next thirty-five years carrying cargoes across the Baltic. During World War II she smuggled arms for resistance movements and refugees. In 1980 she had foundered in a severe storm in the Channel Islands and then a young couple, Nick and Jane Broughton, bought her and *Zebu*'s new life began. We found our support ship in Hull. A 1,900-tonne former factory vessel, built in West Germany in 1965, she had been converted into a North Sea oil exploration vessel, equipped with submersibles. She still retained the distinctive features of a stern trawler and the massive A-frame across her after-deck, originally used to haul nets up a sloping stern ramp, could lift mini-subs. Her cavernous hold could stock expedition supplies and the former submarine base could be converted to house landing craft. Owned by J. Marr & Sons of Hull, it was Hull City Council and the Department of the Environment who bought her for us. Her new name became *Sir Walter Raleigh* or *SWR* for short. Many companies offered to help equip her and a refit committee was formed in Hull under the driving force of Councillor Jim Mulgrove. The people of the city soon took the ship to their hearts, no one more so than Alan Marr, the enthusiastic Chairman of J. Marr & Sons. I invited Mike Kichenside to join us again and captain the ship.

As the United States committee had been allocated forty per cent of the venturer places, I paid particular attention to their problems. The determination and persistence of Ann Smith and Mark Bensen in North Carolina held Operation Raleigh USA together, and around the globe other marvellous friends gave up their time to help. On the operational front we were desperately short of qualified staff. Encouraged by the Prince of Wales, the US Defence Secretary, Caspar Weinberger, kindly agreed to second members of the American armed forces. Australia, New Zealand, Panama and Portugal followed suit.

In January 1984 the Prime Minister, The Rt. Hon. Margaret Thatcher, was our guest of honour at a luncheon organized by David King. Mrs Thatcher and her husband, Denis, became keen supporters. It was thanks to Denis Thatcher's powers of persuasion that many oil companies helped finance the running costs of the flagship. Whilst David worked flat out at the fund raising, I concentrated on expedition planning and logistics. The lights in our HQ, now at London's St Katherine's Dock, were rarely out.

There were local difficulties in approaching the proposed host countries for various projects. All the liaison and reconnaissance teams who toured the world did sterling work but I found that, in dealing with the US in particular, the greatest difficulty was getting the inhabitants of one state to cooperate with those of another.

I made many visits to Texas where Prince Charles had played polo and sown the seeds of the idea for Operation Raleigh. On one trip I arrived to be given complimentary accommodation in a luxury downtown hotel. I had been flying all day and was tired. The thought of dinner with thirty guests was distracting, so, as I was ushered to my penthouse suite by the proud manager, it was not easy to demonstrate an appropriate amount of enthusiasm. He rushed about singing the praises of the hifi, the TV, the fridge full of champagne, the four-poster bed and other accessories that added up, had I been paying it, to $400 per night. Finally came the tour of the bathroom, by which time I was barely awake. The taps were golden and there was even a golden razor; but the only device that really intrigued me appeared to be called the 'gazooza'. Finally the manager backed out, smiling. I was left with the four-poster bed, the champagne, the fruit and the 'gazooza'.

Now cursing the forthcoming dinner, I undressed and was heading for the shower when I decided that the 'gazooza' might make an interesting alternative. Bottles of perfumed bath essence were at hand and, vaguely remembering the manager's instructions, I climbed into the empty bath and anointed myself with one of these pungent preparations. It seemed the next move was to turn on a golden tap on the wall, which I did. There was a few seconds' delay, during which time I gazed about in anticipation. I didn't have long to wait. Without warning, jets of icy cold water erupted from at least six points, some of which unfortunately were directly beneath me. Immediately the bath oil, with which I was covered, produced a swirling mass of bubbles. Unable to withstand one particular jet that was giving me an involuntary enema, I tried to escape only to be struck in the face by another geyser. The water was now painfully hot and the steam level had increased to such a degree that I could no longer find any means to turn the confounded thing off. By a Herculean effort I slithered over the edge of the bath but attempts at standing were thwarted by the bath oil, and I fell flat on my back. Whilst lying winded in this ridiculous posture, I perceived a charming black maid in her sixties peering at me through the steam.

'You gotta problem, sir?' she enquired.

'Turn the bloody thing off, please!' I cried.

By now the entire room was one gigantic bubble bath and I was slipping and sliding around the floor like a stranded sea lion. The maid calmly pressed a well concealed button and handed me a towel. I glanced at my watch and realized that within ten minutes I had to be making a major speech to an elite Houston audience. As I muttered some heartfelt thanks my heroine left, saying 'Yessir, those jacuzzi can be mighty dangerous – you'd never get me in one.' James Bond films thrive on such scenes.

Whilst raising support in Australia David King and I visited many schools. At Scotch College in Perth we were accommodated in a room off a boys' dormitory, the pupils all being on holiday. Following a splendid dinner with the headmaster, we returned to our quarters and I tried to make a credit card call on a school phone to Britain. It was imperative that I get through but the telephone had no number on it and although I was using a valid credit card, the operator simply refused to connect me unless I gave her the number from which I was speaking. In desperation I cried, 'What would you do in a real emergency, suppose an airliner dropped on this place?' After several minutes' pleading and explaining who I was and that I must speak to the Ministry of Defence in London, she very reluctantly connected me.

Back in the room, David was already in bed when I returned ranting about the Australian telephone system. I was about to turn out the light when the door burst open and the room filled with burly policemen. Seeing two middle-aged gentlemen tucked up in the boys' room, they looked rather surprised.

'Well now,' said a bull of a sergeant who was carrying a shotgun. 'Which one of you lovely geezers claims he's Colonel John Blashford-Snell?'

'That's me,' I retorted.

'I suppose you have an MOD Identity Card by chance,' he rasped sarcastically. I produced it and he looked perplexed. 'Blimey,' he said to his colleague, 'I do believe it is him. And who is this then?' he asked pointing at David, who passed an impressive little blue folder over.

'Superintendent King, Interpol,' he stammered.

'Gentlemen, I'm very sorry to bother you. There seems to be some misunderstanding,' and they were gone.

'The old card comes in useful sometimes,' yawned David, who had indeed been a police officer. Next day we learned a lunatic was at large in Perth and had murdered several people. He often disguised himself as a serviceman! The telephone operator had alerted the police. I wonder what on earth the Australian coppers' report must have said!

As D Day approached there was one little problem that no one seemed able to solve. The Prince had mentioned it to a defence minister, generals had muttered about it in the Rag, and Judith reminded me of it daily. Who was to look after my salary? Four and a half years was rather too long for the hard-pressed Finance branch at the MOD to pay a colonel whilst on an expedition. Raleigh simply couldn't afford it. When I was preparing to sell my house, a staff officer called me. 'We've just had a memo from 10 Downing Street. It just says: "Blashford-Snell, pay him."'

On 4 September 1984, Her Royal Highness Princess Alexandra won everyone's hearts when she commissioned the ship in bright sunshine. We were almost ready.

Zebu was the first to depart and on 11 October 1984 she sailed from Tower Pier, London, with arch sea-goon Sir Harry Secombe at the helm for a few minutes. Aboard were sixteen venturers and nine professional crew under the watchful eye of Captain Peter Masters. 'America next stop,' cried Sir Harry as her square sails filled and she left for the open sea and four years of adventure.

Meanwhile in Hull, field director Charlie Daniel, with whom I had shared exciting times in Oman, was working his teams around the clock to have *SWR* ready for departure on 13 November. By the dawn of that day, miracles had been achieved and the Prince of Wales gave us a wonderful send-off. To the cheers of a large crowd, *Sir Walter Raleigh* sailed for New York by way of the Channel Islands. As with Operation Drake, it was a close-run thing. Even as the Prince was speaking to the crowds from the upper deck, welding was in progress on the other side of the ship!

Operation Raleigh

NEW YORK GAVE US a great welcome, and, thanks to the Prince of Wales being interviewed by Barbara Walters on her *Twenty-Twenty* TV show, eleven million Americans heard all about the operation. The phone lines to our US office in Raleigh, North Carolina, were jammed.

The North Atlantic in November is no place for fair weather sailors and it had been a crossing few would ever forget. 400 miles out from Britain the sea was spectacular and, as the ship rolled and pitched, spume blew off the wavetops in the biting wind. The course was taking her straight into the seas, so that she surfed down one roller then came to an almost complete shuddering stop as the bow vanished into the next in a cloud of spray with fifty-foot waves breaking right over her. Suddenly a particularly violent roll hurled one of our two landing craft off its rails in the stern hangar. The situation was serious: about eleven tons of craft with two Suzuki vehicles on its deck was being swung around like a toy. The chains which had held it in place had come loose and had to be tensioned before any serious damage was done. After several hours most of the movement had been controlled using blocks, and it was safe to reach the chains between the two craft without running the risk of being crushed to death. When the weather abated, came the task of jacking the trolley back up onto its rails. Later the Third Officer, Chris Mahoney, went off forward to the heads and suddenly rushed back into the mess and grabbed the fire extinguisher. He had been steadying himself when the ship rolled and had burnt his hand on the bulkhead; all the clothes in the drying room had caught fire after a waterproof fell on top of the heater. The plastic clothing was giving off acrid fumes and the heat was intense. Nearby cabins were evacuated and it took two extinguishers to get the blaze under control.

Next day the disasters continued: Charlie Nicklin and Ted Seymour were doubling up all the wires and chains on the landing craft after the emergency job the previous night. Conditions in the hangar deck were uncomfortable, with the freezing wind howling around and water splashing across the deck. Matters were made worse by the fact that the massive hydraulically operated stern gates were not completely closed. Using a crowbar, Ted was holding them together while Charlie attempted to lash them securely. With the movement of the ship this was proving difficult, and suddenly an ear-piercing scream filled the hangar deck. Charlie had got his thumb caught between the gates and they slammed shut, completely squashing it. Jane Dunbar, the ship's Orcadian doctor, had the unpleasant task of stitching the stump together. A fuel leak was only stopped by Charlie Daniel and a muscular Territorial Army lass, Cathy Davies, lying on their backs in several inches of oil and water in the bilges to remove a pipe.

Another fault was repaired in New York, but in harbour with the festive season in full swing, Chase Manhattan, one of our enthusiastic sponsors, held their Christmas party on board and many members of the Explorers' Club came along. We all felt rather proud of the SES's Scientific Exploration Ship.

Rolling banks of freezing fog greeted us on arrival in North Carolina where a banner read 'Welcome Sir Walter, you're only 400 years late', but the Southern hospitality and the bonanza of gifts, including four twenty-one-foot Carolina skiffs, more than made up for the weather.

It was now time to start the land operations and after a quick call at Miami to pick up incoming Venturers we sailed into Grand Bahama Harbour to be met by 'Union Jack' Hayward and his Port Manager, John Hinchliffe. The sky was blue and the sun shone as we got down to a host of scientific and conservation projects on land and underwater.

We were joined by a group of American juvenile delinquents from an organization called Vision Quest. My colleagues thought I'd taken leave of my senses when I invited these young criminals to join us, but it was an amazing success. They arrived aboard the organization's schooner *Western Union* and were quickly integrated into our team creating a new national park. Most of them had suffered as a result of child abuse and responded very favourably to kindness and understanding. Our Venturers became their big brothers and sisters.

The main underwater project in the Bahamas was a coral reef survey on which we tested an amazing sub-igloo, a clear perspex underwater house, kindly loaned to us by our Canadian chairman and leading diving expert, Dr Joe MacInnes. Eight feet in diameter, this air-filled sphere enabled up to three divers to swap information on the seabed. We assembled Iggy in fifty feet of water off Grand Bahama, the main problem being that it needed nine tons of ballast to hold it down. Mark Bensen solved that by rummaging around the island for some old car engines to cut up. They made our smart igloo look a bit unsightly, but they did the trick, and Iggy proved a fascinating and useful addition to our equpment. It caused a few surprises too. Early one morning two divers went down to prepare for the day's activities and found to their surprise that Iggy was already occupied: staring out at them was a large barracuda. The American Venturer, by graphic demonstration, urged on his British colleague to grab the fish by its tail and pull it out, 'See, like that, easy.' To his utter astonishment, he did, and got away with it. The barracuda promptly chased the American!

But there were hazards above the surface too. We had with us a Recce Section of the Royal Scots Dragoon Guards led by David Allfrey, a most resourceful officer. One of his corporals was strolling quietly back to his quarters having enjoyed a convivial evening in a waterside bar when he was set upon by three thugs armed with knives. In spite of his short stature he was immensely strong and possessed a high qualification in martial arts. Experience in the back streets of Glasgow had fitted him well for such an encounter, but even I was surprised when the local police phoned to say they had arrested him for causing grievous bodily harm to three peace-loving Bahamians. Later it transpired that when the first robber had attacked, the NCO had seized him by the ankles and used him as a club to down the others. Then he had knocked on the door of an expatriate's house and asked if he might telephone the police so that his assailants, none of whom could walk, might be retrieved from the roadway. However, the Bahamas were overrun with drug smugglers and there were several occasions when I thought SWR's well-stocked armoury might come in handy.

Our flagship proved her worth when conducting amphibious operations. The Merseyside County Council had built us two robust water jet powered landing craft, Prince William and Prince Henry, and they gave us the capability to land stores over beaches. Two Avon seariders could cope with really heavy weather and we also had a fleet of alloy assault boats, inflatables and skiffs.

On 31 December 1984 we were landing a party on the reef-strewn shore of Cat Island. Although the sun was bright, a heavy swell was running and each roller threatened to slam the landing craft up against the ship's hull. Most of the Tac HQ staff were also helmsmen, as were the ship's officers, so we took turns at driving the boats. It was really exhilarating, and everyone came back wet and smiling. I adored handling the seariders and apparently reminded everyone of 'Mr Toad'. Though everything went surprisingly smoothly despite the swell, unloading proved a slow process. As the day wore on it became clear the job wouldn't be finished before dark, so a lithesome, bikini-clad Venturer was commissioned as a mobile, nubile lighthouse. Given a flashlight, she was sent to stand on the rocky headland to guide craft in. At 2130 hours the wind freshened. It was imperative that the flagship sailed at dawn to make the next rendezvous so the message went to the party ashore: 'Sorry – you've had your lot – see you in a month.'

'OK, we'll manage,' they sent back, 'and, by the way, Happy New Year!'

We had quite forgotten it was New Year's Eve, and had also quite forgotten about the mobile, nubile lighthouse, still flashing away from the headland. However, Charlie Daniel, gallant as ever, took *St George*, the big searider, in to collect the poor girl, who was frozen stiff and very hungry. As she waded out to the boat, a water snake slithered across her feet! Oh, well, at least it was a little different from the London solicitors' office where she usually worked. After that, the New Year was well and truly celebrated, many times over, as it occurred in all the home countries of those present. Amazingly the ship stayed on course, and I took the opportunity to telephone our World President, Walter Annenberg, in California via satellite and exchanged greetings with the guests at his party, who included the President of the United States!

Meanwhile having taken a southerly route across, *Zebu* was now supporting a diving team searching for lost treasure ships in the Turks and Caicos. It was hoped a major discovery would boost the economy of these impoverished islands. With them was Keith Jessop, who had gained fame and become a millionaire after his successful recovery of the gold from HMS *Edinburgh*, sunk off the coast of Russia in 1942. Keith, whose treasure hunting company had a contract with the local government, was to direct the search for wrecks along the south side of the Caicos Bank.

A great cheer went up from *Zebu* as *SWR* sailed into the anchorage. It was only on rare occasions that the two vessels met. Led by Barry Moss, who had been with me on Operation Drake in Kenya, the Turks and Caicos expedition was very successful. The divers found no fewer than fourteen wrecks. Although none carried gold, they did discover one cargo of copper coins and numerous cannon, and also salvaged a complete fifteen-foot USAF target plane which bore the interesting but, as it turned out, totally untrue legend: 'Finder Will Be Rewarded'!

The scientific research had gone well. There had been some interesting caving, the old Militia building on Grand Turk had been renovated, and a basketball court for the locals had been constructed at Bottle Creek. A large supply of sports equipment, collected in Britain, had been presented to the local high school, and it was obvious that the expedition had made quite an impact on this little community. I was especially pleased things had gone so well as this was our first major Raleigh expedition to be led by an ex-Young Explorer. There had been a great many difficulties for Barry to overcome, not least avoiding complications caused by the drug-trafficking in the islands. As we left, we heard that the Chief Minister and several colleagues had been arrested in Miami for drug-related offences!

Thanks to Dr Armand Hammer, Occidental Petroleum had kindly offered to bunker the ship if we called in at Galveston and thus a few weeks later we enjoyed a brief visit to Texas. The hospitality was overwhelming and when we docked, Charlie Daniel, who had flown ahead, was there to greet us with lorries loaded with provisions and an escort of long-limbed ladies.

Our next series of expeditions was in Belize and Honduras. Once again *SWR* was invaluable in supporting the land based teams, but Mike Kichenside had already warned me that it would be a tricky operation at the entrance to the Black River on the infamous Mosquito Coast. As far back as the 1700s the Black River bar had garnered for itself a reputation as a graveyard. In 1732 a handful of English colonists had tried to establish themselves here. A small British enclave on an otherwise Hispanic coast, the ill-fated colony had been twice burned and finally abandoned. I stared across the line of breakers to where the shore lay, a thin swathe of jungle pressed beneath a sky of leaden grey.

We anchored around 3 p.m. It had taken us some time to locate the narrow break in the bar that marked the lagoon entrance. Guiding ourselves in by the smoke of an unseen village, we spotted the two bright orange panel markers set up by our advance party. Having been here on an earlier recce I took an Avon searider to gauge the strength of the surf and land a small beach team who would provide shore support and radio communication during the unloading. It was a rough trip, but the boat handled well, climbing high over the top of one wave to slam down into the trough of the next. We rode the surf for the last 200 yards, a muddied green surge crested in dirty white. Through the spume of the breakers I could make out brown sand to our starboard, and to port the unbroken green of mangrove. The lagoon entrance remained hidden until we were almost on top of it. We burst over the bar, scattering spray and found ourselves suddenly in quiet water. On either side the mangroves fell away to reveal clearings of palm and fruit trees; in the centre of each was a thatched-roofed hut. I turned the bow in towards one of these clearings where our advance party stood waiting. The Avon nosed in beside a row of dugouts, beaching on a narrow strip of sand that fronted the clearing, and we stepped ashore onto the Mosquito Coast.

Still strewn with half-buried cannon, Fort Wellington had been built back in 1748 to command the entrance to the lagoon and protect the infant British colony from Spanish attack. After the last Britons left in 1786, it was re-christened Fuerte de la Purisima Concepcion and re-armed to defend the newly-formed Spanish settlement. Its guns, however, stood silently pointing out to sea at 2 a.m. on the morning of 24 September 1800, when hostile Indians under their leader General Tempest swept out of the jungle, putting the town to the torch and massacring all but a handful of its inhabitants. It was this blood-soaked patch of ground that thirty Venturers from America, Britain, Hong Kong, Japan and Oman were to call home for the next three months.

Light was fading rapidly and there seemed little chance of our getting any stores ashore before dark. In Central America the gentle twilight of more northerly latitudes is replaced by a swift and violent sunset sliding into starlit blackness. The advance party fell asleep to the mingled roar of the howler monkeys and the surf.

For centuries rumours had circulated of a 'Lost White City' hidden deep within the mountainous jungles of Mosquita, one of the many El Dorados which haunted the early Conquistadors and lured so many of them to their deaths. Cuidad Blanca had been the subject of search and speculation for the last 400 years: local legends spoke of it lying somewhere in the 16,000 square miles of wilderness which lay over the mountains to the southeast of the expedition's camp. Our archaeologist maintained a healthy degree of scepticism, doubting that a white-walled city of palaces and temples could still exist undiscovered even in so remote a region. Yet even he was eager to see what ruins, if any, lay on the far side of the mountains. So a seven-member patrol set off upriver in search of 'the last great lost city of the Americas'.

They never found it. Instead, their searches revealed something in many ways more impressive. When they staggered back into base camp they brought with them reports of not one but a series of ruins, stretching from the coast to the uplands. This was to be our first indication that the Black River/Rio Paulaya region, long ignored as an archaeological backwater, had been the home of a sophisticated pre-Columbian culture similar in many respects to that of the neighbouring Maya. Experiences previously unimaginable – a patrol stumbling into a green-lit jungle clearing to face a massive stone altar; a girl wakened in the middle of the night by a puma brushing against her hammock – became everyday occurrences. They were not, however, without their price. The damp heat of the rain forest brought on jungle rot, tiny blisters that with time spread into open sores three to four inches across. Insects were a hazard too. On the coast the major problem proved to be jiggers, small flea-like animals, which burrow into the skin of the foot to lay eggs. The only effective means of removing them was to make an incision next to the white, pea-sized egg sack and then squeeze. But in the interior the botflies were the real menace. They lay their eggs on the proboscis of mosquitoes so that they may be injected by the mosquito into a host. Once beneath the skin the tiny larva, whose head is built on the same lines as the bit of an oil drill, forces its way deeper and deeper and begins to swell until it is about the size of a maggot. We found that the only way to remove them was to smear the area with Vaseline and cover it with adhesive tape. Starved of oxygen, the larva backs out of the wound and can be drawn painfully the rest of the way.

Red-bearded Mark O'Shea, our eccentric Irish herpetologist, attracted considerable attention from the 'locals' due to his penchant for slithering under the raised floors of the local houses in search of boa constrictors. One afternoon I took him by boat into the mangroves at the edge of the lagoon. Suddenly he let out a whoop and scrambled up a tree. On the top branch two eight-foot black and yellow snakes were entwined in matrimonial bliss. Rudely interrupting Mark seized one and dropped it down into the boat beside me, where it hissed with rage. By now the second reptile had bitten our intrepid hunter several times. However, he returned, triumphantly proclaiming his catch as 'thunder and lightning' snakes, 'mildly venomous'.

The archaeological and scientific work went well. We explored the former British colony of Roatan. *Zebu* was assisting this archaeological and diving project and we encouraged venturers to undertake community tasks. One young lady, a member of our Royal Family, was to hit the headlines later in life, but whilst with Operation Raleigh she was a deeply caring and hard-working girl. Marina Ogilvy decided that the little town of Coxens Hole should be cleaned up, so she painted a collection of old oil drums blue and white and put on a message in Spanish exhorting the people to use her rubbish bins. When I came to see her work I was met by the Mayor, in dark suit and bowler hat. Strangely no great improvement resulted and I asked the Mayor why the rubbish was not being put in the bins. 'Well, Sir,' he replied, 'see, dey is Royal trashcans and we is ordinary folk.'

In the operations centre on the ship we often heard the radio traffic of other vessels in the area. Off Black River we picked up an unusual language that seemed to be booming through from a large banana boat lying nearby and apparently talking to a station in the jungle.

'What's that?' I asked a linguist on our staff.

'Russian,' she said without looking up from the charts.

A few days later *SWR* sailed for Costa Rica to support another expedition. Having a day in hand, Mike Kichenside dropped anchor for a spot of diving at Edinburgh Reef, a series of coral outcrops off the coast. Later US military intelligence asked me if I could shed any light on a strange incident. A Nicaraguan gunboat had gone tearing out to the Edinburgh Reef to intercept what they believed to be a CIA ship but the Hondurans, in whose territory the reef lies, were alerted to this incursion by 'spy in the sky' satellite. They despatched fighter aircraft and sank the gunboat. Checking the dates, I realized we were the 'CIA ship'.

In Costa Rica we were in a more peaceful area and I visited a science camp where one of our aerial walkways was being constructed in the forest canopy in a wildlife reserve. Even snakes were protected here. A venturer who adored reptiles had a live *fer-de-lance* that he had rescued when it was about to be decapitated by a local. He had been keeping the snake in his British Airways day-sack with which all venturers had been issued. Alas, he could not remember which one was his! Eventually, however, the right bag was discovered and I took a long-range glance at the creature coiled therein. The previous week he had witnessed a Costa Rican forestry worker, bitten by one of these killers, neutralize the effects of the venom by drinking an infusion made from the leaves of a local bush. Now our scientists were collecting samples of the plant in hope of isolating its medicinal properties. At another site a similar *fer-de-lance*, when not gazing libidinously at a coil of the expedition's electric cable, insisted on escorting senior research officers to the loo, which they found a trifle off-putting!

Keith Hamylton-Jones, who led this expedition, was a former British Ambassador in the country. When I visited him in San Jose, his HQ was packed with venturers, so one afternoon we sought the peace and quiet of a nightclub to hold a meeting on the science programme. Maps were spread across the tables and the scientists presented their problems. The proprietor brought beer and we became absorbed with the conservation of the rainforest. Time went by and when the club opened, topless bar girls wandered over to see what it was that so distracted four bronzed explorers. Growing weary, the ladies chose to sit on the laps of several of my colleagues. When I asked one of our number if he could, in simple biological terms, describe the importance of his research programme, he sighed, 'Just look at those nipples.' The meeting was then adjourned.

Another expedition had returned to Caledonia Bay, where with great skill Mike edged *SWR* in between the reefs and to anchor clear of the sandfly and mosquito-ridden shore. There were some old buildings on the airstrip and two Panamanian soldiers had come ahead to clean out the vegetation. But to my horror I found the walls had been knocked flat, leaving the expedition homeless. 'You blithering idiots,' I tried to say in Spanish, 'all we wanted you to do was tidy the place up.'

The men looked grave and waving their arms cried, 'Boom, boom!'

Eventually an interpreter arrived and explained. 'They're trying to tell you a big earthquake collapsed the buildings yesterday.'

More work on *Olive Branch* brought up bones from the saltbeef barrels that the Cuna thought were human and this nearly caused a major upset. We also lifted three cannon onto *SWR* and decided to take one back to the Panama Museum. As we chipped away at the coral encrustations, there was a loud hissing and the unmistakable stench of gunpowder. We backed away, as, with a 'poop', a cannon ball appeared at the end of the barrel. The release of pressure on the breach when the gun was raised from thirty feet had caused it to be forced forward.

At Acla we discovered the foundations of a circular tower which is believed to be the oldest European stone structure yet unearthed on the American mainland and this caused international interest. I was preparing to take the British Ambassador, Terry Steggle, and some friends down to see this when an emergency message flashed through to the Ops Centre. Michael Williams, a British venturer, had been sliding down a grass slope on a Colombian island, when he had pitched over a ledge and gone headfirst into a rock, sustaining terrible injuries. General Jack Galvin, the region's US Commander, was a good friend of General Mogg's and thankfully he had instructed his staff to give us every support, so when I called for a Medevac, a USAF C 130 loaded with doctors was on its way in minutes. Meanwhile Terry handled the diplomatic clearances required to fly a British casualty from a Colombian island to Panama in an American aircraft.

Initially the first aid administered by his colleagues kept him alive until the Colombian emergency services could take over, but as we stood around the flagship radio, I saw our senior medical officer, Jane Dunbar, looked grim. 'He hasn't much of a chance,' she confided, as our US Navy radio officer recorded the details of Michael's deteriorating condition. We needed a top brain surgeon if Michael were to live. I remembered meeting one at a Kiwanis Club lunch and called my pal, Billy St Malo, who raced out in his speedboat to collect the man from a holiday island and got him to the airfield just as the C 130 touched down. It was this timely rescue and the skill of the Panamanian surgeon, still in his shorts, that saved Michael's life.

For our next phase, both ships passed through the Panama Canal, *Zebu* sailing on to Hawaii and *SWR* to Peru, where she arrived just as a customs strike was starting. The result was that all the rations and stores were held in bond. Nevertheless, we gave them fifty cents per venturer per day and told them to get on with the projects. Living off the land they achieved miracles of improvisation and, after several months, when the food was eventually released, the upcountry teams said, 'Don't send it, we're enjoying the challenge.'

A new team of US servicemen arrived and amongst them was a Yeoman of Signals. 'You're just the chap to sort out my UHF problems,' I said as he put down his bags. He looked a little blank and, knowing there were often different nomenclatures used by our nations, I explained the difficulties with our Ultra High Frequency ship to aircraft radio. He still looked puzzled so I said, 'Well, I expect you will be used to much more sophisticated equipment in the US Navy.'

'I don't use any of this gear,' he said slowly.

'What do you use?' I asked.

'Flags,' he replied.

So now I was without a Chief Signaller but he made a good public relations officer.

Originally I'd planned only three expeditions in Chile but, after seeing the excellent opportunities open to us amid the mountains and fjords of the south, this was extended to four. However, due to the severity of the southern winter, our first three-month expedition was to take place in Chile's northern regions, an area which surely must rank among the world's wonders. Soaring volcanoes, stark lava fields and huge, rolling dunes make a startling contrast to a seemingly endless desert. The immense Atacama runs for over 600 miles, with many vast areas where it has never rained in recorded history.

Alas, our first Chilean phase threatened to begin badly. Many of the proposed projects never materialized or fell through only days before the expedition's arrival. Perhaps the Chilean committee had expected too much of us, coming, as they saw it, from a host of relatively wealthy nations. There were other problems. The country is divided into twelve regions, each virtually self-governing, and we soon discovered that arrangements made in Santiago are not always effective 1,500 miles away. Planning ahead in South American countries doesn't always ensure the end result, and we were confronted daily with what came to be called the 'South American factor'.

Thankfully the problem of our tasks was solved by the National Park Organization, who, having a surfeit of work and a very tight budget, welcomed our offer of labour with open arms and stepped in at the last moment with new projects throughout Chile. Our expedition extended for almost 1,000 miles, covering sixteen project sites, and the barren, almost uninhabited, northern wasteland made the distances seem even greater. Furthermore, to the discomfort of several venturers who'd brought clothes designed for perhaps more predictable desert weather, the Atacama was freezing cold.

By now *SWR* was anchored off the small port of Mejillones, with a mixed crew of British Army, Portuguese, and US Navy personnel, plus our splendid merchant seamen. Wide beaches and spectacular rock formations stretched along a coast which reverberated to the roar of explosions as the local dynamite factory tested its wares. Oddly, these blasts seemed to have no effect on the pelicans whirling sleepily but endlessly above the ship in the clear cold air. Fat sea lions barked at our divers, seeming to invite them in for a swim, so they were delighted when we started on an oceanographic survey of the bay, clearly under the impression that the supply of human playmates had been laid on for their benefit.

The flagship was due a refit and, working ahead of us as usual, David Allfrey had discovered that at Puerto Montt in Southern Chile there was a shipyard where labour was $1 per man per day. Thus I set up Tac HQ in a rented house in Antofagasta and despatched *SWR* south. Nick Horne, my highly efficient Operations Officer, linked us by radio to the expeditions in Peru, Bolivia and Northern Chile, so the work started. I had arranged to pre-dump material for the projects and David Allfrey's Scottish soldiers went around depositing the necessary rations and equipment. Speaking Spanish in thick Glaswegian accents, they had left strict instructions with one particular mayor and a local café owner, in whose store they left everything, that 'on pain of death' they were not to mention to anyone the whereabouts of the kit, except, of course, to people like themselves.

Three weeks later a group, under the leadership of an Australian Army officer, arrived to begin their project and collect the stores. Despite enquiries in best Sydney Spanish, no one in the village would admit to any knowledge of them. Not surprisingly, frantic messages flashed across Chile and, believing that everything had been stolen, I contacted the regional commander. Troops were despatched forthwith, police ordered to investigate, and the entire village was subjected to a veritable inquisition. At last the stores were discovered, exactly where the recce team had left them.

'Se Escosia say we are to tell no one,' explained the perplexed mayor, 'except people like them – and they were very fierce men.'

Many centuries ago the remote desert oasis of San Pedro de Atacama had been the centre of a flourishing Paleolithic civilization based within impressive rock fortresses built upon the steep mountains that almost encircle the green valley. Thousands of ancient graves scattered throughout the hills were beginning to yield their secrets. An extraordinary museum, set up by the late Father Gustave Le Paige, contains numerous mummies, skulls, stone-age tools, jewellery, weapons and wood carvings. The mummies, many with their hair intact, were found still clad in their fine burial clothes.

Directed by local archaeologists we helped with the excavations, and in fifteen days recovered twenty-nine pre-Columbian mummies, many perfectly preserved. It was fascinating work. Discoveries included the graves of important warriors, buried with their weapons and a llama, presumably as food for the afterlife. Some men carried a pouch of drug-taking implements on their belts! One of our most extraordinary finds was a large basket containing an earthenware pot which, when opened, held a cake at least 1,500 years old.

Later we were to explore nineteenth-century battlefields, where the arid, salty soil had preserved the dead exactly as they had been buried in their uniforms. However, there were also lethal relics of earlier border wars and poorly marked minefields were a constant hazard if one strayed from a well-used track.

In September 1985 we moved south down the enormously long, thin country to rejoin *SWR*. Chilean lakeland is one of the least spoilt places on earth. Stretching for hundreds of miles, scores of emerald lakes glitter amidst beautiful mountains. This is a land of snow-capped volcanoes, deep woodland meadows and small peaceful villages. There are flowers by the acre, great pine forests and awe-inspiring waterfalls. Puerto Montt, capital of the region, lies on a flat plain beside Reloncavi Bay, overlooked by the perfect cone of the Orsono Volcano. Here our flagship lay at anchor, already swarming with eager Chilean workers, hammering, scraping, painting and welding.

The next expedition, still under New Zealand SAS Major Stuart Grey, had its HQ a further 400 miles south at the sprawling frontier city of Coyhaique, capital of Chile's eleventh and least known region. Referred to locally as the 'End of the Earth', the wild, untamed beauty of Chile's Austral zone is breathtaking, a rugged extravagance of nature. Blue glaciers, mirror-black lakes, snowfields, ragged rows of mountain ranges and volcanoes join a seemingly endless coast of bays, channels, inlets, fjords and islands. Flying high above this splendid wilderness I saw few traces of man. A lone track,

perhaps, and maybe an isolated Indian hut or fishing village. This was
real frontier country as the American West must once have been.
Over a third of all Chile lies here, yet this immense wilderness holds
less than three per cent of its population. The incredible terrain, the
weather and the miles of uninhabited land offered us wonderful
opportunity for adventure. Situated at the northern tip of the
Patagonian Icefield, the massive glacier of San Rafael, isolated and
wild, provided an awesome setting for one of our southerly projects.
The only building amidst this wilderness was an abandoned hotel
offering a spectacular view of the glacier left empty by the lack of
visitors and it became one of our bases.

Following their successful project with us in Panama, Dr Harry
Brown came again from California with his SEE International
ophthalmic team to operate on cataract victims. Thanks to Charlie
Daniel's excellent work in Santiago, the customs passed through the
nineteen boxes of medical equipment without comment and within a
few days the team was hard at work in the expedition area. With
cooperation from a local Chilean ophthalmic surgeon and assisted by
venturers, Harry and his colleagues set about their sight-restoring
mission. In four days of intensive surgery, often working for sixteen
hours at a stretch, they gave back sight to seventeen people and
provided hundreds of pairs of free spectacles to poor people who
would never normally have such a service. It was a rewarding feeling
to be part of such a humane project.

There were some strange incidents. One ninety-year-old gentleman
was led back to bed after his cataract operation by an attractive
American venturer, Linda Walters. As soon as he was between the
sheets he muttered something, leapt up, grabbed Linda and gave her a
smacking great kiss. Not understanding Spanish, she asked someone
whether he was trying to express his thanks for the operation.

'Oh no,' said a Chilean nurse, 'he just likes pretty girls and now he
can see them again.' An elderly lady examined by Harry's wife Baillie
was found to be wearing spectacles fitted with plain glass. She
cheerfully confessed they did her no good – she wore them for the
trend!

After one session I showed a video film I had made of this intricate
micro-surgery to the crew but the sight of it in Technicolor was too
much for all but the most hardened. However the Chileans really
appreciated our assistance and all the tasks being done for the
impoverished pioneers of this challenging land and we received much

hospitality. Knowing I enjoyed shooting, the locals invited me on a boar hunt and, providing that I produced the weapons, they would find horses and hounds. So it was that Pablo Calderon, our liaison officer, and I flew to an isolated, but beautiful lakeside community known as Lago Verde.

The mayor, a twenty-five-year-old graduate of Santiago University, accommodated us in his simple wooden cottage and everyone gathered to admire the rifles and shotguns: I could have sold my .357 Smith & Wesson revolver for a huge price. That night a pre-hunt party was held in the village hall. Apparently I was the first Briton they had seen and, whilst some of the loveliest ladies I have ever met flirted outrageously with me, the menfolk toasted Mrs Thatcher and suggested all sorts of horrors they would like to inflict on General Galtieri. By 4 a.m. few were sober, and as we were to start at dawn I slipped away to prepare the guns.

To my astonishment the hunt did assemble roughly on time. Sad, shaggy horses with sheepskin saddle cloths stood in the drizzle as we mounted up. A pack of ferocious dogs skulked around us, snapping and snarling. The *carabineros* and I dished out weapons and ammunition. Then we were off looking for all the world like a John Wayne posse. A hundred yards beyond the last house a lone goose flew over our heads. With a roar like the opening barrages of El Alamein the Chileans discharged everything they had at it, from the saddle. Chaos ensued as their terrified mounts reared and bolted, some depositing their riders amongst the hounds that tore round in circles biting each other in the absence of anything else to kill. It was a pure miracle that no one was shot.

Once the hunters had caught their horses and the dogs had been lashed into silence we reassembled. It was quite clear that our ideas on hunting did not correspond, so via Pablo I delivered a short speech praising their spirit and courage and recommending some weapon training.

'But in England you hunt with the horse and the dog,' they argued.

'Yes, but not with the gun too,' I explained. 'We shoot on foot.'

'Chileans go nowhere on foot,' retorted an old sage.

However we progressed and by noon had shot a couple of ducks, two hares and one of the hounds.

'Now we eat,' cried the mayor as we flopped down beneath some convenient firs to sip *mate* tea and drink litres of heavy red wine,

which had been held in great green demi-johns on the packhorses.
The mayor's groom had plucked the ducks as he rode and roasted
them with commendable speed. In the early evening we sighted a
boar and with a fusillade of shots the field galloped after it. Pablo and
I decided pursuit was pointless and dangerous and walked our horses
to the night stop. One by one the hunters came in, scratched to blazes
by the thorn and with a host of tales. The pig, clearly a jet-propelled
monster, had finally eluded them but not before it had charged them
all in succession, or so the stories went. That night we ate the hares
and drank more red wine around the fire whilst a *vaquero* mournfully
strummed his guitar.

My hangover was not improved by riding into a low branch next
morning and being knocked off to howls of mirth from my colleagues.
For several days we rode through brush and bamboo higher and higher
into the Andes, and suddenly we came to a clearing across which
stretched an old wire cattle fence. The expedition dismounted and,
lining the fence, urinated with great relish across it. Clearly this was
a custom, perhaps Chilean hunters always pee over fences, as
waggoners in England would relieve themselves on the wheel of their
cart, I thought. 'That's an interesting ritual,' I remarked as Pablo
remounted.

'It is not a ritual,' replied my swarthy pal, 'we do that out of respect
to you, Englishman. Over the fence is Argentina.'

By now Raleigh's finances were at a low ebb. In setting up the
Operation we had taken bids from all countries wishing to partici-
pate. Australia had asked to send 240 venturers, Oman 100, and the
United States committees, not unreasonably, had said they would
like to bid for 1,500. Now, fourteen months into the venture, it was a
different story. For a wide variety of perfectly understandable
reasons, many of our national committees had not been able to fill
their quotas, and although our expenditure was well within budget
our income was falling far behind. Every possible measure had been
taken to bridge the gap and we had raised the UK quota from 375 per
year to 660 in the first twelve months. But there is only so much cash
in dear old Britain and we simply could not generate any more funded
venturers from home.

Zebu had ably supported the expedition in Hawaii where an active
volcano had rather dramatized events and our plans were well-
advanced in the Pacific and Australasia. Whilst we were winning the
battle at the front, we urgently needed support at the rear, and so

Charlie Daniel and I returned to Britain to spend the first part of 1986 supporting our overworked CHQ.

On a boiling hot Christmas Day the venturers of the second Chilean expedition poured on to the flagship for a momentous party. Fit, happy and confident, with new-found friends and a host of tales to tell, they'd soon be on their way home. With the day drawing to a close an American pastor joined me in conducting a carol service on deck. I managed to distract his eyes from the bow where some scandalous female venturers were sunbathing topless. In the service we took the theme of peace on earth and said Sir Francis Drake's prayer:

> O Lord God, when thou givest to thy servants to endeavour any great matter, grant us to know that it is not the beginning but the continuing of the same unto the end, until it be thoroughly finished, which yieldeth the true glory: through him who for the finishing of thy work laid down his life, our Redeemer Jesus Christ. Amen.

As the last carol died away across the sunlit blue waters, I was reminded that this was just the end of Operation Raleigh's beginning. There were still three years to run and many, many more young people round the world to take up the challenge.

Around the World

'NEVER FEAR, MY BOYS, we'll all go to hell together.'
These words of encouragement, growled by HMS *Pandora*'s
master of arms early one August morning in 1791, were almost
the last that the imprisoned mutineers from the *Bounty* ever heard.
But as the ship which held the captives began to sink to her grave on
the Great Barrier Reef, the boatswain's mate opened the wooden cell
and most of the men scrambled out and plunged into the foaming
ocean.

This great saga of the sea had begun in 1787 when HMS *Bounty* was
sent to Tahiti to collect breadfruit plants for the growing slave
population in the Caribbean. Finding the attractions of the Tahitian
ladies greater than service under the infamous Captain William
Bligh, the British sailors seized the ship and started the most
notorious mutiny in naval history.

Led by Fletcher Christian, the mutineers put Bligh and eighteen
loyal crew into an open boat off the island of Tonga. Then they sailed
back to Tahiti where the 'pirates' rejoined their ladies, many of
whom were pregnant. However, Christian with eight shipmates and
a number of local men and women sailed to Pitcairn, an uninhabited
island, which, he knew, was wrongly marked on the charts. Their
chances of ever being found were slight but they set fire to the ship as a
precaution and, as far as the world knew, it had simply disappeared.

Perhaps maligned as a leader of men, Captain Bligh was, however,
an acknowledged master of the sea. Set adrift in an open boat, he and
his crew reached Timor in forty-one days, having navigated *Bounty*'s
tiny launch 3,618 nautical miles through terrible seas and the Great
Barrier Reef. Their bold sea run is still a record. On return to England,
Bligh acquainted their Lordships of the Admiralty with the news of
his ship's fate. They were not amused.

Meanwhile, Fletcher Christian's paradise had soured. Quarrels with the Polynesians led to blows and all save two sailors were killed. By 1808, when the first ship called at Pitcairn, only one Englishman was alive to tell the tale, kept company by a large 'family' of women and the descendants of shipmates. These were the founders of the colony that exists to this day, and to whom our flagship, *Sir Walter Raleigh*, brought much-needed supplies and fuel in August 1986. It was a strange fact that as our gleaming, 2,000-ton exploration vessel rode at anchor in the turquoise seas of the tropical isle, she was linked through history to the wreck of the *Bounty* eight fathoms below, since the home port of both ships was the city of Hull.

In 1790 the Royal Navy had come to investigate the *Bounty*'s disappearance. HMS *Pandora*, a twenty-four-gun frigate captained by Edward Edwards, arrived at Tahiti in November and found the fourteen mutineers foolish enough to have remained in their lovenest. They were dragged aboard *Pandora*, clapped in irons and incarcerated on deck in a hastily created wooden cell, called Pandora's box, with only two small gratings, secured by bolts. The heat was so intense that the sweat 'ran in streams to the scuppers and soon produced maggots . . . ' They had little chance to bid fond farewells to their women and children who stood in canoes holding their babies aloft, howling with grief as the man of war sailed for England and the inevitable courts martial. The only sign of *Bounty* was an anchor that Captain Edwards hauled aboard as evidence.

It was late in the day. Sailing for home on a westerly course, *Pandora* sought a passage through the Great Barrier Reef near what is today Cape York. She struck the knife-edged coral wall hard, hurling crew and captives alike onto the deck. During the frantic effort to save her, two of the ship's pumps broke: she sank at sunrise at a spot now known as Pandora's Entrance. Thirty-one sailors and four of the mutineers drowned in the Coral Sea. The ninety-nine survivors, including ten mutineers, swam to a nearby cay where they erected sailcloth tents against the relentless sun. The mutineers had no such luxury. Their skins were lily white from five months' confinement in Pandora's Box: without protection they would die agonizing deaths. Midshipman Peter Haywood, one of the prisoners later to be pardoned, recorded, 'We had to bury ourselves up to the neck in the burning sand which scorched the skin entirely off our bodies . . . ' The hapless band that had survived the relentless forces of the sea and sun had yet another test ahead. Like Bligh, the sailors managed to row to

Timor and eventually reached England. Some of them need not have bothered. Six mutineers were condemned: three were hanged at the yardarm.

Pandora rested under the waves until 1977 when Australians Ben Cropp and Steve Comm, aided by RAAF anti-submarine aircraft using an aerial magnetometer, located the wreck in only fifteen fathoms of water. The local museum's Curator of Marine Archaeology, Ron Coleman, followed up the discovery and soon well-preserved artefacts were brought to the surface, including the surgeon's watch. One of the earliest timepieces to have a second hand and a stop-watch control, it has now been restored to near working order.

In 1986 a larger expedition was planned to visit the historic wreck. A large support vessel with a recompression chamber was needed for the forty divers who would take part, and Nigel Porteous, now our Queensland Chairman, suggested that we cooperate with the museum in this exciting venture. Whilst *Sir Walter Raleigh* had been crossing the Pacific I had flown ahead to set up my Tac HQ in the bush near Cairns and it was here that Charlie Daniel, Nick Horne and I pored over the charts. Mike Kichenside was handing over as skipper to Tommy Smith of Brisbane, who knew the reef pretty well and we had a very experienced mate, New Zealander John Parsloe. *SWR* was the perfect vessel for the job. The six-week expedition would provide information of great value for our hospitable Australian friends, and at the same time offer some really advanced diving for ex-venturers.

The crew, which included young men and women from Operation Raleigh and US and Royal Australian Navy personnel, needed all their skills for the challenging project. *Zebu* could support the expedition with sixteen venturers and nine crew, while back in Cairns Nick and my superb adjutant, Major Hawk Freeman, organized sea planes to resupply the expedition. Again we experienced the unstinting generosity and enthusiasm of Cairns as a great many companies and individuals donated supplies.

Back in England our Advisory Council, fighting for funds, feared this expedition would break the bank. My protestations about covering the cost through the museum's fee and local sponsorship were to no avail. Even when I pointed out that it would be cheaper than keeping the ship in port I received little encouragement. It was the old problem of a committee on the far side of the world not fully appreciating the situation. However, *Sir Walter Raleigh*'s owners were the SES who were ultimately responsible for the whole operation. The Operation Raleigh Council was simply an advisory body and, having secured the backing of the SES for this project, I had no option but to ignore the advisors. It did not make me very popular, but the enterprise went ahead, fully sponsored in Australia, as I had promised.

Charlie started the *Pandora* project whilst I handled the rest of Raleigh by radio from Tac HQ. We had a large team preparing to fly to New Zealand and there was much clearing up to be done following the Queensland expedition. However, eventually Peta and I dragged ourselves away from our desks and squeezed into a tiny single engined 'push me-pull you' seaplane. Skimming over the dun-brown coast we headed out across a vast expanse of turquoise sea for the small white dot on the edge of the reef. We hit the water with a fearful crash and waves came right over the canopy so that for a moment I thought we'd gone straight under, but several crashes and bounces later we came to a halt beside the ship. On board there was sad news. The previous night the ship's popular Able Seaman, Neil Carmichael, from the Isle of Lewis, Scotland, had disappeared whilst on anchor watch. The weather was calm and warm and the ship was stationary. In spite of intensive searching, no trace of him was found and it can only be assumed that he fell overboard whilst attempting to adjust a mooring line on a boat secured astern. The tragedy will always be a mystery.

We had relocated the wreck and work was in full swing when I dived next day, but as we were preparing to go down from one of the large inflatable tenders there was a bump. Something nudged us. This was odd as we were in open water. I glanced up and my jaw dropped, for only thirty feet away a huge dorsal fin was moving slowly towards us. 'Look,' I hissed and Jasmina Hilton, one of our diving instructors, cried, 'It's a whale shark,' and leapt in, grabbed the fin and went off for a free ride. Nellie, as we christened her, was twenty feet long and massive. She visited us frequently and often nudged the grey Avons; perhaps she thought they were a mate. We had no worries about this harmless monster, but there were plenty of other much more dangerous predators around to keep us on our toes. A school of 'bronze whalers' gave me a bad turn in relatively shallow water and I must confess a shark is the one creature that really makes my hair stand on end.

Pandora is 'the most significant wreck in the southern hemisphere', according to archaeologist Dr Margaret Rule, Research Director of the Mary Rose Trust. A museum officer added, 'We are only scratching the surface of this remarkable wreck which will give us an unrivalled collection of late eighteenth-century naval artefacts and much more information about shipboard life of the period.' Certainly it was clear that *Pandora*'s officers had been enthusiastic collectors, for stone implements, wooden clubs, cowrie shells and carved fishing lures were found in abundance, one of the finest collections of datable ethnographic material in the world. Captain Edwards' underwater cabin also yielded historical treasure. Parts of sextants, hour glasses and what appeared to be a complete flintlock pistol were brought to the surface. Soon *Sir Walter Raleigh*'s deck was covered with bottles, plates, wine glasses and even a stone water purifier. Human bones were also found, the sad remains of the thirty-five who met their graves when *Pandora* sank in the Coral Sea. On the seabed was the *Bounty*'s anchor, which was to have been used in evidence, and there was also the massive galley stove, sitting square on the foredeck area. Here sailors once dipped for lumps of salt pork and now a large moray eel stands guard.

We also took the opportunity to study the wildlife of the sand cays in this remote area for the Queensland Parks and Wildlife Service. Jasmina and I joined a group of venturers counting green turtles and booby birds on one cay. As the sun set massive lumbering turtles heaved themselves out of the ocean, like amphibious tanks, and came ashore to lay their eggs, having to complete the task and be back in the water by dawn, to avoid being cooked in their shells by the intense heat. Their wanderings disturbed the colonies of booby birds who wheeled and screamed above us all night. We counted hundreds of turtles on this tiny islet alone, and watched as exhausted they dragged themselves back to sea to brave the sharks waiting for weaklings in the shallows.

The publicity resulting from the *Pandora* project was immensely helpful and did much to show the Australians that we were not just a group of 'poms' out for ourselves.

From my base at Cairns we supported expeditions in PNG and the Solomon Islands. Perhaps it was just as well that Colonel John Swanston, a senior Army doctor, led the PNG expedition. Sickness had not been a great problem so far but in the tropics the toll began to rise in spite of all the medical precautions. Ann Tweedy, a charming and most accomplished American writer, had joined us in Chile to help with the writing of the Raleigh books. Ann was a great friend to us all, spreading good cheer wherever she went and in a most unassuming way integrating herself into every group she visited.

When I visited PNG I found a wide-ranging medical programme in progress with the SEE team restoring sight and Professor Conrad Gorinsky using teams of venturers to collect data on traditional medicines. They recorded over 500 remedies. Undoubtedly some would save lives in the future, but the ingredients were enough to make a highstreet chemist nervous: ants, bark, soil and fungus were all part of the bottomless reserve of biological treasures. I was told that red and black ants crushed together release something like formaldehyde to relieve fevers. There was also a riverside plant, a relative of the iris, whose root helps to cure diarrhoea and stomach problems, and a tree bark which makes an excellent anaesthetic, good for everything from toothache to a night's sleep.

In the Solomons Youth Worker David Parker was leading another expedition that also carried out medical work and in addition built a very useful Red Cross Centre. As I set off to visit them the news was grim. Over 100 people had died in a savage cyclone and more than 100,000 were homeless. In three days of wanton destruction 'Namu's' winds had reached 100 knots. The jungle had been ripped from the hills and entire villages torn apart. International response was immediate. The venturers on Guadalcanal, one of the hardest-hit islands, had immediately joined the relief effort. Their tireless work very probably saved lives and as I reached David's base camp the island postman rushed in with a telegram. It was addressed to David Parker, 'The Leader, Operation Raleigh, Gizo Red Cross, Solomon Islands', and read: 'Please convey my best wishes to the local community and my congratulations to all members of the team on their good work.' The telegram was signed simply, 'Charles, Patron'. This was just one of the many encouraging messages and letters that the Prince of Wales sent to us in the field.

As *SWR* went in to Brisbane for her annual refit we commenced operations in New Zealand, where I was able to see our youngsters doing great things for the National Park Authority. Under the direction of my friend, polar explorer Charlie Burton, and later Tony Walton, the venturers built trails, bridges, and huts amongst the beautiful lakeland of South Island. I had selected the area following an earlier visit to see the place in which my parents had started their married life. Now it was especially pleasing to see the results. One of the staff was Falklands hero Simon Weston who led a conservation task on a remote island trying to trap rats that threatened the rare kakapo. Simon had been with the Welsh Guards when the ship *Sir Galahad* was hit by Argentine bombs and was terribly burned on his face and hands. Nevertheless, this courageous soldier had decided 'life was for living' and volunteered as a signaller on Operation Raleigh. He was a great inspiration to the other staff and venturers.

Meanwhile another group was busy in Tasmania and I arrived there at Christmas, their height of summer, and staggered off in a quite unseasonal snowstorm to find a team working on Cradle Mountain. As night approached, I realized we were not going to reach the venturers' camp that day, and I was thankful to see an emergency hut ahead, a welcome shelter from the storm. As we entered, Joel Schmiedeke, my new and cheerful USAF adjutant, did a classic housesearch worthy of any private eye. He didn't have far to look. Inside was a large but moving sleeping bag. Joel poked it cautiously and the heads of a honeymoon couple emerged.

'G'day,' said the man. Joel asked if he'd mind sharing the nuptial bedroom with four weary travellers. 'Make yourselves at home, mate,' grunted the Aussie, disappearing back into the bag. Twelve hours later the pair were still inside and had not once left their cocoon.

'What stamina these Australians have,' remarked Rodrigo Noreiga, our Chilean mountaineer, admiringly.

Next day we trudged on and saw wallabies hopping about un-hindered by the snow. Australia is a strange and wonderful land!

We always included disabled youngsters among the venturers and in Victoria one young man in a wheelchair complained to me that the axles had rusted badly. I passed his complaint on to the manu-facturers who were mystified but sent out replacements. A year later I saw some photographs of this lad in his chair, forty feet under-water, doing a marine biological survey! No wonder the axles rusted.

Many of our tasks were aimed at helping Aboriginal communities and there were some especially interesting conversations between our black youths and the Aborigines. Seated around a fire beside Lake Tyers, Victoria, one evening the leader of the community talked with a black British university graduate. 'Tell me,' said Chief Murray Bull, 'is there much good grazing land in Manchester?'

After some thought and a sip from his tin of Fosters, the young man replied, 'It's getting in short supply.'

The chief pondered on this, then commented, 'I suppose the white folk took it.'

More deep thought until the venturer replied, 'Yes, you could say that, but we call them the city council.'

These unsophisticated folk have many problems, and especially with their children. It isn't heroin, coke or pot that Aborigine parents worry about. It's petrol sniffing. Cheap and readily available, petrol can be sucked from the tank of a car, outboard or even a lawnmower. The short-term effects are dizziness, violence and addiction. The long-term effects are brain damage and death. The children have cause to worry too. Their parents can usually find the money for alcohol, and eventually the entire family suffers from the disease which often leads to more violence, homelessness and early death.

Paula Urschel, an energetic American from the SEE team, conceived the idea of a counselling programme while she and I talked to the Aborigines in Western Australia. In July 1987, with the blessing of the Australian Government, she returned to the Northern Territories under the auspices of Raleigh with her team of paramedics. One volunteer was an old friend of mine, Eric Niemi, a biology teacher with many years of experience in counselling young people, who had also been with us in Panama and Costa Rica. The other two were counsellors for young people and families suffering from addiction. Both American Indians, they had seen their own tribes suffer many of the same problems the Aborigines now face. The situation is fraught with political and emotional issues. Too often, for example, the addictions of any people in the world are regarded as a feature of their personalities. Our aim was to work with the Council for Alcohol Programme Services and the skilled team at the Gordon Symons Centre near Darwin, where we hoped to take an active counselling role and to exchange ideas.

During the summer months Paula's group lived in villages and towns and 'went bush' for weeks on end in the remote areas. They would be the first to recognize how limited their help could be, given the enormity of the problem. But help they did, and their contribution could stem the growth of the addiction in a few cases. Without such assistance there is a widespread fear that the twin addictions of petrol and alcohol will not be defeated, and that 30,000 years of 'the dreaming' could evaporate with this generation. It was a wonderful sight to see a Red Indian in full head-dress discussing the problem with a war-painted Abo chief!

Thanks to some marvellous fund raising by Walter and Lee Annenberg, our financial situation was looking healthier. However, to keep us on the straight and narrow I was most fortunate to get the help of Tony Nowell, formerly Managing Director of Guinness, Malaysia, on secondment. He usually wore a rosy smile and did not look much like an accountant, but by golly he was good. I also had a new Chief of Staff, Geoff Straw, an efficient former Fusilier, who took on the running of the CHQ. Political events and wars in Sri Lanka, the Persian Gulf and India had necessitated drastic changes in the sea-going programme and as most of the remaining expeditions were inland the ship would return a year early. So we decided that when she completed her Australian tasks she would sail home via West Africa. *Zebu*, however, was heavily committed to sail training and would continue. Venturers were still pouring in and in 1987 we had projects in Australia, Malaysia, Japan, Indonesia and again in Chile. *Sir Walter Raleigh*, resplendent in a new coat of paint, swept majestically into Fremantle Harbour. Along the quays, boats were gathering for the world's greatest yacht race, the America's Cup.

The starting-gun also signalled the imminent beginning of *Sir Walter Raleigh*'s voyage home. For the run, Tommy Smith handed over to his friend, Captain John Fisher, Scottish-born but long of Adelaide. Adrian Turner, the purser, who had sailed from London aboard *Zebu* at the beginning of Raleigh, was one of the many former venturers in the crew. Indeed, we kept finding our 'family' growing. Raleigh was becoming a way of life! Steaming out of Fremantle Harbour on a hot, dry day in March, the ship's horn sounded a final thank-you and farewell to Australia. Ahead were the infamous Roaring Forties, notorious for their storms, grey beards and freak waves. The fronts thundered across the south of the Indian Ocean from Cape Horn with nothing to stop them. As if in defiance of the sea, the ceremonial ship's bell in the Prince of Wales bar rang vigorously as she pitched and rolled. Some of the most seasoned sailors felt uneasy and almost all were sick, but they need not have feared, for even in a sixty knot gale the stout vessel took the sea in her stride.

Sailing via Capetown and St Helena, to pave the way for *Zebu*'s visit, *SWR* came to Sierra Leone to join in the little country's bi-centennial celebrations. Richard Snailham and I spent a few days investigating the interior with a view to future expeditions, but after a humid night in a dilapidated rest-house, with a nest of cobras for company, I had to admit there really wasn't much left to explore here.

On the afternoon of 19 June, *Sir Walter Raleigh*, as freshly painted and powdered as her sixteenth-century namesake, sailed into the inner harbour of St Helier, Jersey, and to a huge welcome at the pier. Then on to Guernsey, through the North Sea to Lowestoft and finally, the Humber estuary. In three years the grand ship had done 43,143 nautical miles and made 117 ports of call without one serious breakdown, quite an achievement for any twenty-two-year-old, and a great tribute to those who maintained her. The anchor was weighed for the last time on 30 June at 7.30 a.m. The ship made upstream to the dock basin of Hull where HRH The Duke of Gloucester, a member of the Scientific Exploration Society, came to welcome her home.

The City Council and hundreds of friends, families and ex-peditioners were on the quayside cheering and shouting con-gratulations. As *Sir Walter Raleigh* sailed majestically into dock, British Aerospace jets wheeled and dived overhead and the twin cannons boomed a final salute. I felt a little sad but rather proud and when, a few months later, we sold her for a very good price everyone was happy.

For twelve years SES had been planning an expedition to Tibet, which had originally been part of the Raleigh programme. But in 1986 when all was gloom and doom at CHQ some of my colleagues felt it might prove too costly, so although it encompassed Raleigh's aims I ran it directly under the auspices of the Society. I hoped in this way to remove a source of aggravation, for I felt that a rift was growing between those who wanted Raleigh to be a youth development programme and the explorers who sought to use challenging expeditions to promote leadership in young people. Thus I left the show in Geoff Straw's capable hands and headed for Tibet.

We had wanted to raft the Bramaputra but the Chinese required a million dollar fee. 'We just want to run it, not buy it,' remarked Sapper Colonel Henry Day, who had been negotiating with the Chinese on our behalf. In the end we settled for a cheaper option, Mt Xixabangma, which at 26,000 feet is the world's thirteenth highest mountain. It is also the greatest Himalayan peak within China, of which Tibet is part. Sharing borders with Bhutan, India and Nepal, it is a mysterious land of awesome mountains, deserts and lakes. For centuries Tibet has been shrouded in secrecy and closed to outsiders, but by 1984 the 'Roof of the World' was opened to foreigners.

We set out in September 1987, at the end of the monsoon, when there is normally little snow below 16,000 feet. Our team of thirty-four was drawn from four countries. Two tough and resourceful American ladies, nurse Paula Urschel and banker Pamela Stephany, were members of previous Raleigh expeditions. The British contingent consisted of soldiers, scientists and climbers, some of whom were also Raleigh veterans. Imperial Chemical Industries (ICI) became our major sponsor and sent a young executive, Ivan Hui, from their Hong Kong office. Speaking Mandarin, he was to prove a valuable member of the expedition. The Swires Group backed us too, and sponsored Chung Kin Man, an experienced Hong Kong mountaineer, and another asset on the language front. Through efforts of our chief scientist, Dr Henry Osmaston, the Chinese Academy of Science provided two scientists. An interpreter, liaison officer and Tibetan driver also joined us from the Chinese Mountaineering Association. One of our goals was the encouragement of Himalayan mountaineering, and Henry Day selected ten young aspirants to join his team and gain experience of climbing at higher altitudes.

The science group also included three young researchers plus a newly-qualified nurse, my twenty-three-year-old daughter, Emma. As patrons we had our good friends, General Sir John Mogg and Eric Hotung. Indeed, it was Eric's generosity that made it all possible. No one could pronounce Xixabangma (Shisha-bangma), so we code-named it Jade Venture. On 11 September we began our long trek from Kathmandu to Tibet. The heavy monsoon had caused serious landslides along the Friendship Highway linking Nepal to China, and the road was impassable by vehicle for some thirty-two kilometres before the Chinese border.

Most of us acclimatized to the altitude by marching northwards over the mountains. British mountaineer Julian Freeman-Attwood together with Lance-Corporals John House and Jim Kimber with 178 porters carried four tons of stores up the valley of the Bhote Kosi. I met them winding their way over the landslides. Each man bore a large box with the label 'Jade Venture' and an ICI logo.

Filing up a narrow mountain path, we came upon some American tourists who watched the procession with interest.

'Tell me, sir,' said the elderly gentleman. 'What's ICKY?'

'ICKY?' I replied, somewhat puzzled.

'Yeah. I.C.I. on each box.'

I quickly explained that ICI manufactures, amongst other things, fertilizers and explosives.

'Looks as if you've enough to fertilize the whole of China, then blow it up,' retorted the American.

At that point John House walked past carrying a steam lance which is used to drill holes for scientific measurements in glaciers. The evil-looking lance bore a strong resemblance to a weapon from Star Wars. On it the words 'Made by British Aerospace', who also manufacture missiles, were clearly visible. To contribute to the confusion, John wore a T-shirt inscribed 'Jade Venture – the Empire Strikes Back'.

'I get it,' the American winked. 'The CIA has companies like ICKY. Good luck to you, young fellow.'

Perspiration poured off us as we continued the climb up the high, steep slopes, picking off tenacious leeches that dropped from every tree, bush and shrub. It was a fit, lean group which finally reached Tibet.

The climbing and scientific groups had got to Tibet at about the same time. However, once across the border there were more landslides and, at Zhangmu, we were narrowly missed by a rockfall. No sooner had we traversed a slope when boulders the size of houses crashed down the mountain. Thirteen people had already been killed at this spot. We now understand why our interpreter, Wei Jian Kong, kept crying 'Hully! Hully!' Gratefully we clambered aboard a sturdy lorry, which, in spite of its obsolete design, was to prove a reliable runner in the weeks ahead. Glad to be off our feet, we happily endured the drizzle as the open truck wound its way through the precipitous gorges once known to the caravan traders as 'The Gates of Hell'.

Far below us the rapids of the River Po roared a greeting as the cold, white water tumbled from the great glaciers of the Himalayas to the plains of India. At the little town of Nyalam, old stone buildings and tin sheds provided a backdrop to the partly-built hotel at the junction of two rivers. Now at 12,000 feet, we puffed and panted as we set up camp in the icy wind.

From here Henry Day would start his climbers on the twenty-mile march to their base at 16,000 feet. After long negotiations, a train of yaks was assembled to carry the stores, and later even diminutive donkeys were used. Waving off the climbers, the academic team turned its attention to the job ahead. It was, to say the least, ambitious. With our Tibetan driver, Basna, and his faithful old truck, we set out to investigate the archaeology, botany, ecology, geology and zoology on the northern side of the mountain. We still felt the effect of altitude, but the scenery made us equally breathless. Army composite rations yielding 4,000 calories a day kept our energy levels high.

On our way up the mountain we paused at a small monastery some five miles north of Nyalam. A serious young monk ushered us into a low-ceilinged cave which, some 900 years before, had housed one of Tibet's best-loved religious masters, the poet Milarepa. Like many Tibetan monasteries, it was destroyed during the 1966 Cultural Revolution but has since been rebuilt with Chinese Government funds. Dr John Davies, an old Raleigh hand, advised me on our altitude stops and at 14,000 feet we paused at the village of Yalan. A low hill ahead was crowned with ruins. 'Ah, a lost city,' joked Pamela. We camped by the road and were soon surrounded by grubby, grinning children.

Scanning the pictures in my wildlife books, the children claimed to have seen wolves, bears, wild goats, blue sheep, snow leopards and even the Yeti. Our diminutive guests departed as the sun dropped behind the hills and the temperature followed suit.

The next day we explored and mapped the ruins of what appeared to be a fortified monastery. The massive walls had suffered fearful destruction about which the villagers knew nothing, except that it had happened long ago. Checking historical records, we guessed the monastery had been a victim of King Langdarme who tried unsuccessfully to eradicate Buddhism some 1,100 years ago.

The Lalung Leh pass at 17,000 feet marks the limit of the South Asian monsoon. At the top we had breathtaking views of the snowclad Himalayan range. Next we passed into a wasteland of dry, gravelly hills and soon came to the barren Tibetan plateau. A vast landscape of windswept grasslands and desert stretched between snowcapped mountains.

Settlements in the region are few and far between. The inhabitants of this rugged land are self-reliant nomads. Their homes were sturdy tents, warmed by dung stoves, and herds of goats, sheep and yaks surround the camps. At Lake Paiku we saw convoys of yaks, like troops of tanks, advancing across the arid plateau. The lead beasts flew red flags, religious rather than political symbols. On the plain were wild asses, gazelles, woolly hares and what appeared to be a fierce crossbreed of wolf and dog. Moving about the region, our studies continued in an area where few foreigners have been. The sun shone and at midday the temperature usually reached 70°F. Henry Osmaston, who at sixty-five was one of the fittest of the team, and Jonathan Cook, a young geologist, even managed a swim in the chilly waters.

Henry and the research assistants took several yaks and moved to the remote Dasuo glacier that flows north from Xixabangma. At 20,000 feet they discovered fantastic ice pyramids over 150 feet high, standing in rows like huge dragons' teeth. These strange formations are only found on the north side of the Himalayas and the Karakoram mountains and these were the largest Henry had ever seen. He also discovered some extraordinary, and as yet totally unexplained, footprints in the snow. Unlike those of a bear, and closer to a human foot, the prints disappeared into the vastness of Tibet. There was no sign of the creature that had made them, but the scientist captured the intriguing tracks on film.

We also needed yaks for the next part of the expedition up the southeastern side of Xixabangma. Overnight their price doubled! Clearly, they must be the most profitable cattle in the world. Although yaks appear large, clumsy creatures, they move with surprising grace, trotting quickly on their dainty hooves up the narrow trails, their flowing hair waving in the breeze. Said to be the most efficient, all-purpose animal in the world, they provide their owners with butter, meat and milk, as well as wool, clothes and tentage. Their dung dries quickly in the sun and is used as fuel and building material, but they can be ill-tempered and obstinate. I noted the caution with which their handlers approached their sharply pointed horns. In our train were also several dzo. A cross between the yak and domestic cattle, the dzo is smaller but carries the same load as its big brother.

As we plodded up a gently sloping valley, the pace was that of a pleasant, easy walk, giving us time to enjoy the magnificent scenery and observe our surroundings. The whistles of the herdsmen steering their beasts became for us the strange music of the mountains.

In the early afternoon we reached a major obstacle. A huge moraine rose 1,400 feet above a fast-flowing river. We were already over 14,000 feet high and, in the thin air, it took us an hour of puffing up an ill-defined path to reach the cairn, bedecked with prayer flags, at the top. Beyond the crest lay the intermediate base and we camped amongst piles of ration boxes, the emergency store. Next day, after a steady climb through boulder fields, we reached Henry Day's main base, with its yellow tents nestling among the rocks in the shadow of the mountain. At 16,500 feet and only some 5 miles from the summit, this was to be our home too.

On 17 October lead climbers, Luke Hughes and Stephen Venables, were already part way up the virgin east face of Xixabangma that rose at a sixty-five degree angle from the glacier below. Meanwhile, John Davies and I used the lightweight Avon inflatable to begin a hydrographic survey of the clear, cold lake at 16,952 feet above sea level.

'You'll be dead in a couple of minutes if you fall in,' said John cheerfully as we launched the craft. Later we discovered that we had unwittingly established the world altitude record for rowing a boat!

Everything was going rather well. The climbers were making good progress and Jonathan's geological specimens and botanist Clare Roberts' plant collection were increasing rapidly. We had also spotted several clusters of blood-red garnets. The rest of us concentrated on studying the wildlife, including the tiny tailless rodents that we fondly called Tibetan mice.

Our only link with the outside world, the BBC, brought news of a hurricane in Britain, but our minds were on our own weather as ominous dark clouds swept up from Nepal. As dusk fell the temperature registered below 0°F. The first flakes of snow began to swirl about the tents. Later that night the storm struck and raged for the next thirty-six hours. It was bitterly cold and pitch black inside our little tent. Emma's breathing was laboured and rapid. I was having difficulty too. Is it the altitude, I wondered, but we had been above 16,000 feet for several weeks and were fully acclimatized. Reluctantly pulling my arm from the warm sleeping bag, I rolled down my glove and glanced at the faint luminous dial of my wristwatch. It was 0300. Funny, I thought, it's very quiet outside, no wind. My shoulder touched the tent wall: it was solid. Not just frozen stiff as usual, but as solid as concrete. I remembered that it had been snowing lightly as we turned in. Now we were virtually entombed.

'We've got to get out. Get dressed quickly!' I shouted.

'Oh, Father, why must you always do things at three o'clock in the morning?' came my daughter's sleepy reply.

There was no time to be lost. Pulling on thick socks, over-trousers, boots, balaclava and overgloves, I turned to the entrance. The tent door was frozen solid too and it took several strong pulls to open the zip. A wall of snow cascaded inwards. Now we heard the wind and, digging through the snow with our mess tins, cleared a way to fresh air. My torch beam reflected off the flakes driven horizontal by the fury of the storm. Nearby I heard cries and laughter, but in the blizzard I could see nothing. Suddenly in a brilliant blue flash of lightning, I saw that the girls' tent had collapsed. With amazing good humour they staggered to the more robust army mess shelter. In base camp everyone dug to save tents and stores, whilst on the slopes of the mountain, the climbers kept a wary vigil for the ever-present threat of avalanche.

Camp Two was totally buried and the precious video camera and much of our best film were lost. At 20,600 feet, four mountaineers were marooned for three days. Our advance science camp was cut off on a distant glacier. The deep snow, shortage of fuel and the fact that no yaks could possibly reach us, soon changed the expedition into a battle for survival. The mountaineers evacuated most of their camps and Henry Osmaston's party had an epic escape from their glacier in what was, by now, a full-scale blizzard. They were lucky to reach base camp with only mild frostbite.

To make matters worse, a petrol stove exploded in our mess tent and Annabel Huxley, a member of the science group, and I were only saved from serious burns by the rapid action of Paula and Emma, who hurled us, flaming, into a snowdrift. Our demi-paradise had become a freezing hell. Eventually the storm passed and, as the sun shone, temperatures rose again. However, we now had to contend with a six-foot blanket of soft snow. We'd have given much for a pair of skis in our retreat! As the sun swung past, we trudged along a high ridge now tipped with a razor edge of blown snow. Claire, weighing only 100 pounds, was carrying a seventy-pound pack. She would never abandon the botanical specimens. I've seldom met such an uncomplaining, resolute person.

A French climber coming up from Nyalam warned us that another storm was predicted. We radioed this news to Henry Day and wondered how on earth they would get out in even more snow. Near intermediate base we again met leading Polish climber, Wojtek Kurtyka, and his friend, Halina Sickaj, whom we had first encountered in Nyalam. These marvellous people shared their ninety-three per cent proof 'mountain tea', a greatly appreciated brew.

I listened to the BBC and the news of the stock market crashing a world away, and then stepped outside to gaze one last time at the moonlit landscape. Scanning the mountain face before me I saw something move. It looked like a couple of foxes, but at dawn Wojtek showed me fresh wolf tracks. Finally reaching the town, we learned of the tragedy caused by the blizzard. People had frozen to death in buses trapped in the high passes on the Lhasa road; villagers had died of hypothermia; and several expeditions had lost men in avalanches. A group of Tibetans watching us hobble in shook their heads in amazement that we had survived our stay on Gosainthan, the Sanskrit name for Xixabangma. It means 'The Abode of God'.

We had only to reach Kathmandu. The road along which we had driven forty days before was blocked in a hundred places by landslides and the twenty-five-mile walk through the 'Gates of Hell' was littered with mud, rocks, trees and tangled telephone wires. It was after dark when Wei Jian Kong and I, our frostnipped feet hurting like hell, stumbled into a hut on the outskirts of Zhangmu. There we found Emma and Jonathan, who provided a welcome dish of noodles. Refreshed, we traversed the worst landslide of all, guided by a drunken Tibetan and fading pencil torch.

'If we could see where we were going, I don't think we'd do this,' I remarked, as we scrambled over the loose rubble and around cascading waterfalls.

After a night in a dormitory at the local hotel, we crossed the frontier into Nepal. Disappointed tourists waited in vain for permission to enter Tibet, for following the Lhasa riots, foreigners were banned once more. Chinese hostility seemed to be displayed by the roar of a nearby explosion that sent rocks flying around us. Our newly-acquired Nepalese porters dropped the baggage and fled for their lives, whilst we sheltered beneath our packs and prayed that the Chinese Army engineers would cease blasting.

Another long march and a few lifts later we reached Kathmandu, where my old friends, Jim and Belinda Edwards, took us in and provided a wonderful feast. I needed it. I had lost twenty-six pounds!

On the mountain Henry Day's team had gone back up the east face. Stephen and Luke came tantalizingly close to the summit but were turned back at 23,950 feet by strong winds. The team had spent the night out in temperatures of minus 32°F in a snow cave – without sleeping bags. Although the summit remained unconquered, the climbers did complete a new route up the eastern face and had succeeded in climbing the 23,950-foot summit of Pungpa Ri.

It had been an epic expedition in itself. The yaks never did reach the base camp and all our heavy equipment was cached in the hope that it might be collected the following spring, but we never returned and I guess the Tibetans did very well out of us! The successes in both mountaineering and science, and the close liaison with the Chinese Academy of Science, boded well for future cooperation. Miraculously, everyone got home safely, although several had frostbite.

Feeling very fit, I went on to visit the Raleigh expedition in Pakistan, which my former PA, Sue Farrington, had done much to set up. Veteran explorer David Bromhead was in charge here and Ann Tweedy was gathering material for the Raleigh books. It was proving a tough expedition and, as I arrived, David was sorting out a little problem of a Japanese girl having her bottom pinched by a frisky Pakistani. It almost resulted in his being stoned to death!

The plan was for the whole operation to end in April 1989 but by 1988 many thought the operation too successful to close. I was due to return to full-time military duty, and the SES Council, although rejoicing in the success, had grown weary of the endless fund raising and inevitable petty squabbles that always seem to occur when large numbers of unpaid volunteers become passionately involved in an ambitious project. A study was commissioned to examine the best way forward, but suddenly we found that a group with support from a large American company was, in effect, trying to stage a takeover bid. Unfortunately those representing them were too heavy-handed and immediately battlelines were drawn. The press generally sided with us, 'the little chaps', and sadly the Prince of Wales himself became drawn into the dispute. Had the SES Council been approached in a different manner, I feel we would happily have agreed to hand over Raleigh, but the certain way to stir the British is to threaten them and this resulted in an unseemly conflict. Eventually the opposition backed away and we decided on the future.

With some gentle persuasion from the Government, which had invested considerably in our scheme for Inner City youngsters, the MOD agreed to my remaining on loan to Raleigh until the end of my military service, provided I did some school and university lectures to aid recruiting. This suited me well, but I knew the venture would continue to need sound business management after Tony Nowell and our other commercial helpers left. The SES debated the issue and decided that the best answer was to set up a separate charitable body to take over. I had got to know Graham Walker, an astute and charming Northern businessman, who had backed the British entry for the America's Cup races in Australia. A somewhat shy man, he was extremely good with youngsters and indeed was truly young at heart himself and also very successful. Graham accepted the challenge and formed the Raleigh Trust and I agreed to stay on, at least until the end of my army career.

Entering this next phase we needed new areas to explore and I began to call my chums around the world. Peter and Val Enzer encouraged me to consider Zimbabwe, whilst Brigadier Joe Singh, now Chief of Staff of the Guyana Defence Force, was eager for us to go there. Cameroons had long been in mind and there was still plenty to do in Chile and Pakistan. An expedition in Alaska helped to clean up after the *Valdez* oil spill and our Canadian committee ran a fine project in the Arctic. We even organized a small expedition in Britain providing community aid. Portugal, our oldest ally, hosted another and no fewer than three expeditions took place in Kenya. Furthermore the Iron Curtain was looking shaky, and I began to work on plans for Siberia and, encouraged by Lord Glenarthur, then Minister of State, we also considered Mongolia. In line with our sea-going tradition we had used the Jubilee Sailing Trust's *Lord Nelson* to carry the venturers to and from the Bahamas, where Tony Walton ran more projects. The return of *Lord Nelson* fitted in well with the end of phase one.

On Monday morning 3 April, the sun was just beginning to penetrate the grey clouds as Vic Rudge, our stalwart Hampshire Coordinator, and I climbed aboard the launch to greet the ship. Beneath the towering cranes lining the quayside, a crowd of well-wishers waited in the chilly breeze. Ahead, silhouetted against the distant horizon, was the tall ship. Her masts stood out like church spires amongst the squat container vessels ploughing furrows up the Channel. Her rigging was alive with venturers furling the sails; it was a scene that could have happened a hundred years ago. Three hundred metres from the dock, her cannon boomed seven times in stentorian salute. Flis Bowden, our movements officer, in her Territorial Army role, answered with the shore gun as cheers rang out; sirens blared and welcoming banners waved in the wind. The press swarmed over the vessel and Vic had arranged a splendid reception with the backing of the Mayor of Southampton. Another ship had come home.

Next day an exhibition of our artists' work was opened at the National Army Museum by the Minister for the Arts. Another guest was the great explorer Wilfred Thesiger, who had assisted us in Kenya. He viewed a portrait of himself, done by one of our venturers, with approval. It was a great tribute to the efforts of our Art Director, Ley Kenyon, who worked tirelessly to get his protégés into the remotest parts of the world where they painted and sketched in jungles and swamps, often with only a stub of a candle for light.

The art show was just one of the events which celebrated the end of the first stage of Raleigh and the beginning of the next. Four days later, over 3,000 venturers, international representatives and supporters piled into London's Royal Albert Hall for a grand reunion, organized by Geoff Straw and Bill Bellars. Peruvian venturer Sandra Echegaray Samanez spoke on John Dunn's popular BBC radio programme and our press office excelled itself, fielding interviews across the country. As evening drew in, people from many lands arrived at the Albert Hall. Some wore black tie, others sported expedition T-shirts and jeans, and a number of two-legged lions were seen being chased by gorillas. Knightsbridge had never seen the like. Tony Walton, just back from Zimbabwe, acted as Master-of-Ceremonies, our padre, Olympic canoeist Basil Pratt, said prayers, and, against the din in the cavernous hall, I reviewed the progress of the 'Raven Rations Survivors' Club'. Graham Walker, our new Chairman, spoke of his hopes for the future and read a congratulatory message from Prince Charles. A multi-projector audiovisual show splashed across the screen; afterwards, the party dissolved into splendid informality.

General Sir John and Lady Mogg were in the thick of the disco dancing. Everyone scoured the circular maze of the hall's corridors looking for companions who had come from as far away as Pakistan, Australia and Singapore. Hawk Freeman flew in from Colorado, and Clive Barrow arrived straight off the plane, still covered in the dust of Kenya. In the programme was a glowing tribute from Prime Minister Margaret Thatcher who had given consistent and enthusiastic support. It was a night no one present will ever forget, a night which made us recall the achievements of this extraordinary band.

Of course, we had encountered a host of problems during the

previous four years. The venturers faced their own trials to raise funds for their expeditions, but few of them knew the battles fought by CHQ and the international committees to maintain the vital cash flow. Sending expeditions to the ends of the earth often means long and costly negotiations with governments, expensive reconnaissance trips and the necessary boats, trucks, rations, tents, and equipment. If, as sometimes happens, political conflicts force us to cancel arrangements, a great deal of time and money has been spent for naught. Then there is the cost of insurance, of recruitment and selection tests and expenditures on research, communications, rent and wages raise the bills to alarming proportions. With careful economic planning, however, we had managed to use a bit more black ink than red, and it was time to look ahead.

More and more venturers were sponsored by their companies, convinced that the challenge of strenuous tasks and demanding projects would prove a good investment. Thanks to Sir Peter Morrison's powers of persuasion large numbers of young were sponsored by the nationalized industries. The success of the inner-city venturers had led the British government to send members of the Youth Training Scheme with us, although this meant increased instruction and guidance by the staff. One group of industrialists told me that they judged a young person's time with us as the equivalent of holding a university degree: 'Many people have paper quali-fications, but very few have practical experience of group man-agement, problem solving, teamwork and tackling projects under difficult circumstances. We know that all the men and women who have been on Raleigh have that experience.' Without a doubt, throwing together young people of different backgrounds, colours and creeds before they have developed any unshakable prejudice does much to foster international understanding.

In maintaining our global links, it was necessary to take care that words in one English-speaking country were not misinterpreted in another. I received some very funny looks when, during a TV broadcast in Raleigh, North Carolina, I talked about 'venturers humping their rucksacks over the hills'. In another instance, I remember the Lord Mayor of Hull missing a step or two as he danced with American Jenny Bond who casually remarked that the North Carolinians 'so enjoy shagging that they hold contests for it'. Apparently 'shagging' is a dance common to their coastal regions.

But everyone understood the broader language of the goals of

Operation Raleigh – the development of leadership and character. People from all over the world shared hardships and returned to their own countries to help the disabled, the sick, the elderly and the unemployed. They are all answering the final challenge of Drake and Raleigh: 'What can you give back to your community?'

As our numbers grew, it became necessary to give more guidance to those returning from the rigours of expedition life. Roberta Howlett produced a booklet entitled 'Been There . . . Done That . . . What Now?' In particular, we formed a close association with the Duke of Edinburgh Award Scheme which operates all over the world and recognizes various levels of achievement attained by young people. This kind of follow-up is vital, and it is good to see how many venturer support groups have been established by the young people themselves. The overwhelming enthusiasm to help others generated by Raleigh expeditions is equally strong in other parts of the world. I have seen it as I tramped through the heather to see Venture Scotland's bothy – a remote hut in the Highlands. I saw it again as I watched venturers launch their hot-air balloon *Spirit of Kitty Hawk*, on a stormy night in North Carolina.

The young lions were beginning to lead the pride.

SEVENTEEN

New Directions

'LOOK OUT!' CRIED the startled accountant as the tusker bore down on us. Needing no further bidding, the chairman, the doctor, the banker, the journalist and I plunged through the bush. Happily, the elephant lost interest and left us, adrenalin pumping, to draw breath and laugh at our headlong flight.

This was just one of the many experiences indelibly stamped on the memories of the twenty-four members of Operation Raleigh's first executive expedition, ranging in age from twenty-seven to sixty-nine, when they volunteered to spend four weeks in southern Africa on the aptly named 'Kalahari Quest'. Irreverently nicknamed 'the wrinklies' by the seventeen to twenty-five-year-olds who usually took part in our expeditions, these mature explorers were to experience the same thrills which made Raleigh so memorable for the young.

The scheme came about because venturers returning to their companies found their superiors did not appreciate what they had done during their expedition, nor how the experience might fit them for greater responsibility. So they suggested executives should see them in action in the field. 'Fine,' said the sponsors, 'but we need to give them the sort of experience offered to younger people. We want something to stimulate and remotivate them and provide opportunities to develop teamwork, decision making, problem solving, innovative and creative thinking, planning, controlling and time management, and, above all, to give them confidence in their own abilities.'

Professor John Adair, my colleague from the days of the Sealed Knot, and one of the world's foremost experts on leadership in management, believed the Raleigh experience could do all of this. He suggested that by taking executives overseas to face challenging projects, we could provide the cloak of excellence in management training while doing much to overcome the day-to-day stress and pressure of the commercial world.

Thus the Executive Expedition was launched. Within hours a secretary rang to ask if we would take her chairman to the North Pole for a year!

We picked a team from varying occupations, skills and backgrounds, from Britain, Botswana, Eire, France and the United States and from companies including the Bank of Boston, British Gas, ICI, Guinness and Vickers Medical Division. Compatibility is vital on expeditions and, to check this, applicants endured an assessment weekend at Sherborne Castle, Dorset, Sir Walter Raleigh's former home.

Final briefings over and kit issued, we boarded a British Airways flight for Gaborone, capital of Botswana. Each executive had a particular role. Eleanor Rogers, company secretary of News International, was the botanist, while Jerry Shively, formerly chief executive of Johnson Wax, was in charge of video filming and canoeing.

Our Botswana chairman, Louis Nchindo of Anglo-American, enthusiastically welcomed the team, delighted that so many top business people should be visiting his country, which, as big as France, is still little known outside Africa. Then, guided by author and Kalahari expert Mike Main, we set off to seek new archaeological sites and study the fauna and flora of the country. By dusk on day one, our column of land cruisers had reached Kubu, a crescent-shaped rocky island about a kilometre long situated in the Makgadikgadi Pans. This vast ancient lake-bed was the setting for Wilbur Smith's bestseller *Sunbird*. Here we made camp, assembled the microlight that had been towed up from Johannesburg and then settled to watch the flaming red sun sink behind the grotesque baobab trees that stood sentinel on this lonely shore of a sea that dried up long ago. It was like sitting on the beach waiting for the tide to come in, but that had not happened for 1,500 years. Mike said of this place, 'None will forget the deep-rooted and tranquil magic of that extraordinary island, lodged like a pearl on the shore of a limitless sea, where the land and sky at evening merge, inseparable, into a symphony of muted colours. To stand here, on the rim of nature's palette, is to stand on the edge of another planet – stark, simple, silent and beautiful beyond words. No soul was untouched.'

BOTSWANA

At this site, directed by Tom Huffman, Professor of Archaeology at Witwatersrand University, and Alec Campbell, who had been director of Botswana Museum, we mapped an ancient walled enclosure and examined over 200 strange cairns. Tom postulated that the cairns could have been schools at which boys were initiated into manhood and taught how to farm, fight and hunt, before entering regiments. But rumours of another ruin nearby prompted us to dispatch Philip Welch and his microlight, with Alec riding piggyback, on a dawn mission. The sun had hardly risen when they were back with the exciting news of significant ruined walls, around a metre high enclosing some seven hectares, at the edge of the pan. Arriving at this new site we found pottery scattered everywhere and discovered a cowrie shell which had originated in the Indian Ocean, probably carried here as currency. Ruins of buildings in the enclosure and the absence of cairns fascinated Tom who had studied the Zimbabwean Empire for over twenty years. He believed that the walls are of thirteenth-century origin and once belonged to this empire. Was this another lost circumcision centre or the remains of a once important city? We shall have to await future excavation to learn more.

The next task lay on Botswana's western frontier. Jon Foulds, chairman of the Halifax Building Society, led his team to the Tsodilo Hills and managed to locate some previously undiscovered rock paintings. Meanwhile, the rest of us drove many dusty miles westward to explore caves near the Namibian frontier in search of more archaeological sites. Vast colonies of bats inhabit these caverns which were discovered in 1932 and are said to be the lair of leopards and the site of a great treasure hidden by an early settler. Sadly we made no dramatic finds, but to sit in the total silence and darkness of the caves was a thought-provoking experience. After a day's exploration in the baking sun, there was little time for rest, with meals to prepare, punctures to repair, reports to write, and equipment to service. However, a bottle of specially brewed, extra-strong original Irish Guinness, even if a trifle warm, did much to restore our health. The entertainments officer, Eamon Murphy, Dublin sales manager for Guinness, kept us well supplied. Indeed because some bottles had broken in the trucks, we were awash with it! Rations were canned or dried, supplemented with fresh beef and delicious local sausage. Several of us became addicted to the tough salty biltong made of dried buffalo meat which we sliced and chewed like gum.

The nights were often bitterly cold and insurance company chairman, Robert Rose, woke on several mornings with frost on his woolly hat. However, we did have one splendid hot water bottle, Mike Main's enchanting Jack Russell, although Pamela Stephany said that a dog's cold nose worming its way into her sleeping bag felt rather like a mamba! Travelling across the Kalahari, ancient baobab trees, on which early explorers had carved their names and used as post boxes, were among the few landmarks available to us. However, navigation was no problem as John Lyons, a New York electronics engineer, had brought along a new device, known as a Magellan, which uses four satellites to determine its position within three metres. Another useful item of twentieth-century technology was a Pilkington image intensifier, with which we could see in the dark and count game at night. Some of our fresh meat had gone rotten and we put it out as hyena bait, then sat to watch with this device. After a short time Helen Foulds exclaimed, 'I can see something moving. It's large and white.'

'Where, where?' we questioned.

'Oh, but I think it's Jerry,' she exclaimed.

Indeed it was, for he had taken his shovel and sought privacy to commune with nature in the darkness. Such are the problems of squatting, even a hundred yards away, when the camp has one of these infernal machines!

The final phase took the expedition into the Okavango Delta where the moist air revived us after the dry, dusty Kalahari. Crocodile and hippos shared the waterways, moving noisily among the papyrus reeds, while the great fish eagle's yodelling call echoed overhead. Our muscles ached from the effort of canoeing, and blistered hands bore testimony to the roughness of the homemade paddles. Eamon had thoughtfully deposited a supply of 'six-packs' in shallow water so that we could refresh ourselves with a cool Guinness. Later on we overheard two Australians in a bar in Maun saying, 'Unbelievable – haven't had a beer for days and we reached down beside the boat and there was a bottle of Guinness – bloody amazing.'

Whether on foot among big game or being poled silently through the reed beds in dugouts, our trip was a journey through another world, and the final supper at the Victoria Falls in Zimbabwe completed the magic.

Writing to me afterwards John Campbell, our management trainer, said:

The scale of everything you undertake is so much bigger on an expedition to a remote place, the distances are longer, the scenery more magnificent, the flora and fauna more exotic, the very timelessness of it. And so it is with the experience. There is no doubt that management development using the outdoors is immensely successful in Britain – mine and other companies can testify to this. But there is something very different about doing the same work in the wide open spaces of the Kalahari, perhaps reviewing the day under a baobab tree, or examining leadership styles after some key decisions around a camp fire in the Okavango Delta. The reality of the situations, the need for decision and the interplay between people is inescapable. There is no hotel room to retire to in comfort and hide away, there is just the reality that tomorrow is another day when tasks have to be completed and the journey continued. So from a management development viewpoint it is an exhilarating environment in which to work. People do learn, do discover new resources in themselves, and new perspectives on a wide range of issues. It is not an experience from which people return unmoved. In many ways it is this personal quest which participants will value most on reflection, the fact that they have had a good opportunity to reconsider their priorities and recharge their batteries and all this on top of examining their leadership, decision making and interpersonal skills.

The impact on the individuals was certainly profound, and they returned home thoughtful, re-motivated and, in many cases, suffering post-expedition blues, but clearly the concept worked. So I decided to repeat it in another land.

In 1987, on my way to Tibet, I lunched with friends in Kathmandu. 'It's said there's a mammoth-like beast living in a remote stretch of jungle alongside the Karnali River,' smiled John Edwards, filling my glass with ice cold beer.

'Rubbish, they're extinct,' I retorted.

'Of course, but something big is frightening the pants off the people and messing up their crops,' said John.

'Get a few facts and we might have a look for your giant one day,' I laughed.

Three years later a bubbly young lady who had been with me on Operation Drake burst into my London office. 'I took this a couple of months ago from a canoe on the Karnali,' announced Sarah Bamfylde proudly, handing me a photograph of what appeared to be a very fat bull elephant with a massive bump on his head and a heavy bearded tail.

Experts could not explain the bump. Some thought it might be a tumour resulting from a bullet wound, but all felt the subject worth investigation. Thus began the Karnali Quest and so the next team of executives went to Nepal in 1991 and, travelling by river, foot and elephant, did valuable scientific work, but although giant footprints were seen in the jungle, we found no monsters. However, reliable witnesses convinced me that a large beast did exist in the remote Bardia forest.

Thus we returned in 1992 flying into Kathmandu with high hopes. Seven of the original group were joined by seven newcomers. Ages ranged between twenty-eight and fifty-five again with a wide variety of professions. Chief Inspector David Warren of the Humberside

Constabulary was the ornithologist, whilst Rod Barnes, landlord of the Jolly Woodman at Burnham, was studying the rare Ganges River dolphin, and Sheena Cox, who managed Our Price record shops in London, was researching the flora. Everyone had different responsibilities and John Hunt, General Manager of Marks and Spencer, Belfast, was to make a video film and specialize in elephants. He trained by running the New York marathon! With luck, we might catch a glimpse of the strange beast, but I was not relying totally on luck and had arranged for trackers to scour the area for weeks before we arrived. Our work was also to take in a wide-ranging survey of fauna and flora for the Natural History Museum and the Nepalese Wild Life Department so there would be plenty to do.

Tiger Mountain, a company noted for its conservation interest and expertise in handling clients who want to climb Everest, had the

THE KARNALI AREA

arrangements in hand when we stepped off our plane. We were to
fulfil one of my ambitions, to explore the little known Karnali River
Gorges with Avon inflatables en route to the remote forest, and forty
porters had already carried the boats over the mountains. Two days
later and 200 miles westward we de-bussed and started the long trek to
the Karnali canyon. Climbing up and down the foothills for three
days got us much fitter. The route was mapped, discoveries recorded
and the bird list grew longer as Inspector Warren's binoculars picked
up our feathered friends. However, there was apprehension as we
approached the river. It had never been navigated at low water and
the rapids would be obstructed by huge boulders. 'It may be
technically more difficult, but the force should be down,' confided
Megh Ale, our chief boatman, as we sipped Kukri rum by the camp
fire. Even he seemed concerned. Few of our team had ever been
rafting but all could swim!

We hit big water on the first morning and, hearing the roar of the
cataracts, checked helmets and life jackets, digging our feet under
thwarts. 'Paddle together,' screamed the helmsman, as Avons slid
down the slope into the wall of towering waves. Freezing glacier
water cascaded over us as we bounced through foaming torrents. The
exhilaration was tremendous and tension gave way to joy as, wet but
unscathed, we hit rapid after rapid. The gorges reminded me of the
Blue Nile: I hoped there were no bandits. One especially dangerous
obstacle forced us to lower our craft, unmanned, on lines, but in eight
days we navigated sixty-eight cataracts, charted the river, caught
fish for science and the pot, as well as counting birds, crocodiles and
mammals. Still no sign of giant elephants.

We were the first foreigners to enter several villages, but everywhere smiling people greeted us. Perhaps this was due to the locally
grown marijuana, but they were jolly friendly. One declining tribe,
the Raji, had until recently been hunter gatherers, believing it taboo
to grow crops, but sadly deforestation has forced them to become
labourers. With pitiful thanks they accepted our gifts of biscuits and
salt and told us they had heard of great creatures in the jungle to the
south. I wondered if they meant rhino or something larger. On 7
March a huge fish-eating crocodile watched us cruise out of the last
great gorge into the jungle-covered valley and, as the sun set, we
found five lovely ladies awaiting us on the bank. Honey Blossom and
her sister, Luksmi, had come with three younger elephants to carry us
on the next phase of the quest. With raised trunks they trumpeted a

welcome. In the days ahead we would come to love these lumbering jumbos as they transported us through the dark forest. Whatever we found they must face the danger with us. Tents up and steaming mugs of tea served, we sat in the warm evening listening to the news from the trackers who had been working ahead.

'Only last night tulu hatti, big elephant, destroyed a banana plantation two hours from here,' reported Pradeep Rana, the naturalist who was to direct the hunt.

'How big?' asked Zimbabwean company chairman, John Cochrane.

'The footprints are very large, you must see for yourself,' said Pradeep.

'I'll go,' volunteered the enthusiastic Marks and Spencer man.

'Any snakes?' enquired our red-headed Irish herpetologist, Mark O'Shea.

'Too cold yet, perhaps a little later,' the Nepalese assured him. Mark looked sad; he lived for snakes!

That night I slept fitfully, constantly awoken by Honey Blossom's insistent calls. 'God, what a noisy beast.' My dreams were little comfort. There was something massive, something malignant, perhaps even supernatural, always lurking just beyond vision in the dense vegetation. I wondered what on earth the next day would bring. Perhaps Honey Blossom was having nightmares too.

Clutching his tape measure, John Hunt left at dawn and, moving through the dripping grass, soon picked up fresh tiger spoor and the track of a large rhino. Then his Nepali tracker pointed out a vast circular print in the mud. 'Tulu hatti,' he hissed. It was very fresh and water oused into the impression as they measured the diameter. 'Twenty-one inches, multiply by six for the shoulder height . . . wow, that's ten foot six,' whispered John, calculating the size of the beast by a tested formula. 'A very big elephant.' The Asian elephant is smaller than its African cousin, the largest is thought to have reached eleven feet one inch. Cows grow to around eight feet and can weigh a little over four tons. Most bulls have tusks, which can exceed nine feet, whereas cows do not, although they can grow short tusks.

In the dark next morning, festooned with binoculars and cameras, we hauled ourselves up our jumbo's tails into the stout wooden howdahs. Three explorers, a tracker and the thanet, or driver, to each beast. Our mounts breakfasted on balls of grass filled with saffron rice which they stole from a canvas-covered pile. As we climbed aboard, their great brown eyes watched patiently. 'Why is it that the largest and strongest animal on earth willingly takes orders from mere men?' we asked, knowing that a flick of the trunk could break our backs. There is a strange bond of respect, even love, between man and elephant, but I knew that Luksmi had broken her thanet's back with her trunk when he had been operating on her foot some years before.

Moving at around two miles per hour we entered the cuckoo grass, twenty-foot stalks brushed past, brightly coloured birds dipped from tree to tree and spotted deer scampered away as our unstoppable transport plodded forward. At the river the ladies pushed down the bank, then, tucking in their hind legs, slid gracefully down on their bottoms. Like five fat cruisers in line ahead, they entered the swirling water; leaning into the current, feeling the way forward, the girls had no difficulty with the crossing. Elephants love water. Walking further on, someone dropped a lens cap. The jumbo picked it up with her trunk and passed it back. We began to wonder who was in charge.

A flash of orange was all we saw as the tiger left the last of its kill and, with a defiant snarl, looped away through the reeds, but our hearts beat faster. 'They'll never believe this in the Tottenham Court Road,' said a lady manager from London, the beating of her heart almost echoing through the forest. Only a week before the ladies had surrounded a tiger on a kill and in a couple of bounds the cat had clawed its way up an elephant's trunk. The surprised thanet hit it over the head with his stick and it leapt off. Asian elephants are thought to respond to orders in Hindi which sometimes causes problems for the Nepalese. A young elephant was on a training trip in Bardia with Pradeep Rana when they came across a large tiger which charged. The thanet gave what he thought was the appropriate command and to his horror the elephant sat down. However the tiger skidded to a halt, looked rather puzzled, and stalked off.

We picked up the previous day's tracks and headed into the mist that still hung amongst the sal trees at the forest edge. Suddenly the ladies stopped. Their ears came forward like parabolic reflectors and the deep rumbling purr of elephants' communication by low frequency sound began. There was something ahead of us. Our eyes strained into the thin mist. Our sharp-eyed policeman saw it first. 'Look,' he muttered, pointing forward. I saw nothing, then the grey background I had assumed was sky beyond the trees began to move. It looked like an enormous pile of rocks sliding silently through the forest, then a huge creature emerged. Its great domed head, heavy tusks and bulbous body gave it the appearance of a fat old gentleman with spare tyres and double chin. A thick, serpent-like trunk sought our scent. No one spoke, but our elephants trembled and our cameras clicked. 'My God,' gasped John Cochrane, as I reloaded my Canon (camera not gun!). Looking up I could scarcely believe my eyes. A second grey mountain was moving into view, even more massive than the first. His enormous tusks curved upwards, and his huge head carried an even higher dome. 'What on earth is it?' whispered someone.

'Mammoth?' said another softly, and I could see how that legend had grown up. It was as if one had been seeking the Yeti, and suddenly met it, but this chap weighed at least six tons.

'He's in musth, we must be careful,' warned Pradeep, indicating the yellow discharge running down the big bull's face from a gland behind the eye. Knowing this condition even makes domestic elephants extremely dangerous, we backed away.

Flapping their ears, the ghostly apparitions approached, pausing only to pluck some choice branch or seize a trunkful of grass. The giants were fifty yards away and our mounts were shaking with fear. They too had never seen anything like this before, but the thanets spoke gently, coaxing them to retreat slowly across a dry riverbed. However, we wanted good, clear pictures, so we returned, and found the monsters feeding in a shady copse. To tempt them out Chan Chan Kali, a sexy young thing, was persuaded to trumpet to the bulls. 'A mating call,' exclaimed Pradeep.

'I hope not,' commented John Davies, our medical officer. But the shrill cry that would have woken the dead had no effect.

'Just our luck to find a gay elephant,' mused my assistant, Sally Cox.

Measurements of the footprints show Raja Gaj or King Elephant, as our trackers named the big fellow, to be approximately eleven foot three to eleven foot six at the shoulder, whilst Kancha, the younger beast, was around ten foot six. I knew they must be amongst the largest Asian elephants ever discovered, but could not explain their strange shape nor why they existed in this remote valley.

For ten days we followed them, sometimes meeting in dense jungle and other times in the tall grass along the river. We stalked each other in a slow-moving game of cat and mouse. Gradually they seemed to become more interested in the ladies and came to meet us when we approached. Did they realize there were humans there too? One day even our girls forgot this when Luksmi suddenly lost patience with a young elephant, charging her and butting her much to the alarm of the riders. The great bulls looked on as the two trumpeting females thundered through the bush. They seemed to say 'what on earth are you silly women playing at?' But for most of the time they regarded us with amused indifference, although when they were together, Kancha acted as an escort and forced us away. At other times they would show off, dusting themselves with clouds of dirt or wrenching over stout trees. There were rumours of a third bull but we did not see him, nor for that matter any cows. That remains a mystery, but with six hundred square miles of forest, who knows what is there.

The BBC World Service news had just ended and I had closed my eyes when Pradeep started beating on my tent. 'Come quickly, John. Raja Gaj is here,' he hissed.

'In the camp?' I exclaimed, wrapping on a sarong and grabbing a torch.

On the moonlit path to the elephant lines I found the boys agitated and frightened.

'Big elephant has taken Honey Blossom,' wailed one.

Sure enough her tethering chains were broken and I knew she could not do that herself. How on earth could a six-ton kidnapper walk undetected into a camp of forty people, I asked myself as we set out to find her. Just inside the forest I shone my flashlight on a black mass and called softly, 'Come along, Honey Blossom, be a good girl.'

It turned and I faced two enormous curved tusks. Thirty feet away stood Raja Gaj. His piggy eyes reflected the light, then, ears forward, he came shambling at me in a deliberate charge. But as I flicked off the torch, he stopped. Elephants have poor sight and the wind was coming from him. Quietly Rod Barnes pushed an image intensifier into my shaking hands. Now able to see in the dark, we stood silently watching him in the green electronic light trying to locate us. His long thick trunk sniffed the air. I could see Honey Blossom just beyond the tusker. 'Get everyone among the boulders by the river for safety,' I whispered to Rod as the thanets advanced with torches of burning grass. For a moment the raider stood and I thought he would charge again, but then, with a snort, he wheeled and, pushing over a two-foot-thick tree as if it were a match stick, disappeared into the darkness. Before Honey Blossom could follow, her thanet climbed up her tail and onto her shoulders, driving her back to camp. A disappointed lady and a brave man! I returned to the camp fire, looking ridiculous in sarong and flip flops and poured myself a stiff Scotch.

Our work continued. Mark found his beloved snakes and collected an impressive fifteen-foot python, a beautiful black and rather lethal cobra and other highly dangerous reptiles, all to be released after study, measurement and the milking of venom. The bird list reached 200 specimens seen and Rod saw his dolphins.

John Davies, our doctor who had accompanied me on many expeditions, was noted for his dry wit, shaggy dog stories and quiet professionalism. This time most of his patients were animals. A large python, nibbled by a tiger, was stitched up whilst it writhed in Chris Burke's firm grip and then we had a really big casualty.

Chan Chan, our foxy lady, held up her foot, as a dog will lift a paw with a thorn in it. 'John,' I called, 'we've got an interesting little job for you.' Lying the young elephant down, her thanet pointed to a bamboo spike, deeply buried in the sole of her right foot. Clearly it was going to be extremely difficult to dig out. However, whilst her handler sat on Chan Chan's head and whispered soothing words into her great ear, John set to work. 'The forceps are no good,' said the doc, 'I need some pliers.' Luckily my Swiss penknife, the one essential item that comes everywhere with me, includes a small pair, and using this, he pulled at the splinter. Chan Chan curled up her trunk as one may grip the arms of a dentist's chair and great salty tears ran down her cheeks. She was in considerable pain. As John worked, I watched that coiled trunk anxiously knowing what Luksmi had done to her keeper during a similar operation. A blow from this iron-hard muscle could easily kill. At last the four-inch spike was out and John cleaned the pliers. The patient stood up and tested her foot. Well-satisfied and grateful, she put out her trunk and stroked the doctor's back. Tears came to our eyes. However, on the last day, Kancha, the smaller tusker, suddenly emerged from the jungle and charged Pradeep's Land-Rover, just to remind us that not all elephants are friendly.

Our success was entirely due to the Nepalese who live with and love the elephants and wild beasts of the forest. Their Hindu God Ganesh is said to be reincarnated in the elephant and we prayed that this would ensure their protection from poachers, but the size of that ivory is a great temptation for an impoverished peasant with a hungry family.

When news of our discovery reached the outside world, there was immediate interest and John Hunt's film was shown by CNN worldwide television. Raja Gaj was thought to be around fifty, and

Kancha in his late thirties. Elephants can live to seventy so they are not old, and the reason for the massive size and strange shape is still under discussion. Some suggest they are survivors of a herd that has existed in isolation for many years and may be mutants caused by inbreeding. Other experts urged a survey of the surviving wild elephants of Nepal. However, the speculation was over and perhaps we can arrange for some female elephants to be introduced. Otherwise these great bulls may be condemned to a sterile existence and their genes never passed on.

Back in Kathmandu I found ele-experts Iain and Oria Douglas-Hamilton on their way home from the Tokyo CITES conference at which the contentious question of the sale of ivory had featured. They had gone to Bardia and found only dung and footprints: the enormous grey ghosts had disappeared again into the vast forest. Perhaps our executive explorers were just lucky, or maybe they had used their initiative and enterprise to solve a problem far from the boardroom. But I knew we must preserve these unique creatures before some ivory-hungry poacher kills them.

So it was when I returned to Britain that I sought support from my friends in conservation. Hardly had I started when a fax arrived from Peter Byrne, hunter turned animal defender, who for some years has been protecting another large elephant 100 miles further west. He wrote how, shortly after we left the area, this huge elephant, heavily in musth, had left a reserve and, doubtless in great pain, wandered into a populated area. The locals, resettled hill people, do not understand large wild animals and when their dogs attacked the intruder, he panicked, crashing through the settlement killing three villagers and several buffalo. According to a witness the giant tusker had speared a bull buffalo from its back to its chest, hurling it fifty yards, before returning to his herd in the sanctuary of the reserve. The outcry can be imagined, but realizing it would be tragic if this awful accident were to lead to the destruction of these noble creatures, I asked friends of the King of Nepal to help. He did and the tusker was spared. So SES set up a fund for a detailed study and we began to plan our return, but that's another story, and now my attention turned northwards to the curtain that was rising on the Soviet Union.

As Peristroika spread, new and exciting challenges became apparent in Siberia, a land I doubted I would ever see unless as a prisoner-of-war, and after some correspondence with interested Russians, I flew out to investigate the possibilities. Aeroflot had kindly provided me with a first class seat and I felt like a member of the presidium as we winged our way over the endless forest and steppe. Sensing that a meal was about to be served, I lowered my tray table from the back of the seat in front. It flopped down on a broken hinge, refusing to stay upright. Pressure on the call button produced the stewardess, one of Russia's leading lady weight-lifters, who glowered at the offending table, then with a flash of inspiration, grunted 'moment' and headed for the galley. Ah! gone to fetch her tool box, I thought. A few minutes later she returned, wrenched the table back into its fold away position, put a bottle of warm champagne on the seat beside me and commanded, 'Drink.' Perhaps that was the answer to all problems in Russia! Finally our meal arrived. Two doorstep-thick slices of bread separated by a thin smear of fish paste, wrapped in cling film. My neighbour, who appeared to be an important official, inspected his sandwich with the care of a connoisseur, then rang for the weight-lifter to whom he indicated that there was something amiss. Seizing the plate, she stamped off towards the economy section. I watched, fascinated, as she plucked a plate from a red-faced peasant woman, peeled the sandwich apart, nodded in satisfaction, exchanged it for the official's meal and marched back. All seemed happy although the peasant looked a little sad. I had discovered one of the differences between First Class and Economy travel. In First Class you have butter in sandwiches, peasants do not.

At Irkutsk I was greeted by our new committee and treated to a whistle-stop tour of the region. One evening I was left to my own devices and, following their directions, decided to join a dinner party in a beer cellar. My hosts were holidaying East Europeans. No one spoke English, but with the help of a dictionary we managed to communicate. The menu included a dish from each country represented at the dinner, but, sadly because they only learned I was coming at a late hour, it had not been possible to include an English course. However, pointing to the buxom waitresses at the far side of the restaurant, they explained they had found some T-shirts bearing English children's songs. 'Ah,' I remarked, 'nursery rhymes.' As the waitresses approached I saw that a cartoon was emblazoned on their ample bosoms. To my astonishment the caption read: AIDS KILLS, DON'T BE SILLY, GET THAT CONDOM ON YOUR WILLIE.' Apparently a free issue from the World Health Organization!

EIGHTEEN

In the Hoofprints of
Genghis Khan

'WELCOME TO MONGOLIA, COLONEL,' said the almond-eyed beauty in the black leather mini-skirt as she brushed aside a lock of long black hair that hung over one eye. 'I am here to look after you, my name is Minjin,' (which means Beaver) she smiled. My God, I thought, this must be a KGB trap. But there was no opportunity to flee as my damnably attractive escort led me out of the airport to the waiting Volga. Somewhere from behind came the rest of the greeting team including Sean Hinton, a young musicologist, who was to become my most valued adviser over the next two years.

Travelling into Ulan Batar, Minjin briefed me in perfect, but somewhat Victorian English.

'Where did you study my language?' I asked.

'In Moscow. I do hope it is correct.' I assured her it was, perhaps just a little quaint. 'Oh, the tapes were very old,' she replied.

By two that afternoon I had explained what Operation Raleigh was all about to a dozen Mongols and was repeating it for the Minister of Education. The planning for this expedition had begun eighteen months previously when a Mongolian Government delegation had visited London seeking closer ties with Britain. After almost seventy years of Soviet domination, Mongolia, landlocked and sandwiched between Russia and China, was likely to become truly independent. However, the departure of 400,000 Soviet troops and the probable withdrawal of Russian aid was going to cause immense problems in a land roughly the size of Western Europe with a population of only two million and few natural resources. The Mongols needed new friends.

Slightly to my surprise, the Minister appreciated the value of hordes of Raleigh venturers invading his country and suggested we fly to the most remote aimag or province to see if we could carry out a series of community aid and conservation tasks there. Thus, Minjin, Sean and I found ourselves jostling to get aboard a well-used Mongolian Airlines (MIAT) Antonov 24 airliner. The seats were utility and not designed for fifteen-stone colonels, but we were soon winging westward over the rolling sands of the Gobi. Frozen lakes and snowcapped mountains passed beneath. The other passengers stared at us with mild curiosity. My neighbour, a small lad, picked his nose thoughtfully and watched everything I did.

At Khovd bright sun and a bitter wind greeted our arrival. On the tarmac a short, smiling gentleman advanced and introduced himself as Mr Terbish, rector of the local Pedagogical Institute. He was to be our host and later to represent Operation Raleigh in the region. Here the arid Gobi (desert) meets the Altai Mountains. In the far northwest the Tavan Bogd range extends across the border with China, Mongolia and Russia. The highest peak, Mt Huiten (15,300 feet), dominates an area of alpine magnificence. The sharp ridges of the mountains with eternal snowscapes are the birthplace of glittering glaciers leading down to sparkling emerald lakes.

Khovd city with some 20,000 Mongols, Kazakhs and other racial groups is the capital of the aimag. Apart from the government building and a colourful theatre the place was drab and dilapidated. Warmed by a bowl of boiled mutton and some soggy rice in the hotel, we began the long round of briefings. We explained about Raleigh, and local officials outlined their own needs, including medical help, the construction of refuge huts for travellers, bridges, biological studies and above all English teachers.

Within a few hours I was ready to see something of the countryside and over the desert we bounced in an old Russian jeep with a singing driver. Quickly I realized I was in an area that few if any westerners had ever visited. There were unclimbed peaks, unnavigated rivers and tales of wildmen. By 11a.m. next day I'd seen enough to know that this was a place for an expedition, but it would be no picnic.

The only transport would be the short sturdy Mongolian horse and the heavily-built Bactrian camel. A double-humped, ill-tempered beast whose disposition is not improved by the wooden nose-peg inserted through its nostrils to which strings are attached for steering. The horse-saddles would be a problem. Made of wood to fit a small dwarf, they would cause grave discomfort and perhaps serious injury

MONGOLIA EXPEDITION

to the average European male. We decided to seek venturers with small bottoms who could ride well. A few 'jeeps' and trucks might be available and the ancient biplane at Khovd airport was said to fly.

The Altai rose from the desert to over 14,000 feet. Armagu (13,200 feet), Tsasan-Sume, Irvis Tag and many unnamed summits tower upwards above the source of large rivers including the Khovd, one of Mongolia's longest. The mountain lakes offer a quiet retreat for numerous varieties of birds, including swan, geese and other water-fowl whilst golden eagle, buzzard and kite glide above.

Although it was now cold and dry, Terbish told me that, when the rains came in the summer, the desert turns green, providing lush pasture for the cattle, goats, horses, sheep and yak of the nomadic people. Being a biologist he was eager to tell me of the wildlife, which included the vigorous mountain sheep or argali and wild goat or yangir, and even the rare snow leopard. Wolves, he explained, were known to attack domestic animals and there were also bear and deer in the region. Being far from the moderating influence of the oceans, surrounded by mountains and situated at a relatively high altitude,

Mongolia has a climate of extremes that can produce severe, unpredictable weather as we were to discover.

The Mongolian food is traditional and has remained unchanged for centuries. Meat, occasionally beef or more usually mutton, is the main dish. It is boiled as small pieces and served with rice imported from China. Nomads have no time to grow vegetables and we were told that 'grass is for horses, meat is for men'. The fat is considered the best part, and guests will be given generous portions and expected to down great lumps of it with relish, but 'Talkh', a tasty bread, and 'Arul', a hard yellow cheese made from camel, cow, goat, or sheep's milk, are also eaten. I could see our western-trained stomachs might have a few problems. Mongols drink salted, milky tea or 'suun chai' by the gallon. It contains more cow or yak milk than tea and, very often, a large dollop of rancid butter is added as a delicacy. Apart from staples such as flour, rice and tea, which are purchased at towns, the nomadic families produce their food from their own herds, just as their ancestors did in the time of Genghis Khan. To my taste, the diet, which is the same for all meals, is exceedingly bland and I knew we would need to bring our own spices and dried vegetables. 'Kumiss' or 'Airak', fermented mare's milk with a slight almond flavour, is the principal drink. However, it has a very low alcohol content, which cannot be said of the vodka!

Back in Ulan Batar, the Minister gave his approval for a full-scale expedition in 1992, but the country was in turmoil and great crowds gathered in Suhbaatar Square demanding democracy. It was an eerie experience, standing amongst them facing the lines of unarmed soldiers guarding the Parliament and wondering if tanks were waiting in the sidestreets. The orderliness of the mass demonstration was most impressive. A crowd of some 12,000 people sat quietly in the square with banners displayed whilst a big bass drum beat a remorseless thump, thump, thump, like some giant clock ticking away metonymically. Hour after hour, day by day, the crowd came to sit and stare at the Parliament. Was this what brought down the walls of Jericho?

The Russians in our hotel were obviously worried and, early one morning, I found myself awaiting our battered Volga on the steps. Beside me stood a bemedalled Soviet General, impatiently looking for his vehicle. Our car was approaching when the Russian moved forward and I feared he was about to take it.

'I think that's our car, General,' I said.

The great man spun round. 'Ah, English, how do you know I'm a General?'

'Because I'm a British Army Colonel,' I retorted.

'At the Embassy, I think,' said he.

'No, actually I'm with the Ministry of Defence in London.'

'So what are you doing in Mongolia?'

'Planning an operation, General,' I replied, but his car had arrived and, as his aides swept him away, he gave me a long, penetrating look. Heaven knows what he told the KGB!

My final job was to set up a local committee and we were fortunate in getting Mr Ch Ganbold as Chairman and the backing of his Peace and Friendship Organization.

Back in London, I set about fund raising for the expedition and thanks to my friend, financial journalist Lorna Bourke, obtained some very valuable help from the Save and Prosper Group, which enabled us to buy Mongolian tents and saddles. Meanwhile Richard Branson had set up a scheme on his Virgin Airways to collect passengers' loose change at the end of flights and with this we financed the TB vaccination programme.

The following year Pamela Stephany, British businessman Brian Henslow, Sean and I did a complete recce of the northern part of the region, whilst Ann Tweedy and another team examined the southern area. Recruiting was going well with lots of small bottoms, mainly girls, applying.

In the mountains there were tantalizing tales of almas or the yeti. The male was said to be six to nine feet tall and the females five to six feet. Heads were somewhat pointed and the body covered in reddish grey hair. We were told that the creature walked upright and had enormously powerful back legs allowing it to leap up to three feet vertically in a standing jump. The footprint, similar to a human's, is often larger and wider. The body shape is that of a heavily-built human and females are said to have pendant breasts, which, it was said, they toss over their shoulders when they run! It seems they are afraid of water, but not fire. There are stories of almas being found asleep in gers or warming themselves by abandoned fires. There are also tales of their kidnapping children and female almas kidnapping male hunters, whom they then rape. Generally they seem to be very shy and usually run away from man. Although they do not appear to speak, they are said to emit a high-pitched squeak or shrill cry.

Reports of almas in western Mongolia are more numerous than in most areas of the world where they are alleged to exist and there are many who readily admit to having seen them. I learned that since my last visit, an almas was said to have been seen in the Khovd River Gorge, but fled when called to by hunters. Although it may be a myth, the almas is very much part of Mongolian folklore and a number of eminent Soviet and local scientists have spent much time and effort researching the mystery. The morning after a discussion with some nomads in the mountains, I was shaving, stripped to the waist. The local children watched in fascination and then, pointing at the hair on my chest, said 'almas'.

There followed a year's planning in Britain where, ably assisted by my super PA, Sally Cox, and Sean Hinton, we set up the first major western expedition to Mongolia for over fifty years. Sir Bob Reid kindly offered the help of British Rail, but the collapse of the USSR and the problems of getting a multinational group down the Trans-Siberian Railway curtailed our plan to go out by train. This was a great shame as I'd quite looked forward to going up to the ticket office at Victoria and demanding, '120 tickets to Ulan Batar, please.'

The advance party flew out in April 1992 under the leadership of my second-in-command, Squadron Leader George Baber, RAF. Con-tainers of everything we needed had been sent out by sea to China and thence by rail to Ulan Batar. George's first task was to get these forty tons of stores and rations across the Gobi to Khovd and set up a base camp. Corporal Tony Martin, a Commando Sapper, soon had five Mongolian Army trucks loaded and, with three other British NCOs, set off on a thousand mile drive. The Mongol drivers reckoned to stop at every ger en route for vodka, women and song. How they reached Khovd in five days was a miracle and a fine example of the leadership qualities of British NCOs.

When Sally and I arrived with the main body of the staff in May, George had a splendid tented camp set up at the foot of the Altai Mountains beside the shallow Buyant River. It was still cool and the wind would whip up sandstorms and even play havoc with a sturdy ger.

The Mongolian economy was deteriorating at an alarming rate. Food and fuel were rationed and construction materials like gold-dust. However, Mick Ponting, our vet, had procured a herd of horses and several camels. Sean had borrowed a battered old Russian GAZ jeep and George had an agreement for the hire of the Antonov biplane. The local telephone company, to our amazement, produced a radio phone that could link us to the outside world.

Simon Hamilton, formerly of the Kalahari Quest, was our treasurer and had spent four months begging for goods in Britain and the store ger was filled with gifts including some home-brewed beer and wine-making kits from Boots. As local drinks only consisted of vodka and fermented mare's milk, these were especially welcome.

I went back to Ulan Batar to collect the venturers. Sixty-six from abroad and twenty from within Mongolia. I also met Gerald Brown, the Anglican Archdeacon for the enormous area from Oslo to Ulan Batar. He needed no persuasion to accompany us and hold a Whitsuntide service in the field. This must certainly have been the first Anglican service ever held in that remote region.

Whilst in the capital I had tried to buy some frying pans and spent hours going from one understocked shop to another. At last one assistant claimed she had what I needed, but, strangely, she brought back a trumpet. She looked so disappointed when I declined that I gave her the equivalent of the few pence that she asked and roused the camp with badly-played reveilles thereafter.

The flight to Khovd with MIAT was quite an eye-opener for the young. We had chartered the plane so we got on first, then the stand-by passengers were loaded into the luggage bay, next small children were passed around to sit on our knees and, finally, a few strap hangers came aboard to stand in the aisle all the way. The loo was out of commission, so, after two hours, we landed at a settlement, aptly named Moron, where everyone tumbled out to relieve themselves on the grass before flying on to Khovd.

To prepare the venturers for the expedition, George had organized a week's training in everything from river crossing to Mongol etiquette. So schooled in local niceties and on how to survive in this stark land, our teams deployed. We organized the expedition into seven groups and the Field HQ (FHQ). Between six and twelve venturers made up each group with a small number of staff. Although we used a motley collection of old Russian trucks to deploy the teams, the only permanent vehicle on the expedition was an ancient and unreliable 'jeep' at FHQ. Horses and camels were used almost everywhere as were our feet.

The tasks included river exploration by Avon inflatables, fauna and flora studies by horseborne parties and a scientific team on the vast Black Lake. There was a 220-foot suspension footbridge and a refuge hut to be constructed. Two medical teams would administer community medicine and handle the vaccination programme as well as the eye operations. In the high mountains at the junction of the Chinese, Mongolian and Russian borders the mountaineers aimed to climb new peaks and study the animals and plants. Our final report, named the Wainwright study after a famous British Lake District guide, was to include as much information as possible about the area, its people, fauna and flora. I was very conscious that being the first westerners in the area, we had a great opportunity for real exploration, as well as helping the people. The way the Mongolian economy was deteriorating, it could be a long while before others came here and, when they did, our work would be invaluable. At the same time I felt we were privileged to be here and must make a point of respecting their culture and traditions.

Each group was named after an appropriate historical figure, so we had Tenzing (mountaineers), Drake (the Black Lake), Brunel (bridge builders), Genghis (the horse team), Livingstone and Nightingale (medical) and Nelson (the river explorers). All were linked to FHQ by radio.

Food was rationed and in short supply and we guarded our stocks with an armed policeman, for whom the local police chief charged us $11 per week, of which we gathered the constable received only four! As the situation grew more desperate, there was a marked increase in violence and we suffered several robberies. Sadly Mongolia was no longer a place where you could rely on the honesty of the locals. We had brought vegetable seeds from Britain and I dug a small plot outside my tent and labelled it 'The Garden of Eden'. As a lady of easy virtue who helped in the camp assisted with the digging, some joker had added 'dug by the whores of Babylon'. To keep down the rodents in the ration store, I encouraged a stray black cat to adopt us and named him 'Cooking Fat' after Ann Tweedy's ginger feline in Britain.

The Mongolian Army had kindly lent us some marquees but, for the most part, our camp consisted of the traditional gers, circular felt-lined tents built around a wooden lattice-work frame. The Buyant river flowed within a few metres and provided water, which we boiled and sterilized most religiously. From his office at the Pedagogical Institute eight kilometres away, the good Terbish and the local government did all they could to support us with the province's limited resources.

On 13 June the teams deployed. Tenzing headed for the heights of Tavan Bodg, whilst Tony Martin led his merry band to the mosquito-infested lake. The horses of Genghis and one rather reluctant camel named Basil went northwards to the Khovd River gorge and White Table mountain. Tan Chi Chiu and Richard Tan, our energetic Singaporean military doctors, trucked southwards over the mountains to Bulgan Sum, leaving Dr David Clayton's team to screen cataract patients in the Khovd area.

The rafters motored to join the upper reaches of the Khovd River that would take them into the great gorge and Mick Christy's Brunel team, the nearest group to FHQ, trotted off to their bridge site in fine style. Suddenly Base Camp was very quiet, the sun shone and the temperature began to rise. I planted my vegetables, issued strict instructions on the watering and drove out to watch the river explorers descend the cataract at the bottom of the Khovd River gorge. When I had first seen this placid river in 1991, I had no idea that it contained such a formidable set of rapids. For 600 yards a torrent of foaming white water rushes out of the canyon. The powerful stoppers and 'holes' are a real challenge for even experienced rafters, but there are no major obstructions and a vehicle track ran along the bank. Thus, it was an ideal setting for the venturers to experience the thrills of the exhilarating sport we had pioneered with our Avons on the Blue Nile. However, there were spills as well.

White water expert Mark Herriott took the first boat down and the other two followed. Screaming with excitement the paddlers fought against the tossing, tugging waves that towered around them.

'So far the Khovd has been a bit of a doddle,' remarked Rob Leppard from Croydon, 'but this is the real stuff. Big water roaring around you, flinging your neoprene craft about like a cork in a tempest.'

'Like riding a wild roller craft,' said Su-Ann Lim from Singapore.

The last raft, helmed by Mike Metcalfe, a tough and popular Geordie, had just started down when it hit a huge standing wave that catapulted it over, flipping the crew into the racing foam.

'I thought I was drowning as I spun round and round under water – it was terrifying,' said a shaken teenager when I talked to her later.

That evening, as the cliffs of the gorge turned scarlet in the sunset, I relaxed catching plentiful Arctic char that swam in the turbulent waters before joining the venturers for a fish supper under the stars. Tsogt, a young Mongolian, had brought his guitar and played Beatles' favourites learnt entirely from listening to the BBC. What an experience this was for all of us, but especially the young. One day they would tell their grandchildren how they were the first westerners in Outer Mongolia. Ann Tweedy had her tent up by the river and, sharing a plastic mug of Scotch, we talked of Aberdeenshire, the reconnaisance trips and the years of effort that had gone into making this particular dream come true. High above us the argali rams fought for possession of ewes, their great horns crashing together with a sound like rifle shots. It was another world.

A complaining Basil woke me at dawn. Camels have an extraordinary vocabulary and the ability to express it at both ends of the body. The Goretex bivvy bag had kept me warm and dry and within minutes I was downing hot sweet tea before scouting ahead to find the route for Mick Ponting's horse-mounted group that was to ascend the mountains on its wildlife survey. A day and a half later we reached the hidden valley Pam and I had found the previous year. But now it was later in the season and scores of gers dotted this Shangrila. Herdsmen came galloping, eager to see the strangers.

Some hours later we rode to a ridge at 10,000 feet to view a huge corniche where Mount Somboros' snowfield dropped into a vertically-sided glacial valley. Returning to camp, a rider thundered towards me. Topol, my solid bay, plodded on and I paid little attention to the newcomer. But he raced straight at us and with a great cry of 'John', flung his arms about my neck almost dragging me from the saddle. It was Nokhoijav, head of a family of Oh-ulds, who had befriended me on my last visit. He begged me to come to his ger, but the hour was late and, instead, we persuaded him to accompany us to our camp where a 'hot rock' supper was being prepared by other locals. So whilst we drank tea a whole sheep was chopped up and placed in a large milk churn full of heated stones. The evening grew cold as we pressed the chunks of fatty mutton to our lips and, through one overworked interpreter, told each other of our lives since we had last met.

Nokhoijav's family were well, the herd had multiplied and, through his radio, he had learned of the dramatic events in Moscow and Ulan Batar. He had known we would return, it was a good omen he confided; now all would improve in Mongolia. Why, we had even brought the vet that we had talked of and medicines too. It was as well because one of the nomad's horses had been savagely mauled by wolves and, next day, all Mick's skills were called upon to save it. Later, seated on low stools, we lunched in Nokhoijav's ger. All the family was there, it was a great reunion, but alas, Ann, photographer Ian Robinson and I had to go back to the plains. As leader of such a large enterprise, there was never time to linger, but I promised to return.

As the expedition progressed the Mongolian economy declined further and by Naadam, the three days of national celebration in July, the situation had become extremely difficult. Fuel was in such short supply that MIAT had ceased its internal flights. With great difficulty we got Harry Brown's surgical eye team in and out of Khovd. However it was worth the effort for they restored sight to sixty-three people and did much good work. Ann just got back to Ulan Batar and Richard Snailham who was to take over as writer only just made it. With him came his wife, Chris, a trauma doctor, who was to prove invaluable.

At Naadam it began to rain but we entered into the spirit of the games with venturers taking part in the archery and wrestling, although with little success. The twenty-five-mile horserace started hours late and we spent a damp day in the desert awaiting its finish. When the bedraggled horses and their exhausted young jockeys cantered in it was something of an anti-climax.

Bob Rose and John Lyons, who had been with me in the Kalahari, somehow got themselves to Khovd, but as they arrived a real drama hit us.

I'd just finished watering my vegetable garden when the dreaded words came crackling over the radio from Tavan Bogd. 'There's been an accident.' Julian Freeman-Attwood's tense voice gave me the facts. Lindsay Griffin, one of Britain's finest climbers, was moving through a boulder field as they returned from a visit to the summit of Mt Huiten. Without warning a huge granite rock had toppled over pinning him to the ground and mangling his left leg. His colleagues, Julian and American Ed Webster, had descended by a different route and were already cooking a meal at their tent. Lindsay was alone and unconscious. When he came to, the top of the trapped leg had turned purple and gone numb. To restore the flow of blood, the climber managed to drag a rope from his rucksack and lasso a higher rock. Thus he made a sort of pulley system and raised the rock a fraction of an inch. As the pressure was reduced the blood flowed back into the shattered limb but with it came excruciating pain.

Back at the tent it was now 1830 hours; the accident had happened around 1500. Puzzled by Lindsay's long absence the other two retraced their route looking for him. But it was not until 2000 that, hearing faint cries, they found him. It took three more laborious hours of work with elaborate pulley systems to shift the boulder and haul the stricken man out. His leg was pulped with multiple compound fractures. For the next fifteen hours they struggled in darkness to descend 1,000 feet to a flat area where Julian thought a helicopter could land. Here they put him in a tent by a stream and, leaving him with rations and pain killers, set off to get help.

It took all the next day and most of the following night, struggling over snow-covered crevasses and a glacier, to reach their base and the vital radio. They had been going for fifty-one hours, without sleep and little food.

'Can you get a helicopter as quickly as possible?' pleaded Julian.

'Leave it to us. Get some sleep and I'll call you in three hours,' I told him, wondering where on earth I'd find a helicopter that could reach Lindsay before his wound, the wolves or the cold overcame him alone on the mountain.

Sean was already phoning the Ministry of Defence in Ulan Batar when George brought in the detailed maps. After five minutes' scrutiny we looked at each other and I said, 'My God, they've carried him down into China.'

'The Army says that they have helicopters but there is no fuel west of the capital,' reported Sean.

'See if MIAT can help,' I snapped.

'But John, there's no fuel.'

'OK, but give them a call anyway,' I retorted.

'Then it's the Antonov Two,' said George, referring to the ancient Soviet biplane that stood in the airstrip. I knew it could land at Bayan Olgiy, some seventy-five miles east of Mt Huiten. From here a truck could carry a rescue team to the base of the mountain, then it would be, with luck, two days' march to Lindsay. There was fuel for the old plane and although it was a forlorn hope we despatched some eager venturer climbers with Army medic Andy Herrod, and Jan Kennis, a Belgian surgeon.

Sean burst in; he always did. 'It's MIAT,' he cried. 'They've called to say there is a chopper and they reckon they can get fuel, but,' he lowered his eyes, 'it will cost US$26,000.'

Sally interjected, 'The insurance company will cover that.'

'Send it,' I said, praying it would get there in time.

It was next day before the huge MIL 8 transport helicopter reached

Khovd and George, his airforce interest aroused, was there. However it quickly became apparent that MIAT's information about fuel was incorrect. There was none in Khovd. So the pilot, Captain Nyamaagiin Jambaldorj, and I dashed off to see the Premier. Mongolian bureaucracy grinds slowly and it is not easy to burst in on even a provincial Premier at short notice. However, within a quarter of an hour we were explaining our predicament to the heavily-built official. Nyamaagiin and our liaison officer, Chuluumbaatar, spoke quickly. They knew what to ask for so did not waste time interpreting for my benefit. At last the Premier nodded gravely and, sending for the keeper of the strategic fuel stocks, the city's last emergency reserve, he generously released a ton. It was 4 p.m. before it had been trucked to the airport and the helicopter was airborne.

Meanwhile Sally was arranging an ambulance jet with SOS Services in Hong Kong and Bob Rose, himself a pilot, was investigating our local airport's navigational beacons, whilst in Ulan Batar the British Embassy was seeking clearance for this unprecedented flight. I had sent George and Sean with the helicopter, plus Chris Snailham as the doctor and Richard, her husband, who himself had once fallen 1500 feet down a mountain in Ecuador and knew what it was like to be rescued. Another team of venturer climbers went as stretcher bearers. There was nothing else we could do but pray.

Every hour's delay increased the risk of infection and the possible loss of Lindsay's leg. Lying alone in his tent, he sipped water from the stream, swallowed pain killers, but ate nothing. He never really expected to see a helicopter. When the MIL 8 thundered over the base camp ger, the biplane party, who had marched non-stop, was just about to start up the awful Potanine glacier. 'Here comes the school bus,' yelled Ed, as the bulky machine, quite unsuited for mountain rescue, lumbered into sight and, leaping aboard, he guided it to Lindsay's tent, some ten miles' distance at an altitude of 10,800 feet. In the thin air this was the extreme limit for the groaning, juddering chopper, but somehow Nyamaagiin coaxed it upward. At 12,800 feet, the flaying rotor carried them over the col and they saw the blue tent on a ledge just below the crest. Still too heavy and too high to hover, the captain made five attempts to roll land onto the ledge, but each time the boulders defeated him. Eventually he dropped the rescuers two miles away. But as they set out for Lindsay, the aircraft whirled away. Wonder where he's going, thought George, as he raced for the tent. Inside Lindsay greeted them and consoled our stalwart RAF officer on the disappearance of his helicopter.

Night was coming as the team dragged Lindsay to a clearer patch of land and waited. There was no sign of the helicopter. At the base camp Julian was almost frantic with worry. What could have happened? Had they crashed? The consequences were too awful to contemplate. At FHQ Bob opened a bottle of special vodka. 'I think we all need a little drink,' he said as we crouched by the radio.

At 2100, to George's intense relief, he heard the heavy throb of the aircraft returning. The pilot had to jettison more weight so he had flown to a lower altitude, landed and, to save fuel, had shut down his engines whilst he allowed time for the casualty to be moved. Then, after restarting, he had removed the heavy batteries and returned. With Lindsay safely aboard, he collected his batteries. It was all an incredible act, balancing weight, fuel, overcoming altitude and the advancing darkness to snatch the horribly injured man from what we now knew must be Chinese territory.

As the 'school bus' landed at Bayan Olgiy airstrip, the engines cut: they were out of fuel and no more was available. Commandeering a van, the medics rushed Lindsay to the local hospital. The only operating table was the hospital director's desk and there, working with Swiss Army penknives, Chris and Jan cut away at tattered clothing and near rotting flesh. Bone was sticking through the skin as they operated.

'Splints?' asked Chris.

The Mongol nurse shook her head sadly. 'No splints.'

'Not to worry,' grinned Sean hacking up the director's filing cabinet with an ice axe.

Back at the strip they found the chopper connected by a hose to an Aeroflot airliner collecting emigrating Kazakhs. Nyamaagiin had swopped five bottles of vodka for 100 gallons of fuel, which would get him to Khovd.

A great grin spread across Lindsay's emaciated face as I stepped aboard. 'Sorry about all this,' he muttered, 'but John, I have something very important to tell you.' As we waited for the Lear Jet from SOS Services Hong Kong, he told me of sighting a large auburn-coloured creature that seemed to walk upright in the mountains, not far from where Julian had spotted some strange tracks, quite unlike snow leopard or bear, that appeared to have been made by a biped.

It was late July before I could visit Tavan Bogd myself and see the extraordinary Alpine scenery, quite unlike anywhere else I had been in Mongolia. Few outsiders had seen these incredible mountains before our expedition and, as we rode through the swirling mist on our shaggy ponies, I found it difficult to imagine any large creature living in this land of snow, ice and swamps.

However, on 10 June, Julian, his colleague Ed Webster and Lindsay had crossed the vast Potanine Glacier and put up a camp near the Alexandroff Glacier, 500 yards from a charming little peak named Snow Church, that rose on the Chinese border. The next day snow and wind prevented climbing but the following morning the weather cleared and they set out for the north face of the mountain. Suddenly they became aware that someone or something had been there before them, for only 250 yards from the tents, they saw a strange set of tracks. Pointing out the detail on the ground, Julian told me the story.

'Looking to the east, we could see the tracks had come over a col down onto our Alexandroff Glacier, right across its head between our tents and Mount Snow Church, and finally over the col into China. In the crisp morning light we could see roughly a mile of tracks,' he explained. 'We first thought they were made by a bear but the configuration was oddly in groups of three and ridged up slightly on one side. We wondered if it could be a biped, walking on two feet and touching the snow with one hand.'

We knew these tracks must have been made between 2000 hours and 0600, otherwise fresh snow would have obliterated them.

'Most mysterious,' said Richard Snailham, as we climbed the steep grassy slope behind Julian's ger to examine the spot where Lindsay's sighting of a creature had occurred. The Terbishes came too and being biologists, took an interest in the plant life. Pulling up a bunch of small red flowers, Mrs Terbish said, 'We use for coughs.' Funny, I thought, as we wandered amongst the rocks looking at the ground, someone's been here before picking these plants and also the wild garlic. But we found no tracks on that bare hillside. Gazing north into Russia and west to China, I shook my head. A few years ago I could not imagine, even in my wildest dreams, being here, especially as a British Army officer. How the world had changed! Now even the almas seems possible!

On returning to Britain, Daphne Hills, a zoologist at the Natural History Museum, kindly examined the evidence for me and felt confident that the tracks were those of a quadruped, almost certainly a carnivore. She said, 'Mammal tracks differ according to gait and speed; when using certain gaits an individual's hind foot will be placed in the same position as a preceding forepaw, leaving only a single mark for both feet. This is very common and results in various unexpected combinations of foot marks. This phenomenon is seen in at least three carnivore families and looking at examples of tracks a wolverine seems the most likely culprit.' However, I could find no record of the existence of wolverine in the Altai, although they are known around Lake Baikal, but in this little explored region, who knows? Without more evidence, one can only guess.

By chance I was able to investigate the sighting in the Khovd River gorge where in April 1991 an almas had been seen by two men. One of these, Gansukh, was my driver for a while and gave me a convincing account of a biped, approximately nine foot tall, covered with reddish hair. As a result Ann Tweedy was able to obtain the negatives of the photographs of these footprints. They were size sixteen!

Gansukh, a taciturn, dour man, was a hunter of some repute. He had seen the creature walking and running 500 yards away and knew it was not a bear. 'Never did it move on four feet,' he said seriously, as he dictated his account slowly and deliberately to me. However when Ann tried to tape his tale for the BBC World Service, he clammed up. 'I cannot speak more, it is a state secret. We have been forbidden to talk of it.'

Our own scientific research was concentrated on the Black Lake, where Tony Martin's troops struggled to study the prolific birdlife beset by swarms of mosquitoes. Visiting the teams in battered old 'jeeps', Richard and I had some incredible journeys, and throughout the region venturers had many lucky escapes when crossing rivers swollen by unusually heavy rain.

The country had now completely exhausted its stocks of aviation spirit, and as there were no MIATS internal flights, the only way to get back to the capital was to travel by lorry, 1,000 miles over the desert. Whilst preparation went ahead, the Brunel group completed its bridge and, taking the Khovd Commissioner with us, we went off to open it. Named Irons Bridge in recognition of a kind donation from the actor, Jeremy Irons, it looked very fine when we arrived at the site. Speeches were delivered and ubiquitous vodka bottles produced by the Commissioner, who drank rather a lot of it! Then Ian Robinson wanted a group photograph, so he arranged the team across the span, including Mick Ponting and his horse, Caesar. As our guest of honour was now a little unsteady on his feet, I kept him at the end, which was just as well. Suddenly there was a sharp crack; a locally-made clamp had given way and one of the main wire cables ran through the anchorage. The decking tilted over, venturers grabbed the handrail and Caesar performed a graceful leap off the bridge onto the bank as if he did it every day. But poor Ian, festooned with cameras, did a backwards somersault into the river. The Commissioner made another speech saying it was no one's fault and that such things often happened in Mongolia. Ian poured the water from his cameras and Mick Christy cursed the local clamp manufacturer. It says something for Mandy Grey, the young British Rail engineer who had directed the building, when she bit her lip then said, 'OK, let's get it repaired.' Ten days later, whilst the rest of us were motoring across the Gobi, she and her team finished the job and managed to get seats on the last plane out of Khovd.

The convoy worked well, although I had to run it in a military style. Tony Martin acted as Sergeant Major and at our regular comfort stops yelled, 'Girls to the left, boys to the right.' The Mongols always got this wrong which caused some consternation. At night we made a tight circle of trucks and slept within. Sentries watched for prowling robbers but the six-day journey was largely uneventful until we reached Karakorum, site of a famous city built in 1220 by the great Khans. By 1586 it had been ravaged by Chinese armies and a monastery built on the site and it was this that we had stopped to see.

Camping in low trees by a river, we visited the magnificent temples and shrines, many of which are being restored. The sky grew black and then the howling wind brought clouds of swirling sand, closely followed by torrential rain, thunder and lightning. Sheltering in a temple entrance I heard a different sound, 'Rump, rump, rump', then an indistinct whisper followed after several seconds by a 'Crump, crump, crump' overhead.

'What on earth's that?' I asked one of our Mongolian Army captains.

'Thunder,' he replied.

Then, as the rain fell in rods, it came again. From my days in the anti-aircraft regiment I knew the sound of guns. 'That was artillery,' I protested.

'No John, just thunder,' my friend insisted.

Back at camp the noises came again, but this time it was louder and I could hear bits of shrapnel falling in the trees.

'Get under the trucks,' I cried.

Everyone thought I had gone mad until Royal Engineer Corporal Paul Hardon drove in. 'You won't believe this,' he said, 'but there's a load of civvies firing bloody great ack-ack guns skyward at the edge of a wheat field back there. Are we under attack?'

Back in Ulan Batar I told the tale to our Mongolian Defence Department friends and asked if they had an artillery unit at Karakorum.

'Oh no,' said the Colonel, 'those are the weather guns. They shoot chemicals at the clouds to prevent hail forming and destroying the crops. That is an important farming area.' As the hungry people of the capital fought for bread it was easy to see how vital the success of Mongolia's sparse agriculture will be in the future.

By contrast two days of packing and partying gave the venturers a splendid send-off. The reception laid on by our most supportive Ambassador Tony Morey and wife Agni at the residence will never be forgotten by the young. 'I never knew the British were so jolly,' commented Sylvie Jonckeau, our delightful French member. Tears poured down many a face as the international venturers bid farewell to their Mongolian colleagues at the railway station. They had shared much over the past ten weeks and for most, the world would never seem the same again. As the well-laden train pulled out, heading across the Gobi for Beijing, we waved frantically and my thirty-three tugrik trumpet sounded for the last time. Sean and I were left with a sad group of young Mongols standing in the drizzle. The perilous state of their economy does not bode well for their future. I wondered if we were right to have given them a glimpse of a lifestyle beyond their reach, but hopefully it will encourage them to use the western advice and help to full advantage.

In Suhbaatar Square, by the statue of the national hero, an old Mongol was trying to sell a pair of fox cubs, but there was something odd about them. They were huge. Sensing my interest, my interpreter said, 'Wolves, they use them for guarddogs in the city, there is much crime now.'

What an extraordinary country. I'm sure there is much more to discover here, and hopefully one day I shall return to the land of Genghis Khan.

EPILOGUE

AS THE GREAT BALLOON rose from the grassy field, a cheer went up, but this time I was on the ground waving. Victoria, our younger daughter, waved back and hurled her bouquet which was neatly caught by her bridesmaid, Cara. Julian Matthews, my new son-in-law, wearing an old family flying helmet saluted from the basket as they drifted away across the Dorset countryside. The post wedding party, with chariot racing and tug of war contests, went on into the small hours and when Judith and I sank into bed the disco beat was still pounding from the marquee. 'Youth is a state of mind,' she groaned. But it had been a memorable day.

I think it was this event, even more than my retirement from the Army a few months before, that signalled a new beginning to me. For almost forty years my job has really been to build teams to tackle arduous tasks, overcome obstacles and solve problems. Those who have taken part were at times tired, hungry, cold and wet, or hot, thirsty and covered in sores. Sometimes they have no idea what is happening around them or where they are going. This is when the strength and flaws of character will show. So I have always looked for people to head the various groups, whom I believed would go on leading under the worst conditions. Such men and women need to possess unusual ability and understanding to knit together a team which in turn must have confidence in its leader. Thus I feel that, although one should not ignore setbacks, if one is seen to despair, group morale will deteriorate rapidly. I believe that expedition officers must display cheerful, reasoned optimism and by their enduring courage press on when lesser men might falter.

The selection process is terribly important. To find out if someone possesses courage I try to discover if they have fear, for one who does not fear can have no courage: they do not need it. Such folk do exist and can be frightening company, often leading their comrades to take unnecessary risks.

Next, I see if the candidate has willpower, because in very many cases I believe courage is simply resolute willpower. But as well as sheer physical courage, there is the moral variety, the sort that will lead one to make an unpopular decision or stake all on your own judgement. Strangely, those who appear to possess unbounded bravery do not always display moral courage. On the other hand, I have never known a person who has moral courage to be found wanting in the face of physical danger. The Duke of Wellington's advice to leaders to be 'cool in crisis and decisive in action' still holds good. Being a leader is a lonely business, and too often one's own thoughts are of little comfort when there is no one around to boost your confidence. Those who lack confidence in their own abilities tend to be oversensitive to criticism.

On an expedition I occasionally find myself listening to two internal voices. Perhaps they represent two sides of my personality. One complains and moans urging me to rest, to turn back or take the easy way out. Fortunately, the other is more forceful and able to suggest alternatives when plans fail. This voice tells me to cheer up and keep going. At times of crisis I have witnessed a confrontation between the two personalities in my dreams. Sometimes the image is so vivid that different courses of action advocated are played out as if on a TV screen. I have even found it possible to replay the scene, sometimes on a different night. At one time I thought I must be going round the bend, until I met a very normal sort of chap who had exactly the same sort of experiences under stress.

Team members must also be selected carefully. I usually look for people who are cheerful, compatible, unselfish and tolerant. Both mental and physical toughness are important, but a person who tends to be overcompetitive can be very disruptive.

Loyalty to the leadership and to the aim of the expedition is vital, but under stress and strain there is always the person who will grumble and knock the system. This is inevitable. Indeed, they may need to criticize in an effort to satisfy their ego and restore their own self-confidence. Whatever the reason, anyone who disintegrates the group under stress is a bad influence and should be removed at the earliest opportunity, before he infects others.

I have always gone to great lengths to build up the team's pride in its achievements so that it becomes self-motivating. My greatest mistakes in man-management have been when I have failed to sack someone usually because I've been too soft-hearted. But there are a few around who have never forgiven me for removing them when they transgressed.

The difficulty facing the overall leader is to select the people with the right characteristics, but the system used on Raleigh has proved most successful for both young and old.

Unfortunately, expeditions attract prima donnas. Although a confounded nuisance on a prolonged venture, they are fairly easy to spot. Their vanity and self-interest usually give them away. On the rare occasions when I have met such characters, I have found that they are often bad mixers, or will usurp the leadership and can become quite irrational. In extreme cases they become rather exhibitionistic and complain bitterly of persecution if they do not get their own way. Masochists sometimes join hoping for the opportunity to prove themselves. Being an idle chap who believes that any bloody fool can be uncomfortable if that's his want, I also regard such people as a potential danger to a team.

I have found that political and religious extremists, or for that matter anyone with strong views, can cause friction. But I have absolutely no doubt that faith can help one to overcome difficulties. My own view of religion is that it is best described as a bank account, into which one must pay regularly so that in times of need you can withdraw. But you cannot arrogantly demand to cash a cheque when you need a miracle: it is very much up to the 'bank manager' to decide on the timing and amount of his support – although one hopes that by maintaining a credit balance he might be better disposed to assist. Of course not all explorers believe in a god, and I have known many who claim to be atheists or agnostics. Whether someone has or has not a religion only really concerns their selection for an expedition in that it is quite useful to know if you have to bury them! Even so, whenever possible I encourage simple services to be held on Sundays. Apart from being appreciated by some members, I feel it has moral value and helps us to retain a sense of time. Congregation numbers are usually poor at the start of an expedition, but increase in proportion to the tension. There are few atheists before a battle!

For many years I was against taking girls with us. I felt that, human nature being what it is, they would be an unwelcome distraction and would not really pull their full weight. However, I soon discovered that there were many advantages to having women members. In Darien there were five girls in the team and they showed themselves to be mentally as tough or even tougher than the men. I found that their inbuilt capacity for survival more than made up for their limited physical strength.

As far as sexual distraction is concerned, it is a question of selecting your ladies carefully. They know most men, and explorers particularly, tend to be a red-blooded lot, but in the end it is the female who calls the tune and if you have the right sort of women, they will keep even the most ardent suitor at bay until the task in hand is completed. On Drake and Raleigh the number of girls wishing to take part surprised us and I see no reason why women should not fill all roles on expeditions today. They tend to be more caring and sympathetic and are useful listeners for worried men to pour out their troubles. But one of their great assets is that they add tone. Men are often inspired by the women's good example and are far less likely to be petty when they are around.

Over the years the expeditions with which I've been involved have raised well over £20 million. It is never easy but I would recommend all aspiring leaders to cultivate those vital qualities of communication and the ability to inspire, for without these one will never sell the project or persuade others to follow. Broadcasting, lecturing and writing are all tools of the explorer's trade, but it is one's moral standards, integrity and expertise that will win the respect of the team.

Explorers tend to be conservationists and there are few tasks more urgent than the protection of the environment, the tropical forests, wildlife and the oceans. The search for traditional remedies for disease awaiting discovery is another tantalizing subject. I can assure those who fear they have been born too late that there is still plenty left to do as the technology increases. We can now dive deeper into the oceans and spend longer in space and the inflatable river boat, which we helped the Avon Rubber Company to develop, has opened up whole new areas.

As far as I am concerned, it is curiosity that drives me on. I have no particular desire to conquer a peak or to be the first man to complete some particular feat. Although I must confess that even if the challenge is not of primary importance, I still derive satisfaction in striving 'to seek, to find' without yielding. But it is the quest for the unknown that is paramount. Therefore, I believe that I am justified in using every possible aid to achieve the aim and solve the problem.

I know it has been said that, with the huge amount of equipment, manpower and technical expertise, it is hardly surprising that SES has got through where others have failed. But I am not in the exploring game to find out something about myself or to compete with others, and do not feel compelled to obey any self-imposed rules for physical challenges.

However, one must remember that expeditions may endanger your health. For the novice, the experience can be an introduction to negative aspects of one's personality easily suppressed in normal daily life. With appropriate counselling and support, this can be a journey of self-discovery leading to increased confidence and a more enlightened attitude to others.

Seasoned adventurers recognize a condition I call post-expedition blues, the symptoms of which are similar to bereavement. This is triggered by the loss of one's newly-found 'family' of expedition friends and suddenly being cut off from the excitement on return home. Routine and a mundane lifestyle aggravate the condition and for many it is cured only by involvement in another challenge. Explorers also face isolation from family and colleagues, who have no concept of their intense experiences: they are often perplexed by the indifferent response to their stories, and the explorer may end up silent and withdrawn. The envy and resentment of the uninitiated, who imagine that one has been on a jolly picnic or at best some self-inflicted masochism, is also common. Dr John Davies, with whom I have been on many trips, advises one to spend several days enquiring about the day-to-day problems that have occurred in your absence, before slowly beginning to recount your experiences.

Operation Raleigh had been the culmination of many years' work by thousands of people and, in spite of all the battles to keep it going, for the most part I had enjoyed it immensely. Under the new Trust it will live on, but I felt it needed different skills to sustain it as a permanent body. Like Kipling's explorer when the railway comes up from behind, it is time to move on. I had achieved my aim and must press forward to the next horizon. So I handed the reins to Jamie Robertson-Macleod, who served the cause since the start and has plenty of experience of raising sponsorship. I left him with a good team of administrators and expedition leaders and turned my attention to my first love, exploration.

Julian Matthews, his enthusiasm fired by an upbringing in the Rhodesian bush and his experience on Raleigh in Guyana, had caught my disease and, with several like-minded friends, we formed

Discovery Expeditions to cater for the growing number of older folk
now seeking challenge and worthwhile endeavours in remote areas.

I could not leave the youth scene completely, and I continue to try
to help the young, especially the really deeply underprivileged in
whom the spirit of adventure has yet to be instilled or redirected.

Whenever I need to remind myself that 'Youth is a state of mind', I
read Kipling's poem:

'There's no sense in going further – it's the edge of cultivation,'
So they said, and I believed it – broke my land and sowed my crop –

Built my barns and strung my fences in the little border station
Tucked away below the foothills where the trails run out and stop:

Till a voice, as bad as Conscience, rang interminable changes
On one everlasting Whisper day and night repeated – so:
'Something hidden. Go and find it. Go and look behind the Ranges –
'Something lost behind the Ranges. Lost and waiting for you. Go!'

INDEX

INDEX 367

Crookenden, Major General Napier 72, 177
Cropp, Ben 305
Crystal Mountains, Zaire 205
Cullaville, Northern Ireland 150–1
Cultural Revolution, China 315
Cuna people 137, 138, 139, 143, 229, 237, 294
Cutler, Corporal 29–30
Cyprus 22, 27, 28–43

Dahlak Islands, Red Sea 120
Daily Express 212
Daily Star 276
Daily Telegraph, The 76, 173, 174, 178, 189
Damgaard, Adrianne 176, 202
Daniel, Charlie 162, 164, 167, 285, 287, 289, 290, 299, 302, 305, 306
Darien Gap (El Tapon) 237
  British Trans-Americas Expedition (1971–72) 120–48, 229, 360
    recruits team 122, 124–6
    reconnaissance 122–3
    preparations 123–30
    air reconnaissance 130–2
    conditions in jungle 132–7
    recruits Indians 138–9, 141
    crosses Atrato Swamp 144–7
  Chevrolet Expedition 142
  General Motors Expedition 123
Daru, Papua New Guinea 248, 249
Darwin Research Station 239
Dasuo Glacier, Tibet 316
David (zoologist, Blue Nile Expedition) 96, 101, 105–6, 109
David Gestetner 178, 196, 203, 236
Davies, Alun 185, 201, 206
Davies, Ben 259
Davies, Cathy 287
Davies, Dabber and Paddy 213
Davies, Gordon 256, 259, 263
Davies, Dr John 315, 317, 335, 337, 362
Davilla, Pedrarias 230
Day, Colonel Henry 312, 313, 314, 316, 317, 318, 319
De Leon, Sergeant 141, 143
Debra Marcos, Ethiopia 62, 78, 79
Desert Rats 44
Devil's Race, Papua New Guinea 241
Devil's Switchback, Panama 141
Devon and Dorset Regiment 83
Dhofar, Oman 154–61
Dhofar Brigade 156
Dinsdale, Tim 271, 272, 276
Discovery Expeditions 363
dolphin, Ganges River 331
Donald, Sergeant Major Ian 149–52, 156
Donald, Margaret 152
Dorman, Richard 202
Doughty, Thomas 227
Douglas-Hamilton, Iain and Oria 338
Drake, Sir Francis 215, 216, 218, 223, 225, 227–9, 239, 279, 302
du Parc Braham, Colonel Julian 120
Duke of Edinburgh Award Scheme 324

Dulverton Trust 221
Duna people 245
Dunbar, Jane 287, 295
Dunn, John 322
Dunnett, Sinclair 194
Durey, Captain Ernie 125, 176, 185, 214, 262
Durrell, Gerald 186

Eade, Spencer 211, 212
Ecuador 213
Edinburgh, HMS 289
Edwards, Belinda 319
Edwards, Captain Edward 304, 307
Edwards, Jim 223, 319, 330
Egypt 264
elephants 198, 262–4
  quest for King elephant 330–8
Elgon Mountain, Kenya 262–3
Elizabeth I, Queen 227–9
Elizabeth II, Queen 78, 147
Ellis, Sapper 42–3
Enzer, Peter 211, 321
Enzer, Val 321
Enzo 274–5
EOKA 29, 31, 34–5
Esso 222
Esson, Frank 238, 254
Ethiopia 55–71, 73–113
Europa airship 264–6, 273–7
Everett, Sara 238, 239
Explorers' Club, New York 125, 229, 287
Eye of the Wind 222–6, 233, 238, 239, 240, 254, 264–6

Falklands War (1982) 309
Farrington, Sue 320
Faulkner, Captain 7–8
Fawcett, Colonel 120
Festorazzi, Dick 177, 185
Fifi (nurse, Zaire Expedition) 192
Fiji 240
Firquat, the 160–1, 171
Fisher, Captain John 311
Fletcher, Brigadier Jack 156
Fletcher, John 92, 96, 98, 101–2, 106, 110, 112
Fly River, Papua New Guinea 249
Fonteyn, Dame Margot 238
Force Publique 189
Ford, President Gerald 216
Foreign and Commonwealth Office 125
Forester, Lord Cecil and Lady (godparents) 55, 58
Fort George, Inverness 269–70, 273
Fort St Andrew, Panama 229–30, 234–6
Fort Wellington, Belize 291
Foulds, Helen 328–9
Foulds, Jon 328
Francisco (muleteer, Darien Gap Expedition) 143
Freeman, Major Hawk 305, 322
Freeman-Attwood, Julian 313, 350, 351, 353, 354
Frewster, Noel 242–3

Officer Training Corps 4, 18–19
Ogilvy, Marina 293
okapi 198
Okavango Delta, Botswana 329
'Old Dairy, The' 255
Olewale, Tatty 249
Olive Branch 235–6, 294
Olivetti 242
Oman, Sultanate of 153–72, 301
Operation Aphrodite II 39
Operation Darien *see* Darien Gap Expedition
Operation Drake
  launch of 215–18
  selection tests 218–21
  search for vessel 221–2
  expedition sets sail 222–6
  in Panama and Caribbean 229–39
  scientific research 233, 237, 278
  financial difficulties 239, 240
  in Papua New Guinea 240–54, 279
  encounters 'lost' tribe 244–7
  search for Artrellia 'dragon' 248–53
  in Indonesia 253–5
  in Kenya 256–64, 290
  in Italy 264–5
  voyage ends 266–7
  reflections on 278–9, 360–3
Operation Raleigh
  planning, recruiting and equippping
    279–85
  fund-raising 280–2, 301, 305–6, 311, 320, 323,
    344
  scientific research 280, 290, 294, 314–15,
    346–7
  in USA 287–7
  in Caribbean 287–80
  search for 'lost white city' of Mosquito Coast
    290–3
  in Costa Rica 293–4
  in Panama 294–5
  in Chile 296–302
  in Australia 303–11
  in Solomon Islands 307–8
  SWR's voyage home 311–12, 321–2
  in Tibet (1987) 312–20
  dispute over future of 320
  art exhibition 322
  reunion at Albert Hall 322
  company sponsorship 323
  guidance to returning Venturers 324
  executive expedition to Kalahari 325–30,
    346
  executive expedition to Karnali River
    330–8
  in Soviet Union 338–9
  in Mongolia 340–57
  reflections on 360–3
Operation Raleigh USA 281–2, 286, 301
Oran, Sapper, 30–1
O'Shea, Mark 292–3, 333, 337
Osman, Dan 232–3
Osmaston, Dr Henry 313, 316, 318
Our Price Records 331

Outward Bound 51–2, 208, 212–13, 215

Page, Peter 157, 161
Paiku Lake, Tibet 315–16
Pakistan 280, 320, 321
Palo, Colombia 143, 144
Pan-Am 223, 242
Pan-American Highway 120, 123, 129, 146,
  147–8
Panama 121, 123, 124, 125, 126–42, 229–39, 282,
  294–5
Panama Canal 121, 239, 295
Pandora, HMS 303–7
Paphos, Cyprus 35–7, 39–42
Papua New Guinea (PNG) 240–54, 279, 307–8
Parker, David 308
Parsloe, John 305
Pasha, Emin 198
Pass, Gerry 203
Patagonia, Chile 299
Patron, Major Alberto 144, 146
Paulaya River 292
Pelican 227
Penny, Andrew 60
People's Front for the Liberation of the Occu-
  pied Arabian Gulf 155
Peru 295, 297
Peta (Operation Raleigh, Australia) 306
Philip, Prince 78, 178
Philippines 22–3
Piccolo Abbai River, Ethiopia 62
Pike, Alice 173
Pike, Gavin 89, 91
Piriati River, Panama 138, 139
Pitcairn Island 303–4
Plymouth 223–4, 228
Pogaian people 245
Ponting, Mick 345, 349, 355
Port Moresby, Papua New Guinea 242, 248
Porteous, Nigel 279, 305
Portugal 282, 321
Potanine Glacier, Mongolia 354
Powell, Bob 189–90, 206
Pratt, Basil 184, 202, 207, 322, 349
Prince Henry 288
Prince William 288
Puerto Montt, Chile 297, 298
Pungpa Ri Mountain, Tibet 320
Pygmies 193, 198–9
Pyke, Magnus 235

Qaboos, Prince, Sultan of Oman 155, 221
Qarau, Sam 184, 199
Queen's Gallantry Medal 207
Queen's Own Hussars 184
Queensland Parks and Wildlife Service
  307

rainforests 237, 292, 293–4
Raja Gaj (King elephant) 335–8
Raji tribe 332
Raleigh, Sir Walter 279, 280, 326
Raleigh Trust 321, 362

John McNeil was b
nautical Engineeri
During 25 years i
founder of one of the UK's leading systems companies and
chairman of an international software house. Currently, he
is chief executive of a community enterprise business in
Dumbarton.

His first novel, *The Consultant*, was serialized for television
by the BBC. It was followed by *Spy Game* and *Little
Brother*. He has written several television screenplays
including *Crossfire*, a thriller serial about the troubles in
Northern Ireland.

He lives in Helensburgh, the setting for this novel, and has
a deep and passionate love of Glasgow, the setting for his
next.

'*HOOLET* IS A BOOK OF UNSETTLING
SURPRISES . . . DISQUIETINGLY EROTIC
AND DETAILED TO PERFECTION'

Campbell Armstrong, author of *Jig*

HOOLET

John McNeil

CORGI BOOKS

HOOLET
A CORGI BOOK 0 552 13489 9

First publication in Great Britain

PRINTING HISTORY
Corgi edition published 1993

Set in 10/11pt Linotype Plantin by
County Typesetters, Margate, Kent

Corgi Books are published by Transworld Publishers Ltd,
61–63 Uxbridge Road, Ealing, London W5 5SA,
in Australia by Transworld Publishers (Australia) Pty Ltd,
15–25 Helles Avenue, Moorebank, NSW 2170,
and in New Zealand by Transworld Publishers (NZ) Ltd,
3 William Pickering Drive, Albany, Auckland.

Reproduced, printed and bound in Great Britain by
Cox & Wyman Ltd, Reading, Berks.

For my son, Rufus

Then catch the moments as they fly,
And use them as ye ought, man:
Believe me, happiness is shy,
And comes not aye when sought, man.

ROBERT BURNS

Will he come, at nightfall, intent on killing?

The last of the sun falters on the far-flung hills beyond the Gareloch. We enter that timeless hinterland between day and night. Silence all about us and not a whisker of movement on the braes behind or the black loch waters below the empty moor.

Murdo sits close by. With his gaunt frame and weather-beaten features, he might be carved from rock. From the corner of an eye he sees a look of doubt cross my face. We are going nowhere – indeed in all honesty there is no place on earth I would rather be at this instant. We are meeting no-one. No appointment has been made, no hour of arrival agreed beforehand. Yet I am struck suddenly by that most irritating and inescapable of modern afflictions; I cannot help myself. I check my watch.

'We've nae lang tae wait,' Murdo says, softly reassuring.

In his two and seventy years, Murdo has never been a split second late for any event he considered important, and he has never seen need of a watch. Not until mankind in its ignorance invented the clock, he has been heard to say, was there such a thing as unpunctuality. He can tell now, from a mere glance skywards at the grey evening light, that death is only moments away. He knows where and when before it happens.

He first saw the hoolet over this tract of heathland four nights ago. Male short-eared owls are slightly smaller than females, and Murdo was certain this was a male. Young and adventurous – one of this year's brood, by the look of him – in search of some territory to call his own. Every bird of consequence is known on the estate here, certainly every bird of prey – the two pairs of hen harriers, the various short-eared and

7

long-eared owls, the barn owls, the buzzards. This was a stranger, a new arrival from outwith Murdo's beat: he surmises from a lonely glen somewhere to the north. The hoolet appeared without sound or warning, precisely at sundown, swooping brazenly down to the heather only a few arm lengths from where Murdo stood. He seized a vole and severed the head, treating Murdo's frozen attempt to blend into the background with a leisurely stare, enquiring and fearless, before winging away with his catch low over a forestry track.

This was fine woodland once, before the trees were felled. One of these days it will be woodland again. And so, in the dour Scottish conviction that everything worthwhile is lost in the past or yet to come, the locals persist in calling it a wood. For the moment, a plantation of spindly new conifers and birches, no more than knee high, offers the perfect hunting ground: warm nesting for voles and fieldmice, with scanty cover from the air.

As it happened, Murdo was here the following evening, engaged in the tedious task of checking the saplings for blight. Exactly as at first sighting, just when the sun dipped in the waters of the Clyde, the hoolet swept in – within a matter of feet, so Murdo swears, of the original place of execution. And the bird stared as before, for as long as before, then flew off with slow silent wing beats on the identical flight path he'd followed previously.

A gamekeeper's days and nights have more hours than most of us could stomach: to return without good reason to the same corner of the estate on three successive days is an almost impossible indulgence. But Murdo's curiosity got the better of him. Anticipating awkward questions from the factor up at the big house, he made his excuses. 'If ye're needing me,' he said, 'I'll be where I am. And if not, I'll be someplace else.' Making a detour this way last evening, he was rewarded with a repeat performance. A virtuoso staging of Death at Sundown for an enthralled audience of one. The hoolet, he told me when I chanced by his cottage this morning, is one of the most intelligent of birds. Having found a winning formula, this shrewd young bird will stick by it to the letter, perhaps for

8

several weeks, until he picks the territory clean. Would I care to see for myself?

There is still time, a few last moments, to consider the hunter versus the hunted, to ponder where my sympathies lie. I regard myself as civilized, shrinking more than the average at any hint of violence, at the faintest sight of human blood. Yet here I am, waiting with eager expectation for a bloody act of violence. The short-eared owl is a serial killer, slaying mercilessly on a mass scale across his chosen patch of country. Why do I admire his clinical skill, his speed and his power, but spare no tears for the hundreds of voles he will kill and devour in a single month? I offer no apology. This is nature, raw and simple. The hoolet kills to survive. He kills without malice. His victims are chosen for no other reason than that they are there as he passes. His aim is the quick clean kill, and a good many of his prey die the death I would wish for myself, struck down in an instant without pain or forewarning.

Murdo seems neither to speak nor move, but in some mysterious way breaks into my thoughts. I comprehend, with nothing being said, that I must look to my left.

The hoolet has come from nowhere out of the gloaming, so close to us, so unexpectedly large at this short distance, I catch my breath. He dives relentlessly to earth, at one and the same moment seeming to hover without effort while choosing where to strike. I have the light-headed sense of seconds stretching into long minutes: I am watching a slow-motion replay of several evenings past. Does the spectacle of death, I wonder, excite some primal instinct, set the adrenalin pumping so that not the slightest action escapes my avid gaze?

The hoolet mantles his catch with outstretched wings of fluffily innocent beige. We hear the tearing of sinews, a muffled crunching of tiny bones – he has no need for silence now. I feel a breeze suddenly on my cheeks, a taste of night blowing in from the Firth. He chooses this moment to leave, carrying off a wee bundle of fur whose twitching tail laments the loss of its head. We watch him wheel, take the updraught and melt away like a ghost in the gloom.

'Well?'

9

No answer is expected. This is Murdo's way of saying he told me so.

We share a smile. We share the special satisfaction of seeing a prediction come true. The hoolet is wild and free, his way of life untouched by ours. But we were here, waiting, ahead of him. For a brief interval we saw events in his life unfold before they ever occurred, before he chose, freely, to enact them. Such moments are rare and I find myself mightily glad of that. How boring life would be, how unbearable, how frightening, if it were always this predictable.

THE SEDUCTION
OF CAROLINE

One

We saw no owl that cold October evening. I stamped my
feet, swore now and then at the obstinacy of nature, and
shared a quarter bottle of scotch with my brother Gordon.
The grouse on the whisky label, Gordon remarked finally,
was the only bird we'd be seeing this side of midnight.

Wind-swept, chilled to the bone, it seemed strangely
perverse to realize just then that my weekly newspaper
column has never made mention of whisky. I had decided
for reasons which now elude me that my trusted friend and
guide Murdo would not, while on duty so to speak, think
it proper to resort to a dram. And since, in the columns of
'Highlander's Diary', Murdo and I are inseparable,
neither have I ever been known to touch the stuff. What
my readers make of this, I can only guess. As I picture
them, for the greater part they live out their lives in
English cities. They work the routine of offices, struggling
through the traffic-choked streets, the sweaty crush of
buses and tubes, to the bleak solitude of the suburbs.
Their knowledge of the Highlands extends little beyond
what wisdom I impart weekly, and what television provides once a year at Hogmanay in the shape of kilts and
bagpipes. Do they imagine that Murdo and I venture into
the wilds with only our staunch Scottish wills as protection
against the bitter climate? And that we return in the grim
night hours to plates of porridge oats, made plainly with
water and sprinkled with salt? I make no such claims in
writing, but nor can I plead wholly innocent if certain
impressions, shall I say, are given. The country happenings of my diary are not the truth, the whole truth, I
discover in occasional outings with Gordon, they are what

readers desire them to be. An escape to the grandeur of glens over Saturday morning breakfast.

The setting was far from remote as we waited vainly for the owl, but it did not suit me to say so in that week's piece. House lights shone by the score in nearby Helensburgh and closer to, below the hill where we stood, in the village of Rhu. Across the Clyde, orange sodium street lamps gleamed along the coast, from the headland at Gourock for mile after mile inland. Glasgow threw a faint halo against the clouds from somewhere far off over the fells. This is where the Highlands meet the Lowlands, where the last true wilderness in Europe ends and civilization begins, in the form of pizza parlours and haggis with chips, distant idle cranes that once made ships, and a nuclear submarine base protected by armed guards and razor wire. Owls do indeed hunt here, and there is a different column to be written about nature lived out against a backdrop of high-security floodlighting. Another day, maybe. My mood at the time was solitary, I felt irrational sparks of anger at odd moments. I needed to write of small violence in a lonely place, and I knew that having done so I would feel all the better for it.

Gordon had sighted the owl the previous weekend. It came down among some small new trees, too far off for him to see whether it had taken a catch. He thought it might have, he said – there was no sure way of telling. The days were beginning to draw in for the coming of winter. The sun was close to setting, and what he would, only a week or two earlier, have considered afternoon was now early evening. He was typically vague about the time. Somewhere around six, he thought. Yes, he had looked at his watch, only to find he'd forgotten to wind it. He misunderstood my irritation on hearing of this, presuming that I considered exact timing to be crucial in tracking down the owl. The gold Rolex was my father's: he had two sons and just the one watch. So there was a choice to be made; I bear no ill-will over my father's decision. But, having inherited the watch, Gordon might at least treat it with suitable respect. Not thinking, he wears it for rough shooting, for trekking through mud and over jagged rocks. I have been staggered to see the Rolex plunged into icy water as Gordon drank from a mountain stream. And he might at the least, at the very least, bother to wind the bloody thing now and then. One of these days, the right moment will come to say all this. Meanwhile, I was able to find private satisfaction, to even the score, by taking revenge on Murdo, Gordon's other persona. I condemned him to a lifetime without a watch.

Does this seem petty? I hope not. We are brothers. We are doomed by the ties of blood. There is almost no act we can do for one another which is not tainted by a sense of obligation. Little can be said between us, however slight or passing, which does not hold some deeply lurking significance. So, if I sometimes bury what may seem to be niggling pin-pricks of resentment between the lines of my newspaper column, I have good reason. Why cause dissension by saying to his face what I can say secretly in newspaper articles he professes not to read?

He had phoned me that morning to mention the owl. A sighting of no great interest, but maybe I was short of ideas for this week's column? I was, frankly, going quietly frantic for want of ideas. By pure inspiration I thought to ask if he'd seen this particular owl before.

'God knows,' he said. 'One owl looks more or less like any other.'

'Not to Murdo,' I said. 'He has ways of telling. Old country ways.'

'Fuck Murdo!'

'Think for a minute. Is this a new arrival or a regular? Does it nest on the estate?'

'What would you prefer?'

'What I'd prefer, Gordon, is not to invent what's supposed to be real life.'

He took, I must say, a reflective pause so lengthy it was worthy of the fictional Murdo. 'I think,' he resumed, 'I

15

think this might be the owl I saw a couple of weeks back. But I'm not saying it is.'

'In the same place?'

'More or less. The same wood, anyhow. Highlandman's Wood. Over near Rhu.'

'When was the first sighting? Round about the same time?'

'Roughly the same. After lunch and before supper. That good enough for you?'

'Didn't you say once that owls sometimes hunt to a set pattern? Flying to a kind of timetable?'

'I've seen that happen, yes.'

'Around six o'clock, you said. Let's play safe and get there by five. It would help in future,' I added, 'if you'd use some more accurate means of time-keeping than a fucking sundial.'

'Five this evening, you mean? Not a hope, Sandy.'

Patiently, I explained the tyranny of deadlines, making clear the aversion newspapermen have to seeing columns of blank space under their by-lines. None of this was new to him.

'Tam McFadden,' he said, 'will no' be very pleased wi' me.'

In my world, estate managers count for nothing. Features editors, on the other hand, are greatly to be feared.

'Compared to Bill Nicolson,' I said, 'Tam McFadden is a mere wee pussy-cat.'

So, with familiar reluctance, he committed to show me where. We found ourselves exposed to the elements, given no shelter by the dwarf trees against an unfriendly wind from the choppy seas out beyond Arran. My mind was occupied for a time with words to describe our immediate surroundings, which in all honesty amounted to not very much. *Dreich? Wasty? Fusselbare?* We had only ourselves and the Grouse for company, and the promise of our final retreat to the pub. It's possible, I suppose, that we could instead have been enjoying the warmth of my log fire or

16

Gordon's ancient coal-stoked Aga. Gordon could be quizzed on the owl, his rural knowledge plundered, the article written. Inconveniently, my early grounding in crime reporting leaves me no such easy options. I have the newshound's awkward vice of needing to see for myself, to breathe in the atmosphere. Moreover, some wise advice from my father has stayed with me for over thirty years, as has the memory of the harsh beating that came with it. If you're going to tell a lie, he'd said, at least be sure it's ninety per cent truth.

There is also entertainment to be had on these occasions from seeing how long Gordon can last out before turning the conversation to his inevitable, perennial topic. He differs profoundly from Murdo, in age, in dialect, in his inability to maintain a silence worthy of the brooding hillsides. Murdo would never talk of sex. Gordon can talk to me of little else.

'This new woman of yours,' he began.

'What woman?' I said with convincing lack of guile.

'The bloody new one.'

'All my women are new,' I said, 'in the sense that few of them last for very long.'

'The long-legged one. The one you said has long legs.'

'Most of them have long legs. I have a particular liking for long legs. I mean,' I said, beckoning for the quarter bottle, 'who given a choice between legs that can barely get a decent grip round you and long, fantastically long, smooth legs able to enfold you several times and still stroke the nape of your neck with her toes – who'd be so dumb as to choose some runty wee lassie.'

'You bloody know which woman I mean!'

We tend to have this problem. It derives, I suppose, from my refusal ever to divulge names. I have always considered that to recount sexual experiences is natural, uplifting, a pleasure in its own right of a quietly rewarding and even faintly erotic kind. To remember, to retell, is, after all, to re-experience. But to mention names is to indulge in mere gossip.

17

'Do you mean,' I enquired helpfully, 'the woman I'm sleeping with now or the woman I shall be sleeping with next?'

'Yes,' he said. 'That one. That bloody one.'

'Ah.'

'Well . . . ?'

I gazed at him guardedly as if he was a foreigner asking directions in the street. What, exactly, was his question? He swore at me in an unhostile, brotherly fashion. I professed confusion, some of our earlier conversation was repeated. We invariably do this. All sex requires foreplay. I enjoy winding him up; I am sure he relishes what is to come all the more for having it withheld, for being further aroused, though he would maybe not make this admission.

'Exactly what,' I said, to move matters on, 'do you want me to tell you about her?'

'Anything. Any fucking thing. Damnit all, Sandy, all you've ever said is she's got long legs.'

'She's tall to go with them. In beautiful proportion. She has quite startlingly green eyes. Her hair is red, real Scottish red hair, vibrant and lustrous. Aged about twenty, I would say. Young enough to be my daughter, if I'd started screwing as early as I should've. Her breasts—'

A gulp at the whisky stopped these recollections. After which I wiped my lips much too slowly with the back of a hand.

'Yes . . .' he urged.

'Her breasts are quite simply perfect. She is, Gordon, even as we speak, at her very pinnacle, at the crowning moment of her life. Like an exotic flower coming into bloom. She is just, exactly just, at peace with her breasts. Not long ago, I imagine, they were still too new, she was too self-conscious of them. Regrettably too soon, because of their generous size, she'll begin to worry that they're starting to droop. But right now she wears them with pride. They are not newly arrived, growing at awkward moments, getting in the way. They are part of her. She loves them dearly, more than any other part of her body.

18

She no longer wants them groped or grabbed at in furtive corners. She wants them admired, adored, gently caressed, stroked and brought to arousal. To be treated, in other words, as so far only she has been able to treat them.'

'Bullshit,' Gordon said, after a surprisingly long period of thinking this through. 'Blicker and hash. You're all bloody talk.'

'If you say so.' I fell into an unconcerned silence. I felt his eyes heavily on me as I started up to a hilltop in search of flapping wings.

'Phyllis,' he said with a profound sense of loss, 'has no bloody tits to speak of. None at all.'

'She never did,' I reminded him. 'But that was hardly, was it, the reason you married. I mean, only a fool would marry for tits.' Here I threw in a suitable pause. 'Even for very large tits. Though if they *were* very large maybe a man would be only half a fool for being tempted.'

'The trouble is,' he confessed, 'the older you get, the more things like that matter. I'm not complaining, I wouldn't want Phyllis any other way. I just wish sometimes she had really big tits. A fucking enormous pair. Then she'd be perfect.'

'You'd like this latest woman of mine,' I said subversively. 'Any bigger and they'd be a problem, a danger to navigation. But they do seem to suit her terribly well.'

He signalled for the bottle. Then I took a further turn at the dwindling contents. We commiserated. On setting out we'd reckoned on only a brief foray. We had looked at the sky, he'd held a wet finger to the air. We'd judged ourselves to be embarked on a quarter-bottle evening, and our country instincts had been badly awry.

'This woman of yours . . .' he said, and waited.

My watch showed the time to be coming close to six. 'Right now,' I said, 'she's not long arrived back home. To her nice, small but neat, single room which I'm told is decorated in an all-over shade of pink. Not cheap pink. Not garish. Not adolescent. A mature, womanly shade of pink. A wonderfully alluring colour for a bedroom. A ripe,

19

fleshy colour. A nude-looking room, very close in shade to the colour of her breasts.'

'Fucking bullshit,' he murmured, in a tone of total belief.

'The very breasts,' I continued, 'which at this very minute she has bared and is examining from every possible angle in her dressing-table mirror. They need no support – they seem suspended in space, full, curving and luscious. She's looking, running her slender fingers over them. And thinking that the moment is ripe for someone like me, a connoisseur of breasts, to enter her life. To breathe over them as deeply as she is breathing. Don't get me wrong . . . these aren't crude juvenile imaginings on her part. She's not thinking full-blown sex, not yet. She wants nothing more than a pair of strong but delicate hands in her life. Someone else's fingers.'

'How do you know?'

'How do you mean?'

'You said right now. How do you know?'

'How do you bloody think I know?'

Gordon considered the question for a while. 'You've followed her home?' he guessed, eyeing me very strangely.

'Of course I've followed her.'

'Bloody pervert . . . you've peeped in her window.'

'Listen . . . she goes into the house. Soon a light comes on at a window. Then I get no more than a glimpse of her before she draws the curtains. I've no opportunity to peep! Besides, it's a first-floor room, too high to see into. And, incidentally, I follow, I see what I see, I never pry. I stand where it's legal to stand, never intruding or hiding. So I don't pry.' I've no objection to being accused by Gordon of perversion, since, perversion being something he would dearly love to indulge in, he means this as a compliment. But I glowered anyway. And, I would guess, sounded sorely offended. 'I do not,' I pronounced emphatically, 'stoop to prying. But I've seen just enough of the room, from a decent distance. I've seen the walls, and they're pink. There's a big mirror against the window, a dressing-

20

table mirror. That's all I needed to see. I *know* what she gets up to in that room, what rituals she performs. I can say with certainty, because I've studied her closely for several weeks. I've watched her, observed what she does and where, how she fills her days. She has few secrets from me. I know her every move.'

'Even behind closed curtains . . .'

'Don't doubt it. She's like all women, a creature of habit. Observe some of those habits and you can safely infer the rest. She is,' I said, throwing an arm about haphazardly, 'very much like this owl of yours, except a great deal easier to find.'

He pondered this for some considerable while. 'You might have something there,' he concurred. 'Phyllis is quite alarmingly predictable. Mostly I find that comforting but every now and then I could resort to murder.' He considered further. 'I like my dinner ready on the table, I've got used to being told about muddy boots and the floor's just fucking washed. I quite like a new cotton dressing gown every fourth Christmas. But I wish, my God Sandy how I wish, I had some other reason than venison stew and sex for knowing when it's Friday.' He laughed the strained plaintive laugh of admitting the joke was on him.

'This Miss Long Legs of mine,' I said in consolation. 'This Miss Exceedingly Long Legs—'

'This Miss Divine Breasts—' he enjoined.

'—has a ten-minute walk from her place of work to the fleshy pink room she calls home. She leaves the shop a few minutes after it closes at five thirty.'

'What shop? You never mentioned a shop.'

'The shop where she works.'

'Where she *works*?'

'As a shop-girl. Which is, if you must know, one of the things I find most tantalizing about her.'

'A bloody shop!'

'Something wrong with a shop?'

'Everything, Sandy. Legs up to her chin, fantastic tits.

21

Wonderful deep green eyes, was it? And I'm supposed to believe she works in a fucking shop!'

'All the more exciting for her, wouldn't you say, when a mature man of the world appears on the scene. A writer for a great national newspaper, a classy address in Upper Helensburgh. I don't go in for clichés – I shan't say "Let me take you away from all this." But I shall, you can be sure, think of something that appropriately expresses how lucky she is to have me.'

'One of these days,' he said wistfully, 'some woman somewhere is going to say no. And the world will fall in on you.'

'Impossible. I take great care in choosing the women who'll say yes.'

His eyes narrowed quizzically. 'In Helensburgh, this shop?'

I nodded casually.

'Funny I've never seen her.'

'Perhaps you have.'

'I'd remember if I had. I've a remarkable memory for large breasts. There's damned bloody few, I'll tell you, in the shops down in the Burgh. On younger women, I mean, women under fifty.

'Interesting,' I said. 'Very revealing. That tells me a great deal about you. About you and Phyllis.'

'In what way?'

'It tells me,' I said with calculated cruelty, 'about the kind of shops you never go into. The sort of shopping you have no need of.'

'And what's that supposed to mean?'

I glanced from habit at my watch. Swiss, gold and a dependable keeper of time, though inclined in damp weather to cloud badly under the glass. It came to me, down a line of unknown ownership, from a stall at the Glasgow Barras. I have no knowledge of its past but I can state with assurance that its history is not mine, not a family history. Very occasionally, with Gordon at my shoulder, I glance at the watch and, instead of reading the

22

time shown, drift into bitter futile thoughts about other earlier times. I fail to notice the hands.

'This bloody owl,' I swore eventually. 'This bloody owl you promised.'

He gave me a stare of long and detailed scrutiny. I have said I never reveal names. He also knows well how far I can be pushed on other points of detail, the degree of revelation beyond which I judge it wise not to proceed.

'I don't like this story of yours,' he said finally. 'I like the girl. I shall probably have wet dreams about the girl. No probably about it, I promise myself I shall. But the shop is a total let-down. If she owned the shop, maybe I'd buy all this crap. If she even ran it, a clever young manageress. But a bloody shop-girl!'

'It's not a story.'

'Oh, yes . . .?'

'I never tell stories.'

'My God!' he exclaimed.

'Not about women.'

'Well I,' he said, taking the final swig of whisky away with him for some several feet, 'shall be the judge of that.'

His turned back was a rebuke and a challenge. It was intended to be. I could tell I was being urged to justify myself, and was forced to consider carefully whether to let matters ride or whether to respond, to admit more to Gordon than I ever have in the past. I am prepared to share experiences with him. But there it ends. What I have always dreaded is that he might some day blunder into parts of my life where he doesn't belong. That he might be tempted to see for himself, to check whether what he hears is fact or fiction. He and I look, it's often remarked, astonishingly alike. But whereas I fit naturally into the small-town landscape – I am, quite happily, a small-town person – Gordon never appears anything but the game-keeper he is. He belongs in the country. Put simply, I can loiter on town streets with impunity, Gordon cannot. He would stick out a mile, which might be extremely inconvenient.

I decided after some reflection that I know him rather well. He is surprisingly shy of women – which is why, it can be supposed, he is so enraptured to hear tell of what he considers to be my boldness. I concluded it was most unlikely he would dream of entering this particular shop. Nor, I was sure, would he think of peering in at the windows.

'She works,' I said, 'in a lingerie shop.'

He turned on his heel. 'A what!'

'Underwear. Silk pyjamas. Brassieres, knickers and flimsy nightwear.'

'My God,' he breathed, 'that's brilliant. Absolutely brilliant.'

'Eh?' I uttered.

'Inspired.' He closed his eyes rapturously. 'Oh, yes. I can see her in a lingerie shop. Oh, yes.'

'It's true,' I protested. 'Every word.'

'Until a minute ago,' he said, 'it was all bullshit, a fucking tissue of lies. But . . .' He grinned broadly and lobbed over the empty bottle. 'But this talk of brassieres is brilliant. Everything fits suddenly. Of course it's true. How could I doubt it.'

'There's more,' I said, greatly encouraged.

'You've actually spoken to her . . . begun the campaign?'

'In a way, yes.'

'Och, come on, Sandy . . . either you have or you haven't.'

'I haven't engaged her in true conversation. Not as the next man in her life. Not as lover or suitor or seducer. I'm not ready for that. I haven't yet worked out my opening lines.'

I paused, and he correctly guessed this to be a puzzle for him. His brow furrowed. Gordon, bless him, is one of those people who clearly reveals when he is thinking.

'A bloody customer!' he deduced. 'You went into the shop. In your filthy boots and Barbour jacket, your hair up everywhere. Looking like a fish out of water among the frilly knickers.'

'Looking remarkably suave and well groomed, as it happens. And also, I hope, suitably anonymous.'

A stare of detached assessment from him as if we were strangers. He seemed to find my appearance unremarkable, unmemorable. So he murmured reflectively, perhaps deciding that a plain but rugged face must be an advantage in the pursuit of women.

'I did not,' I continued, '*wish* to be remembered. She mustn't be aware I'm preparing the ground. When we meet, meet properly that is, she must believe it to be for the very first time. With me so far?'

He nodded, gesturing me to continue.

'I wanted to see her close to. In a shop you can do that, it's nothing unusual. You can stare at the goods. We're perfect strangers but there I was, only a counter's width away, able quite naturally to have my fill of her. She has a little fleck in one of those great green eyes. It looked oddly like a tear forming, like something I'd said had touched her deeply. She has, Gordon, the most appealing fragility because of it. A tall girl's legs, those wonderfully mature breasts, yet child's eyes, about to cry with delight when the right words are said. Too much makeup, for my liking, far too much. But then I saw why – a couple of slight swellings under the powder on her cheek, just below the ear. She's very young, that's her problem. The same height as me, looking me straight in the eye, but still plagued with the odd pimply spot. Which she tries to cover. I found that immensely appealing.'

'Were you looking or buying?' Gordon asked.

'I bought a nightdress. Long, black and see-through. Shockingly expensive but I decided she'll be worth it. I intend to see that she's worth it.'

'You actually bought a fucking nightdress!' Gordon's tone showed his credulity was strained.

'An apt description,' I answered evenly. 'I have someone in mind, as a matter of fact, a woman whose taste runs to black. She'll waft in from her bathroom wearing this madly romantic gift. Very seductively, I dare say. I shall immediately peel it off. And I shall then, without question, fuck her. For a very long time. Forty quid of fucking. I believe in getting my money's worth.'

Gordon gazed at me with genuine appreciation. He is touchingly free of envy. He has decided, I think, that most, perhaps almost all, of what I tell him is genuine. If he was devoid of all doubt, I suspect he might be green with jealousy, perhaps even vindictively so. But a corner of doubt gives him the freedom to listen without rancour, to have proxy sex without guilt. Gordon is immensely, bafflingly, tediously faithful to Phyllis. I give him, I believe, his only access to the adultery he craves but will never venture.

'I had to find some way,' I continued after something of an interval, 'to entice her out from behind the counter. There was a rail nearby of these scandalously scanty robes. I went over, she followed. She stood so close – this was early morning, just after they opened – I could smell the toothpaste on her breath. I could smell soap on her despite a hefty sprinkling of perfume. She has long, beautifully manicured nails. She baths and cleans herself scrupulously because, I'll swear, she sees this as the sure path to better things. Don't scoff at shop-girls, Gordon. This is a young woman with high aspirations.'

His gaze held the dreamy hopelessness of a man falling in love with the wrong sort of girl.

'Her voice is intriguing,' I went on. 'I can't quite place the accent. She has a mature, slightly husky tone, a bit breathy, if you know what I mean. She's definitely from these parts, more or less, but not Helensburgh. There's a hint of Glasgow in the blurring of some of her words. Maybe she comes originally from Dumbarton, but I'm not entirely sure. Whatever, she's gone to some pains to hide her beginnings. It's not an affected accent, not pretentious but it's the voice of where she's going, not where she came from. She's squeaky clean, Gordon. She showers morning and night. She's even scrubbed and sanitized her voice. Fascinating, don't you agree?'

'Voices don't do much for me,' Gordon said. 'I've never been much of a voices man.'

'She asked what size of lady the nightdress was for. I replied did she mean height or . . . I made breasts in the air with my hands. Both, she said, in this sanitized, not quite Glasgow accent. I remember thinking . . . you've never seen me before, but I'm a walking encyclopedia on you, lassie. You've got a flesh-pink bedroom, pink pimples in secret places. You've got green leather boots, and I don't mean the boots you're wearing now. A green not unlike the emerald of those lovely flecked eyes. And I also thought, wait for this one, we've hardly said a word to one another and we're already talking breasts.'

'That,' Gordon opined, with affirmative nods of his head, 'is one hell of a way to start a relationship.'

'The lady, I said, is about so high.' I held a hand roughly level with my chin in demonstration. 'And a rather petite 36. She's particularly fond of black.'

'You're confusing me. Which woman's this suddenly, about five foot six and partial to black?'

'You know damned well who!'

'The one with an insatiable orifice at both ends of her body?'

'Regrettably,' I said, 'I know only one woman answering to that description.'

'I wouldn't have thought,' he returned sourly, 'she kept her clothes on long enough for it to be worth your while buying a negligee!'

I raised a hand to solicit his patience. 'Miss Long Legs chose a nightdress from the rail, held it against her body so I could see the style. She twirled around, stuck out a hip. She put her head at a come-hither angle, then did a most unexpectedly audacious thing. She shone her white teeth at me and licked them, fully twice, with a kind of pantingly slow provocation. A pink moist tongue, very large and muscular. And a delightful hesitancy about the licking, like she'd practised for night after night in front of that mirror but never actually tried it before on a man. I'll

27

tell you, Gordon, she is no mere shop-girl, she's a future bloody marketing manager. She could sell crotchless knickers to the Moderator of the Church of Scotland.'

He could find nothing to say.

'And I remember thinking at the time, and trying very hard not to disgrace myself with an erection, I remember thinking . . . this is my next mistress. She has just chosen for me, and displayed, a sexual offering to my present mistress. My final parting gift to the woman she will replace. Thank you, madam, the bonking was incredible, but goodbye. The eyes are greener elsewhere. I remember thinking, I've never before pulled off anything quite as intricately and perfectly schemed. This marvellous creature, Gordon, doesn't just behave as I predict she will, she has the capacity to surprise me.'

'Then she's not predictable,' he said.

'Far from it,' I told him. 'Having surprised me once, I know what to expect next time.'

Not long after, we decided to throw in the towel. The owl had not obliged. Night was on us, the sky black, the louring clouds scudding, torn by the wind into shreds. The hills had grown bare with the passing of day, grey and granite hard, cut with deep shadows of murky foreboding. A pale new moon was rising out of our seeing behind the peninsula at Roseneath, and cracks of silver glinted like icicles on the blustery Firth of Clyde. We made passage, on the downhill track, through a herd of fatly impassive cows. Mist steamed from their nostrils and flanks, they stamped and snorted and shuffled, a sweet strong odour of cow dung and urine swelled up in the night as we pushed our way by. After the tasteless clean air before, I breathed gladly in as I would a joint of hashish. The warm organic taste filled my lungs, the smell stayed on us like ripe sweat long after the cows were far behind. The country smell seemed to communicate some primitive rural lore to me, a message came on the wind. Murdo, I saw with sudden clarity, would call the owl a hoolet. He has a remarkable wealth of natural knowledge, of facts and wisdom and apposite phrases, passed down to him in a long lineage of fathers and sons. How such snippets of understanding as he cares to impart reach me, I am never entirely sure. Sometimes, I can almost believe in him myself.

A fire was burning at the Ardencaple Hotel, the lochside bar was mercifully empty, the jukebox silent. Gordon warmed his back and I my front. He licked his lips, contrived to look parched, and gazed expectantly, as he had every right to do.

'Sorry,' I said with an impoverished gesture. 'Not a bean on me.'

He was apoplectic.

The nightdress, I explained. My planning had been thorough, I had called first at the bank. But there are times and tides in every man's love life, and this was wholly new to me, a high-water mark of sexual spending. I had never before bought a transparent black nightdress. It had cleaned me out.

'You had forty quid with you? And you spent the lot?'

'It seemed,' I said, 'more than sufficient. She really is disgustingly good at selling.'

'Not a bawbee more? Not a tin farthing?'

Ruefully, I nodded. 'But think of it this way,' I said. 'I drew forty pounds from the bank. How did I divine that was exactly the sum I'd require? She chose the nightdress, the price was forty pounds. By what instinct did she guess that was precisely the amount I was prepared to spend? Sometimes,' I added, more for my own hearing than his, 'my romances run so uncannily on rails it's distinctly disturbing.'

Gordon bought doubles of whisky, with pints of eighty shilling as chasers. His was a decent malt, he declared, but mine was Teacher's – the Englishman's idea of a scotch – and let that be a lesson to me. He gazed far into the flaming coals and began to laugh.

'Forty fucking quid,' he roared.

'Something wrong with forty quid?'

29

'In banknotes, paid in ready cash?' His eyes held a light of gleeful triumph. 'This mature new lover, this lounge lizard from along the Clyde . . . does he pay like a man of substance? Does he flash his credit card, his gold American Express? Does he bollocks! He deals out readies, grubby Bank of Scotland fivers.'

'Credit cards,' I answered, 'carry names. The name is there, on the till receipt, long after you've left the shop. I'm not ready to tell her my name. Nor have I made up my mind whether to give her my actual born name. Sandy Blair Douglas might not sound her idea of the perfect man. I might, perish the thought, have to be someone called Gary.'

He sighed and spat in the fire. 'You're a slippery bastard,' he said amiably. 'You always were. You'll probably slither into your grave.'

My cue to remind him of some pertinent facts. 'I've got an ex-wife,' I said, 'who hates me, a daughter who's forgotten me, a bank manager who despises me, and an editor so brutishly illiterate he thinks "columnist" is a four-letter word. I'm told constantly I can't string one sentence in front of another, that I can barely write a full stop. So—' I paused for breath and a draught of the eighty. 'So, in the midst of this struggle to survive, is it to be wondered that I bask in my one wee glimmer of sunlight. I put vast effort into wooing women. I have an inner eye for women, the instinct to arrive the very moment they need someone most, and to leave not one second after our passion cools in the chilly breeze of reality. I watch a woman's every move, and plan my countermoves accordingly. I am perfectly well able, Gordon, to distinguish between the prestige of a credit card and the anonymity of cash.'

He shrugged inconsequentially. 'She'll still remember you.' He thought further. 'Probably,' he added with a faint air of hope.

'Maybe I'll seem vaguely familiar. But she won't remember where we've met. Shop-girls don't. Their

30

customers are merely a procession of faceless strangers.'

He gazed for a while on the flickering coals. 'A bloody adolescent!' he muttered in a scornful tone. 'A pimply young lass who sells knickers for a living.'

Then he clasped me to him, a bucolic, boozy, brotherly hug. Breathing scotch in my face, he laughed loudly. 'Sandy,' he said, 'you have the uncommon gift, the singular ability, to bring very great shame on the family.'

Thinking back, I realize this was the last time I was to see him laugh, at me or with me, for several months to come.

Two

She lived in an old mansion of some considerable size and
pretensions, overlooking the conifers of Hermitage Park.
An unsmiling house, with the grey stone walls and slate-
roofed porch of a Calvinist's manse. Clumps of weed
pushed up through the gravel drive and pools of moss lay
yellow on the shaded swards of grass. There was a child's
swing in the grounds, and sometimes kids' bikes strewn
out under the larch trees, but I never saw sight of any
child. By night, the porch lantern glowed dimly, an aura
of gloom prevailed – the house seemed perpetually gripped
in the Sabbath of one of those remote Western Isles where
drink is forbidden and the talk is of sin.

Her room was rented – she went there too immediately
after entering the front door, behind the closed curtains
the light remained on for too long into the evening, for her
to be other than alone. A visit to the town's library, study
of the voting register, suggested two lodgers shared the
house with a rather large family called Donaldson. One of
the names was ideal for her; a poet could not have chosen
better. To read it, murmur the syllables, was to conjure up
a vision in the mind of those Gaelic green eyes, that mane
of red hair, the mountainous country of her wonderful
breasts. But the other name spelled disaster. Not
McCrone! Surely not. I stared in dismay at the register.
Not Margo McCrone! It became possible for a while that
I'd simply call the whole thing off. I can forgive almost any
fault in a woman. Except bad breath, chewed fingernails
or a ghastly name.

I might almost have missed noticing, but the vital clue
was there, plainly to see, on the receipt she handed me for

the nightdress. Normally, I place shop receipts tidily in my wallet – there are thankfully few purchases that cannot, with astute fabrication, be paid for by the taxman. But not wishing to advertise an uncomfortably bare wallet, the receipt went, insouciantly crumpled, into a pocket of my Harris Tweed jacket. Only when walking home, uphill on Sinclair Street, did I think to look. My intention was, I suppose, to remind myself of my madness, to shake a head glumly over my inability to claim as legitimate work expenses anything bought from a business called *Sweet Dreams*, then to throw away the evidence that a woman, a girl in a shop, had got the better of me. But there it was, on one of those electronically printed tickets which regard no small detail of the transaction as too negligible to record. Date, time, amount tendered. I had been served, the receipt said informatively, by Caroline.

Suddenly dead in my tracks, I gazed at the cash ticket, and almost turned back then and there. I could barely wait to see her again. *Caroline Sutherland*. The idea occurs that I said her name aloud. Talking of her to Gordon later that same day heightened my need of her. If it had not been for my newspaper deadline, I'd have been back at the shop as its doors opened the following morning. The nightdress was too small, the colour the wrong kind of black, the lady had other garments like this – they tended to shrink in the wash. A surfeit of pretexts crowded my mind but the awful knowledge of that deadline was like a bucket of cold water. My ardour drenched, I passed the day at my word processor.

Caroline Sutherland was proving to be good for me. This was apparent from my stimulated mood as I settled down to write, from my general air of well-being. I don't, any longer, fall in love. I neither go weak at the knees nor jittery in the heart. These are youthful symptoms, I have suffered them in my time, but at the rather advanced age of thirty-eight I have, thank goodness, developed immunity to them, natural resistance. Women, the right women, are to be gazed at, fawned over, fondled and entered.

They are, in special moments, to be given gifts other than fine words. But they are not to be fallen in love with. They are not to be trusted with dominion over men. They misuse their power to control. I know this to my cost.

However. To be in love with the beauty of seduction is a quite different matter. To see the sublimely melting effect of saying just the right thing at exactly the right bedroom moment, to lay a hand without spoken guidance on precisely the bodily spot where a woman conveys tele-pathically she desires it to be placed, to hear of a woman's alibi to her husband: that she has explained a sexual assignation with lies she would be deeply ashamed telling to save the lives of her children – all of this is mentally orgasmic. It is a galactically vast distance from the adolescent frissons of love. Younger men believe they can experience these things. They delude themselves.

Moreover. Friends sense a change in me when I'm engaged on a fresh seduction. They comment how well I look, my jokes are said to be funnier. It has even been remarked, though I was somewhat concerned to learn this, that my eyes burn brighter. That I look in love. The difference being that my brain doesn't spin, my wits aren't dulled night and day by foolish romantic thoughts. On the contrary, my mind grows sharper. I need less sleep. I can, wonder of wonders, write without anxiety or anguish. I can string one sentence in front of another.

In due course, a suitable pause in my telling about the Hoolet will allow explanation of my problems with writing. They were, I realized much later, closely con-nected with events as they unfolded. For now, suffice it to say that in the recent past I had totally lost my ability to handle written language. My recovery had been slow and painful, costly in mental and material terms. Now, quite suddenly, I found myself able to construct ideas in my head, then to set them down, more or less as intended, via a screen, on paper. Much of the improvement I laid at Caroline Sutherland's door. Greater things still could be anticipated from our actual liaison.

The article was written by early afternoon. I faxed it to my paper in London. Such was my confidence while I awaited the response, I needed no medicine from 750 millilitre bottles. My dog, Flora, put her head in my lap. Her legs are lanky, her build stocky – big as a dog should be for a man living alone. Containing an interesting mixture of breeds, she has the intelligence of a good pedigree hound and none of the disgraceful manners of mongrels. She is the only female, I record with gratitude, who can see clearly into my mind. She knew the day had gone well, and looked forward eagerly, dribblingly, to dinner. We shared baked beans with something cold and left-over as we sat revelling in the lazy passage of time.

After an hour the phone rang.

'You are, you idle bastard,' Bill Nicolson said, 'tolerably readable when you write about blood and guts.'

High praise, coming from him. The Highlands, I replied, were satisfyingly filled with such stories. I could send him plenty more of the same.

'I'm changing "outwith",' he said.

I was momentarily lost.

'You said this hoolet thing was from outwith Murdo's beat.'

'So I did.'

'I'm changing it to "outside".'

'Can I ask why?'

'Needless fucking vernacular, that's why.'

'It's a Highland Diary,' I retorted. 'Murdo is a fucking Highlander.'

'Oh, yeah?' he said. 'Well I asked Chic Glennie. And he says the Highlands are Gaelic. This is Lowlands talk.'

'Helensburgh is Highlands *and* Lowlands. We sit on the boundary between lingerie shops and miles of nothingness. We've got the last supermarket worth calling a supermarket between here and Fort William. We speak our minds and we speak any damned way we think best.'

'My readers,' he declared with metropolitan finality, 'will think it's a fucking spelling mistake. I'm fucked if

I'm printing words that look like we've got our fingers in a twist.'

Before closing time at five thirty that evening, I was positioned across the road from *Sweet Dreams*. The shop flaunted its showcase of satins, silks and nylon between the blood-red joints of a butcher's and the blank silver windows of Roxburgh, Hamilton and Finlay, solicitors. Not far distant was Colquhoun Square, the neat, prim, extremely proper hub of the town, with a lawn for each point of the compass, a memorial to someone important and dead, nearby glimpses of the omnipresent Clyde, and the stern stony hand of God – the West Kirk, which to my irreligious eye seems actually to be placed at the north. The pavements were bustling in the slow, uncrowded way of small towns, the road lined with vehicles in no great haste to get home. Clean-shirted business types playing at farmers, seated high in four-wheel-drive wagons with tractor tyres and cow fenders, not the slightest spattering of farmyard mud. Small Rovers driven by inoffensive seeming little men with hats for fishing, gloves for walking and clubs for golf. A gruffly revving coach from the submarine base at Faslane, hunched-up naval ratings staring through a fog of cigarette smoke and grimy glass. And taxis, ordinary saloons with dents and rooftop phone numbers, more taxis than seems feasible for a not very large town not especially near anywhere else. I gazed into an estate agent's, watching the facing shops in the window. I felt at the heart of all things that matter, at the George Square, the Piccadilly Circus, of my universe, and in especially buoyant spirits.

Caroline emerged, impossible to miss. She stood a good head higher than any of the women in the street, and many of the men. She made her established route homewards; I set off in pursuit on the opposite pavement. Soon I overtook, adopting the ploy of following from the front. At a road junction, she caused me minor heart failure: expecting her to turn, *knowing* she'd turn, I took a right at the corner ahead of her. I was already some distance up hilly Sinclair Street before risking a casual glance over the shoulder. No sign of her! Hurriedly, I doubled back to the junction. Which of two alternative directions had she taken? Indecision struck, hollow and nagging, at the pit of my stomach; I felt at a cross-roads in my life. Losing her was not the problem – she could always be followed another day. No, the problem was whether I could guess where to find her. Whether I was capable of reading her mind.

Ahead, a short way along Princes Street, my eye was caught by the signboard at Central Station. My pace quickening, I went there and entered. No Caroline, and a guard's whistle shrilling: a train was about to leave. I ran to the platform, squeezing through the doors of the rearmost carriage as they hissed, sliding to.

Where was Caroline? Nowhere to be seen in this part of the train. Rust-stained, riveted like a beached ship, the sombre bulk of a gasometer slid by the window. The town thinned. In dying sunlight, the Clyde flashed small bright sparks of asdic, phrases of reassurance. She was, don't be faint-hearted, somewhere ahead in another carriage. It stood to reason.

As she'd left the shop, I had noticed, without consciously noticing, she was embarked on a journey of some purpose, not just going home. An unaccustomed firmness to her step, and yes she had checked her watch. Where on other days I had felt in special communion with her – the lack of pace in her travels, the meandering leisure to be seen in her thoughts – today I'd sensed a distance between us, the very real danger she might slip away. And she had made herself ready for evening. Suddenly, I could recall subtle differences in her make-up and hair. We'd been a street's width apart, traffic fumes between us, but I'd *seen*, be quite sure of it, the perfume she wore that evening. Not the sweet fresh pinky scent of yesterday, a musky nocturnal smell.

She was going out. She was going to Glasgow. The station is a terminus, no other direction was possible, her destination inevitable. I stared out past tiny houses, pocket backyards, to smile privately at the wily Clyde. Caroline had beaten me to the train. Now I was ahead of her again.

She was in a forward carriage. The train halted at Craigendoran – I ambled down the platform to discover her. I took a facing seat at a suitable distance for seeing without being seen. But, though I stalked her like a hunter, my caution was unfounded – she looked at no-one in the compartment, examined no faces. Nor, at a guess, was she much aware of farmhouses, or the unfolding green meadows, the broad lazy river lapping beside the track.

Her head was turned to the window. Her hands played without agitation, no sign of impatience. No book to help pass the time – I made a mental note to give little emphasis to books in our forthcoming conversations. The lipstick was freshly applied, dark wet and crimson, a shade too lurid. I forgave her the brashness, it was of slight consequence. After nightfall, I've found, women of her age lose all sense of suitable colours, their taste deserts them. A glittery brooch, neither cheap nor expensive, was pinned to a breast. And her breasts, now I gave them long if distant scrutiny, were more full than ever before, marshmallow tender, fleshily swollen – one of those feats women of nineteen or twenty seem able to accomplish at will. Sad to relate, her breasts are not quite as large as I'd given Gordon to believe. As with fish that escape, the top speed of a treasured new car, breasts are prone to exaggeration. It is expected. Had I correctly described their size, Gordon would have assumed them to be smaller. They were still, let it be said, very desirable breasts. They were far from inconsiderable.

Watching her breasts, a restrained watching with vacant and weary eyes, no question of a stare, the realization hit me that she was out on a date. Why had I taken so long seeing the obvious! Her lipstick, the dressy brooch. Then a further, insidious moment of revelation. She hadn't returned home before setting out. She hadn't bathed or showered. Any wash was cursory, in whatever small basin might be found at the back of the shop. Not a rendezvous with a new man, then. He must be someone close, met in the offhand informality of long acquaintance. Of similar age to her, probably. Uncouth, certainly. A Glasgow lad who liked a hard day's sweat on a lassie. Someone for whom she felt no need to wash.

I might have let jealousy gnaw at me but for a touch on my shoulder.

'Ticket . . . ?'

A conductor stood there. I must still have had vacant fatigue in my eyes.

'Have ye no' gat a ticket?'

Queen Street, I said, searching for change. And took consolation in speaking with no prior thought.

This confidence, my utter conviction in her stopping place, lasted all of thirty minutes. I had told Gordon of her capacity to surprise. She is a paradox. Doing the expected, the habitual, she gives great satisfaction. Departing from the path laid out for her in my forecasts, she creates tingling moments of acute excitement. Her habits are there to be learned. Never, however long Caroline lives, will she have a more dedicated pupil.

She left the train abruptly at Yoker. Caught briefly on the hop, nearly trapped by the train doors, I was quickly close behind once more. On her trail, I followed into outer city byways as bleak, barren, unwelcoming as the sheep tracks of Glencoe.

Yoker is no douce watering-hole such as Helensburgh. The prosperous centre of Glasgow is but a few train stops further, a foreign and faraway place. The tenement streets are not narrow but bear in. The pavements not strewn with rubbish, but litter the brain. Few graffiti are to be seen, but the stone walls seem scrawled with political slogans, cries of anger, appeals for help. Ocean liners once rose on the shipyard stocks, noisily, proudly, above the rooftops. High cranes still loom, dark and skinny against the sky, as poignant, bowed and useless as unemployed

39

welders on corner pavements. Yoker has an antiseptic new shopping palace on its doorstep but knows this is not its future. It has an illustrious history, and like so much of industrial Glasgow clings to it for want of better. Abandoned on the highway to destiny . . . clapped out, corroded, its engine stolen.

This is where she came, glorying in the name of Caroline Sutherland. And I should have seen, as we stepped from the train, the obvious fact this told me.

She turned a corner, into a street of lofty stone buildings, big Glasgow windows. The city has, like any other, its undercurrents of status, its marks of social standing. When scrubbed clean as these were, tenements are always imposing, built like rocks for a thousand years, their closes – communal entrances – tiled and echoing, often bare of front doors. However, height is all, storeys tell a tale. The plush middle classes got three floors, a vista of trees, perhaps river views of the Kelvin. Here were four floors, no glimpse of green foliage; from carved Victorian pediments, TV satellite dishes looked blankly to the sky. Tenements built for the toiling classes, who live in them still. Very few cars. People going nowhere.

A bowl of catfood on the pavement. Sitting close by on a doorstep, a lean woman in a thin floral frock of Co-op fabric. She was of an age when tenements were boundless, the street outside was your living room. She sat watching as her cat ate its supper.

Caroline passed. Nods were given and quickfire greetings between neighbours. On the move – Caroline neither changed her step nor stopped. She pleased me greatly by giving wide berth to the cat. She vanished at a doorway.

I approached the woman, my shoulders bent. Certain streets warn you not to walk tall.

'How are ya doing, hen?' I said, not a trace of Helensburgh about me.

'Oh, ay,' she said in reply. Her eyes never left the cat.

'Ah'm with the *Glasga Herald*.' I fumbled at several

40

pockets, praying my bluff wouldn't be called. 'Want tae see ma press card?'

'Dinna bother ye'sel.' Glaswegians are the most trusting people on earth. They are suspicious of nothing but cleverness.

'Ah'm doing a piece, hen. On Yoker, on the kids about. My editor wants a piece doing—' I admitted a sigh close to a laugh of despair, '—on youth employment. Work opportunities for the young.'

'Then ye'll no' be doing it lang.'

The cat rubbed against my leg. I betrayed no indication of my hatred for cats. 'Yon lassie,' I said. 'Verra tall, a glamour puss on stilts.'

Her eyes came up to meet me. 'Ah'm only set here,' she said, 'minding ma business.'

'Never saw her from Adam,' I said. 'And never will again. Tae tall to ma way of thinking, hen. Ah prefer them wee. Wee and slender like you.'

'Och, you! Wouldnae trust ye wi' ma cat.'

'Ah want her in ma wee notebook. Nae harm done, agreed? A few questions, an interview wi' the press. Look, Ah could foller her doon the street, hen. Ah dinna need you.' I threw myself at her mercy. 'But Ah dinna ken which bloody bell tae ring.'

The woman rose, straightened her frock. 'Ah've nae got all day for the likes o' you,' she said, presenting her back.

'A lassie wi' a job is all Ah'm after. She's got hersel an office job, bae the look of her. That's nae dole money, hen. The fancy dress, the fancy lipstick.'

She turned to show a sour face. 'Oh, Carol's gi' hersel a guid job, all right. Nae money for her mither. Plenty for hersel.'

'Carol?'

'Carol. Yon tall lassie wi' big ideas, big as her leegs.'

'Carol's short for . . .?'

'Short for Carol.' The woman fixed me with a fierce, beady glare. 'Ring forty-five an' ask for Carol. Carol Logan. Ask her tae tell ye o' her big job. Air hostess wi' an

41

American airline. Oh, ay, a real high flier yon Carol. New York taeday, Hong Kong taemorra. Ask her tae tell ye hae much money they gi' her. And ask hae much she e'er thinks tae gi' Janey and Norman Logan.'

I went in at the close Caroline had entered. I waited there, bare cold stairs spiralling up behind me, until the woman was gone from the street with her cat. Pointless, though I considered doing so, to ring the doorbell, snatch a glimpse of the apartment, then claim a mistaken address. No more need be seen. I knew her origins. My sense of intimacy with her, oneness, was all enveloping. She could have no other secret as private, personal, hidden, and I had found it.

Another thought, quickly rejected, was to stay till she left. She would remain only an hour or two. Tea and biscuits, family small talk, lies about Hong Kong. Her dead eyes, her empty staring on the train, made sense now, the visit meant nothing. How frequently did she make these trips? As rarely as was decently possible. To her, returning to Yoker went far beyond a brusque call on her parents, it was an unwanted exhumation: the digging up then reburial of Carol Logan. I wanted very much to study her on the return trip, to see the solemnity gone from her girlish face, a weight lifted, a duty done. She'd buy a magazine to read on the train . . . I knew without question which magazine, I wanted my full new mastery of her affirmed. I wanted to watch her journey, to see her change before my eyes. From Carol to Caroline, Logan to Sutherland. She exceeded my wildest imaginings. I had invented none of her, she had invented herself. I wanted to see the covert smile, the inner relief, as she arrived back at Helensburgh. The end of the line.

But there are streets where I am not invisible. I caught the next train home.

Three

Time to commence the end-game, to begin coming out in the open.

Before, I had kept to the shadows, our lives never touched. Caroline had shown little sign of ever seeing me, no hint of remembering, none of dwelling on my features. Now I intruded into her daily routine, our paths crossed at regular moments. It became my purpose to be seen, gradually taking shape, on the outermost edges of her day. We had small things in common, we shared regular habits of the most unremarkable kind. My morning walk to work intersected hers; in the ever-darker evenings of late autumn what more natural than a further brief encounter on the return journey home? We passed in opposite directions: heading away from the shops and offices in town to the rarefied heights of Upper Helensburgh, I could be presumed to have a professional position, something out of the ordinary. We had the same easy attitude to employment – while her feet showed no great enthusiasm for reaching the shop, I exuded a quiet relaxed air of power, my time my own, a job free of anxious glances at the clock, work that began when I chose to arrive and not a minute sooner. At close of day, our lack of hurry back revealed a touching sameness to the gaping hole in our social lives. We neither of us had partners to do our shopping, at different times we were to be seen with plastic supermarket bags. Avoiding the obvious, mine was from William Low and hers from Gateway – awaiting a red traffic light, Caroline appeared to spot the bag as we stood facing across Princes Street, and was perhaps left wondering whether I knew something she did not about lower prices, superior brands of cheese. She brought a short-lived but much appreciated improvement to my financial affairs. Discovering she banked at the Clydesdale, I moved my account there, freeing myself for a few short weeks from the tiresome clutches of a manager who had learned more than was good for either of us about my immediate prospects. The day came when Caroline was in one counter queue as I shuffled along nearby in another. Her awakening gaze stayed on me: she cannot have failed to notice that while she was withdrawing cash, I held a bundle of notes and a paying-in slip. Money, it must be said, drawn from my account earlier that same Friday morning.

As to one of us following the other, the stage had been reached in our tentative dalliance where, the tables turned, Caroline must start tailing me. A Wednesday afternoon, half day closing at the shop. Making an early way home across Hermitage Park, she turned at a meeting of pathways to find herself behind me as, after a lunchtime blow of air, I began briskly back to my architect's desk, my business telex and numerous phones, my sketches of brave new landscapes, my practice as an inspired manipulator of bones. Alas to say, she did not stay on my tail. Her curiosity was stirring but not yet aroused. My planning demanded that she must think herself the hunter: she would pursue me, speak our first shy words together. So far, all I had won from her was the beginnings of a stilted smile. She needed more time.

I did not wholly abandon the shadows. Another unseen side of me continued watching Caroline, her secret moments. I remained ever alert to the unexpected. Like the hoolet, I came out at nightfall, silently covering my private stretch of ground. Flora would walk with me down to the grey stone mansion by Hermitage Park. A willing collaborator, she would sniff for what seemed hours at the gatepost. Held by the leash, tied to the spot, I not unreasonably turned my wandering attention to the house, the light at an upstairs window. Since the curtains were forever drawn, no-one happening to pass had any reason to doubt this behaviour. But with the curtains drawn, the room beyond them a closed mystery, I had my own rush of doubts.

My affairs, I hasten to explain, are rarely this protracted. None had ever involved such extensive planning. One splendidly informal obsession had its beginnings in a bus shelter, grew irresistible on a ride to the other side of town, and came to a hot and sticky conclusion in an identical shelter so near naval housing that I could, had I been so inclined, have watched that evening's episode of *Take The High Road* and inferred much of the dialogue. Caroline, however, was not of the crude and available kind. I had never expected an easy conquest but she began to seem, especially in lonely lamplit streets, utterly beyond reach. I fell to wondering if I was wasting my time. Reading my mind, Flora lost all interest in the gatepost, and was more anxious by the day to turn for home.

Caroline came, naked like Lady Godiva, to the rescue.

The night this happened, I teetered on the verge of not going. A chilling shroud of drizzle lay over the town as I peered out from my upper window. The Firth was an endless icy sea, no orange lamps to be seen on the facing shore. Through dank drooping trees, the road down the hill caught the progress of headlights, glistening and black like a drenched umbrella. My breath misted the glass. Flora, whose life is to be envied for its simple decisions, took one quick look and gave her opinion, rolling sad eyes, lying dead and heavy as a stone dog in front of the blazing fire. She came under sufferance, on the strict understanding this was to be the very last time, an end to this nonsense.

Caroline's curtains were open. The room was revealed, pink and empty of movement. Rosy subdued light from a low lamp somewhere threw a long thin straggling shadow across a wall and over the ceiling.

Her timing was consummate. A bare cabaret stage, the audience waiting, holding its breath. Then she made an entrance, came centre stage. Slowly, as if to an exotic beat of music in my head, she unbuttoned her blouse, it slid in a silken caress over her tall body as it slipped to the floor. Her brassiere was lacy black, full to bursting. She turned away to the backdrop, smooth young shoulders outlined against her own high and dancing shadow. We heard the music together – hips swaying in time with it, she loosened a hook, let the brassiere fall away. A long while to gaze at the splendour of her back, slender and soft. Then she faced the window, pushing forward first one shoulder then the other to bounce her wondrous breasts.

Undressed, some women look merely bare, stripped of decoration. Others, let it be said, seem pathetically naked. Precious few, and Caroline was one of these few, are deserving of nudity – clothes are wasted on them. Matching flesh and nipple pinks, a glowing bloom to the skin, an adornment of finest curled hair, abundant curves moving where they will, each in their own sweet time, nothing bony or coarse or sagging. From the gateway to the house, I saw her at the ideal distance, in the most flattering of lights. Any pimples, unsightly blotches, evaded my eye. Her skin was flawless, her breasts a glimpse into paradise.

An owl cried out from a tree behind me, a sound not like a bird at all, a shrill whistle, oddly human. I looked up into the branches, could see nothing. When I gazed back to the house, the curtains were drawn. The music was dashed from my head, but the curtains danced on to a dying strain, shifting slightly to and fro until the house fell still and nothing stirred at any window.

I swore roundly. I've had cause before to swear at owls. Hoolets never behave as you want them to.

Back at my desk, a log fire glowing brightly across the room, I switched on my word processor to complete the seduction of Caroline.

We met, where else, in Hermitage Park. She became ensnared by Flora's leash, we fell to talking. She lived

46

close by, and invited me back. Within the hour we were in her bed. She was taken aback, overwhelmed, by the abrupt change in me, the relentless tide of ferocity. She pleaded, in a voice begging to be ignored, not to be driven to such noisy heights of passion – there were children in the house. The whole town must have heard us.

To remind myself, the plan was kept for future reference. I saved it in my computer memory, among old correspondence, entreaties to lawyers, the dead and dusty history of a divorce; beside newspaper articles, printed and rejected; alongside plausible excuses to an inglorious procession of accountants; in an ever-growing litany of seductions which passing months had seen, with the inevitability of season succeeding season, progress from fiction to the realms of reality. I intended calling the file *Caroline*. My little machine demurred, noting without courtesy on its screen that I was permitted no more than six characters, alpha or numeric. So I did what I should have done, and entered *Carol*.

A smile came over me. The best sort of smile, unbidden, unthought of, discovered in an absent moment putting a gleam on a serious face. My word processor is scratched, abused and misunderstood, has seen and bears the marks of kicks, punches and spilled coffee. What is told at the keyboard, I would tell no living person.

It shared my carnal knowledge of Caroline. Even the secret of her real name.

A SMALL MURDER

Four

The telephone rudely awoke me, the sun not yet up.

'Is that you, Sandy?' Phyllis said.

I mumbled a reply: 'Call again in an hour and it might be.'

'We've had a fox, Sandy. Gordon's out after the wretched thing.'

'Then it's as good as dead.'

'He said you'd be wanting to hear. For one of your articles, he said. Blood and feathers everywhere. He knows you, Sandy . . . how you like writing with a pen dipped in blood.'

'I don't use a pen. I have a machine, Phyllis. One of these days,' I ventured through a yawn, 'I shall buy a machine to do my writing for me. And I'll have no need to ever leave bed.'

'He also said – can't think why I'm telling you this – it'll do that doolie some good seeing the hours honest men are about their business.'

Keeper's Cottage is on Lomondside, a low gear scramble up a narrow wynd, the old farm loan into Glen Cairn. On three sides the surrounding hills crowd in, on the other they frame a vista of Loch Lomond and its islands that city people would willingly die for. To the far horizon, Gordon's is the only house to be seen – he has the world at his feet and can think all of it his. You find a low building of white-washed stone, once three cottages, an untidy yard to the front, straggling outbuildings along the boundaries, gaping doors of rotten timber, windows bare of glass – empty buildings while the odd remnants of farming equipment they might have sheltered lie strewn everywhere, rusting in the open air. At what remains of the gate, a sign is drunkenly propped, advertising VENISON FOR SALE AND WILD RABBIT WHEN AVAILABLE. What hidden talent as an entrepreneur led Gordon to paint this in his unsteady amateur hand, then place it beside a track whose only visitors are walking the hills or lost? Gordon sells his game to hotels and restaurants hereabouts. He is wise not to depend for a living on what Phyllis optimistically refers to as passing trade. Because any stranger tempted by the sign would dare venture no further than the gate, with its sight and sound of the dogs. Gordon shares my Douglas blood, the family love of dogs. But to excess. He has the Scottish disposition to extremes – what is not beggarly must be done to overflowing. His yard is ragged with dogs, stinks of them, resounds with barking. Big gundogs, tiny terriers. Smooth and shaggy dogs, anchored by chains, secured with string, or roaming free. An expensive red setter found wandering a campsite and costing nothing; a disreputable lurcher he bought for a fortune to rescue from certain death. As I drove into the yard they began a howling to raise the rooftops. Making for the cottage door, I put my life in Murdo's hands, trusting in a wise adage that might be valid or conjured in my head. *Fear only those dogs who stay silent.*

Phyllis came out to the yard. She seems always to be mopping her hands after washing the dishes. Her face is too thin and she has an unfortunate fondness for dresses patterned like tablecloths that make her chest seem even flatter than it really is, and show more than one wants of her gawky legs. Against which, her smile is comforting, her eyes benign, she carries everywhere the homely kitchen smells of burning peat and crusty baked bread.

Her gaze wandered over my Barbour jacket, green and slovenly, the hole peeping from a crumpled sock, my scruffy boots with soles like tank tracks. 'For a minute there,' she said, 'I thought you were Gordon back already.'

A kiss with my usual detachment on her bony cheek. 'Where is he?'

'Gone to earth by now.' She sighed heavily, running fingers through her hair. 'God, how I detest foxes. What use are they but to plague us and our few wee birds.'

'Gordon, I mean . . .'

'Up at the Plantation. D'you know it, the far side of Meikle Muir?'

More or less, I said, and her parting nod to the forest track got me going the right way.

Gordon sat slumped on a fallen tree, head bowed, a rifle across his thighs, gazing with a sad and helpless kind of fury through the wire fencing of a compound. He looked in on a scene of utter devastation. I thought him like a forlorn foot soldier, the last survivor of some battle to the death. He seemed at first not to realize I was there, which gave the opportunity to look at him longer. I intended carrying this picture of Gordon back home with me, though I quickly decided Murdo could never take attack by a fox so deeply to heart. He has more pity than Gordon and is less pitiable.

The wire enclosed a half acre or so of bracken; woodland behind and the shoulder of hill gave some semblance of shelter. It should have been a safe haven. Inside were feathers, claws and legs, plundered bodies and severed heads. More dead pheasants than at a good day's shooting – I doubted if counting the bits and pieces would tell how many. A stench of fresh damp death hung in the air. Heather rustled in a wayward breeze, feathers tossed and blew like autumn leaves.

'How many?' I asked.

'Ninety odd. Ninety in there, two at best eaten.' He gazed round at me, raising a shaky finger. 'Don't say, don't fucking say, the bitch must've been hungry.'

'I've said nothing.'

'People like you write crap. We're the only creatures on God's earth that kill for the fun of it. We kill for gain, for jealousy, for scraps of land and the wrong religion. The only animals who do, isn't that what you put in your London paper? Rubbish about animals never killing except from hunger.'

'I've never said any such thing.'

'I've seen more killing in these hills than you've had hot dinners. And I've a mind to do some killing myself.' He rose resolutely to his feet, snapping the bolt on the rifle.

'How many foxes was it?'

His eyes frightened me. Staring square into mine, they held a light of smouldering anger the like of which I'd never before seen in him. Such was the rage he seemed ready to kill me. Not the first time by a long way I've been out with him shooting, but this was different. Though I tried to look away, my eyes were trapped by his. I felt as a man must feel when he's about to be murdered.

'One,' he said through his teeth. 'Just the one.'

For an instant I forgot the question to which this was the answer. 'One fox, you mean?'

He nodded slowly. 'She dug a way in somehow. Foxes get in a frenzy, an orgy of murder. The birds can't break free, the wire becomes an enemy, a deadly trap. It goes on and on and on, so long as there's a pheasant still living.'

He marched off. I hurried at his heels. 'A bitch, you said.'

'A vixen.'

'How'd you know?'

'I heard her. First the dogs barking, so I came out to see. She gave a cry at the moon to boast what she'd done – got that for your grubby notebook? The dogs lost their heads then. They hate foxes, vixens send them berserk.'

'Why?'

'Because, you headcase, vixens are where the foxes come from.'

We headed over rough country. A crumbling dry-stone wall barred our progress. On the other side, Gordon took an overgrown footpath towards a clump of trees.

'Are we tracking her?' I asked.

'Call it what you like. We're going where she is. Not the

way she came, I don't give a fuck whether she went over the burn there or round the fucking moutains.'

'Is she in those trees?'

'Probably. Silly bitch gave a final howl from this direction. I can think as she does, work out where she's built her lair.'

'My purposes would be better served,' I said, 'if we tracked her.'

'Murdo on his hands and knees, nose in the heather . . .'

'That sort of thing. A bit of a chase, if you're with me. His sharp eyes spotting broken blades of grass. Maybe using a dog, hot on the scent. One of those bloody dogs of yours that eat you out of house and home, and do damn all but bark.'

'I don't need a dog. She'll smell a dog coming.'

'Won't she smell us?'

'She'll smell us and hear us. Especially your heavy feet. Like a damned regiment on the march.'

I tried moving more lightly behind him.

'But she won't smell this,' Gordon said, touching his rifle.

We came to the trees, crouching low to seek the cover of a thicket. Gordon fell very still. I followed the line of his eyes.

All about were the russets, gingers, golds and earthy browns of the season, the fern hues of autumn, the colours of a fox. At first I missed the vixen on the rim of a clearing, so perfect was her camouflage. Then I caught the alert glint of her eyes staring directly towards our hiding place. She saw us before we saw her. Murdo whispered quietly in my imagination – a fact of nature that you may catch a male fox unawares but never a female, the first you will ever see of a vixen is her fearless eyes on you.

Gazing harder, her raised ears were discernible against dry undergrowth, and the pointed profile of a nose. Caught in the act of eating, her jaws ran dark red, the fur sticky. Her stare unwavering, she flicked the tip of a tongue over her lips as if to destroy the evidence.

She hypnotized me. I locked away her memory, complete in every detail. She sat posing while I painted her in the landscape of my mind. I quite forgot Gordon beside me, my ears were closed to the click of his rifle. I had in turn hypnotized her. She heard no sound, had no warning.

Part of her head blew away below an ear, which stayed high and listening. The spark went in an instant from her eyes. Did she fall or did the bracken reach out to claim her? She vanished as I looked, dead brown into dead brown. Only then was I aware of the deafening report of the rifle, and jumped at the shock of it.

'Dust to dust,' Gordon said, as if in prayer.

'What would Murdo call her?' I asked. The vixen was deserving of some wayside epitaph, she needed a name.

'For Christ's sake!' Gordon exclaimed.

'I've read of foxes being called Laurence.'

'Tod, sometimes.'

'Over in Berwickshire they're called Charlies. I can't call a vixen Laurence or Charlie.'

'Greedy bitch,' he said, going into the clearing. 'Stupid bitch. Fucking bitch. Take your pick. Put one of those in your paper, a rare breath of honesty.' Grasping the tail, he threw the fox over his shoulder and began back the way we came. 'The dogs heard her. They can have her.'

We clambered over a fence for a short cut, a crow's flight home. Threads of chimney smoke beckoned over a planting of conifers, the air was scented with pine and peat. With Gordon's cottage close by, I was suddenly reluctant to have walls around me. I felt as people do who see too little of country dawns, madly intoxicated by the daring of being about so early, under a fresh and seductive spell.

'Fancy a drop of bevvy?' I asked.

He grinned. 'You've got the flask, then. We'll make a ghillie of you yet.'

He settled on a rock for a swig at the hip flask. Before us was a wide and clear new morning. The inches – the islands of Lomond – floated like scattered rain clouds on the limpid blue sky of the loch. He voiced his wonder as if this was new to him, quite oblivious to having destroyed any small part of an idyllic small world. Then he retreated into his own thoughts, holding his tongue for rather too long between kinfolk.

'My long-legged woman,' I said. 'This woman of mine with the long legs. She's gone into show business.'

He pretended not to hear.

'She gave me a debut performance last night. My God, what a performance! I saw her breasts.'

'You did what?'

'Did? Very little, I'm afraid, except stare with my eyes popping.'

'What, at her window?'

'She didn't draw the curtains this time. Quite deliberately so, I'd say. And the way she took off her bra, wiggled her bare tits at me, looked pretty damned blatant.'

'Sandy,' he said, closing his eyes tight, 'I love your tits at night-time—'

'*My* tits . . . ?'

'Your tits. Her tits. The tits you throw at me morning, noon and night. Night's fine by me, Sandy, tits are great at night. I don't even mind tits at noon with my sandwiches . . . I've the rest of the day to dribble and drool. But not now, understand me, not at seven o' fucking clock in the morning.'

'Personally, I can't think of a better start to the day than tits. Especially these tits. They are, Gordon, the high Munros of Scottish tits, mountainous peaks, towering pinnacles.'

He groaned. 'Listen to me, will you? I'm over the hill, the wrong side of thirty. I don't wake up any more stiff and ready for it. All I want these cold mornings is to roll over in bed, get some sound sleep for once, and the only hot thing on my mind is breakfast.'

'Fine,' I said. 'Just don't ask me to tell you next time I'm round.'

57

'You'll tell me whether I ask or no'.'

A change of tune was clearly called for. I lay back in the ferns, hands cradling my head. I gazed at the sun peering over the Trossachs, and told him how Murdo spoke to me as if in a séance. A distant ancient voice, often hard to interpret. 'What he's saying now,' I conveyed, 'is there are forgotten places in Dunbartonshire where they still talk of vixens as Mollies. He was hunting a fox who killed his pheasants, he came on this Molly in a clearing. He raised his rifle, squinted through the sights. What he saw brought a pause. The Molly hadn't in fact carried off one of Murdo's birds, she'd caught only a rabbit. So he uncocked his gun and spared her. The time may come when he'll be forced to kill her, but today she was on Murdo's side – ridding the land of a pest. They went their separate ways. He'd found the wrong fox.'

'My fox escaped, is that what you'll write?'

'This one did . . . Murdo's fox.'

I felt the hard muzzle of a gun pressing against my forehead.

'One of these days you'll go too fucking far,' Gordon said, altogether too quiet and collected. I had the unhappy recollection of hearing him once say he hunted in anger but fired in deadly calm. 'Don't rob me of my pride,' he said, very low with something of a hiss. 'I've damned little else I value so highly.'

'Then don't point guns. Proud country people know better than to point guns.' Carefully, I pushed the barrel from my head. 'For fuck's sake!' I practically yelled then, 'it's only my bloody job, telling stories. You hunted a fox, you shot a fox. Where's the story in that, the interest!'

He was standing above me, staring down, blocking the sky. 'The gun's not loaded, what the hell d'you think.' He aimed upwards, tightened his finger on the trigger. The explosion cracked my ears, echoes clapped back from the craggy hills, 'Well, I never,' he said with a disclaiming shrug. 'Still, where's the interest in an empty gun?'

*　　*　　*

Phyllis had eggs frying on the range, square breakfast sausage and sizzling bacon. She sat with us at the kitchen table, domestic and attentive in an apron. No plate for herself. In Phyllis's articles of faith, cooking is for women and eating for men. I have put away whole banquets of food under her roof, but seldom if ever seen a morsel pass her lips.

'Sandy's been peeping at breasts,' Gordon said suddenly.

'Has he now?' she said, inclining her head at me.

'Bare breasts. Young women undressing in the privacy of their own homes.'

'Only one woman,' I pointed out. 'Though she has enough meat on her for several.'

Silence reigned for a while. Then Phyllis pushed back her chair, wiping thin hands on her apron. 'There's work to be done,' she declared curtly, and seemed to melt from the room.

'Why did you say that?' I demanded from Gordon. 'What the hell did you say a thing like that for?'

He shrugged, staring at the door after her. 'Does a woman no bloody harm sometimes,' he murmured, 'to be reminded of her deficiencies.'

In recent experience, none of my articles had been written so swiftly. Caroline gave boundless inspiration, the prospect of seeing her made words freely flow. I wanted her in my sights again, the sooner the better. A kind of hunt fever had taken hold of me that morning. I needed to be out and about, back on the chase.

Somehow, time lost all meaning. The *Diary* piece was faxed to London. When after what must have been a couple of hours no answering call had come through, I knew the article was flawless. The most lavish acclaim Bill Nicolson can bestow is to have nothing whatever to say.

For only the first time since sleep was disturbed that morning did I think to look at a clock. I had been too productive for my own good. There is sound sense in slow progress, I informed Flora. It was just gone four in the afternoon, more than an hour to go before Caroline would quit the shop. My sunless study seemed like an office suddenly, no place to remain when work is done. My feet were itchy to be on the move. Other itches troubled me – a glossy centrefold of Caroline, naked at her window, tantalized my memory, hard and exquisite longing stirred in my pants. 'Damn,' I muttered. I had to be gone from the house but felt like a wanderer with nowhere to go.

We went for a drive, Flora grandly by my side on the passenger seat, gazing out in superior style at dogs on pavements, as if to claim she'd invented the motor car and good riddance to plodding paws. We cruised down long straight avenues with verdant grass verges, between trim lines of cherry trees and hedges of holly, past mansion after secluded mansion, intimations of old money, more leisurely days. We went by way of streets that would be boulevards if only a little broader. We followed our noses, taking turnings we often take, other turnings that promised novelty, and, finally, a turning we hadn't taken in several weeks. Down one of the narrower streets, West End of town, where upstart new bungalows intrude into broad green acres, the lawns of long dead industrialists – cremated owners of steelworks, buried builders of ships.

I stamped on the brakes. The squeal of my tyres turned a policeman's head.

His was one of several blue uniforms congregated outside the MacRae's ranch house. Police cars were parked with untidy urgency on and off the gravel sidewalk. In the driveway, almost hidden by a BMW convertible, a plainclothes man crouched, searching the flowerbeds.

The MacRae's had two BMWs, a garage vast enough for both and probably numerous others. They were, by my modest standards, filthy rich. They had wrought iron behind the dimpled glass of their front door and floodlights that exploded on of their own volition, dazzling the eyes of anyone foolish enough to approach under darkness. The house delighted, would you believe, in the

60

name of an English golf course. Theirs was new money, plentiful crisp bundles of the stuff, with no subtle pretensions to being thought of as old.

I went over. 'What's the problem?' I asked of no policeman in particular.

'Nothing you need bother about,' someone said.

'If it's a burglary . . .'

'Planning on leaving your car there, sir? Cluttering the street?'

'I'd rather park in the drive here but the gate's blocked. Careless parking, constable. A bad example to the lawful.'

'Know the MacRaes, do you?'

'I'm a friend, yes.'

All heads turned. I had instant attention. 'Calling at the house, were you?' another asked.

'Passing, as a matter of fact.'

'Any idea where we can find Mr MacRae?'

My hesitation must have been all too apparent. 'In his office,' I answered doubtfully, seeming to think. 'Somewhere on King Street. Can't remember the number, I'm afraid.'

'If not . . . ?'

'He's building some new houses along by the Gareloch. You could try asking there.'

They stared, eyes narrowed, suspicious and threatening as only bulkies can be when they have you outnumbered. I held out a rather dog-eared visiting card from my top jacket pocket. 'Any chance Sergeant Grant's around?' I enquired, floundering for a name.

'Press!' came a dark mutter. 'That's all we need, the bloody Press.'

'Know him, d'you, Sergeant Grant?' another enquired, an uncomfortably short distance from my face.

I stared in turn. 'Only in the context of police harassment.'

Sergeant Grant was summoned from his prone position in the flowerbeds. An intimidating presence, the scalpel-sharp scrutiny of a surgeon, the muscular build of a lout, he looked me over without recognition, took lengthy regard of my apology for a press card and gave the eventual admission of a nod. He knew me but could not remember from where. Nor could I quite recall the circumstances – social, I thought, a far remove from law breaking, and, since his florid complexion betrayed a healthy liking for pints, probably somewhat connected with bars.

'Mr Douglas,' he murmured. 'Ah, yes now. What can I do for you, Mr Douglas?'

'What's the problem here?'

'Asking as Press or a friend? My colleague here tells me you were calling at the house.'

'I'm not a crime reporter, Sergeant. A simple columnist, remember? I write about wildlife.'

'Ah yes,' he said hazily, giving no hint of remembering me from Adam.

'Strictly as a friend, I'd like to know the meaning of all this.'

'Are you a friend of Mr MacRae, Mrs MacRae, one of them in particular?'

'Tell me,' I demanded, 'of what exactly am I suspected? The crime of passing?'

He looked at me for a surprisingly long time. 'Mrs MacRae,' he said, watching keenly, 'has been done away with.'

My knees must have given under me. Presumably he had some justification for seizing my arm.

'Murdered . . . ? Aileen's been murdered?'

'Very thoroughly.' His face came very close, the grip grew tighter. 'Aileen, you said . . .'

My reply sounded distant, someone else's voice. 'That's her name, Sergeant.'

'Oh yes, Mr Douglas, found that out by now. Haven't exactly been wasting our time.'

'And her husband's called Duncan. We were that close . . . first-name terms and dinner once in a blue moon. Just him and me and Aileen and a dozen or so others.'

'All right, all right. Murder done and you're the first one passing. Bit of curiosity's only natural.' He let go, consenting to my release.

'How was she murdered?'

'Very nasty. Hard to recognize the face of the victim – nasty. Young coppers throwing up at sight of it – nasty. Signs of a break-in round the back of the house, a broken window.'

'Oh my God,' I said. 'Poor Aileen.'

'Any help you can give finding the husband?'

'Sounds like you've tried the obvious places.'

'All we've found so far is a voice, presume it's his, on the office answering machine.'

'You don't, I hope, suspect Duncan . . .'

'Any reason I should?'

'The way you said "the husband" just now. A certain lack of sympathy.'

'Next of kin, Mr Douglas, all I meant. He needs to be told.'

'He's converting an old warehouse in Glasgow. Apartments for the up and coming.'

'Any idea where?'

'In the Merchant City, that's all I know. They're probably not to my taste and I couldn't afford them if they were.' It's not my practice to confess to penury – the situation called for putting as much social distance as possible between myself and the MacRaes.

'Where are you staying, Mr Douglas? Purely for the record.' He shrugged at the tedium of paperwork.

'Same address as my car,' I replied, nodding at a constable whom I'd seen taking note of the number-plate.

Grant squeezed my arm, not being companiable. 'That's what I like to see. A man able to keep his wits about him in the thick of tragedy.' He took a backward step, rubbing hands briskly with an air of finality. 'No reason to keep you, not if you're passing.'

Sitting in my car gave scant opportunity for mourning

the dead. My hands took it on themselves to begin shaking. I tried to recollect the last time I'd seen Aileen MacRae – my befuddled brain could only wonder how nasty was nasty, how dire must violence be to get policemen vomiting. I tried to picture her but my mind stayed resolutely blank. Perhaps I feared I'd visualize a face battered beyond recognition. Morning seemed suddenly an eternity away, the day a confusion of senseless killings. So I sat at the wheel in a kind of dumb stupor, while Flora stared at me, didn't like what she saw and began to whimper.

Through the windscreen I became aware of prurient faces under blue police caps, Sergeant Grant rocking with ponderous inquisition to and fro on his heels. I turned the car in the tight width of the street, bumping into verges like a learner. I returned, wanting to be noted doing so, the way I'd arrived. Among a host of motives was a sudden and quite unsought desire for damnation to policemen. The very last thing I wanted was to give a hint, any clue to the wary, where I was heading next.

Five

Success is other people's country, package trips to a land I can gawp at but never be permitted to settle. I've seen enough of success to know it isn't my destiny. Success means indigestion and heart attacks, long hours of phone calls I'd want over in minutes and meetings with people I'd run a mile from, in pursuit of acquisitions I'd pay every penny I own not to possess. Success pleases no-one, including those who have it. There are unwritten rules to success understood only by the successful, and contradictions, baffling to me, which seem to those who abide by them so normal they must live in another world. Take Duncan MacRae, whose success is such he has no idea how much he earns, only how much tax he is paying. He sends the children to school a long way off in England while insisting on a berth for his yacht virtually on the doorstep. He joined a golf club for the exercise, then pays a caddie to do his carrying. He boasts of buying at cut-throat discount for his business but pays through the nose for the hi-fi and fabrics that fill his home. He can never know, as I do, the dignity of failure, only fear of it. The more he has, the more he has to lose. I speak from the moral high ground of one who sees what he condemns at the safety of distance. I could write whole theses on success, a professor whose profound learning derives from long study but no personal experience whatsoever.

Duncan's success renders him as predictable as the hoolet. Most days I can say with some certainty where he will be, what he is doing. I was not ahead of him that fateful afternoon but nor was I very far behind. And I proved to be a good sixty minutes ahead of the police.

Come November, his yacht is hoisted on to a trailer at Rhu Marina, carried in processional manner a few short streets, and left on temporary stocks sailing tall over his ranch house. There it will stay till Easter, the spring voyage back to the sea. Plenty of the same is to be seen in various dry moorings around the town – winter in Helensburgh brings vessels inland to the safe anchorage of bungalow driveways.

On Tuesdays, after a heavy lunch of land deals and claret, he is invariably at play – letting others win, being allowed to win, dependent on who is buying from whom – on the hillside fairways that straddle the Old Luss Road. Saturdays are spent in their entirety, rather conspicuously it sometimes seems, at his office near Colquhoun Square, while Sundays he is at pains to have you understand are not regarded as days of rest. Thursday afternoons however are his own, set aside for the solitude of open waters. He takes a portable phone along, voluminous correspondence and planning applications – but work is done out of sight of the shore. He needs some pretence at well-earned leisure. Duncan has become so successful he is a slave to success.

Late afternoon on a Thursday, a few days yet to November. So I drove the convenient stone's throw from Duncan's house to Rhu Marina. His berth was empty, as expected. I made the pleasant discovery that my hip flask was still in the car from that morning's fox hunting. Flora settled into snoring slumber while I made ready for watching sails in the sunset. My window wound down, I breathed a salty wind flirting with the tides, turned my ears to the jangle like cow bells of rigging on masts. Far from the stares of policemen there was freedom at last to think of Aileen. Desolate and numbing sadness began to take hold of me, an overdue tear welled, warm and prickling, in the corner of an eye. Then I caught sight of the *Akwa* full beam ahead. She was dead in the water no more than a hundred yards or so out in the Firth.

I jumped from the car.

Sails furled, the yacht looked to be at anchor near a buoy. A figure appeared on deck, Duncan's burly shape, his quick movement, the sense of purpose in all he does, with more than the hint of a strut. I yelled through cupped hands but lost the battle with shrieking gulls and the clamour of rigging. He vanished just as quickly again in the forward cabin.

In his hut on the quay, the dock-master reclined at full stretch at a desk submerged under charts. He had the colour and wrinkles of a prune, the blue jersey of a seaman. Sea boots planted on a window ledge, he sucked reflectively on a pipe, scanning the water traffic outside. The window had streaks of green algae; he stirred forward to rub a patch clear of condensation and it seemed as if he was peering into an aquarium. The smoke from his pipe stank of seaweed.

'Mr MacRae,' I began. 'The *Akwa* out there . . .'

'Aw being seen tae. Nae cause fer worry. He'll nae sink.' He showed a toothy smile. 'And he'll no leave any of us here, ye ken, since he'll no be sailing awa.'

'Is there something wrong? With that tub of his, I mean?'

'*Tub?*' He scowled at my lack of respect.

'Yacht, then. Sailing boat.'

'Yon's a thirty-three footer, Moody built. She's an offal braw wee craft.' He squinted out, offering an opinion with slow shakes of the head. 'Ah ken Duncan MacRae an it's nae ta do wi' him e'er. He'll put tha blame on her, nae doot, or say tha tide were in when it shouldna be. Any damnfool thing ba' bad skippering. Fer aw her fine whig-maleeries, tha ocean radar frae a bloody battleship, ye ken, a sailing craft like tha's only as guid as tha hand a' tha helm.'

Translation is perhaps advisable from this point. Much pleasure is to be had in the perambulations of my countrymen, the cadences of what even to me is sometimes foreign speech. I revel in the empty richness of barside crack, the resort to a score of words where one, heaven

67

forbid, would be an abundance, the ability to construct long and poetic sentences solely from vowels. But each thing to its own proper place. Enough to convey that my frustration was considerable, though diplomatically concealed, that the tale was a lengthy time in telling but that time was in any case, as I was reminded in several variations, of little consequence just now – I was going nowhere and, with its propeller firmly snagged, neither was the yacht.

Why had I come to the marina? Until this moment I'd assumed as a friend, though not entirely without the feeling there might be other more sceptical motives. But when the truth came out about the propeller I fired a string of questions. From old habit as a reporter? Playing the detective? Even now I am not sure which. Some of one, most probably, and a bit of the other.

How did the propeller come to be snagged?

After the shortest possible voyage, while sailing out from the marina. Duncan cut too close to a mooring buoy and fouled an underwater cable. No excuses, he was running, sails down, on the auxiliary engine. Happens all the time. Landlubbing bloody sailors.

But isn't he a skilled yachtsman? Examinations passed and some kind of certificate?

Oh sure. Like passing your driving test means cars never crash.

When had this happened – this maritime accident of such amazing convenience? I did not, of course, complicate matters by asking in quite these words.

About, let's see, a couple of hours ago now.

I checked my watch, then pressed the point further. Exactly when?

A log was consulted and, another convenience, the time revealed to the very minute. Duncan had radioed over the emergency channel, the call logged at two thirty-six p.m.

Couldn't he free the propeller himself?

Said he tried and not a chance without diving gear.

Then what?

He was offered marine call-out, some people from Garelochhead with an outboard and wetsuits. Immediate service for a fast sixty quid. Or he could wait, twiddle his thumbs and the dock-master himself would come to the rescue when his shift finished at six. Slower service, regrettably, but amicable and only half the price.

So Mr MacRae decided to wait?

See for yourself. That's him out there waiting.

He was, I suggested, not short of a few bob. He'd always struck me as the kind to whom time meant money.

Ah, that's as may be on land but time runs slower at sea. Folk don't buy sailing boats to get places fast, mostly they plain don't sail anywhere. Duncan had said over the radio he'd been planning to heave-to anyway out in the Firth, get stuck into some business documents. Might just as well work where he'd fetched up, what was the difference?

No dinghy on the *Akwa*?

No need, a berth right by the jetties, walk straight on board.

Could he swim to shore, if he was so minded?

Him? More likely to drown in gin and tonic.

But was it possible?

Well now . . . You can't get certified to sail single-handed unless you can swim. High tide at the time, no strong currents, so not a difficult swim. The water was damned cold though, so why swim? Why radio for assistance if you're intending to swim? Why, having once reached land, do the return leg straight back again? No, definitely not. Mr MacRae was the sort to pay others to do his swimming for him.

Did he remain on board from the time he called over the radio?

Where else?

But was he *seen*? Was he in sight the whole while?

He was below decks presumably, working on those documents he talked of.

But the *Akwa* stayed put, visible slap bang ahead through a strategic window? Stuck firm – this time I spoke my thoughts – in just about as handy a spot as one would wish.

Mr MacRae, I was informed, was one of life's privileged, those fortunate few blessed with luck, money, a clean set of sails and a regular siren of a wife. Should Mr MacRae ever be shipwrecked, he'd go down in calm seas, in a few inches of water.

After much pipe sucking over price, I was permitted hire of a rowing boat, and paddled out to the *Akwa*, calling several times for Duncan as I drew near. He came from the cabin, gave a quizzical smile and caught the rope to pull me alongside.

'A point of etiquette,' he said. 'Out here I answer to the name of the vessel.' A strong hand dragged me aboard. Duncan has the muscles of a boxer. He has self-made man written all over him, with fight in his eyes and restless feet. 'And another thing . . . however much you flap your oars like that, you'll never get airborne. I know ducks manage but they've had more practice.'

The paddle out had been spent deciding what to say, how to break the news. I found myself lost for words, my prepared phrases forgotten. He has this effect on me. However hard I try otherwise, conversations with Duncan are invariably on his terms.

'If you were hoping for a sail . . .' he said, shrugging carelessly.

'I was told. At the marina.'

'Who was it, Sandy, wrote of messing about in boats?'

I gazed lamely at my feet, lacking the courage to look him in the face.

'Come on, don't let me down. Boats are dandy, boats are fine. But only for messing about in.' He snapped his fingers. 'Who the hell was it said that? Name's on the tip of my tongue.'

My brain refused to focus. I could only spread my hands, admitting defeat.

'Some literary expert you turned out to be,' Duncan chided. 'Still, whoever said it, he must've been driven to bankruptcy by sailing. There's fuck all you can do with boats, believe me, but mess about. Either the weather's too bad, the hull needs painting, or you're bloody stuck. I feel, I'll tell you, Sandy, like selling this stupid wreck, calling a marine broker this very minute. I mean, when you add it all up, capital and running expenses, work out the piddling few times you even make sea . . . the cost per hour of sailing's bloody ridiculous.' Duncan takes perverse pride in relating both the extravagance of his luxuries and what little regard he has for them, at one and the same moment.

Evening light spread a black oil-slick sheen on the Clyde. Street lamps lined the shore like embankment fishermen, their heads bent, casting with lines of gold into dusky water. Embers of sunset put a ruddy glow to Duncan's face as he waited, head askance, for some explanation of my being here, and his unnaturally black hair gleamed as if smeared with brilliantine.

'Your hair's wet,' I said.

He touched a hand to his head; its wetness seemed to embarrass him. 'Had this bright idea of cutting the prop free. You know me, Sandy, simple mind, seize problems by the throat, assume everything's easy. A rude awakening.' His shoulders lifted in a shrug. 'Problem one, breathing under water. Problem two, slicing through twisted steel hawser with a galley bread knife.'

'I'd like a drink,' I said quickly. 'I'd like both of us to have damned great drinks.'

'I was on the verge of offering,' he said, a trifle offended. 'I never for one minute assumed you splashed all the way out here except for a free drink.'

We ducked into the cabin, where he filled two tumblers at a brass and mahogany bar. Duncan owes no allegiance to any favourite bevvy, he drinks as time and occasion demand. I was offered a mighty measure of dark rum, while he sat facing me with another, his legs crossed on a bench of brown leather, faintly amused, watchful and questioning.

'Aileen's dead.' I heard myself say.

'What? She's what?'

'I'm not sure how to tell you this . . .'

'Aileen dead . . .' His hands began to tremble. Inexplicably my mind wandered. I stared at the rum spilling from his glass, dark patches forming on light blue trousers, and imagined I saw blood.

'Have a drink,' I pleaded.

'She can't be. Not Aileen.'

'Murdered. A break-in of some kind.'

'At the *house*!'

'A window broken. Round the back, I think they said.'

'When!'

'A while ago. I came straight here. For heaven's sake, does it matter when?'

He was instantly on his feet. The glass shattered against a wall, thrown in blind frustrated anguish. 'I asked her to come today,' he moaned. 'A blow of fresh sea air. If only she'd come!'

'Don't blame yourself. She never comes. She gets seasick. Aileen,' I said, slipping correctly into the past tense, 'hated sailing.' I took a feeble sip of rum, oddly conscious I'd consigned her in a few short words from living to dead.

His back was turned to me. He seemed to be staring shorewards from a porthole. 'How?' he asked, his voice broken. 'How was she murdered?'

'Please . . .'

'Tell me it was quick.'

'I didn't ask. And the police didn't tell me.'

He turned slowly. 'The police . . . are the police there? Did someone call the police?'

'You've got a phone,' I reminded him. 'Why not call them, at the house. They were asking for you. Best if you call right now, tell them where you are.'

He lifted the portable phone, began pressing buttons. 'God, no,' he said, gulping for air. 'Not Aileen, murdered.' The phone fell to the cabin floor. Covering his

72

mouth with a hand, he rushed through a door, along a narrow gangway where I heard him retching his guts out. He was a long time gone. He sounded like a man dying a slow and agonizing death. He may, for all I know, have been gone as long as the two years, roughly, since we met, because it was to those years that my thoughts turned in a turmoil of snatched and muddled recollections. I refilled my glass and sat in a kind of trance, not once giving a thought to Aileen. Duncan MacRae has this ability to dominate. I had no choice in our friendship, the decision was his alone. Friendship is something he trades, to be bought cheap and used for profit.

Strange to relate, I have no memory of our first meeting. A call came from him out of the blue, claiming we'd got on like a house on fire, agreed to meet again one of these days, and exchanged phone numbers. He proposed lunch, saying this would be on him. When I hesitated, he gave a great laugh – a suddenly alarmingly familiar laugh though I was unable to put a face to it – and elaborated, not lunch on him personally, you understand, business expenses. He'd been a bit frugal of late and this was a thoroughly bad thing all round. For the company, his accountant, the VATman, the Inland Revenue. I'd be doing him a very great favour and so on and so forth. The die was already cast when I rather too readily said yes. He was an utter mystery to me, a voice and laugh over the telephone, yet he understood me well enough for his first success at manipulation. He had a grasp of my psychology. He knew, in a phrase he is fond of, which hot buttons to push. I'd have said no to lunch on a stranger. But lunch on someone else's tax claim was beyond my power to resist.

His choice of restaurant was wildly prodigal, his flattery endless. I had till then never suspected such luxury was to be found in Glasgow. I should, of course, have known better, from the opulent splendour of carved stone edifices, the credit card stickers on discreet glass doors, but I ate from convenience in the same bars where I drank, and believed in my ignorance that the lavish hotels served scampi in breadcrumbs, that the grand sandstone buildings were home in these straitened times only to insurance companies and banks. So I fumbled like a schoolboy out on a treat, while Duncan had the airs of some rich and distant uncle. We sat at table linen so spotless white it must be thrown away when the meal ended. Large menus were presented with small polite coughs. There was lengthy eloquence in the description of dishes that found no echo in explaining the cost – my menu nowhere made mention of prices.

I had come unprepared for such riches. Duncan however was far from slighted by my appearance.

'What I envy about you, Sandy, is you're not a slave to convention. You're a writer, free to make your own rules. You don't wear a tie because this is your choice. As for me, I'm a slave to expectations. And, I mean to say, I don't even look my best in a pin-stripe suit.'

Over five courses and wines from, if memory serves, the two hemispheres and three different countries of the Mediterranean, he described a life balanced permanently on the brink of disaster. Financial failure always loomed, somehow with one bound he always leapt free. A business gypsy, he said of himself, wandering as the whim took him from one deal to the next. Property today but who knew what tomorrow – he'd heard there was big money to be made out of satellites. He found further cause for envy in my lack of ambition, though I had so far said very little, certainly nothing of myself.

'Ambition is a curse,' he said. 'Ambition is discontent. It's sleepless nights and the nagging desire for a better mousetrap. I will tell you in all honesty, Sandy, where the world would be without ambition. We'd be living in caves, hunting like hungry wolves. But we'd have no exhaust fumes, we'd be free of phones and departure lounges and television. We'd be damned sight happier men.'

He frowned when the bill was presented, needing to run

the point of a gold pen several times down the column to be sure the total was right. 'I bet you're one of those smart-arses,' he guessed, 'has read every book under the sun, knows who wrote what. So who was it said there's no such thing as a free lunch?'

'Go on, enlighten me,' I said, a sinking feeling in my stomach.

'Haven't the bloody faintest. But a profound truth, nevertheless.' He glowered and demanded the manager. We sat in uncertain silence, I felt the heavy burden of luxury, until the manager swept over with a stoop of concern and hands that looked ready to wring.

'Cameron,' Duncan said, 'I'd like you to meet a friend of mine, Mr Sandy Blair Douglas.'

We shook hands with the polite indifference of those who will never meet again.

Duncan gazed through a haze of cigar fumes, as if expecting some comment from me. I drew on my Havana, thinking the taste too strong and the smoke rather close for comfort to the smell of burning bank notes. Eventually the penny dropped. The price of the meal was friendship. Only later did I realize that he hadn't told me as such to my face, this would have implied an intimacy that was frankly beyond him – he'd made a form of public announcement.

I pursed my lips at the manager.' Mr MacRae confided in me,' I said, 'that he's had better food at McDonald's and better service from British Rail.'

'Then we shall have to try harder,' Cameron said, looking me straight in the eye. 'Next time we have the pleasure of seeing you.'

When he withdrew, I treated Duncan to a frown over the table. 'My friendship's not to be bought with a mere lunch,' I said, then took a long pause and gave a bloated smile. 'But for wines like these I'll willingly sell you my soul.'

He laughed uproariously, the same somehow possessive laugh I'd heard on the phone and on another occasion before that. I remember thinking it not unlike a dog barking, a sound of warning.

My rambling apartment caused him considerable confusion. I was alone among his circle of friends in not owning property. The sheer audacity of this took him quite by surprise. I was wise to rent, he'd say on some occasions. Property was a millstone, happy the man with no mortgage and some other sucker to mend the roof. Other times, he'd profess deep concern for my welfare, promising to save me from my own stupidity, tutting over ways to offer a special deal on one of his new houses.

'Who'd give me a mortgage?' I asked once.

He pondered the impossible. 'Think of it this way,' he said finally. 'There's no better friend than the bank that refuses you credit. They're saving you from financial embarrassment. I'd never lend you money, Sandy. Why? Because I'd hate to ruin a good friendship.'

He took to calling round at irregular intervals, with bottles of whisky to make himself welcome. He'd seen my light burning, he'd say, and could tell I was alone and wanting company. He would usurp my favourite armchair and invariably steer conversation to talk of business.

'I've had this amazing idea,' he said late one evening. 'I shall cut out the middlemen. I'm damned if I'm selling houses through agents any more. I shall sell direct to the market. I'll do my own advertising, hire my own salespeople for the sites. Temporary staff, when the houses are gone so are they. Chic young women on low basic pay but high commission, payment by results. Inspired, eh? Utterly brilliant.'

'What's the point?'

'The point, Sandy, is to make more money.'

'Sounds simple enough . . .' I agreed.

'All the best ideas in business are simple.'

'. . . but not brilliant. It can't be both, brilliant and simple.'

He sighed sadly. 'I should know better than expect

76

you'd understand. Your trouble is, you're no business-man. To make money in this world, Sandy, you need the simplicity of a child and the brains of Einstein.'

'Tell me,' I said, 'why do you come here like this? Why do you invade my peaceful evenings, only to lecture me non-stop how little I know about money? I never think of money, Duncan, except when you barge in, yet somehow I survive, believe me I get by.'

A disarming smile from the stolen comfort of my armchair. 'I come here,' he said, 'because I can try out ideas without fear you'll steal them. I can ask your advice and not be lumbered with a damn great bill. You're the only man I know, so help me, Sandy, who isn't a rival or a supplier, an accountant or a fucking lawyer.'

'I wasn't aware I offered advice. Or that you'd take it if I did.'

'You're my grand plan for the future,' he pronounced. 'I can't go on forever selling executive houses – I need to broaden my base. You, Sandy, are the nearest I get to the common man. If I can sell to you, I can sell to anyone. You're going to help me crack the mass market.'

'Me?'

'You.' He gestured grandly as if conferring a prize.

'You will only ever sell houses to people like yourself,' I retorted. 'Executives who want to live in ghettos with other executives. How can I help you? I'm cheap and you're expensive. But I'm cheap cheap, Duncan, where's you're expensive cheap. And expensive cheap's in a class of its own.'

His face darkened. 'What in hell's name has got into you tonight! I drop in for a quiet chat, a friendly few drams. I don't want hassle, I can do without fights over whether I know my own business. I get enough hassle, I'm telling you, I've had a fucking hard day. There's a tough world out there, anyone ever tell you, with people forced to shovel shit for a fucking pittance. All right for you, holed up here all cosy and smug.' Looking suddenly alarmed by his own agitation, he rubbed a hand to his brow. 'I wonder about you sometimes,' he said, sounding hurt. 'I wonder if you've any idea what friends are for.'

Mostly, however, we did not argue. He would try to provoke me but I'd refuse to respond. He sought praise for his ideas, I swallowed my pride and gave it, even when I couldn't see the merest shadow of an idea, any hint of originality. Because somehow he always seemed to turn up just when the world was at its bleakest and most hostile. In which circumstances, I suppose, whoever arrives at your door bearing bottles of scotch is definitely a friend, the best friend imaginable.

Many months passed before he made mention of Aileen. He never talked of a wife, of having a home. I assumed, if the thought occurred to me at all, he lived in hotels and airports.

'Dinner this Friday,' he said. 'All right with you?'

'Friday's fine. Expect me and my biggest doggy-bag.'

'Don't let me down by wearing a tie.'

'An informal dinner . . . ?' This did not fit my understanding of him.

'My dinner's are very formal. But you, Sandy, will not be. You'll be the only one not wearing a tie. I want to show you off.'

'You can rely on me,' I said, 'I only wear ties to weddings and funerals.'

He gazed at me in a mood of appraisal. 'I've been telling Aileen about you,' he said. 'She'll be seriously rattled to discover you exist. Frankly, she doesn't believe I actually know a writer.'

I made private prediction how dinner would be. My accuracy proved awesome. Duncan had the house I expected, furnished as I knew it would be. Great swags of curtain at the windows, crystal chandeliers with brass dimmer switches, kitchen cabinets that looked like the paint had run, and a glossy new Steinway whose whole presence said it had never been played. The house smelled hygenic and out of an aerosol, like a motel bathroom, and

78

the mushy feel of the carpets reminded me of cinema foyers I knew as a kid. He had the guests I expected, very correct and stuffy in dress, vague and guarded in stating what they did. 'I'm a sort of banker, I suppose,' one said. 'Oh I dabble,' another said. 'Any damned thing, ye ken, that'll mek an honest shilling.' And Aileen was much as I expected. Rather younger than Duncan – in her early thirties, I guessed – beautiful without being striking or tempting, as if it was a beauty bought in bottles. She said very little but laughed in all the right places – even when it was plain, from a certain weariness at the back of her eyes, she'd heard a joke of Duncan's one time too many.

'Aileen thinks you're great,' Duncan told me subsequently. 'A natural story-teller.'

This surprised me. I could not recollect Aileen noticing me, not once the entire evening.

He came, out of the past, out of the narrow gangway, his face ashen, his legs shaky.

'For a while there, I had myself believing this was some ghastly trick of yours. Wouldn't put it fucking past you.'

'Sit down,' I said, and fixed him an exceedingly large drink.

'This has come as something of a shock.' He was staring straight through me. 'One of those times, I guess, when one's strength of character is put to the test.' He lifted the telephone. 'The moment I call the police, my life's no longer my own. I'll lose control. Questions, formalities, grubby pressmen like vultures at my door. I'm right, aren't I?'

'I imagine so.'

'Well then . . . I grant myself one last request. Time, Sandy. Time to set my affairs in order.' He put the phone down in an act of defiance.

I must have given some indication of disapproval.

'I've fired plenty of people in my time,' he said, eyes blazing. 'Playing the hard man, hurting inside but never showing it. That's the way I am. My wife's been murdered, you can guess how I feel. But I'm not falling apart, understand me? It's instinct, Sandy. It's instinct to hold my feelings in check, keep the show on the road.'

'What affairs did you have in mind, to set in order?'

'A lawyer, for a start. Don't you agree, I should contact a lawyer?'

'That depends. Are we talking wills or defence.'

'I don't find that particularly funny.'

'It wasn't meant to be.'

He threw his hands wide in appeal. 'Listen,' he said, 'every fucking lawyer I've ever been to always feeds me the same glib excuse. Dear me, Mr MacRae, why didn't you consult me sooner? Well, not this time! For once, I'm getting a lawyer before the shit starts flying. I know nothing of murder, Sandy, except it must be a legal nightmare. I mean, insurance policies, for Christsake. I don't even know if murder counts as an Act of God.'

'Tell me if I'm right,' I said with heavy sarcasm. 'Since you're this hard outside, you must be really hurting inside.'

He seemed not to hear. 'Who else do I need, apart from a lawyer?'

'I rather think you'll have your hands full with the police.'

'They'll take care of the medical side, I suppose?'

'I should think so, yes.'

'Did you ever deal with murders, Sandy? As a reporter?'

'A few in my time.' A stabbing in Govan, someone kicked to death in Easterhouse. A different class of murder, I almost said. But I stopped myself, at the same time wondering whether murder was any respecter of class, was it any more pleasant to be murdered in Helensburgh?

His questioning continued. 'Is it up to the police when the date is set for the funeral?'

'For heaven's sake!' I buried my head in my hands.

'Has it occurred to you, Sandy, sitting there in judgement on me . . . has it for one minute crossed your mind this might be my way of coping, of staying sane?

That I might be doing any fucking thing I can to keep my brain on an even keel?'

'I'm sorry, Duncan. I hadn't thought of that.'

'I had a list of questions in my head. Things to organize. Now I've forgotten them all.' His eyes were very wide, there was a catch in his voice.

'Funerals,' I said. 'You were asking about funerals.'

He crossed the cabin, opened a drawer and started a feverish search. 'Pencil,' he muttered. 'Pencil and paper. We should be writing this down, making a list.'

I steered him like a lost child back to his seat. 'The police, Duncan . . . call the bloody police. God knows how long I've been here but you should have called by now. They'll wonder why.'

'Because I'm afraid,' he blurted.

'Of what?'

'Blood. And death. I'm not the bravest of men, Sandy, not when it comes to death.'

'Aileen's dead. Sitting here won't alter that fact. Sooner or later you'll have to go home. And she'll still be dead.'

He stared helplessly at me, his shoulders hunched. 'I bet you thought I was tough all through. Thick skinned and thick natured.'

'What I think is neither here nor there.'

'She's still alive to me, in here.' He touched his forehead. 'And as long as I'm floating away from shore, she stays alive, to my way of thinking.' He began to cry, tears streaming down his cheeks. His eyes turned red rimmed, his cheeks reddened, his lips grew red and swollen. He looked battered and bruised with innocence. 'I don't want the police, I don't want an inquest, I don't want the rituals of death. I remember my mother passing away, God rest her. She wasn't truly dead, I could believe she was living, till they showed me the coffin.'

'Give me the phone,' I said. 'I'll call them.'

Duncan wiped a sleeve to his eyes. He held out the phone but not quite within my reach. There was a shrewd gleam in his look. The puffy redness drained from his face. Just as suddenly he was his old self again. 'One last question,' he said, 'then you can call them.'

I nodded agreement.

'You're a reporter . . .'

'I *was* a reporter.'

'But you know how reporters operate . . .'

'In cases of murder, is that what you mean?'

'Will they come to the house? Telephone? Follow me around?'

'Aileen was young and beautiful. You, Duncan, are rich and successful. You'll be referred to as a tycoon. Your house will be photographed, they'll call it a palatial residence and exaggerate the value by a factor of two or three. This yacht will appear on front pages with dark references to something called a champagne lifestyle. The tabloids will parachute into your garden, they'll tunnel into your cellar. They'll camp in packs on your doorstep – they'll wait with cameras for weeks, years if need be, for that one time you come out wearing a smile or a shifty look. Refuse to answer questions and they'll make "no comment" sound an admission of guilt.'

'How do I handle them?'

'Do what comes naturally. Be yourself.'

'This is hardly a natural situation.'

'I'm not clear what you want. Vicarious fame? Morbid stares? Pictures of your building sites in the papers, free advertising for your houses?'

He held his head high as if my remarks were unworthy of comment. 'I'd like to be left alone,' he said simply.

'Ah . . .'

'I'd like not to be bothered by seedy reporters. Not to be libelled. Not to have Aileen's name dragged through the mud.'

'You want to bore the press into giving up . . . but without inciting them to fury . . .'

'Exactly.'

'Then get your solicitor to deal with them. Tell him you've no story to tell and you don't need money so offers are a waste of time. Your only feelings are deep grief for Aileen and a natural wish for the killer to be brought to justice. The Press will quickly tire of your solicitor – he'll be dull, he isn't a suspect and he'll be in the way. Meanwhile, make yourself as scarce as possible. Don't play golf, eat in restaurants or have fun. Work, but not near uncurtained windows. Don't reply when the phone goes or the doorbell rings – change the message on your answering machine, telling friends you'll call back, anyone else is to call your solicitor. If you see any men with cameras creeping round the garden, call the police, they'll come down like a ton of bricks on invasion of privacy. I don't know, Duncan, whether the police are going to like you, but they'll like reporters a damned sight less. Otherwise, play nice, act hurt not angry. Don't drive your car at reporters and don't slam doors in faces – they're used to it but they'll take a natural delight in revenge. Here's a thought – send out flasks of hot coffee first thing in the morning and late at night. This is not the action of a guilty man and, who knows, round about the third or fourth day you might even get them feeling a bit guilty that they're bothering you.'

'You have no idea,' Duncan said, 'how reassuring all this is, how helpful you're being.'

'Now, an important point. They'll want photographs. Photos of Aileen by herself and Aileen with you, the loving couple, preferably with expensive worldly goods in background, house, cars or yacht.'

'What do you suggest?'

'It all depends. Do you care particularly what pictures they print of Aileen?'

'I'd rather they didn't print anything.'

'Any compromising shots you're aware of? Aileen stretched out topless on a holiday beach? Or at a party, arms wrapped round another man?'

'Nothing. Nothing like that.'

'Are you sure? Think, Duncan. I mean the kind of photos that look silly fun in an album but not so funny under a tabloid headline. Murdered Woman's Nights of Abandon. You sure there's nothing like that?'

He reacted angrily. 'Do you know what you're saying, for fuck's sake! What the fuck are you trying to do to me!'

'This was your idea,' I reminded him.

'Sorry. So it was.' He sagged. The life seemed to go out of him. I have never quite been sure of his age and Duncan, who shows no mercy in his remorseless probing of other people's lives, had always suffered loss of hearing whenever I made tactful enquiry. Now he looked suddenly every day of forty-five. I had the strangest sensation that for the first and only time since we met he wanted nothing withheld from me. He would bare his soul, I had simply to ask. We were finally true friends. I played with the idea of asking directly: had he murdered Aileen? I felt sure he'd give an honest answer. At the same time, I realized that the act of asking would be an admission of doubt, suspicion of guilt, an accusation he'd killed his own wife. And our friendship would be over on the spot. 'What are friends for,' he'd bemoan, 'except to believe in you when you most need trust.' So I said nothing. Friendships are as fragile as marriages – and as perilous to shatter. You never know when you'll need them.

'Well, what d'you suggest I do?' Duncan enquired. 'About photos?'

'Nothing,' I replied. 'Not a damned thing. That'll force the Press to go hunting, to relatives, Aileen's old school and so on. Which takes a bit of pressure off you. The wily fox scatters the pack.'

'Is that really how you see me?' he said, rather shocked. 'Like a wily fox?'

'You need be more worried,' I said, 'what the police think of you.'

He made an effort at pulling himself together. He breathed in, puffed heavily out, and straightened his shoulders. Then he handed me the phone. 'I'm as ready as I'll ever be,' he said, as if doubting his own words. 'Do the friendly thing and call them, would you? My bloody hands are all ashake.'

I rowed him inshore. We heard the police cars coming, sirens blaring from afar and more squeals from tyres than there are street corners in the whole of the Burgh. Headlamps raked the marina car park like anxious searchlights. The cars screeched to a halt by the jetties.

I had come, better confess it, to judge his innocence or guilt. From ship to shore, I had my answer. Duncan had surprised me, as he so often does, by behaving like Duncan, thinking only of himself, forever planning. As one business sank beneath him, he'd be inexorably planning the next, not an hour of sleep lost, and he cares a good deal more for business than ever for Aileen. But murder? Surely no murderer could have, would have, acted as he did.

But mine is one of those lives where nothing stays certain for very long.

Rowing the final strokes, I peered up at the lights flashing their call of blue murder. Broody and prying silhouettes loomed over us from the quayside, every way of escape covered – the entire force, so it seemed, of the Strathclyde Police.

It did not look as if I was delivering up an innocent man.

Six

I will gladly admit to being nostalgic – growing older is the most serious blunder the majority of us ever make. So Helensburgh suits me very well. The town is well defended against change and has a fortress mentality to fashion. Yes, there are nuclear submarines, but where mercenaries should be, well outside the city gates. The holiday English come by with their maddening caravans, and coachloads of Japanese in search of Rennie Mackintosh, yet they leave nothing behind except litter and money, take little from us but postcards. Our stalwart clock tower shows faces to the tradesmen of three main streets, another to the Firth in case Clyde steamers should still be passing, and the town ticks slowly to the same unhurried time it has marked for close on a hundred and fifty years.

Don't misunderstand me: I don't spend my life in dreaming. Then again, I see little point in leaving my bed before ten – Helensburgh is tolerant of a relaxed attitude to hours. Nor do I yearn much for the past. I have a video recorder and a vacuum cleaner, I wear out coffee machines the way salesmen wear out tyres, and the telephone is my lifeline to means of paying for the coffee. But Helensburgh permits a precarious hold on some of the finer things of long-gone days. For one thing, they don't build houses like this any more. For another, someone's solicitor made a mistake about my rent, and though I wait with foreboding, the day of reckoning has yet to come.

My apartment sprawls over the entire upper floor of what local estate agents, with blithe indifference to the absence of vineyards and swimming pools, insist on calling a villa. To the Glasgow banker who built the house in the 1880s, this was a country retreat, a weekend cottage. Most people today would think it a palace. Up wide stone steps off the sweeping driveway, my own enormous front door opens on a hall befitting a gentleman's club, marble floored under a high domed ceiling. The mahogany staircase is the stuff of grand opera. Visitors have been known to believe the whole house mine; unless they are chasing debts it seems heartless to disillusion them. The family below in the lower villa has the run and expense of the garden – from every window of my upper villa I have the advantage of better views, panoramic vistas over nearly two acres of private ground. I can see lights twinkling over the Clyde and sheep grazing on barren moorland and snow on mountain tops well before winter and long into spring.

I have more rooms than I have furniture to fill them. My first idea on taking the place was to migrate like a nomad – as each ceiling crumbled and fell in, I would up sticks, moving ahead of decay to another grand salon. I reckoned without the obstinate durability of Victorian craftsmanship. Then I designated rooms for different purposes but no guests came to the guest room, my daughter's room stayed cold and deserted, overhead mirrors proved impractical for the stately chamber I planned for seductions, Flora forsook the world's most elaborately plastered kennel for the comfort of my bed. So I sleep and screw in one vast room and eat, work or watch television in another, where there is either a warm log fire or bright southern sunlight. Down a broad corridor of arches and musky panelling, doors stay firmly closed. I haven't any idea what, if anything, lives behind them but for some reason, nothing I say, people who call stare that way with unspoken respect, seeming to imagine they conceal some storehouse of priceless treasure. The rooms are, however, far from wasted. They give me a sense of space. It is possible, maybe even inevitable, to go quietly mad in a city, living alone in a single small room. I have no such claustrophobia. I am solitary but enjoy my own company. When loneliness threatens I have the safety of many places to run to, and I think of the emptiness of old rooms not as evidence of being alone but as offering the comfort of friendly ghosts.

When the doorbell rang, I was in the bathroom. The floor is the same ancient lino I found when I came, the walls are tiled up to the ceiling, a band of bilious green on the grimy-looking white you see in old lavatories. Pipes run in unlikely directions over the cracked tiles, there is a faint odour reminiscent of garlic, and I am reminded as I soak in the bathtub of somewhere deep in the bowels of a grandiose but fading French hotel.

For rather a long time, I'd been staring at myself in the mirror. I saw staring back at me not my own face but Duncan's, his eyes thrown wide in an appeal to be understood. A blink or two and Aileen was in the mirror, her face drained white, her eyes open but lifeless in the bewilderment of sudden death. The bathroom is forever cold, condensation runs down the tiles and clouds the mirror. I rubbed a patch clear and looked full into a new set of eyes I did not for a moment recognize as my own. I was permitted a brief insight of surprise, confusion, a manifestation of deeply realized pain I never expected to see in myself. The doorbell rang again, prolonged and insistent. I and my reflection gazed warily at each other as if we were strangers. Closeness to death can have this numbing effect, this sense of being close to one's own death. I had a weirdly disturbing feeling that the bell called me back from something dangerous. Not for some considerable time had I felt so out of control.

Sergeant Grant was at the front door. Little more than two hours could have elapsed since I'd left the marina. For a man of such sluggardly manner, he was hot on my heels.

'Will you come in?' I spoke not in invitation, leaving the decision to him.

'Just a few more questions, Mr Douglas.' He stepped

inside and trampled his feet on the doormat. He had a tired and crumpled look about him as if it had been a long day. An already big man, his corduroy jacket was at least a size too large in a colour that clashed with the trousers. 'Funny thing about doorbells,' he said as I led up the opera house stairs. 'Guilty people answer you very fast. Odd that, don't you think? Bit of a give-away.'

'Was I fast?'

'Ages. Thought I'd be ringing all night.'

'Well, then,' I said.

'Some guilty people keep you waiting ages, that's the problem. The cunning ones, those that don't panic. Not an easy life this, Mr Douglas. Full of conflicting behaviour, more doubts than certainties.'

'Sounds like life in general, Sergeant.'

'Indeed so,' he agreed. 'There you have it.'

We entered the study, where he and Flora exchanged looks of distrust.

'Does he bite?'

'Only if you call her a he.'

'Ah,' he said. 'Not much of a guard dog, is she? Bit subdued. A stranger in the house, and no barking.'

'Flora seems unaware she's a dog. She prefers cars to walking and my dinner to dog food. She'd smother burglars with wet kisses so long as they come with bags of sweets.'

'Not much use, then,' he said, risking a cautious stroke.

'On the contrary. I'd be lost without her.'

'Oh ay? Interesting. Very interesting.' He drew down his brows in a forensic gaze, as if I'd made an unseemly confession.

He accepted my offer of tea, and I returned with the tray to find him nosing openly round the room. Flora sat watching, tail happily wagging.

'You do very well for yourself,' he said, indicating all about him. 'Very well indeed.'

'Mind if we get to the point of your visit?'

He drew back the curtains for a peer out at the night.

'I'd give my eye teeth for a view like this,' he said. 'Tragic consequence of being in the police, you don't have views. The houses you visit have views, some of them, houses like this. But not yourself. CID overlooks the head-quarters car park, and not a single colleague of mine has a place with a view. Me, personally, I stay in Dumbarton. All I can see is the backs of houses and smoking chimney stacks. The chimneys at Ballantine's, know where I mean? Fair puts you off spirits, Mr Douglas, take it from me, the smoke and stink of whisky making.'

'In what way can I help you?' I persisted.

He took a chair and shovelled sugar by the spoonload into his teacup. 'Sorry to be a nuisance over this, but you did say, am I remembering right, you'd no idea where Mr MacRae was to be found?'

'Correct.'

'And it was you telephoned us from his yacht . . .'

'Correct again.'

'Having done what in the meanwhile? Driven round town searching for him? A kind of one man patrol?'

'No. As a matter of fact I went straight to the marina, more or less.'

'More or less . . .?'

'Meaning I didn't drive round town.'

'Let's see if I've got this right . . . You told me you didn't know where Mr MacRae was. Turned out you did know.'

'I was driving past the marina. I spotted his yacht. Pretty easy to spot, Sergeant. If you'd been passing, you'd have seen it too.'

'If I'd been on the lookout for a yacht . . .'

'I wasn't looking. It was stuck in the Firth, plain to see.'

'Slipped your mind, did it, to mention he's got a yacht?'

'I don't recall being asked such a question.'

He gave vent to a heavy sigh, wearily rubbing his chin. If it's true we become like the things we love, the Sergeant resembled a slap-up supper, beefy fingers as thick as sausages, a face the colour of cheap red wine. He puckered his lips at the taste of the tea and stirred in a further help-ing of sugar. 'You happened to be passing the house . . .'

'So I've already told you.'

'Then you happened to be passing the marina . . .'

'On my way where I was going.'

'Which was . . . ?'

'Nowhere, Sergeant. I was simply out for a drive.'

'Pretty quick to the scene of the crime. Even quicker getting to a man we were anxious to find. You see my difficulty?'

'Frankly no.'

'Coincidences like that happen to you much?'

'All the time.'

His eyebrows rose sharply.

'I used to be a newspaper reporter,' I said.

'So I gather . . .'

'Quite a good one, I'm told. Some of us develop the knack of being – how can I put this? – around the right stories at the right time. Call it intuition, call it coinci-dence, maybe I can't break old habits. I go where my nose leads me.'

'You planning to write a story about this?'

'Certainly not.'

'You quite sure about that, Mr Douglas? The dock-master tells me you quizzed him pretty thoroughly.'

'I'd describe it as idle conversation.'

'Questions such as how Mr MacRae's yacht came to be stuck. How long he'd been out on the Firth. Was there any chance he'd swum back, seen or unseen. Etcetera.' He consulted a notebook to the accompaniment of loud sucking noises. 'Wasted as a writer if you want my opinion, you should have been in the police. Exact same questions I asked him myself.'

'Like I said, old habits.'

'Mmm,' he murmured dubiously, squinting hard at the notebook.

'You mentioned CID . . . Are you a Dectective Sergeant?'

'Thought you'd remember that, from when we first met.'

'Is this some kind of official questioning?'

His head shook far too readily. 'Goodness me, no. See here, I'm not taking notes, I haven't issued a caution. We're very strict, you know, how these things are done. Police and Criminal Evidence Act.'

'Exactly why I asked.'

'But it seemed to me, seeing we're on nodding terms, that we've met so to speak, you'd have no objection to clearing up a few misconceptions.' He munched noisily on a biscuit, picking the crumbs from his teeth.

The shortbread came from the bottom of a tin I'd unearthed at the back of a kitchen cupboard. My biscuit tasted stale so I tossed it over to Flora. Sergeant Grant reached out quickly to impound the last remaining piece on the tray.

'In what way can I help?' I asked.

'Why didn't you call us, when you spotted the yacht?'

'It didn't occur to me, I'm afraid.'

'Never entered your mind?'

'Duncan's wife had been murdered, remember. I thought it best a friend should break the news.'

'Not a job for the police, in your view . . .'

'If it was your wife, who would you prefer? Some stranger calling in blue uniform?'

'Quite. I mean I understand what you're saying. But there's two sides, you see, to breaking bad news. There's the telling of it. And there's the seeing of it . . . How the dearly beloved reacts to the news. Are you with me?' He watched closely, sitting very still. A big brute of an inquisitor with a piercing gaze I could feel digging into me, the keen enquiry of a quick little man.

'I was thinking,' I said, 'only of Duncan.'

'An uncharitable mind might conclude you robbed us of vital information. Interfering with evidence, in a manner of speaking.'

92

Considering it wisest not to reply, I stared back the best I could.

'How did he take it, when you told him?'

'He was badly shocked. He cried. He was violently sick.'

'But in no hurry to get home, to find out for himself . . . yet such a dreadful thing, his own wife murdered in their bedroom at home.'

'Is that where it happened, the bedroom?' The words uttered themselves.

'See what I mean,' he said on a sly note of triumph. 'How did it happen, where did it happen? The very first questions on everyone's mind, the answers we're all of us after and the quicker the better. But not, it seems, our Mr MacRae.' He disposed of the shortbread, smacking his lips. 'Enjoy your rum, by the way?'

'What rum?'

'Something I heard on the car radio. Two used glasses, I think they said, found out on the yacht. No way of telling, I'll agree, whether they'd held large or wee measures, but a regular funeral wake by the sounds of it.'

'Look, I poured him a drink, I was in bad need of one myself. We talked for a while, as friends do in such situations. I consoled him.'

'Did he ask how she'd been killed?'

'Or did he know already, is that what you're implying?'

'A simple enough question, Mr Douglas. Did he ask?'

'I think so. Yes, I'm sure he must have. I couldn't give an answer, you'd omitted to tell me.'

'Anything else he asked?'

I remembered Duncan's talk about consulting a solicitor. To disclose this would be a form of betrayal. He'd talked to me as a friend, said things he'd never have said to a policeman, behaved in a way the police might misconstrue. Briefly, I fooled myself I could claim nothing more was said, that we'd clung together like children and cried our eyes out like babies. But Grant's intensely alert stare continued boring into me. I had to confess to something.

'He asked my advice on handling the Press.'

'Did he, now . . .'

A bad mistake, from the whistled intake of breath. He looked at me, head intently to one side, as Flora does when something juicy is afoot.

'Natural enough, wouldn't you say? I'm a journalist. He's prominent in these parts, a reasonable assumption he'll be hounded.'

'But he asked? This wasn't your idea, mention of the Press came from him?'

'I can't remember precisely. I might have raised it first.'

'And what advice did you give?'

'I told him to deal only through a solicitor.' There, I'd mentioned a solicitor, shouldered the guilt. 'I recommended not handing over any photos of his wife. I told him to lie low and if his privacy was invaded to call in the police.' Our eyes clashed. 'I promised you'd offer him every protection.'

'Good thinking,' the sergeant said grudgingly. 'From one who should know. From the first pressman on the scene, I mean. Who's hired a boat rather sharpish and advised how to keep the rest of the Press at bay. And, stake your life on it, asked God knows how many prying questions.'

'It wasn't like that,' I protested.

'Whatever you say,' he replied.

The phone chose that moment to ring. He indicated I could answer, with a sweep of a beefy hand, as if the phone was his.

'Harry Harper,' a voice said.

I was taken aback. News editors had little cause to ring me any more. 'Yes, Harry,' I said, only too aware Sergeant Grant had seen my surprise, the tightening of my shoulders. Fiddling with the phone, I found a way of presenting my back, although it did not seem wise to speak as quietly as I wished.

'Seen on the wires there's been a murder in your town, Sandy.'

'Yes . . .'

'Care to do me a few words? Wife of some local big wheel, I gather.'

'Not much of a tale to tell, Harry. Why not lift it straight from the wires? You don't need me.'

'Our man on the spot,' he said. 'Bit of local colour won't come amiss.'

'A small murder in a small town. I'll waste my time writing beautiful prose, you'll spike it.'

'Try me. I didn't know you could still write beautiful prose.'

'Look, Harry, do me a favour and pass on this one. The thing is, I knew the murdered woman.'

'Getting better by the minute.'

'Her husband's devastated. All he wants is to be left alone.'

'My heart's bleeding,' he said. 'Listen, Sandy, hear it bleed.'

'He'll be fucked about something dreadful by the tabloids. We're supposed to be quality, this isn't our scene. Just small town people, Harry. She doesn't even rate an obituary.'

'Listen, will you. I saw the wire and said to Bill, doesn't Sandy live in Helensburgh? I mentioned murder, and know what he said? Right up Sandy's street, he said. There's hacks need fifty fags a day to write and there's hacks need a skinful. But Sandy's a blood and guts man. He'll turn a non-story into several paras, murder stalks the Scottish streets. More fiction than fact maybe, but nothing actionable.'

'Don't do this to me,' I pleaded. 'Don't ask me to write about friends.'

'I pity you,' he said. 'Only hack I've ever heard of who claims he's got friends.'

Sergeant Grant gazed accusingly at me as I put the phone down, the kind of look that says more than words ever can.

'You heard me,' I said. 'The very last thing I want is to write this story.'

He stared hard, scratching his chin. 'What I heard, if I heard anything, was only half of what was said.'

'Isn't it illegal, listening in on people's conversations?'

'Coincidence, Mr Douglas. I just happened to be passing.'

Taking up paper and pencil from my desk, I resumed my seat, facing him head on. I hadn't yet decided whether to do a piece for the paper; the notion of getting my own back on the Sergeant was, however, distinctly appealing. And I wanted desperately to learn more. I was still greatly troubled why Duncan had shown such reticence in calling the police. Perhaps I believed that hearing more would provide some explanation.

'Don't suppose,' I said with studied nonchalance, 'you'd mind answering a few questions?'

He laughed without humour. 'You've got the cheek of the devil, give you that.'

'How was she killed?'

'Come on, be reasonable!'

'Brutally, that's what you told me earlier.'

'She wasn't shot, I'll say that much.'

'Knife or blunt instrument?'

'One or the other, think I can safely say that.'

'Why won't you be more precise?'

'Because I can't say for sure till I see the medic's report. Because we're looking for a very dangerous man and the less said the more likely we are to get a conviction.'

'Why so sure it's a man . . . ?'

'Certain facts of the case lead us to that conclusion.'

'Such as the fact she was killed in the bedroom?'

He appeared reluctant to answer but finally nodded. 'Location comes into it, yes. And the method of killing, the probable strength of the murderer.'

'Was she sexually assaulted?'

'Now, that I can't judge,' he said. 'Not being a medical man, not having seen the report.'

'But was she dressed or undressed?'

'Middle of the afternoon, Mr Douglas. Why would she be undressed?'

'Is that when she was killed, this afternoon?'

He scowled, angry with himself. 'I never said that. Go printing that, you could be badly wrong.'

'But you discovered the body this afternoon . . .'

'As you saw, Mr Douglas, with your own eyes.'

'And you'll have checked certain obvious details on arrival – before the doctor came, and Scenes of Crime were called, no need to wait for the report – because, Sergeant, you're the sort to notice little things, like how long people take answering doorbells. Forget thermometers, you'll have felt how cold the body was and checked for signs of rigor mortis. Bet you've made a note whether the blood had time to dry.'

'We were at the house not long after four. All I'm prepared to say is she was killed some time before then.'

'Why all this secrecy? Is Duncan MacRae on friendly terms with the Chief Constable or something? The same lodge, maybe? Are they into bowler hats and rolling up trouser legs?'

His face went purple, he leapt from the chair. 'I don't like you Press people,' he spluttered. 'Never have. You've got big mouths and gutter manners. My Chief Constable, for your information, insists we act all sweetness and light to the media, enlightened bloody times, same as to wayward kids who'd benefit, believe you me, from the taste of a copper's hand. My job's catching criminals, Mr Douglas, murderers, thieves and scum. What's yours? Inventing lies and digging dirt?'

'Can I quote you on that?'

He made a conscious effort to pull himself together. He dropped weightily back in the chair, the floorboards creaked. His big hand dabbed a handkerchief that had seen better days over his beetrooty face. I hadn't noticed until then how much sweat he had on him, and deduced it wasn't the Press he hated but being questioned. People who ask questions for a living hate being questioned themselves. They've learned there's no such thing as an innocent answer.

'I'll strike a deal with you,' he proposed. 'I'll tell you all I'm free to say. Then an end to all this, agreed? Anonymous sources, a wee birdie told you. I was never here.'

Terms accepted by exchange of rather stiff nods. As a peace offering, I poured him another tea, though it was now very cold.

'Entry to the house was made from the back, out of sight of the street. Mrs MacRae had been taking a bath by the look of things, maybe with a tap running she didn't hear the breaking glass. You seem surprised . . .' His head sloped at an inquisitive angle.

'In the middle of the afternoon?' I said.

'Enough bottles around, shampoos and the like, to start a chemists. Lady of leisure . . . maybe she spent her days in the bathroom, lazing and beautifying, how would I know. Or with the husband out sailing, maybe she expected the kind of company ladies take baths for. Time, as they say, may tell.' He slurped the cup empty. 'You do not, Mr Douglas, make the best tea I've ever had. And you should change the shop, if it isn't a liberty to say so, where you buy your biscuits.'

'I already have,' I said. 'That shop closed years ago.'

'Where was I? Ah yes, bathrooms and break-ins. Was it a burglary that went wrong when she disturbed the intruder, or did he enter intent on murder? We can't be sure yet. But she was attacked in her bedroom, wearing only a bathrobe. The weapon might, I'm not going to be more explicit, have been one of the tools a house breaker would be carrying. No indication of anything being taken from the house but we'll need Mr MacRae to confirm that. Hardly to be wondered at . . . our man's not going to hang around looking for safes and jewel cases when he's just done in the lady of the house. But here's an oddity . . . he found her car keys and opened the car out on the forecourt. The keys were still in the ignition, the driver's door left wide open. Was he planning to steal the car for his getaway and did some movement in the street frighten him off . . . someone going by or a passing car? No clues yet on that one – it's a quiet street as you'll know and we've no reports yet of anyone being sighted. A neighbour coming by saw the car door open, got no response at the house and gave us a 999.' He seemed puzzled to find himself still gripping the handkerchief and stuffed it into a pocket. 'Fair enough for you?'

'You might have this buttoned up in a matter of days,' I suggested.

'Seen something I've missed?'

'I was wondering about fingerprints on the car keys . . .'

'Let's wait for what Scenes of Crime come up with.' He became worried by a new possibility. 'But what if there's only two sets of prints? His and hers. Any idea whether Mr MacRae ever drove his wife's car?'

'When it suited his purposes. There are business deals where you want the cachet of a big car, others where it's better to appear . . .' The word that came to mind seemed so damning of Duncan I made vague gestures instead, indicating modesty.

'. . . Inconspicuous?' he said for me.

'If there are just the two sets of prints, you've got a problem,' I responded swiftly. 'Duncan has every right to handle those keys.'

'And if so, we've no way of determining when he touched them last. Might've been this afternoon, could equally well have been earlier. Just moving his wife's car, say, to get his own car out of the driveway.'

'Suppose she was sexually assaulted . . .'

'Murder's too ordinary for the papers, is it?' he said. 'Need the titillation of sex to add some spice to your story?' His body however belied the flippancy in his voice. I don't think I imagined a slight stiffening at mention of sexual assault, the beginnings of a clench to his fingers.

'Just suppose. Don't you have all kinds of infallible

99

means of detection now, genetic fingerprinting and the like?'

'Are we talking body excretions?'

'You tell me.'

'If he's been so obliging . . . if, Mr Douglas . . . and I'm careful in speech so note I've flashed that *if* at you in glowing neon letters . . . well we've got him, sooner or later. Open and shut case. But what if, even bigger neon lettering, made in Scotland from girders, such body fluids as may be found should belong to the rightful husband. Before setting sail, he bade fond farewell to his lady wife, she never had time for her bath. Suppose that's his story . . . what then, you ask?' He sagged from carrying the cares of the world. 'More doubts than certainties, as I told you before. Husbands may be suspects in cases of murder, I only said may. But husbands, Mr Douglas, can legitimately do things, stick their fingers and protrusions in places, other people may not.'

'Quite,' I agreed.

'Any more bright suggestions?'

'What's your guess about time of the murder?' Seeing his brow knit tight, I submissively spread my hands. 'Not for publication, just personal curiosity.'

'What you mean, Mr Douglas, is was she murdered before or after two thirty-six this afternoon . . .'

I produced my most innocent expression.

'. . . assuming,' he continued, 'the dock-master showed you the same log he showed us. Which he did.' A weary lack of caring crept over him, he sagged in the chair. 'To my mind, purely going on appearances, I'd say no more than an hour before we arrived on the scene. Putting time of the crime at three o'clock or thereabouts.'

I had to be out of the house that night. With Flora at my heels, I went where my feet carried me. We took a clockwise route from the garden gate and I guessed immediately, without making any conscious decision, where my feet would lead.

Helensburgh's streets run as straight as Parisian avenues. North of the house the way is blocked by the railway, the track of the West Highland Line. Going south you come eventually to a forced turning at the banks of the Clyde. So my walks are easy, along the paths of a grid. Clockwise or anticlockwise, any four corners get me back to the house, and within the boundaries of railway and water I can wander for only minutes or to the far reaches of the town. Every town should be this simple, perhaps that's why Helensburgh living is so uncomplicated. No alleys to speak of, no hidden crannies, no cheap bright lights but nor in the darkness is there any sense of menace. The tall hedges speak of cosy seclusion and massive stone walls take the chill edge off an occasionally bitter wind.

The Clyde was ahead as we set off. The whole universe shimmered overhead in a pitch-black sky, lights shone across the black water and the lights of a small vessel moved like a spacecraft across a constellation of tiny and infinite stars. We dawdled in our usual fashion. Flora sniffed at trees and I sniffed the clarity of a fresh nocturnal breeze. Nothing much happens on these walks since with the whole town preparing for bed, the same unchangeable sky, there is nothing much to see. Except Archie, who lives I know not where but is always following for some of our travels.

Archie is a beagle of sorts. He has taken a particular liking to Flora. His wet nose coming from behind has the unfortunate effect of awakening in Flora an interest in dogs. A great deal of yanking at the lead always ensues when Archie appears and I've developed a unique style of martial art: flailing kicks that look lethal without ever actually landing. Flora then spends the remainder of our walk gazing up at me in such forlorn hurt and misery I am forced into wondering how tolerable life would be without sex. I have even wondered whether Archie is her reason for sometimes climbing on my bed to deliver a warning stare, the jealous regard of a rejected mistress, at whoever I happen to be with. I kicked out at Archie with untypical vindictiveness that night, almost inflicting serious damage. I had no desire to be reminded of sex. Nothing was further from my mind.

We came to the Clyde, my feet set course for Rhu. I saw the blaze of floodlights out on the water well before we reached the marina. The *Akwa* lay where I'd last seen her. Police frogmen were diving around the yacht, more dark and shiny figures plunging and surfacing by a dinghy anchored closer to shore. I had no idea what they were searching for. I pondered whether they themselves knew and if it was sharp or blunt.

On arriving back home I made no delay in phoning Gordon. It must have been very late by then, judging from his sleepy response.

'Would you do something for me?' I entreated. 'You probably won't be asked this, no reason you should be, but if you ever are, I'd be awfully grateful if you'd say we spent a bit longer hunting that fox this morning than we did.'

'Why the hell should I?' he mumbled.

'You'd save me a great deal of needless confusion.'

'How much longer did you have in mind?'

'Say till teatime. Let's agree I left you about three thirty in the afternoon.'

'Who is it won't be asking me?'

I took the plunge. 'The police.'

His silence unnerved me. Few things unnerve me more than unasked questions from a face you can't see.

'There was a murder,' I said. 'Don't know if you've heard.'

Impossible for him not to have heard, but he gave no answer.

'Aileen MacRae,' I said. 'I'm not asking for an alibi, just some brotherly protection.'

'Did you do it?'

'Of course I bloody didn't!'

'Swear you didn't do it?'

'On our mother's grave, Gordon. On anything and everything sacred.'

'One of your women, wasn't she?'

'Why the hell,' I said, 'do you think I have a problem?'

He made no comment for what seemed like minutes.

'Well . . . ?' I begged. 'Will you help?'

'What time did you say?'

'Three thirty in the afternoon. Not exactly then but roughly, a bit suspicious if we're too exact about time, if our stories match too closely. Let's suppose you happened to look at your watch a short while after I left the cottage, that's how you remember.'

He fell into another disturbing silence.

'Did anyone call round during the day? Anyone see you, anyone who could say I wasn't there?'

'I was off in the hills. No-one saw me.'

'Well, then . . . what's your difficulty, what've you got to lose?'

'Phyllis would have to tell the same story . . .'

'She'll do anything you ask.'

'All right,' he agreed after a great deal of thinking.

I thanked him profusely.

'Aileen MacRae,' he said, with an edge to his voice. 'What a woman she must have been. Lips like wild roses and a suck like an industrial vacuum cleaner.'

'Stop . . .' I said.

'The woman you bought the nightdress for . . .'

Which, thank God, I thought, I never gave her.

'The woman you were planning to be rid of . . .'

'To say fond farewell to. Not get rid of.' Even as I spoke, my talent for prediction sent a cold shiver running down my spine.

For her parting gift, I'd chosen black.

103

Seven

Hours had been spent fighting the memories. Finally, in a mood of weary resignation, I surrendered myself to Aileen. Bewildered by her death, secure in the knowledge she was dead, I surrendered myself more completely than I ever did when she was living. Pulling cool bed linen up to my face, feeling Flora's warm weight on my feet, I let my mind travel the shadowy shelves of my past, selecting albums, delving in pages of recollections, encountering snapshots I had forgotten I'd saved. Her voice reached me and I was reminded how bothered I'd once been to discover a woman whose most appealing feature was how she sounded rather than how she looked. She had a bedroom voice, she'd died in a bedroom. It seemed fitting I should wait until now, to remember her in bed.

She was always desirable from the moment I first set eyes on her. However I did not at first desire her as a mistress. Forget all else, she was Duncan's wife. I have suffered enough from marriage to see little cause for respect of other men's marriages. But I am happy in simplicity and Duncan's world was far removed from mine, I wanted no part of it. Any passing ideas I entertained about making play for Aileen were quickly dismissed. She was a closed book to me. She made polite conversation, she was a household fixture, part of the furniture. But one thing for sure, Aileen was probably the most expensive feature of the house – I could never afford her. I saw no personal shame in realizing this fact. Women are, on the whole, better cheap than expensive. I like salt with plenty of vinegar on my chips, the boisterous crudity of seaside holidays. I like the coarse clutches of working women, the intoxication of crumpled sheets soaked in cheap and tawdry perfume. I had a belief born of ignorance that expensive women excite the eye but not the body. I might have retained my rough and innocent instincts had Aileen never worn her little black dress.

She sat facing me at dinner one evening. We were washing down prime Aberdeen Angus steak with a red Bordeaux as old as I was, while discussion raged on the sheer impossibility of earning any kind of living from business. Someone called the Small Businessman was much on everyone's mind. He was maligned by the masses, abused by those in power. He had more children than Mother Hubbard, all to be educated at his own expense. He was an outlaw to government, bureaucrats were everywhere to track him down and deliver him to the workhouse.

I made one of my few contributions of the night. 'Seems to me only fair,' I said, 'that small businessmen should have small incomes. Otherwise, let's face it, words have little meaning.'

I achieved my desired result of a shocked silence. It has always seemed to me that if I cannot contribute to a conversation then the next best thing is to kill the conversation stone dead.

Aileen leaned very slightly towards me. 'What have you got against small businessmen?' she asked in her rather breathy voice.

'Nothing in particular. I'm entirely impartial to small businessmen. I think they're as undesirable as big businessmen.'

'Why? Be honest, Sandy, aren't you being your usual unrealistic self? Easy to be sweeping about things you know absolutely nothing about. You don't employ people, you don't take risks. You don't, as we do, put every last bean into new ventures that might fall flat and leave us penniless.' She might have been her husband's mouthpiece.

'Businesses,' I declared, 'mostly sell us things we don't

105

want. And the things we actually want, products we really need, they contrive to make at exorbitant cost. Look at Duncan. He hires architects and lawyers and planning consultants, interior designers and kitchen designers and landscape designers. Who pays in the end? The poor suckers who buy his houses. Did Beethoven need a marketing department to sell his symphonies? Did Rembrandt have fleets of salesmen on the road to flog his paintings? Did Christopher Wren put full page adverts in the paper: buildings designed here?'

'Aren't we, Sandy dear, being unnecessarily *artistic* tonight?' But she leaned even closer across the table, parting the little black dress over her neat and rounded breasts, speaking very low as if we were alone together. This was the first moment I noticed the unmistakable breath of bedroom in her husky insinuation. She gave a tinkle of a laugh and clapped her hands, a cue to someone else, who knew the rules better than I did, to embark on a fresh complaint. A very personal and private laugh, I thought it, deserving better than to be shared at a crowded dinner table.

Just a few more words remained to be passed between us. When leaving the house, I held on to her hand longer than ever previously, looked with the detachment of an art connoisseur and remarked on her dress, saying how well black suited her. Then the occasion went the way of harmless flirtations, into oblivion. Aileen never entered my mind and I might have forgotten her little black dress. Except Duncan telephoned only two weeks later. Profuse apologies about the short notice, and yes he didn't need telling I'd be bored to tears by the talk, but would I mind saving his life and enterprises from ruination? Dinner tonight, everything arranged, and Aileen had just this minute realized there'd be thirteen at the table.

'Are you superstitious?' I asked in some surprise. I'd always assumed black cats would avoid crossing his path rather than the contrary.

'Me, Sandy? Hell no. But it's like your dying moment,

106

that quick last prayer to God. Why tempt providence?'

Aileen seated us. The business suit facing across the table promised a forgettable evening. Cursory nods to one another – I have never found interests in common with grey men in matching waistcoats. Just as quickly, Aileen expressed the dismay of a hostess: the suit was far too close to his wife. Whisking him well out of range, she took his place. For the rest of the evening she then said not a single word to me, never once let her eyes meet mine. I became filled with admiration for the skill with which her gaze could be switched from one end of the table to the other yet not come my way in passing. Some diversion would intervene – a blink of the eyes, the food on her plate, attention to a guest, the pressing need to replenish someone's glass. Our chairs facing and only feet apart, Aileen rendered me non-existent. I have begun seductions myself by the ruse of studiously ignoring the very person I most wish to stare at. This trick has rarely been played on me, certainly never with such elegant disregard.

Probably she wore a different black dress. Though it looked much the same, I doubt whether Aileen approved of wearing any dress twice to a social gathering. The neck was cut low at the front, she was wearing no bra. I looked my most bored that night, my eyes grew glazed. Any smile on my lips came from the politeness of not really listening and if I was noticed to gaze fixedly ahead, mine was the vacuous gazing of a late invited guest who would rather have been elsewhere.

For her part, Aileen encouraged and welcomed my staring. I was a while in reaching this conclusion but her motive in ignoring me eventually became inescapable. She indulged as never before in animated conversation, she leaned to one side then the other to catch what was said, a vase of flowers needed adjustment, she had to rise slightly and reach low over the table. But she never caught my eye. The perfect hostess, she caused me no embarrassment. All others forgotten, I gorged myself silly, a solitary feast on her breasts, the best meal I'd enjoyed in ages.

Time was, days of my youth, when I agonized irrationally over the breasts I wished to be buried in. Big or small, round or pointed? Was firmness a virtue, preferable to soft and yielding flesh? Did I prefer grapes or mushrooms – the golden ripeness of exposure to sunlight or the cool pallor of a damp white skin? Travel, as so often, broadened the mind. Breasts, I was to learn, are as varied as lands and cultures. I became an explorer, a world traveller, thirsty for the stimulation of new uncharted territory. I wanted no fixed abode. The best breasts are those yet to be discovered, the only breasts of no interest those I've touched for too long.

I also learned the mystery of breasts and women's willpower – women like Aileen, I mean, who use the talents that nature bestowed. Breasts can be flattened or curved as occasion requires, rendered demure or voluptuous. Some women can alight on a man with their breasts, as precisely as directing the line of their eyes – the way Aileen contrived that night. I watched her dress open up over her breasts when she moved, displaying enough for arousal but never sufficient for full satisfaction. I gazed in rapture at their shapely delights. I marvelled at the shadowy chasm between them, a woman of gentle foothills and deep quiet valleys. I wondered if they were tanned from being bared on a yacht floating far from eyes like mine, whether their lubrication, the sheen catching the flickering candlelight between us, was due to some exotic lotion out of one of her many bottles or tiny beads of perspiration brought on by the heat of my stares. Because she basked in my stares. At times I would look away at whoever was talking, then glance quickly back at Aileen, to catch a slight stiffening of her back, the admission of a sudden glow to her breasts as they rose, parting the little black dress.

'You're unusually quiet tonight,' Duncan said from the head of the table.

'Just for once,' I answered, 'thought I'd leave the provocation to others.'

Thereafter, the seduction began with Duncan. Married women mean two sets of habits to be learned, so I studied his movements before turning to Aileen's. Missing him by minutes at his office, I spent an anxious time with his secretary comparing diaries, for an appointment I then postponed on second thoughts. Discovering the regular pattern of his days came as a considerable relief. I had not relished the idea of tailing Duncan around – his BMW was more than a match for my clapped-out Volvo and he drove like a maniac. But if I was still in any doubts as to the wisdom of an affair with Aileen, his diary persuaded me otherwise. Where did he ever find time for her? She was a neglected flower in a forgotten garden.

Aileen showed only passing surprise when I called at the house the following Thursday – the surprise, I'm inclined to believe, of wondering why I hadn't come sooner.

'You're out of luck, I'm afraid,' she said. 'Duncan's away sailing. He always goes sailing on Thursdays. No weekend yachtsmen, you see. Fewer boats to bump into when he tacks and furls or whatever it is he does.'

'Damn,' I said. 'Driven all the way over for nothing.' I dropped my voice and moved into the doorway. 'Don't tell him I said so but the reason I've come is that amazing old scotch of his. Did he buy the distillery when it closed down?'

'Oh, what scotch is that?'

'The name slips my mind. But I'd recognize the bottle.'

She threw the door wider. 'Better show me, Sandy. The things men drink, I'm a total dunce.'

The bar in the living room had enough stock on the shelves for a small country pub. I chose the oddest shaped bottle in sight. Aileen was easily persuaded to sample a drop, then held out her glass for more.

'Don't ever come again,' she said, a finger wagging. 'I never, but never, drink during the day.'

We sat in her cool cream room, a decent distance apart on cream leather settees. Her slinky black track suit clung close to her body, curves gave evidence she wore nothing underneath. Her suit matched the glossy black Steinway behind at a window, and her peachy smooth complexion somehow suggested that, like the piano, she might have music in her but had never been played. She flicked a finger to her glass, making it ring. Something in the sound caused her to laugh, a little nervous laugh younger than she was. She reclined but not at ease, as if gazing over at me was like awaiting an outcome that might be good or bad. As if, I decided, in looking at me she was already thinking of pregnancy tests. So I flicked my own glass and grinned the danger of ulterior motives at her as the tinkle rang out over a vast cream carpet.

'Well, then,' she said. 'Here we are. The idle rich and the idle poor.'

'Am I? Idle and poor?'

'You're always saying so over dinner.'

'I have never admitted to being idle.'

'True enough,' she conceded.

'Nor have I ever described myself as poor. All I've ever done, as a lesson to those fat cats you think of as friends, is make the point that wealth does not bring happiness. Not the most original moral, I'll agree, but a surprisingly novel idea to most of them – despite the fact they could be paraded as adverts for the desirability of being flat broke.'

'Sorry I spoke,' she said archly.

'I won't deny being a bit short of ranch houses. I don't have one BMW, let alone two. I am feckless and yachtless. But I am not poor, Aileen. I've never claimed to be poor. Poor is a state of mind.'

She tried several expressions, widening her brown eyes in pity for the destitute, fluttering dark lashes at my presumption of her extravagance, arching in tolerant amusement the small and mobile red mouth I'd already decided would be a sensational success at absolutely anything it attempted.

'Those are not my friends, you know, that you meet at dinner.'

'Very well, then . . . Duncan's friends.'

'They're not that either. Just business people, Sandy, men he owes a favour to or wants a favour from.'

'Plus their wives . . .'

'God yes. Their awful wives.'

'And what am I? A token something or other served up with the wine?'

She frowned in genuine puzzlement. 'To be perfectly honest, I'm not entirely sure.'

'Duncan's never thought to explain . . . ?'

'Why should he? People come, people go. All that's expected from me is to look like he can afford whatever they're offering.'

'And to act like they're terribly interesting?' I suggested.

She struck a theatrical pose on the sofa. 'Oh yes. Terribly, awfully, dreadfully, downright appallingly interesting.'

'Then you must be something of an actress,' I said.

'The very best.' She held the crystal tumbler to her face and flicked it again, reacting with rather childish contentment to the *ping*. Her coquettish smile at me through the tumbler was altogether too sweet, too quick, too conveniently screened by a veil of cut glass, a harem smile, too much of everything I wanted from her all at once for any of it to be trusted. I recalled that she'd chosen to sit close at dinner, just as today it was her choosing that sat us nearly a room's width apart. She used closeness to flaunt herself and distance to stay out of reach. She was something in an exclusive shop window, all I was permitted was a nose pushed hungrily against the glass.

But then she frowned, blinking at a shaft of sunlight hitting her face. After partially drawing the curtain at a window, she joined me on the settee. We were at either end of a not especially long seat with Aileen turned towards me, an arm draped carelessly over the back. I smiled cautiously in encouragement, she lolled her head and parted her lips.

My self-control amazes me now, thinking back. I well

remember being greatly confused. It would have been all too easy to make a grab for her, and the afternoon might have passed pleasurably enough. Aileen was intrigued by my arrival, flattered by my interest, and having fun. But she was not swept off her feet. She was in her own house and resolved on full command of whatever transpired. Figuratively, the door was ajar for a glimpse of her bedroom, today at least she would not be throwing it open. Her breasts had brought me to the house and only her breasts were there on offer. They were suddenly not enough. It was not my hands that throbbed in stiff and painful longing for Aileen – her gaze fell openly to my crotch, her eyebrows lifted slightly, she permitted herself the provocative musing of a twitch at the corners of her mouth. In that instant I felt older than my years, and wished desperately for the simple appetites of adolescence, the safe sex of licking at nipples and messing my pants. I felt old and greedy, in no kind of mood for being teased. And the impotence of old age saved me from myself. The fever subsided that had threatened to burst the veins in my pulsing temples; I was as cockily proud of being rid of my erection as I would once have been at calling one up.

So I raised my empty glass. 'Do you mind if I have another?'

If she was taken aback when I rose from the settee, she hid it well. 'Help yourself.' She gestured to the drinks.

When my glass was topped up, I leaned against the bar, an elegant raffish lean from the days when cigarette smoke was romantic, when bars were not for slouching at, when staircases were sweeping symphonies of white marble. I gazed at her across the impassionate distance of a room, exuding gallantry, a man who could be trusted not to take advantage of a lady unless she is at her most vulnerable.

'Do you ever go sailing with Duncan?'

'Never. I get seasick.'

'So what do you do while he's away sailing? How do you pass your days?'

112

'Here at home, mostly. The way we women do.'

'I don't see you somehow with a floormop and bucket.'

She was suddenly and surprisingly angry. 'Damned right, Sandy, my time's my own. I've got the money to do whatever I please. So you tell me . . . how do you imagine I while away my time?'

I answered with a languid shrug. 'Haven't the faintest, Aileen. Maybe that's what I find so attractive, your air of mystery.'

She came over to me, held her manicured hands so close I feared she'd scratch out my eyes. 'First I spend an hour each morning working on my fingernails. Then two hours hard labour making something of my face. Pretty good face, don't you agree, worth twice the effort on my nails? Then I've got the whole afternoon free to think of nothing better than the clothes I'll buy next. Well, is that an enviable life, or isn't it?' She was staring wildly, her nose only inches from mine, and seemed on the verge of crying. I must have taken too long replying: I'd no idea what she expected from me. Tears sprang to her eyes.

'I think it's a remarkably beautiful face,' I said, with insufficient thought.

Her hand swung without warning. Her slap landed like a punch, rocking my head. 'Fuck you!' she said. 'And I was stupid enough to think you'd understand.'

I rubbed my stinging cheek. 'I'm not exactly house-trained, Aileen. What comes next? Do I hit you back or demand an explanation?'

She turned her back on me, then marched, head held high, over to the Steinway. After lifting the lid on the keyboard, she settled with a flurry of wriggles on the piano stool and, giving a last defiant glower in my direction, began to play. What she played was not exactly concert standard but it was well above average for Helensburgh sitting rooms on a weekday afternoon.

'Who composed this?' she demanded.

'Chopin,' I said.

'Oh really? And here's dumb little me thinking that's a

113

brand of perfume.' An adroit change of composer. 'Any ideas on this one?'

'Debussy.'

'God, you're a disappointment!' she fumed.

'Isn't it Debussy?'

'Of course it's fucking Debussy. My God, wasn't I wrong about you?'

'Care to tell me why?' I asked, baffled by the ways of her sex.

'I'm clearly not the woman you thought I was. Which means, Sandy my love, you're not the man I thought you were.'

Forgetting I was there, she began the 'Moonlight Sonata'. Her face was very pale above the high black collar of the track suit, her hands ivory on the ivory and black of the keys. I sat listening for a while, believing her altogether too perfect. Whether it was the music or sight of her that went to my head I really can't say, but I found myself thinking a famous phrase, my answer at last to the means of seduction, words so corny I burst out laughing. Aileen stopped playing and turned, wondering what was wrong.

'Do you do this every Thursday?' I enquired.

She nodded absently. 'And Tuesdays he's off playing golf. So that's my day for learning Italian.'

My gaze wandered the room when she resumed playing, over the carpet, the wallpaper, curtains and leather settees. Everything was cream except Aileen and the Steinway, and the yellow dapples of sun on the crystal chandelier.

'Why don't I take you away from all this?' I whispered to her in my thoughts.

This time I avoided laughing. Seduction is no laughing matter; the serious planning of it denies the luxury of premature celebration.

The Saturday following, just two days later, I called in the afternoon. Aileen wore a simple black cashmere sweater, her tight trousers styled like jeans were neither denim nor cheap. A lot of money had gone into the way she looked – as if she didn't care a hoot for clothes but clothes cared desperately for her.

'You've missed him again. He's driven over to Edinburgh.'

'He spun me this yarn once about weekends in the office, the trials and tribulations of business . . .'

'Usually, yes.'

'. . . but it was locked and dark so I thought I'd try here.'

'This was one of those meetings that crops up sometimes. You must know by now what Duncan's like.'

'He's meeting some investment people, did he say? I saw the appointment in his diary.'

Aileen fluttered a little, undecided between closing the door in the face of impertinence or opening it further to the admission of gossip.

I lowered my voice, looked surreptitiously round at the neighbourhood before proceeding. 'Investment people? In Edinburgh of all places on a Saturday afternoon? Admit it, Mrs MacRae, high finance is not the cushy existence it once was.'

'Are you implying something about Duncan?'

'Me? I've got my faults, Aileen, but implying things is not one of them.'

She stepped to one side. 'Coming in, or what?'

'No. You're coming out.'

'Am I?'

'I want you to show me his houses. I've a sudden urge to become an executive. To have five bedrooms, an en-suite bathroom and what is arguably – how does the brochure go again? – the best loch view in the West of Scotland.'

'Wouldn't you rather Duncan showed you?'

'He'll tell me the houses are wonderful. You might not. You might even tell me they're rubbish and save me making a dreadful mistake.'

'It's Saturday, Sandy. The site closed at lunchtime . . .'

'You don't say . . .'

'. . . and I haven't any keys.'

'Then we shall resort to house-breaking.'

Her face lit up at the thought. 'Your car or mine?' She grinned like a kid who'd been promised a treat.

A candid nod of the head to my clapped-out Volvo. 'Don't spare my feelings,' I said. 'But is that what you'd call transport for an aspiring executive?'

The building-site was deserted for the weekend, exactly as she'd said – I'd earlier watched the workmen leave. A big sign declared the desirability of these exclusive villas, the entire lexicon of the property seller's art. Prestigious, unprecedented in quality, traditionally built, lifestyle enhancing, idyllic in location, breathtaking in concept. There was a progression of development along the private road, from a bare shell at the entrance to a finished show house with fluttering flag at the highest point of the land. Styles were plundered from anything and everything an executive may dream of sequestering – manor house beams over doors posing as Georgian, corner towers with pretensions to Highlands Baronial, an afterthought of Tudor leading tacked on to the double glazing. A clutter of scaffolding and filthy equipment, rutted mud everywhere – it hadn't rained in days but it has always just been raining on building sites. Past some old trees, the last remnants of a mansion house garden, yacht sails bathed in the Scottish siesta of a drowsy summer sun.

Aileen picked her way along a boardwalk of planks to peer in at a showhouse window. Remembering the burglar alarm, she shook her head suddenly at our folly. It must surely be switched on.

I pointed to another house, not yet completed, with roof and windows but no front door. Giving a shrug as though already losing interest she nevertheless followed me in.

Our feet resounded on bare floorboards. Electric wires protruding from fresh plaster, a hole in the wall where the fireplace would be, a smell of sawdust and wet mortar. I kicked up some dust, to watch the particles swirl like tiny sequins in a peep of sunlight. The bareness of the house excited me hugely but Aileen's only response was to sigh to herself as she brushed a smudge of woodshavings from her sweater.

'The living room,' she announced with a crook of the hand.

'Very desirable,' I concurred.

'Odeon curtains there, mirrored cocktail cabinet in the corner, plaster ducks flying on this wall here, and something Regency with brass handles, about here I think, to hold the stereo.'

'I'd prefer the room left as it is,' I said.

'Some executive you turned out to be,' she answered, appearing ready to leave.

'This house, Aileen, has everything I want from a residence.'

'You're easily persuaded.'

'It has the attraction of being empty. You look, as a matter of fact, especially desirable in humble surroundings. Bareness suits you, you look less like a luxury fitting someone else installed.'

A tinge of colour came to her cheeks. 'Aspiring executives, Mr Douglas, don't think highly of empty houses.'

'Then show me the bedrooms,' I said. 'Where I and my many offspring shall rest our weary heads.'

Our eyes met. She nodded a thumb towards the staircase, where the lack of a handrail did not promise an easy ascent. 'Help yourself,' she suggested. 'I shall stay here and be grateful for having a bungalow.'

But, fulfilling my expectations, she climbed up some while after, remaining coyly in the doorway as I paced an upper room, measuring out the shape of a bed.

'Safe to come in,' I said. 'It's only a bare room, for heaven's sake. I'm boringly conventional in my attitude to bedrooms – quite harmless without a mattress and sheets.'

She entered with the suggestion of a sway to her hips,

chin held high. I cupped her face in my hands. 'I am also a liar,' I said. 'Not to be trusted in bedrooms.' My lips brushed gently on her small and precious mouth, still buttoned tight in exhortation to enter boldly if at all. My head bent over Aileen's, her modest height came as an invitation, an act of submission, the allure of her fragrance brought my instant conversion to the subtleties of expensive perfumes – all they required was to be breathed in counterpoint to fresh cement and drying plaster.

She hit me with a swing I never saw coming, the identical punch she'd used before.

'Well fuck you!' she snapped. 'Neither am I.'

She stormed from the room, leaving me to the bruised ruins of a shattered plan. I gazed from the window in search of consolation, saw only rusty scaffolding, the flapping tarpaulins of a roofless house. But I saw her car still standing on the churned up mud and it gradually entered my battered mind that I hadn't heard her feet clatter down the wooden stairs. Traipsing a narrow corridor, over a carpet of plastic sheets, I came into a room where she stood completely naked, her mouth curved in a Mona Lisa smile, her slim bare shoulders framed by some trees outside. A better room, at the rear of the house – I'd given too little thought to being overlooked from the road. Her clothes were neatly folded on the window ledge; even in an empty house Aileen found time for the niceties of her wardrobe.

She wrapped her arms round me, poked a warm and probing tongue in my mouth. 'I do not make love in stranger's bedrooms,' she murmured between kisses. 'Or in motels or hotels or the back seats of cars. I am not that sort of woman. I make love, if I make love at all, in my own bedroom. I'm a Calvinist brought up to the strictest ideals.'

Then she removed my clothes. No hurry or fumbling and an almost maternal expression so virtuous in its attentions she might have been undressing a baby. She was on her knees, removing my trousers when she gazed up with rounded eyes.

'I hope you've a suitable sense of surroundings,' she said affably. 'Foreplay is simply not on.'

I entered her standing, my palms pressed in support against a wall. She clung to my neck, swinging her legs up to clasp my waist. I licked her closed eyes, salty streaks of sweat from her cheeks and a trickle of dribble that squeezed through her teeth. She burned me like a furnace while her breasts felt cool and moist, her hard nipples seeming to claw at me as if clutching the hairs on my chest. All the while she talked – it was the memory of her voice that most stayed with me later. A deep voice full of panting, words out of order, words she never finished except in a kind of sigh, meaningless words and sometimes no words at all, just the feel of something said in her hot breath on my face. It was a language I wanted to learn, I knew it would take a long time learning. I felt in that first mindless abandonment to passion I truly wanted to make love to Aileen for the rest of my life. Her voice frightened me then, I felt threatened by it. I felt I could fall deeply and hopelessly in thrall to the sound of her. I knew this was crazy and this frightened me more. Being aware of the madness of passion is the sure and only warning of something akin to love.

'Don't talk,' I said.

'You fucking make me talk.' Steamy panting in my ear.

I bit her very hard on the neck. 'You'll wake the neighbours,' I said.

A stage came when we collapsed to the floor, I prone on my back and Aileen crouching above me. Droplets of sweat swelled into globes on her raw red nipples, I held out my tongue to catch them falling.

'Next time, we're doing this in my bed,' she said, expelling a great and exhausted sigh.

'Is there going to be a next time?'

'Unless I die shortly . . .'

'Thursday afternoons?' I guessed.

'You are harder work than Chopin,' she said, swaying in time with her laboured breath. 'But clearly far from dead.'

* * *

In a multitude of small ways my life became enmeshed with Duncan's, his habits governed mine, I became trapped by his success. The house was his, as was the bed and the wife. I took comfort with Aileen in the certainty of his trips on the yacht, we shared an anxiety that no constancy is for ever, that a change in weather or mood might bring him prematurely back. This lent, I suppose, a certain urgency to our love-making which in the early weeks was part and parcel of the affair. But it was his shadow that darkened the bed and his schedule not my spent energies that drove me from it as afternoon gave way to the fears of twilight. I rediscovered the great paradox of love with married women – that they promise variety but deliver routine, and therein lies the ending of every affair.

We fell quickly into the happy treadmill of routine, some of it of our own choosing, some betraying Duncan's unseen hand. I discussed this with Aileen one day to her great amusement – errant wives, she said, were like spies, the juiciest secrets lay hidden beneath the cover of unremarkable lives. She christened our relationship a B and B romance, for Baths and Binoculars, the baths being her preparation for my arrival, our shared cavortings in the shower before I left . . . and the binoculars, well I brought those with me for the occasional check on dangers from shipping.

At various times, Aileen would rise in no particular hurry from our bed to scan the Firth from the bedroom window. Rhu Marina was hidden by rooftops but there was an uninterrupted view for four miles of water to the far shore, and clear sight of a headland round which Duncan always voyaged in his dependable adherence to habit. We watched him once on his way out to sea, a good twenty minutes under sail, and Aileen opined that there could be few affairs in history with such a generous margin of safety. She'd lean in sublime nakedness, elbows on the window ledge, my old army-green binoculars raised to her eyes, a smile of touching innocence playing on her lips.

After a while I came to believe she wanted to see Duncan making an early return, that she needed the added excitement of danger.

'Do it,' she urged one day as she was staring out.

'Do what?'

'It,' she said, her voice going husky, and wiggled her naked bottom at me.

I took her from behind, unceremonious and fast with animal thrustings. She moaned quietly, gripping me hard but never once lowering the binoculars. She complained in the very instant I climaxed – less of this clumsy jostling, mister, couldn't I see she was trying to look? Then she turned, dropped to her knees and began licking me clean.

'No time for a shower, darling,' she said in an even tone. 'Duncan's on his way into port.'

I'd have claimed the world record for dressing had I not buttoned my shirt in the wrong holes and come painfully close to castration with my trouser zip – but she clung to me for what seemed an eternity inside the front door. Her dark eyes closed, a dreamy expression crept over her face.

'You have no idea,' she whispered, 'what it's like to have your lover up you as you stare at your husband's face. He looks so happy out there, playing at sailors.'

I asked her in bed one afternoon if Duncan had lovers.

'Gosh yes, I should think so. Businessmen do, don't they? Secretaries and the like and silly young women.'

'Is he having an affair with his secretary?'

'Have you seen her?'

'Just the once.'

'Would you want an affair with her?'

I might, I said, but not if I was Duncan. Damned good legs and a scandalously short skirt, but she had charge of his diary and most of his life. An affair with her would be to forswear all others – a mistress with her hands on your diary must be a worse encumbrance than having a wife. No offence meant, I said, but she had asked.

'Duncan's so ridiculously predictable,' she said.

'Don't criticize his most endearing feature,' I answered in his defence.

'He spends fifteen minutes in the bathroom each morning. He's tidy, he's clean but he's not what I'd call scrupulous. But some mornings he's in there for ever. Scrubs his teeth till the gums bleed and dabs a different brand of aftershave behind the ears. Those, my darling, are the days he always phones later to say the meeting's dragging on till midnight or there's fog on the motorway and tragedy of tragedies he'll never make it back.'

'Do you mind?'

'I've got you, Sandy. Why should I mind?'

'What about before? Before I came along?'

'We neither of us existed before then.' An affectionate kiss, fond and sincere, followed these words, but there was a plaintive echo of pain in them. I wondered at the time whether she was saddened by years of housebound loneliness or harking for a lost and former lover, but I knew better than to ask and we never again made any allusion to having lived or breathed before we met.

In the golden days of a carefree autumn, Aileen took me to lunch at a restaurant I might have imagined her to own, so well did she match its chic composure. A glorious smoulder of sunlight flooded the windows, a freshness of flowers and whites, no dim secluded corners for the midday preludes to night-time intrigues. Her treat, she insisted, and hang the expense. She was dismissive of my anxieties, my immediate reaction that any restaurant where expense was an issue meant Duncan would surely appear – we would have food every bit as good as in the centre of Glasgow, in the anonymous concealment of a city suburb. Duncan never came here, she assured me, neither did she. As a break to the established pattern of our meetings, this was a Tuesday, and when we arrived in Bearsden the name of the restaurant suggested a fond farewell, a nostalgic parting of the ways. October. We had reached the autumn of our affair, she'd become bored with

Thursdays and bed. As my coat was taken by an effusive waiter I admired the poetry of her gesture. I imagined the heat of our passion now warm and mellow on my face, the fierce clutch of our couplings loosening, becoming brittle and falling underfoot. I was also saddened, as one should be by fine poetry. Lunch with Duncan had brought her into my life. Now – because in some way or another he'd presumably pay for her excesses – it was at a lunch on him that I'd lose her. I grew morose and apprehensive. I wanted neither to let go of Aileen just yet, nor the tidiness of losing her in such a fashion.

Elbows on the table, she rested her chin in long ivory fingers. 'It's October,' she said. 'And so is the restaurant. Aren't I clever?'

'Your choice of restaurant, Aileen, is elegant, cool and sophisticated. The very opposite of the way you make love.'

Her laugh rang round the room. 'Our very first October.'

'So it is.'

'How long have we known one another?'

'Do you mean how long since you lured me into that empty house?'

'I wasn't aware, Sandy darling, that hot eyes at dinner parties counted as knowing one another.'

'In that case, three months,' I said.

'Forgotten so soon? It was a Saturday, actually. Making twelve weeks and four days. Why are you so ready to forget four of our precious days together?'

'Because I'm every bit as sentimental as you but not as good at arithmetic.'

'We shall come here every year, the first Tuesday in October. I shall buy you a madly extravagant annual lunch. I've decided this will count as our anniversary.'

My surprise must have been all too apparent. She buried her chin in her hands, her eyes bright and mischievous. 'I'm not a summer person, Sandy. Summer bores me in that tedious little town. I like warm beds and

123

the days growing short and everything brown outside the window. I refuse to accept that I met you in the summer. Let's pretend we're meeting today for the very first time. I'm only just emerging from my summer hibernation . . . Thursday will blow your tiny mind.'

'Why wait? Let's skip the meal and rush home after coffee.'

'Sorry,' she said. 'I don't believe in mixing business with pleasure.'

'Is this a business lunch?'

'A planning meeting. Future strategy for the partnership.' Her voice deepened, heavy with conspiracy. 'Duncan, damn him, puts the bloody boat into winter mothballs any time now. You must, my clever darling, dream up a winter hobby for him. Something a long way off with overnight stopovers. Can't you persuade him the golf is better in Portugal? He'll charge it all to expenses, anyway.'

'How about a single-handed voyage round the world?'

'Perfect,' she breathed, not seeing this as the joke I intended.

Aileen, I believe, was the only woman I've known who never broke a promise. Her breasts kept their promises, her voice never lied in its promise of bed. And, true to her word, that coming Thursday did blow my mind. We were left drained and delirious. In a blur of brain damage I have a feeling there was no part of the house with the possible exception of ceilings where we did not screw in frantic celebration of Aileen's autumn. On the bed, under the bed, in the shower and on the Steinway, where Aileen found the inspiration to thump out with her toes a rhythm in march time. I put our ardour down to the lengthening shadow of Duncan falling over us, the awful knowledge we'd be losing our Thursdays. And something more drove me to hitherto unplumbed depths of sexual desperation. When Aileen promised a future of Octobers yet to come she meant it with all her heart. We'd agreed tacitly to

124

having no pasts before we met, nor had we ever envisaged a future. Affairs are only ever of the present. Once they stretch ahead they transmute into something else, serious, unsettling, no longer simple. To look beyond the coming Thursday was to stare over a precipice into the bottomless pit of a life invaded. Aileen, who had asked nothing of me but afternoons, suddenly demanded eternity.

Though I gave no clue to my feelings, I left her that day in the mental disarray of a man whose marriage is collapsing about him. And it was as I drove home past Hermitage Park that I caught my first sighting of a girl whose legs were longer than those I'd just left, whose breasts were considerably bigger. Which I took as the solace of an omen.

That was to be the last time I saw or made love to Aileen. The next Thursday I pleaded near death from a cold, the Thursday after, Flora needed the urgent ministrations of a vet. Aileen was the very essence of sympathy; convinced she believed me, I detested the lying. Affairs begin with deceptions but are finished by lies. The feeling grew stronger that all was over between us.

However, I made no excuses when the next Thursday came around. Keeping my options open, I dithered, prevaricated, torn between two women. I went late to the house, undecided even as I entered her street whether to call. And that was when I spotted the police.

Aileen had been expecting company that afternoon: Sergeant Grant conveyed the fact she'd been taking a bath. Did she hear a sound in the house and, thinking nothing amiss, imagine it was me? Was there already a new man in her life, or the unexpected reappearance of that lost and former lover whose memory had briefly brought pain to her voice?

Not Duncan, though. Shocked and confused by her murder, of course my suspicions fell first on him. But he was too much wrapped up in his own concerns to have any heed for Aileen's. I'd taken the frequent precaution of checking for myself through the binoculars, and stared blissful ignorance full in the face.

I rose from the bed, switched on my word processor. Calling for *Aileen*, I relived her seduction, played out on the screen. Very close indeed to events as they'd transpired, although I'd described them on a Friday, the day before we went to the building site. Not yet understanding her as well as I believed, I hadn't foreseen her flighty independence, that she'd choose the bedroom, that it would be Aileen not me who so steady handedly peeled off our clothes.

I couldn't bear suddenly the idea of sharing her with a dumb machine. Affairs improve in the human memory, maturing with age like a vintage wine. Computer memory freezes them in time and nothing good should be remembered as it was, not quite, or why else have spirit, imagination, why suffer the indignity of growing old? This is why I never keep love letters, my justification in answer to sentiment for never writing them. Hidden in a drawer they become memorials to something dead, while memories keep the breath of life in those few precious moments when life was worth living. I wanted Aileen always available in the fading, changing fantasies of my thoughts, where new and ever more adventurous love-making was a constant challenge to my inventiveness, the continuation of her promises. Duncan could remember her only as a wife, I'd had Aileen as a mistress. Mine was the better future with her, and mine the greater success.

Furthermore, I was greatly troubled by the discovery that the act of making love, so evocative to recall, could seem furtive and sordid when set down in words.

Erasing her from the computer, I kept her all to myself.

Eight

It was Aileen's fate to be murdered at just such a time when no wars were being waged anywhere with white faces or oil, no nuclear power stations went crazy, no football teams were bought or sold by avaricious millionaires, no prime ministers died or were deposed, and no topless models had enticed themselves into the beds of royalty. A fleeting tragic stardom but one, I rather think, that might have appealed to her exhibitionist streak, and murdered women are, I was relieved to read, treated with whatever respect is commensurate with banner headlines. She was, after all, the wealthy wife of a worthy local businessman. By no common standards of censure could she be said to have asked for it.

The Scottish tabloids, fiercely nationalistic in their reporting of murder, gave Aileen the star treatment, solo appearance on the front pages. A miscellaneous supporting cast crept into the billing with their English cousins, the *Sun* sharing her story with lurid pointers to an inside page – a scandal to do with the French ill-treating British donkeys. Photographs of Aileen showed a far younger woman, as if she'd done nothing worth recording in recent years, their fuzziness suggested a touching lack of clarity to her life. Her pictures denied the slander of violent death – she looked plain and far from rich, she seemed ordinary, decent and honest with perhaps a propensity to sadness, a convent girl who left the house only for gardening or visits to church. I learned she was thirty-seven years old and had a degree in history from the University of Stirling, facts I had neither guessed nor been told by her. There was more than a whiff of garden wall gossip to the tabloid reporting of Duncan's auspicious whereabouts at the time of the murder, but legal advice, I discerned, had been expensively taken – the hideous drama of his being so close was emphasized rather than what the cruel minded might refer to as his opportunity, one paper going so far as to suggest that but for the unhappy moderation of tides and weather he might have saved her.

The quality papers were more subdued, the *Herald* for some reason finding room for a photo of Duncan's new development near Glasgow Cathedral, and the *Scotsman* making minor reference to his financial connections with their home city of Edinburgh. And my paper, an English quality, not greatly moved by murder, except terrorist or political or of those too famous to be wholly ignored? My restrained version of the news was relegated to page six, where I was pleased to note the miserly few column inches were more or less as written and carried no by-line. I doubted very much that Duncan was included among those who were stripping the shelves bare in Helensburgh's newsagents that morning, but I did not, nevertheless, wish him to think I was making any capital from the misfortune of a friend.

Impossible, of course, to stay away from Aileen's house – its morbid magnetism could be felt across the length and breadth of the town. I held out manfully until noon, then gave up the struggle, wishing I'd gone sooner: I'd always gone there in the afternoon and wanted to cast off old habits that might betray any connection with Aileen. Flora led the way in an uncharacteristic rush of tugging, as though she smelled murder in the air and was eager to see for herself. To her disgust, I took a circuitous route down the street where I'd always parked my car on Thursdays, well away from the ranch house and the possible rumours of neighbours. I was greatly cheered to see that by pure good chance, in a town of quiet and largely unparked streets, I had chosen a spot not far from the library, where a car could be left for hours without exciting interest or speculation.

Two constables stood immobile at the gates to *Wentworth*, displaying the kind of boredom policemen attach to what the rest of us see as thrilling. On the facing pavement a sizeable crowd had assembled to gaze in fixed and hungry fascination at the house, though its lack of any visible indication of mayhem must have been sadly disappointing. There was, presumably, an aura of murder, the exhilaration of whispered guesses. Which window is the bedroom, is that her BMW, will the husband appear, or better still a shrouded body? Some, and not all of them pressmen, held cameras; the occasional flash sent sparks of drama falling short of the house. Reporters formed a clique apart from the others, a huddle of anoraks and Barbours, the forethought of thermos flasks, a sour atmosphere of waiting too long and expecting nothing but a change for the worst in the weather. There was only one face among them that I recognized – I did a smart about-turn and thought I'd escaped without being seen. But a voice caught up with me before the safety of a nearby street corner.

'Sandy! Sandy bloody Douglas!'

I turned. 'Fancy seeing you here, Jack.'

We devoted a moment to casting dyspeptic glances over our wretched fortunes, our fall from grace. It is the destiny of crime reporters to expect great things of one another in the flush of youth, to be made miserable by seeing a mirror held up to one's own despairing later years, the squalor of association with crime, the unhappy ending of wholly unsuitable newspapers. Jack Moffat and I had once taken bets on which of us would win the Booker and which the Nobel Prize for Literature. I had never thought to see him in the dismal clutches of the Scottish *Dispatch*, nor he to see me, his mournful expression said, scraping an uncertain living from the comings and goings of owls. I should never have gone to the house. A past I'd believed far behind me had suddenly caught up with a vengeance.

'The word is you knew her,' he said.

'Small town, Jack. Casual acquaintance, like I know the

butcher, the baker and the girl at Victoria Wine.'

'Quick to the scene, I hear. Out on the yacht doing a nifty exclusive with the husband. Spelt with a capital P for prime and an upper case S for suspect.'

'I was offering the succour of friendship, nothing more. Haven't you heard, Jack, I'm no longer in the business of trading in others' misfortunes?'

'Come on, Sandy . . . I read your tight-lipped piece. Not a mention of being ahead of the pack, no proud boast of being first man into Port Stanley. What are you keeping up your sleeve?'

'Maybe the earth-shattering news that any hack who thinks Duncan MacRae is a suspect is chasing the wrong story. And likely to get a nasty addition to his expenses under the heading of libel.'

'You think so, huh?'

'Don't you?'

'Me, Sandy? Allergic to alibis, always have been.'

'So what's your big theory? MacRae swam ashore?'

'Could have done. He's a strong swimmer.'

'Inside information or wishful thinking?'

He smirked with the vanity of superior knowledge. His face had become gaunt and lined since I'd seen him last, his eyes sunken in retreat from lingering too long on the seamier side of the human condition. But the smirk was exactly as I remembered: bad habits stay forever young.

'There's a traditional New Year's dip at the marina,' he said. 'Ever been?'

'I've heard of it. I'm usually too hung over from Hogmanay to want out in the cold watching nutcases jump in freezing cold water.'

'My sentiments exactly. Fucking madness, breaking the ice for a swim in the middle of winter. What are they trying to prove? Bravery, stupidity, virility? Freeze your fucking prick off, more like.' He moved nearer, hunching his shoulders to keep the confidence between the two of us. 'But Mr Duncan MacRae has a penchant for the cold and wicked. He's one of those nutcases of whom you speak

130

. . . plunges in with the best of them at Rhu, a few lengths of freestyle round the icebergs, emerges red as a lobster proclaiming it's good for your health. Every New Year's Day, Sandy pal, did he ever mention it?'

I couldn't recall hearing Duncan allude to this, which probably meant he hadn't. Strange, since he had an inordinate liking for tales of his prowess, and could elevate a morning's walk up Ben Vorlicht into a feat surpassing the ascent of Everest.

'A significant fact, this?' I said, appearing to restrain a yawn only out of politeness.

'Very bad news for alibis, even to a mind as trusting as mine.'

'So he swam from the yacht? Underwater, presumably, so as not to be spotted.'

'It's possible, Sandy. All I'm saying is he could have done it.'

'He arrives on land soaked to the skin, wearing only swimming trunks. Now what?'

'His flash BMW's right there in the marina car park. He does a quick dash home . . .'

'Then the car seat will be dripping wet . . .'

'Not necessarily, not if it's leather.'

'Velour actually, Jack. And it wasn't wet. It so happens I looked. And, sadly for you, saw a very dry and spotless interior. A rather Germanic interior, it seemed to me, suggesting that the only crime Duncan MacRae ever commits is breaking the speed limit.'

His contemplation of me was a study in indecision. First he was admiring, then dismayed at being beaten to a story, and finally a picture of regret in his realization there had been no story in any case.

'So you thought to check . . .' he said, finding immediate need of a cigarette. He didn't offer one and I doubted that he cared whether I smoked or remembered that I didn't.

'A purely precautionary move,' I said. 'In case other papers make a mess of the facts.'

131

'He could have covered the seat,' Jack said in riposte. 'With one of those plastic thingamies they use in garages.'

'Then the police will doubtless have found puddles of Clyde water on the carpets. We shall be hearing anon, as they say.'

'Ah,' he muttered, becoming downcast.

'Besides . . . if he used his own car to get home, why did he try to take hers after doing the deed?'

'You're a bloody pain,' he moaned, 'same as you always were.'

'And why was the bonnet of his car stone cold, like it hadn't been driven in hours?'

'You checked that too?'

'Indeed I did.'

His feet shuffled somewhat, he puffed without gratification at his cigarette, his desolate eyes held a bleary longing for a drink. He sought the commiseration of a new and scandalous thought.

'It's plain old rape and murder, then. By an unknown assailant.' His hands gave this the benefit of enormous headlines. 'Who is still at large,' he added, and cheered up enormously.

'*Was* she raped?' I enquired with no particular show of interest.

'Sort of.' Now he grew defensive.

'Come on, Jack, what the hell's a sort of rape?'

'All will be revealed when I'm good and ready.'

'Tomorrow's *Dispatch*?'

'Maybe. Depends how deep I have to dig in the proverbial graveyard.'

'Was there a press conference I missed, a police briefing someone forgot to tell me about?'

'Private sources,' he answered smugly.

What I particularly disliked about Jack that afternoon was the recognition in him of those very qualities I most deplore in myself. There must be a mould somewhere in which newspapers cast the characters of those they most wish to use and shame. I don't look remotely like Jack, can't drink to anything like the impossible extremes he can, have only once to my knowledge screwed the same woman, and to my eternal relief did it first. But we have a shared disregard for clothes, doggedness written all over us, and an identical smugness when in sole possession of something newsworthy, however trivial. He was decidedly not spinning me a yarn. It seemed only fair that I should reciprocate in like manner.

'I have sources too,' I said.

'Not this one.'

'Mine gave me a photo of Mrs MacRae. Exclusive and recent, well lit and sharply focused. She looks very rich, very beautiful and extremely prone to rape. The sort of woman, Jack, even the hardest of bastards would weep buckets over.'

'The further you sink,' he said, 'the better your lies get.'

'Trouble is, it's wasted on me. My London rag has no great interest in murder, as you'll have noticed.'

He stamped his cigarette underfoot. 'My car awaits,' he declared, grabbing my arm in eager entreaty. 'To take you and your filthy hound any place of your choosing in this stuffy hole of a town.'

His was not an old saloon, maybe for all I knew even a comparatively new and costly model, but he'd reduced it as he did all his cars to a slovenly state of mobile anarchy. The puny capacity of the ashtray was an insult to his consumption, the front seat wells were ankle deep in dog-ends. At the back, a mess of chewing gum, sweet papers, ice cream wrappers, smeared chocolate and stains of mucous green slime brought new meaning to the concept of family motoring. In spite of which, Jack still found the proud ownership to complain roundly about having a dog on the back seat.

'Well?' I asked. 'What exactly is a sort of rape?'

'When I've seen the photo,' he retorted.

His misery returned briefly in my study. He sat with a glass of scotch, gazing everywhere as I searched between

133

piled up books on a shelf where I had a vague recollection
of leaving the photo.

'Christ,' he exclaimed, 'do you write for your rag or
publish it?'

I looked over my shoulder. His head was turned
upwards, his stare at the ceiling was frankly incredulous,
as if he'd never seen such height and ostentation and
couldn't believe his eyes.

Aileen had given me the snapshot early in our affair. An
omission on my part: I should have foreseen that she'd
expect me to ask – she took it for granted I'd want some
memento of her. A faithful if rather soulless likeness,
capturing her dark and slender good looks, suggesting in
her direct and faintly amused gaze at the camera a
humorous nature, an independent streak to her character.
What was missing, of course, was her voice. No photo
could do her justice: if the camera didn't lie about Aileen
nor did it tell enough of the truth. Which lifted a sudden
weight from my mind. The photo could with clear
conscience be surrendered up to the tabloid press. It
showed an attractive woman any man of spirit would want
in his bed, but nothing about her said she'd be ready to
consent. Quickly I thought to check the back and found
no inscription. Briefly, deliciously, the photo spoke with
that breathy and seductive voice of hers. Wanting what
marriage didn't provide, she'd said, was not the same as
wanting to be done with marriage. She'd give freely of sex,
allow stolen moments from her life, even the compliment
of a wistful yearning for me at times when I wasn't around.
What she'd never do, let's be level-headed about things,
darling, was put this in writing.

The photo was snatched from my hand. Jack had come
up behind me as I fell into reverie.

'Where did you get this?' he demanded.

'Sound provenance,' I replied. 'Legally and reputably
obtained. As if you care one way or the other.'

'Sure this is her?'

'See its value?' I pointed out. 'All those pictures of her

134

this morning yet it's like you're seeing the victim for the very first time.'

'I asked if this is her, Sandy . . .'

'Want a signed affidavit?'

'Not a bad idea, knowing you.'

'Well you'll have to take my word. That photo didn't come from me. I'm signing nothing.'

He made a weak pretence at being on the point of refusal but his lustful expression told the true story. He'd sell his soul to the devil to possess Aileen. I felt oddly proud of her – even in death she had the power to bewitch.

To clinch the deal, I poured another whisky into his glass. He went through a period of twitchy doubting then, as if wondering whether he could honour the bargain. This problem he resolved by thrusting the photo out of my reach for ever in an inside jacket pocket. He tipped his glass at me, took a lengthy and savoured taste and became as near happy as his presence of doom would allow.

'What I mean by sort of,' he began, 'is not rape as you or I would do it.'

'Quite,' I said, since he stopped for some reason and I had no wish to argue.

'Not that I ever have,' he continued. 'But the object of rape, it seems to me, is consummation. To put it in and get it off. Am I being clear?'

I merely nodded for more.

'Otherwise, why go through all the hassle? Might just as well go to bed with a naughty book and a box of tissues, right? I mean, rape's a serious business. Either do it properly or not at all, leastways that's my view and I'm making allowances, Sandy, for the fact that your average rapist isn't exactly the lad next door. Now as I understand it, as I'm led to believe, he got it in all right and rape there was, up to the moment of coming. But then he went all bloody Catholic on her, seems to have done a quick withdrawal. Came everywhere on her but in her. More than usually virile by all accounts, went off like bloody Mount Etna.'

He looked over to where I sat in a state of dazed schizophrenia. Part of me was bitterly regretting having begun this, another part cried out to hear more, to learn the worst. I could think of no humanly decent reason to let him continue, no ready means of asking him to stop. A husband, I thought, might need to be told every sordid detail, a lover should have the right to be spared them.

I managed to find a steady voice. 'Presumably, Jack, rape takes as many forms as there are ways of screwing.'

'Very probably so,' he agreed. 'The big difference is, screwing does not normally bring on an attack of death. At least not, for all that I've tried, the way I screw.'

'Hold on. Are you saying she was dead when this happened?'

'As I've heard all this, and early days remember, post mortem yet to come and the men in the white coats still sticking litmus paper in test tubes . . . forensics could be in for a sticky problem – excuse my pun. Was she alive during the rape? Did he forget his condom and go suddenly sweet and considerate, decide to spare her the risk of pregnancy? Or was she dead at this stage? See where that avenue leads us, Sandy. Because your necrophiliac is a whole new class of rapist, I mean mad as a bloody cuckoo. The kind that goes round raping dead bodies is likely, believe you me, to think spurting all over them is the normal way that sex is done. Now I'm not guaranteeing my source is the world's greatest expert on forensics, because he isn't. But he's been around, shall we say, for a good few years and the way he tells this—'

'—Around in the police?' I asked.

Jack spread his hands, claiming to have no idea. 'Maybe,' he conceded. 'The thing is, it could be difficult to say scientifically whether she was dead when he did the hot gushes all over her. At least that's what I'm told. Meaning a headache for our friends in blue. Are they after an ordinary nutter, a fairly normal rapist if there is such a thing? Or a real fruitcake, a laddie who doesn't like his women alive and doesn't exactly go a bundle on them when they're dead? You see, Sandy, playing amateur psychologists for a moment, there's apparently a well known angle to this business of where you want your sperm to end up. The rapist who comes inside a woman is conceding her domination over him, leaving proof she made him do it. His is the greater physical power but sexually she is the stronger. The fruitcake, on the other hand, is showing his total contempt. He's obsessed that women are out to control him. His victim desires his manly sperm inside her, that's his hang-up, so he leaves it outside. She doesn't deserve what he's got to offer.'

'Whose is the theory, Jack?'

'A shrink at the University. Reasonably reliable, we use him sometimes for background.'

'Is this kosher?'

'Is the photo?'

'Look, all you have to do is show it to her hairdresser, or at any one of a dozen local shops. They'll confirm that's Aileen MacRae.'

'I know. And nor do I pay dud money for good merchandise.'

'Then the police have got the murderer's signature . . .'

'And how. Written in copious splashes of sticky white ink.'

'Still think it was Duncan MacRae . . . ?'

He showed nicotine stained teeth in a grin of shameless connivance. 'Bit of a waste of all that underwater swimming, I'd say, to go leaving a calling card at the scene.'

'So why were you acting earlier as if you thought it was him?'

'Because, Sandy pal, it was my miserable bad luck to be born a fucking Scot, not somewhere like Miami where they have a home delivery service for murders, and the weather's kind to tired and frozen feet. This is a good murder so far – money, a yacht and a rare touch of class. I don't want it spoiled, see my point, by some nameless young lager lout with tattoos and a fucking social worker. Don't kid me you and MacRae were close buddy buddies. Be honest, wouldn't you like it to be him?'

'No,' I said. 'In all honesty I don't want it to be him.'

Nine

'Her husband's a friend,' I volunteered. 'At least he seems to regard me as a friend. I've never really worked out how best to think of him.'

Isobel Lockhart, who comes once a week to clean my apartment, had picked up the *In Memoriam* card from my mantelshelf. She is too placid and unenquiring to ask directly, so I considered some explanation advisable. She shook her head sadly that such a terrible thing could happen, dusted vigorously underneath as if this was her sole reason for having picked up the card, then returned it to the shelf. I formed the clear impression she was consumed with curiosity, absolutely dying to ask more, but the appearance of the black-edged card perhaps carried religious overtones for her – Isobel is an avid churchgoer, devout and trusting in beliefs – and she'd decided a respectful silence was called for.

A week had gone by, the town held its breath. No newspaper has ever found the courage or words to announce when a story is dead. The nearest I saw to candour came on an inside page of the *Dispatch*, where I thought to read no further than a small, disheartened admission of defeat: MACRAE KILLING – HUNT CONTINUES.

Meanwhile, Duncan had moved in great secrecy to bury Aileen. The Press had given up haunting his gate, making a police guard there no longer necessary, though any scent of a funeral would have brought reporters running in droves. So he'd acted, I assumed, much as he would with a covert business deal. There was even a touch of under-cover high finance about the card. I was reminded rather

of those tersely clandestine advertisements on the city
pages – which not being an investor I've never quite
understood – announcing, as a matter of record only, that
shares in such and such a company have been taken up by
a motley collection of banks. It had been the family wish, I
was informed, for Aileen Fiona MacRae's funeral service
to be conducted privately. As previously provided, she
had been laid peacefully to rest at a much loved church,
which the card omitted to identify. No flowers please, but
a donation could be sent to her favourite charity, the
Scottish Society for the Prevention of Cruelty to Animals.
To my growing list of new knowledge about Aileen, I now
added her middle name, the surprise that she knew what a
church was, let alone loved any, and a hitherto unsus-
pected soft spot for animals. I reflected, as occasionally
before after a burial, that one too often learns in death
what would more usefully be known of the living. When
we'd lain together sometimes in bed, wondering what to
say next to each other, perhaps we might have shared an
interest in dogs or a passion for exploring old churches.
Who can say? Duncan's card came as a sharp reminder
that an affair is between strangers, a meeting of bodies not
minds.

'I'd appreciate it,' I added, 'if you'd make no mention
of seeing that.'

'What, me?' Isobel said.

'Idle words have a way of travelling,' I pointed out. 'I
get the feeling Mr MacRae doesn't want any talk of a
funeral reaching the Press.'

Isobel sniffed loudly in response. Seeking revenge for
this slur, she pounced with a great deal of muttering on the
tops of some books, choosing to ignore my frequent
instructions that libraries should have a patina of dust, a
long tradition through the history of literature.

I watched from my armchair, musing over the mysteries
of women, their ability to be several utterly different
people wrapped up in a single body. In Isobel's case, a
plumpish body of such unprepossessing domesticity that

140

without a duster or Hoover to hand she seems to be missing a limb. For a time, I'd believed her to have no interest beyond things that could be cooked, vacuumed or laundered. Then one day she'd taken an old leather-bound volume from my bookcase of classics, fretted loudly over the state of its cover, and grown dewy eyed as she dipped into the pages.

'Do you like *Jane Eyre*?' I asked.

'I've always been keen on the Brontës. Charlotte and Emily.'

Hastily, she'd closed the book and replaced it in the case, as if I'd caught her slacking at work.

'Any particular favourite?'

'Hard to say, Mr Douglas. They're all so good, it's difficult to choose.'

'Which other authors do you like?'

'Jane Austen. Dickens. And I'll tell you who I'm really going a bundle on right now . . .' She stopped abruptly, blushing a bright red.

'Yes . . . ?'

'I only read,' she said then. 'I've no opinions to speak of. Whereas you're a writer. Books are your business.'

'I wish they were. But would you like my professional opinion on *Jane Eyre*?'

'Rather not, if you don't mind, Mr Douglas. You'd probably ruin it for me.' And she pressed a foot on the Hoover button, an end to frivolous chatter.

Isobel concealed a brain behind that bovine and chubby face of hers, with its assortment of guileless expressions. As I was to discover, she was active in numerous community affairs. She would cajole money out of me for an endless succession of worthy causes, for all of which, on enquiry elsewhere, she was the local leading light. But she did not converse. I developed several theories to explain this reticence. She was naturally shy. Or her husband beat her and she distrusted all men. Or she'd had an old-fashioned upbringing – I was her employer, living in a grand part of town, she knew her place. Whatever the truth, her lack of communication irked me at various times. I took it personally. I wanted to believe the fault lay in her, a nagging suspicion however placed the blame squarely with me.

Isobel's other mystery was to do with appearance. The strange phenomenon, to put it succinctly, that when she first began cleaning for me I'd have been hard put to say she had an appearance at all. Later, with familiarity, came a vague set of impressions to do with cheerful smiles and a double chin that was jolly despite not seeming appropriate for a woman so young, and of large dresses, never quite in fashion, that I imagined she obtained through her many charities, probably making the Christian gesture of paying at least twice what anyone else would be asked.

On this particular morning – here's the mystery – she'd arrived with an appearance meriting a second glance. Actually, a number of longish stares, as it happened. Not an especially feminine or enticing appearance, but somehow wholesome, a lot more woman than the average – she made up in quantity what she lacked in other departments. The mystery deepened when, on closer examination, I could discern no visible difference whatsoever in Isobel from the last time I'd seen her, or the time before that. This has happened previously, just when I'm at my most vulnerable. Maybe it's to do with losing someone. Nature does indeed abhor a vacuum.

I considered, as I followed her movements from my chair, that the most plump and domestic of bodies can exert a bafflingly powerful allure. Whether I get an attack of hunger for the plain and ordinary, as a gourmet might for a taste of homemade pie, or whether Isobel has an occasional flush of hormones is not something I've managed to resolve. Entire months can go by when she is just the cleaning woman, a species devoid of sex, then I am struck by an immediate and overwhelming urge for exactly the kind of ample compliant flesh Isobel is blessed with in abundance.

Sex was much on my mind that day. I was horrified to

calculate that my last bedding of Aileen had been – what? – a full four weeks ago. And Caroline was lost for ever. As I'd trailed her dutifully towards Hermitage Park a night or two earlier, she'd spun rapidly on her heel for a withering glare brimful of warnings about calling the police, and who the hell did I think I was! A moment's rueful self-pity as she stormed off into the park – how, when we'd finally come face to face, remarkably near the spot I'd planned for our meeting, could she confound me with such a look of contempt? But thereafter any regrets I nursed were for the weeks I'd wasted on an ill-fated affair. Might as well face facts, the unhappy realization we were never meant to be. Quite simply, Caroline had proved too young for the subtleties of an adult involvement. But she left a hole in my life. I was marooned in an empty present, confronting a lone and uncertain future.

So I went to my desk, switched on the word processor and, while Isobel buzzed the Hoover over my threadbare carpet, I wrote of putting my hand up her skirt, where the moist warm welcome that awaited brought such instantaneous relief I emitted a deep and satisfied grunt of fulfilment. Fortunately, because of the Hoover, she seemed not to hear.

One of my most inspired seductions. It was like those Old Masters where the painting contains within itself the same scene, only smaller. And presumably so on into infinity. My scheme was that the seduction on the screen should be an integral part of the actual seduction, my invitation to fuck. Isobel would come by with the Hoover. I'd flatter by asking her advice, a writer needing help with his grammar. As she read the words on the screen, I'd smooth my hand gently over the twin globes of her rounded backside, down past the hem of her skirt on to a thigh such as I dreamed of, a Rubensesque thigh, a man-sized helping of womanly flesh. And there my hand would pause a while, provocative and tantalizing, as she read of the downward meanderings it had already travelled, my intense longing for her luscious thighs – soft but sturdy

143

gateposts, I'd written, the entrance to all I desired – before she then read further, moving ahead of my actions, learning of the artistry and invention in a writer's fingers before this was actually revealed, experiencing through words the slow upward slide of my caress and the easing open of her legs to invite the entry of my creative probings. At which moment, just as foretold, her legs would indeed ease open, such is the magic of eloquent words.

Isobel tidied the room oblivious to all this, humming quietly to herself in a drone not unlike that of the vacuum cleaner. Sometimes I needed to gaze across and check details. She was about thirty, I presumed, one of those women so intent on a husband and home they make the leap straight from podgy adolescence into their cosy ideal of married middle-age. My writing gave her a youthful glowing face, the somewhat slimmer waist she doubtless yearned for. Since she wore no stockings, I praised the natural beauty of her skin, went into raptures over the silken bareness when I stroked that dream of a thigh. Full breasts, rather on the shapeless side, which I decided not to mention. I gazed over as, back turned to me, she stretched to a high shelf, her skirt riding up over pale plump legs. An athlete's legs, I wrote, the very incarnation of graceful power. And it occurred to me, seated at my desk and seducing her with such confident virtuosity, that the words were there on the screen plain to see, she had only to glance in passing, and that I hadn't felt so relaxed, as deliciously satiated, in weeks. Since, in fact, the last time I'd screwed Aileen. I found a new and daring excitement in seducing Isobel while she shared the same room in complete ignorance of being seduced. A feeling not unlike the euphoric fatigue, in every muscle of the body, that comes with a sexual climax. I wondered then whether writing about seduction was as much as I ever needed. Whether, possibly, the real thing would come a poor second best and silken bareness turn to flabby disappointment.

But there is no accounting for urges of the flesh. Stealing another swift look over the shoulder, I saw Isobel now on a chair to dust the tallest of my bookshelves. She'd hitched up her skirt, her legs were naked and, at full reach, their muscular thickness was all too apparent. My head went dizzy at the thought of their tight and clammy grip about me, and I simply could not imagine how I'd ever considered her plain, how we'd resisted each other so long, squandered so much time.

Would it have happened this way? Would it have happened at all? I honestly think so. I had only to invite her over to where I sat, commence the flattery, begin sliding my hand over her plentiful thigh.

But I made the fatal error of allowing Aileen briefly into my consciousness. Back to the clutches of working women, I thought, and for a fleeting moment, with my attention on Isobel's diligent dusting of books, I harboured a doubt whether sweaty couplings on my desk could hold a candle to the soapy fragrance of Aileen after a bubble bath. I remembered her cool slimness in fresh laundered sheets, the scent of lavender polish as we'd screwed on the Steinway.

Isobel wobbled precariously on the chair, her cleaning cloth fell to the floor, swirling a cloud of dust in a beam of light from the window. An awful jolt to the memory – for all its variety, sex with Aileen hadn't extended to the wearing of gloves! *Why hadn't I remembered before!* There must often have been more of my fingerprints in her bedroom than Duncan's, and in far more eyebrow-raising places. How often was the house dusted? And how thoroughly?

I jumped up. 'Got to go out,' I muttered.

'Don't mind me,' Isobel answered as she climbed rather heavily down from the chair.

I found her a spare door key. 'See to the mortice on the front door, would you, as you leave? Otherwise my insurance counts for nothing.'

'Quite right too. All the valuables you've got to steal.'

Isobel is too good natured for sarcasm but she indulged in the droll flicker of a smile.

'And don't let Flora get out. She's got a thing going with a sex-mad hound called Archie.'

Isobel looked at me full, frank and very wide eyed, not a thing she usually does. Her smile changed from drollness to a grin of titillation, lips sufficiently parted to reveal pointed and – I was startled to find – surprisingly predatory teeth. If I'm not mistaken, she also flounced her hips more than was decent.

'Mean old you,' she cooed. 'For all you know, poor wee bitch is dying for it.'

In view of which, I had a quick change of mind. Instead of discarding what was on the screen, I saved it for a later day. Maybe Isobel had noticed the way I sneaked glances at her that morning, quite possibly my state of high arousal transmitted to her, triggering something in response. Who can explain these instant awakenings between the most unlikely of couples? I preferred to believe in the sheer unstoppability, the inexorable momentum, of sexual attraction once set in motion.

Isobel might not know it yet but I'd already seduced her. The act was as good as done.

Ten

It had been Duncan's house when I first came to call. Perhaps because it was so exactly what I expected of him, I felt badly let down. I was going through a phase of wanting to be rid of him from my life, and if our friendship was to be worth continuing I needed him to surprise me, to be less conventional, something other than a small town businessman. I well remember my deep disappointment at the suburban dullness of the house, its failure to rise to the heights of vulgarity. Secretly, I wanted a house I could loathe, a tasteless monument to the making of money, spectacular, brazen and hideous, a house that socked you in the eye in the grandest tradition of self-made men. I'd have rather admired Duncan for something Gothic and truly awful. Certainly it was tasteless, but only in the sense of being an average sort of dwelling, without any style. It looked the type of bungalow a bank manager might aspire to, except a good deal bigger, while the flat expanse of forecourt was somehow commercial in appearance, as if visitors were expected to park, transact their business and quickly leave.

On that first visit, I'd stopped my car somewhat hesitantly at the gate and, as if sensing my hostility, the lights had flooded on, instantly blinding. Subsequently, I made a point of coming on foot having parked round the corner: my old Volvo didn't look right with the house, a misfit among the Mercedes and Jaguars. Arriving thereafter at night, I played a game with the lights, seeing what distance I could sneak up the drive without being detected. I never got far. Like Duncan, the house was ever alert, impossible to catch unawares.

My attitude mellowed with further visits. I came to think of it as the MacRaes', home to Duncan and his wife, a regular hang-out for dinner and drinks. The house went up considerably in my estimation. I regarded it as a country club, no more attractive externally than these modern clubs tend to be, the members a dull and stuffy bunch, but the dining room served passable cuisine, the bar was outstanding, and the accounts department so miraculously remiss they never remembered to send out bills.

Then, finally, came those halcyon days when it was simply Aileen's, our love-nest, and if I could still not bring myself to view the house as an architectural triumph, my pulse beat faster as I sauntered up the drive. I even fell to thinking it not such an eyesore after all. Once, looking back as I left in an especially exhilarated mood, Aileen and the house became as one in my mind, desirable, costly and recumbent. A name occurred to me for the style – Scottish Horizontal. And, for that one and only time, I envied Duncan his money.

But now? Curtains were tightly drawn at the windows, the forecourt empty of cars, a woeful air of desolation. The house had the appearance of being boarded up, closed for the season, a sad and abandoned relic of better times, of past pleasures, like a failed roadhouse, something in a resort town nobody much came to any more. Of all the emotions it had stirred in me, I had never expected the place to evoke my sympathy. Had it become a mausoleum to Aileen? The reclusive hideout of a wealthy eccentric? I couldn't decide.

Driving in at the entrance, I saw that the street was deserted except for a tradesman's van several houses along. By now, I presumed, cars no longer stopped openly outside although some, probably, slowed to a crawl as they passed in keen and morbid contemplation. I almost expected a FOR SALE sign, and assumed, since none could be seen, Duncan had concluded that while murder excites interest it has a depressing effect on price.

148

No answer after several lengthy rings at the door. I could hear the bell jangling inside, distant and hollow. The house seemed empty. Were the BMWs gone elsewhere or parked in the garage? In a last attempt, I put my mouth to the letter-box and shouted for Duncan, calling my name. Then a sound of footsteps from the hall before the door opened a crack.

'If you don't feel like visitors,' I offered, 'you've only to say.'

'Grateful to see a friendly face for a change.' Duncan peered out like a hunted man. The door widened further, he stuck his head through the gap. Only when he'd stared suspiciously in every direction at the street outside did he consent to admit me.

'They've been phoning day and night,' he said. 'They push notes in at the door. Rattle the letter-box and shove in their scruffy bits of paper.'

'The Press, you mean?'

A resentful nod. 'Offering me money for interviews, for what they call my story. Can you imagine . . . the very last thing I need, their money.'

He looked terrible, as if he hadn't slept or shaved for days, and smelled strongly of drink, not the convivial smell of a night on the town, a stale sour stink I recognized only too well which comes out of misery, solitude and losing count of bottles. But he brightened considerably once I was in the house. His usual hospitable style became apparent: he insisted on helping me out of my Barbour, carrying it off to the cloakroom in the manner of a brisk and fussy manservant. With a great deal of sweeping open of doors, he led me to his airy den overlooking the rear garden, where funereal gloom gave way to bright windows and, on the patio outside, a fountain splashed merrily into an ornamental pool. Having made me comfortable in an easy chair, Duncan then departed for quite some while, returning with a generously filled glass in each hand. I guessed he'd run through his stock of clean glasses and had to do some quick washing up.

'Sandy, you old devil,' he enthused, pushing a whisky at me. 'So good to see you.'

'And you. Bearing up well, I hope?'

His face grew long and troubled. 'Ever had that feeling of being the last man left in the world?'

'Once or twice,' I confessed.

'Far from pleasant, believe me.'

'I'd have come round sooner. But one can never be sure in these situations. I didn't want to intrude.'

This sentiment clearly appealed to him. 'You know, you're probably right,' he said. 'Here I am, stuck in the house, feeling sorry for myself, wondering if my friends are ostracizing me. And maybe they're all being bloody decent, not calling round out of consideration.'

'Almost certainly,' I agreed.

He played with his drink. 'Did you mind terribly,' he enquired, 'not being asked to the funeral?'

'I understood your reasons.'

'The few times I've been out it was like a fucking motorcade behind, the Press in hot pursuit. That wouldn't have been right, cameras and flashbulbs at a burial. So the police consented to help – I went roaring out of the drive, no warning or anything, and they quickly blocked the street to stop anyone following.'

'How was the service?'

'Bloody miserable, if you must know. That awful organ music, the smell of candles, the minister droning on in his dreary voice. I've no time for the Kirk – death's a depressing enough experience as it is. I only did it for Aileen's sake. She used to joke about funerals, Sandy. I've only been to church twice, she said, once for christening and once to get married – I owe them one more time. But it's not as if she was looking down from on high to give her approval.' He fell into a short introspective pause. 'Do you believe in the hereafter?' he asked cautiously, looking suddenly doubtful.

'No,' I answered.

'Me neither,' he said sadly.

We exchanged nervous glances, each expecting the other to speak. Meaning to smile, we merely twitched our mouths across the room. Conversation eluded us. So Duncan flopped into an armchair, where he slouched in the downcast manner of a man who wanted no other company but drink. My attention wandered out through the window to the playful fountain. Sparkles of winter sun glinted on the tumbling cascade and the jaunty sound struck a discordant note, too carefree, I felt, to be entirely proper so soon after tragedy. Then I cautioned myself it was the very normality of the sound I found disturbing; what Duncan must need right now, more than anything, was a break in the silence, the cheerful splash of water enlivening the house.

'Know the worst thing?' he said.

'What's that?'

'Having an alibi. You'd think, wouldn't you, that'd put an end to gossip and speculation. Oh, no.'

'There are times,' I said, 'when people can be very heartless.'

He nodded in a dispirited fashion. 'You're good with words, Sandy. Any idea what *alibi* means? In precise terms, that is.'

I had learned early in our acquaintanceship that Duncan has a way of posing certain questions, a guarded look about him, when he'd rather I didn't know the answer. I believe he only places a value on knowledge when, as with money, he possesses it while others do not. In a conciliatory mood, I gestured to hear his definition.

'It means, literally, being elsewhere. It means proof of not having done the deed.'

'Surely no-one seriously believes you—'

'It does not mean,' he interjected venomously, 'an excuse, a fabrication, a wicked lie. My God, you've no idea the anguish that fucking yacht's caused me! What's a man to do, for fuck's sake? No alibi and I'd understand accusations being made, I could hardly complain. But an alibi . . . that's even worse. You're a schemer, a

151

cold-blooded wife killer. As good as a plea of guilty, am I right?'

'Small town gossip,' I said. 'From small minds with nothing better to think of.'

'Exactly what I feel! Ignorance. And the cure for ignorance is education. I've been sitting here, alone but resourceful, telling myself that I'm not actually suspected . . . it's not Duncan MacRae who's misunderstood but the word *alibi*. I'm merely the victim of illiteracy. So I shall go round the town secretly placing dictionaries at people's bedsides. Like a benevolent Gideon, see what I mean? Then God will smile on the righteous.'

'Glad you can see the funny side of this,' I said.

His mouth drew tight in a bitter line. 'There's no funny side. None whatsoever.'

A train rumbled by in the near distance, a railway whistle shrieked. Duncan's garden overlooked an open field of scrubland bordered on its far side by an embankment carrying the West Highland Line. I never once saw cows grazing in the field, only sinister gatherings of hooded black crows, and when I'd first visited the house, heard the nearby idling of a diesel engine during dinner, almost the gruntings of some monstrous animal, I'd thought it strange Duncan hadn't chosen a more congenial site. But the line is infrequently used, hours can go by between trains, and on my trysts with Aileen I developed a fondness for their noises off, the whistles and clanking, the oddly old-fashioned sense of adventure railways can still convey. I'd promised Aileen a trip on the sleeper; we'd screw all the way north to Mallaig as the train rushed headlong through the night. Promises, promises, she'd said, but without any intention to rebuke, because promises between us were made to be broken. So they might as well be fine promises.

Thinking of Aileen served as a reminder why I'd come to the house.

Duncan had drifted meanwhile into a kind of daydream. He seemed hardly to be aware as I extracted the empty glass from his fingers. I found the living room in semi-darkness, its curtains drawn, and poured a stiff whisky at the bar there. On my way back, I paused by the grand piano. A fine film of dust dulled its usually burnished surface.

Duncan stirred himself as if from a slumber, readily accepting the drink.

'Is anyone looking after you?' I asked.

'Do I need looking after?'

'Frankly, this house could do with a good dusting.'

'I expect it could.'

'Don't you have someone to clean for you?'

'I used to have, a regular cleaning woman.'

'Used to . . . ?'

'She won't come here anymore, not after what happened. Squeamish, I suppose, the way women are.'

'Was she any good?'

'That was more Aileen's department than mine. But she always struck me as conscientious.'

'The reason I ask is, I've got a woman who cleans for me. Pretty reliable, and only charges about half the going rate. Her husband's in the navy, you see, she does it for pin-money. Want me to mention that you're looking for someone?'

'This sounds like something my secretary should organize for me.'

'How many days a week are we talking about?'

'She used to come every morning. Not weekends, of course.'

'A quick flap round with the duster, or hours of thorough cleaning?'

'How would I bloody know!'

I had already decided the wisdom of not pursuing this line of enquiry further when the phone gave two rings, then fell silent again. Besides, I'd learned enough – the piano had told all I needed to know. My fears about fingerprints had proved groundless. Dust is a natural partner to my existence, I am used to having it round me.

Whereas Aileen was incorrigibly bourgeois, a housewife at heart, addicted to the smell of polish. She would never have allowed that layer of dust, not a corner of the house escaped her attentions. I was instantly confident that no trace of my visits ever survived the following morning's cleaning sessions. And quite possibly that's the way she'd wished things to be. I've often thought that people who insist on excessive tidiness are in search of something, maybe themselves. As if they want no yesterdays, nothing left of the past.

Shortly, the phone rang again and Duncan answered. He listened for a moment, becoming puzzled before offering the receiver.

'For you,' he said.

'Detective Sergeant Grant here,' the caller explained.

'Yes . . . ?'

'Just wondering, Mr Douglas, if it's not too much trouble, whether you'd mind coming in for a chat?'

'To the police station?'

'I don't believe you've met my boss, Detective Chief Inspector Turnbull . . .'

'No, I haven't had that pleasure.'

'He reckons you could help with one or two points, sort out some niggling questions.'

'Is this an official invitation?'

'How do you mean exactly?'

'Would you advise that I bring my solicitor along?'

'Entirely up to you, Mr Douglas.'

'Can I refuse to come?'

'Certainly you can.'

'Except you'll then invite me more formally, am I right?'

'Well, it'd raise a few eyebrows here, your refusing, Mr Douglas. Why would you want to go doing that?'

'When did you have in mind?'

'No time like the present, is there? Want me to send a car or will you make your own way over? We're at Divisional Headquarters, Dumbarton.'

'I'd rather you didn't send a car,' I said in reply. 'I'm not sure I'd trust you to bring me back.'

When this conversation concluded, I began an explanation but Duncan would hear none of it, saying he'd known before answering the call that this would be police business. The two initial rings had been their idea – he'd needed some way of knowing when it was safe to pick up the phone. What with the bloody Press, he said, ringing at all hours. And the crank calls, weird voices on the answering machine, people not wanting to be recognized or people who were just plain weird. And I'd be amazed, he said, how many heavy breathers.

'They'll ask you about me and the yacht,' he predicted. 'About why we talked so long, and whether I acted distraught.'

'I've already been through all that with the police.'

He shrugged unemotionally. 'I get the impression I didn't behave as a grieving husband should . . . as the police in their greater wisdom *think* I should. I'm the fucking husband, I said the other day . . . till the day your wife is fucking murdered, I'm the fucking expert on how to behave.'

'How did they know I was here?' I wondered.

'They're outside in a van, watching the house,' he said, breathing a burdened sigh and throwing up his hands, as though, like taxation, this was a hazard of business.

'For what reason?'

'Car spotting. Writing down numbers. A bit of a long shot, if you ask me, but they're checking everyone who drives by.'

'The killer's hardly going to be so stupid, surely . . .'

'Exactly what I said. But curiosity might get the better of him, that's what they're hoping . . . it's been known before. Ever heard of the villain returning to the scene of the crime? I thought that was a cliché but sometimes it happens, so they tell me, the compulsion to come back becomes overwhelming. He's a psychotic, apparently. At least, that's the latest of several theories.'

155

'Well, of course he's a bloody psychotic!'

'Very probably so, Sandy, but have you any idea how commonplace psychotics are in this quiet little town of ours? The first thing the police did was question known sex offenders. Any idea how many? Five, maybe? Six?'

'About that kind of number,' I guessed.

'Fifty-three! Fifty-three in what they call the immediate area – men with past records of rape, child abuse, indecent exposure and God knows what other sorts of perversion. Yet they're free to roam our streets!' His chest puffed up in a display of righteous indignation. He looked ready to march on a demonstration, a worthy citizen forced into protest. 'But they're only the tip of the iceberg,' he continued. 'One of the neighbours, across the road there, reported she'd seen a taxi pass the house that afternoon. I assumed it meant nothing, a taxi going by, Helensburgh's full of taxis. But next thing I hear, the police are questioning every driver working the town. And it turns out there's cab drivers with criminal records! Can you believe this? They've done time in prison and the fucking council gives them a licence to pick up our women on the streets, collect young weans from school.'

'It's well known,' I pointed out. 'A regular scare story in the local rag. But we're talking about petty crime, mostly, not psychotic behaviour.'

'Then why did the police take so many statements from taxi drivers?'

'Maybe they were checking whether one of them saw anything suspicious in the street.'

Duncan snorted indignantly. 'Not the way I heard it.' He was staring wildly, a hoarse croak had entered his voice.

'A diverse list of suspects,' I observed. 'Known sex offenders. And taxi drivers.'

I ventured a regretful smile, a sad comment on the investigation so far. Duncan was uncertain at first how to take this reaction but eventually conceded a despairing sigh.

'Clutching at straws, aren't I?'

'Frankly, yes.'

'I want the bastard caught, Sandy.'

'Of course you do.'

'The trouble is, the police don't seem to know whether they're coming or going. They haven't a clue.'

'They must have something to go on, surely? What about fingerprints?'

'No such luck. He didn't leave any prints.'

'How can they tell?'

'From smudges on the broken window, apparently, and objects he touched. Seems he wore thick rubber gloves. They have ways of telling these things. It's all to do with forensics.'

So I need never have worried after all! But I was mindful not to show my intense feeling of relief.

Duncan took note of my reflective silence. 'Is something wrong?'

'The police,' I answered quickly. 'Won't do to keep them waiting.'

He escorted me to the hall, retrieved my coat from the cloakroom, assisted me into it with solemn courtesy. Maybe the deep shadows in the curtained hallway emphasized the hollows under his eyes, the stubbly gauntness of his cheeks, but he looked suddenly old and very tired. He shook my hand, imploring me to come back soon, promising I'd find him in better spirits.

'Can you see yourself out?' he asked, in a voice so meek it hardly seemed his. 'I try to keep well clear of the door.'

'Perfectly understandable,' I said.

His shoulders bunched defensively, while he gazed at me in a plea for salvation. 'Is it? I'm beginning to think, Sandy, I'll never go out again. And this is the very last house, in all the world, I want to be stuck in.'

157

Eleven

Dumbarton means little more to me than a name on signposts, a place to pass through, unheeded, on the drive to Glasgow, an urban sprawl of dual carriageways, a tedious succession of roundabouts. It is a town without a heart, entirely outskirts – you leave it behind with the puzzling sensation of having missed something. The beauty of the Clyde is scarcely visible, and a king's ransom of bonded whisky lies hidden in drab windowless rows of warehouses resembling aircraft hangers. Every official demand I receive originates in Dumbarton – it is the county town, a town of bureaucrats, its main business the filling-in of forms, the asking of questions, the sending-out of brown envelopes. In keeping with this dedication to clerkdom, Police Headquarters could easily be mistaken for a branch of the county offices, whose manicured grounds and dreary civic style of building it shares. I felt my status diminished by having to come here, an inhabitant from an outlying hamlet unceremoniously summoned to the local seat of power. I arrived in no spirit of ready cooperation.

Sergeant Grant came to escort me from the entrance hall. He shook my hand with a rough sweaty grip.

'How's that dog of yours keeping?' he enquired as he led upstairs to the next floor.

'Stuck at home,' I said. 'Probably wondering what's happened to me.'

'Guarding the house, I expect. In her friendly fashion.'

'Are you interested in dogs?' I asked, in a similar conversational vein.

'In men with dogs, you might say. Take a person like

158

yourself, Mr Douglas, who's otherwise living alone. Seems to me a dog is a substitute, a form of company without the commitment.'

'I've tried marriage, Sergeant. It's a very poor substitute for owning a dog.'

'My point exactly, if you don't mind my saying so.' He proceeded ahead down a corridor of closed doors bearing neat wee nameplates. 'What's that dog of yours called again?'

'Flora,' I said.

'Had it on the tip of my tongue!' he responded, and snapped his fingers in a brashly familiar gesture, as if we were old pals comparing girlfriends in a bar.

We entered a room where a lean and sharp-eyed man of forty or so rose from behind his desk to offer the suavely wooden handshake of a diplomat. 'Detective Chief Inspector Turnbull,' he declared in one of those voices that tells a great deal in a few short words. Glasgow accented, no attempt at refinement – almost certainly, I thought, a lad from a working family made good and proud of it. But quietly spoken, and voices like his are usually heard at full blast over the din of shipyard riveting, the roadside clatter of pneumatic drills. I had an immediate hunch he'd bellow when roused, a roar to raise rooftops.

I merely nodded, assuming he must know who I was, and began to sit down. But he clucked his tongue at Sergeant Grant, chiding him to take my coat away to be hung, and then enquired whether I preferred tea or coffee. When the sergeant withdrew on his errand, Turnbull searched some drawers before finding a tape cassette which he contrived with some difficulty to load into a recorder placed on his desk.

'You have to be Jack-of-all-trades in this job,' he muttered. 'Social worker, psychologist and damned recording engineer.' He frowned intensely and sighed to himself. For a while the complexities of the cassette so obviously defeated him I began to doubt his ability to detect the simplest of crimes. Which then caused me to wonder if this was the aim of the performance, a ploy to lull me into a false sense of security. And my very next reaction was to think myself paranoid at entertaining such a notion – why should Turnbull put on any kind of act for my benefit? With an apprehensive face, he jabbed a finger nervously at different buttons on the recorder. He looked so fearful of imminent disaster I began to feel nervous myself. So I tore my eyes away, to gaze absently round the room.

There was the sterile ambience to be seen in those offices in showroom windows which have desks and chairs, perhaps even a painting or two, but no permanent occupants, merely visitors coming and going. Calendars from local businesses hung on each of the four walls – Turnbull had his days and months mapped out before him whichever direction he faced. Indicating, I assumed, a meticulous devotion to schedules, unless he was only being impartial, showing no favour by accepting every harmless offering that came his way. I could imagine why a nearby pub would wish to be on good terms with him, but the suspicious side of my nature was pondering possible motives for a firm of funeral directors to reward the police with a calendar, when Grant returned carrying cups of tea on a battered tin tray. He sat to one side of the office, looked me over with hungry anticipation and gave a brisk rub of his hands, wanting to be down to business. Letting out a victorious 'Ah!' from under his breath, Turnbull finally mastered the controls. He lifted his eyes for a rather sad gaze across the desk. Then he cleared his throat with a muted cough, like a bank manager about to refuse a loan.

'I trust you've no objection to our recording this?' he began. 'It's for your own protection.'

'In what way?' I said.

'Isn't that obvious?'

'I've used a recorder myself sometimes for Press interviews.'

'I'm sure you have.'

'So I could nail my subject with his own words. If we fell out later, I mean, over what was said.'

Turnbull responded with a distinctly chill smile. 'Can we perhaps agree that an accurate record is in both our interests?'

'Might be,' I insisted.

'Quite,' he agreed tersely. 'Point taken.'

'Except, strictly speaking, it can't be in both our interests. If we come to a dispute over accuracy, only the one who's right will be happy. The other – could be you or me – will feel damned stupid he agreed to a recording. See what I mean?'

Turnbull sighed. 'You're a very pedantic man, Mr Douglas.'

'Words are my business.'

'And mine too. You'd be surprised, I think, to learn how often a conviction depends on words rather than visible clues.'

'The wrong word said in an unguarded moment,' Sergeant Grant contributed.

'Or the right one said by someone else,' Turnbull remarked to him. Then gave a little cough against the back of his hand and glanced quickly my way. So I flickered a smile to show I'd noted his pedantry, before saying I'd no objection to a recording – but if Grant had warned me beforehand I'd have brought my pocket dictaphone and we could have been doubly sure then, taken a recording each.

Turnbull peered at his watch. He touched a button on the recorder and started to speak. The time was 12.20 p.m. on Thursday the First of November. He was Detective Chief Inspector Colin Turnbull of L Division, Strathclyde Police. The interview was taking place in his office at Divisional Police Headquarters, Dumbarton. He would now ask those present to identify themselves.

'Detective Sergeant Donald Grant,' the other said.

'Alexander Blair Douglas,' I said in turn.

'Also known as Sandy, is that correct?'

'Yes.'

161

'What age are you?'

'Thirty-eight.'

I was asked for my date of birth and home address.

'Are you in full-time employment?'

'I'm a writer. A newspaper columnist.'

'You are going to be asked questions about the murder of Aileen MacRae in Helensburgh on the afternoon of Thursday the 25th of October this year. You are not bound to answer. This interview is being tape-recorded and may be used in evidence. I'll begin by pointing out that you are attending voluntarily. You may leave at any time.'

'Thank you,' I replied for no obvious reason.

'You were noted to arrive at the home of Mr and Mrs MacRae shortly after four p.m. on the afternoon of the crime.'

Turnbull paused for an enquiring look, so I shook my head.

'Can I ask you to answer verbally? I can't record a gesture.'

'I was passing, not arriving. There were large numbers of police at the house. I stopped, naturally enough, to ask what was wrong.'

'You had no business at the house that afternoon?'

'No.'

'No intention of calling?'

'None.'

'If there'd been no police in attendance, you'd have driven straight by?'

'Correct.'

'I understand that you told a constable at the scene you intended driving in at the gate but the police cars outside prevented you doing so.'

'I might have said something like that, yes.'

'So you weren't simply passing. You were planning to call at the house.'

'It was a flippant remark. Rather a lot of police cars blocking the entrance, you see.'

'Didn't I understand you to say earlier, before we began recording, that you use words with care?'

'Not, it seems, when talking to policemen.'

Turnbull pulled a face, dismissively raising his eyebrows.

'Can it be noted for the record,' I said, 'that the Chief Inspector has just made a facial gesture indicating disbelief.'

He sighed.

'And sighed in exasperation,' I added.

'How long have you been acquainted with the MacRaes?' he asked, in a voice now under iron control.

'Not terribly long. Roughly two years.'

'A close friendship?'

'Not especially. Duncan called on me at home sometimes and I called on him.'

Turnbull inclined his head towards Grant. 'What did Mr MacRae say to you, Sergeant? In describing Mr Douglas's motive for rowing out to the yacht.'

'A very dear friend, sir. Going to the yacht was a caring gesture. Other so-called friends he could think of would've run a mile from bearing bad news.'

'Duncan is effusive,' I explained. 'He exaggerates, as businessmen often do.'

'You called on him sometimes, you say. So why not that afternoon?'

'He wasn't at home, was he?' I replied. 'He was on his yacht.' And immediately realized I'd made a mistake. A quick resolution to myself to take longer in answering in future, to think carefully first.

'Can I ask how you knew that?'

'I didn't, not at the time. But he runs a successful business. I wouldn't expect him to be home during working hours.'

'You were driving past. You might have said to yourself – let's give it a try, see if my pal Duncan's in the house. Maybe he's got his feet up for a change and is absolutely dying for company.'

'I'm not in the habit of dropping in. When he wants me round, he gives a formal invitation. To dinner, usually.'

'Did he invite you today?'

'I'm sorry . . . ?'

'You called on him before attending this interview. Whose idea was that, his or yours?'

'Mine,' I said. 'He's suffered a terrible loss. I wanted to see how he was, let him know he's in my thoughts.'

'Very considerate of you, Mr Douglas.'

'A normal thing to do, in the circumstances.'

'You might think so, yes. But you're the only person so far to have called and offered condolences.'

'And what do you conclude from that?' I asked. 'Except this is a cruel and heartless world we live in.'

Turnbull tapped the tips of his fingers together and delivered a stare of thoughtful scrutiny. 'Well for one thing,' he said, 'the conclusion that your friendship must be closer than you'd have me believe. More as Mr MacRae described than as you portrayed it.'

'Entirely possible,' I agreed. 'I'm rather inclined to undervalue my friends.'

'You not only took the trouble to call, a humanitarian act I'm sure, you had the insight to do so on a Thursday. The day of the crime, one week later. A sort of tragic anniversary, in a manner of speaking . . . a day when Mr Douglas could be expected to be in special need of consolation.'

I held a steady face, made no reply.

'Was that, by any chance, the reason you went?'

'I believe you said I can refuse to answer questions?'

'Certainly.'

'Then I refuse. My reason was to do with Mr MacRae's bereavement. It can have no relevance to your investigation.'

'Your prerogative to think so.' Turnbull opened his hands angelically. 'Let's turn to Mrs MacRae. An oddly inadequate term, housewife, if the photographs I've seen do her justice. But there you are, that's what she was, a

164

housewife. Mercifully free of the need to earn a crust, often alone at home.' He paused pointedly. 'Ever consider a social call, dropping in for a chat?'

'Yes,' I replied to see the response. And was rewarded with an exchange of meaningful looks.

Turnbull cocked his head. 'When was this?' he enquired in his softest of voices, but with a quickening of undeniable eagerness.

'I *considered* dropping in, Chief Inspector. I thought better of it.'

'Can I ask why?'

I savoured this question for a moment or so, hoping the recording had captured his evident disappointment.

'Aileen was a marvellous hostess, good fun in company. But a woman, I rather think, of limited interests. Housewife is probably an apt description. I'm not much for tea and cakes in the afternoon, talking about interior decor and flower arranging or whatever else rich women fill their heads with.' As I spoke, I sent up a prayer imploring Aileen's forgiveness.

'Damned attractive woman, though,' Grant suggested. 'The kind some men wouldn't mind being bored by.'

'And married,' I pointed out. 'The kind some of us have more sense than to call on when their husbands are at the office.'

'Candidate for bloody sainthood,' Grant retorted.

Then a silence of some duration followed in which he studied me from under furrowed brows, his head tilting first one way then the other. Like, I thought, a heavy-weight in search of an opening, hoping his opponent would drop his guard. I yawned, stretching my legs, and the chair slid backwards with a gratifying squeal against the floor, setting the needle dancing on the cassette machine. Only a rustle of paper after that while Turnbull checked through some notes. At length he posed the inevitable question.

'Where were you on the day of the murder, immediately prior to your arrival at the house?'

'I'd spent the day with my brother,' I explained. 'He's the gamekeeper on the Cairnglas Estate. He was out shooting a fox. I went along to gather material for one of my wildlife columns.'

'What time did you leave there?'

'Roughly three thirty in the afternoon. I can't be more exact than that, I'm afraid.'

'Your brother will confirm this, presumably?'

'He'll confirm I was there,' I said. 'Whether he'll remember when is a different matter. Gordon's not very good about dates and times.'

'Is that his name . . . Gordon Douglas?' Grant enquired, pencil poised.

I nodded. 'You'll find him at Keeper's Cottage, Glen Cairn.' I made a pretext of pondering awhile before coming up with a further thought. 'His wife will probably remember, though. Phyllis never forgets a birthday . . . whether you take one or two sugars in your tea . . . things like that.'

'Phyllis Douglas,' Grant uttered melancholically, as he wrote the name down.

'You left Glen Cairn at three thirty or thereabouts,' Turnbull said, 'and arrived at the MacRaes' shortly after four. Going direct, that's only a ten or fifteen minute drive, I'd say.'

'I didn't go direct. I went home first.'

'Any particular reason?'

'I planned on writing my article, getting it over and done with. But my dog wanted some air, so I went for a drive instead.'

Turnbull regarded me strangely.

'She prefers cars to walking,' I said in explanation.

'Ahh . . .' Turnbull murmured, stroking his chin.

'Goes under the name of Flora,' Grant recited from the sidelines. 'Black. A funny old mix of breeds, by the look of her. Roughly the size of a labrad—'

'Does your brother have a dog?' Turnbull said, cutting abruptly across him.

'He's overrun with them. A dozen, I'd say. Maybe more.'

A look of surprise. 'Is he a breeder or something?'

I shook my head. 'Gordon's irredeemably soft-hearted. He takes in strays to save them being put down.'

Grant bent low over his notebook to make diligent note of this fact.

'Why do you attach such importance to dogs?' I queried.

'Do we?' Turnbull countered.

'You most certainly do.'

'And what leads you to that conclusion?'

'Och, come on!' I said. 'I was scarcely through the door before Sergeant Grant was quizzing me about my dog. He's amiable enough when he wants to be, but somehow I don't see him making idle conversation.'

Grant made a feeble spluttering noise.

'Not the subtlest of men,' I added. 'But then big men rarely are.'

Turnbull took his time responding. Lips tightly puckered, he ran a peevish gaze over me and the sergeant, seeming undecided which of us at that moment he most wanted to consign to the cells. 'You were a crime reporter,' he said finally. 'Show me how good you were. Let's hear your theory.' Folding his arms on the desk, he issued a faint smile of encouragement.

'You're looking for a man with a dog,' I reasoned. 'But not a dog like mine.' I paused to see if I was on the right lines.

'Go on . . .' he invited.

'Her hair's the wrong type, I suppose. Too straight, too coarse, perhaps, or the wrong colour. Yes, the colour's wrong . . . you're not after a black dog.' Again I paused but he made no response and little could be read into his impassive expression. 'Ah . . . I've got it! You found traces of dog hairs at the scene. Duncan doesn't own a dog, so you're considering the possibility they came from the murderer's clothes.'

'You'd have made a passably good detective,' Turnbull volunteered after a lengthy period of thought.

'I didn't go near Gordon's dogs,' I said hurriedly. 'That day or any day. They're too bloody wild for my liking.'

'Nobody suggested you did, Mr Douglas.'

'Sounded damned close to a suggestion to me. Why else ask about his dogs?'

'Tell you this, Donald,' Turnbull said, turning to Grant with a sigh of sufferance, 'I've never been keen on middle-class crime. They're so damned clever, these Helensburgh folk, too quick-witted. Much more agreeable, don't you think, dealing with stupid villains and dim witnesses?'

'Any time,' Grant said fervently.

'Are we through now?' I presumed, detecting an air of finality about the proceedings, and began to get up.

But Turnbull signalled me to remain seated. He reclined in his chair, making studious perusal of the ceiling. 'This article of yours,' he said. 'To do with a fox, I think you said. Am I to understand it described your brother shooting a fox?'

'Not exactly. It was about a fictional character shooting a fox.'

'But based on what you had seen that day, Thursday the 25th of October?'

'Yes . . .' A minor note of uncertainty was perhaps discernible in my reply because I couldn't foresee where this new line of enquiry might lead.

'So you intended to write that afternoon but instead went out in your car . . .'

'Yes.'

'. . . And discovered there'd been a murder, police everywhere at the MacRaes' house . . .'

'Yes.'

'Your mission of mercy ensued, the sad news delivered to Mr MacRae, sympathy and rum dispensed on his yacht.'

I chose merely to nod.

'Was the article ever written?'

'Written and published.'

'Which is useful from your point of view, one might conclude, since it provides some evidence as to your whereabouts that day. Not proof, I'll agree, but it's a fact in your favour.'

'I'm glad to hear that.'

'When was it published, by the way?'

'The following Saturday.'

'The 27th?' Grant inferred. 'Two days later?'

'I suppose so. Yes, I guess it must have been the 27th.'

'So, we can read this column of yours in a back issue,' Turnbull said, more as a statement of fact than a question. 'If we're so minded,' he added in an off-hand way, giving the impression he had no intention of putting himself to the bother.

'Don't expect great literature,' I warned. 'I'm only a humble hack.'

'But dedicated,' he suggested. 'A true professional. The show must go on.'

'Sorry . . . ?' I answered, becoming unsettled by the change that now came over Turnbull's manner, his steady transfixing stare and sinewy stillness. Quite suddenly he seemed ready to pounce.

'When did you find the time to write this article?'

'I can't remember, exactly.'

'Try, Mr Douglas. Try.'

'It must have been later that Thursday,' Grant offered with no semblance of being helpful. 'Or the Friday. That's if you were to meet a deadline for publication in Saturday's paper.'

'Thursday, I seem to recall,' I said hesitantly. 'After I got back from seeing Duncan.' I was horribly aware of being caught in a trap of my own making. The article had been written that afternoon – when I'd claimed to be with Gordon. I considered coming clean, admitting I'd lied, and quickly decided that would now only make things worse. A kind of righteous anger swelled over me at the irrelevancy of all these questions, the needless invasion of my privacy.

'Well?' I demanded, since nothing had been said for quite some time.

'Let's see if I've got this straight,' Turnbull stated. 'Your friend's wife had been murdered. You returned home and sat straight down to write a column for your paper. All in a normal day's work.' His expression was cast into a frozen mask, thin mouth turned down at the corners, eyes glinting with contempt. I detected a moralistic streak to his nature, someone who'd enforce the Ten Commandments, given half the chance.

'I have to earn a living,' I protested. 'I also find, which is not uncommon, that getting lost in work is the best possible way of coping with painful happenings.'

'Hmm,' Grant grunted in what could as easily have been scorn as agreement. Turnbull meanwhile gave no response at all, choosing to shuffle through his pages of prepared notes. Some of the pages were possibly typed interview reports but I couldn't see for certain and decided I oughtn't to be observed staring. I began wondering whether it was possible to act normally in this situation, whether there was any answer, any action, that could not be construed as unduly apprehensive. And I couldn't for the life of me work out why the hell I was apprehensive.

Finally Turnbull lifted his head. 'We're agreed, I think, that Mrs MacRae was an unusually attractive woman . . .'

See what I mean! What does one say to this? Where might agreement lead? What's the point in denial?'

'Passably so,' I said.

'Vivacious in company'

'Extremely.'

'So it wouldn't surprise you to learn she was having an affair.' These latest questions were recited as facts but with pauses, quiet intervals, calling for answers.

'What makes you think so?' I asked in return.

His hands widened in silent refusal to reveal his source. 'Surprised or not, Mr Douglas?'

'Frankly, I consider it most unlikely.' My cheeks began to burn and with a feeling of helplessness I realized my face was visibly reddening.

Turnbull promptly took notice. 'You don't strike me as a prudish man,' he said, adopting a curious frown. 'Are you deeply religious by any chance?'

'Far from it.'

'Some other reason, then, why you seem to disapprove of affairs?'

'Aileen,' I said, 'struck me as secure and happy. I can't imagine why she'd need to look outside marriage for attention, sex, novelty, any of the usual reasons for an affair. But if you're right and she did, what possible reason could I have for disapproval? That would be a private matter, between her and Duncan.'

Turnbull touched a button to stop the recorder. 'Who do you think?' he asked in a voice of beguiling innocence. 'Purely between these four walls.'

'Are you serious!' I exclaimed.

'You were a regular guest for dinner with the MacRaes. You've encountered a fair cross-section of their friends. Let's suppose, and it's purely supposition, that it's one of those men who was pursuing this liaison with Mrs MacRae. Anyone in particular strike you as likely? Fond glances exchanged, intimate giggles in the corner, that sort of thing?'

'No-one. The idea's preposterous.'

'You disappoint me profoundly, Mr Douglas.' Turnbull looked away in search of a second opinion. 'Don't you agree, Donald?'

'A distinct lack of imagination,' Grant offered loftily.

'Can you do this!' I protested. 'Turn the tape machine on and off to suit your purposes?'

Turnbull chose to ignore my challenge to his conduct. 'Go on,' he urged. 'Cast your mind back in search of wee clues. You're a writer, for heaven's sake, a better observer than most. Who do you reckon?'

'You're asking me to guess? To make accusations

against someone who's probably innocent? I can hardly believe I'm hearing this.'

'To make a suggestion, Mr Douglas, not to accuse. To point us in what might be a useful direction. In other words, to help the police investigate the most serious of crimes.'

'I thought,' I said in dignified yet scathing judgement, 'Aileen was murdered by an intruder, a stranger.'

'That's a possibility, yes. But by no means certain.'

'Then I'll hazard a guess,' I said angrily. 'Dinner guests were Duncan's friends, not Aileen's. It suits Duncan's purposes to invite to his house the kind of people most of us would rather not meet at all, and certainly not over dinner. Financial manipulators whose game seems to be finding lucrative ways of taking money without technically stealing it. Lawyers who, as far as I can tell, operate on the thin dividing line between legality and downright fiddling. Exactly the types you ought to be investigating instead of the time you waste in chasing petty criminals. My guess, Chief Inspector, is that any one of them might have killed her, they're utterly without scruples. But none stood a chance of taking her to bed.'

'Well, now,' Turnbull said from under his breath.

'Interesting,' Grant opined.

'Very,' Turnbull concurred.

'Since you asked,' I said.

Turnbull devoted a few moments to nosing through his written reports. 'I took the liberty of asking a number of these disreputable people much the same thing,' he revealed then. 'And got an equally interesting set of answers. Question: any guest Mrs MacRae devoted special attention to? Typical reply: that journalist fellow, what's-his-name? Another reply: youngish chap without a tie, can't for the life of me remember what he's called. Care to comment, Mr Douglas?'

'Pure speculation,' I said. 'Idle gossip.'

'Quite possibly.'

'Frankly, I'm amazed any of them gave you an opinion

without charging for it. Had any bills yet or do they expect payment in kind, special favours from the police?'

'No need to get vindictive,' Grant said, and shook his head a great deal, tutting his tongue to his teeth, as if mortally offended.

'Unscientific, I'll concede,' Turnbull admitted. 'Not strictly evidence. But a sufficient consensus for me to want to find out more.'

'Has it occurred to you,' I asked, 'that if Aileen took more notice of me than some other guests – and note I said if – the simplest explanation might be I was the only one there not obsessed with money? Making money, hoarding money, spending money.'

'That possibility flitted vaguely through my mind,' Turnbull replied. 'I'll agree you differ in several respects from the rest of Mr MacRae's friends. In dress, for instance, and income certainly, and views on what we'll call politics for want of something better. You're younger, less socially conventional. Any of which might have a curiosity value, shall we say, to a woman like Mrs MacRae, forced to mix in a circle that was not of her choosing.' He joined his hands on the desk and, chin resting on them, looked me over at leisure in a gaze of growing bemusement, perhaps wishing to convey that he could not reconcile his words with what he saw before him.

Declining to respond, I simply stared back.

'Wonder if you noticed,' Grant remarked to Turnbull presently, 'how Mr Douglas sprang to the lady's defence?'

'Indeed I did,' Turnbull returned. 'Positively chivalrous.'

'And the similarity of his refusal to accept that Mrs MacRae might be having an affair?' Grant reinforced this ungrammatical assertion with a meeting of the eyes suffused with significance.

'. . . With Mr MacRae's reaction? I most certainly did.' Turnbull nodded sagely.

Moments of trial occur in life when it is as well to

remind yourself of your own duplicity. Pointless for the police to try transparent tricks of this kind on a newspaper man, we use them ourselves. We state guesses as facts to seek confirmation. We speak practised lies with an air of infallibility. Untruths and part truths and quotes attributed to anonymous others are tools shared by our two trades. I could tell with reasonable confidence they had suspicion without proof. I know only too well the ploy of closing a notebook and setting it aside, of switching off a tape recording to encourage an admission that would otherwise not be made. I've done it myself.

'Are you implying,' I enquired in a voice of hurt feelings, 'that only someone who was sleeping with Aileen – her husband or a lover – would find it impossible to accept the idea of another man having sex with her?'

'Something like that,' Turnbull said.

'Don't you think Duncan has endured enough without being subjected to an inquisition on his wife's fidelity?'

Turnbull was a brief study in stony-faced resentment. Then he gave me a rueful smile. 'Quite so,' he said. 'Which is why, when he assured us she'd never dream of such a thing, I considered it only right not to pursue the matter further.'

He restarted the tape machine. 'Recommencing recording after a short delay to check an apparently faulty cassette,' he intoned. 'Those present and other details are as previously noted. The time now is twelve thirty-two p.m.' He waited a moment, watching in readiness, presumably expecting me to refute this blatant piece of fabrication. But I merely gestured for him to continue.

'Where were you on the afternoon of October the fourth?' he asked, fingertips tapping gently together.

'I've no idea.'

'Perhaps we should have suggested you bring your diary . . .'

'I doubt my diary would help. I don't lead a life crammed full of engagements.'

'The fourth was a Thursday,' Turnbull said, regarding

174

me steadily. 'Does that assist your recall in any way.'

'I'm afraid not. Is it important where I was?'

'Your car was parked in John Street for most of that afternoon. Are we getting any warmer?'

An involuntary 'Ahh,' must have escaped my lips.

'I see we are,' Turnbull murmured. He hadn't blinked an eye for a considerable while.

'If my car was in John Street,' I said, 'then so was I. Which means I was visiting the library.'

'Do you visit the library often?'

'Not particularly.'

'Do you not? I rather assumed a writer must make frequent reference to books.'

'I have most of the books I need at home, a sizeable library of my own.' I then presented as convincing a portrayal as could be managed of a search through a hazy memory. In truth, I was dumbstruck that the police knew the whereabouts of my car, had apparently been showing an interest in me, several weeks before Aileen was murdered.

Turnbull was patiently awaiting further details.

'I've got a vague recollection,' I continued, 'of needing to consult a specialized book on birds of prey. You see, I was planning a series of articles about hoolets.'

'He was at the library,' Turnbull remarked to Grant in a sigh of disappointment. 'I said he probably was.'

'Always the most likely possibility,' Grant replied, his face becoming glum.

'You must forgive us the occasional flight of fancy,' Turnbull asked of me, adopting a conciliatory tone. 'But I couldn't help noticing that it's only a short stroll from where your car was parked to the MacRaes' house.'

'If I wanted to go to the MacRaes',' I pointed out, 'I'd park at the MacRaes', not at the library. If I felt like a stroll, I'd leave the car at home, walk all the way.'

'Exactly so,' Turnbull conceded.

'Logical enough,' Grant agreed.

'Rather a wild theory, I'll admit,' Turnbull said. 'Our

computer, I'm afraid, putting two and two together to make five.'

'Would you mind explaining?' I said.

'All to do with Thursdays,' Turnbull said. 'The computer seems to have a bee in its bonnet about Thursdays.'

By an effort of willpower, I contrived to fix my face in a look of blank incomprehension.

'Mrs MacRae was murdered on a Thursday. Immediately beforehand, she'd taken a bath, applied perfume and make-up. A matter of conjecture, admittedly, but this could be taken as indicating she was expecting male company. Mr MacRae was invariably away from the house on Thursday afternoons, sailing the Firth in his yacht. Safely out of harm's way, if you follow.'

'Tough life, being a busines tycoon,' Grant muttered with surprising resentment.

'Mrs MacRae, moreover, was in the regular habit of visiting a local salon on Thursday mornings for general beautication, the big number on her hair and fingernails. The kind of attention, according to her perky young hairdresser, one might expect of a woman wishing to impress someone on a rather special evening date. Except we have Mr MacRae's assurance that Thursday evenings were generally spent at home. See the glimmerings of a pattern emerging, by any chance?'

'If you say so,' I answered.

'So the computer couldn't help but take note that your car was nearby one of those afternoons. A Thursday again, you see. We put the day into the machine, your name popped out. What we call a positive correlation.'

'I suggest you inform your computer I was in the library. Tell it not to make unjustified guesses. You can also say I think it's got a nasty suspicious mind.'

'Well, sometimes technology helps and sometimes it's a hindrance,' Turnbull said, spreading his palms in denial that this was any of his doing. 'Saves us a deuce of a lot of deskwork, shuffling through notes and the like, searching for connections.' He offered a baleful smile of apology. Which instantly melted. 'Any explanation why the librarian doesn't remember seeing you?'

'Why should he?'

'She, Mr Douglas. Seems you don't remember her, either.'

'I must have been out of sight, reading in a secluded corner. After some peace and quiet, as people usually are in libraries.'

'Yes, it's pretty peaceful there most afternoons,' Turnbull said, gravely nodding his head. 'A branch library up a sleepy side street, not many strangers dropping in.' He found a photograph among the papers on his desk, then spent a while intently gazing between it and me, making visual comparison. 'A good likeness,' he assured himself finally. 'Yet not so much as a stir of recognition when we showed it to this estimable lady librarian. The perceptive sort, in my judgement. Reliable, if you know what I mean.' He passed the photograph to me. 'Don't you agree, a good likeness?'

It certainly was, no denying that, although my face, which wore a slack and silly grin, was rather grainy from being enlarged. The picture appeared to have been taken as part of a group, to judge from a stray hand in the frame and the back of someone's head behind mine. Taken at a festive event, I assumed, most likely in a pub – the kind of festivity where someone you've never met before flashes a camera in your eyes and by the bleary next day you've forgotten you were there, let alone any photos being taken.

'Where did you get this?' I demanded, standing on my rights.

'Oh, much the same way, I suppose, that you gentlemen of the Press get your hands on pictures of murder victims. Like Mrs MacRae, for instance.'

'All above board,' Grant said with a curl of the lips.

'Glad to hear,' I sneered, 'that you're raising your standards to those of Grub Street.'

Turnbull threw a warning glance to Grant, indicating with a flick of the eyes that the tape recorder was still turning. His face going bright beetroot red, Grant came close to retorting but took a grip on himself and stayed silent. He drew the back of a hand across his mouth, licked his lips, and something about him at that moment, his apparent craving for the beer he'd have when this was all over, struck a chord, an evasive wisp of memory. I'd had the impression previously that we'd first run across each other in a bar. The bar in the photo? I wondered. Not that the place or occasion mattered as such, but I didn't much like the idea of the police having clearer awareness of events in my past than I did. Memory seemed very fragile suddenly and forgetfulness a habit one might live to regret.

'Sounds like it's my word against the librarian's,' I said defiantly. 'And since my car was outside the library, circumstantial evidence is in my favour. So where does that leave us?'

'Let's exercise your memory further,' Turnbull said. 'The second of October, two days earlier . . .'

'Which must therefore have been a Tuesday, am I right?'

He nodded and clasped his hands under his chin and hardened his eyes in an intense stare that brought to mind classrooms and detested schoolmasters, and questions being asked to which the wrong answer was an excuse, eagerly sought, to mete out punishment.

'Haven't the faintest idea of my movements that day,' I said, striking a note of levity. 'Doubtless you'll enlighten me by saying where my car was.'

'Are you familiar with a restaurant called October?'

My eyes widened more than a little, but fortunately Turnbull interpreted this as a quizzical response, adding the further information that it was in Bearsden and Mrs MacRae had lunched there that day. Not, it seems, with Mr MacRae.

'Nor with me,' I said quickly. 'If that's what you're asking.'

178

'Lunch for two. She paid. Which implies, we may assume, someone she's fond of.'

'Someone less able than she to foot a hefty bill,' Grant implied, his gaze accusingly on me.

I made rapid assessment of what they probably knew. The lunch bill must have shown up in Aileen's credit card statements: a sure bet Turnbull had checked those. Had he shown my photograph at the restaurant? I've never considered my face much out of the ordinary – a whole month had gone by, would the restaurant staff be able to recognize me? Wearing a reflective frown, I gazed at Turnbull, who gazed back with solemn curiosity in which I discerned none of the unwavering assurance he'd possessed earlier. I decided he was playing a hunch, so I played one of my own.

'The friend was a woman, actually,' I declared confidently. 'And Aileen paid because it was her turn to pay.'

Turnbull was taken aback. 'Can I ask how you come by this information?'

'You said lunch not dinner. Aileen had no business interests, so it couldn't have been a business meal. Which leaves a treat for a woman friend as the only plausible alternative. One of those occasional meetings women seem to go in for. A good long natter while they pick at salads, catching up on each other's lives.'

Turnbull looked to Grant, soliciting his view, but got no response. Grant appeared discomfited, wriggling his broad backside in the chair, as if this possibility had never entered his mind. So I added a quick additional comment to throw them further off the scent.

'Aileen had a romantic streak. Flickering candle-light and low-cut dresses . . . ask anyone who was ever at the house. If she wanted to wine and dine a man, she'd do so over dinner, I should think, give him the full works.'

'Did you have lunch with her, Mr Douglas?' Turnbull demanded. 'Yes or no!'

'I think I've answered that pretty clearly.'

'Can you account for your movements that day?'

'I forget which day you said.'

Turnbull subjected me to a prolonged glare of scarcely concealed irritation. 'Would you be willing to take part in an identity parade?'

'Who's going to be doing the identifying?'

'I'm afraid I can't tell you that, for obvious reasons.'

'Someone from the restaurant, presumably . . .'

'I can neither confirm nor deny that.'

'To protect our witness,' Grant said, with a derisive flash of his teeth.

'So this parade could be to do with some bloody bank robbery, for all I know. Don't I have a right to be told?'

'It's connected with what we've been discussing,' Turnbull returned. 'What more need I say? If you've been truthful with us, you've nothing to fear.'

'Do I have the right to refuse?'

'Certainly. Just as I then have the right of arrest on suspicion. Up to you, Mr Douglas, whether or not we do this in a friendly manner.'

He then waited in steadfast silence, a tactic I could well imagine him employing on timid first offenders, the sort who'd buckle when stared at for a long, long time with not a word being spoken. He froze into immobility, watching from across the desk with a doggedness that said he was ready to sit there all day, the whole damned week if need be. As time ticked by with agonizing slowness, I tried to picture the waiter who'd served us at the restaurant. Tall or short? Brown hair or fair? A total void in my memory, so I reasoned that since I couldn't remember him, he was unlikely to have any better recollection of me. At which point I delivered a smile brimful of innocence and gave my consent, saying I considered it every citizen's duty to help the police. Then for a moment I wondered if I'd been lured into making some dreadful mistake because a crafty grin split Grant's florid face and he smacked his hands together, leaping up from his chair.

'I'll see to things then,' he said. 'Give them a bell at the station. Get them to organize the witness pronto.' He charged out of the room.

'We haven't the facilities here for a line-up,' Turnbull explained. He stopped the tape recorder and rose to his feet. 'So we'll be driving to Glasgow, the station at Maryhill.

'I thought all you needed was a wall . . .'

'And a pane of glass about so big.' He held his hands an arm's width apart. 'A thirty-mile round trip every time I need an ident, over an hour stuck in the car, and they tell me we can't afford a bloody pane of glass! How does that saying go . . . for want of a shoe and so on?'

In something of a daze, I allowed him to escort me downstairs to a waiting police car. Presently Grant came ambling after us to hand over my coat. It had completely slipped my mind.

He remained beside the car as I entered the back seat beside Turnbull. A fair assumption he'd be straight round to Gordon's to check out my story: slyly his eyes avoided mine when he slammed the car door shut.

We drove with precious little said between us. Turnbull turned his head to the car window, regarding progress outside with darting attention, a policeman's incisive stare. He looked closely at older cars – cars not unlike mine – in rank suspicion of minor infractions. A tradesman's van held his eye as we passed: he stared with such intensity I began to think him capable of X-ray vision, detecting stolen goods hidden behind sheet metal impenetrable to the rest of us. We came to the monotonous borders of Drumchapel, where the deprived streets of tenements marched across the fells like a grey regiment of destruction. He peered up certain side turnings, stared away to the rows of terraces blotting the horizon. I could have sworn he recognized which satellite dishes were new since he'd last come this way, and who had mysteriously found the means to replace one second-hand Sierra with another. He looked towards me suddenly, caught my gaze on him and gave a wee nod in the direction of this most unhappy of the city's housing schemes.

'Spent my early days in Drumchapel,' he said. 'Young constable bashing thick heads together.'

'Thought as much,' I ventured.

'Happiest days of my life,' he said, a dreamy expression creeping over him as he looked away again through the window, and I couldn't imagine what he saw, what contented memories of mayhem, to imbue him with such serenity.

'How did you find out about my car?' I queried, not really expecting an answer.

'Parked in John Street, you mean?' Turnbull pondered briefly before an acquiescent shrug prefaced his reply – he saw no purpose in keeping me guessing. 'There was a break-in the previous week at one of the houses. The lady concerned spotted your car outside, called us saying she'd seen it before at the time of the burglary. So we ran a check on ownership. Just routine policework, Mr Douglas. Keeping that couthy wee town of yours a safe place for ladies living alone in big houses.'

We were entering Glasgow on the broad straight avenue of the Great Western Road. He was peering up at a colonnade of high trees, a spreading latticework of bare branches outlined against the sky. A sky the same steely grey as his hard grey eyes, a city colour, and he looked in his element now in the growing bustle of traffic, with double-decker buses shuttling by and the soot of ages etching shadows in the terraced streets – while I was aware of an increasingly lost feeling coming over me. I remembered being told once that to gain the upper hand over someone you should lure them from their surroundings to yours. I swore inwardly at my own stupidity. What cocky bravado, foolish impulse, had led me to consent to this?

'*Was* the car parked there before, by the way?' His attention remained outside, as if the query was of no consequence.

'Possibly. I use the library now and then.'

'This was the Thursday previous, you see. Any particular reason you always go to the library on Thursdays?'

'Sounds to me,' I said, 'as if you're obsessed with Thursdays.'

'With habits,' he said. 'Habits and patterns. We all of us live according to a regular pattern. Even you, Mr Douglas, with no office to work in and no wife to come home to. There's a pattern of sorts to most killings. All I have to do is find it.'

'This killing was random,' I pointed out.

'Maybe so,' he said. 'You and Mr MacRae and poor beautiful Mrs MacRae and most of bloody Helensburgh, all doing what you usually did on Thursdays. While somewhere there's a demented soul who did the very opposite. He was most definitely not where he was usually to be found on a Thursday.'

The facilities for which I'd been brought on a drive lasting some thirty minutes proved disappointing, to say the least. A bare rectangular room brightly lit by glaring fluorescent tubes. A large mirror was set into one of the longer walls – a window, I presumed, through which unseen eyes could stare in secrecy. Fair enough, I told myself – they could play at guessing my identity while I tried guessing theirs.

A motley collection of some eight or so men of about my age were standing in line against the back wall as I was shown into the room. The witness, whoever he or she was, had obviously got one detail right in their description of me: none of the men wore ties. It was immediately apparent that about half of them never did – they probably thought a tie was a Saturday clash between Celtic and Rangers – while the rest were office types, bank clerks and suchlike, who'd obviously been instructed to remove theirs and unbutton their formal shirt collars. I stiffened my resolve, determined to show no nervousness.

Where would a guilty man stand? Somewhere amongst the line-up, trying to lose himself, so I emphasized my innocence by taking up a position conspicuously at one end. What expression should I adopt? Where should I direct my eyes and what, if anything, ought they to reveal? I looked in the mirror at the faces beside me and saw various aspects of boredom. Several of the men showed interest only in their own reflections, none had any appearance of trying to see through the glass, of being curious or concerned over who was concealed on the other side. I gazed in like manner straight ahead, regarding myself without vanity. To the best of my recollection, I'd worn a half-way decent tweed sports jacket that day I'd had lunch with Aileen. Gratifying to note that my old Barbour suggested rural pursuits, a beer and sandwiches man rather than a visitor to smart restaurants in the company of a beautiful woman.

The minutes dragged by all too slowly until, at long last, a constable entered the room. We could go now and thanks, gents, for taking the trouble.

One of the men clasped a rough hand to my shoulder.

'Dinnae bother yersel,' he breathed knowingly. 'Jail's nae sae bad.'

'What, me?' I protested. 'Snatched off the streets to make up numbers.'

'Oh ay,' he said and winked, then nodded at the one-way glass. 'Fucking mirras! Mightae done i' mesel. Wha's tae say.'

'Something to do with an under-age girl,' I said, winking back. 'So they told me.'

'Oh, Ah fucking did tha'!' He roared with laughter. 'Ah def'nitely did tha'.'

On the return journey to Dumbarton, Turnbull was no more talkative than before. Sensing sullen dejection in his silence, I couldn't resist rubbing salt in the wounds.

'Told you,' I said. 'Told you it wasn't me.'

He'd been staring out at nothing in particular. His head came slowly round for a hard gaze in which scorn and fury were equally mixed. 'I don't like you, Mr Douglas. Not one little bit. A big mouth and too bloody full of yourself.'

'Then charge me,' I suggested. 'Under the Unpleasantly Truthful to Policemen Act.'

Muttering something under his breath, he looked away out of the car, up to the relentlessly meagre terraces of Drumchapel lining the fells to our right. 'Nor do I much like that stuck-up wee town of yours.' He pointed a finger. 'See over there . . . crimes of necessity and desperation. Those lads steal because they've no bloody hope of a job. They shoot drugs because they've no bloody hope, period. They beat their wives when they're drunk, do them to death out of ignorance. But when a woman's murdered in a big and fancy Helensburgh house there's no such excuses.' He shook his head soulfully.

'Might have been a lad from Drumchapel who killed Aileen,' I suggested.

He turned to face me. 'Pretty unlikely,' he responded, showing weary disdain at my lack of perception.

'Mind explaining why?'

'Her car,' he said. 'Shiny new BMW, all the extras. They're damned quick, those lads. He'd at the very least have lifted the stereo.'

The day was not destined to end well. To my intense irritation, when I arrived back at the house I couldn't get in. A great deal of digging in the pockets of my Barbour failed to find my door keys. Thinking they must have fallen out in the car, I was hunting under the seats for the second or third time when from inside the house, Flora began howling in mournful protest. A jog to my memory: something to do with Isobel. Isobel and keys. Of course! It all came back to me in a rush: I'd asked Isobel to lock up when she left that morning. I'd been in a tearing hurry, my mind on other things. When I'd given her the spare door key I must have forgotten to pick up my own.

In a sullen mood, I motored over to collect them from her neat wee terrace house on a nearby estate of naval housing.

When I finally returned, wearily, to the flat, my bunch of keys was inside on a bureau in the hall. Most unlike me and perhaps indicative of my wound-up state that day, my mind muddled with a confusion of thoughts, that I hadn't the slightest recollection of leaving them there.

Twelve

Isobel had done her worst. I had left her alone in the flat that morning and she'd been destructively thorough.

Things had been spruced and straightened. Things had been moved. Things which by rights should be the wrong way up had been turned on their heads. Nothing, it seemed, was quite where I'd left it. Some things were gone, ravaged, disposed of – I had to stare and rack my brains to work out what I'd lost. The desk top gleamed; burnished clean of its pattern of intricately overlapping coffee rings it looked new and strange, like somebody else's. The wastepaper-basket was empty. I throw away more words than I keep, I need a wastepaper-basket full to overflowing as reassurance I've been productive; I had a horrid feeling it would take days to fill the damned thing up again.

Meanwhile Flora seemed to have caught my disquieted mood. She lay not in her usual place prone by the fire but in front of the settee in my big bay window, lugubriously rolling her eyes, giving voice every so often to a low and restless whine, as though some unseen presence sat there. I could only conclude that Isobel had done unspeakable things to the loose covers with the Hoover and dry-cleaning fluid.

Isobel had also, I decided, been making phone calls at my expense. The phone rang, and wasn't where it should be. I stretched out a hand to find the receiver several tell-tale inches beyond my reach.

'Just checking you're not in custody,' Gordon said.

'Free as air, thanks.'

'We haven't seen much of you lately. I'll be culling some deer next week. Want to come over?'

'Anything worth writing about?'

'Well, maybe you'll get some mileage out of the way deer react to being shot at.'

'Which way's that?'

'They don't. Remarkably nonchalant, deer, about being killed.'

Promising stuff, I agreed, so we made arrangements to meet. Then I asked what he'd told the police.

'How d'you know about the police being round?'

'My infallible intuition.'

'I spun them the line we agreed, said you were with us that day.'

'And Phyllis . . . ?'

'Told them the same story. But she won't swear it on oath, Sandy, not if this comes to court.'

'Well, it won't. Tell her that, would you?'

'She's got a bad case of conscience since they left, a sneaking suspicion you did the murder. She's been bending my ear all evening, asking why you lied.'

'Because,' I replied, 'if no-one ever lied to the police, we wouldn't need detectives. It makes them feel wanted.'

'I'm not so sure I'd lie on oath, either, if you land yourself in deep shit. So don't count on it.'

'Did they check your dogs?'

'How the hell d'you know that!'

'What did they do? Take samples of dog-hair?'

'There were two of the buggers,' he related. 'Acting like they owned the place. The young one, a constable I think, more or less pushed his way through the door and began firing questions. What's the time? he said suddenly. You know, as if he'd to be somewhere else in a hurry. Search me, I said. Och, ay, he said, well if you don't know the time now, how come you're so certain about the time last week? Pimply wee prat, thought he was bloody Columbo. As for the other one . . . said he'd wait in the car but I could see him through the window, nosing round outside.'

'A sergeant, this one?'

'Ay, I think so. Anyway, all hell broke out in the yard . . . the dogs in full cry, this policeman yelling and shouting. Turns out the lurcher had gone for him. We found him locked in his car, gabbling down the radio. I'll have that mad fucking dog! Fucking dangerous, shoot it myself! This is private property, Phyllis screams at him. Anyone tries to shoot that dog'll have to shoot me first.' Gordon gave a throaty chuckle. 'Only thing he took from here was teeth marks, Sandy. And if that's evidence, he'll be baring his arse in court.'

'Name of Grant?' I said, grinning all over my face. 'Big guy, bit like a boxer gone to seed?'

'No,' he said. 'Lanky sort of fella. Name of Mac-something-or-other.'

Flora was becomingly increasingly vocal. I replaced the receiver to find her attacking the settee. Paws scrabbling, she dug her nose underneath as if she was burrowing down to the flat below. A determined grunt, one last enormous effort that prised the settee up from the floor, before she reversed out, tail contentedly wagging, with something in her mouth. After dropping it on the carpet, she tilted her head at me to convey that, whatever her skills of retrieval, she'd never mastered the trick of pulling the wrappers off sweets.

I stared then. She stared back, ears pricked up in inducement. Slow to react, I must have told myself several times that I never buy toffees. Too late when I dived for it. Flora had finally given up on me and eaten the evidence, wrapper and all.

Isobel sounded distinctly ratty when I rang.

'Course I bloody didn't!' she retorted roundly. 'Think I don't know how to treat dogs, and I'm in the middle of something! Bad for their teeth, toffees. You all right, Mr Douglas? You don't seem yourself today.'

No clear memory remains of the dash across town, to MacIntyre's solidly respectable Victorian pile high on the hillside at Rhu. Just a fragmentary impression that the journey was done in quicker time than the old Volvo is actually capable of.

MacIntyre came to the door with a brandy in one hand, brushing food from his mouth with the other.

'First consultation's free, right?' I got in quickly.

He answered with a great deal of crusty muttering about normal office hours, crowned this with an overburdened sigh, then showed me through a gloomily opulent hall to his study.

'You'll be wanting a bloody brandy, I expect,' he said, sounding cheerful as an undertaker.

'Better make it a large one,' I replied. 'In case you say what I think you're going to say.'

I am ambivalent about lawyers. A doomed presentiment tends to come over me that if their advice is worth having I can't afford it. I am especially in two minds about MacIntyre. He negotiated the lease on my flat so I've always be grateful to him about the peppercorn rent but subject to doubts that he should, surely, have spotted something amiss. Yet his study is even larger than mine, resplendent with old furniture that does not look as if it could be picked up in the kind of establishments where I buy old furniture. He was wearing slippers which slithered on the polished oak floor as he went over to the drinks cabinet, so that although he can't be more than a few years older than me he seemed ancient and shuffling and somehow immensely wise. The leather-bound books lining his walls created an aura of profound learning. I felt, as I never do in his office on Clyde Street, that he might for once know what he's talking about.

'Tell me about search warrants,' I began. 'How do the police go about getting one?'

'They submit a report to the Procurator Fiscal outlining the case against the suspect. Then the supervising officer swears a statement before the Sheriff. That's about it, all very straightforward.'

'What's a case? Do the police have to give details of their suspicions?'

'Well, of course!'

'And say what they're looking for?'

'Why else ask for a warrant?'

'A specific item, you mean?'

'Evidence. Meaning drugs, a weapon, a body. Exactly what evidence depends on the offence we're talking about.' He gave a hopeful, enquiring look.

'Suppose all they've got is a gut feeling? Such and such a person might be implicated, they can't say how. A search might uncover some evidence but they've no idea what.'

'You're talking about a fishing expedition,' he said. 'They'll be turned down flat. The law doesn't work that way.'

'Exactly the reason,' I said, tipping my brandy balloon at him, 'I asked for a large one.'

'Are you going to tell me what this is all about?'

'I was asked to take part in an identity parade today . . .'

'In connection with . . . ?'

'The MacRae murder.'

'Jesus Christ!' he exclaimed.

'Hold on . . . there wasn't a witness behind that screen. It was a sham, a fix.'

He screwed up his eyes. 'Are you saying this parade has already taken place . . . ?'

'This afternoon.'

'And you didn't fucking call me first!'

'What for? I didn't do it.'

'Jesus bloody Christ,' he spluttered, shaking his head in disbelief.

'Look, all they're doing is trying to prove a connection between me and Aileen MacRae. I've no idea why, but unless I'm very much mistaken, adultery's no longer a crime in this country.'

'You don't need a lawyer,' he groaned. 'What you need is a fucking psychiatrist!'

'It was all staged,' I said, 'to keep me occupied while they searched my flat. They can't have found anything

. . . there's nothing to find. So I won't lose any sleep over it.'

He confessed to being lost.

'But it would be nice,' I explained, 'to slam in a suit for damages. Illegal entry and search, infringement of rights, police harassment. Whatever else you can dream up.'

He stared for a considerable while. He emptied his glass in a single gulp and wiped his lips with his sleeve. He indulged in more censorious head shaking. Then he returned to the drinks cabinet, slippers swishing, and replenished his glass. He turned to face me, striking a courtroom pose.

'These are serious charges,' he stated. 'What proof do we have?'

'Sergeant Grant stole my keys at Police Headquarters. They were in my coat pocket. I found them later inside the flat.'

'Not Don Grant . . . ?' A sceptical frown puckered deep lines in his brow. 'You can't mean Don Grant!'

'Don't say "Don" like that. It makes me wonder whose side you're on.'

'He's as straight as they come. Known him for donkey's years.'

'Then where was he this afternoon, while I was being paraded? He sure as hell wasn't at my brother's.'

'Anything else?' MacIntyre enquired in a flat voice. A peculiar, glazed expression came over his face.

'He came round to my place last week. I remember telling him my dog would give a friendly welcome to burglars, so long as they brought her sweets. He made a point today of asking her name again. When I got back to the flat, she was acting strangely. And if Grant wasn't there,' I reasoned emphatically, 'who left that toffee under my settee?'

He made no comment, merely stared.

'Unfortunately,' I confessed, 'the dog ate it.'

'Your word against his, then . . .'

'Afraid so.'

'Anything else . . . ?' he repeated.

'My flat had been searched, things moved. Nothing obvious, but I could tell.'

'Anyone been in the flat, apart from yourself?'

'Only Isobel, the woman who cleans for me.'

'Ah ha . . .' he muttered, throwing his eyes to the ceiling.

'But she never moves things like that. She knows I'll complain.'

He asked again was there anything else?

'I guess,' I offered lamely, 'it's all what you'd call circumstantial evidence.'

'If I was summing up in two words,' he said, 'those aren't the two I'd use.' Slippers flapping, he came over to squeeze my shoulder in a fatherly fashion. His mouth tugged down at the corners as if he was about to cry his eyes out. 'Miserable bad luck about that toffee,' he moaned. Then he lost the battle with himself and doubled up laughing.

I searched the apartment for hours that night as a stranger would see it with fresh and enquiring eyes. Policemen's eyes. The X-ray vision, missing nothing, Turnbull had sent searing through the car window on our journey to Glasgow. I left no paper unturned, peered under carpets, delved into drawers and cupboards and behind the bathtub. Instructive to note as time went by how it became increasingly difficult once I'd picked something up to replace it as exactly as it was. The brain played tricks, memories merged and faded. Which of these books had been on top of the other? Were the pencils kept in the jam-jar on the desk with their sharpened ends upwards? All of them? But I uncovered no evidence, not the slightest shred, to link me to the murder, and I sent a prayer of gratitude winging skywards to whatever divinity had led me to give my only photo of Aileen to Jack Moffatt.

There was the black negligee, of course. Forgotten till that very moment, gone clean from my head. Aileen's size and her favourite colour, but where was the proof as to who it was bought for? Besides, it looked untouched and try as I might I could not imagine that those delicate folds, wrapped between flimsy tissue in the *Sweet Dreams* gift box, had been the work of Grant's great clumsy hands.

Still, no point in tempting providence. I watched it flare on the fire, small glowing charred fragments floating away up the chimney. A last fond burnt offering to Aileen's memory.

Maybe I took comfort in knowing that no smallest part of Aileen remained to haunt me: for the first night in months I slept without dreams of her.

NEXT OF KIN

Thirteen

A peculiar sensation comes over me occasionally that parts
of my mind are not my own. Thoughts bubble up which
are hard to recognize as mine. As if from nowhere, a
sudden memory will flash before me, quite unconnected
with what I'm doing. My memory, of course, but I can't
avoid the feeling it's someone else's. The rational explanation, Dr Galbraith would no doubt convey, is to do with
the inner self, submerged aspects of personality, a
manifestation of repressed and rebellious instincts. Dr
Galbraith is a shrink and much given to explanations of
this kind. The idea of a stranger inside me, driven by his
own weird urges and fantasies, has never greatly appealed
– one of the reasons why Dr Galbraith and I ultimately
went our separate ways. But it was odd how, in the midst
of the most spectacular success of my journalistic career,
whilst a myriad other thoughts and emotions swam in my
head, something he'd said kept coming back to me. That's
the trouble with shrinks: however much you deplore their
analysis, you can't forget the things they say. They dig and
probe at the psyche, leaving sharp splinters of enlightenment festering deep down in the brain. Maybe they change
you, despite yourself. Had I known that, I'd have run a
mile from consulting him in the first place.

Circumstances at the time – leave it at that – had led me
to seek his advice. He counselled the obvious and the
impossible. He told me at ponderous length of failings in
my character I was already painfully aware of and could do
nothing about. He offered opinions about me I didn't want
to hear, and took my protests as evidence that we – he
always said *we* – were finally getting somewhere.

'What would make you happy?' he asked on one occasion. 'What one thing above all others?'

'A scoop. My name splashed under a big story.'

'I don't think so.'

'Are you saying you know better than me what would make me happy?'

'Temporary happiness, maybe. Until you discover this is not what you really want. Then you'll be back, depressed as ever.'

'Why ask me, then? Why do you always imply my opinions count for nothing?'

'OK, Sandy, you know best. So what will you do to achieve this happiness? How will you get your scoop?'

'I can't *do* anything.'

'In other words, what you want so badly, you're helpless to get.'

'It's all a question of luck, being in the right place at the right time.'

'And are you a lucky person?'

'Not on the evidence so far.'

'But you try anyway. You research stories, put in long and arduous hours. You've set yourself a goal that depends not on your efforts but on luck, the fickle fall of the dice. You're one of life's gamblers, Sandy, eternally living in hope . . .'

'Nature of the business, Doctor. What else can I do? Shoot the Prime Minister with one hand while I've got my notebook ready in the other?'

He was frequently so wide of the mark as to be laughable, surmising for example that I expect too much from women – choosing to ignore all indications to the contrary that I expect very little from women but sex. Eventually he arrived at the conclusion that I tried too hard, obsession was the root cause of all my problems. This wee gem of wisdom, by the by, came from a man who, when I asked once for an urgent appointment, made the brusquest of apologies for being so busy, yes even evenings, and suggested Friday week! That was the nub of it, then – the more I reached for success the further away it slipped from my grasp. My marriage, he said, collapsed because I worked too tenaciously at propping it up. I invested too much emotion in relationships to give them room to breathe. My writing had gone to pot from trying over-desperately to find the right words. I demanded too much of people, wanting friends to behave like relatives and relatives to act as friends. He advised relaxing, letting life take its course. When I expressed confusion that striving for perfection could be any sort of failing, he glibly offered the view that I seemed more than usually partial to confusion. At which point, I said I'd been a damned sight less confused before ever seeing him. By mutual consent, from that moment our paths were never to cross again.

A closed chapter in my life, one I prefer to forget. So it was with some surprise and a considerable degree of pique that I found Dr Galbraith's sanctimonious pronouncements returning to mock me. It was as if he couldn't resist rising like some Freudian phoenix from my past to claim victory, gloat he'd been right. I wasn't after a scoop – heaven only knows, I'd long since purged myself of that kind of ambition, of all ambition. I wasn't trying hard. I wasn't trying at all. I was relaxed, letting life run its course, and hadn't left bed that particular morning till well gone eleven. While poor Jack Moffat, with his dogged hunger for headlines screaming in 72-point type, his chronic indigestion, his pickled liver deserving a George Medal for bravery beyond the call of duty – Jack, the luckless wretch, was busting a gut. Nor was I after personal glory when I wrote the story, merely exacting revenge on Sergeant Grant. And on reflection, Galbraith would have claimed that too as vindication of his analysis: as a parting shot he delivered judgement that I had a vengeful streak in my make-up. Take care, he said, or the thirst to get even would be my downfall. And, by God, wasn't he right.

*   *   *

Monday of the following week. Early evening, brisk and bright under the pearly orb of a sailing full moon. The buildings, the Firth, the hazy vistas to the enveloping hills, shone in a wash of luminous grey, same hue as the clouds and the great stone houses. Helensburgh looked adrift in a frosty sea, craggy, remote and marooned in mists. Driving down to the Off-Licence for my weekly supplies, I wound the car window open to savour the wafting odours of coal fires and burning wood and peat – by some miraculous aberration of local government no-one has yet decreed we must have Clean Air, so the winter's air has the tang of a breakfast kipper, fresh from the sea and tasting of smoke. Halted by one of the town's three sets of traffic lights, I paid little heed when a police car sped across the junction. But then another swiftly passed. And after that, fleetingly lit by the skewed beams of my headlights, I caught a glimpse of Jack Moffat in the car immediately behind. A cigarette dangling from his mouth, a determined jut to his jaw, he was crouching agog over the steering wheel. His passenger, a gold ring flashing at the lobe of an ear, face shadowed with designer stubble, seemed vaguely familiar. As the signal changed to green, I finally placed him and went charging after them up the hill. Jack was a dawdler, more often to be seen heading a queue of traffic than following – usually a very long and crawling tail of cars, full of impatient mutterings. Catch him driving in hot pursuit of the police, the *Dispatch*'s most notorious paparazzo at his side, and it's well worth giving chase.

Jack, I found out later, had been nosing round Divisional Headquarters in Dumbarton. Doing a background piece on the MacRae investigation, he'd said, local colour and all that. He'd cajoled Sergeant Grant into sitting at an incident room computer terminal in a pose suggesting dramatic progress. As I heard tell, Grant hadn't grasped this was no hack photographer behind the lens, while his failure to question the use of a telephoto the size of a bazooka might have been connected with vanity.

Quite what choice tit-bits Jack hoped to glean from his shots of computer screens must remain conjecture, because at that very instant an urgent message flashed over the police radio. So Jack was on the spot as the news broke. He had his paparazzo with him, equipped to the eyeballs with available-light film and night lenses and 1000mm telephotos. The sort of luck every reporter dreams of.

I turned after him into the car park at Victoria Hall, an extravagantly proportioned edifice built, as far as can be gathered, in the forlorn expectation that if there's to be an annual pantomime, the entire town will flock forth at a single sitting. It was still Jack's story, for all I cared. I was following for the sheer hell of things and I felt – at least, my rebellious inner self felt – in a capricious mood. A limp banner across the Gothic portico of the Hall announced a coming production of *Cinderella*. I wondered in my mischievous madness if her golden coach had been stolen, or an Ugly Sister slain, or the Fairy Godmother abducted. But the trail led, on foot now, away from the building, between a break in a hedge and into the darkness of Hermitage Park. My thoughts turned to the Brothers Grimm, menacing tales of the Gothic and surreal. The path wound a meandering route under high and brooding conifers, between grottos and mysterious dank huddles of rock, by way of woodland glades wispily veiled by drifting mist. Torch lights glowed across the park like fire flies in the night and, over the tree tops, the dour silhouette of Victoria Hall stood gaunt and jagged against the floating moon – battlements and turrets, steely slate roofs the shape of witch's caps, glinting with evening dew. A rustic bridge of rough-hewn timber spanned a small gorge, with close by a flight of crumbling stone steps down to a coursing stream, the Millig Burn. Signs of hectic activity there, the intense white flare of floodlights, glimpses of police moving beside the burn. That was as much as I could see – a brace of young constables stood guard at a cordon of yellow ribbon strung in a wide swathe from tree to tree, issuing gruff cautions to a rapidly swelling crowd. Casting about, I discovered Jack perched atop a rocky outcrop, stretching to the tips of his toes, craning his neck. I tugged playfully at a trouser leg. He threw out his arms for balance, swaying like a drunken high-wire artiste.

'And Jack fell down and broke his crown,' I said.

'Christ, you!' he scowled, then clenched his eyes shut and mumbled unspeakable curses at himself, as if he'd run like the wind for the last bus and missed it.

Above us, boughs shook on a fir-tree – the paparazzo, clasping an enormous-lensed camera protectively to his chest, was using his spare hand to inch precariously along an upper branch.

'Ooo-yy!' one of the constables yelled up at him. 'You! Bloody get doon frae there!'

'Wasting your voice,' Jack called back. 'He's deaf, poor sod.'

'What's the story, Jack?' I said.

'Fuck you!' he muttered.

'You heard the nice polisman,' I said, seizing tight hold of his leg.

He glowered down at me. I began pulling as though I meant business. 'All right!' he hollered. 'All right, fuck you! It's a girl.' He slashed a finger across his throat.

'Knifed, you mean?'

'How would I know? Fucking dead, that's all I know.'

When I released my hold, he clambered down from the rock, treated me to his entire repertoire of snarls, then went to the cordon, where he flashed his press card at the constable. 'Give Sergeant Grant a tinkle on that wee radio, would you, laddie? Tell him Jack sends his regards and craves an audience.' Taking a grouchy sidelong glance at me, he lowered his voice. So I moved in closer to hear. 'A private audience, all right? We're in the middle of an interview, remind him.'

The constable nodded stoically towards the quaking tree. 'Is yon bloody Tarzan gang to get his hearing back, or no'?'

Jack cupped his hands to his mouth. 'Any luck, Donny?' he bellowed.

'Nae chance. Fucking canvas screens blocking ma view!'

'Then give it a miss, OK.'

Only when Donny dropped down to the ground did the constable consent to reach for his radio. 'Who do Ah say wants him?'

'The Press,' I said promptly, favouring Jack with my most guileless of smiles. 'National and local.'

Nearly half an hour elapsed before Sergeant Grant found time for the Press. Ample opportunity to return to my car for the old Army binoculars I carry everywhere for bird-watching. When I got back to the cordon, the *Sun*'s local stringer was fresh on the scene. Donny the paparazzo had slipped away somewhere with his bazooka lenses into the night.

We ducked under the yellow tape, where Grant led us out of earshot of the assembled onlookers. Jack and the stringer produced pocket recorders. I'd come unprepared. Trawling the pockets of my Barbour, I came up with a crumpled train ticket to scrawl on, but had to beg the loan of a ballpoint pen.

'She's about twenty,' Grant informed us. 'And don't ask was she attractive. Might have been, for all I know, but she certainly isn't now.'

'Name?'

'Come off it, Jack . . . next of kin have to be told, you know that. Looks like she hasnae been there long, maybe only an hour or two. Down by the burn, half in the water. Out of sight of the path but no telling yet if she fell or the assailant tried to conceal the body. Young lad found her, walking his dog after school. Nasty shock for the poor kid. Thought at first the dog had attacked someone.'

'The kid's name . . . ?'

'We've got him at the local station right now. He's only fourteen. I'll give you his name if the parents agree.'

Jack moved away some paces, pulled a portable phone from his pocket and began a whispered conversation.

I asked how she was killed.

'Attacked violently from behind. No obvious signs of a struggle. The poor lassie probably never knew what hit her.'

'Hit with what . . . ?'

'Taken unawares,' Grant retorted crisply. 'Surprised. Violently assaulted. I never said she was hit.'

'Same killer as the MacRae woman?' the stringer wanted to know.

'Too early to say, Robbie.'

'Was she raped?' I asked.

'Her underclothes are disturbed, that's all I'm saying for now.'

Jack's back had been turned to us while he schemed on the phone, but he must have been listening with half an ear. He spun round in a trice. 'What d'you mean by "disturbed"?' he demanded. 'Tights ripped off? Knickers pulled down?'

Grant twisted his mouth into a sneer. 'What I mean, Jack, is she sure as hell wasn't strolling through the park looking like that.'

'Attacked from behind, no signs of a struggle. So she wasn't conscious when he did this disturbing . . .'

'Your guess is as good as mine . . .'

'Same fucking man, isn't it! The same crazy maniac. Likes his women dead when he does it.'

'No comment.'

'Did he come inside her this time or miss badly again?'

Giving vent to a jaded sigh, Grant reached inside his jacket. For a brief while he became all an old-time bobby should be. He'd have been perfect behind the desk of a rural outpost with a black Bakelite telephone and his trusty bicycle propped against the counter. A simpleton's look of wishing to be helpful came over his face as he peered closely, almost short-sightedly, at a fob-watch, tapped it, held it to an ear, then peered again. An heirloom of some value, judging by the formidable chain securing it to his person.

'Look,' he said. 'A few hours yet before you go to press for the morning papers. I'll have a word with the boss, see what we can do by way of a statement.'

And there, abruptly, the press conference ended. A call came ringing across the park from the direction of the burn. The search had unearthed an object which one of the uniformed men held up on a stick to attract his attention. Grant scurried off that way. But not before I'd snatched a quick look through the binoculars.

'Fancy a drink, Jack?' I said, to learn his intentions.

'Got to be bloody kidding!' he muttered, staring intently past me into the distance, his eyes everywhere. Trying to locate the missing Donny, by the look of him.

'Sticking around, then . . . ?'

'Only show in town,' he said.

'There's always the kid. Very observant about knickers, boys of fourteen.'

'What's it to you?'

'Me?' I said. 'Only trying to help. I don't do this kind of thing any more.'

I mooched back to the car in no apparent hurry, wondering what Dr Galbraith would make of my capacity to juggle a profusion of simultaneous different thoughts, to be several people at one and the same moment, to be elated and fanciful and sick to the stomach. Sudden awareness hit that I'd been scribbling my notes on a ticket to Yoker – a dazed feeling came over me of not knowing for a moment whether I'd stepped by some freakish warp of time back to the past or into the future. I stared up at the moon gleaming like a huge pearl button over a Gothic landscape of turrets and battlements, and grinned in sheer delight, feeling like a child who'd wandered into a fairy tale. Several fairy tales. I felt the reporter long dormant inside me stirring into wakefulness. I felt like Rip Van Winkle. I felt I'd been sleeping for years and been kissed back to life. I gazed over to the Hall at the name on the pantomine banner. A poor girl, her clothes tattered, who yearned to be rich. And I'd found her, thanks to the missing slipper. The kingdom was mine. Because what I'd seen through the binoculars was a leather boot and though it was drenched, dripping with water, there was no mistaking that vivid shade of green.

I thrust my hands nonchalantly into my pockets. Jack Moffat's story! My fingers closed round something pointed and hard, and I wanted to laugh out loud. Jack, who in all the years I'd known him hadn't stumped up even a miserly half-pint, had given me a rather expensive-looking ballpoint pen to write it with.

Fourteen

It was my dismal destiny that evening to be plagued by Dr Galbraith. At unsuspecting moments as I put the story together a fragment at a time, things he'd said, strictures he'd laid on me, came like ghostly echoes out of my buried past. Almost as if I was assembling a jig-saw with his hectoring presence at my shoulder, and while I tried to match the pieces of Caroline's brief young flowering, he moved them sometimes for me, claiming the life I was assembling was not hers but mine. And, of course, our lives had become entangled for a few short weeks even though she'd never known it. Several times during the course of that long and hectic evening I had the overwhelming conviction that I was always intended to write her story. Fate had been shuffling the deck for weeks past and was about to deal me a winning hand. Why else had Caroline resisted my advances except to ensure we'd never met? Met properly, that is. What inspired intuition had led me to pay cash for the negligee, leaving no record I'd called at the shop? For what reason other than the guidance of fate had I given her so much of my time? One of my numerous failings, this, the desire to read meaning into life. Galbraith, damn him, was forever insisting life had no meaning. Or did he say something to the effect that only by giving up the struggle to find meaning in life would one finally discover what meaning it actually had? Trying to make sense of his ramblings can still get me confused.

Yes, confused. I drove the short distance from Hermitage Park to the solemn stone house where Caroline had lodged. From the car, I looked up at her darkened window, scanned the other windows where lights glimmered behind closed curtains, gazed the full length of the street from one corner to the other, and become completely and helplessly confused.

My plan was already prepared in outline by then, clever and foolproof. I'd claim reporter's luck. On my way home, as a matter of fact. Just happened to be coming along the street, spotted the police cars at the house, and made the obvious connection. Police all over the park . . . police swarming here . . . an easy deduction, wouldn't you say, Chief Inspector? Home of victim number two, and how many girls could there be aged around twenty missing from that address? From that point on, well, I could work the mechanics out later. Simply a matter of asking the right questions of the right people, I'd assert, getting a lucky break, a lead to her family in Yoker. From who, this convenient lead? Och, come on, Sergeant, fair's fair. I'm not revealing my sources. Privilege of the fourth estate.

Except . . . *where were the bloody police cars!* I stared in utter dismay at the empty street.

I'm not at my best in moments of crisis. Another fucking Galbraithism! I think too fast, he said. I fail to see the obvious. I make assumptions. I'm over-hasty in reaching conclusions and when the facts don't fit I fall apart. All to do with self-confidence, apparently. I don't have any. Either that, or I compensate by having too much. At the risk of confirming his viewpoint, this is not an avenue I'm prepared to develop at any length. Sufficient to say that my brain ceased to function while I sat in a state of virtual paralysis in the car. No idea, not the foggiest, how long I sat there. My head began to hurt, a numbing pain from the effort of trying to think and being completely unable to focus my thoughts – much as I've felt before in times past when I struggled for words and couldn't find any, not a single bloody word. The same recurrent thought crippled me like a hangover migraine, repeating like a record stuck in a groove, over and over and over. All I could think was I'd got the wrong girl. It couldn't be Caroline dead by the burn.

Maybe I'd become so accustomed to failure I couldn't believe fortune when it stared me in the face. Maybe that's why I took so long to see daylight. Of course it was Caroline! It *had* to be Caroline. Confused? Who was confused? The police, bless their plodding cotton socks. A body in the burn and they didn't know who she was!

Night had grown cold by now, the temperature had fallen inside the car. I could scarcely see the street through thick condensation clouding the windscreen. But it wasn't the cold that set my hand shaking, an uncontrollable tremble as I traced big headline letters on the misted glass. S-C-O-O-P. Go fuck yourself, Galbraith. You, too, Sergeant bloody Grant.

Even as I wrote there came one of those eerie occurrences that confirms my belief in fate. At the back of my mind a doubt was taking shape about my carefully worked-out plan. No police cars at the house, so how to explain my knowledge of the murdered girl's identity? Then a sound outside, a short sharp screech from somewhere in the trees. I rubbed a patch of glass clear just in time to glimpse a flutter of wings, a spectral shadow crossing the disc of the high bright moon.

Who told me? A little bird told me. Oh really, Mr Douglas . . . and how did *he* know, this little bird of yours? A hoolet to be precise, Sergeant. Work it out for yourself.

Just like old times. Ring the doorbell. Put on a smile. Lie through your teeth.

They're always watching television, volume blaring to wake the dead. Always a soap opera – are they on the box non-stop or just the times I call? Never watch them myself, life's too drearily like soap in reality to watch actors doing it badly. I've only ever seen soap operas in other people's living rooms and then only for as long as it takes to get the bloody telly turned down. A shouting match till then, which annoys me intensely because it's impossible to lie with any subtlety when you're shouting your head off. And the soap's always left running like a silent movie flickering away in the corner of the room. Doesn't matter whether it's mutilation, death or catastrophe that brought you to their door, you're only worth one eye – the other stays glued to the box. Until first mention of money.

They must buy their carpet in the same cheap warehouse, these people, a nauseous nightmare of swirling browns. They go in for net curtains and mauve emulsion paint and dangling strips of coloured plastic where there ought to be doors. And they've always got wee glass animals on the window ledge, and garish china ornaments won at bingo, and an overflowing stack of buff envelopes jammed behind the clock on the mantelpiece, as though not paying bills is a source of pride, a totem of social standing. They live in the living room, every facet of living. An ironing board blocking the door and clothes drying over the backs of chairs, cans of beer on the floor, dirty plates on sloppy trays. Their DIY runs to starting jobs that never get finished, and what's half done is either polythene or vinyl. Any hour of the day or night bet on a certainty they both look as if they've just tumbled out of bed. He'll be in socks and a vest, she'll be wearing fluffy slippers, caught in the middle of doing something messy to her hair. Gordon thinks me a snob in this regard, but Gordon doesn't ring doorbells at places like 45 Caledonia Street.

Exactly like old times.

Her hair roughly turbanned in a damp towel, Janey Logan squeezed past the ironing board into the living room. Under a drying pair of jeans and a goldfish bowl, a woman with an equally thin sour face and a towel round her head was berating someone on the TV screen. All I've ever gleaned about soap operas is they clearly don't offer escape.

'He's frae the papers,' Janey declared.

210

'Oh ay, wa' paper's tha'?' Norman Logan said, not considering my entrance worth a backwards glance.

At that stage I hadn't decided which paper. So I tried making it understood over the volume that I was writing a series on dreams. 'Dreams come true,' I said. 'A feature we're running on successful young women.'

Norman invited me to kiss his arse.

'Bright young lady, that girl of yours,' I said.

'Carol . . . ?' Janey said, so bemused I wondered how many girls she had.

'We'll pay for the interview, naturally. Big centre spread.' I resorted to sign language, rubbing fingers greedily together over Norman's shoulder.

He zapped the telly into immediate silence with deft use of a remote control. 'Wha's Carol been an' done noo!' he said, facing me with a scowl.

'Doing pretty well for herself, I'd say. An air hostess, seeing the world. New York. Hong Kong. You must be very proud of her.'

'Och, bloody kids!' Norman muttered.

I've called on a score of Janey and Norman Logans in my time. A moment always comes when, initial belief suspended, one or other of them gets it into their head you're probably selling double-glazing. That's the smarter of the two, the person to watch and beware. And it was Janey who planted both hands on her hips and gazed at me sceptically.

'Carol's nae a success,' she said. Her head shook at the very idea. The crinkles gathered on her lined forehead. She shook her head again, wondering what kind of fool I took her to be.

'We've just done a reader survey,' I returned. 'Know how many women under twenty-five want to be air hostesses? Twice as many as want to be Page Three girls. Three times more than dream of running their own hairdressing salons.'

'Carol, ye say . . . ?'

'Why so surprised, Mrs Logan?'

'Oor Carol? In tha papers?'

'She's a born dreamer, right? As a kid that's what she always wanted, a job with an airline.'

Janey confirmed my guess with a nod but her eyes still held a question mark.

'Sweet Dreams, Mrs Logan . . . that's what this feature's called. And we'll be kicking it off next week with Carol Logan. One of those rare young women who made her dream come true.'

'Oor Carol . . . ?' Janey said reverentially.

'Take my word, Mrs Logan, when I write this story your Carol will be big news.' I hesitated. Unable to look her in the face, my gaze became shifty. 'But I'd better come clean . . . Carol's not the reason I'm here.'

A breath escaped Janey's lips, her suspicions confirmed. An astute move, I always think, to get them believing the worst of you. Then a twinge of guilt sets in. And you've got them hooked.

'You're the reason,' I said quickly. 'Mr and Mrs Logan. The ground crew at Yoker, that's what we'll call you . . . the mum and dad behind the scenes.' I helped myself to a chair. 'That's the trouble with today's kids, they never give parents the credit.' I took out Jack Moffat's ballpoint, stared in puzzlement at the floor by my feet. 'Got anything to write on, by any chance? Looks like I left my briefcase at the office.'

Glasgow born and bred, the both of you? I began. What age are you, Mr Logan? And you, Mrs Logan . . . no, not for printing, just for the file. Both at work, are you? Sorry to hear that, Mr Logan, must be a struggle, making ends meet. Get much help from Carol? Well, damned expensive being young these days, money goes nowhere. What with clothes, make-up, boyfriends. Really? You surprise me. No boyfriends, attractive girl like that? Mind describing her for me, your own words, Mrs Logan, the kind of personal touch readers appreciate. Could I check a wee detail, by the way . . . does Carol ever mention Helensburgh? Was it a friend of hers moved there, an old schoolfriend maybe, . . . job in a shop, I heard. Most grateful, Mrs Logan, must have got that wrong, no-one in Helensburgh. Said the exact same thing myself only the other day . . . toffee-nosed place . . . not a patch on Gourock for a trip down the Clyde. Hear about that murder there, by the way? Think they'll catch the guy? Bloody police, couldn't agree more. Reckon half the thieving's down to them. Busy life, Carol's, airports here, there and everywhere. Away for weeks at a time. D'you miss her ever, Mrs Logan, worry at nights is she all right? Just read that back, shall I, a real stickler about quotations, my editor.

'Had a bit of a fight with him over this story,' I told them. 'He wanted to send a staff photographer. I said no, let's keep this sincere, about real people. Any objections to us printing family photos of you both?'

'In tha papers . . . ?' Norman said on a note of wonder.

Janey narrowed one eye, as if that side of her remained immune to blandishments. 'Wha's the deal?' she said.

'The deal, Mrs Logan, is a hundred for the interview and the same again for every photo we print.'

They stared at me dumbstruck.

'We'll have someone round first thing tomorrow with the cheque.'

A monstrous display cabinet, teak veneer and leaded glass doors, lined the wall by the dining table. Lights shone behind the glass on trinkets of leaded crystal and gaudy china statuettes. Janey dug in a drawer there for a photograph album.

'Any snaps of Carol, while you're at it?' I said. Then I agonized over the richness of choice while making dubious noises about the problems of reproduction in newsprint. A cardboard box of peeling holiday snapshots was produced from another room. These brought from me appreciative murmurs about the closeness of family life. Several more photos, mounted in frames, soon arrived from the bedroom.

'My pictures editor will go bananas over these,' I enthused. 'Any special favourite of yours, Mrs Logan?'

She took forever choosing a wedding photo. She'd been a good deal fatter round the face twenty years ago. Plumper in every direction under a full and flowing bridal gown. About six months pregnant at the time, I'd say. Gorgeous dress, I remarked, make it yourself? The hand of the mantelpiece clock counted away the passing minutes as she reminisced about sewing machines. She was working at the factory then, assembling bobbins, got herself a beautiful new electric at staff discount. Wasnae the same these days, Clydebank, since Singer closed doon.

You're out of bloody practice, Sandy, I thought, making a slip like that, giving her an opening to squander precious time. Out of practice in more ways than one – a sudden rush of panic as I wondered what money I had with me. Did I have a fucking bean! Muttering about having to call Carol's boss at the airport, I searched everywhere for the phone number and discovered, thank God, a single crumpled tenner in my wallet.

I stopped at the front door to request a favour. Tearing the tenner in two, I gave Jenny one of the halves, asking her to hand it over if anyone called. Local lad, running an errand for me. Bloody juggler, I am, I said. This feature hardly begun and they're already throwing the next one at me.

'We'll get these all back to you tomorrow with the cheque,' I promised, my arms full of photos. 'And we'll throw in a silver frame for the wedding picture, as a special thank you.'

Not quite like old times. Definitely over the hill. I'd have had the wit, once, to check my wallet before ringing the doorbell.

A couple of streets away, a kid of about ten was cycling in aimless circles on a mountain bike.

'Want to earn an easy ten quid?' I called from the car.

Not pleasant being stared at as a pervert. But everyone has their price, even kids of ten. Maybe especially kids of ten. He stopped cycling in circles.

I showed the half note as a token of good faith.

'All you have to do is watch a door for me. A couple of hours.'

He cycled closer. 'Tha' all?'

'Do what you're doing now, bike up and down Caledonia Street. Keep your eyes on number fifty, but not so they notice you watching, OK?' I handed him the torn note. 'My phone number's in the corner, there. Call me at nine thirty and I'll tell you where to collect the other half.'

'Wa's ya game, pal?'

'They owe three months on the video. My boss thinks they're planning a bunk.'

'Wa's tae say ye'll focking pay up, Jimmy?'

'Half a note, Jimmy,' I said, 'is damn all use to either of us.'

Hermitage Park was still crawling with police. Caroline's street was as silent as a graveyard, not so much as a peep from the hoolet in the trees. I turned a corner into the next avenue, chose a house, one of a terrace, rang the bell. A woman came to the door, peered at a photograph under a dim porch light. I'd chosen a poor snapshot, Carol some years ago. Not even vaguely like Caroline. No, the woman said, didn't recognize the face. I gave her my visiting card, asking her to call if she remembered the girl later. She took it like a pamphlet handed out on the pavement, politely indifferent.

Further along the road, I stopped an elderly gentleman, military moustached, walking a spaniel. We peered together in darkness, the nearest street light some yards distant. He shook his head. What's she done? he enquired. Run off or something? Always doing it, I said, handing him my card with an air of desperation. Always running off. Then I returned home, told Flora she'd have a dinner to end all dinners. Later, I said, good things are worth waiting for. She observed in downcast silence as I switched on the word processor . . .

The sleepy Clydeside town of Helensburgh was shocked by a second brutal murder yesterday when the body of a young woman was found in a local park.

The discovery was made around 5.30 p.m. by a schoolboy, (NAME HERE), 14, walking his dog. Police say the woman had been attacked in darkness and raped. Her body, clothes ripped and undergarments removed, was lying in a burn running through Hermitage Park, only minutes away from the busy centre of town. Such was the frenzy of the attack that one of her thigh-length leather boots was discovered later some distance away in the water.

The murder comes less than two weeks after the rape and murder in her home of Aileen MacRae, 37, wife of a well-known West Coast property developer. Both women were killed in identical fashion. Both, the DISPATCH has learned, were sexually assaulted AFTER THEIR DEATHS.

'A ghastly and vicious killing,' said a senior police officer at the scene of the latest crime. 'No question we're dealing with the same madman. There's a psychotic killer, a DANGEROUS MANIAC, on the loose in this town.'

Local people have been increasingly outspoken about the slow progress made so far in investigating the MacRae killing. Fears were heightened by the revelation that police had still not established the identity of the second victim last night, many hours after the body was found.

Yet the DISPATCH found out who she was. It was EASY. Why couldn't the Strathclyde Police!!!?

The girl was Carol Logan, 20, of Caledonia Street, Yoker. Voicing her grief in an EXCLUSIVE INTERVIEW with the DISPATCH, Carol's mother, Janey Logan, 52, said, 'She was a quiet girl who kept herself to herself. Tall, with lovely red hair. I get an empty feeling inside at the thought of never seeing her again. Like she's flown away and left us for good.'

But Mrs Logan won't be shedding tears, she told us. Not yet. She spoke of her anger that the police were being so slow.

'Makes you wonder,' she said, 'what hope there is they'll ever catch this crazy killer.'

Carol's story has a bizarre twist. The DISPATCH can reveal that the dead girl had been leading an AMAZING DOUBLE LIFE. Claiming to be an air hostess, she told of flying international routes and sharing hotels with the rich and famous. 'We didn't see Carol for weeks on end,' said her father, Norman, 54, an unemployed bricklayer. 'We thought she was soaking up the sun beside swimming pools overseas. Exotic places like Hong Kong.'

In fact Carol, under the alias Caroline Sutherland, was living only a few miles from home, in a rented room in Helensburgh. And in a further extraordinary twist, Carol, described by her mother as a dreamer, worked in SWEET DREAMS, a boutique frequented by many of Helensburgh's wealthiest women. The girl who met a tragic end at the hands of a sex-crazed killer was a shop assistant selling sexy underwear.

'She never told us,' says Janey Logan. 'She never once mentioned Helensburgh.'

Carol Logan's personal life will give few leads to the police. A stunningly attractive, well-dressed young woman nearly six feet in height, she had no special boyfriends. She dreamed, her mother says, of marrying an airline pilot. No-one else would do. Mrs Logan says her daughter even talked on her visits home about the colour she'd chosen for her wedding dress. Her favourite shade of pink.

Nor is Carol's mysterious life as Caroline Sutherland likely to give many clues. The few who knew her in Helensburgh speak of a solitary girl, without friends of either sex, who spent evenings alone in her room.

Last night there was frightened talk in Helensburgh. Local people have given the killer a name. THE HOOLET. A quick and silent creature of the shadows. A relentless stalker of his victims who strikes without mercy by day and by night.

The police, even with the help of the DISPATCH, have a tough puzzle on their hands.

Did THE HOOLET intend killing Carol Logan? Or was

217

he after Caroline Sutherland? Or did he blindly attack a
helpless young woman who just happened to be walking in the
dark through Hermitage Park.

Until these questions are answered, few women along the
banks of the Clyde will sleep easily in their beds.

Nearly ten o'clock by the time Jimmy made contact.
When the phone finally rang, I had all but given up on
him. I swore black and blue down the line.

'Didnae hae focking change tae bell ye,' he said.
'Watching yon focking door, OK. Howmy tae getteny
change when Ah'm watching the focking door?'

'See anything?'

'Na. Nae focking signa innybiddy.'

'Anyone call at the close across the road?'

'Ye didnae say tae watch tha close across the road.'

'But did you see any police?'

'Polis . . . ?'

'Did you see any fucking police in the street, Jimmy?'

'Nah.'

'Sure?'

'Course Ah'm focking sure.'

'Your money's at number forty-five. Ask for Mrs
Logan. And don't say anything about police, all right?'

'Me?' he said. 'Polis? Gottae be focking kidding.'

I called Ritchie Hamilton at the *Dispatch*.

'That story you've splashed over the front page,' I said.
'About the kid and his dog finding a body . . .'

'How the fuck d'you know that?' he spluttered.

'See through walls, me.' I said. 'Clear it. Stick it inside
under the horoscopes. I've the real story for you.'

'What's the corroboration?' he asked, when I'd told him
in outline. No names, no mention of Caledonia Street.

'Me, Ritchie. You have to trust me on this one. Try
corroborating with the parents, any breath to the police,
and you'll blow the exclusive.'

'Dunno . . .' he muttered.

'Fine by me. I'll give it to my blatt in London. Trying to do you a favour, that's all. More your kind of story than ours.'

Heavy breathing in my ear while he thought it over. Wheezes and rasps like an asthmatic old steam engine. He's a sixty a day man, Ritchie. They should play tapes of him thinking over the radio as a health warning to the young.

'I've got every photo of the girl,' I threw in. 'Every bloody photo there is. Best any other rag can do is print artist's impressions.'

We agreed terms. Very lucrative terms. But no by-line, I insisted. Call me a Special Crime Reporter, if he liked. Give Jack Moffat the credit, no skin off my nose. I wanted no recriminations with London, that's all. Then another long and sibilant pause when I spelled out my deal with the Logans.

'Jesus,' he said presently. 'A measly few hundred? How the hell'd you swing that?'

'Tell you some time. All to do with early birds and worms.'

I faxed the story to his office, along with faxes of some pictures of Caroline and the Logans for the first edition. I packaged the photos, phoned for a cab and asked the driver to deliver them, record time, to the *Dispatch* office in Glasgow. They'd pay, I said.

A celebratory mood, heady, intoxicating and more than a little vengeful, settled over me when all was done. I'd given Jack Moffat a lesson in news gathering, evened the score with Sergeant Grant. I'd got my own back on Bill Nicolson for the miserable pittance he pays, never on time, for my weekly sweat and blood. I had the bright idea of ringing Galbraith, shouting 'scoop' and 'success at last, you wanker' at him, and slamming the phone down without saying who I was. What better revenge than confusing the bastard? But his number was gone from my address book, just a torn margin where the page had been. Funny, that. I had no recollection of doing it.

Fifteen

Two tape recorders this time. Two. Both plugged in and ready to go.

What was Turnbull playing at? Did he so distrust Japanese technology he wanted an entire back-up system? Was this his only means of making copies – a cassette for the Procurator Fiscal the minute I broke down and confessed? Was this some psychological gambit, meant to intimidate? Two bloody tape recorders! He registered the calm absence of emotion with which I took note of them as I sat to face him across the grey metal table. I entertained thoughts of a cheerful remark to break the ice. He must have read my mind because no suggestion of a smirk, nothing in my eyes, betrayed any irony – yet a thunderously sullen glower knitted his brows, he looked me straight in the face with a frigid stare of warning. *Don't! Don't utter a damned word.* Nothing actually said, all done by telepathy. So I resigned myself to silence, letting a perfectly amicable comment about doing this in stereo fall by the wayside.

He started one of the machines and recited the prologue. The time was 7.23 a.m. on Tuesday the 6th of November. We were in Interview Room One at Helensburgh Police Station. He was Detective Chief Inspector . . . and so it went on. Ritual. I detest ritual, the pointless mouthing of words in a book. We all knew who he was. Just as, without any explanation given, I could guess why we were in Helensburgh rather than his office at Dumbarton: he couldn't bear the indignity of the Press seeing me brought in for his enlightenment. Not after I'd declined Grant's kind offer of a blanket over my head.

'Alexander Blair Douglas,' I said. 'More usually known as Sandy.'

Sergeant Grant announced his presence, sounding as if he hated himself, hated being here, hated the world and everything in it. I glanced his way, wondering whether it was significant that he always sat in a corner. Defensive body language, arms locked in a tight bundle across his puffed-up chest, legs clenched together. Grant, I observed with quiet equanimity, looked more of a suspect than I did.

'You are going to be asked questions about the murder of Carol Logan, also known as Caroline Sutherland, in Helensburgh on the fifth of November.'

'And I'm not here voluntarily,' I pointed out.

'No.' Turnbull said in terse agreement. He took out a newspaper, that morning's *Dispatch*, holding it up with the kind of distaste he might have accorded to touching someone's dirty underwear. An already tired and crumpled paper – rushed, I could well imagine, in a flurry of angry demands and recriminations from desk to desk, department to department, as though the police budget only ran to buying a single copy. Just one story on the front page. SHOCK SECRETS OF SEX KILLER'S LATEST VICTIM. Early off the presses, since the picture of Caroline in a low-cut party frock was the one I'd sent down the wire. She stared out at me with a blurred look about her, somewhat forlorn, that I didn't recall having noticed when I'd chosen the photo. She seemed bewildered to find herself there, as if she'd wandered by mistake on to the front page, was about to mutter apologies and make a hasty departure. Maybe it was my imagination but her eyes appeared to be raised slightly to the headline above; she seemed unable to comprehend that it had any connection with her. I won't say she pricked at my conscience, that would be going too far. She was dead and her death was news; she was news whether I'd written the story or not. But she looked, I have to confess, like a stranger in the bed, a girl after the night before, wan and

221

bleary in the cold light of a new dawning, and all you could think of was how to get her out of your life without being unpleasant. Maybe I'd have felt differently if Turnbull had shown me a crisp new copy of the paper, if he'd handled it with even a modicum of respect. But I gazed at it in a dumb kind of stupor and after some moments felt much the same about the headline as Caroline did. Maybe if I closed my eyes very tight, wished hard enough, I'd find it was nothing to do with me.

'This your doing?' Turnbull demanded.

'Not the headline. And I haven't read that in print, so I don't know what liberties they've taken with the words. But if you're asking if the story came from me . . .'

'Oh, I am, Mr Douglas. I am indeed . . .'

'Certainly it did. An outstanding example of investigative reporting, though I say so myself.'

Turnbull spoke to the tape recorder like an advocate addressing the jury. 'On being shown a copy of the *Dispatch* newspaper,' he declared, 'today's date, Mr Douglas has admitted writing the front page story.'

'I was asked a question,' I said. 'I gave a straight answer. I did not *admit* to anything. Admitting implies owning up. Are you saying there was any wrong-doing involved, any crime committed, in writing that story?'

'Why we're here so bright and early, Mr Douglas, to establish who did what. Because the way crimes are piling up in this town, I can't tell any more whether we're dealing with you, the Yorkshire Ripper or the bloody Mafia. There's murder, for starters. Withholding evidence from the police. Obtaining goods, namely photographs, by deception. Need I go on . . . ?'

'I'm simply a newshound, doing my job. Just so happens I did it rather more quickly than you did yours. Is that what's bothering you?'

'Where were you yesterday, between the hours of four to six in the evening?'

'At home.'

'Alone?'

'With my dog.'

'Can your dog testify to that?' No hint of humour in this.

'Unfortunately not.'

'Can anyone else?'

'No.'

'Did you murder Carol Logan?' The question tripped lightly, without emphasis, off his tongue.

'Would I have plastered those details all over the front page if I did?'

'An anonymous article, Mr Douglas. You asked the paper not to print your name.'

'For personal reasons, not to hide my identity from the police.'

'You suggested use of another reporter's name. What's that if it's not hiding your identity?'

'Look,' I said, 'you hauled Ritchie Hamilton out of bed demanding who gave him the story. He told you to get lost, am I right? Said to get a court order and you'd still be damned lucky. So Sergeant Grant called his pal Jack Moffat in the walking wounded ward and Jack, assuming he was still coherent from trying to drink the medicine cupboard dry, pointed a quivering finger my way. So come on, are you seriously trying to say I had that story printed and thought you'd never . . . I was a reporter fifteen years, for Christssake, knew Jack Moffat for every damned one of them . . . Are you saying I kidded myself you'd never find out?'

'I was listening carefully. I heard no direct answer to my original question.'

'No, I did not murder Carol Logan.'

'Were you acquainted with her?'

'No.'

'Had you heard of her, whether as Carol Logan or Caroline Sutherland, prior to her murder last night? Her name mentioned, any reference to her in conversation?'

'No.'

223

'Had you seen her at all . . . around the town maybe . . . in the shop where she worked . . .?'

'I don't have a wife who's bored with me. I can't afford mistresses. I'm not in the navy. Which just about counts me out, wouldn't you agree, as a likely visitor to her shop.'

'As you pointed out in this wee essay of yours, a bit slow, we Jocks in the Force, on learning about this young lady. But catching up, Mr Douglas, catching up. We found her handbag early this morning, round about one a.m. Got carried away by the burn, you see, lodged way downstream in a culvert. Contents include one rather bedraggled cheque book. She banked at the Clydesdale. Could have been the Bank of Scotland or the Royal Bank or the TSB or one of those nice friendly High Street Building Societies. But no. By sheer coincidence she used the same branch you use.'

'Just the two of us, you mean? The only customers. Bank of no hope.'

'Likely you saw her there, that's what I mean.'

'Ask the manager how often he sees me. I've got an aversion to banks. My wallet is allergic to banks.'

'Ever see her, then, in Hermitage Park?'

'Not that I'm aware of. I walk my dog in the park sometimes. I may well have seen her there.'

'But you don't remember seeing her . . .'

'Clearly not.'

'A stunningly attractive young woman, to use your own words in the *Dispatch*. Do you not have an eye for the ladies, Mr Douglas? This rare young bloom in the park, and you never noticed?'

'I'm usually lost in thought when I'm out walking. A thirty-ton truck could be bearing down on me and I'd hardly notice.'

'Nearly six feet in height, so you say here. Funny thing about height . . . don't know about you but it's the very tall women I tend to remember, and the pretty wee women who would fit in your pocket. Average women, they're the ones I'm blind to. How about you? A good hard think . . .

224

sure you never saw her, not once round the town? Legs all the way up and head in the clouds?'

'If I ever land in the dock for anything, Detective Chief Inspector, I'll hire you to defend me. You're doing a damned fine job. Quite right, I would remember her, a girl like that. Since I don't, we seem to have established pretty conclusively that she and I, both rather solitary souls, never clapped eyes on each other.'

'You were in Hermitage Park last night, after the body was found. Sergeant Grant saw you there, spoke with you. Correct?'

'Correct.'

'At which time, you tell us, you had neither seen nor heard of Carol Logan . . .'

'Correct again.'

'Did you see the body at all?'

'No. All I saw, briefly and at a distance, was a woman's leather boot.'

'Torn off in the struggle, you say here in the paper. Who told you so?'

'I've got eyes and a pair of binoculars. I saw one soaking wet boot. Pretty unlikely, in my experience, that the police had removed it from the body. So I made certain assumptions. Was I wrong?'

Turnbull was deaf to the question. 'Anything about that boot say Carol Logan to you?'

'How could it? It was just a boot.'

'Are you smarter than the police, Mr Douglas? Says here in the paper, you are. In as many words.'

'I'd make a lousy policeman. You'd probably make a lousy reporter. You approach problems one way, the police way. An area of ground to be searched, you search every square inch. Questions to be asked, you go house to house. I can't do that, there's just me and my notebook. So I'm forced to take short cuts. It's not systematic but sometimes it pays off.'

'And while we were working our way inch by inch down the burn, did you take one of these short cuts of yours?

225

Did you get to the culvert ahead of us? Find her handbag, by any chance, Mr Douglas? Is that how you knew who she was? Are you that damned bloody smart?'

'No, I didn't find her handbag. Stupid of me not to, now you point it out. All last night, I couldn't work out why she was such a mystery to you. The fact is, it never occurred to me that everything with her name on had been washed away down the burn.'

Turnbull thrust the newspaper across the desk at me. 'Take it,' he growled. So I did. 'Need to read any of that?'

'Such as . . . ?'

'Words,' he said, gritting his teeth. 'Words like EASY. Why was it, Mr Douglas? Why was it easy?'

Come, come, I said. We were both professionals. I wouldn't expect to learn his trade secrets, why was he enquiring into mine? A mute answer, conveyed by a vague shrug of the shoulders. I enjoy the economy of small gestures. Sometimes I wish I could write whole articles with just winks and nudges and shrugs.

'Frankly I think you undersell yourself,' Turnbull said. 'Work bloody miracles, you do. Six o'clock last night you'd never met nor heard of Carol Logan. You never caught sight of the body. Yet by twelve minutes past ten, the time you hired a taxi to the *Dispatch*, you've toddled off to Yoker, lied your way to an interview with the parents and conned them out of photos. We hadn't found that handbag yet. We didn't have one name for the girl and you'd come up with two. Easy, Mr Douglas? *It's fucking impossible!*'

'Unless I killed her, you mean?'

'Now you're being smart,' Sergeant Grant observed. 'First bloody thing you've said that makes sense.'

I looked over at him, bunched on his chair in the corner. Our eyes met. Surprising to see such disappointment in the watery melancholy of his gaze, as if I'd fallen in his esteem. Presently he frowned, his chin pulled in against his chest, when it became apparent I was gazing at him in an exactly similar manner.

Rolling back my cuff, I stared ostentatiously at my watch. 'You can hold me for six hours,' I reminded him. 'Then you either charge me or run me back home.'

'Expect to be here that long?' he replied.

'The way you're going about this, yes. Your show, do this any damned way you like. Save us all a lot of time, though, if we came straight to the point instead of all this beating about the bush. Why not simply come out with it? Ask the obvious question.'

'And what question's that . . . ?'

'How I knew who she was.'

A smile began curling at the corners of Grant's mouth, wistful and contrite. A petty criminal's smile, as though he'd been caught in the act but what the hell, he'd done worse in his time. He felt his mouth misbehaving and wiped it, stillborn, from his face. 'Then tell us, Mr Douglas,' he said caustically. 'Wouldn't want to keep you if you've other things planned.'

'All ears,' Turnbull said.

'I went home last night. Home to my dog and fireside slippers. Shows how keen I was to break this story, right? I didn't hang round the park to see what you found in the bushes. I didn't trail Jack Moffat down here to pounce on Dougie Watson, fourteen, and his pooch Ben. Home, Sergeant. Where I wrote a short and unsensational piece for my regular paper. Girl found dead, police suspect link to MacRae killing. Bottom of page two, if I was lucky, and my fool of a news editor calling up later to ask where's Scotland? Then I tried pouring a dram and the bar was dry. So I began pulling on my coat. That was me, Sergeant, going where I'd been going when I spotted your police cars roaring up the hill. Out to the Off-Licence. Evil personified.'

'This story got a point?' Grant enquired.

'The phone rang. A voice asked if I was Mr Douglas. I said yes. "She's Carol Logan," he said. "45 Caledonia Street, Yoker." Then he rang off.'

Turnbull had been fiddling with a pencil, acting bored

but tolerant. He froze in the instant, staring at me, pupils like saucers. The pencil was somewhere between one hand and the other – I couldn't quite see why it didn't fall. He looked to my detached and amused eye like an action shot on a sports page, a disaster about to happen.

'A voice . . . ?' he said eventually.

'A man, that's all I can tell you. I didn't take much notice at the time, to be honest. Just those few words spoken, then he was gone. Someone playing silly buggers, I thought at first. All he said was *she*. Who was this *she*? I was out of the house, half-way to the car, before it clicked who he meant.'

'He called you? You're saying he called you?'

'Well, someone certainly called me. And he was well-informed. Turned out she *was* Carol Logan.'

'He said that, Carol Logan? Not Caroline Sutherland?'

'Just the one name. Carol Logan.'

'That's not whose body we found, Mr Douglas. Who she really was, the name on her birth certificate, is beside the point. She was killed here, not in Yoker. Here she was Caroline Sutherland. The only identification she carried with her said that's who she was.'

'Then maybe he didn't know that, threw her handbag in the burn without peeping inside. Or maybe he was showing how clever he was – look at me, I've discovered her secret. He gave me no chance to ask.'

I've thought a great deal about lies. Because reporting's a lie, fiction's a lie, most of life's a lie. As a kid, I told kid's lies, fibs. I lied as kids do mainly out of fear and didn't much care whether the lies were silly, pathetic or risible, so long as they saved me. Now I care. I want lies to be proud of. A sign of maturity, the sophistication of one's lies. I do them in all shapes and sizes, from *ad lib* to labours of love. I'll toil for hours, making them smooth, well-honed, convincing, unbreakable, baroque, embellished, magnificent. I strive for the literary pinnacles of story-telling, where lies are a high form of art. It grieves me sometimes that it's an art only I can appreciate, but there you have it, lies are invisible, subliminal, they must go undetected. I've learned when to lie and when not to. How to tell a lie and not be found out. How to be caught telling a small lie to get away with a bigger one. When to be plain and when to be fancy. I've learned to construct a lie so the parts mesh together like an intricate piece of clockwork, then take it apart again, bit by bit, down to the last wee detail – because that's what the people you tell them to may do, brood on lies, lose sleep over lies, as they seldom will with truth. I've discovered that women believe lies if they're to do with love, and men if they're to do with practically anything, especially women or other men; that women need lies to be what they're longing to hear, while men must be scandalized, shocked, caught unawares.

As Turnbull evidently was.

'The guy called you . . . ?' he murmured in something of a daze, and slowly, cumbrously, wagged his head. He didn't want to believe me, but he did. His face told all. The further you stretch belief, I've found, the more belief you get.

Grant stirred in his chair. He looked utterly perplexed and totally lost, as though my explanation was too simple to grasp. Uncomplicated people can be a pain. They prefer their lies complicated. They have a necessity, I suppose, to place faith in things they don't understand.

'Why'd he call you, Mr Douglas?'

'No idea. He didn't say.'

'Why d'you think?'

'Because I work for the papers, why else? He wants publicity. Killers of his sort usually do.'

'Then why you? No aspersions intended but you're hardly first choice, see what I'm saying. I mean me, if I wanted to make the *Dispatch*, I'd call Jack Moffat.'

'Could be he tried and Jack's pocket phone was busy. Could be he reckoned that if Jack thought the kid and his dog was big news, there were better ways of making the *Dispatch*.'

'Know him do you, recognize the voice?'

'I don't think so.'

'What d'you mean . . . think? People call me on the phone, I can tell straight off if it's a voice I know. We get these weirdo phone calls all the time. *That raid last week, Mr Grant, the betting shop in Alexandria . . . I'd take a look under So-and-So's mattress if I were you, you might be surprised.* And there's a hankie over the phone, the voice is all high and squeaky . . . but I say to myself, hel-lo, wonder who Mrs So-and-So fancies all of a sudden that she wants her old man back in Barlinnie.'

'Was that a question?' I said. 'Or do tape recorders bring out the raconteur in you?'

'You sounded, Mr Douglas, unsure if you knew him or not.'

'Just a few words, then he was gone. I told you, it was some while before I realized the significance of what he'd said. I wasn't really listening to the voice. I wish I had, but I didn't.'

'A stranger, then. Someone you've never met.'

'I assume so.'

'Got your phone number, though.'

'I'm in the book, Sergeant. Under Douglas. And call it vanity if you like, but I'm there in bold print with the word *Writer* tagged along behind.'

'So you're leaving the house after this call,' Turnbull interposed. 'The penny drops. You can't remember the voice by now, right? Just the fact it's a man . . .'

'Not young, not old, that's about all I can tell you.'

'Local accent?'

I shrugged apologetically. 'No idea. But possibly Scottish.' Turnbull waited, inviting some explanation of my uncertainty. So I said: 'Most times I hear an English accent on the line it's some hassle or other with my paper. But this call . . . as he began speaking, when he checked my name, I don't remember thinking it was a call from London. So perhaps he's from these parts and I noticed that subconsciously.' I gave Turnbull the credit for being more informed on memory than I was. 'Just an average voice, I imagine. Like you were saying before, average people are the ones you forget.'

'But you remembered what he said. Carol Logan, a name you'd never heard before. Her address in Yoker and everything.'

'Went in one ear and out the other, as a matter of fact. I stood there outside the house like an idiot. Couldn't remember a damned word of it.' In re-enactment, my fingers snapped in a succession of clicks. 'Kathy something, I thought. No address, nothing.'

Turnbull leaned weightily on his elbows. He wore an ambiguous look of rapt attention. Impossible to tell now whether he believed all of this or none of it. 'Called you again later, did he?' he offered in a subversively helpful suggestion.

I dismissed his help with a shake of the head. 'I'd written it all down on my jotter. From habit, I guess. You know how it is, pick up the phone with one hand, grab a pencil with the other.'

We stared at one another then. No longer strangers exactly after brief collisions of encounter, we knew each other like old enemies, we knew each other not at all. As if, I thought, we gazed with the bars of a grille between us, seeing some parts clearly while others were hidden. He stared, then he stared harder, seeming to want the bars to melt so I'd be revealed in my totality. And I discovered, with the all-seeing eye of instinct, that his stares bespoke no suspicion or subterfuge, only confusion. He continued to stare. The bars confounded him, closing in all around. He found himself trapped.

'So you went to Yoker,' he said.

'Yes.'

'Occur to you, did it, to get in touch with us first?'

'No. I wanted to find out what the name and address meant.'

'You didn't consider it your duty to leave that to the police?'

'It was an anonymous call, no mention of murder. I was

following a hunch . . . Where's the law that says I have to share my hunches with the police?'

'Thought cross your mind, did it, to share your suspicions with the Logans? The dead girl's parents, for heavens sake!'

'I didn't know the dead girl was Carol Logan, not for certain. What are you saying, I should have distressed those people? What if I'd been wrong, got them distraught over nothing?'

Turnbull folded his hands together, propped his chin on them and closed his eyes. He seemed to be praying silently for strength. 'At what point,' he asked, eyes firmly shut, did you become sure Carol Logan was the girl in the park?'

'This morning, when Sergeant Grant used his boots as a door knocker.'

'Don't piss me around, Mr Douglas!' Eyes screwed tighter. A renewed prayer for deliverance.

'The Logans described Carol, showed me some snapshots. She was tall. I'd seen a large boot, long in the leg. Not easy to tell the colour, I'll admit, fished out of the burn in darkness, but it looked like green leather to me. And Carol had green eyes. I thought it a strong possibility she was the girl.'

'Any thoughts of telling them so?'

'Yes, I thought about that.'

'Then why didn't you tell them?'

'Because the way I deliver bad news is by printing it. Because it's your job telling them, not mine. Because I broke the news about his wife's murder to Duncan MacRae. And Sergeant Grant tore me off a strip, said I'd interfered with possible evidence. Said you like seeing the face when you bear sad tidings, to check any signs of guilt. That enough reasons to be going on with?'

Turnbull opened his eyes now, narrowly, for another of his long enquiring stares. 'What kind of monster are you, Mr Douglas? Buggered if I can understand, buggered if I can. This is an ordinary couple, their only child has just

232

been murdered. And you lie your way into their home, calmly sit there spinning cock-and-bull stories, acting as if Carol Logan's still alive and well and in fucking Hong Kong. You obtain their photos by deception – and by God the Fiscal's going to be getting a report from me on that. Want to hear what she did, Mrs Logan, when I was there at four this morning – hoping to hell I turned up before the rest of the Press got wind – wept buckets, needed to see and touch a picture of her daughter. She couldn't do that one wee thing, weep in pity over a fucking snapshot. You'd walked off with her albums.'

'For the record,' I stated, 'I did not lie my way in. I said I was writing an article about Carol. True. I said she'd be big news. True. I agreed a payment for the interview, payment will be made. I asked to see photographs, and when a sum was mentioned, Mr and Mrs Logan fell over themselves insisting I carted away the lot. Now you can write all that down for the Fiscal if you're so minded but I rather think he'll suggest you save your best efforts for finding the killer.'

'This Hoolet . . .'

'An apt name, don't you think?'

Turnbull stabbed at the STOP button on the tape recorder. He snatched up a phone from the table, jiggled the cradle in fury. 'Anyone round this fucking morgue!' he spat. 'Or's the fucking kettle locked up till the day-shift! Yes, fucking coffeesir. Three fucking coffeesirs. Black. Very black. Colour of my mood, that's how black.' He banged the phone against the recorder at the precise moment he touched the START key. I guessed this was to drown out any click on the tape.

Grant displayed conspicuous serenity. In fact, the angrier Turnbull grew the more droopily composed his expression became. There's nothing policemen like more from their superiors than bad temper directed at someone else for a change.

'The Logans say anything to you about Caroline Sutherland?' he enquired.

'No.'

'Another of your hunches, then . . . ?'

'As it happens, yes. They said she was abroad. So what was her body doing in Helensburgh? I asked if she'd ever mentioned Helensburgh, they said no. Something struck me as odd about this story of her being an air hostess – for a start, no bottles of duty free in the flat, no big bottles of perfume for her ma, no British Airways napkins on the sideboard. So I tried some theories on myself. My first thought was she might've been shacked up here with a married man, wanted it kept quiet from her parents. Something else struck me . . . she was killed early evening, about the time most people go home after work. So maybe she had a job in the town. And since she was killed in the park, it was possible she lived somewhere near by. Pure speculation, but I tried showing her photo round the neighbourhood. The usual thing, ringing doorbells, stopping people in the street. No luck till I found an old biddy walking her dog. That's Caroline Sutherland, she said, and pointed out the house. Said they used to chat sometimes in the park. Nice as they come, she said, most young folk won't give you the time of day. She told me about the lingerie shop – couldn't recall the name, why should she, but down by the Square, she said, so I went to see for myself. Lonely young lady, she reckoned – mention any programme on the television and Caroline had seen it. Terrible waste, she said, spending your best years goggling at the box.'

'Take her name, this old biddy's?'

'No. Should I have done?'

'Make me a happier man if you had.'

'Ask around if you don't believe me. I was calling at houses, leaving my card. You'll find plenty who remember seeing me.'

'Call at the house while you were at it? This house she pointed out to you.'

'You know I didn't.'

'Why didn't you?'

234

'Because I had my story by then. Carol and Caroline. Obviously the same girl.'

'Don't you believe in cross-checking your facts? I thought you newspaper people always did that.'

'I wanted to make the first edition, time was running out. Ritchie Hamilton was prepared to back my hunch.'

'Front page story, and it's only a hunch . . .'

'That's all it was. No hard facts, no withholding of evidence.'

'Whereas if you'd called at the house, and they'd said yes, that's her, Caroline Sutherland, it wouldn't be hearsay any more. And maybe they'd have noticed she wasn't in her room, worried over where she was. Might even have called the police. Getting warm, am I?'

'I confess, Sergeant. I did a shoddy bit of reporting. Yes, I should have called at the house. Now what? What section of what act have I broken?'

There was a time, long years gone by, when I'd sat in a bar somewhere in the East End with Jack Moffat. One of those bars with spit and sawdust for floorcovering and a boisterous, invigorating violence in the choking haze that warmed and cossetted like a blazing hearth. Jack, I recall, tottery on his stool, his tongue oiled by a joyful succession of hauf and haufs, turned his mind to philosophizing about success. We'd talked about decent apartments, then money, then women. In that order. Drink was a staircase, a dizzying upward climb to the unobtainable. Now we'd reached success and beyond that lay only oblivion.

'There's two kinds of fucking victolry,' Jack said, measuring every word, a look of pride coming over him at the completion of each sentence. 'There's the physical and the interrectual. You can knock 'em out cold or you can lay 'em fucking stupid. Know what I'm saying here?'

'Sure,' I said uncomprehendingly.

'Boxers knock 'em cold. Polyfuckingticians on platforms knock 'em cold, right? *Wham!* Out on the floor. Crowd on their feet, cheering their fucking heads off, right?'

235

'Right,' I said, flailing a punch through the air to show my understanding.

'But the interrectual knock-out, right . . . shut the buggers up, see what I'm saying . . . nothing but fucking silence. Isnae tha' great, Sandy, you illiterlate bastard? Take no prisoners, victolry of the fucking battlefield, smoke drifting over the vanquissed. Silence of death. Jesus, tha's somethen . . . the verbal knock-out. Power of ya mind over theirs. Lay 'em cold. Revel in the fucking silence.'

And they gave me a silence to be savoured, Turnbull and his lugubrious sergeant. Long enough to remember Jack on his stool, clear as if it was yesterday. And to muse over the iniquities of alcohol. Why if drink could touch Jack with such wisdom, wasn't he by now the wisest man who ever lived?

Turnbull cut into my errant thoughts. 'Whose idea, calling him the Hoolet? His or yours?'

'Mine.'

'Sudden flash of inspiration . . .'

'I suppose so. Where do ideas come from?'

'Said to yourself, two murders, this is a big man now. Can't call him just "the killer" any more. He needs a nickname, a catchy phrase, something for readers to remember him by.'

'When you can tell me his real name, Chief Inspector, I shall be delighted to print it.'

'What d'you people call it, a story with legs? Expecting this story to run and run, Mr Douglas? Think he'll stop at two?'

'More in your hands than mine, wouldn't you say?'

'Last night, was this, your flash of inspiration?'

'As I was writing the article. Why?'

'Not the day before? Or last Friday, say?'

'There weren't two murders till last night.'

A transient smile softened Turnbull's stern features. He lifted a hand in a gesture of condescension. 'Of course. Foolish of me.'

The smile re-emerged across the room, where Grant held on to it longer. 'No need for a nickname,' he declared, 'not with the one murder. I mean, who'd write about the Hoolet, fearless killer of one woman.' He relished the smile, folding it round his lips.

Turnbull leaned in my direction on the scratched metal table. He picked for a moment between his teeth with a thumbnail. Fixing his hard grey eyes on me, he said, 'Last night, then. Must have been last night. After the second murder.'

'Is this leading anywhere?' I asked. It occurred to me that I ought to be troubled by their gleeful behaviour but ignorance came to my defence; I couldn't work out why they were suddenly so smug.

'An *aide memoire*,' Turnbull announced. 'A sin of the past come to haunt you.' He started the second tape machine, idle all this while.

A moment passed before I recognized the voice as mine. I'd never heard one of these police recordings before and was so perturbed by the fuzzy sound that to begin with I scarcely heeded what was said. They must prepare these machines specially, years of research into getting the tone muffled, the echoing hollowness, the criminality imparted to voice and inflexion. A voice speaking from the dock, from a prison cell, some limbo for the guilty and condemned.

'I've got a vague recollection,' I heard, 'of needing to consult a specialized book on birds of prey. You see, I was planning a series of articles on hoolets.'

Then Turnbull speaking. 'He was at the library. I said he probably was.' Spoken closer to the microphone. No hollow echo. All fairness and sweet reason.

He stopped the play-back and leaned at ease in his chair, arms casually folded. 'The date in question was October the fourth. A trip to the library weeks before these murders. And you're planning – quote – a series of articles on hoolets. What shall we call this, another hunch? Or remarkable foresight?'

'I wrote an article at the time. About birds, not murder. It's there in print, my "Highlander's Diary".'

A cutting of the column materialized in his hand. 'A serial killer,' he recited, 'slaying mercilessly . . . Why do I admire his clinical skill, his speed and his power.' He looked up. 'Who are we describing here, Mr Douglas? Man or bird?'

'You're taking the words out of context.'

'Really?' He read aloud from the *Dispatch*, in a tone of accusation. 'The Hoolet. A quick and silent creature of the shadows.' His eyes fixed cruelly on me. 'The word "Hoolet" was in your head, presumably? Association of ideas.'

'It's called a metaphor,' I said. 'A somewhat blunt instrument but entirely legal.'

'As presumably was your use of the phrase "serial killer". Some good few weeks, let's note, before we had an actual such killer in this town.'

I tucked my arms together, crossed one leg in a relaxed manner over the other, and countered his stare with round eyes, a hint of ridicule. 'What would you like me to tell the Press?' I enquired. 'If they should ask at the door, I mean. That I was here for questioning? Or for an oral examination in literature?'

Wisdom is not the exclusive preserve of Jack Moffat. On occasions, I've had my own sparks of profound insight. That night in the East End bar, for instance. In all fairness, this was not foremost in my mind when Turnbull went purple in the face, pounded the table and sent the telephone flying. I felt an empty fluttering in my stomach. I was beset with the unreasoning fear of a kid caught lying. I wanted desperately to be anywhere else. But some small part of my brain stayed cogent. Perhaps that part of me kept its sanity while the rest was crumbling into disarray. Or perhaps it was the sane and normal thing to feel panic setting in, and it was a kind of madness to be able, despite all else, to observe Turnbull, watch the moods flash over him, and yet have a care for what he put me in mind of. Still . . . what I'd proposed to Jack was that everyone could be summarized in a single word, their whole character encapsulated. If you couldn't do that, I'd said, either the person was a mystery to you or they were schizophrenic. Jack's wife was a bitch, enough said. Jack himself was a pig, get the idea?

Turnbull, I thought, was like the weather. West Coast weather. Changeable, unpredictable, dour one minute, chilly the next, suddenly mild with sunny patches. And then what? A storm swirling up fit to dampen the spirits.

'My problem,' he thundered, 'is he killed Carol Logan! If he'd killed Caroline Sutherland, I could begin to understand. Two women from Helensburgh, both killed in Helensburgh, that makes sense. But according to you, he killed some mixed-up wee lass from Yoker. Nothing in her handbag to say she was from Yoker, nothing in her pokey wee room. So how did he know? *That's* my problem, Mr Douglas, this crackpot phone call of yours.'

'Just your word for it,' Grant observed, a stoic on the sidelines.

'That's right,' I said. 'Just the two of us to say he called. Him and me.'

The coffee arrived, black and with too much sugar, borne into the room by a woman constable, very business-like with a face not pretty enough to be a distraction and a sense of purpose in her stride. Sturdy young legs and sensible shoes. I view policewomen much as I do horses, cautious about what kind of kick they have. I wondered suddenly if it was a mistake, given the circumstances, to be seen staring at legs. But Turnbull was checking the tape counter, ensuring the cassette wasn't near its end. While Grant, his eyes reduced to slits as though they were shut, was peering in admiration at her calves, seeming to listen, as if to music, to the pianissimo rustle of stockinged thigh against thigh. Catching my eyes on him, he gave a veiled wink. I feigned the shock of a puritan.

The coffee heralded a change in the weather. The storm passed on. As the door closed once more, Turnbull mellowed somewhat. The promise of a balmy patch between the clouds, with the threat of frost still present in the air.

'No reference in your article to this call,' he said.

'No.'

'Quite a story, that. Killer Calls Ace Reporter.'

'That's as maybe. But then I'd be news. And I prefer the quiet life.'

'He called for publicity, you said.'

'And I denied it to him, up to a point. Responsible journalism, wouldn't you say?'

'Who did he kill? you say in your report. Carol Logan or Caroline Sutherland? Or a random murder, a girl in the park? But we know he killed Carol Logan, Mr Douglas. Why not say so?'

'I prefer what I wrote. Makes for a better story.'

Turnbull smiled then, disarming and agreeable. 'Funny sort of reporter,' he mused. 'There's going to be media people all over my patch from now on, newspapers, telly, you name it. They'd give their eye teeth for a chat with this . . .' He paused then conceded defeat, no use disputing the name of someone else's baby. '. . . Hoolet,' he resumed. 'Yet you say nothing.' He paused further, appearing to face a dilemma. 'I'll give you the benefit of the doubt, Mr Douglas. This is a raw deal you've given me in this muck sheet, the police being slow and all that crap. But there's big brass up at Pitt Street would say I had it coming. Broke the truce, they'd say, gave a newsman a rough ride, put him on parade for the MacRae case. Bloody asking for trouble. So I'll come clean with you, see if that clears the air. I don't think you did these murders. To my way of thinking, there's an odd kind of logic in what you've been saying. This man's mad. But not your kind of mad. Not the kind of mad to announce to the world who he's killed, the same time shitting a brick on the police all over page one.'

'Nice of you to say,' I murmured.

'But Don thinks you did it. Both women.'

'Do you?' I said, turning to Grant.

'Oh, ay,' he said happily. 'Plain as a pikestaff.'

I've heard, we all have, about the nice man and the nasty man. Was this a new variant on the technique? Get the big jovial type to play nasty, while the natural bastard acts on your side? All the harder to decide since they both sounded totally sincere. Perhaps, I thought, we were all lying, a three-handed game of lies.

'Mind telling me why?' I asked.

'Certainly I mind!' he retorted.

'He says you're everywhere in this investigation,' Turnbull offered considerately. 'Always quick to the scene and full of surprises. And another thing . . . he's been talking to Caroline's landlady. He tells me – this right, Don? – our Miss Sutherland had a feeling she was being followed these past few weeks, dirty old man in a raincoat brigade, and he'll be nagging me stupid over that, won't you, Don?'

'Like a hungry dog, sir.'

'. . . planned for weeks, he'll be saying. So it wasn't a random killing. Meaning our first murder won't have been random, either. Connections, he'll say, what's there in common between Aileen MacRae and Carol stroke Caroline?'

'Apart from the weapon,' Grant contributed. 'And the sexual trademark.'

'Would you like my fingerprints?' I said impetuously. 'And blood maybe? Want me left alone in a room with a test-tube and my vivid imagination?'

'Kind of you,' Grant said. 'We were going to ask.'

'Connections,' Turnbull continued, as though he hadn't been interrupted. 'And he can only find one so far. Doesn't know what to make of it, me neither. But early days yet. Tenacious as buggery, our Don, a bulldog, if you must know. He'll gnaw away at it day and night till it's solved.'

He broke off there, willing me to ask. So I denied him the pleasure.

'First to the next of kin,' he said. 'Beat us to it both times. Like you knew exactly where to find them.'

Then he smiled. A real lie of smile. Trusting and trustworthy.

Questions for hours about the voice on the phone. My fingerprints taken and a sample of blood. My indulgence was craved. The six hours were up and I was of course free to leave, but would I consent to help further with police enquiries? No euphemism intended, Mr Douglas, help, be of real assistance, anything to catch this bastard.

How could I refuse? A police car, blue lights aflash, siren theatrically howling, whisked me to the University of Strathclyde, where a tweedy expert in Linguistics, who had lately enjoyed lunch, risotto on the evidence of his beard, played more than a hundred mysterious voices in an office that smelled of something mouldy, perhaps books. City voices, country dialects, village incantations and seashore twangs. He laid claim at one stage to being a connoisseur of voices, he tasted them as a vintner does wine. He knew which particular Clydeside street, even, spawned a certain style of speech. He could recognize the seed stock of a tongue, whether fathers and fathers before that had been rooted in the same soil.

I disappointed him profoundly. Everyone listens to voices! he said, can't bloody not. Darkness outside the windows by now, an impatient hum of home-bound traffic oozing through the glass. For Christsake, he complained, the voice is the medium, how can you take in the message without some vague idea, some bloody thing, for Christsake, about accent, timbre, social class. Think, would you. Educated or uneducated?

I'm a writer, I replied. I only listen to the words.

Sixteen

A quiet town, they call it. What they mean – in their pressed white pants at the Bowling Club, in their flowery hats at Sunday Service, in kilts and maternal blue as they marry off their daughters – is that this is a place where nothing should happen. Nothing you couldn't, with a clean conscience, hire a photographer to snap, and stick in an album.

Indeed for many years the local newsheet, the *Helensburgh Advertiser*, has displayed great skill in constructing indignant headlines from the inconsequential, the ordinary and the practically non-existent. In desperation one week at the paucity of news, it was reduced to leading on the SCANDAL OF TOWN PAVEMENTS, a sorry tale of an elderly citizen falling flat on her face. Weeks later, the theme had to be revisited: OUR SCANDALOUS PAVEMENTS – ANOTHER FALL. When the town awoke one Friday to find an ominous headline warning of a SHARK ATTACK! the commotion was quick to abate, families took once more to their dinghies on the Clyde. The victim, it transpired, had once stayed in Helensburgh, though not for very long. She had survived. The shark was in Australian waters at the time.

Small discontents, then. A history of minor moans and trivial tattle. If any of Helensburgh's great and good ever craved excitement, expressed a longing for something, any damn blasted thing, for the Lord's sake, to *happen* round here, they'd be the very first to protest if anything actually did. So the murders changed the town. Only for a while but it seemed, as is usual in the midst of momentous happenings, that the change was for ever. The first murder had been a novelty, the foundation of gossip, a basis for huddling in shops and on corners, a reason for that oddly proprietorial pride in being at the focus of tabloid attention. The second murder induced shock. The whole town went into trauma.

By day, fear was in the eyes. Women regarded men in the streets with shrunken glances and accusation. Even ministers of the kirk, I heard, found themselves objects of suspicion, good is only a flip of the coin away from evil. Men thought it best not to look closely at women, and, as tends to happen in trying to appear innocent of what you haven't done, went shifty in the feet and villainous in the face. On my much delayed expedition to the Off-Licence, I counted a dozen of all ages who could have been rounded up for questioning on the damning testimony of their eyes.

By night the streets emptied of townspeople and filled with police. They patrolled in clomping pairs. They sat in cars by the kerbside, engines running for warmth; the plumes of exhaust rising in the chill black air gave them an aura of expectancy, a readiness to pounce at the fall of a body, the muffled choking of a scream. They watched eagle-eyed, recording and collating vehicle movements on each of the roads into Helensburgh: along the Clyde from Dumbarton; beside the Gare Loch out through Rhu; over the Blackhill Plantation to Luss; and even those who'd previously been aware there were only three ways of entry to the town felt suddenly stranded – if the Hoolet's one of us, it was murmured abroad, we're trapped here with him. Fleets of unmarked police cars and vans were rumoured to be hidden and cruising, the glint of moonlight on nightsights was spotted high on a church bell-tower – an influx of 999 calls told the police only that their own men looked murderous in the dark. They began the task of trawling every dwelling place in the town, questioning males over the age of sixteen, and some who were younger but looked sufficiently sturdy to kill. Doors were usually reluctantly opened. Quite whether they hoped to achieve anything by this buzz of activity I found hard to determine. Perhaps it was simply public relations, they had to be seen to do something. Public relations is what you inflict on the public when you can think of nothing else.

I felt splendidly apart from the general fear and outrage. I had in no small part changed the history of a place on the map. I felt elevated, I suppose, as people do who make history, above it all, entitled to watch events unfold from a lofty distance. The word was quickly out that I'd written the report in the *Dispatch*: as far as I could tell, Jack Moffat let this slip in the bar at the Imperial, the news spread like a bushfire through the parched undergrowth of rumour. I had the sense of being stared at in the street, pointed out, though I could never actually see this being done. Other more sinister stories must have been voiced: no-one in shops seemed ready to look me direct in the eye. But I quite enjoyed the fame, such as it was, and remained untroubled by infamy. Helensburgh has its dusty pantheon of celebrities – Logie Baird, Jack Buchanan, Deborah Kerr – who'd packed their bags in search of fame. I'd remained faithful to the town; fame had come calling on me. I began contemplating what glowing epitaph the grateful burghers would inscribe on my tombstone.

My only rumblings of discontent – because there's always some black cloud to mar every moment of glory – were over the town's future. The awful idea came to me that this kind of collective shock was like the discovery of sex, like a first erection, like finding pimples on your face, like being hefty enough suddenly to punch your father and not be punched back. The shock of growing up. I suspected I'd wake one day to find that, overnight, Helensburgh had become a big town. Where murder was commonplace and nobody noticed.

The one other who remained aloof from the pervasive paranoia was Gordon. We Douglases have stubbornness and rivalry in our blood – since I was involved, he was damned if he'd raise an eyebrow. He didn't dwell on the newspaper sensationalism, he never reads the daily blatts. He seldom watches the news on television; enough worries of his own, he says, without being burdened by the misdeeds of mankind. If he'd a mind to stare at a woman, and sometimes he had, he'd bloody stare, why the hell not! When the taproom banter turned to murder in his local at Luss, he'd steer it adroitly on to country matters. He was no stranger to violent death. If it wasn't wildlife being slaughtered, he wasn't a bit interested.

Seventeen

He woke me like a berserk cockerel in the dank grey
stillness of dawn. Daybreak was a dull white crack
opening in the sky against the eastern hilltops, a door ajar
to a drizzly new day, and persistent stars still flickered
bravely in the firmament. Gordon stood in the courtyard
beneath my bedroom window, flapping his elbows,
crowing up to the heavens. His filthy Land Rover coughed
and juddered, spewing out vapours of diesel that gathered
like a marsh mist above the gravel and swirled about his
feet. Phyllis says we're each as crazy as the other. Mine is
the stupidity and ulcers of hopeless fortune seeking, the
madness of traffic, the senseless pushing of crowded
streets. Leastways it was. Now, she says, I'm just plain
empty headed from having no ulcers to justify my
existence. While Gordon, I've heard her declare at
different times, is daft as a cuckoo, silly as a mule, mad as
a charging bull. When he saw me finally pull the curtains
aside, he leapt on to the running board where he perched,
scrawny neck at full stretch, flapped his elbows more
frantically still and crowed at the top of his voice. King of
the fucking farmyard. One of these days he'll expire,
Phyllis thinks, of something unseemly, like foot and
mouth disease. Me, I'm urban crazy, she says. Whereas
Gordon is country crazy.

I lifted the window to hiss a muted warning: 'Want to
wake the whole bloody neighbourhood!'

'Time they were bloody up,' he called back. 'Time
honest folk were about their business. Cock-a-doodle-
dooooooo-oo.'

'Something on your mind?'

'Killing, Sandy. Death to the old and infirm.' He hopped on to the ground. Exhaust fumes scuttled like kicked-up dust. 'Dear Sandy,' he said, aiming an imaginary rifle between my eyes.

I stared out drowsily. The sky was lightening, the cleft above the hilltops growing perceptibly wider, a glister of gold beginning to break through. Dawn comes uncommonly fast to unfamiliar eyes. I was in a mood for darkness to linger.

'Waited damn nearly an hour for you on Tuesday.' He gave a casual shrug to show his time was of no more consequence than mine. 'Busy man, my brother, I said to Phyllis. Something must've cropped up.'

'Christ!' I exclaimed. '*Deer!*'

'They're up on the fells, if you're interested. Grateful, I dare say, for the stay of execution.'

I said I'd be down, and dressed in a hurry. Thick socks rolled over my stalking breeches, an Arran sweater the colour of unwashed fleece, a hipflask filled to the brim with Famous Grouse stowed in the poacher's pocket of my Barbour.

Flora lay curled on my bed, deep in the rapture of unfeminine snores. She didn't so much as blink an eye when I left, even though I stamped my boots to get the blood circulating, and must have disturbed the slumbers downstairs.

'Sorry about the other day,' I said in the Land Rover. 'I forgot.'

'You forgot . . .'

'A wee matter of being arrested.'

He merely nodded, taking this as sufficient excuse.

'To do with the murder,' I said. 'In Hermitage Park.'

He nodded again. 'I heard about that.'

'How did you hear?'

'Why? Think I don't hear things?'

'I'm curious, that's all. Did you finally get round to mending your crystal set? Read it in the newspaper your fish and chips were wrapped in?'

'From the fucking police, that's how!' he said, a black scowl contorting his face. 'A girl gets battered, and I'm made to give account of myself. How's that look, fingerprints taken, searching questions in front of the wife?'

'Depends,' I suggested with a smile, 'whether she trusts you or no'.'

'Very tall, this girl, so I heard. She'd a job in the town, selling knickers and such.' He twisted his head to stare at me. Fortunately the lane was deserted; he seemed to be steering by ear, the sound of hedgerows snapping on mudguards and doors. 'They didn't mention the size of her tits. Big, I guess, tits you could swing on. A lost opportunity, raping a girl with small tits.'

'Somewhat early in the morning for subtlety,' I said.

'Out on bail, are we?'

'No charges preferred. My offence, such as it was, seemed to be the crime of superior knowledge.'

'Did you tell them you'd been watching her, staring in at her bedroom window?'

'Simple people, policemen. I don't think they'd understand.'

'Think to tell them you went shopping for underwear? And she held the see-through nightie against her big tits, giving a come-hither smile?'

'Better I didn't. Likely to cause no end of complications.'

'Weird goings on in the town, I was saying to Phyllis. Nae sooner does Sandy buy a nightdress for one of his women than her head's bashed in. Then bugger me if the girl he buys it from doesn't get *her* head bashed in. Either there's something lethal about the stuff they sell in that shop, I said, or our Sandy has some explaining to do.'

'What are you implying?'

He hadn't taken his eyes off me. Branches and twigs racing at us through the windscreen and the tyres gouging gobs of earth from the verge. 'I was out shooting rabbits Monday afternoon,' he said, an uncongenial tone. 'Showed the bloody police the pot of stew to prove it. Out on my ownsome, Sandy, man enough to carry my own dinner home. So don't look to me for any lies this time round, any more of your fucking alibis. I want no part of this.'

I gripped the steering wheel with one hand, gave a yank to swerve the Land Rover to the opposite side of the lane. This had the effect of getting Gordon's attention back where it should be. He has never liked me putting him in his place. Brotherhood, he prides himself, allows room for only one man in the driving seat.

'I'm in the clear,' I said. 'My movements accounted for, thanks very much.'

He seemed disappointed. Gordon reminds me at times like this of my bank manager, or a minor god from mythology, which is much the same thing. He wants, needs, help sought from him. He dispenses it unwillingly, if at all.

We took a hidden turning, civilization left behind, climbing with a whine of gears towards a glen in the near distance. A sign, toppled over by the dry-stone walling, warned of a ROAD UNFIT FOR MOTORS. The lane closed in to single vehicle width, a route to nowhere that finally gave out in a dying gasp of a dead end. Gordon braked violently, gesturing for me to open a rusty farm gate. Then we skirted a ploughed and desolate tract on a poor excuse for a road, two deep ruts over a minefield of pot holes. Rain had puddled in boggy green pools, mud splattered like ink blobs on the windshield. The wipers smeared arcs of impenetrable murk across the glass, the Land Rover bucketed like a dinghy in a gale.

'I've given the killer a name,' I said.

'The Hoolet. I heard.'

'It seemed only fair. Since we're on speaking terms.'

'You and him . . . ?' He sounded doubtful.

'He phoned me the other night. Convenient really. Otherwise I'd have had difficulties, shall we say, explaining how I knew so much about Carol Logan.'

'Did you tell the police?'

I nodded emphatically. 'A whole new dimension to the case, one of them said. It casts revealing light on his personality. We are dealing here, Gordon, with an attention seeker, someone desperate to be noticed.'

Gordon lapsed into the silence of inner thoughts. The windshield was opaque by now; he stuck his head out of the side window every so often, where it became freckled with mud. The Land Rover pitched and yawed. He proceeded in slow bottom gear for the next quarter mile or so, as if navigating a course in choppy seas.

'Anyone you know?' he asked eventually.

'Just a voice. Remarkably normal, all things considered. Not a murderous voice, if you know what I mean.'

'Where did he call from?'

'Hardly likely to tell me, was he?'

'From a call-box, an ordinary phone, what?'

'I don't remember noticing.' I took close regard of his face. His lips drawn down in a pensive line, cheeks rippling where his tongue was digging inside his mouth. A sure indication that Gordon is hatching a surprise when he sucks at the back of his teeth and tries, with a look of mild astonishment, to work out what he had for breakfast.

'Can't they trace calls?' he suggested. 'Check your records at the exchange and see who's been phoning you? The actual numbers and everything.'

'News to me. What makes you think so?'

'When I ask for an alarm call, the exchange knows my number without me having to say.'

'You sure?'

'Marvels of electronics,' he said, looking unduly pleased.

He left me to my misery. A little while later, after some frenzied exercise of memory, I cheered up considerably.

'He was in a call-box,' I declared. 'Funny you should ask because it never occurred to the police.'

'Keeping their powder dry,' he muttered ominously.

'Definitely a call-box.'

'Best if it was,' he agreed. 'Harder to track him down.'

'I had someone ring me that very evening, from a box in Yoker. A kid, no-one they're likely to find. So if you're right, and they're able to check, well . . . it confirms my story.'

'I worry about you, Sandy,' he said, his voice burdened with genuine grief. 'You're like some unweaned wee animal. Nae fit to face the world without me bottle-feeding you.'

'I'd have thought of it anyway,' I replied. 'Sooner or later.'

'The fuck you would,' he said.

It is a constant source of amazement to me how empty Scotland is. We left the Land Rover in a hollow, struck out on foot over a muir of heather and ferns, and within minutes I was lost. Helensburgh could not have been far distant beyond the fells that surrounded us, but in which direction? Highland hills can be like the moon, their far sides a mystery, sunless and barren. We made our way along a randomly wandering narrow trail, a deer path indented in places with hoof prints, carrying the tell-tale signs of animal droppings. Wind whistled through the crags above our heads, fine drizzle blew cold and prickling against the back of my neck. The sky was a majestic expanse of leaden silver that seemed low and close where it touched the ridges, limitless to the far horizons. Lean Douglas firs grew impossibly, soaring and ancient, from the infertile rootings of rocks. I felt my whole body awakening, becoming vibrantly alive, and would have found an awesome perfection in this windswept emptiness. But Gordon strode ahead of me, pausing sometimes to stoop, like an Indian stalker, for evidence of activity on the track, and I couldn't keep my eyes off his rifle. Shooting would be idyllic, poetic even, if it wasn't for guns.

A high-velocity rifle with a precision telescopic sight. The high speed for a clean kill, the sight to reduce the risk of injury. I have always thought it anachronistic for a man of Gordon's temperament to employ such an advanced and fearsome weapon in the slaying of helpless animals. He should outwit them the way he tracks, by the exercise of primitive skills. He should strike swiftly and painlessly with his strong bare hands. I think he knows this. That is why you can tell what he's hunting by the way he carries the rifle. When he is killing in anger, bringing down retribution on a fox, he totes his gun in a kind of cold ruthless anger, gripping it tight and white-knuckled, pressing it close and ready to his side. But when he is forced to kill from necessity – a mission of mercy, as he prefers to say, a hind with a shattered forelimb, a stag going blind – he holds the rifle as if he wants no part of it, as if he is enduring an unwelcome companion and would rather be alone. Sure, he grasps the rifle firmly, because of its value. But he holds it at a slight distance away from him. Then his balance is upset over ditches and stony paths. He leans away to the other side a little, stumbling sometimes. He looks as though the gun has attached itself to his hand and he can't be free of it.

When he aims and fires, however, he is without diffidence or remorse. Best do this properly, he always says, or not at all. The humane way, he says, they don't feel a thing. He always speaks as if to justify himself, and I used to think he spoke for my benefit, a countryman explaining country habits to an ignorant intruder from the town. More recently, though, I have come to believe he is addressing himself. I suspect that death troubles him more than he cares to say. He wishes it weren't so easy to kill. When he squeezes the trigger he is confronted, inescapably, by the fragility of life. His constant worry is whether something that can be so easily taken can be worth very much. Hunting, he says, is a pagan pastime. He offers a little prayer before he fires but I get the distinct impression that each bullet destroys some small part of his wavering faith.

We had been scrambling uphill. He stopped for breath, for an excuse to be rid of the rifle for a while. He leaned it, stock down, against an outcropping of limestone and moved, probably unaware of doing so, some feet away. He stretched out his arms with a great yawn of release, gazing up to the sky.

'So the police,' he declared, 'will think the Hoolet's from Yoker.' As if there had been no break in our discourse.

'They'll think he used a call-box in Yoker,' I said. 'Not the same thing at all.'

He ruminated over the difference for several long moments. 'How can you injure eight hundred people with a single bullet?' he asked then.

I sighed. Out and about, he's prone to blathering. His talk, now I come to think of it, tends to reflect the character of his surroundings. A rough clamber of a conversation on days such as this, full of abrupt turns, sudden changes of views. Best go along with him or you get left behind.

'Taking injury in its broadest sense,' he prompted. 'Discomfort inflicted. People made cold and hungry . . .'

'Haven't a clue.'

'There was a gamekeeper last year,' he recounted. 'On an estate up north, doing what we're doing now. He took aim at an old stag. The stag was on a precipice, outlined against the sky. Behind, a long way off, out of focus in the sight, was a line of pylons. The shot missed and took out a power cable. He couldn't have hit that cable, at that distance, if he'd been trying. But eight hundred people, so they say, were without electricity for a whole weekend in the heart of winter.' He paused briefly. 'That's why, Sandy, you'd best make damned sure before you pull the trigger what else is in your line of fire. Bullets don't always land on target.' He dug round his teeth with his tongue, chewed noisily for several moments on whatever small morsel was retrieved. 'Your lies,' he continued, 'are bloody stray bullets. They ricochet. You shoot wide. You know not what injury you cause, pal.'

I made a reply ready but left it unsaid. Gordon is prone

to moralizing when he hunts, it must be something in the mountain air. His face grows saintly and doom laden, hair-shirt holiness, when he preaches on the errors of my ways. His sermons should be heard, like all sermons, in silence and quickly forgotten. He preaches, I imagine, as preachers do, not for the good of sinners but to make himself feel better.

I offered him the hip-flask and he took a long sup then smiled a happy grin and slipped the flask into his pocket. His eyes closed as he licked his lips. Nothing like a stiff drink straight after Sunday Service.

The deer were somewhere ahead when I felt the drizzle like icy pin-pricks on my face. I hadn't noticed the change of direction but now we were approaching upwind. Gordon wrinkled his nose, sniffing the air, though I doubt that he actually smells his quarry. He does this to impress me. He locates them, I surmise, simply through instinct. If he'd only say so, this would impress me more.

He signalled me down and we dropped side by side in the heather. About a score or so of roe deer were grazing on a brae about a hundred yards to our front. A plantation of young firs framing the herd to our left and a rugged rockface to the other side. We had come on them unawares, by the only route giving a clear line of fire. He tracks with the pitiless logic of a wild animal.

'Which would you choose?' Gordon asked.

I scanned the deer through my binoculars. One deer looks much like any other to me. Little point in guessing, so I said as much.

'The doe fourth from the right. See her?'

'Yes.'

'Seven or eight years old. She doesn't move as fast as the others. Going stiff in the joints. From an old injury, probably, to one of her legs.'

I studied her with the glasses. 'How can you tell? She isn't moving.'

'See that distinctive flash on her forehead, the shading

255

on her flanks? I've had my eye on her for some weeks now.'

'Sounds like premeditation . . .'

Gordon shrugged his shoulders. 'And come he slow,' he quoted solemnly, 'or come he fast, it is but Death who comes at last.' He screwed an eye to the rifle sight. 'Got her centre of your glasses?'

'Yes . . .'

'Then get her to one side. Watch the reaction around her.'

Delicate and timid creatures, I thought sadly, and she was quite the most beautiful among them. Her head was down as she foraged in the undergrowth. I willed her to remain that way a while longer, to turn her back on us and be spared. But she raised her slender neck, revealing trusting eyes, huge and dark, and I wondered why mere slowness of movement deserved such a savage penalty.

'Best do it then,' I heard murmured beside me.

The doe buckled at the knees, then fell where she stood. There were others in the herd within only feet of her. They stiffened briefly as the shot rang out, ears pricking up. Then they bent their necks once more to resume grazing. She lay dead in their midst, at their feet, the fact was unnoticed, unheeded.

'Jesus!' I murmured.

Gordon rose to his feet. Then the herd moved in a trice, taking to their heels with nervous dashing elegance. When we got to the body, I saw a small round hole just above the eyes, only a trickle of blood, a glistening black snail's trail on her lustrous coat. Gordon handed me the rifle to carry, and hefted the deer on to his shoulders, her lifeless legs draped round his neck.

'There's women for you,' he said. 'Callous indifference to one of their own kind. Dash off in panic at the sight of a man.'

The sky broke suddenly. Rain fell in sheets, slanted by the wind. It ran in cold streams down our faces as if we were weeping floods of tears. Dangling on Gordon's back, the doe stared at me with glazed dead eyes. I ought, I suppose, to have cried a little in reality. But to what purpose? Who but me would notice a few small drops in an ocean?

He shot two further deer that morning. The rains were relentless; he muttered grumpily at the vapours clouding the gunsight. He had an explanation, an excuse of sorts, for the choice of each victim. I forget them now but if he was acting as he said for the good of the herd maybe he's to be believed. Countrymen have the advantage over the rest of us when it comes to the dealing of death. We cannot question rural ways. Nature, we're told, has no place for sentiment. All I can say is that I felt alone in my ignorance. Time went by and no inner voice spoke to guide me to wisdom. I must have left Murdo behind on this occasion. Or perhaps, for once, he'd chosen not to come.

Driving back, bumping along the rutted track, Gordon requested me not to mention the murders in front of Phyllis. She was alone most days, he said, the cottage was pretty remote. She was keeping a loaded shotgun in the kitchen and woe betide anyone who thought she wouldn't use it . . . even so, why play on a woman's anxieties?

Something had been troubling me all morning. I could no longer keep it to myself. 'Who told you their heads were bashed in?'

'Eh?' he said.

'The two women . . . Aileen MacRae and Carol Logan. You said their heads were bashed in.'

'Did I? Figure of speech, Sandy. I mean, murder's murder.'

'Did the police say?'

'Must have done.'

'They said nothing of that to me. And I'm damned sure they didn't tell Jack Moffat. There's been no mention in the Press. Plenty of speculation but no hard facts about the way they died.'

He creased his forehead, thinking back, but at the same

257

time irritated at having to justify himself. 'It was the young one, bloody Columbo, same one as came before. I said I'd be damned if I'd give my fingerprints, bloody police state was this suddenly! And he said, couple of women get their heads bashed in, who are you, Mr Douglas, to complain over civil liberties?' Gordon glanced in my direction. Then he smiled faintly at the idea of being privy to inside information. 'Was he speaking out of turn?'

'Being careless, by the sound of it. Did he say anything else of interest while he was shooting his mouth off?'

'Maybe.'

'Such as . . . ?'

He brought the vehicle to an abrupt halt, switched off the engine, then sat quietly cogitating. Finally he turned to me with a look of injured pleading. He resembled one of those children, wide-eyed on a beach, who thinks he may be lost, is wondering how lost you have to be before it's all right to squeal in panic.

'He asked Phyllis for her date of birth.'

'So . . . ?'

'Twelfth of April. Then he asked when was our wedding anniversary. Eighteenth of June. No call for you to be getting special presents then, he said. Bit early for Christmas.'

I sat very stiff and still.

'Without a word, Phyllis got up and left the room. She came back with a cardboard box. Black, done up with a silver ribbon. Seductive wrapping, Sandy. I mean it's like destroying a provocative dress, but you can't help ripping it off.'

I muttered an imprecation.

'Is this what you're after? she said. Because if so, why don't you bloody say! Then she took out the nightdress and asked did he want to come up to the bedroom, watch her put it on, check was it her size? I did the choosing, she said, and my husband paid. Dull old married couple splashing out once in a blue moon. My idea, she said. An anniversary present, as a matter of fact, anniversary of our first ever fuck. Anything else you want to know? Bloody devastated, he was. Left with his tail between his legs.'

A long time passed before I found my voice. Then all I could manage was 'Why?'

'I wanted to see her,' he confessed weakly, 'this latest woman of yours. The enormous tits, the sexy fucking smile.' He paused in contemplation of his own folly. 'Not in your league of deception, Sandy, guess that's how the police found out. See, I paid by cheque. Address on the back and everything.' His hands were fastened in a sweaty grip on the steering wheel, he dropped his head. 'I hadn't decided, that's the funny part, whether to give it to Phyllis for Christmas or be rid of the blessed thing. Bury it, drown it in the Loch.'

'I burned mine,' I said, a facile remark.

'Never mentioned it to Phyllis,' he murmured, 'not a word.'

'Houses belong to wives,' I suggested hopefully. 'There are no safe hiding places.'

'I guess not.'

I offered the solace of a smile. 'Good job it was her size, then.'

He stared away into the far distance. His gaze, mobile and twitchy, seemed on everything and nothing. Lost, no question about it, and in desperate search of a familiar face.

'A good deal taller, actually,' he said. 'And not nearly so flat chested.'

When we resumed the drive homewards, I considered asking whether he'd done the same with my other women. With Aileen, for instance. Whether I'd said sufficient to identify her, bloody boasted too freely, and he couldn't resist taking a look for himself.

But I kept these thoughts hidden. For the very reason, I suppose, I never ask women if they love me. What good can come from questions to which you don't want to hear the answer?

*　　*　　*

No, I did not wish to see him skin and joint the carcass. I'd
take his proficiency with a knife for granted. The killing, I
can tolerate. I might even confess to the decadence of a
thrill at seeing death come so quickly; there is something
indecently beguiling in seeing the precise instant at which
the spirit departs a living thing. But even in death, the
deer was still beautiful – I couldn't bear to witness as she
was sliced into meat. So, saying he'd see to it later, Gordon
hauled her from the Land Rover to the back door of his
cottage, where he dropped her in a bundle beside the step.
Perhaps he hoped I'd do some of the carrying, but when I
made no move to help, he lugged the remaining two bodies
to the door without a word of complaint. His many dogs
set up a dreadful howling. They sounded, I thought, like a
pack in full cry.

We were soaked to the skin. We left our boots beside
the Aga, draped our Barbours over the fender to dry.
Phyllis joined us at the table, seeming preoccupied, to be
making conversation merely out of a sense of obligation.
Her presence is demanded in the kitchen, she believes,
something served up with the food. She ladled out steaming stew, which we devoured ravenously. Rabbit stew, she
said, as though my palate couldn't be relied on. How is it,
the rabbit? she enquired solicitously. Gordon had bagged a
couple . . . when was it? . . . Monday evening last.
Repetition of *rabbit* like the refrain of a prayer, and
uncertainty in her voice, which I thought odd. So I looked
at her and she promptly averted her gaze.

Her days are indistinguishable, one following another.
How, I've heard her say, if hours drag so slowly does time
fly so fast? They work six days of the week, she and
Gordon, and on the seventh they walk, whatever the
weather, in their Sunday best to the wee kirk in Luss.
Then it's a change of clothes and back to work, same as
usual. Yet I remember only dates while she never forgets a
single day, as if her life is so unremarkable its every
nuance must be clung to. There's always some small event

260

she treasures in her memory, rain in the morning or unseasonal sun or a robin hopping red-breasted on the fence round the yard. Two Tuesdays ago, she'll say, wasn't that when we saw those geese flying over?

Excellent rabbit, I said, best breakfast I'd had in years.

In all probability, I concluded, she was trying to sound convincing. She thought that memories are meant to be vague, the more uncertain their recall the more readily they're taken as gospel.

Gordon had work to do. Ministry returns of some sort in his tiny back office, and how he hates paperwork. I offered to ring for a taxi but Phyllis would hear none of it, insisting on driving me home. Blow of fresh air, she said, throwing me my coat. A chance to see the bright lights and temptations of town. Becoming a regular Sodom and Gommoraburgh these days, and she gave a saucy wink.

Considering this was Phyllis speaking, in her unfashionable scuffed brogues and shapeless winter coat, the prospect sounded like a gateway to sin. The thing is, the hip-flask bumped my side as I pulled on the Barbour, and it felt hollow. Not yet twelve noon and between us Gordon and I had polished off the best part of half a bottle – me on an empty stomach. If she'd asked should she bring the scanty nightdress, I'd have probably said yes.

Eighteen

She needed the driver's seat right forward, ridiculously close to the steering wheel, appearing small and frail and altogether too threadbare neat for the agricultural robustness of a Land Rover. I feared she'd demolish the gatepost as she shot with a surprising burst of speed into the road outside the yard. But the turning space was limited: either she judged the manoeuvre to perfection or luck was on our side.

She asked what I'd be writing about the morning's expedition and I took the easy option of an honest reply. Phyllis is one of those rare beings, a woman to whom lying is far more trouble than simply coming clean. On the few occasions I've toyed with an evasion, the perceptive suspicion has been evident in her face before it was ever spoken. Or so I've imagined. Why this should be I have never quite fathomed. She reminds me uncannily sometimes of Miss McCreadie, a forbidding teacher who was the bane of my young schooldays. Her grey hair, swept into a dourly puritanical bun, was cast iron, her terrifying stare as stiff and unbending as her back. It was whispered in the playground that she possessed a sixth sense for deception, she could recognize a fib quicker than we could tell Rovers from Austins. An elderly spinster, Miss McCreadie: what free man would have survived more than a few hours of that withering scrutiny? She taught me to spell and the rudiments of grammar. Unintentionally, she also drummed into me the invaluable lesson of looking warily at eyes before giving voice to a lie. Some eyes have a special kind of glitter and are not to be fooled. Phyllis has just such a beady glint when she stares. In idle moments, I had fallen to wondering what priceless lessons were there, lying in wait, to be learned from conversations with Phyllis. Unfortunately, I'd always found that type of staring too damned uncomfortable to endure for very long. Like an ice-cold scalpel slicing into your heart.

'I haven't decided,' I answered. 'I may end up writing nothing.'

'Can't you just write what you saw?'

'Ay, I could.' My voice said otherwise.

'Isn't that what you newspaper folk are supposed to do?'

'Only in theory.'

'Isn't that why Gordon takes you out with him, to report on a gamekeeper's work?'

'He helps with ideas, Phyllis. But I never write what I see, not exactly. I wish it were that easy.'

'He shot some deer this morning . . .'

'Three, to be precise.'

'Then why not simply describe what happened?'

'Because I can't think what to say. Gordon fires, one rather lovely animal drops down dead. Does the herd stampede, show any sign of awareness? Do they exhibit fear? Not a bit of it. He could kill the lot if he wished, picking them off one at a time. It's cold, calculating and without a vestige of drama.'

'Which means culling is humane,' she stated. 'And efficient. The animal is in a calm state of mind as it dies. If you shoot a panicky deer, there's adrenalin in its blood, the muscles are full of acids. So you get tough and stringy meat. Can't you tell your readers that? Tender venison means the animal had a painless death?'

'I don't write a food column,' I replied. 'I need a theme and I can't seem to find one.'

She glanced shrewdly towards me. 'Do you disapprove of culling?'

'I didn't think so till now. But I'm beginning to wonder.'

'You are aware, I hope,' she declared, 'that in nature no wild creature ever dies of old age?'

'Thoroughly aware, Phyllis. In fact, I had Murdo say exactly that several months ago.'

'You don't say!'

'Which is the cause of my present difficulty. There are only so many wise things to be said about the Highlands. And Murdo's already said most of them.'

At the foot of Glen Cairn, she joined the main road beside Loch Lomond. White peaks on the lumpy grey water, waves breaking with fidgety chatters along the rocky shore. A sky you could reach up and touch: the slopes of Ben Lomond submerged in the high tide of an inverted sea. Tickles of drizzle on the water and patchy rainfall blowing, windtossed and wispy, in undulating curtains across the Loch. In a lonely rowing boat riding out the swell, a seated figure crouched in doughty patience over a fishing rod. On a tiny bare island, a cluster of stones under watery siege, a cloaked grey heron huddled miserably, staring with grim determination at the dark and choppy surface. This end of the year with its dreich short days there are no booming, flashy speedboats to drive the fish into hiding. Yet I've heard it said about Lomond that when the fish are best the fishing is terrible: the Loch has little mercy for winter anglers, men or birds. I could find no pity for either of them; the morning had exhausted my goodwill for hunters.

'Bloody Murdo!' Phyllis said with sudden feeling.

'You sound just like Gordon,' I noted.

'Or he like me,' she observed acidly. 'Are you surprised, Sandy, after fourteen years of marriage?'

All the years I'd known her and I'd never seen her drive. Until that moment, Phyllis was a passenger, an occasional utterance from the back seat. I'd have said, if asked to guess, that she'd tootle along the middle of the road, find the engine beginning to stutter and discover she'd forgotten to push in the choke. I'd have said, so help me, she'd need my guidance on which turnings to take. I was convinced that before the journey was out she'd inflict such dire damage on the gearbox we'd be forced to call the

AA. Hopelessly wrong. She drove briskly, confidently. A caravan slowed us where the road bent sinuously, a 'D' plate displayed on the tail and, in the Mercedes in front, serious stolid faces surveying the Loch as if it was there to be enjoyed and by God, come rain or flood, they were going to enjoy it. In our own time, thank you very much, can't you see we're aliens? Bloody Germans, she complained as she shot past, cutting them up – D for Dreadful . . . still bloody here from last summer the speed they're going. She drove, even, with the makings of panache, allowing for the age and condition of the Land Rover. I'd always assumed from my journeys with Gordon that the gears crunched, that's what Land Rover gears did. Phyllis however made fluent and silent changes. And I don't know what magic she worked on the wipers but mucky drizzle dashed against the windows, mud sprayed up from the road, yet the windscreen somehow stayed clear. I imagine she has ways of dealing with dirt – spickness and order follow obediently at her apron-strings. In passing, I wondered what else I didn't know about her, what other surprises she hid. It came as something of a shock to realize that I'd never had the least curiosity about her. She was my brother's wife, she was simply *there*. And probably, because I was Gordon's brother, she'd made no attempt to be other than his adjunct, a devoted, and mostly silent, spouse.

She held her hand on the horn, dropped a gear and charged past a crawling tractor driver. He gave a horn blast of retaliation. She swore quietly to herself, and I've no idea what she said, but it sounded, as only Gaelic can, like lilting music mingled with hellfire.

'Bloody Murdo, as you call him,' I said, 'didn't turn up this morning.'

Phyllis frowned. 'He's only a figment of your imagination, Sandy.'

'He's real to me. He's in here.' I touched a finger to my forehead. 'Psychics have mediums, St Joan had her voices, I've got Murdo. Gordon shows me things, Murdo interprets them for me. Except today, Phyllis, he never showed up. I watched those deer being shot, waited to hear what story to tell . . . nothing.'

'Oh, for heaven's sake!' she said.

'All writers have inner voices. When they don't speak, you can't write. That's all there is to it.'

'But you have to write *something* . . .'

'Why?'

'Don't you have a column to fill?'

'I'm not sure. I mean, yes, I have a column. But I'm in two minds whether to jack it in. How does this sound for this week's Diary? *I quit.* Give me the greatest of pleasure to send that down the wire to Bill Nicolson.'

I couldn't stand the way she stared at me, so I looked away.

'Crime writing pays better,' I said.

'Did they pay you well for that stuff you wrote in the *Dispatch*?'

'As a matter of fact, yes.'

'And what happens when the money runs out . . . ? What will you do then? Live on air and our charity?'

'Well, it's just an idea . . .' I began. Then I stopped, because that's all it was, a distant first glimmering.

'Yes . . . ?'

I made no reply. Without looking at her, I could feel the increased intensity of that mordant stare.

'Your trouble, Sandy, is you've no-one to talk to. You've only yourself. And if you want my opinion, you give yourself lousy advice.'

'Are you offering advice, Phyllis?'

'If you need some. And I think maybe you do.'

'I know your kind of advice,' I said. 'It consists of one word. *Don't*. Don't go out with wicked women. Don't you dare tread muck through my house. Don't spend money, not a brass farthing.'

'Try me,' she said. 'You might be surprised.'

At which precise moment, she took a rapid right turn, cutting sharply across the path of an oncoming car and sliding the Land Rover into a perfectly controlled four-wheel drift that brought us on to the Helensburgh road. So I thought it quite possible she'd surprise me. I am, in any event, not in command of the situation with women I can't lie to.

'Let's be clear, it's only an idea . . .'

'So you said . . .'

'Did you see my story in the *Dispatch*?'

Only the slightest of nods. She'd bought a copy of the paper, read it avidly then thrown it, disgusting rubbish, from the car window on the way home. She'd stolen a look at the front pages while she was buying groceries in the village shop. She'd done her regular stint on the old folks' outing and peered over someone's shoulder in the Council minibus. She wasn't saying how or where but yes, reluctantly, she'd seen the *Dispatch*.

'I had to explain to the police how I came by that information. So I told them the Hoolet phoned me.'

'I see,' she murmured. And I rather think she did, the whole damned thing, every smallest detail.

'It occurs to me he might decide to ring again. And an interview would be worth a heap of money. Exclusive. The Hoolet speaks, our intrepid reporter tells all.'

'What would you ask him?'

'I haven't decided yet. Maybe how he chooses his victims.'

'And what will he say?'

'What he'll say, Phyllis, is something plausible. I don't know what. I'll need to think of a possible connection, something Aileen and Carol had in common.'

She gave me one of those silences that speaks volumes.

'I read minds,' I said. 'And you're thinking *Don't*.'

'Impressive,' she said. 'I didn't know you could do that.'

'Mind explaining why?'

She arched her eyebrows as if this ought to be reply enough for anyone. My God, she was thinking, isn't it obvious? They'll arrest him sooner or later. He'll deny ever talking to you, then you'll be in deep deep trouble. Bottomless depths of dung.

I smiled knowingly at her. Oh yes? I indicated by thought transference. He's mad, a total loony. Who'll believe him rather than me?

'Because it's not true,' she answered, having considered at length.

'But there's only one other person who'll know that,' I pointed out.

'Yes,' she said. 'And somehow I don't think he's the sort who'll take kindly to having words put in his mouth.'

I lie because I trust no-one. And I lie, too, because I know I'm not to be trusted.

An unaccustomed experience, then, to discover I trusted Phyllis. She was, I suppose, so far removed from my ideal of a desirable woman that none of the usual complications came into play. I didn't have the least interest in going to bed with her. I found her wonderfully and comfortably plain. I didn't even have the problem of thinking her so ugly as to be a challenge – and I'll confess to having been so challenged a couple of times in the past. I was briefly troubled by the thought that talking to her, from the heart so to speak, was so remarkably easy – with affectations and delusions and deceptions put aside – that this was probably, in a perfect world, how talking should be in those exhausted, languid intervals between screwing a woman's arse off. But this aberration quickly passed as we conversed. At some stage, I didn't quite notice when, we arrived in Helensburgh and stopped outside the house. Then we sat there in the Land Rover, still talking. For well over an hour I should think. I'd been honest with her, you see. So she was honest with me.

Gordon, she said, would be devastated if I didn't continue with my column. Gordon wasn't just family, he was my *entire* family. He was father to me when I needed fathering, he was a sympathetic mother, he was kindly uncle and maiden aunt. And what was I in return? The black sheep, ungrateful and prodigal.

'Gordon as good as writes your column,' she said. 'Yet you give all the credit to Murdo.'

'It's only a name, Phyllis. Why does it matter which name I use?'

'It matters to Gordon. You hurt him more than you'll ever know.'

'Has he told you so?'

'Of course not!'

'Well, then . . .'

'He's a very proud man, Sandy. Do you really not know that? Your own brother?'

'You're asking the impossible. Murdo's become an institution. I can't change my column suddenly, start writing about someone called Gordon.'

'It's your column. You can do as you please.'

'Does Gordon want to be written about, is that it? Is his life so unfulfilled he suddenly wants some trivial brand of fame?'

'He wants recognition,' she said. 'Not from the public, from you. Damn you, Sandy, you're such a mean bastard. You're like a miser with your pathetic words.'

'They're all I've got in this world.'

'Then be generous with them. Give him just a few wee words of acknowledgement now and again.'

'Not if he asked me on his death bed,' I said.

She stared in astonishment. In pity, too, for me or Gordon or maybe for both of us. And I discovered that at some point during the journey a spell had been broken, things seemed to have changed between us, because I was able to stare back without flinching, as I'd never been able before. The big difference between Phyllis and Miss McCreadie was that Phyllis showed herself capable of occasional pity, and a good deal more besides.

'I might do it, though, if you were to ask.'

'Lord above, you can be so infuriating!'

'*Are* you asking, Phyllis?'

'Yes.' Only a moment's hesitation.

'Then I'll write my column. And one of these days, no promises, I might make some mention of Gordon, Murdo's new assistant on the estate.'

'You might . . .'

'Depends how I feel.'

'You are,' she said, 'even a miser with promises.'

We talked of a great many things. Trust is like sex, exhilarating and addictive and to be tried in numerous ways. I had not talked so freely, so intensely, since my first mad nights of liberation at university, when I was drunk enough to trust everyone and them drunk enough to listen.

'Why,' I asked at some stage, 'did you lie about the nightdress?'

'So he's told you about that . . .' She reflected for a while, sufficiently long to decide no great hurt had been caused by his telling me. 'It wasn't bought for me, you realize. I know where he hides my presents and it wasn't there. He'd hidden it carefully where he thought I'd never look.'

'I rather gathered that.'

'Well if he needed, that badly, to buy a present for some other woman, the fault must be mine.'

'Why?'

'Because I'm his wife, Sandy. If he's looking elsewhere, I must be failing to satisfy him.'

'Is that a sufficient reason for lying to the police?'

'I can't,' she said, 'think of a better one.'

Finally, no apologies given or needed, I made enquiry about the rabbits. They must have been needling my subconscious. It was our open and honest talk about lying, probably, that caused me to think back, remember her uncertainty about the day they were shot and arrive at the conclusion that she'd been hesitant because deception didn't come easily to her.

Tuesday, she said. He'd shot them on Tuesday. He had

270

told her Monday, hoping she'd forgotten and would take his word for it.

'Where was he Monday afternoon?'

She shrugged, neither knowing for sure nor caring very much. 'Out and about somewhere on the estate, same as always. Why should Monday be different to any other day?'

'It's a ridiculous alibi,' I said with half a smile. 'I mean, a pot of stew, for goodness sake.'

'Hardly the best of stories,' she agreed, and rolled her eyes in momentary despair. Then she had a flash of inspiration, her face brightened and she added, in logic that escaped me: 'But at least the police bothered to taste it. That must count for something.'

'What the hell were you thinking of, you two? His advocate rising in court? Members of the jury, I offer in evidence one pot of rabbit stew. Proving conclusively that my client could not have done these murders.'

She gave a forced laugh. 'His idea, Sandy. Not mine.'

'Why didn't you say he was at the cottage?'

'Because he wasn't, and neither was I.'

'So what? Nobody knows that.'

She stared with a dull and contrite gaze, the hard glitter quite gone from her eyes. 'Not exactly true,' she murmured. 'I was with someone else.'

I was feeling around my coat pockets as she turned the vehicle in the forecourt and accelerated away down the drive. I called frantically after her but by then she'd vanished from sight.

A saloon car, in a neutral shade and not recently washed, was parked just along the street from the entrance gates to the house. There'd been cars of various makes, all in unremarkable colours, at about this spot for several days now, and when they got tired of the view up the hill towards Glen Fruin, there was a car, sometimes a van, parked a short way further down the street on the opposite kerb so that they could admire the panorama of the Firth

271

as they sat on their backsides, drinking out of a Thermos and listening surreptitiously to Radio Clyde. I walked over to tap on the glass. The young plainclothes man inside wound down his window.

'I've got an engagement in town tonight,' I said. 'I'm giving a talk.'

'Well aware, Mr Douglas, thanks all the same.'

'My speech is inside, and my change of clothes.'

'So long as you dress decent and talk proper,' he said.

'Just to let you know,' I said. 'I've come out without my keys. So I shall be breaking into the house.'

'S'all right, Mr Douglas. Thoughtful of you to say.'

Disturbingly easy, really. Up a drainpipe, on to the roof of the Gothic porch, a pane shattered and in through the bathroom window. Flora was waiting in the corridor, tail wagging ten to the dozen as if to say she'd known all along it was me, so why waste effort in barking?

My regular bunch of keys wasn't anywhere to be found. I checked the deadlock on the front door and it was bolted, so I had obviously taken my keys with me when I'd departed the house that morning. Hell! I must have lost them somewhere out on the muir with Gordon. Or had they fallen from a pocket at the cottage when I'd slung my Barbour over the fender to dry?

I tried ringing but got no reply. Phyllis, of course, wasn't back yet. And if Gordon was in, he wasn't answering.

Nineteen

Months ago, some local committee or other had asked if I'd give one of the talks in their winter programme. Winter had seemed a long way distant at the time, and the impression was cleverly given of just a few elderly folk foregathered in a chintzy front parlour. So I'd been trapped into saying yes. Since the lecture was for charity, I've a suspicion this was all Isobel's doing.

She was in the very front row of seats, her hair freshly coiffured, a shade too much red colouring applied to her glowing pink cheeks. We had each, in our own way, dressed formally for the occasion. I had donned a tweed sports jacket over my only respectable pair of cords; I'd even shown an iron to the cords despite knowing they'd refuse to take a crease. Isobel was dressed in a tailored suit the exact shape of her ample figure. Not quite what you'd call dowdy, but a depressingly sober shade of black, almost certainly the suit she'd wear to any event she considered important. She sat plumply, gazing up at me with a stare of intense concern. Her face shone above the sepulchral black suit, bearing such an expression of seriousness that I could well imagine her to be at the funeral of someone close and dear. It was as if she thought of me as family and blamed herself for my death.

The *Advertiser* had gone so far as to describe me as 'the renowned local author and columnist', listing the evening under Coming Attractions. Victoria Hall, 8 p.m. Sharp!, posters told the town from shop windows, as though my punctuality was legend. Isobel informed me later that the charity was more than happy with its gate money. Nearly a hundred pounds, she said proudly, and the polis had been especially generous. But then, she ventured, maybe attendance had counted as business and they'd claimed it back as expenses. Over seventy people turned out to hear my views on 'The Press and the Public', braving a night of insidious sleet that made treading the pavements like wading through porridge. How many came because of my association with the murders is a matter of conjecture. More than a few, I should think. The polis were well represented, in the persons of Sergeant Grant and two plainclothes men, who, having tailed me from the house, seemed to have decided that it was no weather to be stuck outside in a car. None of the three gave any indication of knowing quite why they were there, the plainclothes men jutting their chins out squarely in front of them, their eyes pinched and mistrustful as they made detailed inspection of the ceiling, while Sergeant Grant, his bulky frame filling a chair somewhere towards the back of the hall, seemed distinctly sheepish when I gave a cheerful wave of recognition – he gathered in his shoulders, slumped a little and hid his head, trying desperately to be the one thing he never could be. Inconspicuous.

'What is the Press?' I began. 'It's people like me, writing about people like you.'

I threw in a pause to encourage laughter. Not a ripple of amusement. A sea of eyes before me, staring up in blank incomprehension. At the corner of my vision, a crouching figure scuttled forward. A flashbulb fired as the *Advertiser* captured the moment for posterity. I gazed down at Isobel, intending to convey blame for my predicament, but she gazed back, wide-eyed and entranced. Her serious look, her Gosh-Mr-Douglas-you-don't-say look, her mouth slightly agape and the faintest suggestion of a tremble to the lips, so that I found myself wondering what I'd just said that could have been so astounding.

When the hall was empty but for a weary attendant clearing away the chairs, when the lights one by one were being extinguished, I spotted her lurking meekly in the shadows.

'Well?' I asked, going over. 'How was I?'

'Och, nobody expects these talks to be very interesting, Mr Douglas. Still, so long as people dig deep in their pockets.'

'Can I give you a lift, Isobel?'

'Thought you'd never ask!'

Fraser was off at sea, she informed me in the car. Engaged in submarine diving trials out in the Atlantic somewhere. I deduced that Fraser was her husband. I couldn't remember hearing his name previously but she expected me to know, so maybe she'd talked of him before and I hadn't been paying attention.

'Fine time to choose, I must say,' she declared. 'A woman doesn't feel safe lately, alone at nights.' She pressed a hand imploringly to my arm. 'I'm not going home. Not after last night. I kept hearing noises outside.'

'Then where would you like me to take you?'

'I'm open to suggestions,' she said.

I glanced at her quizzically. She formed her full mouth into a kiss, her expression becoming dreamy.

'You should be ashamed of yourself,' I said.

'Is that a promise?' she answered.

I invited her to look at the road behind. 'See those headlights back there? That's an unmarked police car. If you come back to my place, they'll record the time you arrive and when you leave. They'll probably count how many times you use the bathroom during the night. That information will go into a computer in Dumbarton and you'll no longer have a private life. You'll become, Isobel, what the police delight in calling a Known Associate.'

'And what do they call you?'

'A Suspect, I should think. Maybe even a Prime Suspect.'

'Who do they tell?'

'They tell other policemen. Are those the kind of creatures you want gossiping about you?'

'Will they be outside all night?'

275

'I assume so. I see them in the street when I go to bed and they're still sitting there in the morning.'

She closed her eyes and, whatever her secret thoughts, a curl came languorously to her lips. 'Sounds about the safest place to be, then, inside the flat with you.'

How, when I understand women so well, can they be such a mystery to me? Do they, I wonder, surprise themselves? I certainly get this impression at times. At the exact moment when I'm most highly aroused, when I'm drinking the delights of a woman's abandonment, her unexpected proficiency in making love, I can detect, deep down in her eyes – no, not exactly *in* the eyes, somewhere off behind them – I can detect a stunned look, a look of bewilderment, and I sense that she herself is the cause of it. Can this really be me? she is thinking. My God, who *is* this man? What am I *doing* here? I have occasionally considered whether I ever look quite like that at the back of the eyes when I'm screwing. I don't think so. But there again, women are women, so even if I did they'd never say so. They'd probably just smile enigmatically to themselves, go all limp and satiated, and delight in my confusion. Psychologically, of course, they have all the advantages. I can look many things when I'm making love, but not quietly satisfied. Only women can do that. Only women, when the entire planetary system is erupting, fireworks blazing, the 1812 Overture blasting away from the massed symphony orchestras of the galaxy – *with* the accompaniment of real cannonfire – can look ever so slightly pleased with themselves. Let's face it, women are never, quite, what they've led you to believe. This is why sex is so inviting before the act, such an irresistible challenge, and so utterly perplexing afterwards.

Isobel was a case in point. She was clearly dying for it. Plain plump women always are. Can't wait to tear their clothes off and get down to screwing. Quickly and with a great deal of sweaty groping – it's what they're made for. I've known this since I was a kid at school in a class where

276

the girls came in only one variety, plain, and a single size, plump. In later years, confirmation has come by way of several plain, plump women. You cannot be plain and plump and sophisticated. Nor can you make love slowly, delicately, when you are absolutely dying for it, which, face facts, if you're plain and plump you must be.

Isobel, however, must have had a cool brain and a will of iron. She allowed me to remove her raincoat, then sat pertly in an armchair where she requested a drink in a level tone of voice. Whisky please, Mr Douglas, just as it comes. When I sat facing her from my own usual chair, most of the room was between us.

'Do you have any preference,' I asked, 'which of us does the seducing?'

'I'll do it if you like,' she offered, 'but I think, quite honestly, the man should make the advances.'

'I thought about seducing you, Isobel, last time you were here. Seriously thought about it.'

A superior smile. She already knew this.

'But not this way. I mean, a whole room between us, for goodness sake.'

'Then maybe you should head over here.'

I went over to her, knelt on the floor at her feet and placed a hand between her legs, just above the ankles.

Isobel smiled again, very sweetly. She appeared so composed and serene that I found myself wondering, as I explored the hot folds beneath her skirt, whether angels in heaven are plump and wear knickers.

Black frilly knickers. Bought, unless I was very much mistaken, from *Sweet Dreams*.

Thinking back over my life I find precious little to be proud of. In this I am probably no different to any other person who suffers the depressions of private honesty. But there were moments of total unselfishness, charity of the highest order, times when I gave to others with scant regard for what I'd get back in return, and paramount among these I count my indulgence in oral sex. The giving of it, I mean. I gain no pleasure from running my tongue over a woman's vulva. I perform oral sex solely from the goodness of my heart. Whatever advantage my prick has taken of women, my tongue has returned a thousand times over.

Look at it this way. The tongue is not an erogenous zone. It is a taste organ. And the taste of a woman's vulva can hardly be classed as a gourmet's delight. Gordon would almost certainly retort, were I ever to confide these thoughts to him, that I am very far from being a gourmet. But I have sampled escargots and oysters and various Chinese dishes of dubious origin; I can imagine why they appeal to certain palates although they do not appeal to mine. Vulvas are most definitely not haute cuisine. A vulva might look at close range not unlike a fresh and juicy oyster but it leaves an overwhelming impression of stickiness in the mouth and has an aftertaste of urine. So I divert myself during the performance of oral sex. I think of the food I would rather be eating. I think, quite often as it happens, of such delicacies as kidneys and liver, which have a slight similarity of texture and taste but which are far superior to the tongue. And I tell myself that true acts of charity are never pleasant. If they were, believe me, we'd all be generous to a fault.

My industrious tongue set Isobel talking, and once started she seemed unable to stop. She gave a running commentary on our actions. When she'd moaned in ecstasy she put into words for my benefit why she'd moaned. The best tongue in the world, she said. God, yes. Then came the best fuck she'd had since she couldn't remember when. And soon after that, the best fuck ever, honest to goodness. She apologized for being so conventional in her preferences, but did I mind very much if we moved from the floor to my bed? No barrel of fun, is it, Mr Douglas, risking a splinter up the bum. We made the move entwined, each step a thrust, out of the study door and along the corridor. You'll split me from arse to tit you wicked man, God I'm as high as a kite. We came simultaneously as we tumbled together on the bed. Holy Jesus, you're an animal, I could do this for ever to a band playing. She wanted the light out then. Too fat for her own good, she said, blushing all over at my eyes feasting on her naked flesh. In fact I was thinking her not fat at all but Rubensesque, a body built for robust pleasures. She enfolded me in her warm, soft, roly-poly limbs and began groaning. Oh, Mr Douglas. Oh my God, Mr Douglas. I asked her to call me Sandy. Mr Douglas sounded needlessly formal, I pointed out, my face buried between pliant mountains of breasts. Sandy. San-dy. She had to speak my name several more times, trying its sound, before becoming familiar with it. Breathlessly, she thanked me for fucking her, and I was so touched by her gratitude I thanked her in return. Don't be a silly sweet man, Sandy, she replied, and I could feel the heat of her embarrassment in the darkness. I plunged my head into the furnace between her legs and she told me, in delirious intervals between sucking noisily on my limp and exhausted prick, that between her legs was where my head was now situated. God, yes, keep on doing that. Don't stop *ever*. No sooner did a thought spring into her head than she spoke it aloud to me. As if the harder my tongue worked, the harder must hers.

During the night she made a confession. 'Do you know what I used to think, as you sat at your desk writing on that machine of yours? I used to imagine what it would be like to have your head between my legs. Licking me, I mean. I used to wonder whether men who talk as nicely as you use their tongues better in bed. I mean, it's a kind of communication, making love. I'd look at you, when your back was turned, and think . . . does he just poke with it – your tongue, I mean, Sandy – or does he lick his women like he's speaking poetry?' She paused for reflection. 'Have you got lots of women, Sandy? I get the feeling you have.'

'Only one at a time,' I replied tactfully. 'I've never been promiscuous.'

'You can probably tell I'm inexperienced,' she said. 'There was a boy, just the one, before I met Fraser. Then we got married. And there's been just one more since, not counting you. Craig, his name is, a pal of Fraser's in the navy, you know how these things happen what with him being at sea so often. Quick and rough merchants, all three of them, no subtlety. I've actually said to Fraser he knows only two ways of making love, in and out. Got him thoroughly worked up, that did, but he never changed. Och, well, the next time we did it, he was at it half the night. Shove, shove, shove. Seven times in a row, as if he was trying to prove something, but why bother? Like seven cups of stewed tea one after the other, when you've had one, be honest, the others are no different. But Fraser, as I was saying, is a man of few words, and practically every other one of them is "fuck". For someone who talks about it so much, I'm always saying, you're not so bloody hot at doing it. Not adroit with his tongue, Sandy, see what I mean? And that's my point. Might as well have a carrot shoved up you as a thick rough tongue like that. And the same goes for his pal, Craig. Illiterate, they are, in the ways of love. Whereas you stroke me so gently with your tongue. A lick from you, Sandy, is like you're talking to me, saying beautiful beautiful words.'

I ran my lips over her breasts, over both upright nipples, onwards over her soft and bulbous stomach, down through a thicket of coarse hairs with the ripe warm smell on them by then of a cowshed. Her legs opened. Imagining the taste of honey, I licked her vulva with infinite gentleness. She moaned very loudly.

'Hear that?' she said. 'That's me moaning. That's what you do to me, Sandy. Kill me, you will, you and your silver tongue.'

Plump women are more exhausting, this is a fact. I can screw a skinny woman all night but there's something about plump women that saps the energy from me. I fell into deep sleep during the small hours and was drifting through a world of dark and exotic odours when Isobel's scream shattered the peace.

I sat up in fright.

'The dog!' she said, her voice fluttering. 'I put my hand on the fucking dog!'

Soon the door-bell was ringing as if it would never stop, and the insistent thumping of fists could be heard on the downstairs front door.

'*Open up, Mr Douglas! Police! Open up, d'you hear!*'

I threw the bedroom window wide to call down. 'For God's sake! Have you any idea what fucking time it is!'

'We heard a scream, Mr Douglas. What's going on in there!'

'Nothing. Nothing's going on. There was no scream from in here.'

'We'd like to see Mrs Lockhart, if you don't mind. See she's OK.'

Isobel, bless her, had the presence of mind to appear at a different window towards the far end of the house.

'What's wrong with you people?' she shouted. 'I thought the polis were supposed to keep the bloody peace, not break it.'

'Are you all right, Mrs Lockhart?'

'Course I'm all right.'

'Are you sure? Are you quite sure you're all right?'

'Wha's ya problem, wee yin? Are ya deaf as weel as stupid!'

When the plainsclothes men had retreated, I fetched drinks to calm Isobel's nerves. She sat, legs crossed like a Buddha, on the bed and I opened the curtains wide to admit a shining white moon. With the silver light on her, Isobel looked like a great and voluptuous carved statue. Now she seemed not to mind me gazing closely at her body. She held her back proudly erect to flaunt her abundant breasts.

'Do you know,' she said, 'Fraser's only ever talked to

281

me once in bed. Only once what you'd call a real conversation.'

'What about?' I enquired, running the tip of my tongue between her legs.

'Oh, nothing much. Nothing you'd call memorable.'

I insinuated my tongue inside her. 'How long's he away?'

'Not long enough!'

'Would you like to spend the nights here while he's gone?'

'Some nights maybe. I'd better be seen at home now and then. You know how neighbours are.'

'Why not just come round? Any time you feel like it.'

I was lapping at her like a contented cat. It began to dawn on me that I was savouring the taste of her. She tasted strong and aromatic. She tasted the way she looked: big and warm and generous. And mingled with her flavours I could taste the salty cocktail of my own fluids. I've never got round to the extravagance of truffles but I can imagine, I think, what they taste like. Rich and rare, earthy and priceless. I began to gorge like a pig.

'Will I be a nuisance?' she wondered.

'Not unless you scream,' I said.

Twenty

Isobel did scream again – fortunately not loud enough for
the plainclothes men to hear. A muted gargling scream,
trapped at the base of her throat. It was early morning by
then, the time somewhere around seven o'clock. She'd left
my side to visit the bathroom and was almost instantly
back in a flurry, her eyes popping.

'There's a . . . man out there,' she gasped, gathering up
the bedcover to hide her naked body.

I discovered Gordon in the hall. Flora was all over him,
her tail joyfully wagging.

He held up my doorkey. 'Hope you don't mind,' he
said. 'Thought I'd let myself in without disturbing you.'

We had coffee together in the kitchen, Gordon unable to
keep his eyes off Isobel, and Isobel looking uncharacter-
istically pale one minute then going bright pink the next
under his shameless stares. Her unbrushed hair was
sticking up in all directions, there were dark rings under
her eyes from lack of sleep. Her formal black suit seemed
out of place at such an early hour of the day: she had the
appearance of being in mourning and had quite lost her
voice. I tried to draw her into the conversation but all she
could do was nod dumbly or give a sullen shake of the
head.

As for Flora, she slunk away in disgrace after I gave her
a piece of my mind. What good was she to me? Next time,
I said, next time someone lets themselves into this
apartment, the least you can do is bloody bark!

I'd taken his Barbour by mistake yesterday, Gordon

283

explained. He hadn't noticed until this morning when he'd dressed to go out.

'Put my hand in a pocket and thought, hello, whose are these keys?'

'That can't be right,' I said. 'It must have been my Barbour I took yesterday. I felt my hip-flask bumping inside as I put it on.'

He pondered a while then snapped his fingers. 'You gave me the flask, remember? When we were out shooting. I must have forgotten to give it back.'

His gaze lingered hungrily on Isobel. 'Sorry if I surprised you, hen,' he said.

Gordon has never been much of a liar. He neither looked nor sounded one bit sorry.

A vision, he told me after I'd seen Isobel into a cab for home. A fucking vision. A vision to strike a man blind. He'd never at one single time seen so much bare flesh. As if, he said rapturously, all the tits in the world had been piled up naked in my hall corridor. And then, when she'd turned and fled, all the great wobbling arses in Creation, more arses than are in heaven and earth, Horatio. And more cunt than is dreamt of in your philosophy. And pubic hair, he eulogized, long enough to comb into plaits. My God, he declared, I thought only Greek women had hair down their legs like that.

'I dream of women like her,' he murmured in a state of trance. 'I dream of really big tits. Dream and pray. God, you're a lucky bastard.' His eyes grew downcast and soulful. He slumped in his chair and surrendered to misery.

'Why didn't you phone?' I chided him. 'Bloody thoughtless, walking in without saying.'

'Just trying to save you trouble,' he said. 'Putting myself out for you, the way I always do.' He fell silent for a time then spoke with the trace of a sob in his voice. 'You've ruined my life, Sandy. I'll never sleep again without dreaming of those fabulous great knockers.' He looked questioningly at me. 'What did you say her name was?'

'Never you bloody mind about her name!'

He bowed his head. 'Phyllis is screwing someone,' he said. 'Having it away when my back is turned.'

'Not Phyllis,' I retorted. 'Be reasonable. She doesn't do that kind of thing.'

'I found some condoms,' he said. 'Got a splinter in my finger, went to her sewing box for a needle and found some fucking condoms hidden. Well, we're trying for a kid so we never use them. How's this for irony . . . ? She's having it off on the side and she's the one buying the condoms! But who's the sucker that earns the money in our household? Yours truly. So some bastard's stuffing it to my wife and I'm fucking paying for the privilege!'

I mumbled some words of consolation.

'Phyllis is fucking someone,' he said in anguish. 'And someone's fucking Phyllis. As for you, you're fucking more often than I have hot dinners. Seems like the whole fucking world is fucking except me.' He snatched plaintively at my sleeve. 'I've never asked you a favour, not once.'

Quite true, he never had.

'Give me one of your women . . .'

'*What* . . . ?'

'One you've finished with. Hell's bells, Sandy, you've got more women than you know what to do with, more than any man can possibly need. Just one, for Christ's sake. Please! This is me, your brother, saying fucking *please*.'

'I can't do that, give you a woman.'

'Why not?'

'Are you serious?'

'Deadly bloody serious.'

'I'm supposed to pick up the phone, is that what you're suggesting? Sandy here, darling, come round would you and give my brother a good hard fuck.'

'We're alike, aren't we?' he pleaded. 'Same height, same eyes, same hair! If they'll sleep with you, damnit, why won't they sleep with me?'

285

There were tears, real tears, welling in his eyes. So I paused to take stock instead of giving the reflex response I had in mind. I'd seen Gordon cry on only a few rare occasions in the past. He'd done the crying for the pair of us when our father had his final stroke, and we'd both cried buckets by the bedside as our mother slipped into limbo. I'd seen him cry once after a favourite dog was run over, and he'd cried copiously one Hogmanay, he wouldn't say why, when the piper played 'Scotland the Brave'. But I'd never seen him cry for himself. I've been married; I know the bleak despondency of loneliness. It came as a shock to discern such loneliness in him. You don't expect this, somehow, in your one and only brother. I mean, Gordon of all people.

So I hugged him – years since I'd done that – and promised I'd try. No guarantees, I said, women have minds of their own. But I'd give him a glowing recommendation and after that, well, all would be in the lap of the Gods.

I remembered Sheena Campbell suddenly and thought she was probably right up Gordon's street.

'How does a slightly older woman appeal to you?' I asked.

He suspected trickery. 'How old?'

'In her forties. Dark hair, dark eyes. Very intelligent, an academic actually, but screws like a harlot.'

'Sounds too good to be true,' he said.

'For a mature woman, she has the most wonderfully preserved breasts. Her nipples are enormous, the same rich red as her lips.'

He closed his eyes, imagining. He looked childishly pleased, with a silly grin plastered across his face. He begged to be told her name but I said only 'Sheena'. And that seemed to satisfy his curiosity. Gordon does not have an enquiring mind. He gives his trust too willingly. He never thought to question why, if this woman was all I claimed, I was prepared to relinquish her to him.

*   *   *

For quite some hours after he'd gone I sat at my word processor. An entirely new experience, this, planning a seduction for someone else. Eventually Flora came padding into the room to see what was going on.

'Here's my problem,' I explained. 'How do I get Gordon to seduce Sheena Campbell when Gordon, poor sod, has never seduced anyone? Not even Phyllis. She had to make all the moves.'

Flora gnawed at her paws, her tail thrashing the carpet.

'And how do I arrange for Sheena Campbell to be seduced by Gordon when I never got round to seducing her myself? We never actually met.'

From the corner of my eye, I saw Flora tearing at something.

'Though it is perfectly true,' I added, 'that she has extremely good breasts, nipples like plums as a matter of fact, and screws like a harlot.'

I finally turned around just as Flora gobbled a toffee whole in one slobbering bite.

She learns by experience, that dog. This time she'd managed to remove the paper first. We stared at each other then for several long and bemused moments, and in the way animals sometimes do I'll swear she read my every thought. I'd call the manufacturer of the toffee, ask which shop sold them in Helensburgh. Oh those, they'd say, done to special order, those toffees. Funny you asking, sir, almost no-one buys them any more. Hang on, would you, I'll dig out the exact name and address.

Deluding myself, of course. I realized as much as soon as these thoughts hit me, and Flora, helpful dog that she is, could see the sudden look of resignation on my face, could sense the pointlessness of regarding a mere scrap of paper as a clue. Anyway, what's done is done. When she saw me coming, she swallowed the wrapper.

Then, tongue lolling from her mouth, I'll swear she smiled.

CONFESSIONS

Twenty-one

By some mad logic, the Hoolet chose his victims; he did not strike at random. Jack Moffat's first official hint of this possibility came, where else, in a bar in Dumbarton. At the Dumbuck Hotel actually, he was to tell me later. Across the road from the hotel were the shabby bonded warehouses of Ballantine's distillery. There were ponds on the lawns beside the warehouses where flocks of geese floated serenely when they weren't strutting round the premises on twenty-four-hour guard. Using geese as burglar alarms was as old as history, Jack remarked with a casual gesture through the window. The ancient Greeks entrusted their security to geese, as did the Romans. Bloody effective, geese, sirens and storm troopers rolled into one. Why put your faith in technology? he said. Why spend a fortune on electronics when there's old and tested ways of achieving the same ends?

'What's the best protection the police can offer?' he sneered. 'Parking a few lousy cars on street corners! Seems to me the womenfolk round these parts would be a fucking sight safer with geese in their backyards.'

He can be more subtle than you'd expect when he's intent on provocation.

'Oh, ay,' an inspector said. 'And why's that, Jack?'

'Warning. At least they'd get time to dial 999.'

'Well that depends, now.'

'On what?'

'Whether he's already in the house, or no'.'

'He being the Hoolet . . . ?'

'Isnae tha' who we're talking aboot?'

291

'Hold your horses a minute. You saying he knows his victims?'

'Ah'm saying no such thing, Jack. The deafening silence of authority, me.'

Jack claims to have waited close on an hour before following up. Patience is my middle name, Sandy. Questions and drink flowed.

'What's the forensic stuff?' he asked at a suitable moment.

'Who's kidding who, Jack? You bloody know all about forensics.'

'I mean the phrase. I keep hearing this phrase. What do you guys mean on this case when you talk about the forensic stuff?'

'We mean what we always mean. What was found at the scenes.'

'On the bodies?'

'Maybe. Maybe near the bodies. Maybe removed from the bodies. We mean what we found, tha's aw.'

'And you're not saying?'

'Give this man a prize, lads. Fucking genius, this one.'

'It's something you know, right? Something to do with the Hoolet. Hair. Fibres. Semen. You're keeping stumm in the hopes of trapping him, right?'

'Oh, sure, Jack. Just like my head buttons up the back.'

'Are we talking genetic fingerprinting here?'

'Wasting your breath, lad. The secret's as safe as the bevvy in those warehouses oot there.'

'I've got an editor up in town, George. Bastard's going to be asking why I'm so free with the bar bills when you people don't seem to believe in the freedom of the Press.'

'Your problem, Jack.' Said to smirks and general laughter.

'Pints of heavy again all round?'

Good of you, Jack, they said, deftly making room in their glasses. Twist our arms if you're having another yourself.

'Where'd you reckon he first met Carol Logan? Helensburgh or Yoker . . . ?'

Jack was never entirely at ease when interviewing Turnbull. 'Interview' was the operative word, he said with a loser's shrug of recollection. No friendly jars in the Dumbuck, no question of catching him, wearing green wellies and off his guard, in the vegetable patch Sunday mornings. You made an appointment. You called on Turnbull at his convenience. Security locks were opened on doors, then closed behind you with a threatening clunk. He'd sit stiffly, as unsmiling a bugger as you ever saw, the other side of a desk so spotless you could eat your dinner off it, and he'd be spring cleaning as you talked: reaching out every so often to flick away subversive specks of dust with the back of his hand, or seeking out bits of fluff too small to be seen from his grey Marks and Sparks suit. And that office: not a scrap of paper out of place, no ashtrays and he bloody meant it, and the corridors smelling of disinfectant. Those interviews felt, Jack thought, like hospital visits. He got the firm impression, he said – and you know me, Sandy, I'm no shrinking violet – that a death was imminent but you weren't supposed to mention death in there. It wasn't decent.

'Lot of men you've got covering the ground in Yoker,' Jack said.

'Yoker's where the victim came from,' Turnbull riposted.

'Street by street enquiries, I mean. Anyone seen Carol Logan with a man? Any stranger been around recently asking questions about Carol Logan?'

'Routine enquiries, Jack. The hard graft of a murder case.'

'See the thing is, Mr Turnbull, my problem here, is that she was killed in Helensburgh. I mean, let's assume the Hoolet picked her out at random. He's lurking after dark in Hermitage Park. Poor Carol Logan comes by on her way home from work. Short skirt, great figure, terrific legs. What else does he need to know? I mean, come on, rape's rape . . . Who needs a name and a home address? A bash on the head, right, and down to business. See the thing is, I've quizzed her mum and dad, the people in her close, most of bloody Caledonia Street. Marvellous sweet girl, they say, can't understand it. And here the lesson endeth. So what more can they be telling you, Mr Turnbull? Why so much interest in Yoker?'

'Crucial assumption you've made there, Jack . . . about him being in the park and her happening to come by.'

'He was waiting for her . . . ? That what you mean?'

'Well, it's a possibility, one of many. We have to consider all eventualities.'

'But you must have a favoured theory by now. Is that the line you're pursuing . . . he knew her and was lying in wait?'

'I've got an open mind on these matters. Something of a lateral thinker, though I say it myself.'

'Did the Hoolet tell you this . . . he was there waiting?'

'Wish he'd be so obliging, Jack. Don't I just wish.'

'See the thing is, Mr Turnbull, let's put our cards on the table. One of your squad, I won't say who, sort of shot his mouth off the other night. What I heard, strictly entre nous, was that some of your men think you're being a wee bit obsessive about Yoker. Lots of demoralized muttering about chasing Scotch mist up blind alleys . . . not my words, Mr Turnbull, just trying to do you a favour, letting you know what's what. See, to be perfectly blunt, my source went on to say he doesn't believe this story about Yoker. You should've seen my ears prick up on mention of the word *story*. Oh yes, what story's that? I asked. Story, Jack? Who mentioned any story? Never seen policemen look so new-born innocent all of a sudden, Mr Turnbull. Want my advice, Jack – this is a quote verbatim – anyone at Divisional HQ tells you the Hoolet's been in contact, you ask who says so and was this source sober at the time.'

'Someone's been pulling your leg, Jack.'

'How did he make contact, Mr Turnbull? A letter,

words pasted together from newspaper cuttings? A phone-call? A tape recording?'

Jack confessed to me he was profoundly shaken by Turnbull's reaction to this question. Turnbull reached down into a drawer and removed a Bible which he placed before him on the desk. Jack had never before encountered a policeman who kept a Bible in his office. Jack said he hadn't been that near to a Bible in years. Such was the wild look of pious anger in Turnbull's eyes, Jack felt he was about to be exorcised. And he felt, he said, that the floor would probably open under his feet and he'd learn, before his time, the true meaning of Hell.

'I swear to you on this Holy Book,' Turnbull intoned, 'that the Hoolet has made no contact with me, in any way, shape or form. I'm playing straight with you, Jack. You can work for that miserable gutter rag till you're as old as Methuselah . . . that's as sincere a rebuttal as you'll ever hear.'

Jack required some several long moments to gather his wits. 'Someone else, then?' he suggested. 'He made contact with someone else?'

'Not that I've been told. Not to my knowledge.'

Jack made careful note of the fact that Turnbull's denial came after the Bible had been returned to its drawer. He couldn't be sure whether this was by accident or design. But he was still so dazed at being given an answer on oath, by a hard-bitten detective would you believe, that he meekly accepted what he'd been told.

'I took it as gospel,' he said to me subsequently. 'I trusted the bugger, so help me.'

He could reel the facts at you, could Jack. All down in a scrawl in his dog-eared and beer-stained notebook but he could recite them from memory. How many inspectors, sergeants and fresh-faced young constables 'L' Division had assigned to the Hoolet case. How many supporting specialists had come and gone from Scenes of Crime and Forensics, the numbers of psychologists and psychiatrists who'd been consulted on Aspects of Personality. The three psychics whose amazing rapport with *vibrations* had come up with three totally different, but equally nebulous, descriptions of the killer. How many telephone calls had come flooding in, anonymous, confiding, halting in speech, giving first names or initial letters of names or where the Hoolet worked or where he was in the habit of parking his van. Looking-over-the-shoulder voices, Jack would relate, someone's-about-to-walk-into-this-room-at-any-minute voices, know the sort I mean? Warming to his task, Jack would go on to enumerate how many statements had been taken, how many fingerprints fed into the glossy new system at Pitt Street, the pride and joy of the Strathclyde Police. And we're talking telephone numbers here, astronomical digits, censuses no less of entire populations. Put your savings in petrol shares, pal, stick all you've got into shoe leather futures – they're using them, these guys, like they're going out of fashion.

Sergeant Grant, though, was an island of calm in this turbulent sea of activity. Possessed of a shambling gait and deliberate manner, Grant seemed never to be in a hurry. He was always prepared to find time for Jack: they would share the occasional drink together after hours and Grant would chat among other things about intensely private matters, his wife and his kids and the new three-piece suite in his lounge. If he hadn't been a cop, he'd have been damned close to being a friend; Jack had even cadged a tenner off him one night when he found himself short.

They don't, Jack said reverently, make cops like that any more. Grant was innumerate and proud of it. Almost alone among the Hoolet squad, he didn't believe in computers. Just as well too, he was prepared to admit, since his great bananas of hands were too clumsy for those silly wee keys. He kept the essentials in his head and put an outmoded trust in instinct. Dear old Don Grant, Jack came to think, had the makings of a great detective.

'That boss of yours . . .' Jack said one night. 'The only policeman, I reckon, to get a mention in weather forecasts.

Deep gloom in the West, black storm clouds over Dumbarton.'

'You are talking,' Grant confided, 'about a desperately unhappy man. He had the MacRae case all but wrapped up . . . the prime suspect in his sights, just a matter of time and finding the evidence. Sit tight on the bastard, wait till he cracks.'

'No need to mention names, Don, but are we talking husbands here?'

Grant took a protracted draught of his beer. He ran his tongue across his lips, tasting and considering. Jack became convinced that what Grant would say next was wholly determined by the brewer's skill, whether he found the flavour to his liking. By such apparently trivial personal preferences, Jack firmly believes, are secrets spilled or preserved. Scoops have been made, he says, spies betrayed, wars won or lost, by the contents of a bottle.

'Are we on or off the record?' Grant asked then.

'My doctor says I've got terminal amnesia,' Jack replied. 'Soon as something's said, I forget it.'

'Great excitement a few days back. The DCI gets this bright idea of going back to check all the clothes in Aileen MacRae's wardrobe. Bingo! There's this flimsy bedtime creation . . . lots of money, Jack, for not very much. Get the picture? One of those if you've got it, flaunt it, items of attire. And guess where it was bought . . .'

A moment of déjà vu for Jack. He'd been there, he said, more times than he cared to remember. He should fucking know by now not to agree, ever, to answers off the record. But then again, he confessed, if you don't agree, you don't get to hear what you hear. An unavoidable dilemma, another step on the pathway to Hell.

Jack's eyes grew enormous, his voice husky. 'Surprise me,' he said.

'Trouble is, turns out Mrs MacRae bought it herself.' Grant gave a gentle smile of enormous pleasure.

'But it's a connection of sorts, right? Means she'd met Carol Logan . . .'

'She was in the shop on one single occasion. That's a pretty tenuous connection. A real lady of the manor, our Mrs MacRae. And Carol Logan was just a girl behind the counter.'

Jack put his analytical talents to work. 'Was there a label on this garment?'

Grant nodded. They'd have traced the supplier anyway, he said, but this hadn't proved necessary.

'So the husband, say, might have seen the label? It's possible, right?'

'And then what? Decides to kill Carol Logan for selling his wife a saucy nightdress?'

'Sure that sounds crazy. But the Hoolet's a nut-case, Don. He does crazy things.'

'Put yourself in the DCI's shoes,' Grant declared. 'There's a murder and you've got a prime suspect. Trouble is, the killer goes and kills a second girl this suspect never knew, or at least that you can't prove he knew. And there's worse to come. You had the suspect under surveillance at the time of the second killing. And, take it from me, no way he was in Hermitage Park. You're misery personified, Jack. Fame and promotion slip from your grasp.'

Grant smiled from ear to ear, downed his beer and with an expectant look placed the drained glass on the bar counter. Jack was mystified by the hugeness of the smile. Even he, who is as familiar as any of us with the hatred engendered by bosses, could see no cause for celebration in being right up shit creek. I mean, they're a team, the police, he thought. Don't they *want* to catch killers any more?

It took him, he said, several more minutes to work out what the smile meant. He slapped a hand suddenly against his thigh.

'Don, you sly bastard,' he said. 'You've got a suspect of your very own.'

'Won't say I have and won't say I haven't,' Grant responded. And though his grin now grew even broader there was an abrupt look of warning in his eyes to enquire no further. The very reason, Jack thought, why you can't depend on a cop to act like a friend. Just when you most need a demonstration of friendship, down come the shutters and you're staring a policeman in the face.

Now, an aspect of the case had been troubling Jack for quite some time, and this concerned the forensic stuff. There was a grave inconsistency in the various stories he had been hearing from the squad. This was the precise moment, he says, seated in Heraghty's with Grant, when he suddenly saw with total clarity what had previously been apparent to him as only a disturbing shadow glimpsed through a fog.

He knew immediately what his next question would be, but he made a show of having to thumb through his dog-eared notebook. He turned pages and squinted and frowned before locating the elusive passage. You can't overdo this performance, he'll tell you, take as long as you like. Mutter and fuss and look stupid. The vaguer you become, the more likely the other guy is to act in a spirit of compassion.

'Ah . . .' he stated finally. 'Didn't you say something . . . damned if I can read my writing here, Don . . . about the Hoolet ejaculating all over Aileen MacRae . . . ?'

'Me?' Grant replied. 'Unlikely that, Jack. Not the kind of thing I'd say, is it, on the record.'

'Well, someone told me. See I've got it down here. "Came copiously over her abdomen and upper thighs." That's a direct attibution, Don, got it in quotation marks.'

'Not a word I use, abdomen. More of a belly man myself.'

Jack professed confusion. 'Could have sworn I got that from you.'

'Me? Never!'

'We're talking here about the forensic stuff, right? Him coming all over his victims.'

'A wide field, forensics. There's one hell of a lot of evidential material, Jack, comes under the heading of forensics.'

'But you're not denying the Hoolet's a sex maniac . . .'

'Seems pretty certain he is.'

'So he acts *sexually* . . .'

'Goes without saying.'

'Meaning he leaves evidence of a sexual nature . . .'

'Entirely up to you if you want to infer that.'

Jack stared short-sightedly into his notebook then shook his head in remorse. 'Can't read my own fucking writing these days.'

'Not the kind of thing I'm likely to have said, is it?' Grant stated blithely. 'Not on the record.'

Jack always believed he'd have made a bloody fine policeman. Not, he says, that he could have stomached the uniform or the regular shaving, not with his eruptive complexion, or, perish the thought, going into some cop shop, looking around and thinking: this is where I *work*, this is where I shall pass my hellish days. But the pay was a pretty hefty whack and the pension not to be sneezed at. And, he avowed, he had the right kind of brain for detection. He lived and breathed and supped *crime*. He sweated crime through his pores.

The police, he concluded, were all at sea on this one. They were blind and couldn't see. Turnbull and Grant each had their suspects. How utterly misguided, he thought. There was, after all, the forensic stuff. Any time you had a suspect, all you did was send samples of blood and semen off to the lab. All over bar the shouting. Proof positive or not as the case may be.

So they hadn't found him yet, right? Not in Helensburgh or Yoker. Whoever the Hoolet was, and wherever, the police had yet to call at his door. Fucking obvious.

He wrote a short and restrained piece for the morrow's *Dispatch*. Not gloating, he said, merely factual, buried without ceremony on an inside page. He even requested the sub-editor to eschew the use of capitals in the text, and was mildly surprised to see his wishes respected for once. Enquiries continued, he reported. According to police sources, no arrest was imminent.

Briefly it occurred to Jack, as a gesture of friendship, to explain to Grant where he was going wrong. His better judgement saved him from an uncharacteristic act of charity.

I ask questions, he explained to me. That's my life, the only thing I know. Not up to me, is it, to provide the fucking answers.

Twenty-two

It was a dreary December, housebound and empty. If I could hibernate through winter, I'd be a far happier man. The days are all too brief, the nights interminably long and lonely. During the dismal grey twilights that pass for afternoons, I gaze from my window at the denuded trees, the bleak and vacated streets. The skies seem pitiless in their depressing lack of colour, their absence of warmth. Fallen leaves lie strewn, dead and decaying, and when the heartless winds chase them across the dank lawns there seems no joy in their boisterous swirling, only mute pleas to be left in peace. I am seized by an ache of longing for something recently gone – I am never quite sure what, all I can say with any certainty is that it is now lost in the past and I have an inexplicable fear, cold and dark and brooding, that it will never return, even with the all too distant coming of spring. In these moods, I feel not unlike those gaunt trees outside the house. Winter, I tell myself, has stripped me of my living cover, of all vitality. I stand bare and unprotected. Ahead are endless hours with the prospect of only my own silence. A dog, a warming fire, the solitary comforts of a full glass, serve to ease the ache but not to cure it. It's not the damp coldness of winter I dislike so intensely. It's the icy wastes of my introspection.

On one of these crepuscular afternoons, during one of my recurrent fits of moodiness, Sergeant Grant chose to arrive, unannounced, to summon me to another identity parade. Out in the courtyard a driver sat in a liveried police Granada, waiting to convey us to Maryhill. Grant offered no explanation as to the purpose of this second identification and showed no emotion, neither surprise nor pleasure, when I readily agreed.

He came as a welcome breath of human contact. In the car I wondered how many suspects had gone with him to a police station, without a murmur of protest, because he'd chosen exactly the right moment to call.

Standing in a line of supposed look-alikes, I stared ahead at the mirrored glass screen and to my considerable satisfaction discovered in myself not a shred of anxiety, nor any vestige of interest, about who might be hidden behind the glass, studying my features and trying to remember. Remember what? Remember where? That's when I felt the amused beginnings of a smile. I fought it off, clamping my mouth tight. For inspiration, I thought of the statues of saints in cathedral niches, of pictures of Christ. A harsh world this, I thought, in which to be innocent. Innocence is in the eyes. The innocent are serious, too burdened to smile.

Afterwards, when the room had emptied and Sergeant Grant came to take me back to the car, I searched in vain for clues to his reaction. Possibly there was a slight droop of disappointment to his shoulders but he tended to slouch at the best of times. His expression was its usual dour picture of melancholy, offering no enlightenment. In rather formal terms, he thanked me for my cooperation. Then he gave a long and questing look, put his head to one side, screwed up his face in what I took to be a weighing up of options. I was never quite sure with Grant whether thinking was the hard effort he made it appear.

'You a bevvy man, Mr Douglas?'

'Are you offering to buy?'

'Least I can do,' he said cheerfully. 'Doesn't seem right, does it, coming all this way into Glasgow and leaving without a couple of jars.'

'Where will it be, then?' he asked in the car, and raised his bushy black eyebrows and tapped his thick fingers eagerly together as though my choice of pub would reveal something profound. So I proposed the Scotia Bar, as much as anything, I suppose, because it's a haunt of Glasgow's literati, exactly the kind of place he'd *expect* someone like me to hang out. I'd reveal nothing.

The oldest bar in Glasgow, so they claim. A resolute survivor of dirtier, poorer, chirpier times. Only pubs and graveyards can remain unchanged for so long and retain their aura of dignity. Whole streets have been torn down and rebuilt around the Scotia; in this wee corner of the old city time stands still. On the pavements outside, I'll swear the night has the murky dimness of old gas lamps and the air reeks of belching chimney stacks; a stone's throw away, the Clyde burbles lazily of ancient memories where it swills under the Victoria Bridge. Inside, a low curved ceiling of wooden beams and cream-painted planking seems almost to touch your head. The walls are clinkered wood, there are salons like cabins to either end of the long and perpetually crowded counter. A feeling of being inside an old sailing ship, and in consequence the Scotia is the best bar I know in which to get totally, hopelessly stotious. When your head spins it's not your body that's swaying but the pub itself. Throw up and you can place the blame on high and heavy seas.

Grant presented a pint glass and regarded me thoughtfully. 'You're a very obliging man, Mr Douglas, where the police are concerned.'

'Any reason I shouldn't be?'

'We've hauled you in now for two IDs. Not a word of complaint from you. You trot along, meek as a lamb. You never make an issue about your rights, demand a solicitor present. And twice you've been interrogated . . . you never asked for a solicitor then either.'

'Are innocent men supposed to ask for solicitors?'

'No, but they usually do. Especially in cases of murder, Mr Douglas.'

'Then be assured, Sergeant . . . next time you want my

cooperation, I shall kick up an almighty stink. Lawyers will be summoned.'

'I was looking at you earlier, in that line-up. Said to myself, now there's a man with not a care in the world. For all he knows, there could be anyone staring in at him. Endless possibilities, Mr Douglas. Could be a woman says she saw him tailing Carol Logan through Hermitage Park. Or a ticket collector who remembers a man of your description taking the train to Yoker several weeks before the murders. I've found an observant lady who spied a man with a dog hanging around the gate to Carol Logan's house. And plenty others I won't bore you with . . . could've been any one of a dozen eye-witnesses. Yet there you were, cool as a cucumber. And that I find odd. It's no' as it should be.' He stared very hard. A searching, troubled stare in which his many and various doubts were manifestly displayed. 'Well, go on,' he urged. 'Say it. Protest your innocence.'

I merely shrugged, on the principle that buying me a beer does not entitle a man to put words in my mouth.

He could not conceal his exasperation. 'You see, Mr Douglas, we're talking double murder here, as serious a charge as you can get. And even the most innocent of men, when he's been hauled in by the police for the third time, starts to bloody worry. What if, he thinks. What if there's some stupid old cow behind that glass screen imagines she saw me in Yoker. I *wasn't* in Yoker, that's what he thinks, but bloody hell what if? When you've been in the Force as long as I have, Mr Douglas, you get to see a thing or two, believe me. And there's no-one looks as guilty as a guiltless man with the polis on his back.' He paused for rather a long time. 'Tell you what I saw today in that room. A man with nothing to fear. But not an innocent man.'

I had forgotten, as he spoke, where we were. I had ceased to notice the hubbub of bar talk, the warm press of bodies all around, the pall of cigarette smoke and that pub smell, which someone ought to market, of every drink under the sun. I had Grant's steady, enquiring eyes on me.

He talked softly, not raising his voice, making no concession to the din, yet I heard every word. Jack Moffat claims pubs work a spell on those who inhabit them. Nowhere else as public can you be so private. A man's pub, he pronounces, is the unbeliever's confessional. Which is why, when he's after a story, he goes into their pubs, not his own.

Off behind me somewhere in the bar there came a noisy burst of laughter and it broke the spell. For the briefest of moments I wondered if I'd actually spoken the words in my mind. I'm sure Grant intended that I should. He'd paid for the drinks, but the choice of pub was mine.

If only you knew, I'd thought, how much I have to hide.

But I hadn't gone as far as saying this. I couldn't have done. Staring him in the face, I found him awaiting an answer from me.

'So what do you conclude from all this?' I asked.

'Me?' He spluttered into his glass, a self-deprecating laugh. 'All depends, doesn't it, Mr Douglas, which way the wind's blowing, which side of the bed I get up. Some mornings I tell the wife I know who this bastard is, I bloody *know*. Other days she'll ask and I'll say why bloody ask me, I'm pig ignorant, only a bloody sergeant. Just what the world needs, she says. A psychopath being chased by a schizophrenic.'

He lifted his glass above his eyes, contemplating the colour of his beer against the light. Then he drank for a while with the stoical discontent of a man drinking alone. He'd made a confession of sorts; perhaps he expected I'd play along and contribute some admission of my own.

Eventually, though, my silence defeated him. 'This is how I see it,' he resumed. 'Either you killed those women or you didn't.'

'Remarkable,' I said. 'I think policemen are wonderful.'

'Let's say you did, you're the Hoolet. Then you're a careful, cocky bugger. You're not afraid of witnesses . . . you're sure, absolutely certain, no-one saw you anywhere near the scenes of those crimes. They look like the work of a madman, someone out of control, but that's what they're meant to look like. Which makes you cunning, Mr Douglas, and calculating and dangerous.' He was briefly hesitant. 'Care to look me in the eye?'

'Sure,' I said. And when I returned his stare, his imagination got the better of him and he quickly shifted his gaze to the floor.

'So dangerous,' he concluded, 'doesn't bear thinking about.'

'Then don't think about it, Sergeant. The only person I'm a danger to is myself.'

'Which leaves us with our other possibility . . . you didn't do those dreadful things. Not you. How could you, with your dog and that personable smile of yours and your obliging manner, always ready to help the polis. The trouble is, Mr Douglas, my difficulty with looking at you in that light is you know more than you're bloody saying. You've got guilt written all over you. You're *implicated*, one way or another. Damned if I can say how, but you're involved.'

The beer was not to his liking: his glass was pushed to one side, still more than half-full. He gazed about, making assessment of the bar as if it was new to him, and didn't much like what he saw. His forlorn eyes spoke with a damning eloquence. He didn't like the people, their loud opinions, their posturings, my pretentious milieu. He looked as though he could endure any humiliation except the wrong choice of pub; his dejection seemed absolute. He pulled up his raincoat collar to muffle his ears.

'My round,' I said hurriedly. 'Where's it to be?'

He was on the point of leaving and I couldn't bear the thought of being abandoned there alone. Maybe he could tell. I wouldn't put it past him.

The Granada dropped us on Argyle Street, where Grant informed the driver there was no need to wait. 'Hardly official business, this,' he remarked to me. 'Wouldn't want it said I'm one to misuse police transport.' And he slapped me rather hard and with great familiarity on the shoulder. The air of deep gloom had lifted from him and there was the beginnings of a spritely bounce to his step as we proceeded up a narrow and shadowy side street. He winked at me without explanation and laughed as if one or other of us had told a joke. So I laughed too, finding it genuinely funny that, with the departure of the car, Grant was no longer a policeman and I no longer his suspect.

In a matter of moments we were instantly friends.

Don looked, I must say, at home in the Mitre. He was a big man in a very small pub and he slouched contentedly against the bar counter as if he owned the place. The counter of dark-stained wood occupied much of the pub, which he doubtless considered a proper sense of priorities. Probably no more bottles were on display than is usual, but there seemed to be a profusion, an abundance of alcohol; a mirror behind the shelves shone a jewel house glow through ambers and rubies and liquid gold. I imagined his home to be like this, old fashioned and as comfortable as a favourite pair of slippers. There'd be brass plates on the walls, embossed with galleons, and the red leather benches wouldn't be leather at all but plain, hard-wearing, honest-to-goodness plastic. Beside the bar there was a television going which he glanced at idly from time to time, watching the flickers, the way he'd look at an electric log fire. We were scarcely through the door when a bottle of Belgian beer was poured into a tall glass without him having to ask, and I'll bet his wife does that too.

'Life's never simple, is it?' he proposed with a sigh.

'It would be,' I said, 'if it wasn't for people.'

'What I mean to say is, I'm a fairly straightforward sort, not what you'd call complicated. I like my crimes simple for preference. I don't mean *easy*, Sandy, don't get me wrong, I've never been one to shirk hard work. But I like crimes I can understand, miscreants I can empathize with. What it comes down to, I guess, is wanting to feel secure in my own judgements. To me, a crime's simple when I can consider the circumstances and think: aye, I know why he did that, might have done it myself, even, in his shoes. I'm not saying crime is ever justified, that's for the courts to decide. But I need the sanity of some reasonable cause.'

He stared into some far-off distance beyond the pub walls. 'Remember the MacRae case?' he said, as if it was years ago.

I nodded too readily. I nodded again, slowly, with the weight of a painful memory.

'We met outside by the gate . . .'

'So we did,' I said, after appearing to think.

'I was in my element then,' he said. 'I could see motives. A whole heap of motives, I'll admit, but nothing out of the usual. To be perfectly honest, I didn't trust the evidence of a break-in. You get a woman done in, and there's a sexual angle more often than not . . . jealousy, anger, conjugal frustration. A swanky house, pots of money, you take a damned quick look at the will. See, to me, Sandy, all the paraphernalia of forensics, all the modern technology, isn't how you solve a case. You solve it up here, based on experience.' He tapped a finger to his forehead. 'Forensics are how you give proof to the courts.' He gazed at me and through me. 'Know what experience is?'

'Tell me,' I said.

'Experience is a way of seeing. And those that can see can also go blind. I never, in a million years, expected another murder. Och, all the signs were there, the brutality of the attack, that broken window, the aborted theft of her car, but experience said they were planted . . . we had a Domestic on our hands.'

He pondered, his features cast in a look of shamed bewilderment. The full extent of his naivety seemed only now to be sinking in. 'Next thing, there's the Logan killing. Panic stations . . . suddenly we're dealing with an Ugly. No more collating our notes on bits of card, the computers get wheeled in, recriminations are flying left, right and centre. And my boss, smarmy bugger, rubs my nose right in it. Regular church-goer, our DCI Turnbull, forever invoking the Almighty. Well, Don, he says, we've got an Ugly. Let's face facts, it always was an Ugly . . . we should have seen that from the start. Hindsight, I said, putting up a defence. And he looks down his fucking nose at me and says: Hindsight, Don, is God's punishment to the blind.'

'I assumed it was Domestic,' I stated consolingly. 'At first, I mean.'

'Did you, now!'

'Aileen didn't strike me as a victim. Not of a common killing, she wasn't the type. The nastier things in life had somehow passed her by.'

Don stared blankly, his mind on other things. His slumped stance over the bar was limp and despondent, his hand seemed glued to the glass. He looked like any of a million men in a million bars, questioning his very existence.

'We also met later in Hermitage Park,' he said after quite some while.

I confirmed with a cautious nod.

'Not what I expected, that one,' he said. 'A blow from out of the blue. Same killer, no two ways about it, an identical modus, no doubts whatever we're dealing with the same man. But now what? Do I kiss my instincts goodbye or go on listening to the voice of experience? Because they're the same kind of murder, Sandy, exactly the same. And yet they're not, the differences scream out at you.'

He'd been back to Hermitage Park, he explained. Several times now, always after dark. He'd found concealment among the conifers, felt the slow drip of rain on his face from the restless branches. The park was alive with the murmurings of night but the loudest sound, deafening to his ears, was the hoarse grate of his own breathing. On the last occasion, a couple of teenage schoolgirls had scurried through – on a stupid reckless dare, he thought. He could have reached out and touched them; they squealed as they ran by, but never saw him.

'I put myself in the killer's mind, Sandy. Along comes Carol Logan through the moonlight. She's a gift, a victim to use that word of yours. Practically every day they get raped, girls like Carol Logan. I felt an erection coming on . . . *his* fucking erection, Sandy. I had to get out of there fast for my peace of mind. I sat down by the Esplanade, in the pissing rain, getting soaked to the skin. Ritual cleansing. I wasn't going home, to my own bath, and taking him with me.'

He'd gone back to the MacRae house, he related. Just the once for this particular purpose. Considerately, Duncan had remained at his office in town, lent Don the keys, so he could hear and feel the solitude. He'd chosen the day and time with care. Early afternoon with winter sunlight streaming in through the windows.

'Deadly quiet,' he recalled. 'But not the outdoor quiet of the park. No movement, no drips of rain. I'm in a bedroom straight out of Hollywood. The bathroom door opens, there's the smell of a bath and expensive perfume. Aileen MacRae flounces in . . . a crack over the head, Sandy, that's all it takes. Then I can bash her brains to pulp, pull the robe over her face and degrade her, no fear of dead eyes staring up at me. I can take whatever perverted pleasures I delight in. I can leave her sticky with semen, where semen belongs with women of her sort, where I can *see* it, Sandy, oozing down her silken belly, over her shapely legs. Except, Sandy. Except. I'm in the killer's mind and I find myself thinking . . . hang on! I'm the Hoolet, a creature of night. I hide in parks, among the trees. I don't belong here, in a swanky bedroom, the bright middle of the afternoon. Sorry to trouble you, Mrs MacRae. I'm off!'

'He's mad, remember,' I said. 'Why should he behave the way you'd expect?'

'*Because* he's mad, Sandy. He's possessed of a muddled, hurting, frightened and frightening mind. But when he kills, he has a *reason*. He is compelled by a single obsessive thought. There's a clarity to his madness, no inconsistencies.

311

And because he's mad, Sandy, that fucking mad, he shouldn't fucking confuse me.'

I ordered drinks, more of the same, and for several minutes neither of us spoke. It was a silence without awkwardness, the shared and mellow silence of friends. Catching my eyes on him, he offered a slight, frank smile, as if inviting me to read his thoughts, he had nothing to hide. Later I emerged from some mental meanderings to find him, unashamedly, staring at me. I opened my mind to him, presenting no resistance, but he grew distant and sad. His narrowed gaze was beset with doubts: he questioned my good intentions; I wasn't playing fair with him.

Yes I was, I replied with a look. Any failure of understanding was his.

We moved on as the evening progressed. He needed a blow of air, a change of scene. Pubs, he declared, slapping his hefty hands together, were made for travellers, men without roots. Somewhere in this bloody town, he said, there was a pub you could leave with more hope than you went in with, and one of these days he'd find it.

I hailed a passing cab and set the driver on course for South Side.

'Do you have reasons for what you do?' Don enquired.

'Not always.'

'But usually you do . . .'

'I imagine so. I hope so.'

'A reason for writing?'

'The best there is, to scrape a living.'

'A reason for staying where you do?'

'Don't breathe this to a soul, Don, but the rent's ridiculously cheap.'

'A reason for fucking Mrs Lockhart the other night?'

We were crossing the river. I gazed down, watching the brash lights of the city reflected in dark and eddying currents, watching reflections break and shiver and fit themselves falteringly together again as ripples slowly spread, going nowhere.

312

'Isobel wanted to be fucked. I didn't wish to disappoint her.'

'Didn't bother you there were police sitting right outside?'

'It didn't seem to affect my performance, Don, so I guess not.'

'Trying to prove something to us, by any chance?'

'Such as . . . ?'

'Such as . . .' he repeated. He was staring down from the window on his side of the cab, although we were over the bridge and there was no river below now, no reflections to contemplate. '. . . That you do your fucking in bed, Sandy. A normal, healthy kind of guy, not the kind that hides under trees in the darkness. No hypocrisy about you . . . when you fuck another man's wife, you shout it from the rooftops. If, for instance, you'd been fucking Aileen MacRae, you'd have been happy to say so to the police.'

'Sounds plausible,' I said.

'On the other hand, could have been due to circumstances. Say, for the sake of argument, your sexual urges got the better of you. They're very strong, these urges, they take you over. An inconvenience, having the police outside, but you couldn't help yourself.'

'That, I have to say, sounds far less likely.'

'Any possibilities I've missed . . . ?'

'Maybe I simply felt like a fuck . . .'

He digested this before the acceptance of a taciturn nod. 'The simplest is always the most likely,' he conceded.

Considering it was simple, he took an awfully long while arriving at this conclusion.

My choice this time was the Old Toll Bar on the road to Paisley. I admire its dour and spartan optimism, its opulent absence of affectation. They were shabby wee men, Glasgow's working Victorians, runty and downtrodden. They liked their ceilings stupendously high: if the day ever dawned when they could walk tall, by God

they'd have the headroom to do it. They liked their wood
sumptuous, shades of darkest brown; their only riches
were colour. They liked soaring mirrors crowding the
walls, ornately engraved with promises: see your grimy,
boiler-maker's face swim groggily in a sea of Very Old
Vintage Port and Brandy and Champagne. They supped
on Black and Gold, the Aristocrat of Whiskies, washed
down with Younger's Celebrated Ninety Shilling, and
whatever became of that? There's something profoundly
religious about the baroque gantry rising tall behind the
bar, with its great proud casks, stained treacle brown
and banded with iron – to be gazed up at in awe while
conversing in hushed and respectful tones. By rights,
there ought to be spit and sawdust on the floorboards,
but they've gone the way of the runty wee men; to spit
on the floor now would be like spitting on somebody's
grave.

I tried to remember whose round this was, which of us
had paid for the cab. Given the circumstances under which
I'd left home that afternoon, I hadn't, to be blunt, come
funded for a binge. Some quick figuring brought the
depressing conclusion I'd already spent several quid more
than I'd come out with, but, there again, I've never been
much good at mental arithmetic. My hesitation on
reaching the counter must have been apparent: Don
insisted on buying the next few rounds. His treat, he said
bounteously. Then, on a bench, in a corner, he sat quietly
beside me taking his own counsel, drinking in the
surroundings, nodding thoughtfully to himself from time
to time as though, merely by bringing him here, I had
redeemed myself.

Occasionally, he'd peer without apparent involvement
at the television set mounted up near the ceiling against a
window of leaded glass. Restive images, from somewhere
alien and mysterious, as though the century outside was
trying to force its way in. Beyond the bar counter, a fruit
machine flashed aimless messages which customers stead-
fastly ignored. Looking over that way, Don sighed

without much caring, the sigh of experience, a policeman's despair over any lost cause.

We'd stay South Side, he proffered, emphasizing the sybillants as he hailed our next cab. Our tongues had loosened by this stage, and, being aware of their looseness, we were both becoming slower in speech, articulating our words with more than usual care.

The cab made a circuit of Queen's Park. We were decanted at the Boswell Hotel, which Don insisted, for some reason never revealed to me, on calling the Country Club. A haven for serious imbibers, this, with so many hand-pumps at the bar it looked like a signal box, and a blackboard declaring, for those who care about such things, the Original Gravities of this week's Guest Ales. Caledonian Golden, 1043. Belhaven, 1041. The bottled beers were a museum collection: beers concocted from the most unlikely ingredients; beers from countries I didn't know brewed beer; beers from countries I didn't know existed any more, or maybe they were simply very old beers. You could have drunk your way round the globe; it would have been cheaper and more enjoyable than an airline ticket.

Don rasped his hands together with a swish. 'Fancy a strawberry ale?' he said. 'I get a sweet tooth round this time of the evening.'

He was astonished to learn my ignorance of strawberry ales. 'Then we shall educate you, Sandy,' he announced for all to hear. 'We shall partake of a tasting.'

I heeded a chorus of alarm. My head, my stomach, my pocket joined in protest. I demurred but he would hear none of it. So we repaired to a table where, after whispered discussions at the bar, over a dozen bottles were brought of various shapes and sizes. A raspberry lambic as companion to the promised strawberry, wheat beers, rice beers, beers made in monasteries, beers that were reticently Dutch and aggressively Teutonic, beers aged and tended beyond the dreams of most wines.

Don sipped something dark and potent. He wiped the froth from his lips. 'I was in here a few weeks back,' he said. 'With some pals, doing a gallop through real-ale country. Must've had eleven pints, and didnae like any of them. Bloody wonderful evening.'

Was this Sergeant Grant laying down a challenge, or my good friend Don issuing a warning to be on my guard? I'll confess to not really caring.

'My record is fifteen pints,' I said to cover both possibilities. 'Though I don't recall clearly, so it might have been more.'

He was muted and thoughtful over this feat. During the subsequent sampling of several bottles, his only approximation to speech was an 'Mmm' here, an 'Ahh' there, a dismissive 'Errmm' annunciated after a great deal of agonizing.

Then he said: 'That Dr Galbraith's an odd cove . . .'

'He's a bloody shrink,' I explained.

'Never had need of one, Sandy, so I wouldn't know.'

'Went to talk to him, did you?'

He made a contrite nod. There was a job to be done, nothing personal; he expected I'd understand.

'Tell you much, did he?'

He wagged his head with careful solemnity, as though fearing that incautious movement would shake it right off. 'He claimed professional confidentiality or something of the kind. Well, I knew he would, Sandy, but no harm in trying, is there?'

'That's the only decent thing I ever heard said about him.'

Don focused a not very steady gaze on me. 'What's that phrase you journalists use . . . off the record? Between these four walls, Sandy, off the record, so to speak . . . if that phoney shrink of yours had told me anything, what might he have said?'

'Sorry, Don, I'm claiming professional something or other, too.'

'You can't, Sandy. You're not a bloody shrink.'

316

At the time, by this advanced stage of our revels, the argument sounded convincing.

'Did he mention why I was under his care?'

'Nothing, bugger all. Lawyers, shrinks, social workers . . . wouldn't give you tuppence for the lot of 'em.'

'I couldn't write, Don, that was the problem. Fucking inconvenient, if that's the only work you can do.'

'Och, come on . . . you? Never!'

'Couldn't write a fucking word.'

'So you saw a bloody shrink? Would've been simpler, surely, to buy yourself a dictionary!' A chuckle began and was quickly extinguished. 'Sorry,' he said, 'no offence meant.'

'None taken. Find it hilariously funny myself sometimes, thinking back.'

'So what caused this, your inability to write . . . ?'

Arms studiously folded, he looked across the table with more than a semblance of interest. I felt – how shall I say? – the subject of genuine concern. I had the feeling that if Dr Galbraith had ever looked at me in quite that way, if he'd shown even a spark of common decency, some good might have come from our encounters. I thought, too, that if we'd had our sessions in a bar – no black-framed certificates bearing down from the walls, no photos on a mahogany desk of that pompous wife of his, her three Siamese cats and two point five ghastly offspring – the learned doctor might have made some claim to understanding human nature.

'I was a crime writer then,' I said.

'I know,' Don said, with a look of knowing everything.

'I was going through problems at home . . . arguments about money, about the house, why was I staying out all hours . . . the usual things.'

'Arguments about sex . . . ?'

'By then, there wasn't any to argue about, Don.'

He nodded sympathetically.

'I'd go to work at the paper, from all that personal turmoil into everyone else's turmoil. It seemed everywhere

I went the streets were deep in shit. You must feel much the same in your job sometimes . . .'

'Indeed, I do.'

'Well, this brilliant solution came to me one day. I'd dignify my work through the quality of my writing. I'd elevate crime to the very highest literary plane. In short, Don, I had only to sit down at a typewriter to make the whole world a better place.'

'I have always,' he said approvingly, 'admired aspirations.'

'Looking back, I became compulsive, but I wasn't aware of that at the time. I'd write a piece about a street brawl, some vicious stabbing or other. I'd reread, the phrases were inadequate, it sounded oh so sordid. I was describing, accurately, what had transpired, but I couldn't see that, Don. So I'd rewrite, change the words around, move a paragraph here and there. I'd make the victim more pitiable, the transgressor more vile. I'd take an entire day, maybe two days, putting a minor story on to paper. I began blaming the words . . . I was choosing the wrong words. I'd sit staring at the typewriter for hours at a time, trying to find that single, correct, masterly phrase which would express what I wanted to say. I'd have the entire story in my head, all the details, the arguments for making our laws tougher, why flickknives should be banned and poverty abolished . . . all I needed was the right fucking words. And when you get into that frame of mind, Don, take it from me, the words flit away. Your vocabulary shrinks, you forget how to speak. You can only write in silences and grunts. You feel the story is bottled up inside, trying to escape. And the stories pile up, all that shit accumulating in your head, and you'll never be fucking free of it.'

'So you consulted Dr Galbraith . . .'

'Dr Galbraith,' I stated scathingly, 'had his words. They didn't help me with mine.'

'Ahh,' Don breathed, as if this explained everything.

'At which point, my brother stepped gallantly into the

318

breech. Gordon has always, I rather think, considered my prior birth an accident of timing. He holds the touching belief that, of the two of us, he is really the older and most wise. It's all a matter of genes, he says. He took me under his wing because, Don, that's what elder brothers do.'

Don reflected for several seconds before nodding with consummate understanding. A nod that had in it none of the condescension, the infuriating smugness, of a professional shrink.

'His analysis was devastatingly simple. Since crime was shit, I should no longer write about crime. If I, Sandy Douglas, was lost for words, I should let someone else speak the words for me. I'm inclined to think, Don, he had himself in mind for the role, but he couldn't bring himself to propose this . . . you see, Gordon may consider himself older and wiser, but he *defers* to me, he can't help himself. That, too, is in the genes. So I invented Murdo. I began my Highlander's Diary. The cure was instant and miraculous.'

'But you still have a compulsion to write about crime . . .'

'Why do you say that?'

'That business over Carol Logan.'

'A regrettable lapse.'

'Not, if I might say so, on the highest of literary planes.'

'I wrote the story as it was. In the style it demanded.'

'Compulsions are strange things, Sandy . . .'

'They're compulsive, Don.'

'. . . For instance, if another juicy crime was to come along tomorrow . . .'

'I'll write what my editor instructs me to write. In that sense, and that sense only, would I feel compelled.'

He reflected, stroking his chin. 'But don't you still have the desire, an urge deep down, to pull off that great piece of writing? You've found the words again now. All you need is a suitable crime. A series of murders, say, as heroic as your talents.'

'You have a nasty mind, Don . . .'

319

'I'm only trying to empathize here,' he retorted. 'Just trying to gain some insights.'

'No. I would not murder someone merely in order to write the story. OK?'

'How about murder for some other reason?'

'Only when I'm very drunk. And then only policemen.'

He smiled warmly. 'Aye,' he said. 'Me, too.'

For a period of a minute or so, Don meditated over what he'd heard, pulling his face into shapes, plucking at his lips. At length, he ventured that I must owe Gordon a great deal.

'Well, he certainly thinks so,' I said.

'Do you? Do you think so?'

'Yes,' I said. 'I probably do.'

'Would you lie for one another?'

'In other words, would we invent an alibi?'

'Now I didn't say that!' he protested. 'We're only talking in generalities here.'

'Gordon is a man of exaggerated principles,' I answered obliquely.

'And are you?'

'Definitely not, Don. How dare you even think so!'

'Let's see if I've got this straight.' His face underwent all manner of contortions. To all appearances, he was having great difficulty in keeping his eyes open, let alone think straight. 'You'd lie for Gordon. But he wouldn't lie for you. Is that the gist of it?'

It occurs to me now that my friendships are fragile and transient for precisely the reason that I can never, quite, take them for what they seem, never, quite, be rid of the suspicion there must be a catch. I looked at Don as he faced me across those empty remains of my education, and, try as I might, could not avoid seeing a policeman in plainclothes. He had cloaked himself in a disguise of amiability, in the bluff familiarity of a life-long pal. And I argued to myself that, even if I were wrong, doing him a grave misjustice, he deserved the answer he'd get. Whoever asks a man if he's a liar can expect only a lie in return.

'You've hit the nail right on the head there, Don,' I said.

He relapsed at once into his habitual desolation. All the drink in the house would have brought no respite.

He looked like a policeman whose entire case has collapsed around him. Like someone who'd just lost a friend.

Twenty-three

Once midnight struck I entered a dream. I dreamed I walked on the moon, with great slow strides of my weighted feet. I dreamed the streets tilted and swayed with a lurching, drunken motion. I dreamed that Grant had a face of rubber which grew sillier each time I looked, his enormous crescent smile becoming impossibly broad. I dreamed of a taxi taking shape from out of a billowing mist and I think, though I know this sounds crazy, that the figure at the wheel was the Invisible Man – he wore a jacket with the collar turned up, a gangster's trilby with the brim rolled down, but he had no face, at least none I can recall.

In the dream, Grant melted clean away, swallowed by his smile like the Cheshire Cat. Somewhere between the Country Club and Helensburgh he simply vanished. One minute he was there, the next he was gone. Logic tells me this must have occurred in one of those streets of austerely respectable stone dwellings which could be practically anywhere in Dumbarton – but I have no clear recollection. Nor can I remember him bidding goodnight; just as well, perhaps, since I don't remember saying any words of farewell to him.

Also in the dream, after what seemed an immeasurably long journey, down a darkened road of infinite twists and turns, I was spirited from the taxi to my doorstep where, in a moment of sublime surrealism, I offered the invisible driver money I didn't have, which he gruffly refused to take, saying, in a disembodied voice, that things had been taken care of.

Usually my dreams are uncluttered with duty or

hygiene. I don't, as in this dream, run ice cold water from the tap to douse my face, or stare for ages into mirrors at the bloodshot whites of my eyes. I am unaware of any previous dream in which I was sick – my bathroom, seen dimly through the haze which seemed to cloud every room of the apartment, appeared so dreamily spotless that, desperate to protect the lino, I dropped to my knees and buried my head in the lavatory pan. I'd had dreams before in which Flora was with me, a presence felt, trotting obediently along behind as I went off on some foray of seduction. But I had never before dreamed of Flora begging for a walk, imposing guilt, telling me by means of sad looks and pitiful whining she'd been neglected for *hours*, her bladder was bursting. So I responded to duty. I applied my groggy thoughts to the task of attaching the leash to her collar. She dragged me headlong down the stairs, out into the night. I felt the bliss of a cold wind blowing. The sky was pitch black and filled the slumbering streets. I dreamed of being lost in the stars.

I awoke after some unknown passage of time to find myself sprawled full-length on a bench. A moment's disorientation before recognizing the surroundings as Kidston Park, a knot of public grassland jutting into the Clyde. The village of Rhu lay beyond my feet, Helensburgh behind me, Venus shone down from immediately overhead – I took great pride in being able to locate myself in such cosmic vastness. Flora was just visible on the foreshore, inspecting flotsam washed in by the tide. Not a whisper of wind now; the Firth was immense, placid and polished. A Milky Way of lights on the opposite coastline, their images gleaming, sharp and shimmerless, in a surface so heavy and still you could have walked on it.

Was the submarine another dream? I still don't know. Black, evil and bulbous, with a dull shine on it like gun metal, it slid close past the promontory towards the sea in utter silence. The wake swelled behind, skittered along the beach, noiselessly turning shingle like a breeze rippling through corn. Uniformed officers stood immobile on the conning tower; from its innards an upward glow of yellow cast deep and disturbing shadows across their stony faces. A sailor stood in splendid isolation on the flat deck towards the bows; I imagined him to be surfing through the darkness. I held my breath, waiting for his momentum to run out, his balance to falter, and the treacherous water to swallow him up. But he was still there at attention as the vessel turned and, black against black, was suddenly gone. I breathed freely again, feeling that some awesome threat had passed by in the night, leaving the town unscathed.

I was sitting on the bench, staring after the vanished surfer, when a vehicle turned behind me into the car park. Two policemen came over, no attempt at banter. Their actions were guarded, their hooded looks a mixture of caution and contempt. When I insisted, demanded as a right, that Flora was delivered home first, one of the constables took my keys to lead her inside, while the other remained with me in the squad car, and his angry eyes, watching via the driving mirror, would have killed me if they could.

The worst part of a nightmare is the beginning, when you see it coming. As the dream starts to turn nasty, you decide it's time to wake up.

And you can't.

Twenty-four

Turnbull was alert, bright of eye, conspicuously smooth-chinned and exuding a faint aroma of surprisingly feminine after-shave. Not a crease about him, whereas Grant seemed to have slept in the same clothes I'd seen him in last, to have slept, badly, in his skin. His face had the jaundiced ashen pallor of a corpse. As to his crumpled, bunched-up exhaustion – if Marcel Marceau ever mimed a groan, that's what Grant looked like. He looked exactly the way I felt.

On this occasion, I was not granted the comparative luxury of Turnbull's office. Inquisition took place in a starkly bare interview room in which every sound had an edge, a ring of meaning: chairs scraped, papers hissed as they were turned, questions came with a hard echo of accusation, and my answers resounded in their emptiness and futility. Nor was Grant seated, as previously, in a mid-way position by the wall, where I could delude myself he was acting the umpire, ensuring fair play. He sat facing me, behind the metal table at Turnbull's side, where they appeared, differences notwithstanding, a formidable coupling. They shared common cause and the same ill-humour: when his face wasn't buried deep in his hands, Grant's stare matched Turnbull's in its burning intensity.

The session began with the tape-recorder off, for motives which were soon to become apparent.

'I'm prepared to be reasonable,' Turnbull said in opening. 'To give you a second chance.'

Grant, head slumped, muttered something about a truce.

'To offer a truce, if you will,' Turnbull said, picking up

the cue. 'Refresh my memory, would you, about the afternoon of October the 25th . . .'

I could feel the queasy approachings of a hangover. My mind was a blank. I repeated the date but it meant nothing. My past seemed lost and I feared for the future.

'That was a Thursday, Mr Douglas . . . the day Mrs MacRae was murdered.'

'Ah, yes,' I said, giving a glazed stare.

'You spent the day with your brother, if I remember correctly. He shot a fox . . .'

I acquiesced through a haze.

'You left your brother's cottage in Glen Cairn at approximately three thirty in the afternoon. You returned home, to Helensburgh, where you wrote a newspaper column about that same subject . . .'

'Yes.'

'Your movements are therefore accounted for at the time of Mrs MacRae's death . . .'

'So it would seem.'

'Do you wish to change that story, Mr Douglas?'

'No.'

'Quite sure about that?'

'Getting me drunk, Detective Chief Inspector, does not make me stupid. All it does is turn your sergeant there an unhealthy shade of grey.'

'Sergeant Grant,' Turnbull stated evenly, 'is an exceptionally stupid man.'

'Stupid as they come,' Grant muttered from somewhere in his hands.

'As am I. I am an imbecile, Mr Douglas. I shall, when this enquiry is wrapped up, personally bust myself back to constable. I shall tramp the beats of this division for evermore as a penance. I deserve nothing less.' Joining his hands as if in prayer, he addressed his following remarks to Grant. 'Confession, Don, is good for the soul.'

'Purgative, sir.'

'That's the only respect in which I envy Catholics . . . their elevation of confession into a sacrament. You confess. You are forgiven. You are then free to go on sinning just as before.'

Now he began the recording. I learned today's date, the number of the interview room, that the time was some few minutes past four in the morning, and, through the brief acts of speaking our names, I discerned that Grant's hangover was more advanced and painful than mine.

I would be asked questions, Turnbull said, about the murder of Aileen MacRae in Helensburgh on such and such an afternoon in October this year.

'You transmitted an article that day to your newspaper in London. Is that correct?'

'Yes.'

'Are you aware that fax machines attach a date and time to messages?'

I must have looked uncertain or shocked.

'Take it from me, they do. I checked with the newspaper late last evening. According to their records, your transmission that day, the day of Mrs MacRae's murder, was at twelve fifty-one p.m. Do you accept or dispute that time?'

'If that's what they say,' I replied.

'Does your brother have a fax machine at his cottage?'

'No.'

'So the message was presumably sent from your home?'

'That's where my machine is. I've never claimed otherwise.'

'Has there been any confusion about your movements that day? Did you perchance send the fax then return to visit your brother?'

'No.'

'Now, in an earlier interview with the police, on the First of November this year, you stated that you left your brother's cottage at three thirty in the afternoon. You told us, will you confirm this, that your article was faxed to the newspaper that evening, some while after you had been seen by Sergeant Grant at the MacRae residence.'

'I believe that's what I said.'

327

'So you must have been mistaken about the time of your fax?'

'So it would seem.'

'Your brother and his wife must similarly have been mistaken about the time you left Glen Cairn?'

'I can't answer for them.'

'But it looks that way, doesn't it?'

'You'll have to ask them.'

'Your accountable movements that day are therefore as follows. You were at your house in Upper Helensburgh at twelve fifty-one p.m. Shortly after four, you were seen at the MacRaes'. Where were you between those two times?'

'At home. I must have been at home.'

'Any witnesses to that . . . ?'

'No.'

'. . . Can you think of anything that might confirm your presence at home during that period?'

'Afraid not.'

A faint and sardonic smile as he said: 'You didn't, then, send any other faxes you've omitted to mention?'

'No.'

Turnbull declared an end to the interview and turned the recorder off. A sudden solemnity descended on him. He studied me for a while in the utmost seriousness, as though his sense of victory was so overwhelming he could take no pleasure from it.

'See what I mean about confession, Mr Douglas? I'll wager you feel better already. Wouldn't be at all surprised if you're wondering why you didn't come clean about this weeks ago. I've lied at times myself, not ashamed to say so. And even small lies cast long shadows, over yourself, over others. Poor old Don here, you've had him stumbling round in the dark, couldn't see straight for want of trying. And now, Mr Douglas, you've finally let the light back into his life. And into mine. The Good Lord be praised, I feel we're getting somewhere at last.'

He commenced the recorder again. Declaration of our

328

names sounded like a role call of the sick and dying. Questions this time would be about the murder of Carol Logan, also known as Caroline Sutherland.

'Just a formality, Mr Douglas, to tie up any loose ends. In a previous interview with the police you stated that between the hours of four to six on the evening of November the Fifth you were alone at home. Let's be clear, it was during those hours that Carol Logan was murdered in Hermitage Park. Do you wish for any reason to change your previous statement?'

'No.'

'Has any means of confirming that you were at home come to light since that interview?'

'No.'

Turnbull let loose a sonorous low sigh, of relief, of a task accomplished, of heartfelt thanks to someone up above. It was as though the air he expelled had been within him for weeks. For the second time that morning, he brought the recording to a halt.

'You confuse me, Mr Douglas,' he said. 'If you could lie once, over Aileen MacRae, why not lie again in this instance?'

'No idea,' I admitted.

Grant raised his head for a pained gaze of censure. His eyes were half closed against the fluorescent light, and he winced a little as he spoke, as if someone was yelling in his ears. 'Didnae need to, did he? Same killer in both cases . . . since he didnae do the first murder, a safe assumption he could no' ha' done the other. Two alibis for the price of one, you might say.'

Turnbull gave this protracted thought before conferring a nod of agreement. He started to record yet again and I paid scant regard to his words. We hadn't moved location. The slow passage of minutes was of no particular consequence: I'd nowhere to go to but bed and little hope of seeing that for quite some while yet.

I found Turnbull staring oddly towards me. He repeated something he'd already said.

'. . . Would you like a solicitor present, Mr Douglas?'

'No.'

'Are you sure? One can be provided if you've insufficient means.'

'I don't approve of charity to solicitors.'

'Entirely up to you, Mr Douglas.' He relished the drama of a pause. Eyes languorously closed, he filled his lungs with a deep and long-held breath. The flats of his palms rubbed and twisted one against the other; I imagined some wee living thing between them being squashed with exquisite torture.

He resumed, beginning to say: 'Mind telling me where you were earlier today between the hours of . . .'

'*What*!' I said, sitting bolt upright.

'Beg your pardon . . . ?'

'Questions about *what*?'

'Och, very fucking nonchalant,' Grant said, 'pretending not to hear! Very cool, very collected, very fucking sanguine.' Or maybe memory serves me poorly here and he didn't actually voice this: it was conveyed with a look.

'You'd like me to repeat . . . ?' Turnbull said.

I nodded with urgency.

'You will be asked questions about the murder of Isobel Lockhart in Helensburgh between the hours of ten p.m. last evening and two thirty-five a.m. this morning.' He observed me closely, distrusting that my hearing could be so bad, my shock so profound. His stare became cautious: he suspected trickery.

'Isobel? Isobel *murdered*?'

'You didn't know? That she'd been murdered?'

'How could I? How the fuck could I!'

'Do you wish to reconsider . . . about a solicitor, I mean?

'You tell me . . . do I need a solicitor?'

'Well, now . . . that's for you to say.'

'Your man Grant,' I said, pointing a finger, 'wouldn't give tuppence for solicitors.'

'Are Sergeant Grant's views of any relevance?'

'He told me so last night. As a matter of fact I was with him until the early hours of this morning.'

Turnbull arched his eyebrows, pursed his lips, as he would to a blatant lie.

'If he denies that,' I stated in cold fury, 'I'll demand a fucking congregation of solicitors. I'll want judges and law lords and commissions of enquiry. I shall produce a dozen bar owners and the entire beer-drinking population of Glasgow as witnesses. Plus . . .' I added without any great conviction, '. . . one taxi driver who will attest that Sergeant fucking Grant was a fucking sight more pissed than I fucking was. As . . .' I added further, 'he clearly still is.'

'I see,' Turnbull remarked unemotionally.

'What I mean is, I don't need a solicitor. Not unless you're trying to fit me up.'

'I've already told the DCI I was with you,' Grant said with a look of hurt innocence.

'The sergeant,' Turnbull stated, 'will be making a full statement about his movements yesterday and early today.'

'Good. Can I go now?'

'In a hurry, are you?' Grant enquired.

'I'd like to be alone somewhere so I can cry over Isobel. Is that all right by you?'

Turnbull clasped his hands on the table. 'Any idea what time the sergeant left you?'

'Ask him!'

'I can't say precisely,' Grant admitted. 'Some time before one in the morning, I should think. Maybe a quarter to.'

'Then ask the taxi driver!'

'I've got a man trying to locate him right now,' Turnbull said. 'And afterwards, Mr Douglas? What then? What were your movements between approximately one in the morning and the time you were arrested at Kidston Park?'

'I was out. I was walking my dog.'

'Always doing that, aren't you?' Grant muttered, intent

331

on revenge. 'Any time women get murdered in your town, a sure bet you're out walking your bloody dog!'

Turnbull chose to ignore this outburst. 'For nearly two and a half hours?' he said, pulling a wry face. 'Freezing cold weather, the dead of night . . . ?'

'I needed a blow of air.'

'Anyone see you?'

'Probably not.'

'Happen to bump into your brother, did you?'

'Not that I remember. I fell asleep on a park bench.'

'Anything else you'd like to tell me?'

'Such as . . . ?'

'Whether, for instance, your perambulations took you past Mrs Lockhart's home on the Churchill Estate . . .'

'I doubt it.'

'Forgive me, but you sound uncertain . . .'

'The fact is, my dog did the walking. All I did was follow. She's not usually in the habit of going to the Clyde by way of the Churchill Estate, that's all I can say.'

Suddenly the interview was over. Turnbull ejected the cassette from the machine, inscribed a few terse notes on the label, then rose briskly to his feet. 'I've a locus to visit, Mr Douglas. There's a police surgeon examining intimate parts of Mrs Lockhart's body . . . parts I presume you are very familiar with. I've got clever people from Scenes of Crime picking bits of brain off the three-piece suite. There's the usual forensic stuff I shall be trying very hard not to puke over. So you'll understand why reports to the Fiscal about wasting police time, spelt A-L-I-B-I, are not for the present exactly high on my list of priorities. But I shall neither forgive nor forget.' He pushed his face into mine. 'Don't waste my time any further. Not with stupid questions. Like do you *need* a solicitor? The legal profession of Scotland, Mr Douglas, in its entirety, will be making a fat living from you for years to come.'

He left, with Grant lumbering after, and a uniformed constable, features carved from granite, entered the room to guard me. He moved a chair across the door where he sat, back held rigidly upright and arms tightly locked to enclose bunched fists, as though, without forcible restraint, he would not be answerable for his actions. After several minutes, I asked for what purpose I was being held. He replied without any visible movement of the lips. I asked if Section 2 of the Criminal Justice (Scotland) Act denied me the right to sleep on the floor. He said I could do whatever I bloody liked on the floor except piss or crap. Or wank on it, he added, and his teeth bared suddenly and his knuckles showed white.

So I was in a virtual coma there, curled in a foetal ball, when Grant returned just minutes within the statutory limit of six hours.

'You can go,' he declared. 'All right?'

Then he turned smartly on his heel and went. He did not, I presumed, wish to see my reaction. Or give me the pleasure of seeing his.

The daylight seemed unnaturally bright as I emerged from the building. Then came another explosive glare in my face and I realized a camera had flashed. Jack Moffat was waiting there on the steps with his paparrazo. He had on a grubby anorak; in the bitter cold, his nose shone bright red out of the shadows of his hood. He stamped his feet and blew on his hands. Jack can look frozen stiff in the height of summer, come winter and he'll teach Eskimos a trick or two about forbearance. He trades in doorstep pity.

'Been helping the police, I hear.'

'You know me, Jack. I've a helpful nature.'

'Anything to say?' he asked, not looking too hopeful but with notebook quickly to hand.

'No comment.'

'Christ, wouldya listen to this guy?' Jack muttered. 'Thinks he's some kind of fucking celebrity!'

I stared in dumb confusion towards the car park, trying to collect my thoughts about where I'd left the Volvo. Perhaps I had a vain expectation that the police would at least have provided the means to get home. I considered begging Jack for a lift but the very idea was preposterous. So, with the intention of finding a taxi, I began a trek to the road, and found walking easier than expected: you put one foot at a time ahead of the other.

I paused after several tentative steps, turned, and called back: 'Is it true, Jack? About Isobel Lockhart?'

'Jesus,' he said, beating his hands to his sides. 'Some help you musta bin.'

The taxi driver made a rapid tour of Helensburgh's churches. I wanted somewhere to pray, I explained, and he stared in a leery, one-eyed manner as though this was the weirdest request he'd ever heard.

But doors were bolted, the kirks all locked in grim desolation. There were hours for worship, hours for coffee, and not many of either. When I was a kid and had no appetite for praying, I could have found sanctuary in a kirk any hour of the day or night; now I had a desperate hunger for whatever praying I could get, but God, it seemed, had the morning off. Instead, I directed the taxi to a hardware emporium on Sinclair Street, where I bought a bundle of candles – some traditional form of burnt offering was the very least Isobel might expect of me.

As the cab then headed up the hill, I felt hot tears trickling against my cheeks. Not for her, not for the moment. How immensely depressing, those great locked doors. How demeaning to traipse past copper saucepans and Pyrex dishes and bottles of bleach in search of a candle for the dead.

Twenty-five

I lit several candles in turn, watched each of them burn, obsessively intent on the merest curl of flame, on the slow dribbles of molten wax like tears down the deathly white stems. I was consumed by misery, beset with doubts and confusion. Only one thing was sure and in desperation I clung to its certainty. This was a story I had no wish to write. No wish whatsoever.

I thought of Aileen, and her neat pert breasts swelled in my mind, the nipples pink, fragrant and flagrant. I could see, could imagine, why she'd been murdered. I thought of Caroline, and, so help me, my hands seemed to run the long shapely length of her legs. Under my fingers I felt, through the taut silkiness of her tights (this is *crazy*), the bristles of pubic hair . . . no question here, I thought, no question at all, why she was murdered. But my thoughts turned to Isobel and at that very instant – swear to God this is true – a candle spluttered out with a brief final flaring; it was as if, when the flame died, I was plunged into a bottomless darkness of the mind. I couldn't see *why*, couldn't begin to grasp what she'd ever done to deserve such violence. I pictured her in my room – turn from the desk now and she'd be there – and thought not of sex but of dusters. Memories of Isobel were of vacuum cleaners, floor polish, cloying sweet smells out of aerosols. She was slippers and aprons. She'd no business, no business at all, being in the national headlines. Isobel's place was the local rag – ironing board for sale, perfect condition, call evenings only. She was irredeemably domestic. She should have died of something commonplace in a freshly laundered bed.

Towards evening the phone rang. It was the call I'd been expecting and dreading. With no gesture to small talk, Harry Harper demanded how many words and when? Argument was fruitless, all the reasons I'd rehearsed were dismissed out of hand. I'd known this latest victim? Ace, Sandy. Bloody brilliant, Sandy. Wonderful stuff, this. Very small, is it, that town of yours, or d'you have a knack of knowing these women? Nose on you like a fucking bloodhound. Whadya mean, too *personal*? No such fucking thing as too personal . . . write from the heart.

Whatever became of quality? I protested lamely.

One murder is gutter, he retorted. Two is tabloid. But three? Three, Sandy, is sheer fucking quality. Turbo-powered, leather and walnut, Blaupunkt stereo quality. Any more murders and we'll be doing a photo feature in the mag. Then the line went dead with an abruptness that told me he'd slammed down the phone.

News editors are sharks, in the perilous seas of human misfortune. And lowly reporters like me? All we can do is swim for our lives.

I struck a match to the one remaining candle, did little else for the next mindless hour but stare as it was slowly devoured. Outside my window, night had long since fallen over the town, and when the last struggling flicker of light was eventually gone, I sat in the gloom thinking the residual scent of burning like incense, like a plaintive prayer – as all my prayers are – for forgiveness. Sorry, Isobel. Sorry to the bottom of the heart I shall write from.

I switched on the word processor and began to type. Green letters glowed softly from the screen.

What I remember most is the moon. A bright full moon in a pitch black sky. Like a shining lantern, beaming down on the park. I remember welcoming the light of the moon and at the same time being fearful of it, needing to shrink from sight into the velvet shadows of the trees. Hoolets can see in the dark, they move without sound, they have claws and deadly beaks with which to kill. They can fly safely away under cover of night. I can only act the part of a hoolet. The hiding filled me with foreboding and shame.

I wrote a newspaper piece once about a hoolet. He comes to the same place day after day, the exact same time of the evening. He returns in the twilight, at the promise of blood. Instinct brings him back. There will always, he knows, be a victim waiting.

Precisely on time, Caroline comes walking along the path, no need to look at my watch. I see her tall figure crossing the wee bridge across the burn. Last night there was a bloody kid cycling on the path just as Caroline came by. I spotted him in the bright moonlight and held my breath, moving back deeper into the trees. But tonight I stare carefully in all directions and my pulse quickens as I find we are alone. Just me and her.

I am wearing dark green, the colour of trees. I am dressed like a hiker in green waterproof trousers and a mountain jacket of green nylon. Under that, nothing. The clothes are light and make no rustle of sound when I move. I am wearing plastic gloves. Over my moccasins, I have walking shoes several sizes too large, in case I should leave any footprints. I am glad at feeling so cold in the winter's air – I don't wish to sweat, I must run no risk of leaving any personal traces on her. The police are not clever, local police never are. But back in the laboratories, the men with their test-tubes are exceedingly clever.

Caroline is nearer now. I hear her steps on the gravel. I begin a routine. One, do this. Two, do that. My lips move to the actions but I am scrupulous in not actually speaking the words. From my jacket pocket I take out the first plastic bag. I remind myself to go for the right-hand pocket, though I can feel the weight there, and need no reminding. I take out the hammer and lay the bag carefully on the ground. I have a large stone ready to place on it. There is no wind tonight but I do not chance the bag blowing down the bank and away in the burn. I must leave nothing at the scene . . . nothing I don't wish to be found.

I do not move a muscle till Caroline has passed. She walks

by only feet away from where I stand hidden, pressed tight against the trunk of a tree. Quickly I step out behind her, and before she can turn, long before she can even think to scream, I swing the hammer at her head. She drops without a sound in a heap at my feet.

I have practised this swing with my heavy hammer. I have hit at pumpkins in a firm sideways motion, then examined myself minutely to be sure the pulp has splattered away and there is none on me, not the tiniest of specks.

I drag her body between the bushes, towards the burn and into a wee clearing out of sight of the path. No thorny branches here which might inadvertently scratch my skin. None of the blood they find will be mine. Now for the other pocket, left-hand side. I take out the second of my plastic bags and set it down at the base of a tree, out of harm's way. I remove my clothes, slipping the trousers down over my big walking shoes. I place these also at a suitable distance. Then, naked, I smash in her head. I remember giving Aileen seven very hard whacks but Caroline needs only six whacks to achieve the same effect. I think she has a softer skull and I wonder for a moment if this is because she is younger.

She also has coarse pubic hairs, dark in the silvery light. They are not fine and clipped in a neat triangle like Aileen's. Nor does she have the fragrance Aileen had, a smell of perfume and bath oil even in death. Caroline smells of blood and cheap perfume and I think, while I was beating in her brains, she had the presence of mind to shit herself. I squeeze the dog sperm out from the plastic bag and over her belly and down between her legs. I am careful not to touch! I use the plastic to smear it around, to work it into her pubic hairs. Is this mad, or what? Is this a man who despises women? I look up at the moon and it seems to answer. Yes, the moon says. Mad. Really fucking mad. Stark staring bonkers.

Her handbag! I glimpse it suddenly in the helpful moonglow, lying where she fell on the path. I throw it away into the burn. Then I enter the stream, where I take off my outer shoes one at a time, leaving them within easy reach on the bank. I stretch out in the burn, letting the freezing water course over me. I bathe in it, washing away every possible splash of blood or of God knows what else. I had an erection with Aileen, when I was smearing the dog sperm. I had to grab for my hammer bag and pull it quickly over my prick, in case I shot on her body and over the carpet. But not this time. I am limp and controlled. I give thanks again for the biting cold.

No-one has come by! I drag the body closer to the burn. I dress again. I put the hammer into its bag and the sperm bag with it, then place them in a pocket, together with the plastic gloves. I walk away and my moccasins squelch ever so slightly. Should anyone approach, I am ready to melt into the cover of darkness. But, though I stretch my eyes in the park, wishing for the sharp sight of a hoolet, I am thankfully alone here.

I emerge by a narrow lane that passes beside the War Memorial. Now I must cross a road. Not a main road, this one, and I am only a harmless hiker in the clothes I wore earlier. But I fear to be seen now. I fear the white brightness of the moon. So I peer cautiously both ways before crossing the road, and have to force myself not to run. Only a few short paces before I reach the welcome seclusion of a pocket of woodland. A change of dry clothes and shoes is hidden here in a rubbish bag, and a towel for a brisk warming rub.

I make the dangerous crossing of Sinclair Street only after the most careful inspection. I wait for a gap in the passing traffic. I am already free by now of my black plastic bag – I have left it by the side wall of someone's garage where others, identical council refuse bags, are awaiting collection.

I return home down quiet back streets. And there I take a long hot bath and a comforting glass of scotch. After that, I scrub the tub with bleach and leave the water running for an hour. I am nothing if not thorough.

I return to the park then. I have a clean fresh smell about me. When I encounter the police, I look shocked and outraged and innocent.

I am deluded at times, no getting away from it. I am subject to confusions, envy and trivial acts of revenge. I want things I can't have, so I have persuaded myself not to covet them, to *pretend* I don't ache for the unattainable. But I am not fooled. Now I have the bitter frustration of no longer hungering for what is beyond me. I feel unfulfilled since I have nothing to strive for. There is a madness to this, and if suffering these perfectly normal ambiguities of life is mad, I will freely admit to being mad. But violently mad? Murderously insane?

I must have read and reread those stark sentences on the screen many times. And the reason these musings suddenly clouded my consciousness was the disturbing (and, yes, mad) realization that the words were my only means of retaining a grip on sanity. Thank God I didn't lurk in the park. I didn't kill Caroline. I know that, I said aloud. I am sure of that. At least, fairly sure. Yes, reasonably certain.

These are not my words!

To explain. I had turned my mind often to the puzzle of how Caroline met her end. I'd wondered in idleness about the forensic stuff, and tried to make sense of why, if the Hoolet had ejaculated over his victims, as the police seemed to be saying, he wasn't afraid of genetic fingerprinting. I'd listened to Sergeant Grant describing his return to the murder scene, and I'd pictured myself there beside him, sharing his apprehension. The night Caroline died, I'd been in the park, with Jack Moffat and his paparazzo and at least a hundred others: I shall never forget that moonlight, cold and cruel and luminous. So . . . any revulsion I felt was overcome by curiosity. Reading, I experienced a sense of enlightenment, not unlike a dimly recalled memory slowly taking shape. As I read, questions were answered; I had sight of the truth at last through the dull throbbings of a hangover. Ahhh, I thought. Yes! Of course, yes, *that's* how it was done. That's why she was killed near the burn.

I remember, round about the third reading, being suddenly aware that this knowledge was now part of me, indistinguishable from memory. I knew how he thought and how he'd acted. In the entire world only two of us knew these things. Him and me. What defence would it be to claim the words weren't mine? It occurred to me then how clever he'd been to write them.

An hour or more must have passed while I continued to stare at the screen, scrolling up the text, reliving Caroline's death over and over and over. What had caused the words to appear? The most likely explanation, I now believe, is that I'd keyed in some particular word or other as I began to write, and this had resulted in the text being retrieved. If so, when had the Hoolet done this? When had he sat down in my room, at my machine, and typed? Had he been fluent, familiar with keyboards, or picked with slow fingers at the keys? His words struck fear into me but the idea of erasing them terrified me more – there might be hidden clues I'd so far failed to spot, and I was frightened of losing them.

I read till my head swam. Shoes, plastic gloves, mountain jacket. *I return home along quiet back streets.* How home? All the way by foot, or was a car parked in waiting? Does he tell the whole truth or only that part of the story he wants me to read? *I am already free now of my black plastic bag.* In what street was this? Weeks ago, now. Long since collected. In a municipal tip somewhere. Crushed. Buried.

. . . *black plastic bag – I have left it* . . .

My doorbell rang insistently at this point. I found Phyllis at the front door, looking fraught and distressed. A night of biting frost, her panting breath forming clouds in the air, yet she'd come out without a coat. She wore only a thin, shapeless cardigan and, with wild staring eyes, seemed for a moment not to recognize me.

'It's Gordon,' she blurted. 'They've arrested him!'

I led her by the arm upstairs, settled her down beside the hearth and poured a stiff measure of whisky. She gripped the glass with bony fingers, taking timid sips, and gazed at the flames like one of the damned into hellfire. Her lips moved soundlessly as if she had lost her voice.

'This is all my fault,' I said. 'Things will be fine soon, you'll see.'

'How, Sandy? How is it your fault?'

'That stupid alibi of mine . . . when I got you and Gordon to say I was at the cottage. I had to come clean. I told the police it wasn't true. They'll give him a rough ride for a few hours, take their frustration out on him, then let him go.'

She raised her gaze to me, unable at first to grasp what I'd said.

'Same as they did to me, Phyllis.'

'Bloody wonderful!' she exclaimed. 'Bloody fucking thoughtful of you!'

At this instant, on the far side of the room, I suddenly saw the green glow on my word processor screen. Muttering an oath under my breath, I quickly moved over. Then I hesitated, turning my head to look back. She was staring across at me, her face darkened by a questioning frown. Nothing for it but to switch the machine off. The words were immediately gone; only a glimmer of light remained in the centre of the screen, which faded away before my gaze.

'The alibi was his, too,' Phyllis said bleakly.

'How do you mean?'

'They're charging him with the murders, Sandy.'

She was to tell me later that my actions on hearing this were a complete mystery to her. But Phyllis, thank God, is a practical sort. People behave strangely under stress, she conceded. They do the oddest things because they have to do *something*, any damned thing they can. And she forgave me the apparent lapse, since, when I finally returned to where she sat, and cupped her hands in mine, tears were brimming in my eyes – I looked absolutely shattered, she said – and she couldn't for the life of her ever remember seeing me cry. Still . . . she felt the need later, only the once, to make a barbed comment; Phyllis is prudish enough to believe strange behaviour should not go unremarked.

'You and your words,' she said. 'Gordon in the clink and all you could think of, your fucking words.'

I had, you see, practically dived for the switch again, then begun typing letters in a frenzy. ISOBEL. HOOLET. CAROLINE. All to no avail.

She wasn't to know Gordon was foremost in my thoughts. I'd lost his words! Now what? How the hell could I learn why he'd put them there?

The media circus was in full swing. Reporters had gathered in droves outside Divisional Headquarters at Dumbarton. There were photographers by the score with Nikons and aluminium stepladders, kitted for the Scottish winter in desert boots and tropical camouflage. Out of Mitsubishis and Transits, television crews unloaded sufficient equipment to make a De Mille epic. They tested their sun-guns and spots, setting the walls ablaze with a glaring white br'lliance. They squinted against the light and scratched their heads, then plunged the surroundings into utter darkness that sent spots swimming before the eyes. Heights and angles would be readjusted; soon the lights would explode on again and still nothing was right – someone blamed the building. Expectation filled the air under a cover of practised nonchalance. Dog-ends were stamped out and fresh cigarettes cadged; the television men had flasks of scalding coffee; newshounds shoulder to shoulder with other newshounds quaffed deviously as if fearing to share their quarter-bottles. Business as usual inside the premises, where, through the uncurtained glass, lit by harsh fluorescence, police could be seen at desks, moving in no particular hurry from room to room. A pretty WPC appeared at a window; she stared out, impassive and self-absorbed, into a welter of camera flashes: we were all invisible, phantoms in the night.

Around eight o'clock, signs of agitation became apparent among the BBC crew – their evening news went out at nine. The contingent from ITN, who'd always known ten was a better hour for educating the nation, began to look complacent. The men of the printed page weighed the prospect of a statement being delayed past ten, dreamed of tomorrow's headlines, and their smugness was odious. Frantic maydays went out from the BBC van and above the murmurings of idle babble, the metallic clatter of floodlight arrays being moved yet again, the sometime revving of car engines where hacks were seeking respite from the climate, came the sound of strings being pulled in distant high places. Turnbull's emergence into the lime-light very soon after was rumoured to have been prompted by urgent words being spoken in ears. Somehow I doubt this. From what I'd come to know of him, I'd say Turnbull's timing was of his own choosing. He spoke when he was good and ready, not a moment sooner.

And not a word more than he had to. It was the briefest of statements. A man would be charged tomorrow morning at Dumbarton Sheriff Court with the murders of three women. A local man, married and aged thirty-six. Thank you, ladies and gentlemen, that's all I have to say.

Among a chorus of shouted questions, someone suggested the Squad must be cock-a-hoop. Well earned pats on the backs, eh, Mr Turnbull?

'We shan't be throwing any parties,' Turnbull replied in parting. 'Not until due sentence has been handed down.'

All the while, Jack Moffat had, apparently, been standing right behind me. His familiar nasal whine sounded over my shoulder.

'Why is it,' he complained, 'that the buggers with the news, I mean to say these guys with the fucking great stories of our time held in the palms of their hands, never have any *style*. No panache, Sandy, know what I'm saying. I mean, if fucking football managers can be over the moon from winning some lousy match, you'd think that guy could at least crack a smile. I mean, he's just caught the Hoolet for fuck's sake yet you'd think he was reading the shipping forecasts.'

'Wrong there, Jack,' I said. 'That's a man playing to the gallery. You people want drama, he's saying, you can

344

bloody sit on the edges of your seats till nine tomorrow morning.'

'Yeah,' Jack concurred without much enthusiasm.

'At which time,' I added, 'Detective Chief Inspector Turnbull, ringmaster extraordinary, will produce the man we're all dying to see with a blanket over his head. He's giving us two fingers, Jack, loving every minute of this.'

'Yeah,' Jack said again. 'Could be.'

Then he treated me to a long and very personal stare through eyes narrowed to slits, and he smirked with great satisfaction over some secret only he knew. I'm absolutely certain he'd already learned by backdoor means who the local man was, married and aged thirty-six. Never mind that he wouldn't be able to print the name just yet, he knew, he wanted me to see he knew, and that's all that mattered to him. I've always suspected that Jack's idea of a great story is one so incredibly hush-hush only he has discovered it, so secret it can never be told. Maybe that's his problem: he's a newsman through and through, but not in his heart.

I forced an air of bonhomie I was very far from feeling.

'The Hoolet,' I said, gesturing to show the enormity of the headlines. 'At home with his wife and brother. Exclusive. Just think, Jack, what those family photies will be worth.'

The Audi caught my eye when I was on the point of driving away. The Headquarters car park was a mêlée: television gear being hurriedly stowed in the Mitsubishi four-tracks, vehicles jostling to leave, headlamps flashing irate messages about who was here first, and a fog of engine fumes burning red with the glow of brake lights. Through it all, almost hidden in shade by a facing wall, I glimpsed a car I recognized vaguely. It was the kind of spick, cleaned-every-Sunday new that gets changed every year. It had a distinctive registration, but not the owner's initials – that would be nouveau and crass. The letters read R-H-U, as if to claim cleverness from living somewhere you can fit on a number plate. When a parking space became clear beside the Audi, I manoeuvred over there, sat at my wheel and waited.

I mused over Gordon and doorkeys, over the time I'd left his cottage wearing the wrong Barbour. Early the next morning, Isobel had encountered him in the hallway. But we'd only Gordon's word that he was on his way in; he could have been in the flat for ages, sufficiently long to type those words. Word processors are silent; there's no clatter of keys. As for Flora, she knows him well – he'd brought toffees to placate her – she wouldn't have thought to bark. And, of course, Gordon had clapped eyes on Isobel, seen her naked, and gone mad with desire. Give me one of your women, Sandy. *Please!* This is your brother, begging you.

I also mused over the previous occasion I'd lost my keys. I'd discovered the loss soon after leaving Helensburgh police station, and made the natural assumption Sergeant Grant had taken them. But stupid of me not to have seen before that the police don't need to steal keys: they have skeleton sets, locks are no impediment to them. There'd been a toffee then, too; the same intruder at work. When and how had Gordon got his hands on my keys? Think! He's sly and resourceful. The answer would come to me. Give it time.

MacIntyre showed up some forty-five minutes later. The car park was all but deserted by then, just a few straggling hopefuls kicking their heels at the entrance to the building. But he was taking no chances of being spotted; he appeared as if from thin air, probably having left by a back exit and keeping to the shadows around the periphery.

I wound down my window as he was groping in the dark for his keys.

'How does it look?' I asked. 'Grim, or am I being optimistic as usual?'

He squinted, coming closer. 'You may be his brother, Sandy, but you are also, I should point out, a member of this bloody rat pack.' He gestured angrily at the ghosts of the departed.

'Now, listen,' I retorted, 'they won't let me in to see him. Since fucking lawyers seem to take precedence over family, fucking lawyers might at least have the decency to say what the hell's going on in there.'

'Things do not look good,' he confessed with a droop of despair. 'His fingerprints were found at one of the scenes. So the police say, and I see no reason to doubt them.'

'What does Gordon say?'

'Not very much, I'm afraid.'

'How is he pleading?'

MacIntyre sighed heavily. 'I gave him the usual spiel. I said I trusted him, he must trust me. So long as he assured me of his innocence, I'd defend to the best of my ability. In that case, he said, I'm innocent.' MacIntyre sighed once more with all his heart. 'I never like that, Sandy . . . clients who need me to tell them how to plead. Christ Almighty, they've only got a choice of Guilty or Not.'

'Did he say anything about me?'

MacIntyre bent his head towards me, looking baffled and askance. 'I rather think, Sandy, that your welfare isn't much on his mind.'

Phyllis had retired to my bed. She'd grabbed a bottle of Scotch for company and drained it dry. To the best of my memory, there hadn't been much in the bottle, but it will have been a great deal to Phyllis, who hardly ever touches the stuff. She lay on her back between the sheets, lips apart, looking like death, but eerily serene, as if death had come as a welcome release. I'd never seen her in bed before and sleep suited her, softened her facial angles, rekindled in her a kind of fragile youth. Perhaps dreaming is the only time she finds no cause to frown.

As she slept, I searched the apartment from top to bottom. A room at a time, looking in drawers and cupboards and under carpets. I searched for signs of disturbance in any dust, and I was ready if need be to take up every single floorboard.

I had been thinking, on the journey back from Dumbarton, about the black plastic refuse bag. I'd tried to remember the exact words on the screen, and I'd thought about the possibility they conveyed only part of the story. I remembered how Gordon read my newspaper columns on the sly, like coded messages, searching for buried references, and it occurred to me that he might write in exactly that way. On reflection, I had made the dispiriting discovery that I'd read almost nothing in Gordon's hand since we were kids at school and made cruel fun of each other's essays. He jotted down lists now, inventories of wildlife and livestock, brief notes to himself, and that was all. I'd attempted to think the way he thought, and I knew how he spoke but precious little of the thoughts behind the words. I'd wracked my brain until my head ached and the ominous pain was worse, far more terrible, than any hangover. It was an ache of the spirit, a pain of the soul.

But I'd come up with a theory. The only one I could think of that made any sense.

And after a fairly short hunt I found the bag in a bureau drawer, concealed under some light clothes I wouldn't be touching until the summer. Not to be found, in fact, unless you were looking.

So he had, as I'd guessed, told his story truthfully but partially. When I lie, at least I bloody lie, there's an openness, an honesty, in my constant deceits. But Gordon is underhanded, his are lies of omission. Yes, he probably had got rid of the green trousers beside someone's garage . . . and the walking shoes and the mountain jacket. But he hadn't – I was convinced he hadn't – said what he'd done with the hammer.

Inside a small bag of clear plastic was a heavy club hammer, and the dried blood which caked the head in profusion was presumably Caroline's – he couldn't possibly have been in the flat since Isobel's murder.

Blind instinct kept me from touching, getting my prints

on it. I stared through the plastic. I could feel the pulse beating in my temple as I stared. Those minutes were the longest, most unendurably harrowing, of my life.

He wanted me to find it. If he'd intended to plant it on me, implicate me for the murders, he'd have dropped some kind of hint to Turnbull, made a remark about me to MacIntyre, and the flat would have been crawling with police by now.

He's completely and hopelessly mad, of course. But far worse than his madness is his stupid fucking pride. Only once have I heard him say *please*. He'll do anything – any act of desperation or folly – rather than ask for my help.

BLOOD RELATIONS

Twenty-six

She was praying, in church, when I first laid eyes on her. So I came to believe her heaven-sent.

Over the years I must have passed the West Kirk a thousand or more times without any compulsion to enter. But that particular morning the doors were open wide, no service was in progress, and I'd somehow wandered in. God alone knows why. I entered in the defiant spirit of a kid venturing through a lonely graveyard after nightfall.

The woman in brown was kneeling in the pews towards the back of the nave. Diffident positioning, I noted: where I might kneel as a stranger to churches. Her hands were tightly clasped, her eyes raised to the altar in a look of pleading. I sat to one side, across the aisle, and she gave no intimation of being aware of my presence.

Late forties or thereabouts. Comfortably off but doesn't throw her money about. Hair could do with a bit of attention, less severe and matronly, and some advice on clothes wouldn't come amiss: that brown coat was rather dowdy given the general brownness of her complexion. Long fingers, pale and sensitive. She wore no wedding ring yet her features had none of the mute sadness, or the wanton relief, of a widow.

All desire, I suppose, has to begin somewhere, with a first glance that steals subversively back for a second, longer look. There is a perverse attraction in searching for reasons to be attracted: in the right light, perhaps, all women are desirable. But it was her desperate need of prayer which most aroused my interest. She seemed so blameless in appearance, I couldn't help but wonder what she might have done that begged for forgiveness. When

353

she finally departed the kirk, I followed at a distance. I felt drawn by the lure of secret sin.

Let's take the detective work for granted, skip over the assiduous tailing of her little brown Metro, my unaccustomed rising in the dark morning hours to commute at her bumper to Glasgow. Let's take as read the time I devoted to the contents of her trolley at Gateway: her brand of tea bag, the detergent she used, her liking for avocados and greenish bananas; there are women whose characters can be read in a shopping basket, you don't know till you look. Let's not dwell on the geography of her garden, which I came to know intimately, with its spiky rhododendrons, crunchy gravel paths and numerous places of concealment – none of which gave any hope of seeing past those impervious drapes of heavy brown velvet. Trust me when I say my efforts were unstinting. She was forty-nine and had never married. I never assumed she'd be easy.

Her name was Sheena Campbell. She lectured in medieval history at the university. Her quarters there lay down a corridor of High Gothic vaulting, cathedral pillars, Arabic tiles; her door was forever closed and I imagined the panelling inside to be of burnished sandalwood, the walls to be painted a rich shade of brown. No opportunity was to present itself to hear her declaim at first hand, but I eavesdropped at the supermarket checkout – the voice was pleasant though given to monotones – so I believed the student who swallowed my story about doing an inside piece on the campus.

'Och, tha' Sheena!' he said. 'Mother Teresa. No' exactly inspired. Sorta pedestrian, if ye wantaknow. And the kinda bloody feminist wi' a padlock oan her fanny.'

She had airs, was probably born with them. Asked for her address in a shop, she made primly sure they called it her residence. A converted lodge, this, once the home of carriages and grooms, situated to the north, the less favoured side, of one of the rambling old mansions. The Upper Station was close by, but she avoided trains, any form of public transport, preferring her pampered little car, which was housed in a stable fit for a team of horses. Walls had been prettified, the craggy stone almost buried under a jungle of creeper. She'd put in a mock Regency door with coach lamps to either side, installed proprietary double-glazing that screamed of plastic, and turned the entrance courtyard, by means of terracotta pots, some twee garden seats, and a rather sickly vine, into a wistful yearning for somewhere in Greece. About a quarter of an acre of grounds surrounded the lodge, and at weekends a grumpy looking gardener would labour over tasks I found mystifying – digging and turning beds with nothing much in them, raking up charming and seemingly healthy plants from the gravel – while Sheena, in jeans and boots and leather mittens, would devote hours to sprinkling tea-leaves and eggshells on the roots of the creepers and under the vine.

Of all the greenery on display, my favourite soon became the tropical specimen with prickly leaves, third pot along, left of the door. To all appearances, Sheena was a logical person. She liked neatness and order. She had the gardener to do her bidding, and he was surely a dab hand at any odd job. So why play games with the pot? My theory is that every house, somewhere, has an inconvenience there's no point in putting right. You try several repairs, it always goes wrong, you give up trying. Whatever . . . on returning from work, Sheena would park her little car in the stable, turn her key in the front door and sometimes the door would open, sometimes it wouldn't. Then she'd swear, steal a cautious look round, and take a spare key from beneath the pot with the prickly leaves. While this second key gave no guarantee of immediate entry, in the end, after some further muttered swearing, it always did the trick. Maybe the thought never occurred to put the spare on her keyring; maybe she had a dread, peculiar to single women, of losing keys. No matter, these occasional charades endeared her to me enormously. I have an innate suspicion of career women.

So I liked her silliness with keys, just as I took comfort from the fact she was no great shakes at lecturing.

I detected clear signs of vulnerability.

But what did I actually know of her? There was the university, an apparent love of gardening . . . and very little else. Seated in my study, a gale-force wind battering at the windows, I would try to seduce her. Suspecting something was afoot, Flora would pad into the room and I could feel her curious stare striking hard against my back.

I'd be a writer of weighty tomes, we'd share a devotion to scholarship. My words were persuasive . . . I'd see the light begin to sparkle in Sheena's eyes as though hearing me speak kindled a fire slowly inside her. Gently I'd peel off her clothes while at the same time taking off mine – if I knew anything about her, she had confident modesty, we must always be equals. When we lay naked together in her bed . . .

. . . but perhaps books would bore her. She felt a slave to bloody books.

I can see the problem clearly now, though it eluded me at the time. I was an author . . . what could be more natural than acting the author? I found the notion astounding. Its novelty and daring took my breath away.

Seduction, I realize now, can never work this way. Where is the mystery in being as you are? What magic can you weave, what spell of enchantment, by being yourself?

Shortly after this, I was out on a foray with Gordon. Snow lay thick on the ground, and the sun, a pale orb low on the horizon, spread a tinge of gold across the land. Retinues of pine trees wore mantles of white and bowed their branches. No movement but us and the only sound to be heard was a crisp crunching as we trudged through the drifts. Clouds were motionless, frozen to the sky, tracks were buried in the folding white hills, any creatures surviving had gone deeply to ground – when a capercaillie

356

burst without warning across our path in a great flurry of wings, I let out a gasp of astonishment. Watching the bird flap away just inches above the snow, Gordon smiled to himself, as if thankful he'd brought no gun. We were kids out window shopping, he announced, filling his lungs with a massive breath. Peer in wonder through the frosted glass.

'Would you read a woman's diary?' I enquired of him.

'Without being asked?' he said, screwing up his face.

'Well of course. If she asks, there can't be anything worth reading!'

He needed no time for thought. 'Certainly not!' he answered emphatically.

'What if you found it lying around, this hypothetical diary, crying out to be read.'

'So what! You can't help yourself to things simply because they're there.'

I was persistent. 'But what if reading a woman's secrets, which I'll agree is rather sneaky, turns out to be good for her?' In an inspired choice of words, I went on: 'What if it proves to be the key to her happiness?'

He fell very quiet. I sensed his awareness that talk of right and wrong cut no ice with me. He seemed to be searching for some other way to express his misgivings. Eventually his face grew troubled and solemn. 'I keep a diary,' he said. 'Just a few wee words, jottings at bed-time.'

'Really? I never knew that.'

'If I caught anyone reading it, so help me I'd blow their head off.'

'Even Phyllis?' I asked.

A pause in our progress while his brow knitted and he stared afar at the sun-gilded hills. I took his eventual answer to be yes, even Phyllis. He shared a roof with her, and a bed, and the income of church mice. Everyone, however, needs some small corner of their thoughts to call his own. The trouble is, he said, those corners that never see daylight become stagnant and murky. Dark dungeons of the mind, he confessed, where secrets are locked which mustn't, ever, be free.

This was probably the moment when I gained my first real insight into Sheena. I suddenly knew, beyond any doubt, she *must* keep a diary, that she confided in its pages every frustration, every bowel movement, every itch and boil and latent desire.

And I assured myself that words are meaningless unless they're read.

I chose an afternoon when the outside light was failing and she was safely removed to Glasgow. Entry was plain sailing . . . something of a disappointment, if I'm honest, in its lack of drama; none of the siren scent of danger I'd screwed up my nerves to face. I lifted the edge of the earthenware pot, turned the door latch and returned the key to its hiding place. All there was to it! Once inside the house, I felt calm, unhurried. As if, I thought, she'd invited me in.

First I went through the rooms, getting the feel of the place, turning strangeness to familiarity. Off the tiny entrance hall was a chintzy living room not unlike my own, only smaller and neater and with feminine touches – fresh flowers, dashings of lace, china figures in excruciating good taste, and a conspicuous cleanliness that assailed every sense: you could smell and see and touch the absence of grime, you could walk on it, sit on it, a room so virginal I felt compelled to take off my shoes and creep round thereafter in my socks. Sheena was quite obviously a woman you seduced only after spending a fortune at the cleaners.

An archway led to the dining room, spotless and floral; a door beyond that into the kitchen, which to my eyes was sterile to the point of unreason, not so much a place for preparing food as a laboratory where dishes could be examined microscopically, germs discovered and exterminated. No cartons of milk going sour, and in the fridge, the lettuce was crisp, the tomatoes unwrinkled. It was a kitchen I'd have said no person living alone could either want or maintain. Sheena must be married to herself! I retraced my path, serious doubts beginning to form.

She'd built a cosy wee den adjoining the living room. This had been an outhouse once; the wallpaper of pastoral design lay unevenly over lumps in the plaster. To both sides of the little Victorian escritoire, books were crowded from floor to ceiling; I glanced over the many volumes of history to determine whether any of the covers bore her name. None of them did; I became a little more cheerful. As for fiction, she read only women authors – the great classics but not Dickens or Hardy or Walter Scott – had all of Virginia Woolf several times over in a selection of bindings, and betrayed a surprising addiction to Barbara Cartland.

Up the creaking stairs was her bedroom – which I glanced into from the doorway, on my honour, merely to see what it was – and across the landing, a bathroom tiled in lavender, bidet and basin to match. She shaved her legs with a Braun, wore Rochas perfume and used toothpaste for sensitive gums. Nothing in the cabinet of a sexual nature – no packets, flavoured or otherwise, no devices with batteries, no tablets bearing the days of the week. Was she allergic to sex? More hopefully, was she practical and hot-blooded? Did she keep her requisites ready to hand beside the bed? I take pride now in my respect for her privacy – I declined to look. I had, after all, first seen her in church. Begin as you mean to go on.

I began to feel ridiculous in my socks. Returning downstairs, I retrieved my shoes. Then to her little study where I commenced a search of the drawers. I was swift yet unflustered. Correspondence on official letterheads . . . telephone bills, paid on the nail . . . electricity, likewise . . . something from the Inland Revenue in a fat buff envelope; I'd come back to that later.

And there it was! Leather-bound, tantalizingly heavy as it lay within my grasp. At the back of my mind, a fear must have been lurking that I'd find only a slim pocket-sized diary, university issue with a crest on the cover, and nothing inside but appointments.

Even as I began turning the pages, I heard a crunch from outside of tyres over gravel. I shoved the diary back in the drawer, frantically rearranged the papers over it, and froze behind the study door. Was there another way out? Of course! The back door leading on to the garden, small lobby, far side of the kitchen. Bolted top and bottom? Locked? Key left there, protruding from the lock? *Fucking think!*

I heard footsteps on the hall floor, the creak of a door hinge. Then I could only sense a presence in the room outside, imagine her moving towards me over the fitted brown carpet. A clink of glass against glass reached me, the low sound of a drink being poured. Then only silence.

I chanced a cautious peep round the edge of the door.

He was seated with his back to me. A conventional cut to his hair, an athletic neck. He was tall, that much I could see from the height of his broad shoulders above the armchair. Nonchalantly, with all the signs of being at home, he'd tossed a stylish raglan overcoat on to the sofa. I heard the click of a lighter, then he was holding a cigarette exactly as a cigarette should be held, like a thirties gigolo, an elegant accessory poised between two raffish fingers. He puffed rings up at the ceiling with an obvious air of anticipation. His head turned in search of an ashtray, he rose from the chair, and I shrank back behind the door. I pressed my nose to the crack beside the door-frame and he was lifting a vase of flowers for the saucer underneath. As he came back to the chair, I had a full view of his face and was surprised to discover him older than his back had suggested. Fifty or thereabouts, I guessed. But he believed himself younger and had enough money by the cut of his suit that he could probably claim any age he cared and few women would argue. His hair looked naturally dark, he had black brooding eyes. Loose limbed in movement, I noticed, and his mind on nothing very much except whatever had brought him here, yet there was a tangible aura of nervousness to him, a vaguely troubled manner, which I put down to the pressures of business. Soon the smoke from his cigarette pervaded the study, the smell of tobacco filled the house. It was as if he meant to intrude, as if like some wild animal he was putting down his scent to claim the territory. And in that moment, if I hadn't been certain before, I knew he *owned* Sheena.

How soon afterwards she arrived I really can't relate. I remember looking constantly at my watch but anxiously so, not really heeding the time. Perhaps I only imagined that whole hours went by – now I think back, he lit just the one cigarette. Anyway, it was with a feeling of release from a limbo of waiting that I heard another crunch of tyres in the driveway. Then her voice. No note of surprise, but of course she'd seen his car outside, his Porsche or Lotus or whatever it was.

'You're early,' she said in her pleasant monotone.

'Managed to skip a client meeting,' he answered. A voice of substance, Scottish, with breeding.

'Had a tutorial,' she said. 'Students these days are *pathetic*.'

I stared through the gap at the rim of the door . . . I'd long since given up breathing. Lightly, she kissed him on the cheek, then regarded him for a moment with a pensive style of affection as if he'd changed in slight and various ways since their last meeting but she couldn't see how. She fluttered her hands towards the stairs.

'Won't be a moment. Teeth and things after the drive.'

Greetings over, formalities done. While she was up in the bathroom, he discarded his jacket then took off his tie. He considered another cigarette, actually placed it to his lips but after an admonitory shake of the head returned it to the packet – rather too exactly, I thought, with more than a hint of hoarding. I wondered what he did for a living. Something in finance? Insurance? One of those occupations where everything's counted, only so many vices in a day.

Sheena took her time, cleaned more than her teeth. She made a fresh entrance with her make-up repaired, dressed fetchingly in a figure-hugging blouse whose top buttons, no mistake about it, would be demurely fastened on varsity precincts. He rose to meet her, they stood at the centre of the room, within touching distance . . . but not touching though I could feel their desperate longing. Cathodes, I thought, staring hard. Current building up. Sparks about to fly.

'Missed you,' she said.

'Me, too,' he said with a break in his voice.

'How have you been?'

'I'm fine. Katriona's fine. The kids are bloody fine.'

'I don't,' she said, 'wish to hear about Katriona.'

She threw her arms about his neck, clasped him with a sudden eruption of the passion I'd always been certain was in her. He cradled her head against his shoulder, her face was towards me, and I could see the shine of welling tears before they gushed in a torrent down her cheeks. Her eyes were instantly red as if from hours of crying.

'Hate you,' she said. 'Hate you, hate you, hate you.'

This was the only time I ever saw others make love. A careful choice of words, don't think me coy: I'd know a fuck if I saw one. But undeniably that afternoon, an act of love was played out in my presence. There was too much evident pain, the tenderness was too apparent in both of them, for it to be otherwise. To this day I remain uncertain whether my eyes popped most at the love or the screwing.

She took the initiative, no haste in the removal of his clothes, never once fumbling with buttons or zips. Dropping to her knees, she cupped his buttocks in her hands while burying her face in his crotch. His back was turned to where I stood watching; I could see only a red colouration which spread over his skin, rising from his feet, over his shoulders to the nape of his neck.

Then he stripped her with an identical, relaxed assurance, his lips following in the path of his hands. They'd done this before, a great many times; there was still a palpable sense of wonder to his actions as if this was the very first sight he'd had of her body, as if he stood proxy for me, and my eyes were his.

Her breasts were heavy; I longed to reach out and fondle their maturely drooping curves. The nipples were the sultry crimson she'd applied to her mouth, in their tips I could see the quiverings of her heart beat. She had the stomach she should, for a woman of nearly fifty, the beginnings of a sag, and she saw no need to tighten the muscles for him, no reason for vanity – her flesh had bulges, pliant folds, the shape was voluptuous. A thicket of pubic hair, a tangle of gorse and bramble, intrepid explorers only. Damn the cigarette smells still wafting around – I felt participation denied me – when he pushed his tongue between the parting of her legs, the music must have been gypsy violins, the taste dark and strong, her aroma the blackest roast imaginable of rich Vienna coffee.

She led him to the sofa, and when he lay there at full stretch, gazing up at her, her body bulbous and fifty, a provocative smile playing over her lips, I was confounded to see he was still unaroused. Absolutely amazed, actually, and more than a little delighted. His shrunken genitals seemed to bury themselves in shame, a shrivelled walnut almost lost in the undergrowth. I pushed my face against the doorframe, my smile outdid hers in its curls of delight. Only one erection round here, old sport. And I've fucking got it!

Sheena knelt beside him, began licking his thighs, his stomach. She teased the tip of her tongue into his navel and around his testicles. Then she took his prick in her mouth and, as whole minutes passed, I watched the gradual arousal of his body through the changing expression on her face. Her lips began to swell, her eyes to grow rounder, blue veins stood out on her temples, her cheeks developed a fleshy red bloom. When she judged the moment to be right, she slid on to him with a sinuous

363

motion I found remarkably agile, her hands playing with brief dexterity within the nestings of their hairs. Then she was sitting astride him while he lay immobile on his back, leaving the wriggling and bouncing, even the looks of contentment, to her.

'Well, then,' she murmured. 'That's better.'

When it was over, which was a short while longer than being a disgrace, though only just, he had the decency not to light a cigarette. Sheena rolled off the sofa on to the carpet, where she reclined on a crooked elbow and they exchanged satiated gazes, and she fluttered her lashes a little while his eyes begged for more . . . but let me catch my breath darling my God wasn't that *wonderful*.

'Please, Miss,' he said, raising a hand, 'can I go to bed, Miss?'

'What a naughty little boy,' she said. 'Stay behind after school!'

Once they had gone upstairs, I waited only a few moments. Rashly few, on reflection, although, luckily, they had ears only for each other. The front door closed behind me with not too much of a bang, I managed to creep in relative silence over the gravel. Had I looked back maybe I'd have seen what model of car he drove, but I had no such thoughts at the time.

The darkness was profound. Only a few paces from her door, I was engulfed by the night.

'Ever get those days?' Jack Moffat will say, 'when you'd better believe in something? Drabbly days, daggy days, dribble and smuchter. Days the only thing keeps you going is the Power of the Press.'

Not the power to effect real change, he'd say hurriedly, nor the ability to inform in any constructive way. Newspapers don't bring empires crashing down, or deter the more ludicrous excesses of the EEC; they don't catch criminals, and be honest it was Christine Keeler not Fleet Street that sounded the death knell for Macmillan. Newspapers, he'll tell you, never make news, they only report it. They can't form public tastes, merely reflect them. And as mirrors do, he'll add, they generally show things the wrong way round.

But the Press has this power, he insists, to make wee things happen, mysterious things. A useless power, like spoon bending and crop circles, which cannot be explained and exists solely to be marvelled at. You're reading a story, an unfamiliar place name catches your eye. A matter of days later, you look out of a train window and there's that very name on a station platform. You pick up a woman's magazine at the dentist's, glance at the perfume ads. Next thing, your wife is dropping hints about Christmas, and fuck me, Jack says, you can read her bloody mind. There are dark forces at work here. Something magnetic, Satanic, is pushing up from the earth and into the newsroom.

Reluctant as I am to subscribe to Jack's beliefs, I will admit to recalling this pronouncement of his when, only days after the visit to Sheena's, I opened the local rag and there, in a photograph, was the man I'd seen that afternoon. BURGH MAN ON COURSE FOR SUCCESS IN OZ. He wore a wooden smile, as people generally do for newspapers; his arm was round the waist of a remarkably attractive young woman. I stared curiously at her face for quite some time, trying to comprehend why the hell he needed Sheena, and decided I didn't much like her, perhaps this was the answer. Her beauty grew jaded the longer I stared, until all I seemed to see was a toothy grimace for the camera, a look in the eyes that would freeze all passion.

His name was Charles, the rapacious young woman was his wife Katriona. He was forty-nine years old, and she twenty-seven, they had twin daughters aged six. He was a civil engineer. He stayed in Stirling now, and practised in Glasgow, but he'd spent his childhood in Helensburgh, which made him, in the eyes of the *Advertiser*, forever local property. He was said to be thrilled at the prospect of managing the company's office in Sydney, although leaving Scotland filled him with sorrow. A wrench to go, he was reported as saying.

My immediate response on scanning the article was to crow to the rooftops. I poured a scotch, offered a toast to Flora. Got her to myself now, I whooped. Yawning gap in her life. Opposition disposed of.

In the heat of the moment, I must have forgotten another of Jack's pearls of wisdom. Nobody actually *reads* papers, he says. 'Not the papers I write for. Might as well print just the bingo and photies, leave the rest fucking blank.'

To which I will add a pearl of my own. People read what they want to read.

What it revealed under the photograph, what I omitted to notice in my initial euphoria, was Charles's surname. And buried amid the details on his background and family, which my brain couldn't have registered at the time, came the news that Sheena Campbell, the well-known historian who stayed in the town, was twin sister to Mr Charles Campbell, forty-nine, for whom parting would be 'a wrench and a sorrow'.

My waning of interest dates from this time. I had always assumed there was no conceivable act between a man and a woman to which I could possibly take exception. I made the implicit assumption that the more adventurous the act, short of whips and bondage and acrobatics, the more rewarding it would be. I thought no less of Sheena for what I'd seen, and for several weeks following I would close my eyes, think of her nakedness and feel a quickening of desire, if anything even greater than before. But it was a desire solely of the mind, my body took flight. I didn't care to brood on why; I suppose I had no wish to discover, built into me somewhere, a set of rules I disapproved of, a system of taboos I was powerless to break.

I quickly forgot her. Total amnesia. I could pass the entrance to her lodge and not glance inside. Out in the car, I'd draw alongside Metros and barely turn my head.

Forgot her, that is, until the morning when, at my

apartment, Gordon threw himself on my mercy. Quite suddenly I found myself pondering afresh how to seduce Sheena, how to unfasten those top two or three buttons on her blouse, because even Gordon, bless him, if he could progress this far, could lie back and let nature take over.

Nothing she likes more, I thought, than fucking a brother.

Twenty-seven

More roughly than intended, I shook Phyllis awake in my bed, told her I didn't wish to seem inhospitable, but life goes on, doesn't it always. Grief is a luxury, I said with undue harshness, the world doesn't stand still for the likes of us. She had a pack of dogs to feed, and chickens, and probably half the lifestock in Strathclyde to water, groom, put away into mangers. Didn't she have a goat or something that would burst unless it was milked? She arose like a sleepwalker without demurral. Hardly a stitch on her but she seemed not to notice and neither, especially, did I.

I bundled her into my Volvo. The Land Rover in which she'd arrived was parked outside the house; we'd worry later, I said, about getting it back to her, and I made her hand over the keys. Cresting Blackhill on the road to Luss, where town becomes country in the twinkling of an eye, I looked everywhere: into the shadowy concealment of trees, behind the rambling walls enclosing the reservoirs, at the car park, eerily vacant, beside the frosty sheen of the skating pond. No police cars lying in wait, and why should there be? Turnbull had lied about not celebrating just yet, or his men would be ignoring his strictures. Party night, I thought, in the bars of Dumbarton. They had the Hoolet at last, confined to cells under lock and key.

At Keeper's Cottage, I steered Phyllis towards the stairs, then saw no more of her. Her rubber gloves, from under the sink in the scullery, were a size too tight, but they'd have to do; I stuffed them in a pocket. I borrowed a sturdy torch. Out of the jumble of a back room, I helped myself to an old pair of Gordon's waterproof trousers, some clomping green wellingtons, and a hurricane jacket which, though it didn't remotely match the pants, was in a deep shade of blue, the colour of night.

Staying the safe side of the yard fence, I strained my vision in the darkness for sight of Gordon's dogs. Maybe the lateness of the hour subdued them unusually; they stared back sullenly, silently, with every brand of wickedness. I wondered which of them he'd used for the semen – the lurcher, the setter, the wolfhound? – how readily the brute had complied. Was it the same as milking a goat? Damnation, did country people actually *like* doing this kind of thing?

One of them sensed the loathing I felt. From somewhere in the yard, a low and threatening rumble began at the back of a throat. One by one, the dogs took to growling, to spasmodic yelping, and quickly every one of them was barking, baying for blood, straining on the chains that tied them to kennels and posts.

If my eyes had been sharper, perhaps I'd have seen which dog broke the silence. That, I was sure, would be the one. Maybe it barked from a sense of shame, or, out of some perverted loyalty to Gordon, to guard his reputation. No matter . . . the hairs rose on my neck and I practically ran to the car.

I could hear the dogs, like hounds from hell, all the way to Loch Lomond.

He was my brother. I kept repeating that fact, as if, through repetition, I would be spared any challenge to belief, as if, like a child reciting a ten-times table, saying the same thing to distraction would create unassailable truth.

I was his elder brother. I said that, too, over and over until its novelty faded. Then I believed totally that I was indeed the elder of the two, and felt weighed down by the burden of responsibility. Suddenly I could see why Gordon had taken so eagerly to the role when I'd failed to seize it. I began to grasp why men had sons, why mothers suckled children, why grandfathers bounced babies on knees. There was a profound sense of power quite unlike any other, a warm glow inside not of mere belonging to family but of being its source.

I was aware, as never before, of the ties of blood. And I felt none of the irony in that discovery which perhaps I should. It wasn't family blood he'd spilled.

I had no pumpkins in the house to practise swings with the hammer. Besides, night was moving on, and I had little time for such niceties. In retrospect, there was less urgency than I thought – the Hoolet could strike again whenever he wanted; provided Gordon was in police custody, his innocence would be proven. But I had 9.00 the next morning firmly fixed in mind – some sixth sense told me the Hoolet must be on the loose before charges were ever laid at Dumbarton Sheriff Court. There would be a public outcry, an unjustly accused man would be instantly freed. Who else but the Hoolet could possibly know about the hammer and semen? Try, Detective Chief Inspector Turnbull, explaining that one away.

So I made do with grasping the hammer, still in the plastic, getting the feel of it, and striking just a few heavy sweeps through the air. I'd read a masterly guide, the Hoolet's own words: the idea was to not to kill at first blow, merely to render unconscious. The hammer felt lethal and had a life of its own.

Far too timid in the beginning, a blow hardly sufficient to stun. I over-compensated then, could imagine the mess, blood everywhere. Then a more controlled blow which felt to be perfect. I repeated the action, beginning with a slight backswing and curving the hammer in an accelerating arc aimed just behind the ear, a point in space roughly five feet and a few inches above the ground. Next, I held the hammer outstretched in front of me at this same height, touched it to a wall and noted my distance from the skirting board. This was as far, almost precisely three feet, as I must be standing from her.

Then I attached the leash to Flora's collar, dragged her, protesting, down the stairs, and left the house. After midnight by now; I noted the moonless void of the sky, and when I took a breath, the freezing air seemed to strike ice in my soul. I felt as Gordon must have felt as he'd stalked these streets, a manifestation of darkness. My mind grew black as the night and I prayed not to God but the devil. Let me find him, oh great and evil one. Let me, I beg you, find Archie.

I have never since offered such prayers again. But I noticed, how couldn't I notice, that my conventional prayers are never heard, while this one was answered. Perhaps the blacker the deed, the greater the forces which rise up to see it done. Whatever. I had to make two tortured circuits of the neighbourhood – on the brink of losing my mind – before, from out of a garden somewhere, from the foragings of a dustbin, from out of some fetid hole or deep dank cellar, or maybe even from the very lair of Satan, Archie came suddenly trotting along behind us. I turned immediately for home, looked back at him and clicked my tongue in encouragement. He became suspiciously hesitant. When I stopped in my tracks, so then did he. Possibly he scented a trap. A dog of higher morals than you'd expect from his roguish existence, perhaps he thought the offer too good to be trusted, he caught a whiff of prostitution. Walking on, not daring to glance behind, I pleaded with Flora to do her utmost. Her soulful great eyes met mine as she sought to understand. A bounce entered her step, she hoisted her tail high. And Archie's resistance crumbled. I was acutely aware at that moment as we trooped in line, his nose only inches from the root of Flora's tail, of a kind of compassion for his coming loss of innocence. And of unspeakable dread over mine.

Change crept over me. With each action I made, some part of me was shed, and something alien and dominant seemed to take hold. I donned the rubber gloves, the trousers and jacket. I tugged the wellingtons over thick socks. With a feeling of no longer being myself, I sat at the wheel of Gordon's Land Rover. The hammer in its wrap of plastic was in a jacket pocket. Safe in another pocket, in a plastic sachet I'd emptied of rice, was Archie's generous donation of semen. And I *became* the Hoolet. A lucid breed of madness took over, pitiless and sharp as a full winter moon, so remarkably clear in its single-mindedness, nothing on earth would have stopped me.

I drove away from the house in the grim knowledge that if the police flagged me down, made me empty my pockets, a glance would tell them who I was. And I have a suspicion – which I've never dared voice until now – that I'd have used the hammer to save myself.

I parked the Land Rover in the street adjoining Sheena's, just a short corner away from the entrance to her lodge, and covered the remaining distance on foot. I was watchful, the boots made scarcely a sound treading the compliant grass of the verge. Few windows faced the road, all at a goodly distance over high garden walls. Had anyone peered out, they might have glimpsed a ripple of shadow, a rustle of wind down a dimly lit street.

My plan, if you can call it that, was to catch Sheena asleep. She had no phone upstairs to summon help, none I remembered seeing. I'd enter the house, make a sound to lure her down. Not the noise of an intruder – maybe a tap left running in the kitchen – and I'd be lying in ambush behind a door.

But there was a light burning at one of the upper windows. Not her bedroom, that was across the landing; this must be the bathroom. Out of sight of the road, screened by a wall, I waited a couple of minutes, and the light was still on. No problem, I thought, she must be taking a bath, so I proceeded ahead, quiet as I could be in crossing the gravel.

The window was at the side of the house, and the light shone down, making a pool of illumination at the entrance to her courtyard. I had to pass through the light, be plainly visible for a moment, and I made the error of glancing up. A pane of clear glass above frosted glazing; the lamp hung in view from the ceiling. Then, when I continued forward, it was as if I'd stepped into a black hole in space. I tripped over something, went headlong on my face in the gravel. A rake, I think. That bloody gardener!

Heart thumping, I pressed flat against the wall. A drainpipe ran down quite close to my ear, I could hear water inside, gushing away from the bath. Probably the shower was running, and perhaps, with its noise in the room, Sheena hadn't heard me. I waited for a while and no lights came flooding on at other windows, the coach lamps stayed off at the door. Then the courtyard went dark; she must have left the bathroom. Had she retired to bed? Were the house lights all off now or was the lamp switched on beside her bed? Impossible to tell from where I stood . . . I'd chance it, I thought, let myself in. If she heard the door, what difference would it make: I wanted to lure her downstairs. So I claimed the doorkey from under the pot, slipped it into the lock. A final drill before opening the door. I groped inside the jacket, making sure I'd remembered the torch. Then I followed the Hoolet's instructions. Check the hammer in one pocket, the bag of semen in the other. Move my lips to silent words. One, do this. Two, do that.

I turned the key.

Twenty-eight

I waken slowly as if from a dream. Cautiously, I open my eyes. To see nothing. For a terrible instant, I think I've gone blind.

Where am I? In Sheena's living room? On the sofa? Yes, I must be: there are soft cushions at my back, the buoyance of feathers, the touch of silk. The room is in total darkness, mercifully so because my mind begins to clear and suddenly, out of the dream, I remember what horror lies there at my feet. And I am becoming aware now of that smell in the room of blood and mayhem and death. I close my eyes, screwing them tight, as if shuttered behind the lids, retreating to their own darkness, there is some faint promise of . . . of what? A reversal of time? Flight to the recent past? Do I really, stupidly, believe that by the simple act of not seeing, I can obliterate what has happened? Undo what is done? Make none of this true?

But I can't close my nose, find any escape from that smell which insinuates its way into my nostrils, filling my head and swirling like the stink of some medieval battlefield into every cringing recess and cranny of my brain. The smell of fresh blood all around me, sickly and sweet, like that stench I remember, tainting the air, when the vixen made a meal of Gordon's pheasants. Sightless in the inky vastness of the room, I see nothing but red before my eyes. As if, inside my skull, every thought I have is swimming in blood.

Whole minutes pass before I dare to light the torch. Then I can bear only to point the beam at the ceiling. Tremulously, I move my free hand into the light. Smears of blood on the rubber glove! Quickly, my thumb scrabbles at the switch, I flee back to blindness. But the light's still there, tormenting my eyes! I become frantic, rocking my head like a mad thing, trying to be rid of the haunting vision . . . anywhere I look, everywhere, the hand comes floating in front of my face. All too slowly it fades into nothingness, ghostly red fingers, the colour of blood.

I sit in the dark, afraid to move. My lips make twisted shapes, forming words. I try desperately to speak the words aloud but no sound emerges. Now I am blind and dumb. My madness persists, the conviction grows that if the blindness won't bring her back to life, I have only to shake off this ludicrous dumbness and all will be well. If I can only speak . . .

'*I never intended to kill you!*'

I shall say this with every ounce of sincerity I possess. As if, through saying it, breath will return to her battered body. And I remind myself . . . all I intended was a single blow, not too hard, only to stun her, a minor concussion. Then drop the hammer, the bag of semen, and run like the fucking wind.

'That would have satisfied the police, Sheena, can't you see? Positive proof the Hoolet's still roaming the streets. Only the lightest of blows, Sheena, I promise.'

For Christsake, I think, what's a bloody headache between friends! Afterwards, anonymously, I'd have sent her flowers, chocolates, showers of gifts. And Gordon would be free.

But my mouth has the parched muteness of terror, and if any tiny sound escapes my struggling lips it is at best only a faint gasping in the room, like a wretched last sigh of dying.

I sit in the dark for minutes longer until sanity returns. A sanity whose sudden clear perception of the truth is more terrible than any maunderings of madness. I scream inwardly as I have never screamed, my mouth thrown wide, my fists pounding the sides of my head.

Murder! Horror! Blood!

I regain control of my thoughts then. As if the Hoolet inside me has been driven from my brain. The scream has exorcised him.

I have the courage now to switch on the torch, to point its beam ahead, down at the carpet.

Sheena lies sprawled only feet away from me. She wears a dressing gown of black and lustrous satin. It gapes apart, the sleeves are ripped. Under the gown, she has the tattered remnants of a negligee, black and diaphanous. It is low-cut over her breasts, with lacy cleavage, and is cutting into her ample flesh. A nipple protrudes. She has one arm outflung at a twisted angle, the other, its fingers clenched, tries pathetically to cover the bareness of her breast. The negligee has been pulled up over the waist, exposing her lower body. She is not lying as she fell . . . her legs, outstretched on the floor, have been positioned apart, an obscene invitation to entry. Her stomach looks old, the skin pale and ghastly. A glister of oozy fluid runs over it from her navel, down between her gaping legs to form a pool of slime on the carpet. I move the torch a little, hoping the shapeless blob above her shoulders is only a shadow. How many blows? Six or seven or mindless more? Perhaps I can bear to look because no eyes are staring back at me from anything resembling a face.

I send the torch beam searching. Blood spattered everywhere. Blood on the ceiling and drips down the walls. No surface of the room has been spared: in the farthest corner, the light picks out a pattern, flecks and splashes and droplets, like a swarm of insects on the tasteful cream paper.

I find the strength to get to my feet. Carefully, I give wide berth to the body on my way to the door. The torch beam goes ahead of me across the floor; I sidestep any traces of blood. I shine the light up the stairs.

His footprints are red against the pale beige of the carpet. He was wearing the moccasins, I assume, a large size of foot. I follow the prints up and the trail grows fainter on reaching the landing. He tried her bedroom

376

first, just as I did, before locating the bathroom.

The shower is a recent addition, an attachment over a conventional bath. Blood on the floor tiles and a smudge on the rim of the tub where he'd rested a hand. Doing what? Removing the moccasins? And was that the moment he'd heard me outside? He is ready, it seems, for anything. One, do this. Two, do that. Three, place a rake in the dark by the door.

I return downstairs where I pick up his trail again, proceeding into the kitchen, very faint traces of blood now. I have become sufficiently clear-headed to block out, quite consciously, all emotions. No time for anger, no room yet for pity. I have become a hunter. I know every second I remain in the house increases my danger. But there might be greater danger in rushing away. I steady my step, keep an iron grip on my nerves.

A pane has been broken in the back door, splinters of glass are strewn on the floor. This is where he entered, reaching in to turn the key in the lock, and if she heard a sound in her sleep, so much the better; he'd planned, just as I had, to lure her down.

The back door stands open. This was where he left in a hurry, perhaps at the very minute I was coming in at the front. Some drips of blood on the floor, and a print of red on the wall where his hand must have pressed for a moment, taking his weight. For what reason? A change of shoes? Ah . . . he'd been naked, of course, wearing only the moccasins. He'd intended to shower, wash his body clean of blood. And I'd interrupted him. If the shower had been used, that smudge on the bath would, surely, have been sluiced away. So he'd dressed again in the lobby here. In a blind panic, I should think. With her blood still on him.

I don't quite know why I return to the living room. Something tells me I must, even though by now every instinct is screaming to take to my heels . . . every instinct but one. Some third eye has spotted what I, in my state of shock, have failed to notice. Some inner sense is guiding me. Might as well say it, I have a guardian angel suddenly, even here in what must be the nearest you can find to hell this side of Judgement.

I shine my torch on her tightly clasped hand. She is gripping a scrap of newspaper. I prise her fingers apart and the words on the bloodstained cutting are so unexpected, yet at the same moment so familiar, that the beam of light starts to tremble and shake as I read.

> . . . *I offer no apology. This is nature, raw and simple. The Hoolet kills to survive. He kills without malice. His victims are chosen for no other reason than that they are there as he passes. His aim is the quick clean kill, and a good many of his prey die the death I would wish for myself* . . .

My words, of course; I could probably remember the date this column appeared if I put my mind to it. I don't trust myself with the cutting – what if I lose it? – so I eat it. I try to swallow but it sticks in my throat. I chew, grinding my teeth. Then I swallow several more times, scour the back of a hand across my lips, but the taste is persistent. Imagination runs riot. Just the taste of paper, I say. That's all, the taste of fucking paper.

I am on the point of leaving when a train passes somewhere outside. I am crossing the back threshold, following in his tracks, when the throb of a diesel fills the air, then the blare of a railway klaxon. Madness briefly returns, suddenly Aileen seems to flash before my eyes, I am afflicted with a pang of longing for her, suffer the renewed sadness of loss. I feel the poignant regret the sound of a distant train tends to induce in me these days, and I chide myself that we never took the trip we planned on the sleeper to Mallaig. I banish the thought as quickly as it came – its perversity appalls me – and I grow fearful again at my tenuous hold on sanity. Aileen, for fuck's sake, and railway journeys, romantic delusions at a time like this! I am half in, half out of the house, when I freeze into immobility. The West Highland Line . . . how far from here? Maybe only a street block away.

The scales fall suddenly from my eyes. I have been blind and can see. I can see *everything*. The Hoolet, the murders, why he killed. I curse my stupidity, loudly, with venom. If experience is enriching, I must be a millionaire from the regularity with which I curse like this. I'm in a class of my own, hugely gifted, a bloody genius at missing the obvious. I'll tell you candidly that in the entire history of mankind there has been no discovery, no invention ever, I could not have made . . . television, splitting the atom, the digital computer, Tutankhamen's tomb, you name it . . . if only I'd fucking *looked*!

I forget to pull the choke on the Land Rover. The starter motor whines and shrieks in the still night air. When the engine finally turns, as I judder away along the street, I remember that Sheena's key is still in my pocket.

I tell myself this is part of the plan.

Twenty-nine

Resist the mountain views at Blackhill. Travelling the road to Luss, look not at the prospect over the reservoirs to Glen Fruin, but to the other side, and you might catch sight in passing, only a glimpse since it's thoughtfully sited, of the municipal refuse dump. There are no gates, this is one of the few places in Helensburgh that never closes – people from the town choose the most unlikely hours to dump their household jumble, and, at dead of night, a forgotten tribe turns up in nomadic trucks, decrepit vans, people from other and less privileged parts, coming to spirit away rejected fridges and rusty prams, offering a roof to disgusting old mattresses someone else didn't want under theirs.

As I turned the Land Rover in at the entrance, its headlamps swept over a semi-circle of steel skips, overflowing with the garbage the burgh throws out in a day. A ramshackle estate car was parked to one side, and I could see the probing gleam of a torch dipping into a skip. I stopped in the opposite corner of the compound, turned off the engine and lights. Out of view behind the vehicle, I removed the boots, the trousers, the jacket. When I'd disposed of these, dislodging a rotting carpet to cover them, I peeled off the rubber gloves, and shoved them beyond sight or salvage under a mangy pile of books.

The torch meanwhile continued its probing. If whoever he was over there had stopped to look my way, had any curiosity about me, I'd have noticed, the motion of the beam would have flashed a warning. But they see no-one, people like that. Their only concern, I suppose, is not being seen themselves.

The hosepipe came with the flat. There's an outside tap and a coil of rubber tubing so ravaged by age that water sprays madly out of pin-holes along its length. Been there, I should think, since before the house was divided up, the days of chauffeurs and stately radiators, gleaming carriagework that, rain or shine, was washed and polished every day. I've never had much use for a hose: the thick coating of muck is about all that holds the old Volvo together. One winter I forgot to turn off at the mains and when the frosts came I had a glacier down the wall so stupendous its significance passed me by; then the thaw finally set in and the plumber's bill was every bit as spectacular. So I turned it off and left it off. Which meant, when I got back from the refuse dump in the early hours of the morning, some fevered searching of memory before I could locate the stopcock.

I gave the Land Rover a quick hosing down. Then I opened the doors and drenched the inside: the rubber floor mats, the seats, the lot. I played a jet of water on to the driver's seat until the pond on the floor flooded over the door sills. I scrubbed the seat fabric with a brush, then doused it some more. I scrubbed the steering wheel, the door handles, anything I'd touched with the gloves. When I locked up, I left a couple of windows not quite shut; drying would be quicker that way, and when the police came by, as they surely must, I could say I'd been washing the vehicle for Phyllis. Black as midnight out here, Sergeant, didn't bloody notice the windows ajar.

Time to reverse the habits of a lifetime: I sank into a bath filled with a great deal more water than I usually bother with, a miserly splash of scotch in my tumbler . . . the bath as steamily hot as a sauna, sweat pouring off me in buckets, the ancient Ascot spluttering to itself just above my head and ready to blow at any minute. Afterwards, heeding the Hoolet's advice, I left the tap running in the empty tub. Then I dressed in fresh clothes, satisfied myself the binoculars were in the glove compartment, and drove off in the Volvo.

Immediately before leaving the house, however, I made a spontaneous phone call. I'd been thinking in the bath, and under a sudden onrush of doubts, my certainty deserted me. Quite abruptly, my limbs began to tremble, my head to go fuzzy with the heat, and I couldn't tell fact from fiction, deduction from guesswork. I had heard the train and made an instant assumption – now I remembered Gordon's fingerprints and felt utterly lost. Then, a new and entirely crazy idea hit me, the wildest of conjectures from whatever part of the brain sees the world as upside down. I tried to imagine what the Hoolet was doing right that minute, what he'd be thinking. Was he in a bath or a burn somewhere? Hot water or a freezing stream? And I did a mental about-turn, and wondered why we all did that – public, police and Press – thought always in terms of *he*. And why the dog semen? Why, especially, dogs?

Sort of necessary, said my brain with its lunatic logic, if the Hoolet wants semen, and has none of her own.

Ridiculous, of course. But I'd lost my earlier confidence in who he was, had not a thought in my head where to find him.

I must have dialled the number without prior thought. So it was fortunate really I got no reply. God knows what hour of the morning by then, and I wouldn't have had a word to say.

Utter madness to return to Sheena's. Or was it? If her body had been found, I'd have seen the police a mile off. And the street lay empty.

Her car keys were where I hoped to find them, on a hall table beside the front door. I unlocked her garage and reversed the little Metro to where it would be seen from the road. I left the garage door agape, the light blazing inside. I left the keys in the Metro and both doors wide open; the courtesy light stayed on. I returned briskly to the house to switch on the hall lights, every lamp in the living room.

I left the front door fully open behind me, light streaming out.

Thirty

There was a cruel wind blowing. I crouched in the shelter of a hillside overlooking the town and the cold struck suddenly at the pit of my stomach. A feeling of déjà vu swept over me like nausea. I had been here before, waited before. I seemed carried back in time, doomed to an existence of waiting. I heard the heavy tread of impending failure, a funeral procession of hopes.

How much longer?

Last time I was here, Gordon had been standing by my side. As day drew to a close, as my optimism sank with the setting sun, he'd offered the reassurance of clichés. Patience is a virtue. Everything comes to those who wait. Hoolets, believe me, are creatures of habit. Like bad pennies . . . they always come back.

Not a hope. A fool's errand.

Aiming the binoculars at the foot of the slope, I strained my eyes. In the poor light, I could discern the merest outline of houses, vague dark shapes coalescing with shadows. And I remembered the owl. The hoolet that never came. The hoolet that never was. I recalled Gordon's rugged composure as he'd drained the last drop from the bottle. We had waited further. We had attended in hopeful silence as the colour ebbed from the sky and, eventually, as twilight enclosed us, he'd shrugged his lean shoulders as if to say there'd be other days and other hoolets. Country ways, Sandy, patience of a hunter. Maybe I do him an injustice, but I'd convinced myself that his smile, which he'd tried to disguise as pleasure at the panorama spread before us, was occasioned by the non-arrival of the bird. Now I'd be forced to rely on his description of the hoolet, the daily routine of its hunt over moorland. Whatever I wrote, he'd be the author. I was his fucking ghost writer, that's why he smiled.

He's inside already . . .

I could spy no lights at any of the windows. So I slipped the binocular strap from my neck, put the glasses down beside me in the bracken, clasped my hands round my knees, and made a huddle against the cold. The town was asleep. No light could come on, nor any car drive by, without my seeing it.

His speed along the road was the sober side of legal. A little faster and he might have been stopped, any slower would have attracted attention. I saw the headlights as he made a turning from the Esplanade, they cut a flickering path between scattered houses and trees. For a while he travelled the open spaces past the Rugby Club, then the beams skewed in at his gate. All became black once more until a light showed for just a few brief minutes at one of the windows. I didn't need the glasses to see all this, but I trained them on the window – compulsion drove me to trace a path away from the ranch house and over the field behind it. Past a straight run of hedgerow, a railway signal was set at red. I'd flattered myself I was in full command of my senses by now. But the rails glowed dully in the light of the signal, and I stared in a trance, imagining them to be his tracks. A long hot bath and still he was leaving a trail of blood.

He'd been travelling from the direction of Rhu. That was how, at last, I knew where he'd been. For the life of me, I couldn't comprehend why I hadn't seen it sooner. And why hadn't the police? There might possibly be some primitive lifeform, as yet undiscovered, with less brains than me, Turnbull and Grant combined. But I doubt it.

I left the Volvo where I'd parked and set out on foot, the binoculars bouncing against my chest. I was trudging back towards town, down the middle of the road, when a police patrol car stopped to pick me up. They were moving at a fair lick as they skidded past and, tyres screaming, into a U-turn. Why they appeared so surprised, I cannot imagine. They were obviously looking for me.

Grant was a collection of moods to suit the occasion. He sat in solitary foreboding behind the metal table of the interview room. He was prosecuting counsel and judge, jury and prison guard. He was executioner and mortician. And, when he'd seen me hanged, spat on my body in the mortuary and drawn my entrails, he'd shovel the quicklime with gusto in a miserable corner of the prison yard. He was the condemned man . . . as I mounted the scaffold, he'd permit himself the final request of a smile, then never smile again for the rest of his days. He was so awestruck by his prowess as a policeman, his eyes almost popped from their sockets. His failures and oversights, his prevarications and ineptitude, committed all manner of ugliness to his mouth – some force outside him dragged the corners down, tore back the lips to bare his teeth. Four women dead, and he'd caused the deaths of three of them, as surely as I had.

He attempted to say something as I was led into the room, but his mouth could only mime angry words. His clenched fist seemed to shake at me before gesticulating to an empty chair. I sat facing him. He stared for an eternity, burying me in the quicklime. He exhumed the remains, hacked off my limbs and threw the pieces to vultures.

'The Chief is otherwise engaged,' he said finally. 'Urgent business of an ugly nature, he'll be along in due course. Wants everything ready by then . . . except the signature. Particularly anxious, he is, to witness you signing.'

Grant moved a hand to activate the tape machine.

'Before you do that . . .' I said.

He glowered, wondering why they'd abolished burning at the stake.

'Makes no difference to me,' I continued, 'whether the

386

tape's running or not. Might do you some good, though, if it looks like you solved this one all by yourself.'

He bunched a fist and came close to punching me. He began rising from his chair, but decided that a pleasure postponed was a pleasure gained.

'I spent the night in Highlandman's Wood,' I said. 'Out looking for hoolets. Of the avian kind, I mean.'

'Fuck you!' he snarled, and reached as before for the recorder switch.

'I must have wandered off course, easy to do in the dark. Saw the strangest thing through my binoculars . . . someone going into one of Duncan MacRae's houses. Know the houses I mean, that new estate the other side of Rhu? Homes for thrusting executives, Sergeant. Double garage, jacuzzi and expensive views of the Clyde.'

At some point as I was saying this, his hand withdrew from the switch: I think at the mention of Duncan's name.

'Now, why would someone do that?' I said, looking suitably puzzled. 'An empty house at dead of night.'

Elbows on the table, he clasped his hands together, propped his chin on them and regarded me with every conceivable shade of suspicion. But his brain was racing. He was thinking the same thoughts I'd had when I saw the direction the car came from. Think of empty houses and the possibilities are endless. A resourceful executive can work wonders with an empty house.

'I don't mean the show house,' I said, and perhaps overdid the frowns of confusion. 'One of the houses they're still working on. A damned funny time for a tour of inspection . . . think there's a kettle inside for the builders? Maybe he was dying for a cup of tea.'

'This house got a bathroom?' Grant said suddenly.

'Why bother, middle of the night? Plenty of trees to piss on . . .'

He was on his feet now. '*Is there a fucking bathroom!*'

'No idea, Sergeant.'

Lost in thought, he dawdled to a corner. After a long period of mulling, he banged his head rather hard against the wall. He repeated the penance several times before turning.

'See who it was?' he said. 'This someone?'

'Just a figure,' I answered. 'A man's figure. Sorry, but it was bloody dark.'

'Car!' he yelled. 'What kind of car? Did you see the fucking car!'

I must confess to making a meal of my answer. I furrowed my brow and wrung my hands. I got to my feet and paced the room, half expecting that the constable who guarded the door, who was staring with an expression of open-mouthed incredulity, would strong-arm me back to the chair. But neither he nor Grant moved a muscle. I smote my forehead until the cogs unjammed and my brain started slowly to turn. I snapped my fingers.

'He arrived in one car,' I said. 'But left in another. He went off in a big BMW, the kind Duncan drives.'

'His car, you mean? Bloody think! Was it Duncan MacRae's car?'

'I couldn't swear to it. A darkish colour, like his, and probably the same model, that's all I can say.'

Grant departed in haste, only pausing at the door to contemplate me briefly with a look I was unable to fathom. No question there was excitement in his eyes, and a gleam of hungry expectation . . . but was he hoping I was right, or intent on proving me wrong?

'Get him some tea,' he instructed the constable.

'I'd prefer coffee,' I said.

'You're in custody,' Grant snarled, 'not some fucking coffee shop!'

And I wasn't sure, either, whether this eruption of anger was real or feigned. Because the plastic cup I was served promptly afterwards certainly seemed to contain coffee. At least I think so . . . it might have been cocoa. The machine put extra sugar in everything, so the constable said with no pretence at apology. I was about to say this must be policy, they could do with some sweetening up around here, when I saw from his face he'd heard that one before. Nothing I could say he hadn't heard said. Bloody criminals, he thought, rolling his eyes at the ceiling. All think you're so fucking clever. So how come we nabbed you?

The waiting played havoc with my confidence. It had sounded a good story as I told it, but as one hour stretched into two, as I ceased to keep count of time, I began to believe myself a fool. Why hadn't I been content with the truth, said I'd spotted Duncan making a late return to his house? Coming from the direction of Rhu, I could have said, and relied on Grant to infer the rest.

What, Grant? Call himself a detective! He'd had weeks to consider possibilities . . . Not once, bet you, had he given a moment's thought to those empty houses. Very well, then, drop him a hint . . . Why hadn't I made some conversational remark on the houses? I could have suggested that Duncan had been visiting his new development. Just an idea, Sergeant, me playing amateur sleuth. And why had I lied about the car? Why hadn't I simply *guessed* there must be another car?

'He's got a yacht, Don, because you and I haven't. Every house in his street has two cars in the drive. So he'll have three. This is Duncan, remember, anything you can do he can do better.'

Oh, yes? And Grant would have gazed with aggrieved eyes from across the table, profoundly grateful for penal reform. The electric chair, yes, or the gas chamber, garrotting, or the guillotine. Hanging, though, was too good for me.

So MacRae was out late – this is what he'd have said – might have been at dinner with friends. What's your reason, Mr Douglas, do tell, for assuming he called at an empty house? Now me, seeing a man come home at three in the morning . . . very last thing I'd think of, that he'd been taking a bath. Anything particular happen lately to make you think of baths?

It was a good story. An inspired story. Had I been alone

at that moment in the open air, back on the hillside, I'd have staked my life on it. But there's something about police interview rooms . . . I think, as you wait, as the hours drag by, they wind the grey walls slowly in on you. They put drugs in the coffee . . . hallucinogens and pentathol. They play tricks with the lighting to induce depression. Hidden microphones pick up the erratic thumpings of your heart, amplifiers boom it back. The constable is from counter-intelligence, highly trained in psychological warfare, licensed to kill by stony silence. After the passage of hours, I could see clearly why innocent men confess to murder, anything to get out. It was a pathetic story. I didn't believe it myself.

When Grant came back to the room, he sat behind the table, folded his hands together in front of him and regarded me with detached curiosity. I was a specimen of insect he'd never seen before. Worth collecting or to be stamped underfoot?

He had the habit, common to big men, of weighty pauses, gravity oozed from his pores. So he stared until my nerves were at breaking point. Then he continued staring a good deal longer.

'The water was warm,' he said. 'In the tank at the house.'

I made a strangulated gasp.

'Any ideas why?' he said.

'Maybe he needed a bath.'

'Why? Why'd you think?'

'Maybe his heating's on the blink. At home, I mean.'

'I've been clocking up your Brownie points, Mr Douglas. I can just as fucking soon take them away!'

I showed him a chastened face and asked meekly what else he'd found.

'There's plastic sheeting over the floor. You come in at the door, toddle up the stairs, into the bathroom . . . you're on a sheet of polythene all the way, tacked to the boards. Now, the workmen might have done that to protect the flooring, no reason why not, but it's been washed very recently, last few hours, I'd say . . . stairs are soaking . . . and I don't, somehow, see workmen creeping in after midnight to play charladies.'

'Any luck with the car?' I said.

'In the garage. High mileage Volvo, company registered.'

'Anything like mine?'

'There's some might think so.'

'Duncan's company?'

Grant nodded. 'For running odd jobs, site to site, that's what he tells us.'

'The day Aileen was murdered . . .' I began, and seeing what was coming, he closed his eyes in a sigh of tribulation. 'Don't suppose,' I continued, 'you thought to check all the plates in the marina car park?'

'Wasn't the scene of the crime,' he said sorrowfully, and clapped a hand to his chest. Mea culpa.

'Any chance he could have parked it at the marina?' I proposed. 'Say, earlier that morning? He swam ashore from the yacht, drove home in the Volvo, used it to drive back. You examined the BMW, found the inside was dry and assumed he couldn't have swum.'

He looked utterly miserable.

'He's a good swimmer,' I pointed out. 'Never misses the New Year's Day dip at Rhu. I guess he doesn't feel the cold.'

'Bloody masochist, more like.'

'He left the door open on Aileen's car so the murder would be discovered quickly. Am I right?'

'Possibly . . .'

'He'd showered at home by then, it would take only a few minutes to drive back to the marina. The idea was, you'd get the call from an anxious neighbour and find him marooned on the yacht. Better you saw him with your own eyes than hearing from witnesses. Nothing beats a police alibi.'

'Possibly . . .' he said again. Head cocked to one side, he examined me thoughtfully.

'And if anyone had spotted the Volvo near the house, you'd assume it was mine. Was that part of his plan?'

Grant made only a grunt in reply. He narrowed his eyes, worried I was seeing into his thoughts.

'Like to hear my other theories?'

'Got more, have you?'

'Custody's good for the brain,' I said. 'Plenty of time to ruminate.'

He raised both hands, suggestions welcome.

'You were watching his house, an unmarked van out front . . .'

'Not watching,' he said, and his broody shake of the head was at his own short-sightedness. 'Trying to psyche him, play on his nerves.'

'He slipped out the back. Over the field and along the railway line. Then by way of quiet streets to Hermitage Park.'

'Plausible,' he conceded.

'He murdered Carol Logan beside the burn . . . Do you suppose that's where he bathed to clean off the blood?'

His gaze grew distant. 'I sat in the rain,' he reminisced. 'I'd been standing in the trees, where he'd stood. And I needed a ritual soaking. Maybe I was closer than I knew to getting into his mind.'

I nodded and said: 'You told me the murders were the same, yet different. You were right. With Aileen, he was killing his wife, in his own home. He could come and go as he pleased. But the others were strangers. He needed the cover of night.'

'Should have seen that,' Grant murmured. He closed his eyes while shaking his head, and I remembered him saying once that hindsight was God's punishment to the blind. 'Should have bloody seen it,' he repeated, his eyes still buttoned tight.

'After the Logan murder, you gave up watching him . . .'

'The men were reassigned,' he said in a pitiful tone of regret.

'In your shoes, Don, I'd have done the same.'

'Someone else's orders,' he proclaimed, retrieving what dignity he could.

He was almost gone from the room, the door closing behind him, when he returned on an afterthought. He stepped back through the doorway with a kind of lumbering diffidence, as if calling on a house where he might not be welcome.

'About that car, the door left open . . . I thought the same as you, at the time. I'm not so sure now.' Dilemma etched deep lines in his forehead, he scratched hard behind an ear. 'See the thing is, Sandy, why pull the same stunt with Sheena Campbell?' Grant counted the actions up on his fingers. 'He had to drive over to Rhu, take a bath, remove every trace of blood from the plastic, hose and scrub the Volvo. Then hotfoot it home to bed. An hour at least, all that must have taken. No way I can see he wanted the body found quickly.'

'Who's Sheena Campbell?'

He made quick scrutiny of me. For just a second, his eyes clouded over with a renewal of suspicion. Perhaps my question should have been phrased some other way, perhaps I shouldn't have looked so blank and stupid. Reason got the better of him; his shoulders rose and fell as he shrugged off the doubts.

'Tell you sometime,' he said.

Another hour went by. I was brought coffee with biscuits. Custard creams, the constable said with an ingratiating smirk, the sergeant's compliments. The coffee was decent, now, in a china cup, and the sugar came separately, some sodden cubes in a puddle on the saucer. The constable apologized profusely for the accident en route. Opening bloody doors, he muttered, keys and cups, only one pair of hands. When I'd drunk the coffee he began staring, transfixed by the saucer. I didn't take sugar, I explained, not wishing to make an issue of his clumsiness. 'D'ya mind?' he enquired, hand hovering over the cubes, then slouched on his seat in front of the door, happily crunching. 'Sweet tooth,' he confided. 'An' magic in goal. S'how Ah got intae the Force.'

Constables are masters of the small and inconsequential. The date on a motor vehicle licence. The thirteen minutes you've been parked, you'd have sworn was the blinking of an eye. The double yellow this side of the road and what's the time and is it Sunday. The sound of footsteps down a corridor, one step heavy, the other a neat size eight with Italian buckles . . .

He was at attention on his feet before I heard anyone coming, and deftly opened the door on cue. Turnbull entered, with the looming presence of Grant a step behind. Neither man took a seat, they stood in rapt contemplation of me from the opposite side of the table; I inferred that out of belated embarrassment or something of the kind they were waiting for me to invite them to sit. So, of course, I did no such thing.

'We found a comb at Mrs Lockhart's house,' Turnbull said. 'Your brother's, no possible doubt about that. His fingerprints, his hair.'

I made a murmur of surprise.

'Dandruff shampoo,' Grant offered with a sniff. 'Boots own brand.'

'Any suggestion how it got there, beside the body?'

Grant's gaze stayed unblinkingly on me while I searched my memory. As realization dawned on my face, he made a remark in Turnbull's ear, claiming credit, I should think, for my gift of recall.

I explained about the day I'd come home wearing Gordon's Barbour. I'd given a public talk in the town that evening, I reminded them, posters up in the shops and a notice in the *Advertiser* – so Duncan knew I'd be away from the flat. He'd already borrowed my keys and must have made a copy. I'd believed the coat to be mine. Duncan must have thought so too when he stole the comb.

'Remember that time I called on him?' I said to Grant.

'A week to the day after Aileen's murder? You phoned the house and asked me to come over for questioning. Add the journey time to and from Dumbarton, a thorough grilling from you, and Duncan could be sure I'd be away for several hours. He must have acted on the spur of the moment. He pocketed my keys . . . when I got home, they were in the hall . . . I assumed I'd left them behind.'

Be honest, I'd assumed no such thing. I'd been so convinced Grant was the culprit, I hadn't given a thought to Duncan. I had clean forgotten him taking my coat to his bloody cloakroom. And, my God, hadn't he gone over the top in acting the solicitous host! The trouble with Duncan is, that veneer of hospitality is so obviously contrived, his superficiality so transparent, you enquire no further, his character seems skin deep. He's a businessman. He's a success. As Jack Moffat likes to say: success is a lie concealed under falsehood.

Turnbull peered at me perceptively. 'Something else . . . ?' he enquired.

I shook my head. 'Just contemplating my own stupidity.'

I gained the impression that this admission put us all on an equal footing. At any rate, Turnbull then sat down and Grant was quick to follow.

'I'm Glasgow born and bred,' Turnbull mused. 'Thought I'd seen every form of wretchedness till they posted me here. Now I've got tower blocks one end of my patch and crofts the other. Misery, Mr Douglas, and I'd be hard put to say which is worse . . . people piled up like sardines, or people so lonely they could scream.' He gestured past the walls, far beyond the town. 'We get these farmers, out in the glens, remote on the islands, going crackers with shotguns . . . happens all the time, the sickness of isolation. And there's always dogs on the loose. Show me a cottage miles from nowhere with a pack of dogs running wild, I know there's trouble brewing. Now it's none of my business, he's no danger to anyone, but that brother of yours needs looking after. Weak in the head, is he?'

'No more than I am,' I said in his defence.

'Yesterday he was guilty. I told him about the comb, and he was guilty. Why? Because I said so. He *believed* me, Mr Douglas, never seen such faith in the police. And today? I asked him just now how he managed a fourth murder from inside a police cell. I got a question in reply . . . do we have a suspect? Husband of one of the murdered women, I told him, all you need to know. You could see his little brain ticking . . . suddenly he's shouting his innocence. Always like that, was he? Impressionable? Gullible?'

'He has a certain childish innocence,' I said.

'He's been released. There'll be no charges.'

'How about me?'

Turnbull looked me in the eye. 'I'd like your agreement to remain in custody . . .'

'Until when?'

'Until I say you can go.'

'You can't do that!' I retorted.

'I know,' he said. 'That's why I'm asking.'

'Any particular reason?'

'You're a reporter, Mr Douglas. Sometime soon you'll be walking out through that door . . . and there are issues I'd rather not see in the Press just yet. Do I make myself clear?'

Maybe if people trusted me more, they'd speak their minds and I wouldn't misunderstand them. Maybe if I did likewise, they'd learn to trust me. If only life were this simple. Did he really believe I gave a damn at that moment for bloody newspapers! How I Trapped the Hoolet – Reporter's Startling Story. Savagery Of His Latest Slaying – EXCLUSIVE. Oh sure, so exclusive I'd be keeping it all to myself. A few more years of Galbraith, a ton of white tablets, and I might even be sleeping nights again.

Naturally, Turnbull misunderstood my look of shock.

'A lot to ask, I know.' He threw out his hands, and made sad eyes, distressed at having sunk so low.

I signed the form Grant produced from his pocket, a

declaration of voluntary attendance, and I scribbled a rider in the margin stating that I waived my right to leave, I'd go at DCI Turnbull's discretion. Then I initialled this, and when Turnbull read the note he seemed genuinely moved.

'You didn't have to do that,' he said.

In case I changed my mind, I told him.

He began by asking: 'Why did MacRae want the key to your flat?'

'I imagine he thought I was having an affair with Aileen. He was looking for proof.'

'*After* he'd killed her?'

'Not for himself, for you, the police. A whole week had gone by. You hadn't arrested me. And your men were watching his house, not mine.'

Turnbull nodded. 'I take it he didn't find any such proof . . .'

'There wasn't any.'

'Presumably, he had some reason for believing you'd visit his wife that afternoon . . .'

'Yes. It's called a suspicious mind.'

He stared for a few seconds, but in a friendly enough way, without imputation. Then he nodded again, taking my word.

'We found semen on the bodies,' he said.

'I heard from various sources.'

'We can check the origin of semen, Mr Douglas. Are you aware of that?'

'Then you'll find it's not mine.'

'You sound very certain . . .' Grant said.

'I have a good memory, Don, for where I deposit my semen.'

Turnbull wore the wisp of a smile as he rose to leave.

'Like I said to MacRae,' Grant declared. 'If it's not Mr Douglas's semen, Mr Douglas couldn't have left it there.' And his smile was unashamedly broad as he followed through the door.

From then on, the walls stopped slowly winding in. After

397

the third or fourth cup, the constable, who introduced himself as Andie, learned how not to slop the coffee, and it came without drugs. In a gesture of goodwill, he removed the tape recorder. The passage of time ceased to matter very much, except that I'd glance at my watch occasionally to find a whole hour had gone by, then I'd check again after a similar period and only minutes had passed . . . frankly, I didn't greatly care whether this was due to police funny business or not. I tried thinking of Duncan, only to realize that I was beginning to pity him. This was an emotion I heartily disapproved of, so I promptly put him out of my mind. I thought instead of Gordon. In fact, I thought a great deal about Gordon during those long waiting hours. I wished him to be where any half-way decent man should be after release from wrongful arrest – back home with his wife. But intuition told me he'd be sitting in the building somewhere, refusing to budge until he witnessed my deliverance with his own two eyes. And what worried me, felt like an immense weight bearing down, was what we'd say to each other – not what we'd say later, in the police car going home, or when we got stoned out of our minds at his cottage, but our very first words, and what looks we'd exchange as I came into view. How do you look a brother in the face when you've connived at injustice, believed him guilty of murder?

Is there such a thing as telepathy? No sooner had I asked myself how to face him than I became sure, intuition again, that Gordon was at the same instant pondering this very question. Thirty-six years since I heard his plaintive first cry from an upstairs cot, and never in all that time had I experienced the certainty of knowing his thoughts, and of him knowing mine.

I began to hum some tune or other I've heard Gordon whistling at the wind in the glens near Loch Lomond.

Andie the constable looked disapprovingly on. Maybe you have to be drunk or mad to hum tunes in police stations. Certainly, I felt a form of madness was lifting from me, and perhaps, like an exorcised demon, it could be felt in the air.

More hours fled by before Turnbull's return. He came alone, under a cloud of such introspection, his face so long and grave, that I feared something must have gone dreadfully wrong. He sat scrutinizing his immaculate fingernails before lifting his eyes to acknowledge my presence.

'MacRae doesn't want a solicitor,' he declared. 'He wants to see you. Says you're his best defence.'

'Me?'

'Why might that be? What does he want from you?'

'Haven't a clue.'

'Will you see him?'

'The least I can do for a friend,' I said.

Thirty-one

Duncan had dined well. In the stark ambiance of his interview room, bereft of soft lighting, crisp white tablecloths, the cabaret tones of a palm court piano, he had dined alone on at least four courses. The debris of a lavish meal littered the table. Among the plates, congealing with sauces and cream and chewed stalks of asparagus, stood a bottle of what was undoubtedly a rare and pricy claret. He was wiping his lips with a linen napkin. He gestured grandly for me to sit, dabbed fastidiously at the corners of his mouth then gave a bloated belch for which he offered no apology.

Turnbull flicked his eyes to the door; the constable who'd been standing guard made a silent departure. Turnbull took the remaining chair, a few feet distant from us, plucking at his trousers to keep his creases razor sharp. Duncan – who has the instant judgements of a suburban snob – once said I was his kind of man because I had an aristocrat's disdain for trousers. He couldn't go to a bank, wouldn't trust them, where the manager plucked at his pants. He'd hire or fire a salesman simply on the way he sat down. So he regarded Turnbull with a sidelong stare and smiled faintly to himself, as if believing that superior manners would ensure his release.

'Kept some wine for you, Sandy,' he said, raising the bottle. 'Knew you wouldn't let me down. Will you join me?'

'So long as it isn't your usual plonk,' I said.

He poured me a glass, then swept a hand round the room. 'Think I should redecorate? Install a bar, maybe? Paint the walls a decent colour?'

'Planning on staying, are we?'

He leaned towards me, imparting a confidence. 'Here of my own free will. I mean, they haven't charged me. Stay as long as I like.'

'Me, too,' I said.

'Chat all night, then, if we feel like it. Conference facilities provided free.' He held his drink towards me, so I clinked glasses. 'There's a catch, though.' He made a sly nod in Turnbull's direction. 'A distinct absence of privacy.'

'Then I shall watch what I say, Duncan. As I'm sure will you.'

'Plod here says the minute I step out that door he'll charge me. I must suffer the indignity of eating my own food at his lousy table. Seems I'm a free man, Sandy, who may contemplate his freedom but not exercise it.'

I agreed this was utterly outrageous.

'Don't know which is worse,' he declared mournfully. 'The fucking police or the Inland fucking Revenue.' And for a while his attention fell to brooding on his many sufferings at the hands of authority. Then his eyes were suddenly on me with an implication of injury. 'Plod also says you saw me this morning, early hours, at one of my houses.'

'Plod exaggerates. I saw someone. I said I couldn't make an identification. I made that very clear.'

'Not exactly the way I heard it,' he remarked quietly.

'I also said this someone drove off in a car rather like yours. Maybe a BMW but I couldn't swear to it.'

'Couldn't have been me you saw,' Duncan said. 'Impossible you saw me.' He stared with the force of certainty. 'I mean, be bloody honest, you couldn't possibly have seen me. Who's to say you were even bloody there?'

'My car says,' I offered with a semblance of regret. 'Damned thing wouldn't start. And the police picked me up on the road from Rhu.'

He drank some wine. He stared deeply, pensively, into

his glass, then his gaze rested briefly on the glass I was holding. He looked at me with the trace of a sardonic smile, and I gained the clear impression he was remembering that every drink we'd ever taken together was his. He seemed to find some reassurance in this, as if I could be easily bought, as if he'd long ago bought me several times over.

'Out of interest,' he enquired, 'purely so I know where we stand . . . were you banging my wife?'

'I'm afraid so.'

'Then I think,. Sandy, for the sake of old times if nothing else, I deserve some kind of apology.'

'It was a lousy thing to do . . .'

'. . . Hardly the action of a friend . . .'

'I'm truly sorry. What more can I say?'

Duncan shrugged his shoulders without concern. 'We're both men of the world. I've had mistresses. Think I haven't had mistresses? Damn it all, Sandy, if you'd a wife and she looked like Aileen, I'd bloody bang her. And I'd hope, old friend, you wouldn't take it personally.' He lunged at me over the table for a hearty handshake. 'I forgive you,' he said benignly. 'No hard feelings.'

Turnbull clapped his hands slowly together in silent applause. A brilliant performance.

'Plod does not seem very convinced,' I noted.

Duncan was unperturbed. 'Before now, did I ever ask if you were banging Aileen?'

'No.'

'Ever give you any hint I suspected?'

'None. I can truthfully say that.'

'Did Aileen ever say anything to you about me suspecting?'

'Not a murmur.'

'So if Plod wants to base any ridiculous charges on the basis I knew, he'll have a tough time proving it . . .'

'Don't underestimate him. The resourceful type, I'd say.'

Duncan reclined at ease in his chair. 'Shall I tell you his case against me, Sandy? As I understand it, I mean. I'm a good swimmer . . . nobody actually saw me swim the day Aileen was killed . . . but I had opportunity. Happens I own an old car . . . I've got reasons, Sandy, he'll hear them when it suits me . . . anything wrong with owning an old car, anything strange or suspicious? He alleges I was at the site on Gareloch this morning . . . yet his men discovered me tucked up in bed. Sure I could have been there, can't prove I wasn't. But that's hardly the point, is it, old friend? The onus of proof is on him. All circumstantial so far, agreed?'

I nodded reluctantly.

'Then there's the women. Christ, Sandy, I'm not making any accusations, but fair's fair, you'd more reason to kill them than I fucking did. For Christsake, we're talking sexual motives here . . . Which of us was banging half the fucking burgh? Girls and married women and fucking ageing spinsters.'

'Who says?'

'You did.'

'Really? When was this?'

'Och, don't act the innocent suddenly. All those nights we spent, drinking distilleries dry. Always boasting, Sandy. Always telling tales of your sexual prowess.'

'Not very likely, is it, to the husband of a woman I was banging?'

'You were pissed out of your mind. You probably don't remember any of it.'

'Is this part of your defence? That I boasted about women?'

He affected a wounded look. 'If I'm asked on oath, old friend, what can I do but answer the truth?'

'Told you names, did I? Caroline Sutherland? Sheena Campbell?'

His expression grew canny. 'Well, now. Cuts both ways, that, doesn't it? I mean to say, the only way I could have heard those names was from you. And I don't recall you mentioning names, not names as such. Just a catalogue of conquests.'

'Then it looks,' I declared, 'as if neither of us knew those women. So Plod will have a hard time proving otherwise.'

Duncan topped up our glasses, draining the bottle. He was briefly quiet, savouring his wine. Then he planted both elbows on the table, nodding his head for me to move closer. His voice was low, shades of secrecy. 'This Hoolet,' he said. 'Think he's mad?'

'Not in the way he wants us to believe.'

'But a crazed person . . . someone acting under pressure? Someone driven to increasingly frantic acts of desperation . . .'

'Probably.'

'You see, I got to thinking a great deal, alone in that house . . . why Aileen? Why such disgusting violence? And there's only one possible answer, Sandy. Revenge. A wanton and perverted ritual of revenge. But against who? Not against Aileen. Christ, Sandy, I'm not claiming she was a saint . . . I was her fucking husband, I knew her appetites. But would a lover do that? I hardly think so.' His voice was a strained whisper now and Turnbull was crouching forward on his seat to catch the words. 'You were her lover, Sandy. Did she ever provoke violence? Ever give you other than complete satisfaction.'

'Never,' I murmured.

'An act of revenge against me, then? Hell, I'm a businessman, I've made enemies in my time. Given as good as I've got, too, and no fucking regrets. But there's a psychology to revenge, Sandy, take it from one who knows. It's the eye for an eye principle . . . someone cheats you, cheat them back . . . a supplier overcharges you, rob the bugger blind. Know why revenge is sweet? Because of its Biblical purity.' He paused for a moment's refreshment. He dabbed his lips dry then tidied the napkin into neat folds with a curiously religious air. 'Now this was a sexual revenge,' he resumed. 'So it couldn't have been aimed at me. Because I'm the very soul of discretion. Any banging I do gets paid for. Secretaries get holidays on the Costa Brava. Husbands get building contracts. Lassies in business get to hang their frilly curtains in my houses. See what I'm saying? I do not, Sandy, leave a trail of resentment in my wake. Whereas you . . . I mean, face facts, how many husbands in this town, how many parents in Yoker, must be sharpening their knives to cut off your balls?'

'Anyone particular in mind?' I asked.

'Not for me to say, is it?' He gazed at me shrewdly. 'Be extremely helpful, though, if you were to write down all the relevant names for this dumb policeman here. He could then take statements, check movements and motives. Least you can do for me, all things considered, after banging my wife.'

'Look, Duncan, if you're trying to blacken my character, don't bother. Plod already has a pretty low opinion of me.'

'Let's exercise your memory,' he said regardless. 'Let's consider what we know about the Hoolet. He bears a deep and abiding hatred for you – pretty bloody obvious, right? – someone from your past. He's familiar with your habits. He's learned, somehow, about you and Aileen – which counts me out, agreed? He chooses a Thursday, a day I'm away on the yacht, because he doesn't want to confuse matters, throw any suspicion on me. He checks your house, sees your car in the drive. He can be sure you're alone inside, you invariably are . . . so you'll have no alibi. He murders Aileen, creating the appearance of mad sexual frenzy. This must look, Sandy, like the act of a jealous lover. Then he waits. He expects the police to find out about your affair with Aileen. They'll search your house for love letters from her. They'll interview friends she confided in. But he waits in vain. The police fail him. You're still walking free.'

'He should have left something of mine at your house,' I said. 'Like a comb, for instance.'

'I'm sure he regrets that,' Duncan replied with an analytical lack of involvement. 'So he takes the obvious next step . . . he kills another of your women. He checks your car again, on his way to the park. He considers, I should think, leaving evidence near the body this time . . . yes, maybe a comb. But he believes this won't be necessary. He's careful, this Hoolet, he doesn't want to overplay his hand, create any suspicion of a stitch-up. Two of your women killed now, and again you have no alibi. There's no doubt in his mind you'll be arrested. Can you imagine his fury, Sandy? I mean, we're constructing a hypothesis here . . . when he reads that story of yours splashed over the front pages! He thinks you're throwing down a challenge, mocking him with his failure. The police conclude you can't have done it. What, Sandy Douglas? they say. Never! No killer could be that fucking blatant. So you force him to act again. I mean, me, I can even feel a twinge of sympathy for this guy after all his careful planning. We're not talking serial killers here, the maniac the police are looking for. This is just a guy with a grudge, acting out a part, know what I'm saying? And the forces of fate are conspiring against him.

'So he does it again, one final killing. Your car's outside the house again. This time he'll make certain . . . he takes something of yours, this comb you mentioned, and drops it at the scene. But providence, Sandy, is not on his side. How's he to know you're with the police, that you've got the perfect alibi? How's he to guess he's taken someone else's comb?'

'Put that way,' I said, 'I can almost feel sorry for him.'

'Then an even worse twist of fate . . . the police pounce on the wrong man. They arrest your brother!'

Here, Turnbull made his only contribution to this after-dinner repartee. His face expressionless, he recited solemnly: 'I told you that myself. Phoned you to say. Thought you had a right to know, as Aileen's husband.'

'Plenty of people knew!' Duncan retorted. 'Soon as you rang off, I had the Press phoning for comments. Justice finally done, eh, Mr MacRae? He's got a fucking mouth on him, I'll tell you, that sergeant of yours.'

'What happens next?' I asked. 'Hypothetically speaking.'

'Fucking obvious, isn't it! He has to act quickly, prove to the police they've made a balls-up. Probably, I should think, he's in too much of a hurry to check your car . . . he strikes again, Sandy, confident that suspicion must finally fall on you. I mean, who else can it be? I'm only guessing here, but this latest victim is yet another of your women. Give them time, and the police will establish your link with her, some evidence of a relationship.'

'And what if he's wrong . . . there's no such evidence?'

Duncan leaned back, folding his arms. He cast a baleful gaze on me. Then he sighed, sounding tired and dispirited. 'Now we enter the realms of fantasy,' he suggested. 'But then this whole damned thing is crazy. The position I'm in is crazy.' He sighed again, woefully shaking his head. 'Circumstantial evidence, that's all they have, Sandy. All the police can marshal against me is supposition, allegations, might-have-beens and possiblies.' He paused at length. 'Except for my fucking pond,' he said. 'The pond on the patio.'

I looked suitably baffled.

'They found a plastic bag in the water. A hammer inside, Sandy, and some semen. Dog semen, they tell me. I mean, what sort of fucking nut-case is this, uses dog semen? Think I'd do a thing like that to my wife, for Christsake, my beautiful Aileen!'

I gave the answer of a shocked silence.

'And a doorkey,' he said, puffing with outrage. 'A fucking key from some woman I've never fucking met! I mean, see reason . . . if I had a key, I'd have gone in by the door! This guy broke in at a fucking back window.'

I continued to look as if this was all over my head.

'I mean, for Christsake,' he ranted, 'this is me we're talking about here. I'm not some moron from the sticks. Would you tell this bloody lawman, Sandy, who doesn't know his fucking arse from his elbow, that I'm not such a fool as to leave incriminating evidence, hammers and such, round the fucking house? Christ Almighty, we're agreed the Hoolet's a clever bastard . . . think he's going to hold on to the fucking evidence!'

'Perhaps,' I ventured meekly to Turnbull, 'there's been some misunderstanding.'

Nothing was said for some considerable while.

'Hypothesis,' Duncan pronounced then.

'Yes . . .' I answered.

'Total guesswork, heaven knows.'

'Try me.'

'This is a man with a grudge, trying to frame you. He doesn't check your car this last time. Why? Because he's nailed you cold. He's planted the murder weapon on you, hidden it at your flat.'

'Then the police,' I said, 'are welcome to search.'

'The way I see this,' Duncan proposed, 'someone finding themselves in such position – a hammer under the bed or wherever – might do all manner of crazy things. They might, see what I'm saying, accidentally incriminate someone else. Someone who . . . Jesus, Sandy . . . there's not a shred of evidence against.' His hands were sweating. He wiped them on the napkin. He had no thoughts now for its condition and let it fall, crumpled, into his lap. 'I imagine the police would respond sympathetically if this was explained,' he suggested.

'As you say, all in the realms of fantasy.'

'I'm an exceeding generous man, old friend. I never forget a kindness.'

'And I, Duncan, cannot be bought by big promises. Only by lunches and bottles of scotch.'

'All I fucking want, damn you, is a fair trial!'

'We're all equal in the eyes of the law,' I said. 'You'll get as fair a trial as I would have done.'

Thirty-two

Gordon has changed. He has taken of late to smoking a pipe. Seated beside the fire indoors he juts a straight-stemmed briar from his mouth and his appearance is professional, quietly reflective; you might take him to be a philosopher, a writer of learned works. For the open air, his preference lies with a meerschaum, its stem drooping in a curve, and he has developed the habit of leaning on walls and gates as he puffs contemplatively. Looking upon the countryside, his gaze has a knowing but faintly puzzled quality, as if nothing he sees holds any mystery for him, and he cannot quite believe his world is so small. Possibly he talks rather less than before, though not that you'd notice – the only real difference is the pipe. It is as if his hair was beginning to grey, or his back to stoop. Sometimes small surface changes are the only indication of great upheavals inside. I always expected this to happen. He has beaten me to it. He has become middle-aged.

The year began wretchedly. Rain fell constantly, there was ice overnight. The white crags of the mountains held a forbidding look of danger, storm clouds wreathed them, and the lochs swelled heavy and black. I waited in vain for the sun. A week passed, then another; I gazed fitfully from my window believing the town to be locked in perpetual winter. A gale rattled the chimneys, broken branches littered the garden, the lawn turned to moss. There was the darkness of night, the dim pallor of twilight, some-where between the days had been lost.

The weather broke finally. Dawn came late, nearly nine in the morning before the sky began to brighten, and I heard a forgotten sound from my bed. It was as welcome as the olive branch must have been to Noah – the joyful chirrup of birds.

I took Gordon on a mountain trek. Another sign of his premature ageing – once he would have pleaded work, had a thousand and one tasks to perform, but I asked so he came. And he trailed behind while I led, as though he was no match for my youthful energy.

We went into the Arrochar Alps, ascending towards the looming peak of the Cobbler. Along a forestry track at first, between tall pines enclosing shadows and silence. We took a rest on our travels, where machinery lay strewn for cutting and hauling. Over our heads, cables stretched tautly through the trees like a ski-lift and there was a scent of fresh sawn wood and damp vegetation. Gordon sat on an oildrum some feet apart from the fallen trunk I'd chosen. Briefly, Duncan intruded on my thoughts. He'd read my most private imaginings. He'd searched among the files on my word processor, discovered my seductions and believed them, every word. On that first clandestine visit to my flat, he'd learned of my obsession with Caroline and Sheena, while they'd been blissfully ignorant. He knew every intimate detail of my seduction of Isobel before it ever happened. He'd been ahead of me. He was truly a hoolet, and somewhat grudgingly I admired him for that.

I said nothing of this to Gordon. I looked across to where he sat and his eyes met mine with the twinkle of a smile, frank and disarming. There was no awkwardness in our lack of words. He lit a pipe and it was as if, somewhere nearby, peat was burning in the open air.

After we'd scrambled further, I stopped where the view was right. Loch Long lay below us, grey and deep as an inland sea. Miniature houses lined the banks like a string of pearls. Slopes climbed steeply from the valley, the greens and browns of a Highland quilt. You could see the geology, the workings of nature laid bare, mountains cast from the foundries of the earth, boulders sculpted by a million years of wind, deep clefts carved by the craftsmanship of glaciers. The sun was the pale yellow of an early primrose, threads of mist clung like chiffon to the snow on the peaks. And there, off to the east, framed by a gap opening in the hills, was the glint of sunlight on the darkling stillness of Loch Lomond.

It was a perfect place for burial. From the peace of the grave, you could look out on the seasons, observe the grazing and mating of wild red deer. At nightfall there are foxes just in view down by the treeline, and the sometimes glimpse of a wheeling falcon. Occasionally, as the evening dew shines in the faintness of twilight, you might catch sight of a prowling hoolet, and with only the dead in attendance, he may dive and feast by your lonely plot.

I began collecting stones. Gordon took the perch of a rock, relit his pipe and looked solemnly on. His smoke drifted across the mountainside and I imagined it as incense, the performance of a last and mystic rite.

I piled stone upon stone until I'd built a cairn. I checked the view finally, made sure you could squint from its apex through the gap to Loch Lomond.

'Murdo,' I said. 'May he rest in peace.'

To which Gordon added, 'Amen.'

THE END

SONS OF THE MORNING
by Jack Curtis

'GRIPPING . . . A SUPERB BOOK IN ALL RESPECTS'
Express & Echo

Linda Bowman was the first. Nobody special, just a face in
the crowd. Yet someone picked her out, someone with a
high-velocity rifle, someone elated by his own dark power.
Then there was the man on the train; then the young
couple drinking at a riverside pub. It was every policeman's nightmare – a clever and remorseless killer choosing
his victims at random.

Robin Culley is a policeman, and it's his nightmare, but
his instinct tells him that, despite what they seem, the
killings have a motive.

Culley's obsession with the apparently pointless slaughter
leads him into worlds of fear and shadow; from the highest
level of British politics – the Cabinet itself – to the world of
assassins for hire and mercenaries on the run; from a
sinister Arizona billionaire art collector to the dangerous
secrets of the SAS. It threatens those closest to Culley; and
it takes him, finally, to a heart-stopping confrontation
with a psychotic killer on the storm-torn wilderness of
Dartmoor . . .

0 552 13592 5